Medicine, Patients and the Law

Margaret Brazier

PENGUIN BOOKS

PENGUIN BOOKS

Published by the Penguin Group
Penguin Books Ltd, 27 Wrights Lane, London W8 5TZ, England
Penguin Putnam Inc., 375 Hudson Street, New York, New York 10014, USA
Penguin Books Australia Ltd, Ringwood, Victoria, Australia
Penguin Books Canada Ltd, 10 Alcorn Avenue, Toronto, Ontario, Canada M4V 3B2
Penguin Books (NZ) Ltd, 182–190 Wairau Road, Auckland 10, New Zealand

Penguin Books Ltd, Registered Offices: Harmondsworth, Middlesex, England

First published in Pelican Books 1987
Second edition published in Penguin Books 1992
10 9 8 7 6 5

Printed in England by Clays Ltd, St Ives plc
Set in Monophoto Times

PENGUIN BOOKS

MEDICINE, PATIENTS AND THE LAW

Margaret Brazier was born in 1950. She graduated from the University of Manchester in 1971 and was called to the Bar in 1973. She has lectured at Manchester University since 1971 and was appointed Professor of Law in 1990. She is the Legal Studies Director of the University's Centre for Social Ethics and Policy. Her publications include several articles on torts and medico-legal problem and she is the editor of *Street on Torts* and General Editor of *Clerk and Lindsell on Torts*.

In memory of
L. T. Jacobs 1914–85
and
Harry Street 1919–84

Contents

PART III: MATTERS OF LIFE AND DEATH

Preface

Rarely a day passes now without the press or television focusing on some issue of disputed medical practice, medical ethics or medical litigation. The medical profession finds itself in the limelight. Its image undergoes drastic changes. One day the doctor is hailed as a saviour. The next he is condemned as authoritarian or uncaring. The rapid progress of medical science, extending life at one end and bringing new hope to the childless at the other, has thrown up intricate problems of ethics and morals. At every level of medical practice the law now plays a part. The number of actions for malpractice against doctors, once virtually unknown in England, is growing apace. Doctors fear an epidemic of American proportions. Patients find the English legal system obstructive and cripplingly expensive. Nor are patients' grievances limited to the lack of provision for compensation for medical mishap. Increasingly patients demand a greater say in their treatment. The extent to which it is their right to have such a say becomes ultimately a question for the law. Meanwhile, medical progress has created new problems for the law's definition of the beginning and end of life. Research on embryos, abortion, the damaged newborn baby and euthanasia excite lively legal and moral debate. The enactment of the Human Fertilisation and Embryology Act 1990 is unlikely to defuse that debate.

The object of this book is to examine the regulation of medical practice, the rights and duties of patients and their medical advisers, the provision of compensation for medical mishaps and the framework of rules governing those delicate issues of life and death where medicine, morals and law overlap. It is intended to provide a picture of the role of the law in medical practice today and to highlight those areas where the law is woefully inadequate. So in Part I, I consider the general legal framework within which medicine is practised today. In Part II, I look at legal remedies available to the patient injured by, or unhappy with, treatment he has received. And finally in Part III, I examine in detail specific issues relating to the treatment of the living and the dying which have posed awkward problems of law, morals and medicine. Throughout the book I concentrate, primarily, on the provision of health care for the mentally competent patient. I do consider in Chapter 5 the problems arising when a patient is temporarily or permanently mentally incompetent. I do not attempt systematic coverage of mental health law. To do so would be to double the length of the book. The reader should refer to the specialist works on that topic suggested in the bibliography. The book is intended for a wide audience. It is designed to be read by lawyers and law students seeking an introduction to the law relating to medical practice, by members of the medical professions, and above all by the lay public, looking for a guide through the maze of current issues confronting them every day in their daily newspaper. I make no judgement on medical practice in the nineties. I am not qualified to do so. I do evaluate the state of the law and too often find it sadly wanting.

The first edition of this book was to have been the joint project of Professor Harry Street, Professor Gerald Dworkin and me. Professor Street died in April 1984, having worked on early drafts of parts of Chapters 4, 6 and 9. He inspired the writing of the book. His example as colleague and teacher created a debt which I can never repay. Gerald Dworkin's many commitments prevented him from completing his planned share of the work. He kindly allowed me to use the drafts he prepared of Chapters 18, 20, and 21. His wise advice and meticulous reading of other chapters has assisted me greatly.

I should like to acknowledge the help given to me by many of my colleagues in Manchester, from the disciplines of law, philosophy, theology and medicine. Their patience in listening to me as I chewed over awkward problems, and advising me as the work progressed, has been invaluable. In particular I thank friends and colleagues, Diana Kloss, Maureen Mulholland, Tony Dyson, John Harris and Mary Lobjoit, who have given me invaluable advice and support. I must also thank my students, who challenged my views on several occasions and forced me to think again on many issues. I acknowledge the especial efforts of Nina Fletcher in helping me track down materials. I thank all the secretarial staff at Manchester and Southampton who struggled valiantly with so many drafts of the first edition, and my special thanks for this edition must go to Deborah Robey.

No criticisms made in this book are the result of any personal experience of medical practice. The care which I and my family have received from our general practitioners, from Manchester Royal Infirmary and from Withington Hospital, where my daughter was born, has always been of the highest standard.

I submitted the typescript for this edition to the publishers in February 1991. I have been able to make some amendments in November 1991.

Margaret Brazier

Table of Cases

The date in brackets after the reference to a case in this Table refers to the date at which the case was decided. In a number of instances the case is actually reported at a later date, as will be apparent in the full case reference given in the relevant note

Table of Statutes

Table of Statutory Instruments

PART I

Medicine, Law and Society

Introduction

In contrast to most European countries, the law of England is not to be found neatly encapsulated in any Code. The task of the non-lawyer seeking to establish his rights or ascertain his duties is therefore far from easy. The law relating to medical practice is to be discovered from a variety of sources. Parliament has enacted a number of statutes governing medical practice. The regulation of medical practice and the disciplining of the defaulting doctor are entrusted by Act of Parliament to the General Medical Council in the Medical Act 1983. The structure of the health service is provided for by a series of statutes on the National Health Service, notably the National Health Service Act 1977 and the National Health Service and Community Care Act 1990. Those same statutes embody most of the rules dealing with complaints procedures within the NHS too. The Medicines Acts are concerned with the safety of drugs, and a number of other Acts of Parliament will be seen to be crucially relevant to issues of medicine, patients and the law. An Act of Parliament can deal only with the general framework of legal rules. Acts of Parliament therefore commonly empower government ministers to make subsidiary regulations known as statutory instruments. These regulations may determine crucial questions. For example, most of the duties of general practitioners within the NHS are dealt with by regulations and not by Act of Parliament.

Increasingly, too, it will be impossible to understand the legal rules governing the practice of medicine without some reference to European law. In matters within the jurisdiction of the Treaty of Rome, the European Community is empowered to make laws affecting all Member States. This may be by way of *regulations* which immediately and directly become law in the United Kingdom, or by way of *directives* which oblige the United Kingdom government to introduce an appropriate Act of Parliament to give effect to the directive. In 1985 a Community directive on liability for unsafe products resulted in the Consumer Protection Act 1987 which, as we shall see in Chapter 8, radically altered the rules governing drug-induced injury. It must be noted, though, that the European Community is primarily concerned with economic and commercial matters. The extent of the Community's powers to pronounce on ethical questions such as embryo research or abortion is disputed. And the European Community should not be confused with the European Convention on Human Rights. That Convention is a quite separate treaty to which the United Kingdom is a party. The Convention seeks to establish the rights of the individual and does directly deal with questions of rights to life and to found a family. Individuals can petition the European Court of Human Rights if they believe their rights have been violated. Alas, a judgement in their favour has no direct effect in this country, as the Convention is not incorporated into English (or Scottish) law. The Liberal Democrats now say that the Convention should become part and parcel of English law via an Act of Parliament giving it direct effect here. The Labour Party is giving consideration to similar legislation.

Statute and statutory regulations alone, British or European, by no means give the whole picture of English law. Much of English law remains judge-made, the common law of England. Decisions, judgements handed down by the courts, form the precedents for determining later disputes and define the rights and duties of doctors and patients in areas untouched by statute. The common law governs questions of compensation for medical accident, the patient's right to determine his own treatment, parents' rights to control medical treatment of their children and, as we shall see, several other vital matters. I deal with English law. The common law is not confined to England. Decisions of courts in America, Canada and elsewhere are mentioned from time to time. Such judgements do not bind an English court. They can be useful as examples, or warnings, as to how the same basic principles of law have developed elsewhere. Finally it must be remembered that for the lawyer Scotland counts as a foreign country. Scotland maintains its own independent legal system. On many of the questions dealt with in this book English and Scottish law coincide. Occasionally the law of England and Scotland diverges. I confine myself to stating the law as it applies in England and Wales, although I try to point out some areas where the law of Scotland differs from its English counterpart. And the problems of law and medicine embodied in the book are common to Britain as a whole.

CHAPTER 1

The Practice of Medicine Today

Few professions stand so high in general public esteem as that of medicine. Popularity polls of professionals in the press regularly result in doctors at the top of the poll and lawyers near the bottom! Yet few individuals attract greater public odium than the doctor or nurse who falls from the pedestal. The revulsion occasioned by Nazi atrocities in the concentration camps was nowhere as marked as in the case of Dr Mengele. That he used his skills as a doctor, taught to him that he might heal and comfort the sick, to advance torture and barbarism causes horror even now, forty years and more after the end of Nazi rule and when the man himself is dead. The transformation of a supposed angel of mercy into the angel of death makes the blood run cold.

Public passion is rightly aroused by the likes of Mengele. But passion is never far away from ordinary everyday relationships between doctor and patient. Clients can usually remain relatively impartial about their solicitor. If he does a good job they may appreciate him. If he is incompetent they sack him. He will rarely be loved or hated. The family doctor by contrast arouses more intense feelings. For many of his of her patients the doctor is almost a member of the family. He is expected to feel for them as well as provide professional care. When the doctor meets the patient's expectations he will be rewarded by admiration and affection. Woe betide him if he does not. One error, one moment of exasperation or intensity, may transform the beloved doctor into a hate figure. The hospital consultant enjoys or endures a similarly ambivalent role. The consultant, at any rate until comparatively recently, was accorded an almost godlike status. He was a figure inspiring awe in the patient, visiting the ward attended by a retinue of junior doctors and nurses. The consultant's exalted status insulated him from personal contact with the patient and protected him from the sort of complaints voiced freely to nursing staff. He paid a price. Gods are expected to work cures. They are not expected to be subject to human error. When the consultant proved to be human, when medicine could not cure, the patient found it hard to grasp and rightly or wrongly, and often wrongly, regarded the doctor as personally incompetent.

Attitudes are changing slowly. Family doctors are becoming a different breed. Some of them try hard to persuade their patients to see the doctor as a partner in promoting good health. Doctors are urged to prescribe less freely and to talk more to their patients. The good GP is as interested in the prevention of ill-health as its cure. A new generation of consultants is gradually taking over in the hospitals. They are in most cases less grand and more prepared to listen to patients and nursing staff. Entrenched attitudes take time to change. Doctors may be changing slowly, but the perception of many patients has not changed. They still regard the doctor as a miracle worker, and the publicity attaching to and money poured into high-technology medicine reinforce that perception. Stories rarely appear in the press applauding the good work of the geriatrician or praising the community health physician. Doctors in such unglamorous specialities, it is reported, rarely win the coveted NHS merit awards which can boost the senior doctor's salary. Money, fame and publicity are usually reserved for the transplant surgeon, the gynaecologist running a 'test-tube' baby unit, and so on. The medical marvels with which the public are bombarded reinforce the image of the doctor as superman. And so when a member of the public becomes a patient and 'superman' lets him down he is unsurprisingly aggrieved. Nor can doctors entirely blame the media for their image. Doctors decide on who get merit awards. Doctors vote with their feet as to which branch of medicine they enter. Many continue to vote for the glamorous world of 'high-tech' medicine.

Quite apart from the question of medical 'image', there are certain inescapable features of the profession of medicine which will always render the doctor more vulnerable to attack than fellow professionals. The doctor deals with the individual's most precious commodity, life

7

and health. On a mundane level he may determine whether patient X is to be sanctioned to enjoy seven days off work for nervous exhaustion brought about by overwork or classified as another malingerer.[1] At the other end of the scale he may hold in his hands the power of life and death. He is the man with the skill and experience. In his hands, as the patient sees it, rests the power to cure. Only recently have the lay public become more aware that the cure is not always possible. As Ian Kennedy has said, the patient appears before the doctor '. . . naked both physically and emotionally. However unwilling we may be, however well-intentioned the doctor, it is hard to overstate the power which this vests in the doctor.'[2] The price of power is that those who exercise it can today expect constant scrutiny from those subject to it and from the public at large. The age of deference is past.

The power inevitably held by the doctor in our society is matched by the human cost of any error he may make. When an overstretched, overtired accountant makes a mistake he will probably get a chance to put it right next day. When an articled clerk's inexperience lets him down the likelihood is that his principal will notice and correct the error. For the junior doctor who has been working continuously for over thirty-six hours there may be no second chance. Nor, of course, is there a second chance for the patient. The accountant or the solicitor may lose his client money or property. Monetary compensation paid for out of the professional's insurance cover will go some way to placate the client. For the patient for whom the doctor's mistake resulted in disability or death, money is poor compensation. Finding out why things went wrong may be more important to the patient and the family. And inability to find out 'why' may explain the bitterness which attends many claims against the medical profession.

When the price of a momentary error is so high, it follows that concern to prevent error is acute. Every profession has its black sheep. Some are merely incompetent, others are venal. The failure of the Law Society to pursue and discipline its members effectively remains the subject of debate. There is no evidence that the medical profession is any better or worse than its brethren in other disciplines in maintaining and policing standards. Its failures will always attract greater attention. A solicitor who grossly overcharges, fails to keep proper records or

1. Ian Kennedy, *The Unmasking of Medicine*, Allen & Unwin, London, 1981, Chapter 1, pp. 9ff.
2. ibid., p. 8.

conducts his client's business dilatorily will arouse public concern as well as private anger. But the outcry will not reach the same level of passion as that occasioned by reports of a doctor failing to visit a child when the child later dies. The medical profession may rightly claim that doctors make no more mistakes, that there are no more 'bad' practitioners, than in any other profession. The claim is futile. The cost of a medical error is such that doctors will always be expected to be better than others and the standards of the profession as a whole to be of the highest.

Nor are the consequences of a failure in medical skill the only reason for the medical profession's susceptibility to virulent attack. The decisions which face the doctor can so often touch on sensitive areas of moral and religious concern. This is in itself nothing new. For example, until the advent of safe Caesarean surgery doctors could be called on several times in a year to decide whether to save the life of mother or baby in a difficult confinement. Three developments have intensified the modern doctor's dilemma. Technology has given the doctors power to save and prolong life undreamed of twenty years ago. The doctors now have to decide when to use the technology. In many cases life can be prolonged; the question is whether that life is worth prolonging? Secondly, until the middle of this century decisions on life and death were usually made in the privacy of the patient's home. The midwife attending the birth of a grossly handicapped baby decided with the parents whether to attempt to save the infant's life. Only she and the family ever knew that the supposedly stillborn baby struggled to breathe. Today such scenes are played out in the publicity of a busy labour ward. Thirdly, there is no longer any general consensus on the sanctity of life, when life begins, or when it ends, or should end. Abortion, once illegal and hazardous to the mother, can now be carried out safely and cheaply in the early months of pregnancy. The debate on the morality of abortion has not abated. The legality of some abortions in England is unclear. The divide between pro- and anti-abortion campaigners is greater than ever to the extent that in the USA abortion clinics have been bombed and doctors carrying out abortions have received death threats. In this country in 1981, Dr Leonard Arthur, a leading paediatrician, stood trial for murder as a result of his decision as to the management of the care of a severely handicapped baby. His lengthy ordeal ended in acquittal. At the core of the issue was a dispute between medical professionals and within society itself as to the treatment of severely damaged babies. In what other profession would an ethical and professional dispute result in a criminal prosecution of this sort?

The power in the hands of the doctor explains the concern that the public and patients have in its exercise. It places the medical profession in the limelight, a limelight some doctors appear to relish. Nor is the profession averse to publicizing its successes. Doctors cannot then be surprised when failure, incompetence or controversy attract equal notoriety. Alas, the representatives of the profession too often react in an over-defensive manner, so exacerbating the original criticism or complaint. What the profession, patients and the public have in common is a need for: (1) the medical profession to be properly regulated and controlled, (2) an adequate and rational system of compensation for patients suffering injury, (3) effective means of investigating medical accidents, and (4) provision for doctors to be given comprehensible guidance on those areas of medical practice of moral and ethical sensitivity. The extent to which the law does and can meet those needs is the theme of this book.

Regulating medical practice

The regulation of the medical profession is entrusted by statute, the Medical Act 1983, to the profession itself acting through the General Medical Council. The GMC controls medical education and maintains a register of qualified practitioners. Surprisingly, no law expressly prohibits any unregistered or unqualified person from practising most types of medicine or even surgery! A criminal offence is committed only when such a person deliberately and falsely represents himself as being a registered practitioner or having medical qualifications.[3] The rationale of the criminal law is that people should be free to opt for any form of advice or treatment, however apparently bizarre, but must be protected from rogues claiming a bogus status and from commercial exploitation of untested 'alternative' medicine. On its own the penalty for falsely claiming to be qualified is not much of a deterrent, a maximum fine of £5,000. The fraudulent 'doctor' out to make money

3. Medical Act 1983, s. 49; and see *Younghusband* v. *Luftig* [1949] 2 KB 354; *Wilson* v. *Inyang* [1951] 2 KB 799. Unregistered practitioners are expressly prohibited from certain fields of practice, e.g. venereal disease (Venereal Disease Act 1917). And they are barred from holding certain positions (Medical Act 1983, s. 47).

is deterred in other ways. He will not be able to recover his fees in a court of law.[4] If money has been handed over voluntarily where the 'doctor' led the patient to believe he was qualified he may face additional charges of obtaining property by deception and conviction may result in imprisonment.[5] The herbalist and the faith-healer are left free to practise, but they must be honest with those who come to them for help and not pretend to be registered doctors.

Few would quarrel with the liberality of the law where the unqualified adviser limits himself to advice. The nightmare is that some unqualified person might resort to surgery. Any physical contact with a patient permitted by him under the impression that he is dealing with a 'real doctor' will be a criminal assault. A biology teacher who set himself up in private practice in Lancashire was imprisoned for assault causing grievous bodily harm for carrying out gynaecological operations on unsuspecting women.[6] A more difficult question is raised where the patient agrees to surgery by an unregistered practitioner knowing full well that he is not dealing with a conventionally qualified doctor. I would tentatively suggest that a prosecution for assault would still succeed in most cases even if nothing went wrong with the 'operation'. The consent of the 'victim' of an assault is not always a defence when bodily harm is done.[7] The public interest in preventing unqualified persons from engaging in surgery may be sufficient to render the 'doctor's' conduct punishable as a crime.

The General Medical Council

The General Medical Council, the governing body of the medical profession, is composed of fifty elected members chosen by the profession at large, thirty-four appointed members selected by universities and the Royal Colleges of Medicine, and a group of nine nominated members, nominated by the Queen on the advice of the Privy Council.[8] A majority of the nominated members must be lay people. As elected

4. Medical Act 1983, s. 46.
5. Theft Act 1968, s. 15.
6. He was initially sentenced to six years' imprisonment. His sentence was reduced on appeal to eighteen months!
7. *R. v. Donovan* [1934] 2 KB 498; *Attorney-General's Reference (No. 6 of 1980)* [1981] QB 715, 719.
8. Medical Act 1983, Sched. I.

11

and appointed members are required to be registered practitioners the lay element on the Council is minimal. The Council's duties include maintaining the register of practitioners,[9] and providing '. . . advice for members of the medical profession on standards of professional conduct or on medical ethics'.[10] The Medical Act 1983, which defines and delimits the Council's powers, illustrates the importance of the Council's role in relation to medical education and in ensuring that registration is granted only to suitably qualified and experienced aspirants. Over one half of the statute deals with the issue. I shall not go further into the details of qualifications for registration. Public concern focuses rather on the Council's exercise of its powers to require registered doctors to maintain standards. Those powers are perhaps more limited than the public appreciates. The Council is required to establish a Health Committee which may suspend a doctor unfit to practise by reason of physical or mental illness or may make his registration conditional on compliance with certain conditions, for example, he may be obliged to accept medical treatment himself.[11] Elaborate procedural safeguards are erected to ensure that a doctor alleged to be unfit is treated fairly. Complementary to the Health Committee is the Professional Conduct Committee. With this Committee lies the power to discipline any doctor who has been found guilty of a criminal offence in the British Isles or who '. . . is judged by the Professional Conduct Committee to be guilty of serious professional misconduct'.[12] Such a doctor may (1) have his name erased from the register, or (2) be suspended from the register for one year, or (3) have his registration made conditional on compliance with conditions set by the Committee, for example undergoing additional training or attending a refresher course. Once again the procedure is scrupulously fair to the accused doctor and he has an automatic right to appeal to the Privy Council.[13]

9. Medical Act 1983, s. 2, and see ss. 30–34.
10. ibid., s. 35.
11. ibid., s. 37. And see *Crompton* v. *GMC* (*No. 1*) [1981] 1 WLR 1435 and (*No.2*) [1985] 1 WLR 885.
12. ibid., s. 36.
13. ibid., s. 40.

What amounts to serious professional misconduct?

The efficacy of the General Medical Council's disciplinary powers as a means of maintaining standards of competence and care within the profession and in protecting the patient depends largely on what the Council treats as 'serious professional misconduct' and in the penalties imposed on guilty doctors. The GMC is '. . . concerned with errors in diagnosis or treatment, and with the kind of matters which give rise to action in the civil courts for negligence only when the doctor's conduct in the case has involved such a disregard for his professional responsibility to his patients or such a neglect of his professional duties as to raise a question of serious professional misconduct'.[14] Isolated error or even incompetence as such is thus excluded from serious misconduct: so what does meet the bill?

Earlier legislation defined punishable misconduct as 'infamous conduct in a professional respect'. Echoes of that wording persist. Serious professional misconduct is defined in Halsbury's *Laws of England* as conduct '. . . reasonably to be regarded as dishonourable by professional brethren of good repute and competency'.[15] So adultery with a patient or a patient's spouse remains serious misconduct. Drug abuse, alcoholism and fraud join the list. Added to these are touting for custom and a number of offences to prevent unseemly competition among doctors. From the patient's viewpoint two areas of potential misconduct are of prime importance: breach of confidence, which I deal with later in Chapter 3, and failure to attend the patient.

In the GMC 'Bluebook' giving guidance on what constitutes misconduct, neglect of the doctor's duties to his patients is given as the first example of potential misconduct. Yet there is widespread suspicion that doctors who fail their patients are let off lightly. Are there any grounds for this suspicion? First a high degree of proof is demanded before a doctor will be 'convicted'.[16] The charge against the doctor must be proved beyond all reasonable doubt. This is no different from the standard pertaining in any other professional disciplinary

---

14. GMC 'Bluebook' *Professional Conduct: Fitness to Practise* (February 1991), p. 10. Note the subtle but significant change of emphasis from an earlier edition.

15. Earl Halsbury, *Laws of England*, Butterworths, London, Vol. 30, para. 125.

16. *Bhandari* v. *Advocates' Committee* [1956] 1 WLR 1442, PC.

committee, for the doctor may well stand to lose his livelihood and reputation. There is, however, force in the criticism that once 'convicted' the penalty does not always fit the crime. In November 1984 two doctors who had faced the ultimate penalty of being struck off the register appealed against their sentence. One had failed on two occasions to attend two desperately sick little girls.[17] The other had committed adultery with a patient.[18] Her husband instituted the complaint. Neither denied misconduct but they said they should merely have been suspended, not struck off. The appeal hearings revealed that since 1970 no doctor suffered the ultimate penalty of striking off for failure to attend a patient. By contrast, between 1975 and 1984 four doctors out of ten disciplined for sexual misconduct were struck off. Both doctors lost their appeals. But has the GMC got its priorities right in punishing the adulterer with greater vigour than the uncaring doctor?

At the heart of the dilemma lies the notion that it is not negligence, nor an isolated failure in caring, that constitutes serious misconduct. The doctor's action or inaction must bring the profession into disrepute. Hence the emphasis the Council places on adultery and alcoholism. The Council should respond to public feeling. In 1992 the doctor who fails to visit a dying child, brushes off a sick patient as neurotic or neglects the elderly brings greater dishonour to medicine than the occasional adulterer.

Public unrest about the medical profession's ability to police its members led to the introduction of a Private Member's Bill[19] to amend the Medical Act 1983. Nigel Spearing MP proposed a modest reform. The GMC was to be given power to impose its *minimum* penalty of making registration conditional on compliance with stated conditions for up to three years, for example undertaking a refresher course or working under supervision for a while, where the doctor has 'behaved in a manner which cannot be regarded as acceptable conduct'. The GMC opposed this Bill. Doctors, they said, understood what was entailed in serious professional misconduct. 'Acceptable conduct' was too vague a test. The Council itself, it was claimed, had revised its guidelines on failure to attend patients and made clear that the prece-

17. See *Rodgers* v. *GMC*, 19 November 1984, PC.
18. *Evans* v. *GMC*, 19 November 1984, PC.
19. Medical Act 1983 (Amendment) Bill (reintroduced, albeit always unsuccessfully, in several subsequent sessions).

dent of 1984 where the doctor in a bad case[20] was struck off should be a warning to all. Outside the GMC other doctors' organizations are not so optimistic that internal reform can answer the public's concern. The British Medical Association (BMA), an organization representing many doctors, has backed Mr Spearing.[21] The BMA did not regard the revised guidelines on misconduct as sufficient to allay legitimate public concern. What the GMC has done in its latest guidance[22] on professional conduct is to outline a good standard of medical care. The criteria for proper care are unexceptionable. Emphasis is laid on conscientious assessment of the patient, consideration for him, prompt attention and a willingness to take a second opinion. But the guidelines still beg the question as to when departure from the standards set constitutes *serious* misconduct. No solid guidance by way of illustrative example is given to answer criticism that the GMC is too ready to find there has been misconduct, and admonish the doctor, rather than categorizing his conduct as serious; and unless serious misconduct is proved the GMC has no power to take any positive steps to punish the doctor and/or protect other patients.

Moreover, there is a further cause for disquiet. How many complaints ever get as far as the Professional Conduct Committee? Elaborate screening procedures exist to ensure that 'frivolous' complaints are eliminated. All letters from aggrieved patients are first scrutinized by GMC staff. If a complaint relates to an NHS doctor and concerns poor practice rather than personal misconduct such as sexual misbehaviour, the patient will be told that he must first pursue his complaint through the NHS complaints procedures. Only if the doctor is found culpable within the NHS system will the matter then be dealt with by the GMC. The second stage within the GMC is that a complaint is examined by the Preliminary Screener. If the Preliminary Screener, usually the President of the GMC, considers that there is a case to answer, he places the evidence before the Preliminary Proceedings Committee. That committee decides whether to 'commit' the doctor for a full disciplinary hearing before the Professional Conduct Committee.

20. *Rodgers* v. *GMC* (above).
21. *The Times*, 27 June 1985.
22. GMC 'Bluebook' *Professional Conduct: Fitness to Practise* (June 1990), p. 10. And see M. Brazier, 'Doctors and Discipline II' (1985), 1 *Professional Negligence*, 179.

Of course, doctors must be protected against vexatious and sometimes malicious complaints. But has the GMC in its complex, lengthy and secretive procedures got the balance between protecting doctors and protecting patients right? Jean Robinson, who has been for many years a lay member of the GMC, has argued eloquently that it has not.[23]

The GMC has made some effort to respond to public concern. It has acted on a number of malpractices, notably unsafe prescribing practices. Doctors who failed to warn the parents of a child who died of the dangers of the surgery agreed to were suspended swiftly. In 1990 four doctors involved in the sale of kidneys were found guilty of serious professional misconduct and the physician who organized the transactions was struck off the register. Disregard of professional responsibilities led to erasure from the register of two doctors in 1989. In one case a hospital doctor failed twice to attend a new mother and her baby when junior doctors became concerned about their condition. When she did attend she failed to make an adequate examination of the baby, whose heart had stopped beating, and failed to take any adequate steps to resuscitate him.

More importantly perhaps than their more interventionist approach to individual cases, the GMC has recognized the need for some limited structural reform of its procedures.[24] First, it is proposed that a lay member of the Council should be involved in the Preliminary Screening process. Where the Preliminary Screener concludes that the Council should not pursue a complaint any further, the papers and evidence will be reviewed by a lay member of the Council. No complaints would thus be dismissed without some non-medical participation in the decision. Second, the Council is proposing establishing 'performance review procedures'. The GMC remains opposed to Nigel Spearing MP's proposal for a second-tier disciplinary offence of 'unacceptable conduct', and to suggestions from Action for Victims of Medical Accidents to act on the basis of 'professional misconduct', dropping the requirement that such misconduct should be 'serious'. The GMC regards the present procedures as appropriate to matters of discipline. They do now see the need for further safeguards for patients from

23. Jean Robinson, *A Patient Voice at the GMC*, Health Rights, 1988.
24. See the Annual Report of the GMC, 1989, pp. 6–7; and see pp. 8–11, reviewing disciplinary cases before both the Professional Conduct Committee and the Preliminary Proceedings Committee.

incompetent doctors, particularly if those doctors are in the private sector beyond the jurisdiction of NHS complaints or audit procedures. The introduction of such review procedures would require amendment of the Medical Act 1983. It remains to be seen how quickly the GMC will act in attempts to reform their procedures. Have they yet done enough? Publicity may next focus on the Council's power to restore a doctor to the register after erasure.[25] Whether the GMC would find this desirable is open to question. The GMC's role is far from easy. While if it is insufficiently severe with defaulting doctors the Council will become a target of public criticism, should it lapse from strict fairness to a doctor the Council may face legal proceedings by him for breach of natural justice.[26] Yet if the Council wishes to retain pre-eminence in the regulation of medical practice it cannot shirk its responsibility to the profession and the public.

The role of the Privy Council

I have mentioned in passing the right of a doctor to appeal against any decision of the Professional Conduct Committee to the Privy Council. The hearing will not be before the entire Council of politicians, ex-politicians and assorted dignitaries but before the Law Lords and usually one other Privy Councillor. There will be a complete rehearing of the evidence. The system throughout is designed to ensure total fairness to the doctor. The complainant has no right of appeal if he is dissatisfied with the GMC decision. Perhaps he should have, to ensure fairness between patient and doctor. At the hearing the Privy Council examines the evidence in detail, but is unwilling to interfere with penalties or to take a lead in condemning any particular variety of misconduct.[27] In the exercise of general supervisory powers over the GMC the Privy Council does act directly to protect the public. The Medical Act 1983 grants the Privy Council default powers to require the General Medical Council to exercise any powers or duties conferred on it.[28] In this context the Privy Council monitors GMC action, and it is reported that in 1985 the Council in concert with the Department

25. Medical Act 1983, s. 41.
26. *R.* v. *GMC ex p. Gee* [1987] 1 WLR 564 HL.
27. See *Rodgers* v. *GMC* (above) and M. Brazier 'Doctors and Discipline' (1985), 1 *Professional Negligence*, 123 and 179.
28. Medical Act 1983, s. 50.

of Health put pressure on the GMC to extend its definition of serious professional misconduct to include a greater range of omissions to treat patients.[29]

The action for malpractice

Whatever the General Medical Council should be doing, it is not ordinarily concerned with isolated medical accidents, because even the best doctor can err, nor has the Council any power to compensate an injured patient. That is the function of the courts by way of an action for malpractice, that is, an action for negligence. More and more patients are resorting to litigation. The reaction of the doctors has been one of unsurprising horror. Insurance against professional liability began to cost them more and more. Doctors have traditionally belonged to medical defence organizations, professional associations which indemnify them against liability but are not commercial insurance companies. Subscriptions to medical defence organizations rose from £40 a year in 1978 to nearly £1,400 in 1989. More and more was being paid out in compensation to patients. In 1989 one of the leading defence organizations, the Medical Protection Society, announced plans for differential subscriptions. Doctors in 'high-risk' specialties, such as obstetrics, where litigation is common, would be asked to pay £4,000 to £5,000 for indemnity. Commercial insurance companies began to eye the 'medical market'. These events led the Department of Health, which since 1988 had in any case been paying two thirds of their subscription for hospital doctors, to act promptly. From January 1990 hospital doctors within the NHS have been indemnified directly by their employing health authority. I shall assess the effect on medical litigation of this NHS indemnity in Chapter 7. Cynical observers suggest that one immediate effect of lessening the burden on doctors' pockets will be a decrease in complaints by doctors about medical litigation. But the financial cost to them of litigation was never the doctors' only grievance. Distinguished doctors see the threat of litigation as harmful to the development of medicine. They claim it will lead to defensive medicine. Doctors will take the course of action least likely to result in a court case rather than that which they judge to be medically desirable. They cite the experience of the USA, where malpractice actions are epidemic. For example, it has been argued that

29. See *The Times*, 23 May 1985.

the rate of Caesarian birth in certain states has climbed steadily because if the baby is delivered by surgery and proves to be damaged the risk that the doctor will be sued is minimized. Finally, doctors see a finding of negligence against them as a blot on their career. The lawyer may perceive the negligence action as providing a means of compensation for injury, a finding that a man on one day committed an error as all men do. The doctor sees it differently. And so do many patients.

The malpractice action is not any more popular with patients[30] either, once they are enmeshed in the process of law. Litigation is enormously costly. In one claim relating to the treatment of a premature baby who succumbed to near blindness allegedly as a result of negligent treatment, the costs of the action already exceed the amount of agreed damages by over £80,000. The legal process is also beset by delay. The premature baby is 12 now and the case is still not completed. The cards often seem stacked in the doctors' and the health authorities' favour. Even though the health authorities have taken over the task of indemnifying doctors, many doctors still belong to the highly professional defence organizations, and many health authorities still contract out defending claims to the two major defence organizations, the Medical Protection Society and the Medical Defence Union. The claim will in many cases be defended all the way. The burden is on the patient to prove negligence. He must get expert witnesses to back him. There will be no investigation of *why* things went wrong. Instead there will be a gladiatorial contest between lawyers and the experts called as witnesses. The outcome of the trial may depend on whose lawyer asks the right questions.[31] And it is a sad fact that too many plaintiffs' lawyers are not very good at their job. The emergence of the pressure group Action for Victims of Medical Accidents has helped patients, but few patients enthuse over the idea of an action for malpractice as a remedy for negligent treatment. In Part II I look at the malpractice action in detail and consider what changes are necessary in the way the law works. I shall look, too, to see whether, if the malpractice action fails to provide any mechanism for impartial investigation of medical mishaps, other complaints procedures fill the gap.

30. For a damning indictment of the current system of medical litigation, see C. Ham, R. Dingwall, P. Fenn and D. Harris, *Medical Negligence: Compensation and Accountability*, King's Fund Institute/Centre for Socio-Legal Studies, Oxford, 1988.
31. See the forceful views expressed to the American Bar Association by Dr Havard, Secretary to the BMA, *The Times*, 19 July 1985.

The National Health Service

No investigation of the control of medicine in Britain would be complete without looking at the operation of the NHS. I do not attempt a survey of health services law as such; that is done elsewhere.[32] Throughout this book, though, it can be seen that the existence of the NHS and the framework of statutes and regulations which make up the rules for the health service dramatically affect the legal relationship of doctors, patients and other medical staff. Attention will be drawn to these features of the NHS in Part II and in Chapter 16 on General Practice.

NHS statutes such as the National Health Service Act 1977, the Health Services Act 1980, the Health and Social Security Act 1984 and the National Health Service and Community Care Act 1990 are largely concerned with the constitution of the service. Parliament creates by statute the authorities who administer the health service, and provides for the services available and payment to those who administer them. The last fifteen years have seen constant change in the details of the service's administration. Powers and duties have been transferred through different tiers of authorities. The controversial 1990 Act is difficult to evaluate. In its aim to make the NHS more competitive and cost-conscious there may well be implications not just for the way services are provided but also for the quality of those services and the rights of patients. These implications will be evaluated in Part II. One matter must be mentioned now. The Act provides for health authorities to contract with each other and with general practitioners for the provision of services. Section 4(3) makes it clear that such contracts '. . . shall not be regarded for any purpose as giving rise to contractual rights or liabilities'. Disputes as to the 'contract' will be decided by the Secretary of State for Health, not the courts.

Supplementing the legislation is a mass of regulations made by ministers under powers granted them by statutes. Regulations deal with some of the patient's most crucial concerns, for example the general practitioner's obligations to the service and his patients. Finally a mass of literature emanates from the Department of Health in London giving information and guidance to health authorities and to individual doctors. Guidance on matters of long-term general import-

32. See J. D. Finch, *Health Services Law*, Sweet & Maxwell, London, 1980.

ance comes in health circulars. Circulars cover a number of issues affecting patients' rights. The present procedure for dealing with hospital complaints, the new rules on NHS indemnity and the procedure for managing claims by patients are just three examples. Circulars up-dating doctors on medical developments may be crucial to a malpractice action. If a circular has warned of the danger of a particular drug, this may help a patient prescribed the drug prove that the doctor was at fault. Finally, health circulars themselves may provoke litigation, as did the DHSS circular advising doctors on the right of girls under 16 to confidential advice on contraception.

A right to health care?

Ultimate responsibility for the health of the NHS lies with the Secretary of State for Health. The National Health Services Act 1977 provides in section 1:

It is the Secretary of State's duty to continue the promotion in England and Wales of a comprehensive health service designed to secure improvement:
(a) in the physical and mental health of people of those countries and
(b) in the prevention, diagnosis and treatment of illness and for that purpose to provide or secure effective provision of services in accordance with the Act.

Section 3 of the Act imposes on the Minister a further duty to provide to such extent as he considers necessary to meet all reasonable requirements a whole range of services including hospital accommodation, medical, dental, nursing and ambulance services and such other services as are required for the diagnosis and treatment of illness. High-sounding sentiments and expressions of political will, but is there any legal significance in this 'duty' imposed on the Health Minister? Do patients have a right to health care? In 1979 four patients who had spent long periods vainly awaiting hip-replacement surgery went to court alleging that the Health Minister had failed in his duties under section 1 to promote a comprehensive health service and under section 3 to provide the appropriate hospital accommodation and facilities for orthopaedic surgery. The patients alleged: (1) that their period on the waiting list was longer than was medically advisable, and (2) that their wait resulted from a shortage of facilities, caused in part by a decision not to build a new hospital block on the grounds of cost. The patients asked for an order compelling the Minister to act and for compensation for their pain and suffering. The Court of Appeal[33] held that (i) the financial constraints to which the Minister was subject had to be considered in assessing what amounts to reasonable requirements for hospital and medical services; (ii) the decision as to what was required was for the Minister, and the court could intervene only where a Minister acted utterly unreasonably so as to frustrate the policy of the Act. An individual patient could not claim damages from the Minister for pain and suffering. The patients lost the immediate legal battle. They gained valuable publicity.[34] And the courts did not entirely abdicate control over the Minister. A public-spirited patient, resigned to getting no damages himself, might try again for an order against any Minister who he alleged had totally subverted the health service, for example a Minister using his position and powers exclusively to benefit private medicine at the expense of the NHS. Chances of success are not high, and of course the government of the day could always change the law, but they can be made to do it openly and not be permitted to pay lip service to a duty to a health service which may have been abandoned.

None the less, as against the Minister, the Court of Appeal clearly rejected any legally enforceable right to health care actionable by a patient for his own benefit. Does any such right exist against the local health authority? In 1987 the parents of a very sick baby who needed surgery for a heart defect sought to enforce such a right on their son's behalf. They applied to the Divisional Court by way of an application for judicial review for a court order that their son be operated on. The health authority explained that lack of resources and lack of trained nurses meant that the baby kept missing out on his operation to other more urgent cases. The court refused to make an order that the operation be carried out immediately.[35] The parents had no right to demand immediate treatment for their son. The health authority could do only what was reasonable within their limited resources, human and financial. It is difficult to see what else the court could have done. The court could not provide the resources needed to operate on all

---

33. R. v. *Secretary of State for Social Services, ex p. Hincks.* The first instance judgement is reported (1979) 123 Sol. J. 436. The appeal judgement remains unreported but is discussed by Finch, op. cit., pp. 38–9.

34. See Finch, op. cit., p. 39.

35. R. v. *Central Birmingham H. A. ex p. Walker, The Times,* 26 November 1988; R. v. *Central Birmingham H. A. ex p. Collier, The Times,* 6 January 1988 CA.

sick babies. In effect, the judges were being asked to decide that baby X needed surgery more urgently than baby Y, and judges are not qualified to make clinical judgements. The absence of any right to health care has a number of worrying implications. In particular it has the effect of encouraging overstretched health authorities to withdraw services if resources are stretched rather than to struggle on doing their best. For while patients have no right to demand care, once a patient is admitted to a clinic or hospital a duty of care to him arises. If, owing to lack of resources, he suffers some injury resulting from lack of care, he may have a right to compensation from the authority. It will often be 'legally safer' to close an underfunded casualty unit rather than seek to keep going with weary overworked staff.

The courts may have refused to recognize a right to demand care, but they have retained a right to scrutinize the reasonableness of health authority decisions. In *R.* v *St Mary's Hospital Ethical Committee ex p. Harriott*,[36] Mrs Harriott had been refused treatment by the IVF (test-tube baby) unit. The unit's informal ethical advisory committee had supported the doctors' decision not to treat Mrs Harriott because she had been rejected by the local social services department as a potential adoptive or foster mother and because she had criminal convictions for prostitution offences. She challenged their decision in an application for judicial review. The judge held that the grounds for refusing her treatment were lawful. But he said refusal of treatment on any non-medical grounds could be reviewed by a court. It would be unlawful to reject a patient because of her race or religion or other irrelevant ground. A patient denied renal dialysis or surgery because the consultant in charge refused to treat divorced people or Labour Party members might well have a remedy. However, judges, it must be remembered, tend to be conservative and are notoriously unwilling to overturn doctors' decisions.

Public and private medicine

Fifteen years ago private medicine was of marginal interest in England. The trend has been reversed. Private health insurance is booming and luxury private hospitals are mushrooming throughout the country. The morality of public versus private medicine and the medical merits of the two systems are for others to assess. The differences in the

36. *R.* v. *St Mary's Ethical Committee ex p. Harriott* [1988] 1 FLR 512.

operation of the law relating to doctor and patient depending on whether the patient is NHS or private may surprise some.

At the basis of the legal difference between public and private patient lies the fact that the NHS patient has no contract with his doctor or anyone else. The private patient has a contract with his chosen doctor. That doctor must personally carry out any agreed treatment or surgery. The NHS patient may be operated on by any doctor employed by the health authority or NHS trust. He has no choice of surgeon. NHS and private doctors are both obliged to do their best. A contract may impose more stringent obligations. One patient paid £20 for a vasectomy. Nature reversed the operation. The trial judge held that the surgeon contracted to render the man sterile. When his wife conceived again, the surgeon, albeit his surgery was faultless, was in breach of contract.[37] The Court of Appeal reversed that decision, deciding two to one that that contract did not guarantee sterility.[38] Private practice shuddered with relief. The advantages in legal terms by no means always lie with the private patient. We shall see that when it comes to proving negligence the NHS patient has the edge. Something goes wrong in the operating theatre and it is not denied that someone must have been careless. The NHS patient simply sues the health authority, claiming that one of their employees is responsible, and the authority has to pay. The consultant operating privately will not be acting as the employee of the hospital or clinic. If all the medical staff put up a wall of silence and refuse to give evidence, the private patient will be unable to show who was careless and thus must lose his action.[39]

One other matter should be noted in connection with private medicine. The NHS complaints procedures are far from perfect but at least they exist. A private patient who believes that his treatment was negligent may find that the only way to vent his grievance is to sue, even though monetary compensation is not uppermost in his mind. In *Kralj* v. *McGrath*[40] Mrs Kralj endured a nightmare delivery and her second twin died. She sued her obstetrician because she was unable to find out in any other way what went wrong and thus call the doctor to account. Moreover, private patients, who pay increasingly large fees for treatment, are not likely to be deterred from legal action by the feeling

37. *Thake* v. *Maurice* [1984] 2 All ER 513.
38. *Thake* v. *Maurice* [1986] 1 All ER 497, CA.
39. See pp. 157 ff.
40. [1986] 1 All ER 54.

some NHS patients have that they should be grateful for any treatment at all. And if the private patient needs remedial treatment to put right the result of the doctor's negligence, and wants to have the treatment in the private sector, he will need money to pay for that remedial treatment. All these factors perhaps explain why private patients reach for a writ more readily than their NHS counterparts. Finally, of course, the patient who can afford to pay for medical treatment is more likely to be able to afford to pay for legal advice.

The state of the law

I set out earlier in this chapter four objectives for the law relating to the practice of medicine. The regulation of the profession by the profession still falls short of what the public demands. I have indicated that the provision for compensation for injured patients is not ideal, though there have been some improvements since 1987. In Part II I elaborate on this theme and cast doubt too on the adequacy of complaints procedures. The value of the law's role in relation to difficult ethical and moral issues of medicine is dealt with in the next chapter and in Part III. Doctors and lawyers regard themselves as practitioners of ancient and honourable professions. A fraternal respect exists between senior members of the two professions. Judges, we shall see, have been hesitant to criticize doctors but have fewer inhibitions about intervening in other professions. Attacking the medical profession is easy, and in certain circles is becoming a popular pastime. Doctors as we have seen are a vulnerable target. They may doubt whether the law at present serves them well. We shall see that astute lawyers can use the law to keep the doctors out of court,[41] to defeat claims against them, and to prevent investigation of errors.[42] In the long term this may damage the doctors as much as it now frustrates and infuriates aggrieved patients.

Medico-legal problems have a high profile today. Rarely a day passes without media attention to some dispute about the role of the law in the regulation of medicine. This attention comes in diverse forms. It may be a tabloid exposure of medical and legal blunders. A brain-damaged child suffers first at the hands of one set of professionals who allegedly bungle her delivery, and then at the hands of another

41. Chapter 7.
42. Chapter 9.

25

who bungle her claim for compensation. The 'serious' press carry articles on the problems of legislating on abortion, genetic engineering, the care of the dying and countless other medico-legal dramas. Attempts to answer the problems arising from medicine tend to be piecemeal. Changes are made to the ways in which hospital doctors are indemnified, but radical proposals to change the whole basis for compensation for patients are rejected. Parliament legislates on embryo research, and tacks on to that legislation an ill-thought-out amendment of the abortion laws voted on after several separate votes late at night. Meanwhile medical advances outstrip the capacity of the law to deal with them. Increasing numbers of students, law students, medical students and nurses now study medical law. Postgraduate degrees in medical ethics and law have mushroomed. Perhaps these developments in the study of medico-legal problems may lead to a more rational and comprehensive approach to the legal regulation of medicine and the proper protection of patients.

CHAPTER 2

Medicine, Moral Dilemmas and the Law

Medical ethics make news today but are far from new. From the formulation of the Hippocratic Oath in Ancient Greece to the present day, doctors have debated among themselves the codes of conduct which should govern the art of healing. These days philosophers, theologians, lawyers and journalists insist on joining the debate. Outside interest, or interference as doctors sometimes see it, is not new either. Hippocrates himself was a philosopher. The Church through the centuries has asserted its right to pronounce on medical matters of spiritual import, such as abortion and euthanasia, and to uphold the sanctity of life.

The Hippocratic Oath makes interesting reading. Its first premise is that the doctor owes loyalty to his teachers and his brethren. Obligations to exercise skill for the benefit of patients' health come second. Abortion, direct euthanasia and abetting suicide are prohibited. Improper sexual relations with patients are banned. Confidentiality in all dealings with patients is imposed. In 2,500 years these basic precepts of good medical practice changed little. Dramatic change in the kinds of moral and ethical problems confronting the doctor came only in the last fifty years. The art of the Greek philosopher physician became a science to many of its practitioners. Science has given the doctor tools to work marvels undreamed of by earlier generations. Women whose blocked Fallopian tubes prevent natural conception can be offered the hope of a test-tube baby. Women who have never ovulated can become mothers via egg donation. Babies born with spina bifida and other disabling handicaps can be saved from early death by delicate and complex surgery. Soon, some forms of foetal handicap may be correctable by surgery carried out while the baby is still in the womb. And certain genetic disorders may be curable by means of genetic manipulation of the embryo. Ventilators keep alive accident victims whose heart and lungs have given up. Dialysis and transplant surgery save kidney, liver and heart patients from certain death. The list of technological miracles is endless. They have placed in the hands of the doctors powers which through the ages men have ascribed to God alone.

Technological progress has been matched by social change. People are less and less willing to accept without question the decisions of those who exercise power, be they judges, politicians or doctors. Paternalism is out of fashion. Feminists ask why doctors should determine which infertile women receive treatment. Lawyers and philosophers, not to mention parents, wonder why the doctor is best qualified to judge whether a damaged baby's quality of life is such as to make life-saving surgery desirable. The power of the doctor to end life, whether by switching off a ventilator or by deciding not to give a patient a place in a dialysis unit, disturbs us all. These acute moral dilemmas are just as acutely felt by the doctor. His difficulty is accentuated by the fact that the new technology cannot be made available to all those in need. There is just not enough money or resources in the National Health Service.[1] Above all, the medical profession in 1992 faces a society more deeply divided on virtually every moral question than ever before. The public demands a say in medical decision-making on sensitive ethical issues. Yet from the hot potato of whether doctors should help lesbians to have children by artificial insemination, through the debates on abortion to euthanasia, the doctor who seeks guidance from public opinion will discover division, bitterness and confusion.

Questions of medical ethics arise throughout the whole field of medical practice. The ethics of the doctor/patient relationship are discussed in Chapter 3 and throughout Part II. Of the ethical and moral questions before the doctors today the most divisive revolve around matters of life and death and the concept of the sanctity of human life. It is the application of views on the sanctity of human life that is dealt

1. See J. K. Mason and R. A. McCall Smith, *Law and Medical Ethics*, Butterworths, London, 1991, Chapter 11; G. H. Mooney, 'Cost-benefit Analysis and Medical Ethics' (1980) 6 J. Med. Ethics 177.

with in this chapter, and to which I return in detail in Part III of the book.

The sanctity of life: Judaeo-Christian tradition[2]

For the devout Roman Catholic the concept of the sanctity of life is relatively straightforward. Human life is a gift from God and thus is literally sacred. Any act which deliberately ends a life is wrong. Life begins at conception and therefore abortion, and research on or disposal of an artificially created embryo, a test-tube embryo, is never permissible. Indeed the truly obedient Catholic will abstain also from any form of non-natural contraception. Life ends when God ends it. No degree of suffering or handicap justifies a premature release effected by men. Yet even so there remain grey areas in the application of belief that life is sacred. The Roman Catholic Church forbids abortion even when pregnancy threatens the woman's life. But a pregnant woman with cancer of the womb may be allowed a hysterectomy albeit that the child will then die. This is called the doctrine of double effect. Abortion is banned because the only intent of that operation is to kill the child. An operation for cancer incidentally destroys the child but that was not its primary purpose. At the other end of life, the Church, while condemning euthanasia, does not demand that extraordinary means be taken to prolong it. Where is the line drawn? Should a grossly handicapped baby be subjected to painful surgery with a low ultimate success rate? Must antibiotics be administered to the terminal cancer patient stricken with pneumonia? The doctrine of double effect, the application of a distinction between ordinary and extraordinary means to preserve life, have generated substantial literature and debate. Even accepting that areas of doubt exist for him, the orthodox Roman Catholic remains fortunate in the security of his beliefs on the sanctity of life, beliefs shared by many fundamentalist Christians of the Protestant tradition.

Many other practising Christians, who subscribe in essence to the doctrine of the sanctity of life, see further problems once they seek to apply their faith. Contraception is morally acceptable to the majority, and indeed to very many Roman Catholics now. The exact point when

2. See J. Finnis, *Natural Law and Natural Rights*, OUP, 1980; O. Donovan, *Begotten not Made*, OUP, 1984.

life begins and becomes sacred then becomes of the utmost importance to determine the morality of certain contraceptive methods. Abortion to save the mother's life is accepted by many Christians, as it always has been in the Jewish faith. The child's life may deserve protection but not at the expense of his mother's. This step taken, the extent to which the child's life may be sacrificed to his mother's has to be ascertained. Is a threat to the mother's mental stability sufficient? What about the women who suffer rape and conceive as a result? Today there is the question of the status of the early embryo created in the test-tube. These and many other issues have caused dissension and distress in the councils of the Church of England and the other Christian traditions. For example a number of eminent Anglican theologians[3] have found that research on the early embryo is acceptable and raises no conflict within their Christian faith. This stance received the support of the Archbishop of York[4] in debates in the House of Lords. Other Anglicans remain adamantly opposed to any form of destructive research on embryos. Nevertheless the Christian, Jew, or adherent of any religious faith at least enjoys a framework of belief. The sanctity of life has meaning for him because that life was given by God.

The sanctity of life in a secular society

In Britain today the numbers of people practising any religious faith are in a minority. A fair number still describe themselves as Church of England when entering hospital or joining the army. Churches are still popular for weddings and funerals. Thriving communities of Jews and Muslims remain committed to their traditions. But Britain is overwhelmingly a secular society. The majority of the population is uncommitted to any religious creed. How many people retain a general belief in God as the Creator is open to question. For those who do not, what meaning has the sanctity of life? If life is not bestowed by God, on what grounds is it sacred?

There can be no doubt that belief in the sanctity of life does survive the death or absence of religious belief. Taking life is as reprehensible to many agnostics and atheists as it is to the Christian or the Jew. Indeed very many such people have been more consistent in

3. See, for example, Keith Ward, 'An Irresolvable Debate' in A. Dyson and J. Harris (eds.), *Experiments on Embryos*, Routledge, 1989, Chapter 7.
4. HL Official Report, 15 January 1988, cols. 1461–6.

upholding and fighting for the sanctity of life than have certain warmongering Christian priests or those 'Christians' who in America gather round the gaols to celebrate the death penalty's return.[5] But what for a secular society is the basis of the sanctity of human life? In fact for most people who are not philosophers the answer is simple. They share a deep and embedded instinct that taking human life is wrong. Life is man's most precious possession. All other possessions, all potential joys, depend upon his continued existence. An attack on one individual's right to life which goes unchecked threatens us all. Our autonomy is undermined. Our security becomes precarious. The move away from a concept of life as God-given, however, has certain consequences. If at the basis of belief in the sanctity of life is a perception of the freedom of the individual, of the joy that life can bring, then the quality of life comes into account. The right of the foetus to come into possession of his own life, his own freedom, must be balanced against his mother's rights over her own life and body. When pain and handicap cause an individual to cease to wish to live, then he may be free to end that life. It is his to do with as he wishes. Individual choice becomes central to applying the concept of the sanctity of life. No one must interfere with an adult's choices on continued life. Whether any other adult can be compelled to assist a fellow to end his life raises more difficult questions. And the concept of freedom of choice offers little guidance where an individual is incapable of choice. Nevertheless this uncertain position commands a fair degree of generous support. People have an intrinsic right to life. Life is sacred, but not 'absolutely inviolable'.[6] This is the view occupying the 'middle ground'.

Sanctity of life: a different perception[7]

The latest stage in the debate on the sanctity of life involves an attack

5. See the correspondence in *The Times*, 27 August to 2 September 1985, following an article by Paul Johnson (*The Times*, 26 August) calling for a ban on abortion and embryo research but a return for the death penalty.
6. See M. Phillips and J. Dawson, *Doctors' Dilemmas*, Harvester Press, London, 1984, pp. 22–6; and see that same work generally for its support of the 'middle ground' of the debate.
7. See in particular two persuasive and lively works: Jonathan Glover, *Causing Death and Saving Lives*, Penguin, Harmondsworth, 1977; J. M. Harris, *The Value of Life*, Routledge & Kegan Paul, London, 1985.

on the whole idea that 'taking human life is intrinsically wrong'. Life is seen as having no inherent value. Life has value only if it is worth living. Taking life is wrong because 'it is wrong to destroy a life which is worth living'.[8] Side by side with a move to concentrate attention on the quality of life alone comes a redefinition of human life deserving of protection. It is *persons*,[9] not all human animals, whose lives have value. Unless there is capacity for self-awareness, for the individual to recognize himself as a functioning human person able to relate to other persons, he has no life of the quality and kind which must be preserved. Certain consequences follow. A person who can reason must be allowed to judge for himself whether continued life is worth it. A human who cannot reason for himself, who is not a person, may have that judgement made for him by others. Providing painless release for a person who considers his life not worth living, or an individual whose capacity for self-awareness has gone so that he has ceased to be a person, becomes a moral action. The unborn are not persons. They have no rights against their mothers who are persons. Abortion is moral and it may even be considered immoral not to abort a seriously damaged foetus. Research on embryos to benefit existing persons, whether by improving treatment for infertility or seeking a cure for congenital disease, is not only morally permissible but almost a moral imperative. Euthanasia of the hopelessly brain-damaged with no hope of recovery is entirely acceptable and may, in strictly controlled circumstances, be involuntary.

Sanctity of life and the medical profession[10]

No doubt the disparity of views among the general population is reflected in the personal views of many doctors. Doctors, however, actually have to take decisions on the sorts of matters others debate. How far and in what fashion is the sanctity of life a central medical ethic? The Declaration of Geneva[11] includes the following undertaking:

8. Glover, op. cit., Chapter 3.
9. Harris, op. cit., Chapter 1.
10. See R. Gillon, *Philosophical Medical Ethics*, Wiley, Chichester, 1986.
11. For the Declaration of Geneva, the Hippocratic Oath and other codes of medical ethics, see Mason and McCall Smith, op. cit., Appendices A–F, pp. 251–61.

I will maintain the utmost respect for human life from the time of conception; even under threat, I will not use my medical knowledge contrary to the laws of humanity.

When the Declaration was first formulated in 1947, 'the utmost respect for human life' no doubt imported to most doctors a prohibition on abortion, at any rate where the mother's life was not in danger, and a complete ban on any form of euthanasia. The Declaration was amended and up-dated in Sydney in 1968. By 1968 abortion on grounds other than immediate danger to the mother had been legalized in Britain and parts of the USA. Within a decade debate was to flourish within respected medical circles as to whether keeping alive all handicapped babies was right, and whether prolonging the life of the sick and elderly had not been taken to extremes by modern medicine. What then does the utmost respect for human life entail?

What it does not entail, and what has never existed in any code of medical ethics, is an injunction to preserve life at any price.[12] The prevention of suffering is as much the doctor's task as the prolongation of life. Alas, the two cannot always be complementary. The doctor struggling to interpret and apply his obligation to respect life faces a number of quandaries.

The beginning and end of life

An admonition to respect human life would be easier to adhere to if there was uniform agreement as to when life begins and ends. Few biologists now see the fertilization of the woman's egg as the beginning of a new life. They argue that egg and sperm are living organisms and point out that many fertilized eggs fail to implant. The fertilized egg may still split into two, and in rare cases grow not into a baby but a hydatiform mole, a cancer threatening the woman's life. Fertilization, it is said, is just one further step in a continuing process. Acceptance of that view renders acceptable use of contraceptive devices, including the 'morning-after' pill, which prevent implantation. At what stage then does life begin and attract respect? We have noted the argument that the foetus has no status because it is not a person. This appears from observation of medical practice to attract little support among doctors. A growing view appears to be that the foetus as potential life attracts

12. See Phillips and Dawson, op. cit., p. 26.

greater and greater status as it grows to full human likeness.[13] This gradualist perception of the embryo has resulted in the support for embryo research given by most doctors' organizations. The Royal College of Obstetricians and Gynaecologists, the Medical Research Council, the British Medical Association and, after initial opposition, the Royal College of General Practitioners have all backed embryo research up to fourteen, or at the most seventeen, days. No doubt such 'official' and prestigious support for research helped to ensure that Members of Parliament eventually voted to permit research for a period of up to fourteen days in the Human Fertilisation and Embryology Act 1990.

The end of life too has no definite marker any more. It can no longer be equated with the cessation of breathing and heartbeat. Resuscitation techniques to restart the heart still enthrall the press, with tales of the 'man who came back from the dead'. The development of life-support machines to replace heart and lung functions during surgery or after traumatic injury demonstrate that life can go on although the heart has stopped. When then does death occur? A definition of death as the irreversible cessation of all activity in the brain stem[14] is generally accepted within the medical profession although some doctors still occasionally express public doubts. For the lay public the decision to agree to switch off the life-support machine of a relative causes individual anguish, and anxiety occasionally surfaces that a desire for organs for transplantation might prompt too swift a pronouncement of death. These are problems solved by procedures designed to ensure that no anticipation of death is allowed, by reassurance and sympathy offered by medical staff to waiting relatives. The moral dilemma relating to dying arises a stage before brain-stem death. A person may suffer irreversible brain damage, be irreversibly comatose and yet still show signs of some activity in the brain stem. He is not dead according to the current definition of death. Some argue that this definition should be extended to include the irreversibly comatose. For those who regard human life as of value only where the individual can recognize himself as a person, loss of consciousness is equated with

13. ibid., pp. 47–9, 82–5; Mason and McCall Smith, op. cit., pp. 112–14.
14. See Chapter 20 and also Ian Kennedy, *The Unmasking of Medicine*, Allen & Unwin, London, 1981, Chapter 7. And see the *Guardian*, 6 August 1986, expressing disturbing doubts on brain death.

physical death.[15] But is such a move really euthanasia by the back door? The question of continuing to keep alive the unkindly named 'human vegetable' will not go away. It must be faced, not by a surreptitious moving back of the moment of death but by addressing ourselves to the question of whether the doctor may ever kill.[16]

Killing and letting die

I noted earlier that codes of medical ethics have never commanded the doctor to prolong life at any cost. Caring for a patient as he dies in peace and dignity may be the last service his doctor can perform for him. Doctors and nurses tending the terminally ill in hospices are accorded the highest respect. The doctor's obligation to relieve suffering may on occasion cause him to refrain from prolonging life. Asked whether a doctor should invariably invoke every weapon of medical progress to prevent death, people of every shade of opinion would answer, no. For the Roman Catholic the test would be whether 'extraordinary means' must be resorted to in order to prolong that life. Extensive surgery on a dying cancer patient offering him only weeks more life would be ruled out. Antibiotics to cure a sudden, unrelated infection pose a more difficult moral dilemma. Nevertheless for most of us, religious or irreligious, this satirical rhyme sums up our attitude:

> Thou shalt not kill; but needst not strive
> Officiously to keep alive.

We revolt at the thought of a doctor killing a patient directly. We accept and are content to leave to the medical profession a liberty to refrain from further treatment in a hopeless case.

Scratch the surface of this popular attitude and problems and doubts emerge. What amounts to 'officiously' keeping alive? Is the doctor alone to judge when a life is worth living, for example to decide when a patient with kidney disease qualifies for dialysis? Lawyers and philosophers enjoy the endless argument these issues generate. Doctors on the whole do not. They have to provide answers.[17] Where a patient is sane, conscious and an adult, the dilemma, albeit no less distressing,

15. Glover, op. cit., pp. 43–5.
16. See Chapter 21, and also Phillips and Dawson, op. cit., pp. 33–4.
17. ibid., p. 34.

has today a relatively easy answer. The patient should decide whether treatment continues.[18] Indeed the doctor, if he has been frank with the patient, has little choice but to leave it to the patient. He cannot lawfully give treatment without the patient's consent. Once a patient has decided to reject further treatment the doctor must normally desist. Suicide, if refusing treatment can be so classified, is no longer a crime. The freedom of the individual to make his own moral choices where he is able is largely unquestioned.

A more acute dilemma arises where the patient cannot make his own decision. Here the distinction between killing and letting die takes a central role. Asked if a doctor, or anyone else, should be allowed to smother a brain-damaged patient, the average man recoils in horror. But when a parent at the end of his tether does the same to his dying handicapped child he may attract public sympathy and understanding. Public attitudes to what the press call 'mercy killing' are not consistent.[19] Not surprisingly then, the distinction between killing and letting die has not been allowed to go unchallenged. It is subject to a three-pronged attack:

(1) New technology makes the distinction between letting die and killing difficult if not impossible to put into practice. (2) It is argued that there is no valid moral distinction between killing and letting die. (3) Some writers have maintained that directly and painlessly killing a patient may be a morally superior decision to leaving him to a slow undignified death.

The problems posed for the doctor by the technology at his disposal cannot be sidestepped. An accident victim rushed into hospital is put on a life-support machine. All that can be done is done for him. He proves to be irreversibly brain-damaged but not brain-dead. If he had never been put on a machine, then failing to put him on the machine would be allowing him to die. Disconnecting the machine, a positive act, may be seen as killing him,[20] though comatose patients disconnected from life-support machines have lived on for several years in

18. See Chapter 21.
19. Contrast the public sympathy attracted by a divorced mother convicted of the manslaughter of her son, who was dying of cystic fibrosis, with the crowds who gathered to hurl insults and hate at Paul Brown, convicted of the murder of his Down's syndrome baby daughter.
20. See I. Kennedy, 'Switching Off Life Support Machines: The Legal Implications' [1977] Crim. LR 443.

some cases.[21] Into which category, killing or letting die, does not feeding the patient fall? A newborn baby grossly handicapped may never demand food, may be unable to feed naturally from breast or bottle. Is omitting to tube-feed the baby killing or letting die? What about failing to operate to remove a stomach obstruction? Into which category falls failure to perform delicate and painful surgery to relieve hydrocephalus (water on the brain)? The difficulties of applying the distinction in practice can be enumerated endlessly.

So, why not abandon the distinction altogether? In favour of such change of direction are several apparently persuasive arguments.[22] The conception of the value of human life as dependent on self-awareness and the quality of life renders it moral to end a life once self-awareness has gone, or, as in the case of a newborn baby, where it has never developed. A patient still able to reason but living in pain, distress and handicap retains the right to make his own judgement on his quality of life. Otherwise the decision may be taken from him. Once quality of life, not life itself, is the determining factor, it follows that directly killing the patient may be a moral imperative. For if the patient's quality of life is such that life has no intrinsic value, is it not kinder to end that life painlessly than let him drag on for more days, weeks or months in undignified 'sub-human' misery? If one accepts the basic premise that the value of human life is solely dependent on life being objectively 'worth living', then in pure logic progress to acceptance that a doctor may sometimes kill his patient must follow.

Pure logic does not, however, govern most human reactions. Voluntary euthanasia, assisting a patient who desires to die, has a number of committed proponents. Involuntary euthanasia, the doctor directly killing patients whose prospects are hopeless, has very, very little support and virtually none among doctors themselves.[23] The arguments against are dismissed with some scorn by the philosopher proposing a change of attitude. Suggestions that doctors are 'playing God' ought to cut little ice unless you believe in God. Fear that powers to kill may be misused could be alleviated by proper controls. Instinctive revulsion is seen as an uninformed response.

21. See I. Kennedy, 'The Karen Quinlan Case: Problems and Proposals' (1976) 2 J. Med. Ethics.
22. Glover, op. cit., Chapters 7 and 15; Harris, op. cit., Chapter 4.
23. See Phillips and Dawson, op. cit., p. 34, and BMA *Philosophy and Practice of Medical Ethics*, 1988, p. 90.

The distinction between killing and letting die will not go away. Three factors at least militate against any introduction of involuntary euthanasia. First, the conception of life as in some sense 'sacred' in itself has a greater hold on the population as a whole than its detractors appreciate. Few may now subscribe to belief in the God of the Bible, the Talmud and the Koran. Belief in a Creator of sorts is more widespread. Belief that men must set limits on what man may do is deeply ingrained. Killing those who cannot speak for themselves remains taboo. Second, the vision of the slippery slope to euthanasia for the unfortunate and the dissenter operates to deter acceptance of involuntary euthanasia. Today the hopelessly brain-damaged, tomorrow the mentally handicapped, the day after opponents of the government is the fear of many. No elaboration of controls devised by lawyers and politicians will drive away the fear. Finally, and practically most importantly, even if the exercise of judging objectively quality of life is carried out in all good faith, how can it be achieved? Who will sit in judgement? Occasionally that task falls even now to certain doctors. There is insufficient provision for treatment of kidney failure within the NHS. Not all patients who need it can be offered dialysis. Some are left to die. The doctors decide. In Oxford doctors decided to terminate dialysis for a mentally handicapped patient. His quality of life did not justify continuing to treat him while denying others treatment. The public outcry was overwhelming. The doctors responsible were branded as 'murderers' and 'barbarians'. How much greater would that outcry have been had the decision been to kill the patient instantly? And that despite the fact that on one view killing him quickly and painlessly might be seen as 'kinder' than leaving him to die as his system was slowly poisoned by blood which his failed kidneys could not purify.[24]

Sanctity of life and the law[25]

Legislating on moral and ethical issues created fewer problems for the Victorian parliamentarian. Applying the common law posed no dilemma for the judge. He knew what was right and what was wrong.

24. See D. Brahams, 'A Doctor's Justification for Withdrawing Treatment' (1985) Vol. 135 NLJ 48.
25. See Glanville Williams, *The Sanctity of Life and the Criminal Law*, Faber & Faber, London, 1958; P. D. G. Skegg, *Law, Ethics and Medicine*, Clarendon Press, Oxford, 1984; Mason and McCall Smith, op. cit.

The Victorian was unperturbed by doubt, unconcerned by any feeling that his decision should mirror the moral attitudes of society as a whole. Women and the 'lower classes' were deemed incapable of making moral judgements in any case. Additionally the divisions in moral attitude, although they did exist, were not as deep as those pertaining today. Nor were the problems of medicine as complex. Death remained then an independent agent largely beyond the doctor's skill to combat.

Yet, despite the plethora of new ethical problems created daily by modern medicine and the changed moral climate, the law remains relatively unchanged. No statute expressly addresses the fate of the newborn infant with multiple handicap who in an earlier age would have died whatever had been done for her. Every attempt to legislate on euthanasia has stalled early in its progress through Parliament. Governments shy away from legislating, and even pronouncing on medical ethics. The first test-tube baby, Louise Brown, was born in July 1978. It was not until twelve years later that Parliament finally enacted the Human Fertilisation and Embryology Act regulating test-tube-baby techniques and all the consequent advances in reproductive technology. Before that Act, the Abortion Act 1967 stood alone as a legislative attempt specifically designed to tackle developments in medicine and altered moral outlooks. And the Abortion Act was piloted through Parliament not by the government of the day, but by a Private Member, David Steel MP. The troubled history of that Act, a compromise which pleases few, perhaps explains why governments of all political colours shy away from entering the battlefields on sanctity of human life. The debates on embryo research and the amendment to the Human Fertilisation and Embryology Bill which originally sought to reduce the time-limit for abortion[26] unleashed a bitterness and outbursts of vitriolic abuse unknown in even the most hard-fought government versus opposition confrontation.

Political disinclination to engage in debate on the sanctity of life means that to a large extent the regulation of the medical profession on issues of life and death has been left then to the profession itself within the framework of the common law. In drawing up and applying codes of practice on the treatment of the handicapped newborn, the brain-damaged and the dying, the medical profession acts within the

---

26. But ultimately resulted in a 'liberalization' of the law on late abortions; see s. 37 of the Act, below, p. 302.

constraints of the criminal law of murder and manslaughter. The doctor's exposure to the law can be brutal. The law holds its hand from laying down the code of practice within which he works. Struggling to decide on whether treatment should continue he acts within guidelines agreed within his own profession but lacking any statutory force. Ninety-nine times out of a hundred he can comfort himself with the thought that no one will question his decision in these grey areas between living and dying. On the hundredth occasion he may face the spectre of prosecution for murder or attempted murder. The distinction between killing and letting die does not operate in the criminal law to debar a charge of murder. Allowing a patient to die when it was the doctor's duty to treat him, when the doctor knew that and intended that death would ensue, is as much murder as stabbing the patient to death.

The crucial issue once more is what is the content of the doctor's duty? When is it his obligation to prolong life? Left to decide that issue according to conscience and professional opinion most of the time, doctors not unnaturally are resentful that intervention when it comes may take the form of criminal prosecution for murder. Doctors do not see themselves as murderers. Even the most vehement and passionate member of Life, believing as he will that medical decisions as to the care of the newborn are frequently wrong, err too often on the side of withholding treatment, would not place the doctor on the same moral plane as the man murdering in the course of robbery.

The reaction of the medical profession has in the main been that the law should keep out of medical ethics. Proposals to replace the existing and hazy common law with detailed legislative rules attract little enthusiasm.[27] Procedural rules about consultation, reference to codes of practice and the keeping of records of decision-making appear more acceptable. What doctors might really welcome is such legislation which additionally promises immunity from prosecution to the doctor following the correct process. Such legislation would check the maverick. It would ensure that no one doctor whose standards deviate markedly from his fellows could pursue a course of treatment or non-treatment of patients unacceptable to the majority. But it would enshrine in the law a principle that such decisions are for the doctors alone. The rest of us would be excluded from any right to a say on these matters of life and death.

27. J. Havard, 'Legislation Is Likely to Create More Difficulty Than It Resolves' (1983) 9 J. Med. Ethics 18. See also Chapter 21.

'The ultimate decisions about life and death are not simply medical decisions.' This was the view expressed in an editorial in the *British Medical Journal* in 1981.[28] I concur wholeheartedly. The meaning and application of the sanctity of life is not a matter to be left for the doctors to decide and for the philosophers to argue over. The law's involvement to ensure that society's expectations are met is inevitable. The law is very far from perfect in its operation. Reform in a society divided in its moral judgements is hard to formulate. And indeed, detailed legislation is probably undesirable even if such legislation were to be agreed on. The variation in the circumstances confronting the doctor is too great. Rules that would meet every possible medical and social dilemma the doctor may face cannot be invented. The doctor's judgement cannot and should not be excluded. What can be done, if there is a will to do so, is to stimulate greater debate on the codes of practice under which the doctor works. Greater legal and lay involvement in their development should be encouraged. The gap between lawyer and doctor needs bridging. Perhaps amendment of the law of homicide should be considered, so that a doctor alleged to have stepped beyond the bounds of the acceptable in his professional sphere remains subject to the judgement of his fellow men but avoids the horrors of an inappropriate murder trial. Doctors complain that laymen do not understand the full implications of the problems presented by the handicapped and the dying, do not appreciate the complexity of modern medical technology. Only greater openness and a greater willingness to involve those outside the medical profession in decision-making will bring about better understanding. Only better understanding of the problems of medicine will bring about better law-making.

However much any government might prefer to remain aloof from debates on medicine and morals, the developments in embryology and assisted conception have forced the British, and other European and Commonwealth governments, to legislate. There are perhaps four main aspects to the problem of legislating on the implications of modern reproductive medicine. (1) Legislation may be designed to protect patients from possible abuses, to prevent what is generally perceived as an undesirable practice creating risks of exploitation. An example of such legislation in England might be the Surrogacy Arrangements Act 1985 prohibiting commercial exploitation of surrogacy. (2) Legislation may

28. [1981] BMJ 569.

be needed because gaps in the existing law place certain patients and their families in a legal limbo. For example, if A donates an egg which is fertilized and implanted in B who carries and gives birth to the child, who in law is the child's mother? Such questions of family law and status may be complex and sometimes controversial, but a clear answer is essential to safeguard the interests of the children. (3) Developments in genetics and biotechnology create or exacerbate several legal problems. Who owns genetic information, and how should access to that information be controlled? What property rights accrue from body products? If cells from my body are used to develop a remedy to some disease, can I claim the ensuing profit made by a drug company? If a healthy gene taken from my embryo is used and inserted to replace a defective gene from my sister's embryo, to whom does the gene belong? Can human genes be patented? All these questions require a legal answer and, if legislation does not provide the answer, lengthy and expensive litigation will proliferate, as has already happened in the USA. (4) Finally, the most difficult of all aspects of legislation in this area is to decide what kinds of procedures are acceptable in our society. Are there medical possibilities whose implications are such that, though possible, they should be prohibited by law? The United Kingdom Parliament has voted to allow research on embryos up to fourteen days. In West Germany embryo research has been completely prohibited.

Legislating on what is permissible is fraught with difficulty. Emotions run high. Anti-abortion campaigners in 1990 flooded Parliament with model foetuses. Pro-embryo research lobbies played to the cameras with touching and well-timed stories of the joy brought to previously infertile women by their 'test-tube' babies. The scientific possibilities are hard to grasp and science fiction scenarios abound. Test-tube-baby technology creates fears of Aldous Huxley's *Brave New World*. But above all, each side in the moral debate believes they are right and the other is irretrievably wrong. What tends to be overlooked is this. In many ethical debates today there is no answer that will be accepted as unchallengeably right. I may believe that from fertilization my embryo is a human entity endowed with the same moral status as I am and endowed with an immaterial, immortal soul. I cannot prove my contention but nor can that contention be disproved. The question for legislators is not to find a right answer, to achieve a moral consensus, but to determine how in a liberal, democratic society legislation can be formulated in the absence of such consensus. To evade that task is to leave the scientists free rein to do as they see fit. To criticize them with hindsight is unfair and unproductive. Theologians, ethicists, lawyers and indeed all citizens must be prepared to grapple with these awkward moral dilemmas and, probably, be ready to compromise.

CHAPTER 3

A Relationship of Trust and Confidence

Whatever, in connection with my professional practice, or not in connection with it, I see or hear in the life of men, which ought not to be spoken of abroad, I will not divulge, as reckoning that all such should be kept secret.

The Hippocratic Oath

I will respect the secrets which are confided in me, even after the patient has died.

Declaration of Geneva (as amended Sydney 1968)

Doctors, like priests and lawyers, must be able to keep secrets. For medical care to be effective, for patients to have trust in their doctor, they must have confidence that they can safely talk frankly to him. An obligation of confidence to patients lies at the heart of all codes of medical ethics, but comparison of the two quotations above shows that the obligation is not always absolute. The Ancient Greek physician undertook not to divulge that which ought not to be spoken of abroad. He presumably judged what fell into that category. The Declaration of Geneva is much more stringent. *Any* information given by a patient in confidence must be kept secret for ever. A moment's reflection reveals the problems inherent in both absolute and relative obligations of confidence. An absolute obligation leaves the doctor powerless to do anything but try to persuade his patient to allow him to take action when a patient tells him he has AIDS but is still sleeping with his wife, when a mother tells him of her violent impulses towards her baby, when examination reveals that a patient may be a rapist sought by the police. Examples could be elaborated endlessly. On the other hand a relative obligation, which leaves the doctor free to breach confidence when he judges that some higher duty to another person or to society applies, may disincline patients from seeking necessary treatment. This may damage not only the patient but also those very people vulnerable when the doctor treats and does not 'tell'. The wife whose husband goes untreated for AIDS and the baby whose mother seeks no counsel may be more at risk if fears of breach of confidence prevent the husband and the mother getting any help at all than if the doctor treats them in confidence.[1]

I look at the law on confidentiality as it affects doctors and adult patients, and I examine the role of the medical profession itself in enforcing the ethical obligation of confidence. The special problems affecting confidentiality and parents and children are considered in Chapter 15. The vagueness of the law may surprise some. The number of occasions when the law compels the doctor to breach confidence may shock many.

Finally I examine what the patient is entitled to be told. From the patient's viewpoint the doctor's obligation of confidence exists to prevent the doctor passing on information about the patient to third parties. A relationship of trust requires that this should not happen. It also requires that the doctor be frank with the patient. Information about the patient should generally not be withheld from him. How far is the patient entitled to frankness from his doctor? When may he have access to his records? It has been suggested that medical confidentiality has as much to do with preserving relationships of trust and confidence between doctors themselves[2] as between doctors and patients. I do not enter into the historical or philosophical debate. I do, however, attempt to see what role the law plays in defining the doctor/patient relationship.

1. For a lively discussion of the complex ethical dilemmas faced by doctors in relation to confidentiality, see M. Phillips and J. Dawson, *Doctors' Dilemmas*, Harvester Press, London 1984, Chapter 5, 'Secrets'. And see J. K. Mason and R. A. McCall Smith, *Law and Medical Ethics*, Butterworths, London, 1991, Chapter 8.
2. See J. E. Thompson, 'The Nature of Confidentiality' (1979) 5 J. Med. Ethics 57.

Breach of confidence: the law[3]

The present law on breach of confidence has developed in a rather haphazard fashion. The precise legal nature of any obligation of confidence remains uncertain.[4] What is clear is that the judges have shown themselves willing to act to prevent the disclosure of confidential information in a wide variety of circumstances. A duty to preserve confidences has been imposed in settings as diverse as trade or research secrets confided to employees,[5] marital intimacies,[6] intimate disclosures to close friends[7] and Cabinet discussion.[8] Very often the obligation of confidence arises as an implied term of a contract, as is the case with the employee bound by his contract of employment to keep his master's business to himself. But the obligation of confidence can equally arise where no contract exists, or has ever existed, between the parties. The basic general principles of the law on breach of confidence amount to these. The courts will intervene to restrain disclosure of information where (1) the information is confidential in nature and not a matter of public knowledge, (2) the information was entrusted to another person in circumstances imposing an obligation not to use or disclose that information without the consent of the giver of the information, and (3) protecting confidentiality of that information is in the public interest.[9] As well as acting in advance to prevent the disclosure of confidential information, the courts may where appropriate award compensation after information has been improperly disclosed. Finally, once an obligation of confidence is created it binds not only the original recipient of the information but also any other person to whom disclosure is made by the recipient when that other person knows of the confidential status of the information.

Applying the general law to the specific issue of medical confidentiality, no problem arises from the requirement that the information

---

3. See F. Gurry, *Breach of Confidence*, Clarendon Press, Oxford, 1984.
4. See Law Commission Report No. 110, *Breach of Confidence*, para. 3.1 (Cmnd 8388), and see G. Jones, 'Restitution of Benefits Obtained in Breach of Another's Confidence' (1970) 86 LQR 463.
5. Gurry, op. cit., Chapters 8 and 9.
6. *Argyll* v. *Argyll* [1967] 1 Ch. 302.
7. *Stephens* v. *Avery* [1988] 2 All ER 477.
8. *Attorney-General* v. *Jonathan Cape Ltd* [1976] 1 QB 752.
9. *W.* v. *Egdell* [1990] 1 All ER 835, 846, CA.

given by the patient himself or that deduced by the doctor on examination is confidential in nature. Most people do not broadcast their medical problems from the rooftop. Equally it is unchallenged that the relationship of any doctor with any patient, NHS or private, imports an obligation of confidence. In a very early case action was taken to prevent publication of a diary kept by a physician to George III.[10] Much later, in 1974, a judge put the doctor's duty thus: '. . . in common with other professional men, for instance a priest and there are of course others, the doctor is under a duty not to disclose, [voluntarily] without the consent of his patient, information which he, the doctor, has gained in his professional capacity, save . . . in very exceptional circumstances'.[11]

The problematic area of medical confidentiality comes, not in establishing a general duty of confidence, but in determining what amounts to 'very exceptional circumstances' justifying breach of that duty. First, disclosure will always be justified legally when the doctor is compelled by law to give the confidential information to a third party. This may be by way of an order of the court to disclose records in the course of some civil proceedings, or may be under some statutory provision such as those Acts of Parliament requiring specified diseases to be notified to the health authorities. Doctors, unlike lawyers, enjoy no professional *privilege* entitling them to refuse to give evidence in court. I shall return to this later. Second, it is clear that the doctor may voluntarily elect to disclose information in certain circumstances. The general law on confidence, as we saw, required that preserving confidentiality be in the public interest. In early judgements the public interest 'defence' tended to concern disclosure of crime; 'there is no confidence in the disclosure of iniquity'.[12] It is clear now, though, that it is not limited to crime or even misconduct, not amounting to crime, alone. In *Lion Laboratories Ltd* v. *Evans* (which considered the disclosure of confidential information suggesting that a breathalyser device, the Intoximeter, was unreliable), Griffiths LJ said:

I can see no sensible reason why this defence should be limited to cases where there has been wrongdoing on the part of the plaintiffs . . . it is not difficult to think of instances where, although there has been no wrongdoing

10. *Wyatt* v. *Wilson* (1820), unreported but referred to in *Prince Albert* v. *Strange* (1849) 41 ER 1171, 1179.
11. *Hunter* v. *Mann* [1974] 1 QB 767, 772.
12. *Gartside* v. *Outram* (1856) 26 LJ Ch. 113, 114.

on the part of the plaintiff, it may be vital in the public interest to publish a part of his confidential information.[13]

The exact ambit of the public interest defence as it affects doctors remains difficult to ascertain, despite two recent and important judgements in the High Court[14] and the Court of Appeal.[15] It raises a host of questions. Should, or rather may, the doctor inform on any patient whom he suspects of any crime, however trivial? What other circumstances justify the invocation of the public interest to override the patient's interest in confidentiality? The guidance received by doctors in this awkward area still comes primarily from the General Medical Council and I shall consider and assess their rulings. For despite the underlying authority on the law of confidence, the enforcement of the obligation of confidence often rests in practice with the GMC. The civil action for breach of confidence is an excellent weapon for restraining threatened breaches of confidence. It is less effective in compensating the victim of a breach of confidence except in a commercial setting. If a trade secret is revealed by an employee and the employer loses profits his loss can be measured by the courts and appropriate compensation ordered. A breach of a medical confidence results usually not in any monetary loss but in indignity and distress for the patient. It is not clear whether damages for mental distress can be awarded in an action for breach of confidence. The Law Commission has recommended reforms which would allow the award of such damages.[16] Even so such damages may be costly to obtain, and complaining to the GMC is likely to remain in general the preferred remedy in cases of breach of confidence. The role of the law is this. The GMC is not the sole arbiter on issues of confidence. A patient dissatisfied with the findings of the GMC has no appeal from the GMC decision. What he does have is a concurrent right to take the matter to the courts by way of an action for breach of confidence. In this way the GMC's definition of the duty of confidentiality is on every occasion potentially susceptible to review by the courts. The courts, not the GMC, are the ultimate

---

13. *Lion Laboratories Ltd* v. *Evans* [1984] 2 All ER 417, 433.
14. *X* v. *Y* [1988] 2 All ER 648.
15. *W.* v. *Egdell* [1990] 1 All ER 855, CA.
16. Law Commission Report No. 110, paras. 6–106, but see the Scottish decisions *A.B.* v. *C.D.* (1851) 14 Dunl. (Ct of Sess.) 177; *A.B.* v. *C.D.* 1904 7F (Ct of Sess.) 72; discussed in Mason and McCall Smith, op. cit., pp. 196–7.

arbiters of the scope of the doctor's duty of confidentiality. But the judges have tended none the less to look to the GMC's guidelines on confidentiality in formulating the legal rules.[17] They may not endorse those guidelines word for word, but they do accord perhaps undue respect to the rules that the medical profession has formulated for itself. We shall see in this chapter that the ethical standard set by the GMC does not always exactly match legal principles. We shall see that there are occasions when the ethical obligation may properly be the more stringent. That the relationship of professional ethics and law in this country needs much more careful review is the outstanding lesson of the present confusing picture.

Breach of confidence: the GMC

A patient aggrieved by a breach of confidence on the part of his doctor may choose to pursue his grievance by way of a complaint to the GMC. Any improper disclosure of information obtained in confidence from or about a patient can constitute serious professional misconduct on the part of the doctor. Again the crucial issue is: when is a disclosure improper? The GMC gives further detailed guidance.[18] The doctor's duty is to maintain confidentiality strictly save in eight specified circumstances. The death of the patient does not absolve the doctor from this duty.[19] In this respect the doctor's ethical obligation is stricter than his legal duty. The law of confidence probably does not protect the patient's secrets after death. Doctors may disclose information in the following cases.

(1) The patient or his legal adviser gives written consent.
(2) Information is shared with other doctors, nurses or health professionals participating in caring for the patient.
(3) Where, in particular circumstances, on medical grounds it is undesirable to seek the patient's consent, information regarding the

17. See *X* v. *Y* [1988] 2 All ER 648; *W.* v. *Egdell* [1990] 1 All ER 835, 843 and 850.
18. GMC 'Bluebook' *Professional Conduct: Fitness to Practise* (February 1991), pp. 18–21; and see BMA *Philosophy and Practice of Medical Ethics*, 1988, pp. 19–27. And see the (Körner) Report of the Working Party on Confidentiality.
19. The publication of memoirs by Lord Moran, physician to Winston Churchill during the Second World War, provoked a great furore: see Mason and McCall Smith, op. cit., pp. 198–9.

patient's health may sometimes be given in confidence to a close relative.

(4) When in the doctor's opinion disclosure of information to some third party other than a relative would be in the best interests of the patient, the doctor must make every effort to get the patient's consent. Only in exceptional circumstances may the doctor go ahead and impart that information without the patient's consent.

(5) Information may be disclosed to comply with a statutory requirement, for example notification of an infectious disease.

(6) Information may be disclosed where it is so ordered by a court.

(7) 'Rarely, disclosure may be justified on the ground that it is in the public interest which, in certain circumstances such as, for example, investigation by the police of a grave or very serious crime, might override the doctor's duty to maintain his patient's confidence.'

(8) Information may also be disclosed if necessary for the purpose of a medical research project approved by a recognized ethical committee.

The exceptions to the duty of confidentiality as detailed by the GMC leave a fairly large degree of discretion in the hands of the individual doctor to determine when a breach of confidence is warranted. This is unavoidable if any exceptions to the duty of confidence are to be permitted. What we need to consider is how far the categories of exceptions set out by the GMC conform to the likely response of the courts if the issue were to be litigated rather than referred to the GMC.

The first two exceptions to confidentiality raise few problematic issues of law. There can be no breach of duty when a patient expressly consents to disclosure or when, as in the case of necessary communications with other doctors and nurses, consent can be implied.[20] Exceptions (5) and (6) again raise no awkward legal problems. The doctor must be justified in law in revealing information when the law compels him to do just that.

20. Care should be taken, however, even when transmitting information to other medical staff, to ensure that only those who 'need to know' are communicated with, and that they accept the obligation of confidentiality; see *W*. v. *Egdell* [1990] 1 All ER 835, 850. And the amount of information collected for statistical and similar purposes causes some concern for the future of confidentiality.

Disclosure in the patient's interests

Difficulty is first encountered when we look at exceptions (3) and (4). The essence of both is that the doctor should be free to speak with a relative, or, very exceptionally, with some other person, when he judges that the patient is too ill to make decisions as to his own treatment. He may act in the patient's best interests. Two points must be made clear. Relatives of an adult patient have no special status as regards his treatment. Acting in the patient's best interests is not in itself a defence to a breach of confidence. The legal justification for talking to third parties without consulting the patient is that generally he may be presumed to give his consent to such discussions. When a patient is unconscious, or cannot communicate at all, the doctor may reasonably infer that if able he would agree to his family and friends being consulted. Where a patient is very ill indeed, albeit still able to talk, the doctor may again usually assume that he will be prepared for the doctor to speak with his family to obtain their advice and to reassure them. Most people would be only too ready to agree and let their family take part in their treatment. But if a patient places a ban on communication with any third party, the doctor must respect that ban. The patient is entitled to confidentiality and entitled to require that it be maintained even when it is contrary to his interests. The doctor may seek to persuade him to change his mind. He may not override his decision.

Disclosure in the public interest

Exceptions (7) and (8) relate to the general 'public interest' defence available in any action for breach of confidence. The GMC provides in exception (7) for a general exception of disclosure in the public interest, giving the example of informing the police about grave crime but not limiting the exceptions to disclosure of crime alone. They stress that disclosure should be resorted to rarely. Exception (8) concerns a special instance of the public interest disclosure as part of a properly approved research project. I shall leave consideration of this issue until the chapter on clinical research.[21]

I will look now at the circumstances in which a doctor is justified in informing the police about criminal conduct on the part of a patient.

21. See Chapter 19.

He is generally under no obligation enforced by the criminal law to contact the police. Unless a statute specifically so provides, the doctor does not himself commit any offence by failing to tell the police of any evidence he may have come across professionally which suggests that a patient may have committed or is contemplating some crime.[22] A criminal offence is committed only when a doctor or anyone else accepts money to conceal evidence of crime.[23] The major exception to this general rule is section 18 of the Prevention of Terrorism (Temporary Provisions) Act 1989. Section 18 makes it an offence for any person having information which he believes may be of material assistance in preventing terrorism or apprehending terrorists to fail without reasonable excuse to give that information to the police. In the light of the threat posed by terrorism today, the duty of confidence between doctor and patient is unlikely to be seen as a reasonable excuse for failing to go to the police.

In the case of most crimes then, the choice is the doctor's. The criminal law will not penalize him for not informing the police. Will he be in breach of confidence if he elects to do so? The judges early this century were divided on the issue of whether a doctor was justified in going to the police after attending a woman who had undergone a criminal abortion. Hawkins J. condemned such a course as a 'monstrous cruelty' and doubted whether such a breach of confidence could ever be justified,[24] where Avory J. saw the doctor's duty to assist in the investigation of serious crime as always outweighing his duty to his patient.[25] Recent judgements appear to support Avory J.'s view although they deal with confidential relationships outside the medical field. Lord Denning has suggested that the public interest justifies disclosure of any crime or misdeed committed or contemplated.[26] Within the doctor/patient relationship freedom to disclose in the public interest should be more limited in scope. Unless commission of any crime disentitles the criminal from normal standards of medical care, disclosure should be strictly limited. Doctors who reasonably suspect that some other person is at risk of physical injury at their

22. Criminal Law Act 1967, s. 5(5).
23. ibid., s. 5(1).
24. *Kitson* v. *Playfair* (1896), *The Times*, 28 March.
25. Birmingham Assizes (1914) 78 JP 604; see Mason and McCall Smith, op. cit., p. 178.
26. *Initial Services Ltd* v. *Putterill* [1968] 1 QB 396, 405.

patient's hands must be free to act to protect that person. Doctors who discover that a crime of violence has been committed *may* be lawfully entitled to breach the patient's confidence. That is less clear. But in cases of child abuse,[27] rape, and serious violence the risk that the crime may be repeated will generally ensure that the doctor who breaches confidence acts with legal impunity. What the doctor may not do is hand over to the police information on each and every patient who transgresses the law. Parliament has legislated in a number of cases to compel breach of medical confidence. The courts should not be over-zealous to add to that list.

The inherent anomaly in this view may be that a doctor found to be in breach of confidence for disclosing a crime will be condemned by a court for taking steps to combat crime, a moral duty cast on every citizen. The doctor is distinguished from other citizens by the presence of a positive legal duty to his patient. Enforcing his duty to his patient benefits the public as well as the patient. The Court of Appeal has expressly recognized a public interest in the maintenance of medical confidentiality.[28] Medical confidentiality is at the root of good health care. Should the courts, however, find that as upholders of the law they cannot condemn those who help bring lawbreakers to justice, the alternative solution is to rely on the ethical standard of the GMC, that breach of confidence is justified only in case of grave or serious crime. The doctor may not break the law if he discloses details of petty crimes. He may be punished for professional misconduct. The legal and ethical standards do not need to be exactly the same. The relationship between them does need careful thought.

Next arises the question of disclosure where crime is not an issue. The law no longer limits the concept of public interest disclosure to crime alone, nor does the GMC in its ethical guidance to doctors. Defining exactly when the doctor may disclose on this more general basis is exceptionally difficult. Can he report a patient's epilepsy to the DVLC (Driver and Vehicle Licensing Centre) if the patient refuses to give up driving? May he tell a wife that her husband has AIDS? What about the problem of the patient whose genetic counselling reveals a risk that her sister too may be a carrier of genetic disease? In all cases the doctor must first do his utmost to obtain the patient's consent to

27. See Pereira Gray, 'Legal Aspects of Violence within the Family' (1981) 282 BMJ 2021.
28. *W.* v. *Egdell* [1990] 1 All ER 835, 849.

disclosure. If persuasion fails, what may the doctor do? He must balance his duty to the patient against the risk threatening other individuals. It seems clear then that he may in an appropriate case inform any relevant public body.[29] So he may probably contact the DVLC concerning an epileptic patient.

What exactly constitutes an appropriate case for disclosure, and whom exactly may the doctor inform? In *X* v. *Y*[30] a tabloid newspaper acquired, in breach of confidence from a health authority employee, information identifying two general practitioners who were continuing to practise after having been diagnosed as HIV positive (AIDS carriers in popular parlance). The health authority sought an injunction prohibiting publication of the doctors' and their patients' names. The newspaper argued that the public at large, and the doctors' patients in particular, had an interest in knowing that doctors were HIV positive. Rose J. reviewed the evidence about transmission of HIV from doctor to patient where the doctor had received proper counselling about safe practice. He found that the risk to patients was negligible. Far greater risks arose from the possibility that if they could not rely on confidential treatment people with AIDS, or who feared they might have AIDS, would not seek medical help. The judge, granting the injunction, said:[31]

In the long run, preservation of confidentiality is the only way of securing public health; otherwise doctors will be discredited as a source of education, for future individual patients will not come forward if doctors are going to squeal on them. Consequently, confidentiality is vital to secure public as well as private health, for unless those infected come forward they cannot be counselled and self-treatment does not provide the best care . . .

By contrast in *W* v. *Egdell*[32] the Court of Appeal sanctioned a breach of confidence by a psychiatrist. W had been convicted of the manslaughter of five people and of wounding two others. He was ordered to be detained indefinitely in a secure hospital. He could be released only by order of the Home Secretary if he were found to be

---

29. See *Hubbard* v. *Vosper* [1972] 2 QB 84; *Church of Scientology* v. *Kaufman* [1973] RPC 635 (disclosure of matter threatening the health of members of the public), see Gurry, op. cit., pp. 334–8.
30. [1988] 2 All ER 648.
31. ibid., p. 653.
32. [1990] 1 All ER 835; applied in *R.* v. *Crozier*, 3 May 1990, CA.

no longer a danger to public safety. As a step towards eventual release he sought a transfer to a regional secure unit. The transfer was not approved by the Home Secretary and W then applied to a mental health review tribunal for a conditional discharge. In support of his application his solicitors arranged for an independent psychiatric report from Dr Egdell. Dr Egdell's report was not favourable. He judged that W was still a dangerous man with a psychopathic personality, no real insight into his condition and a morbid interest in explosives. Unsurprisingly W's solicitors withdrew their application for his discharge but did not pass on the report to the tribunal or the hospital where W was detained. Dr Egdell was concerned by the fact that his report was not passed on. He ultimately sent his report to the medical director of W's hospital and agreed that a copy of that report should be forwarded to the Home Secretary. W sued Dr Egdell for breach of confidence.

The Court of Appeal first made it crystal clear that Dr Egdell did owe W a duty of confidence. Had he sold his story to the press or discussed the case in his memoirs Dr Egdell would have been in breach of confidence. But the duty of confidentiality is not absolute. The public interest in medical confidentiality must be balanced against the public interest in public safety. If Dr Egdell's diagnosis was right, W remained a source of danger to others and he was entitled to communicate his findings to the director of the hospital now detaining W and to the Home Secretary, who would have the final say on if and when W should be released into the community.

X v. *Y* and *W* v. *Egdell* do not mean that a doctor may *never* disclose that a patient has AIDS, or that he may always disclose findings about a patient's mental health. In each case the powerful interest in maintaining confidentiality must be balanced against the danger ensuing if confidentiality is not breached. Only where there is a clear and significant risk of the patient causing harm to others which cannot be abated by any other means may confidence be breached. Consider this example. A surgeon is HIV positive. It seems that it is not uncommon for surgeons to cut themselves in the course of surgery so that there is blood-to-blood contact between surgeon and patient. At least one surgeon has died in Britain having contracted AIDS from a patient. The surgeon refuses to give up surgery or accept any advice about how to safeguard his patients. *X* v. *Y* notwithstanding, the risk of harm to patients on such facts justifies the surgeon's doctor informing his employing authority and the GMC. But should a psychiatrist in the same role as Dr Egdell discover some relatively harmless abnormality in the patient, not noted by his current carers, he may not without the patient's consent breach his confidence. For disclosure to be lawful there must be an overwhelming *public* interest in disclosure.

Can this *public* interest in disclosure justify disclosure not only to a public body or official but also to an individual at risk? If the 'HIV surgeon' refuses to give up unprotected intercourse or to tell his wife of his condition, can she be warned of the danger she faces? This is a rather more awkward question. In defamation a defence of qualified privilege protects any communication which the maker has a duty to impart and the recipient a legitimate interest in receiving. No defence of qualified privilege as such exists in breach of confidence.[33] The defence is that the public interest demands disclosure. Private interests alone are not enough. But where a genuine risk of physical danger, of injury or disease is posed to any third party then the public interest in individual security may be sufficient to justify disclosure to that person so that he may protect himself appropriately. When the doctor reasonably foresees that non-disclosure poses a real risk of physical harm to a third party he should be free to warn that person, especially if that person too is his patient. And the courts should not be over-zealous to prove him wrong. Similarly, in such cases, if the doctor thinks it more appropriate to contact the third party's GP he should not be condemned. But risk of harm must be established. A simple belief that someone else, spouse or relative, is entitled to information is insufficient. So a husband has no 'right to know' if his wife asks to be sterilized. Parents have no 'right to know' if their daughter of 16 or above seeks an abortion. They clearly have an interest, a legitimate and not merely prurient interest, in the matters at stake. That is not enough. The balance of public interest in confidentiality should be displaced only by danger of physical harm.

The doctor must not forget that at the end of the day the law determines when overriding interests justify a breach of confidence. The law should be generous in deciding whether an individual judgement by a doctor within a recognized category of disclosure is correct. It cannot abdicate responsibility for the overall framework of medical confidentiality. And the role of the law of defamation must not be overlooked. Disclosure of any confidential information, albeit every word is true, may be the subject of an action for breach of confidence. But if the doctor is mistaken and some of the information disclosed by

---

33. Law Commission Report No. 110 (Cmnd 8388), paras. 6-94–6-96.

him proves to be untrue, he may face a further action for defamation. Any statement causing responsible citizens to think less of a person or to avoid his company may be defamatory. Diagnoses of alcoholism, venereal disease and AIDS are all examples of possible defamatory remarks. Suspicion of child abuse is another. In defamation the doctor has a complete defence if what he has stated is true. Additionally he has a defence of qualified privilege if (1) he reasonably believed his statements to be true, and (2) he communicated with a person with a legitimate interest in the relevant information. Informing the police of suspected violence to a child is clearly privileged even if the doctor's suspicions prove to be unfounded. Informing an employer that an employee is an alcoholic is probably not. The issue of whether communication was justified is one and the same in the law of confidence and defamation.

In this most sensitive area of doctor/patient relationships, striking the balance between confidence and concern for others is of the utmost difficulty. One interesting suggestion[34] made to help strengthen the patient's position is that doctors ought in advance to give patients notice of the circumstances which they consider may warrant a breach of confidence. The framework of their future relationship would then be set by the parties involved. The weakness of the proposal lies in the difficulty of predicting circumstances calling for a breach of confidence in advance. And the danger exists perhaps of criminally inclined patients shopping around for a doctor who promises never to 'grass'. That would be scarcely edifying for the profession or the public.

Breach of confidence and negligence

I have suggested that on occasion the doctor's duty of confidence to his patient may be overridden by his duty to safeguard a third party from physical harm. If he mistakenly decides the question of this conflict of duty in the patient's favour, and the risk of harm to someone else materializes, is the doctor at risk of a lawsuit by the injured party? He may well be. For normally where risk of injury is readily foreseeable and a person has the ability to eliminate that risk, or at any rate to minimize it, a duty to take the necessary action will arise. An education authority which failed to ensure that small children could not get out

34. See Paul Sieghart, 'Professional Ethics – for Whose Benefit?' (1982) 8 J. Med. Ethics 25.

of their nursery school and on to a busy main road were found liable, not just to any child on the road, but to a lorry driver injured in an incident caused by a straying child.[35]

In California the student medical centre at the University of California actually faced an action[36] in the courts for failing to warn a young woman of the risk posed to her by one of their patients. The girl's rejected lover sought psychiatric help at the centre. He told staff there of his violent intentions towards the girl and that he had a gun. The staff warned the police, who decided to take no action. The medical centre said nothing to the girl. She was murdered by their patient soon afterwards. Her family sued the University for negligence. The medical centre was found liable for failing to breach their patient's confidence and warn the girl of the threat to her life.

On similar facts an English court would be most unlikely to find a doctor negligent. First the court would have to determine whether in the special circumstances of medical confidentiality a duty to breach confidence could be countenanced. In the case of the education authority held liable for the escape of the infant, their duty to child and to lorry driver was one and the same. The doctor is faced with a stark conflict of duty. If the doctor may lawfully breach his patient's confidence, does he have a duty to do so to safeguard the individual at risk? The courts in England are reluctant in effect to make A liable for a wrong committed by B.[37] So the injured individual would have to satisfy the court that the doctor's knowledge of the risk to him was sufficient to make it 'just and reasonable'[38] for the doctor to be required to act to protect him. At the highest the doctor's duty may be set as an obligation to consider and assess the risk to the third party. The Californian medical staff did their best. They informed the police. The extent of the doctor's duty to third parties in England would appear to be this. He must not ignore any risk to other people created by his patient. He must weigh his duty to his patient against his duty to society and other individuals. If he acts reasonably on the evidence before him in the most awesome of dilemmas, the court will not penalize him if he ultimately proves to be wrong.

35. *Carmarthenshire CC* v. *Lewis* [1955] AC 549.
36. *Tarasoff* v. *Regents of University of California* (1976) 551 P 2d 334.
37. See *Smith* v. *Littlewoods Organization Ltd* [1987] 1 All ER 710, HL. And note the restrictive approach of many American courts to *Tarasoff*; see de Haan, 'My Patient's Keeper' (1986) 2 *Professional Negligence* 86.
38. *Peabody Donation Fund* v. *Parkinson* [1984] 3 All ER 86, HL.

Breach of confidence: law reform

In 1981 the Law Commission, a body appointed to review the current state of the law and recommend reform, published a report on *Breach of Confidence*[39] proposing detailed reforms. Ten years later the government has still not acted on the report. The proposals are to some extent technical and will have more impact in the field of commercial confidence than medical confidentiality. Those proposals relevant to doctors and patients include the following. The action for breach of confidence will lie in the form of an action for a tort, a civil wrong. An obligation of confidence will attach both to information entrusted by the patient to his doctor and to information about the patient confided to the doctor by a third party, for example reports to a general practitioner from a consultant to whom the patient has been referred. Compensation ordered where an action for breach of confidence is successful should include damages for mental distress and any consequent physical or mental harm. The Law Commission rejected arguments that the doctor's duty of confidence should survive the patient's death. They took the view that a law protecting the individual's interest in information entrusted by him to his doctor could not be stretched to embrace his family's privacy and freedom from distress after that person's own death. The ethical obligation imposed by the GMC might properly be more stringent than the legal obligation enforced by the law on confidence.

Compulsory disclosure

The circumstances in which the doctor may choose to disclose information about his patients may concern some patients and certainly creates difficult problems for their doctors. The doctor's dilemma is to some extent solved when the law compels him to disclose information. The number of instances in which this is the case is worryingly high.

First, a doctor must give any information required by a court of law. Privilege, in the sense of being free to refuse to give evidence relating to professional dealings with clients, is something usually enjoyed by lawyers alone and not shared by any other professional colleagues. A doctor can be subpoenaed to give evidence just like anyone else. Nor can he withhold anything from the court. He does

39. Law Commission Report No. 110.

not have to volunteer his views or expertise but whatever questions he is asked he must answer. Just as he can be called to the witness box, so his records can be called up before the courts. The only protection for medical confidentiality lies in the judge's discretion. Judges will try to ensure that confidence is breached only to the extent necessary for the conduct of the trial in progress. The doctor may be unhappy at having to break trust with his patient. He can at least be reassured that he is at no legal risk. Any breach of confidence made as a witness in court will be absolutely privileged against later action by the patient.

One further emergent area of protection of confidentiality should be mentioned. In *D. v. NSPCC*[40] the plaintiff sought to compel the NSPCC to disclose who had mistakenly accused her of child abuse. The court refused to make the order. The public interest in people feeling free to approach appropriate authorities to protect young children outweighed the plaintiff's private interest in unearthing her accuser. Thus there will be some cases where the courts may refuse to help a party seeking to discover who gave damaging information about him to the police or some other body. The courts may find that the public interest outweighs the private rights of the affected party. A similar balance of public versus private interest may also apply where the doctor is not a potential defendant but merely a witness. Particularly sensitive information may be allowed to be withheld from the court in the public interest. The decision is always a matter for the judges, not the doctor. Again the doctor's protection depends on the judge's discretion.

Next, the doctor may be compelled to hand over information to the police or other authorities before any trial commences. We have seen that under the Prevention of Terrorism (Temporary Provisions) Act 1989 the doctor must take the initiative and go to the police. This is unusual. But what a number of statutes demand is that the doctor answers questions if the police come and ask him. If a statute imposes a duty on 'any person' to answer police questions, any person includes a doctor.[41] Again, his profession confers no exemption or privilege upon him. Where no specific statutory power aids the police in their investigation of a crime the question becomes whether, if they believe a doctor holds records or other material constituting evidence of a crime on the part of a patient, they can search the doctor's premises and

40. [1977] 1 All ER 589.
41. *Hunter* v. *Mann* [1974] 1 QB 767.

seize the relevant material. The Police and Criminal Evidence Act 1984 grants police access to medical records but imposes certain safeguards. A search warrant to enter and search a surgery, hospital or clinic for medical records or human tissue or fluids taken for the purposes of medical treatment may be granted only by a circuit judge[42] and not, as is usually the case, by lay magistrates. The judge is directed to weigh the public interest in disclosure of the material against the general public interest in maintaining confidentiality.

Beyond the scope of the criminal law several further examples of compulsory disclosure must be noted.[43] Provision is made for compulsory notification of certain highly infectious diseases and of venereal disease.[44] Interestingly, AIDS is not a notifiable disease in the United Kingdom. The Public Health (Control of Disease) Act 1984 expressly states that cholera, plague, relapsing fever, smallpox and typhus shall be notifiable diseases and makes provision for other diseases to be so categorized at times of epidemic. The government has so far resisted hysterical pressures to make AIDS a notifiable disease. Once again the question is one of balancing the competing public interests, the interest in patients seeking advice and treatment for disease, and the interest in protecting the health of those at risk from infection. AIDS is not in the same league as diseases such as cholera. The cholera carrier immediately places his casual contacts at risk and, if he is untreated, can do little to minimize that risk. Cholera spreads like wildfire. AIDS is much, much less infectious and the patient himself can by acting responsibly at the very least reduce the risk to others. To act responsibly he needs professional help and must not be deterred from seeking that help by fear that his doctor will be forced to 'squeal' to the authorities. It should be noted though that the provisions for compulsory treatment in the 1984 Act have by regulations made by the Department of Health[45] been extended to AIDS patients and HIV carriers, though, to my knowledge, they have been invoked only once.

Accidents at work and instances of food poisoning are notifiable. Abortions must be reported. Details of drug addicts are required under

42. Police and Criminal Evidence Act 1984, ss. 8–14 and Sched. 1.
43. For a comprehensive list see Phillips and Dawson, op. cit., pp. 204–6.
44. The National Health Service (Venereal Diseases) Regulations 1974 make provision for the tracing of sexual contacts but also seek to ensure that the identity of patients and contacts remains confidential.
45. See the Public Health (Infectious Diseases) Regulations 1985.

the Misuse of Drugs Act. Births and deaths have to be notified by doctors as well as registered by families.

Finally, a number of bodies concerned with health administration may require information in the course of performing their functions. These include the Health Service Commissioner (Health Ombudsman), the Department of Health and regional and district health authorities. Examining the individual items on the long list of circumstances when a doctor can be forced to hand over information concerning his patients, many can be justified on grounds of public interest. The trouble is that the list tends to grow haphazardly. Only in the case of AIDS has the question of competing public interests and the validity of private rights been expressly addressed. What is needed is a review of medical confidentiality to examine all instances of compulsory disclosure and clarify when the public interest overrides the general benefit of preserving confidentiality. Legislation compelling disclosure should be express rather than simply including the doctor in a general requirement that any person gives information. Parliament should address the problem directly and not leave it to the judges to interpret ambiguous statutory provisions.

Patients' access to records[46]

I turn now to the opposite side of the coin. Patients are entitled to expect their doctors to keep their secrets. Can the doctors have secrets from their patients? The law of confidence prevents doctors from improperly disclosing information from or about their patients. But what if it is the patient who seeks information about himself? At last patients have been granted limited rights from November 1991 and to demand access to records.

Let us take first the patient wishing to compel a doctor to give him information or let him see his records. The doctor clearly ought to give him any information necessary to ensure that the patient has adequate health care. Should a doctor fail to give the patient sufficient details of his condition or treatment to enable the patient to take care of himself, he may be found to be negligent. If he makes physical contact with the

---

46. See generally on the implications of record keeping for medical confidentiality, Report of the Committee on Data Protection (Lindop Report) (Cmnd 7341). And see the draft Code on confidentiality of personal health information within the NHS DA (84) 25.

patient, for example administers an injection, and entirely misleads the patient as to the nature of the injection, this might even in an extreme case amount to assault. That is the limit of the doctor's obligation. He need not communicate every detail of his examination and diagnosis if such communication is not essential for proper treatment. And in England the courts have adopted a very 'doctor-friendly' test for what degree of communication is necessary for proper treatment.[47]

Next, when can a patient demand to see his records? Until November 1991, the answer to this simple question was confusing. A patient who starts legal proceedings against a doctor or hospital is, and has been for some time, able to obtain a court order giving him and his advisers access to his health records.[48] The difficulties in getting access to health records by any other means prompted some patients who only wanted to know what had gone wrong with their treatment to bring legal actions even though they did not particularly want or need monetary compensation. Where records are computerized, a patient from November 1987 could invoke his right as a 'data subject', under the Data Protection Act 1984, to demand a copy of any information held about him in computerized form. However, regulations made by the Secretary of State for Health under section 29 of the Act provides that access can be refused, if such access is likely to cause serious harm to the physical or mental health of the patient or any other individual.[49] The majority of health records are *not* held on computer. Consequently giving access to computerized but not manual records operated as a powerful disincentive to computerizing health records. Patients' organizations and the Campaign for Freedom of Information lobbied hard for legislation giving patients access to manual records. Without any statutory right of access, patients' rights to see their records depended on complex legal questions of ownership of information and, in the NHS, more mundane questions of who owned the paper on which records were written too.

The first attempt to give patients a right to see their health records within the Access to Personal Files Act 1987 failed. Pressure from the medical professions resulted in health records being excluded from that Act. But in 1990 the Access to Health Records Act, introduced into Parliament as a Private Member's Bill, became law and it came

47. See below, pp. 78–87.
48. Supreme Court Act 1981, ss. 33–5; see Chapter 7.
49. Data Protection (Subject Access Modification) (Health) Order 1987.

into force in November 1991. The Act applies to patients treated in the private sector as well as NHS patients. Under the Act patients may apply for access to their 'health records', but only records compiled *after* November 1991.[50] Health records include any information relating to the patient's physical or mental health '. . . made by or on behalf of a health professional in connection with the care of that individual'. Health professional is defined in section 2 of the Act and includes doctors, dentists, nurses and midwives. Access to health records is not unlimited. It may be wholly excluded if the holder of the record[51] believes that the patient is incapable of understanding the nature of his application for access.[52] It may be partially excluded where the holder of the record believes either (1) the relevant information is likely to cause serious harm to the physical or mental health of the patient or any other individual or (2) that information includes information relating to someone other than the patient.[53] In deciding whether to refuse access NHS authorities are required to consult the health professionals currently responsible for the patient's care.[54]

On the face of it the exclusions from rights of access seem fairly reasonable. A patient whose mental health is fragile and who may be devastated by a full account of his diagnosis and prognosis may be thought to be 'better off' not knowing the true state of affairs. Of course, when he is refused access he may imagine an even worse scenario! The crux of the problem though is the way in which health service authorities, and doctors in particular, will use the exclusions. A patient is diagnosed as having terminal cancer. His doctor decides not to tell him, and advises the health authority to refuse access to records because *he* judges that the patient could not cope with the truth. What can the patient do? Ultimately section 8 of the Act allows him to apply to the court, so a judge can decide if access has been improperly refused. The judges' record on a patient's 'right to know' does not inspire confidence that they will act to check over-enthusiastic medical paternalism.[55] What should not be forgotten is that a patient who

50. See s. 1.
51. Defined in s. 1(2).
52. s. 4.
53. s. 5.
54. s. 7.
55. See *Sidaway* v. *Governors of the Bethlem Royal and the Maudsley Hospital* [1985] 1 All ER 643, discussed fully in Chapter 4, pp. 82–7.

genuinely would rather not know what is wrong with him will never ask for access to his records.

Doctors have in the main resisted patient access to records and are unhappy about the Access to Health Records Act. Why is this so? First, many doctors believe that the 'silent majority' of patients prefer to trust the professionals. This may be so. No one is forced to use his rights under the Act. Second, they fear that patients will be unable to understand records. Perhaps records should be more clearly written, thus improving communications between doctors too. Finally, doctors claim that patient access will inhibit their ability to be frank with one another. A chance remark 'Mrs B. in neurotic state again' will destroy the patient's trust in her doctor. So it may, and so it should. Moreover, sometimes information on records is plainly wrong,[56] and this is particularly true of the 'chance remark' sort of information. 'Mrs B. neurotic because husband is drinking again' may be totally mistaken. The Act will give the patient greater control over his own health care and enable him to play his part in the therapeutic alliance with his doctors which many believe now best maximizes his hopes of recovery. It is a pity that medical opposition ensured that the Act operates only in respect of records made after 1991.

NHS practice

It is important to note that within the NHS crucial decisions on patient confidentiality and access to records may be made not by health professionals but by health service administrators. A manager, not a doctor or nurse, may decide, for example, to allow police access to patient records.[57] I have already examined the role of the GMC in enforcing the ethic of confidentiality. Their jurisdiction is limited to medical practitioners. The UKCC enforces similar stringent ethical rules for nurses. Day-to-day control of the records of NHS patients, in particular hospital records, rests in the hands not of the doctors or other medically qualified staff but of health service administrators. Doctors as well as patients have expressed concern that a patient's notes are seen by an unnecessary number of persons. They complain that decisions as to when to disclose records are taken too often by

56. s. 6.
57. See Pheby, 'Changing Practice on Confidentiality: A Cause for Concern' (1982) 8 J. Med. Ethics 12.

administrators. Administrators are not subject to the control of the GMC or the UKCC. Doctors fear they may be less concerned about confidentiality. Medical staff are outraged too that administrators have been known to let patients see their own records without consulting the patient's doctor.

NHS staff are of course subject to the law on confidence. Information confided by the patient to his doctor remains legally confidential when passed by the doctor to NHS clerks for filing and preserving in NHS files. But the undeveloped and uncertain state of the law makes it a dubious safeguard for the patient's privacy. In the last few years a number of committees[58] have addressed the problem. A draft Code on confidentiality within the health service has been proposed. The Code asserts the fundamental principle of confidentiality between doctor and patient and declares that that principle binds health authorities. Disclosure within the service is justified only if required in the context of the patient's health care. Disclosure to third parties outside the service is permissible only with the patient's consent save in exceptional cases. The exceptions, for example where disclosure is required by law or in case of serious crime, correspond closely to the exceptions sanctioned by the GMC. The innovation in health service practice introduced by the code is that prima facie the decision on disclosure shall always be taken by a medically qualified person and where possible it should be the doctor caring for the patient. The Code will be enforced by the sanction of disciplinary action or even dismissal against staff members who break it. A Working Party on Confidentiality[59] has recommended that in every staff contract an express clause on confidentiality should be included, and has advised that several other practical measures be taken to ensure that rules on confidentiality be respected.

Alas, the draft Code remains in draft. It seems that fundamental disagreements about who ultimately controls information about patients has stalled the process of reform. The health professionals argue that doctors must decide who to tell and what to tell them. Managers argue for greater accountability to the service itself for professional judgements. In the meantime patients' rights enjoy less

58. Notably the Inter-Professional Working Group on Access to Personal Health Information and the Working Party on Confidentiality set up by the Steering Group on Health Services Information (Körner).
59. See Körner, p. 17.

than adequate protection. The Access to Health Records Act effected a compromise. The doctor or other health professional must be consulted. That must be right. The professional responsible for the patient's care is best able to evaluate his state of health, and responsibility should carry correlative rights. But are doctors entitled to the final word? Fears, based on experience, of medical paternalism might cause patients to say no. But the alternative is to entrust patients' rights to managers who more and more are adjured to consider costs as their priority. It is an unattractive alternative.

The problem throughout the area of medical confidentiality and professional secrecy is this. The issues arising within the doctor/patient relationship are unique. The law seeks to force medical confidentiality into the general framework of the law of confidence, privacy and ownership of records. It simply does not fit. The matters at stake are too important for these questions to be left fuzzy and unpredictable. Doctors and patients need to know where the law stands. It may well be that at the end of the day the ethical standard of confidentiality will diverge from the requirements of the law. For example, the profession itself may elect to enforce a higher degree of confidentiality in respect of suspected crime and to maintain the obligation of confidence even after a patient's death. The crucial importance of the continuing ethical debate[60] among doctors themselves must never be forgotten. For that debate to be fruitful, the legal framework within which the profession may properly act must be clearly defined. If the GMC is left to operate its concept of confidentiality in the present state of legal complexity and confusion, we outside the profession must not complain if we do not like their conclusions.

There is a final disturbing aspect to the debate on confidentiality. Patients perceive confidentiality as a means of protecting patients' rights. It seems some health authorities regard confidentiality as designed to protect their reputation and have sought to punish staff who disclosed evidence of poor conditions and patient maltreatment. NHS trusts, it is claimed, have asked doctors and nurses to sign contracts forbidding any discussion or criticism of the hospital!

60. For a view that ethics are more important than law, see J. Jacob, 'Confidentiality: The Dangers of Anything Weaker Than the Medical Ethic' (1982) 8 J. Med. Ethics 18.

PART II

Medical Malpractice

Introduction

In this Part, I examine what general remedies the law affords a patient who is dissatisfied with the medical care which he has received. He may feel that he has not been fully consulted or properly counselled about the nature and risks of the treatment. He may have agreed to treatment and ended up worse, not better. Consequently a patient may seek compensation from the courts. Or he may simply want an investigation of what went wrong, and to ensure that his experience is not suffered by others.

The law relating to medical errors, commonly described as medical malpractice, operates on two basic principles. (1) The patient must agree to treatment. (2) Treatment must be carried out with proper skill and care on the part of all the members of the medical profession involved. Any doctor who operated on or injected, or even touched, an adult patient against his will might commit a battery, a trespass against the patient's person. A doctor who was shown to have exercised inadequate care of his patient, to have fallen below the required standard of competence, would be liable to compensate the patient for any harm he caused him in the tort of negligence.

In short, to obtain compensation the patient must show that the doctor was at fault. And if he sues for negligence he must show that the doctor's 'fault' caused him injury. Three overwhelming problems are inherent in these two simple statements.

First, how do courts staffed by lawyer-judges determine when a doctor is at fault? We shall see that the judges in England defer in the most part to the views of the doctors. Unlike their American brethren, English judges will rarely challenge the accepted views of the medical profession. Establishing what that view is may cause the court some difficulty though. Each side is free to call its own experts and a clash of eminent medical opinion is not unusual.

Second, as liability, and the patient's right to compensation, is dependent on a finding of fault, doctors naturally feel that a judgement against them is a body blow to their career and their reputation. Yet a moment's reflection will remind the reader of all the mistakes he has made in his own job. A solicitor overlooking a vital piece of advice in a conference with a client can telephone the client and put things right when he has a chance to check what he has done. A carpenter can have a second go at fixing a door or a cupboard. An overworked, overstrained doctor may commit a momentary error which is irreversible. He is still a good doctor despite one mistake.

Finally, the doctor's fault must be shown to have caused the patient harm. In general, whether a patient is treated within the NHS or privately, the doctor only undertakes to do his best. He does not guarantee a cure. The patient will have a legal remedy only if he can show that the doctor's carelessness or lack of skill caused him injury that he would not otherwise have suffered. So if I contract an infection and am prescribed antibiotics that a competent doctor would have appreciated were inappropriate for me or my condition, I will be able to sue the doctor only if I can show either (1) that the antibiotic prescribed caused me harm unrelated to my original sickness, for example brought me out in a violent allergy, or (2) that the absence of appropriate treatment significantly delayed my recovery. And in both cases I must prove that had the doctor acted properly the harm to me would have been avoided.

We shall see therefore that the law is a remedy only for more specific and serious grievances against a doctor. It is in any case an expensive and unwieldy weapon. Many patients have complaints, particularly about hospitals, which do not amount to legal grievances. They complain about being kept waiting, inadequate visiting hours, or parents not being allowed to stay with their children. I shall look in this Part at extra-legal methods of pursuing complaints against a hospital or a doctor, and in particular I shall investigate the role of the National Health Service 'Ombudsman'. Nor do I limit my examination to faults alleged against medical practitioners. Many medical mishaps arise from the dangers inherent in certain drugs. I consider the liability of the drug companies and attempts by government to ensure that available medicines are safe. Finally I ask whether the whole basis of the present law of negligence as it applies to medical practice is due, or overdue, for radical reform.

CHAPTER 4

Agreeing to Treatment

There would be very little support in England today, even from the most paternalistic of doctors, for the proposition that every sick adult should be compelled to accept whatever treatment his doctor thought best. No one, as far as I know, suggests that the millions of adults who stay away from dentists out of childish fear and to the detriment of their dental and, sometimes, their general health should be rounded up and marched to the nearest dental surgery for forcible treatment. Few would deny the right of the adult Jehovah's Witness to refuse a blood transfusion even if in doing so she forfeits her life. Medical treatment normally requires the agreement of the patient. The right of the patient, who is sufficiently rational and mature to understand what is entailed in treatment, to decide for herself whether to agree to that treatment is endorsed as a basic human right. The right to autonomy, to self-rule rather than rule by others, is endorsed by ethicists as a right to patient autonomy. How far is patient autonomy recognized and protected by the law in England?

Every mentally competent adult has an inviolable right to determine what is done to his or her own body. I shall look at the law in relation to incompetent patients and children later. A person who intentionally touches another against that other's will commits a trespass to that person just as much as coming uninvited on to the person's land is a trespass to his land. The tort of battery is committed. Where a person consents to a contact no battery is committed. So a boxer entering the ring cannot complain of battery when he is hit on the chin by his opponent. Battery is any non-consensual contact.

How does this tort relate to doctors? Any doctor examining, injecting or operating on a patient deliberately makes contact with that patient's body. Normally he commits no wrong because he does so with the patient's agreement. Should he fail to obtain a patient's agreement at all, should a doctor force himself on a patient, then clearly he commits a battery. But that is extremely unlikely. However, what of the surgeon who correctly decides to treat cancer of the bone of the right leg by amputating that leg and by error amputates the wrong leg, the left leg? Once the error is discovered the poor patient has to endure a further operation to remove the right leg. One patient's notes are mixed up and a woman who was scheduled for and consented to an appendectomy is given a hysterectomy. Both unfortunate victims can sue the surgeon in battery. They did not consent to the operation performed. In a Canadian case a woman who expressed her wish to be injected in her right arm was injected by the doctor in her left. She sued in battery and succeeded.[1]

Of course in all these examples the surgeon or some other member of the hospital staff has been careless. So the patient could normally sue in negligence too. But there are certain differences between the two torts. In battery, a patient need not establish any tangible injury. The actionable injury is the uninvited invasion of his body. This is important. A doctor may on medically unchallengeable grounds decide that an operation is in the patient's best interests. He goes ahead. The patient's health improves. Yet if it was done without consent a battery has still been committed. A doctor who discovered that his patient's womb was ruptured while performing minor gynaecological surgery was held liable to her for going ahead and sterilizing her there and then. She had not agreed to sterilization.[2] A woman who underwent a hysterectomy when all she had agreed to was curettage similarly recovered for battery.[3] The essence of the wrong of battery is the unpermitted contact. There is no requirement that the patient prove that if he had been asked to consent to the relevant treatment he would have refused.

Two other points should be noted. Battery may be alleged by a patient who says he did not consent. On whom does the onus of proof lie? It used to be argued that it was for the defendant, the doctor, to

1. *Allan* v. *New Mount Sinai Hospital* (1980) 109 DLR (3d) 536. Cf. *Wilson* v. *Pringle* (below).
2. *Devi* v. *West Midlands* AHA [1980] 7 CL 44.
3. *Cull* v. *Butler* [1932] 1 BMJ 1195.

prove that the patient consented. Now a High Court judge has said that the onus of proof lies on the patient. He must establish that he did not agree.[4] And what sort of compensation will a patient receive? In negligence we shall see that a defendant is only liable for the kind of damage which he reasonably ought to foresee. In battery the test may be more stringent. The defendant may be liable for all the damage which can factually be seen to flow from his wrongdoing. A doctor who injected a patient in the 'wrong' arm would be liable in battery or negligence for any unwanted stiffness in that arm, for any adverse reaction which he ought to have contemplated in view of the patient's history. He would not be liable in negligence for a 'freak' reaction. In battery he may well be so liable. But judges in England seem eager to limit the scope of battery when it overlaps with negligence. They may strive to avoid subjecting any surgeon to liability in battery.[5] A significant disadvantage too with the tort of battery as a means of vindicating patients' rights is that for this action to lie there must be some physical contact between doctor and patient. A patient who, for example, agreed to take a drug orally, having been totally misled as to the nature of the drug, could not sue in battery. But had the doctor injected him with that self-same drug, an action in battery would lie.

What is meant by consent?

The key to the whole issue is consent. What is meant by consent? It need not be written, although as a matter of practice a written consent form will always be provided before surgery. Consent may often be implied from the circumstances. If a patient visits his general practitioner complaining of a sore throat and opens his mouth so that the doctor can examine his throat, he cannot complain that he never expressly said to the doctor: 'You may put a spatula on my tongue and look down my throat.' A patient visiting Casualty with a bleeding wound implicitly agrees to doctors or nurses cleaning and bandaging the wound. In an American case an immigrant to the USA complained that he had not consented to vaccination. It was found that he had bared his arm and held it out to the doctor. His action precluded the need for any verbal consent.[6]

4. *Freeman* v. *Home Office* [1984] 2 WLR 130.
5. See *Wilson* v. *Pringle* [1986] 3 WLR 1, CA
6. *O'Brien* v. *Cunard SS Co.* (Mass. 1891) 28 NC266.

DOCTORS OR DENTISTS (This part to be completed by doctor or dentist. See notes on reverse)

TYPE OF OPERATION INVESTIGATION OR TREATMENT

I confirm that I have explained the operation investigation or treatment, and such appropriate options as are available and the type of anaesthetic, if any (general/regional/sedation) proposed, to the patient in terms which in my judgement are suited to the understanding of the patient and/or to one of the parents or guardians of the patient.

Signature . . . .   Date . . ./. . ./. . . . .

Name of doctor or dentist . . . .

PATIENT/PARENT/GUARDIAN

1. Please read this form and the notes overleaf very carefully.

2. If there is anything that you don't understand about the explanation, or if you want more information, you should ask the doctor or dentist.

3. Please check that all the information on the form is correct. If it is, and you understand the explanation, then sign the form.
   I am the patient/parent/guardian (delete as necessary)

I agree to what is proposed which has been explained to me by the doctor/dentist named on this form.

to the use of the type of anaesthetic that I have been told about.

I understand that the procedure may not be done by the doctor/dentist who has been treating me so far.

that any procedure in addition to the investigation or treatment described on this form will only be carried out if it is necessary and in my best interests and can be justified for medical reasons.

I have told the doctor or dentist about any additional procedures I would *not* wish to be carried out straightaway without my having the opportunity to consider them first.

A patient for whom surgery or any form of invasive investigation is proposed will inevitably be asked to sign a consent form. In 1990 the Department of Health issued new guidance on consent to treatment and produced new and more detailed standard forms for use within the NHS. The Department's aim is to ensure that health care professionals do appreciate the need for information and give patients the information to which they are entitled. The standard form for routine surgery, investigation or treatment is shown opposite.

Without doubt this new form attempts to ensure that patients appreciate that they are entitled to ask questions and to demand explanations about what is to be done to them. They are not passive recipients of what doctor thinks best. Specialized forms are now recommended for certain types of surgery such as sterilization expressly stating the particular problems of that procedure. But at the end of the day a form is no more than some evidence of what the patient has agreed to. What is important is the substance of what the patient is entitled to be told and has been told. Clearly any action expressly prohibited by the patient, that is, additional procedures that on the form he states 'I would *not* wish to be carried out straightaway', would constitute a battery if imposed on the patient. What sort of authority does the provision in the form about additional procedures found to be necessary and in the patient's best interests confer on the doctor?

This would not affect liability in the cases discussed earlier of the doctor who sterilized a patient, or the doctor who performed a hysterectomy in the course of minor gynaecological surgery. Neither measure was immediately necessary to preserve the woman's health. The doctor is only authorized to carry out further surgery without which the patient's life or health will be immediately at risk. So the doctor discovering advanced cancer of the womb while performing a curettage may be justified in performing an immediate hysterectomy. Delay might threaten the woman's life. A doctor discovering some malformation, or other non-life-threatening condition, must delay further surgery until his patient has the opportunity to offer her opinion.

The use of the standard form is not compulsory within the NHS. In private hospitals and clinics a different form may well be used. What would be the effect of a form within which the plaintiff consented to the proposed operation and any further surgery which the surgeon saw fit to embark on? In the absence of the clearest evidence that the patient fully understood the 'blank cheque' which he handed to his doctor, such a form will be virtually irrelevant. Any consent form is no more than one piece of evidence that the patient did, in fact, consent to what was done to him. If the patient can show that despite the form he did not give any real consent to the procedure carried out, the surgeon will be liable to him.

How much must the doctor tell the patient?

We have seen that for consent to be real the patient must be told what operation is to be performed and why it is to be done. The doctor certifies on the consent form that he has explained the proposed operation, investigation or treatment to the patient. What exactly must the doctor explain? All surgery under general anaesthetic entails some risk. Many forms of surgery and medical treatment carry further risk of harm even if they are carried out with the greatest skill and competence. Patients have argued that if an operation entails an inherent risk then they cannot be said to have given a real consent to that operation if they were not told of the risk. They had inadequate information on which to make a proper decision. They could not give an 'informed consent'. Therefore an action in battery should lie. Alternatively they argue that if an action in battery does not lie, they ought to be able to sue for negligence. The doctor's duty of care encompasses giving adequate information and advice. If he has given the patient inadequate information and the patient consequently accepted a risky procedure and damage did ensue, then the doctor, it is argued, is responsible for that damage. So far, in England, such claims have not fared well!

Let us look first at the argument that if risks or side-effects inherent in an operation are not disclosed then the patient has not really consented at all, and the surgeon is liable for battery. A Miss Chatterton pursued such a claim in 1981. She suffered excruciating pain in a postoperative scar. Dr Gerson proposed an operation. The operation failed to relieve her symptoms. A second operation was carried out. Miss Chatterton was no better and subsequently lost all sensation in her right leg and foot with a consequent loss of mobility. She claimed that while Dr Gerson was in no way negligent in his conduct of the surgery, he failed to tell her enough for her to give her 'informed consent'. Her claim in battery failed. The judge said that a consent to surgery was valid providing that the patient was 'informed in broad terms of the nature of the procedure which is intended'.[7]

7. *Chatterton* v. *Gerson* [1981] 3 WLR 1003. The nature and purpose test for

By contrast, a patient who agreed to an injection which she understood to be a routine post-natal jab but which was in fact the controversial long-acting contraceptive Depo-Provera succeeded in her claim for battery. Her doctor failed the test set in *Chatterton* v. *Gerson*. He obtained her agreement to the injection leaving her totally unaware and indeed misleading her, albeit in good faith, as to the nature of what was being done to her.[8]

Subsequent attempts to claim in battery, where the nature of what was to be done was explained but the risks of the procedure were not, have failed just as Miss Chatterton's claim failed. In 1983 another High Court judge deplored the bringing of such claims in battery. He viewed the proper cause of action, if any, as lying in negligence.[9] And in 1984 the Court of Appeal too added its voice. The Master of the Rolls said:

> It is only if the consent is obtained by fraud or misrepresentation of the *nature* [my italics] of what is to be done that it can be said that an apparent consent is not a true consent.[10]

The House of Lords unanimously endorsed his views.[11] The Canadian courts too see battery as an inappropriate remedy for inadequate counselling. The Canadian Chief Justice has said:

> I do not understand how it can be said that the consent was vitiated by failure of disclosure of risks as to make the surgery or other treatment an unprivileged, unconsented to and intentional invasion of the patient's bodily integrity ... unless there has been misrepresentation or fraud to secure consent to the treatment, a failure to disclose the attendant risks, however serious, should go to negligence rather than battery.[12]

It is easy to understand why English and Canadian courts shy away

---

battery is cogently criticized by Tan Ken Feng, 'Failure of Medical Advice: Trespass or Negligence' [1987] *Legal Studies* 149.

8. See the *Guardian*, 23 July 1983. This case is further discussed in Chapter 17.
9. *Hills* v. *Potter* (*note*) [1984] 1 WLR 641, 653.
10. *Sidaway* v. *Board of Governors of the Bethlem Royal and the Maudsley Hospital* [1984] 2 WLR 778, 790; and see *Freeman* v. *Home Office* [1984] 2 WLR 802, 813.
11. *Sidaway* v. *Board of Governors of the Bethlem Royal and the Maudsley Hospital* [1985] 2 WLR 480.
12. *Reibl* v. *Hughes* (1980) 114 DLR (3d) 1.

from finding doctors liable in battery. The word itself is emotive. Doctors must resent being accused of 'battering' their patients. Conduct constituting the tort of battery will often also constitute the crime of assault. And very, very rarely are doctor/patient disputes the proper concern of the criminal law. However, distinguishing between battery and no battery on the *Chatterton* v. *Gerson* test is not easy. Consider the example of a patient tested for HIV without his consent. He agrees to a blood test preparatory to surgery. He is never told that among the tests to be carried out on his blood is a test for HIV. Did he understand the nature and purpose of the test? He understood what would be done to him and that several tests would be carried out on his blood. It is difficult to say that he did not understand in broad terms what was going on. Of course, had some ruse been employed to obtain his consent the picture might be different. A doctor suspects a patient is HIV positive and wants a test for that sole purpose. Fearing that the patient would refuse consent if asked outright, the doctor uses a pretext for the test, for example a suspicion of anaemia. That patient falls within the *Chatterton* v. *Gerson* test, for his consent was *obtained by fraud or misrepresentation*. The line between battery and negligence is a fine and often illogical line.

The proper cause of action, the courts have said, lies in negligence. But English plaintiffs have fared little better in negligence. The courts have held that the doctor's duty of care to his patient includes a duty to give him careful advice and sufficient information upon which to reach a rational decision as to whether to accept or reject treatment. The problematic issue has been when the doctor is found to be in breach of that duty. Mr Bolam agreed to electro-convulsive therapy to help improve his depression. He suffered fractures in the course of the treatment. The risk was known to his doctor. He did not tell Mr Bolam. Mr Bolam alleged that the failure to warn him of the risk was negligent. The judge found that the amount of information given to Mr Bolam accorded with accepted medical practice in such cases and dismissed Mr Bolam's claim.[13] He added that even if Mr Bolam had proved that the doctor's advice was inadequate he would only have succeeded if he could have further proved that given better information he would have refused his consent to the treatment. The test of negligence was the test of generally accepted medical practice. Other cases in the 1950s were even more favourable to the doctors. Lord Denning

13. [1957] 2 All ER 118.

held it to be entirely for the individual doctor to decide what to tell his patient, even if the doctor went so far as to resort to what his Lordship termed 'a therapeutic lie'![14] It was a matter for his discretion. Another patient was partially paralysed in the course of an aortagram. A court in 1975 found that the risk was real but remote, and as the patient never inquired about risks the doctor had no obligation to enlighten him.[15]

The underlying trend in the English courts was that 'doctor knows best'. Across the Atlantic matters took a startlingly different turn. The doctrine of 'informed consent' was born. In *Canterbury* v. *Spence*[16] an American court said that the 'prudent patient' test must be adopted. Doctors must disclose to their patients any material risk inherent in a proposed line of treatment.

A risk is thus material when a reasonable person, in what the physician knows or should know to be the patient's position, would be likely to attach significance to the risk or cluster of risks in deciding whether or not to forgo the proposed therapy.

The Canadian Supreme Court too rejected the 'professional medical standard' for determining how much the doctor must disclose. Emphasis was laid upon 'the patient's right to know what risks are involved in undergoing or forgoing certain surgery or other treatment'.[17] The Canadian court did allow though that a particular patient might waive his right to know, might put himself entirely in the hands of his doctors. And they said that cases might arise where '... a particular patient may, because of emotional factors, be unable to cope with facts relevant to the recommended surgery or treatment and the doctor may, in such a case, be justified in withholding or generalizing information as to which he would otherwise be required to be more specific'.

The 1980s brought the issue once again before the English courts. Backed by the transatlantic doctrine of informed consent, lawyers tried to breach the walls of medical silence. Miss Chatterton, who as we saw lost in battery, failed too in negligence. The doctor, the judge

14. *Hatcher* v. *Black, The Times*, 2 July 1954.
15. *O'Malley-Williams* v. *Board of Governors of the National Hospital for Nervous Diseases* [1975] 1 BMJ 635.
16. (1972) 464 F. 2d 772, 780.
17. *Reibl* v. *Hughes* (above).

said, did owe her a duty to counsel her as to any real risks inherent in the surgery proposed. He did not have to canvass every risk and in deciding what to tell the patient he could take into account '. . . the personality of the patient, the likelihood of misfortune and what in the way of warning is for the particular patient's welfare'. This standard Dr Gerson had met.

The issue after *Chatterton* v. *Gerson* was who judged what amounted to 'a real risk of misfortune inherent in the procedure'. The English courts have rejected the 'prudent patient' test and opted for the professional medical standard. The case that eventually went to the House of Lords concerned Mrs Sidaway. For several years, following an accident at work, Mrs Sidaway had endured persistent pain in her right arm and shoulder. Later the pain spread to her left arm too. In 1960 she had just become the patient of Mr Falconer, an eminent neuro-surgeon at the Maudsley Hospital. An operation relieved the pain for a while. By 1973 Mrs Sidaway was once again in constant pain. She was admitted to the Maudsley Hospital in October 1974 and Mr Falconer diagnosed pressure on a nerve root as the cause of her pain. He decided to operate to relieve the pressure. Mrs Sidaway gave her consent to surgery. As a result of that operation Mrs Sidaway became severely disabled by partial paralysis.

Mrs Sidaway sued both Mr Falconer and the Maudsley Hospital. She did not suggest that the operation had been performed otherwise than skilfully and carefully. Her complaint was this. The operation to which she agreed involved two specific risks over and above the risk inherent in any surgery under general anaesthesia. These were (1) damage to a nerve root, assessed as about a 2 per cent risk and (2) damage to the spinal cord, assessed as less than a 1 per cent risk. Alas for Mrs Sidaway, that second risk materialized and she consequently suffered partial paralysis. She maintained that Mr Falconer never warned her of the risk of injury to the spinal cord. Throughout the long and expensive litigation Mrs Sidaway's greatest handicap was that Mr Falconer died before the action came to trial. The courts were thus deprived of vital evidence as to exactly what the patient was told by her surgeon and what reasons, if any, he had for withholding information from her. The case had to proceed from the inference drawn by the trial judge in the High Court that Mr Falconer would have followed his customary practice, that is, he would have warned Mrs Sidaway in general terms of the possibility of injury to a nerve root but would have said nothing about any risk of damage to the spinal cord.

Mrs Sidaway's lawyers argued in the High Court that the failure by the surgeon to warn his patient of the risk to her spinal cord invalidated her consent to the operation. This claim in battery failed. The judge endorsed the views discussed earlier that a lack of full information will not render an operation a battery provided the patient understood the general nature of the surgery proposed. The judge dismissed her claim in negligence too. Against his judgement on the issue of negligence Mrs Sidaway appealed and lost again in the Court of Appeal.

Thus ten years after the unfortunate operation which left Mrs Sidaway paralysed, and seven years after Mr Falconer's death, the case reached the highest court in the land, the House of Lords.[18] The paucity of evidence as to what actually happened when Mrs Sidaway and Mr Falconer discussed the proposed surgery rendered the case, as Lord Diplock put it, 'a naked question of legal principle'.[19] What principle governed the doctor's obligation to advise patients and to warn of any risks inherent in surgery or treatment recommended by the doctor? The majority of their Lordships endorsed the traditional test enunciated in the case of Mr Bolam nearly thirty years before. The doctor's obligation to advise and warn his patient was part and parcel of his general duty of care owed to each individual patient. Prima facie, providing he conformed to a responsible body of medical opinion in deciding what to tell and what not to tell his patient, he discharged his duty properly. There being evidence that while some neuro-surgeons might warn some patients of the risk to the spinal cord many chose not to, Mrs Sidaway's case was lost.

The *Sidaway* judgement, their Lordships said, should not be seen as a total endorsement of the view that providing a doctor follows current medical practice in deciding on the advice to give his patients he will be immune from legal attack. The courts retain ultimate control of the definition of the doctor's obligation. First, for Lord Bridge and Lord Templeman the crucial issue in Mrs Sidaway's case was that the risk of which she was not advised was a less than 1 per cent risk, and all the medical expert witnesses were agreed that it was a risk which many responsible neuro-surgeons elected not to warn patients of. Where experts disagree, the courts remain the ultimate arbiter of their difference of opinion. Even where the overwhelming body of medical

18. *Sidaway* v. *Board of Governors of the Bethlem Royal and the Maudsley Hospital* [1985] 2 WLR 480.
19. ibid., p. 497.

opinion accepted non-disclosure of a particular risk, Lords Bridge and Templeman asserted the judicial right to intervene where disclosure was obviously necessary to an informed choice on the part of the patient. Lord Bridge gave as an example '. . . an operation involving a substantial risk of grave adverse consequences, for example [a] ten per cent risk of a stroke from the operation'.[20] Second, for Lord Diplock and Lord Templeman a further vital question in the case was that Mrs Sidaway had not expressly inquired of Mr Falconer what risks the surgery entailed. For Lord Diplock the case is concerned solely with what information the doctor must volunteer. Lord Templeman said Mr Falconer could not be faulted for failing to give Mrs Sidaway information for which she did not ask.

What four out of five of the Law Lords in *Sidaway* were un-equivocally agreed on was the rejection of the transatlantic test that what the patient should be told should be judged by what the reasonable patient would want to know. Only Lord Scarman rejected current medical practice as the test of what a patient needs to be told. He dissented, and in a powerful judgement asserted the patient's right to know. The patient's right of self-determination, his right to choose what happened to his body, was the factor which to Lord Scarman made the issue of advice given to the patient distinct from other aspects of medical care. The doctor should be liable '. . . where the risk is such that in the court's view a prudent person in the patient's situation would have regarded it as significant'.[21] But, albeit the patient's right of self-determination distinguishes advice given from other stages in medical care, advice before treatment cannot be totally separated from the doctor's general duty to offer proper professional and competent service. Thus the doctor, in Lord Scarman's view, should be to a certain extent protected by a defence of 'therapeutic privilege'. This would permit a doctor to withhold information if it can be shown that 'a reasonable medical assessment of the patient would have indicated to the doctor that disclosure would have posed a serious threat of psychological detriment to the patient'.[22] Lord Scarman recognized the right of a patient of sound understanding to be warned of material risks save in exceptional circumstances. But still he too found against Mrs Sidaway. He held that she failed to establish on the

20. ibid., p. 505.
21. ibid., p. 493.
22. ibid., p. 493.

evidence put forward by her counsel that the less than 1 per cent risk was such that a prudent patient would have considered it significant. And the death of Mr Falconer deprived the court of evidence of his medical assessment of her condition and her state of mind.

After Sidaway?

Construed narrowly the *Sidaway* judgement related only to the test for the degree of information the doctor must *volunteer* to disclose. And their Lordships, as we saw, were at pains to assert that the courts were in no way abdicating ultimate judicial control over medical responsibility to give patients sufficient information to make informed choices on treatment. That is the theory. The practice, alas, has been rather different. It seems that, after *Sidaway*, doctors judge what doctors should properly tell patients. Note how in the consent form the doctor states that he has explained the proposed treatment in terms which in *his* judgement is suited to the understanding of the patient. The patient's right to self-determination, to autonomy, is thin in content. Much was made in *Sidaway* of the fact that Mrs Sidaway did not expressly ask her surgeon, Mr Falconer, about the risks and side-effects of the proposed operation. Mrs Blyth asked a lot of questions. She suffered prolonged bleeding after an injection of the long-term contraceptive Depo-Provera. Despite her questions, she was not given comprehensive information on the potential side-effects of that controversial drug. She sued for negligence. The trial judge held that in the circumstances he did not have to follow the *Sidaway* judgement.[23] Mrs Blyth had made express requests for full information, he said, and therefore was entitled to *all* the relevant information about Depo-Provera. The Court of Appeal[24] disagreed and allowed the health authority's appeal. The test of what Mrs Blyth must be told was to be judged by good professional practice. It seems that asking questions makes little difference to the degree of information the patient is entitled to![25]

The Court of Appeal reiterated its support for the 'professional' standard for disclosure in the case of *Gold* v. *Haringey Health*

23. *The Times*, 24 May 1985.
24. *The Times*, 11 February 1987.
25. Presumably 'professional practice' may demand that the doctor says more to the inquisitive patient.

Authority.[26] Mrs Gold agreed to be sterilized, but was never warned that sterilization might be reversed naturally, nor was she told that male vasectomy carries a lower risk of reversal. She sued for negligence after the birth of her unplanned child.[27] Again the trial judge[28] said that he did not have to follow *Sidaway*. *Sidaway*, he argued, applied to therapeutic treatment only. Mrs Gold was not sterilized because of any medical problem but as a convenient means of permanent contraception. In cases of such non-therapeutic interventions, the patient should be given all the information a sensible and reasonable patient would be likely to want to know. The test should be the 'prudent patient' not the professional standard. Mrs Gold fared no better than Mrs Blyth in the Court of Appeal.[29] Any distinction between therapeutic and non-therapeutic treatment was resoundingly rejected. The provision of any health care advice or treatment demanded the exercise of professional skill and so the *Bolam* test must apply. Whether or not the doctor was negligent was to be judged by whether or not in deciding what to tell the patient he conformed to a responsible body of professional opinion. When Mrs Gold was sterilized some gynaecologists did warn of the risks of reversal and discuss the comparative 'safety' of vasectomy as against female sterilization. Others did not, so Mrs Gold's claim was doomed to fail. In *Gold* the patient's right to decide for herself on treatment seems almost to disappear from the picture. Lloyd L J[30] said: '. . . a doctor's duty of care in relation to diagnosis, treatment and advice, whether the doctor be a specialist or a general practitioner, is not to be dissected into its component parts. To dissect a doctor's advice into that given in a therapeutic context and that given in a contraceptive context would be to go against the whole thrust of the decision of the majority of the House of Lords in [*Sidaway*].'

The judgements in *Sidaway*, *Blyth* and *Gold* may be seen superficially as victories for the 'doctor knows best' school of thought. It is dubious whether they represent victories for doctors. If what worries the medical profession is the threat of litigation and a fear that 'informed consent' claims are really just a means of trying to get compensation where traditional allegations of negligence would fail, *Sidaway* is

26. [1987] 3 WLR 649, CA.
27. See generally the case-law on failed sterilization in Chapter 16.
28. *The Times*, 17 June 1986.
29. [1987] 3 WLR 649.
30. p. 657.

unlikely to reduce the spate of litigation. What that judgement does is force a change in the nature of the allegations patients will have to make. Instead of arguing that their doctor has failed to give them the information that they, as patients, consider that they are entitled to, patients will seek to rely on Lord Bridge's assertion of ultimate control over the medical profession. Patients will endeavour to argue *either* that *no* reasonable doctor would have withheld the relevant information *or* that the practice of the profession is so manifestly bad that the courts should intervene to condemn the profession as a whole. Such allegations will lead to even more acrimonious litigation. A Scottish judge has sought to abate the prospect of such litigation at the cost of stifling any legal substance to patient autonomy. Lord Caplan in *Moyes* v. *Lothian Health Board*[31] said that he found nothing in *Sidaway* to suggest that 'the extent and quality of warning to be given by a doctor to his patient should not in the last resort be governed by medical criteria'. Lord Bridge's assertion that judges have not abdicated control over disclosure to patients on that analysis becomes meaningless, and it is to be hoped that in this context the English courts reject the advice of their Scottish brethren.

What price patient autonomy?[32]

To some extent the Court of Appeal's 'pro-doctor' judgements in *Blyth* and *Gold* are understandable. A test that gave the inquisitive patient greater rights than her less vocal neighbour could operate unfairly. Articulate, middle-class patients would be at an advantage. Asking questions in busy, noisy NHS clinics is not easy and some consultants can be tremendously unapproachable. Distinguishing between therapeutic and non-therapeutic treatment would be tricky too. For example, is childbirth, unattended by gross complications, therapeutic or non-therapeutic treatment? The virtual rejection of patient autonomy must be blamed on the *Sidaway* judgement. Their Lordships' notion of patient autonomy seems to regard autonomy as properly respected once the patient has chosen to entrust himself to his doctors for treatment and has had explained to him the general nature of what is to be done. Explanations of risks and side-effects are required only

31. [1990] 1 Med. LR 471.
32. See generally M. Brazier 'Patient Autonomy and Consent to Treatment: The Role of the Law' [1987] 7 *Legal Studies* 169.

when doctors consider such explanations to be in the patients' interest. Why did the English courts decline to follow their Canadian brethren and assert that patients should in the fullest sense define patients' interests? Three reasons seem pre-eminent. (1) Patients do not want more information. (2) Patients could not understand that information if they were offered it. (3) More information would lead to patients 'irrationally' refusing much-needed treatment. None of these reasons are sound.[33] Surveys show that in general patients do want more information. And a right to more information does not mean information will be forced on the unwilling patient. If a patient says, 'Doctor, it's up to you. I don't want to know any more about this operation,' a prudent patient test would not require that he be held down and forced to listen. Patients do have difficulties understanding medical details. The remedy is to teach doctors how to communicate more effectively. As for 'irrational' treatment refusals, once again there is no evidence to support the contention that more information leads to more patients refusing treatment. And how is 'irrationality' to be judged? A woman is told that radical mastectomy will maximize her prospects of recovery from breast cancer. She knows that if she loses a breast her husband will leave her and she knows that psychologically she is unable to cope with the necessary mutilation. Who can say she is 'irrational' if she opts for the marginally less 'safe' option of lumpectomy?

The standard determining how much patients should be told about treatment should be patient-centred. Preferably it should relate not to the mythical reasonable patient but to that particular patient. The tort of negligence is, however, a clumsy mechanism for enforcing a patient's right to information. Battery is inappropriate both because of its emotive nature and because it excludes oral drug therapies. The courts should be innovative and adapt the fiduciary relationship to embrace the doctor and her patient.[34] Within such a relationship of trust the doctor's duty would be to make available to the patient that information which it seems likely that individual patients would need to make

33. See in particular *Making Health Care Decisions*, President's Commission for the Study of Ethical Problems in Medicine, US Govt Printing Office, 1982, and *'What Are My Chances Doctor?': A Review of Clinical Risks*, Office of Health Economics, 1986.
34. Alas, such a proposition was rejected by both the Court of Appeal and the Law Lords in *Sidaway*. See M. Brazier, op. cit., pp. 189–91.

an informed choice on treatment. Such a change is desirable not just to endorse patient's rights but also to enhance patient care. Full participation in treatment by the patient, an alliance between patient and doctor, improves the quality of health care.[35] Interestingly, growing numbers of doctors are moving towards this view. It may be that *Sidaway* will in the end be consigned to legal history by the health care professionals themselves. For if it becomes near universal practice to give patients the information patients want, then following *Sidaway* and *Bolam* that will become the legal standard too. Unfortunately that is likely to be a lengthy process.

Does it matter who operates?

As important to many patients as what the operation entails may be the question of who operates. If a patient agrees to surgery believing eminent consultant X will operate on him, is his consent invalidated if registrar Y operates? Where he contracts with consultant X that he will operate, the consultant is in breach of contract if he substitutes someone else. Within the NHS he would, in the abstract, have to show that his consent was conditional on X operating. He would not have agreed to the surgery if anyone else proposed it. In practice, the standard consent form used within the NHS provides that no assurance is given that any particular doctor will operate. He cannot complain if the registrar operates. Of course if the registrar lacked the experience to perform a particular operation he will be able to sue him and the consultant if harm ensues. He can sue the registrar for his lack of competence. He can sue the consultant for his failure to provide proper supervision and for allowing an inadequately qualified member of the team to operate.

Every now and then suggestions have appeared in the press that medical students are being allowed to carry out minor operations. A story that hit the headlines in 1984 told of a vet who was allowed by a surgeon friend to remove a patient's gall bladder. A patient operated on by a vet will have a claim against the vet however competent he may have proved to be. He agreed to a qualified doctor operating on him. He no more agreed to surgery by a vet than to surgery by the author of this book. If the vet proves not up to the job, the patient can

---

35. See H. Teff, 'Consent to Medical Procedures. Paternalism, Self-Determination or Therapeutic Alliance' (1985) 101 LQR 432.

recover too against the surgeon who allowed him into the theatre and the hospital that permitted such an event. His action against them will lie in negligence. An operation performed by a medical student will give rise to a claim in negligence if the student is not competent. A claim in battery may also lie if the patient was not informed about the proposal to allow a student to operate. He consented to an operation and accepted, if he signed the standard form, that no particular practitioner undertook to operate. But he consented to surgery performed by a practitioner, not an 'apprentice'. Teaching hospitals play a vital role. The public interest requires that medical students train on real people. Nevertheless, any contact with a patient on the part of a medical student requires the patient's consent.

Emergencies

So far in this chapter I have made the assumption that the patient is in a fit state to give his consent. But when the patient is unconscious, treatment may have to be given immediately, before the patient can be revived and consulted. He may have been wheeled into Casualty after an accident. He may have agreed to operation X, in the course of which the surgeon discovers a rampaging tumour needing immediate excision. Surprisingly there is no modern English case in point. In a nineteenth-century case a woman agreed to the removal of a diseased ovary but told the surgeon that she was soon to be married and that he should not deprive her entirely of her ability to bear children. In the course of the operation he discovered both ovaries to be diseased and removed them both. Her claim against the surgeon failed on the grounds of her 'tacit consent'.[36] Despite her express statement prior to her operation, the court found that had she been in the shoes of the surgeon and seen the state of her organs she would be presumed to have agreed to the further surgery.

This idea of 'tacit consent' is still sometimes invoked to justify emergency surgery.[37] The patient, it is said, can be assumed to consent to what the medical staff do to save him. Where the patient has agreed to one operation and signed the standard consent form then this idea has some validity. The patient has in truth authorized further necessary surgery. Where the patient is brought into Casualty unconscious the

36. *Beatty* v. *Illingworth* (1896) BMJ 21 November, p. 1525.
37. *Wilson* v. *Pringle* [1986] 2 All ER 440, 447, CA.

idea of 'tacit consent' is unreal and unwieldy. In other areas of law the courts have recognized a defence of necessity. Applied to medical cases, it can fairly safely be said that the doctor is justified in taking any necessary action to save life and '. . . proceeding, without consent, with any procedure which it would be unreasonable, as opposed to merely inconvenient, to postpone until consent could be sought'.[38] The layperson might well ask why it should matter whether urgent treatment to save a patient's life is justified on the grounds of 'tacit consent' or a defence of necessity. Why should anyone other than a pedantic lawyer care which term is used? It matters because if emergency treatment is lawful because of 'tacit consent', it is the patient who must prove that the surgeon's assumption of consent was unreasonable. With a defence of necessity the surgeon has to prove that his intervention was reasonable and necessary to save the life of the patient or to prevent grave and permanent injury to her health.

Very often when a patient is unconscious or otherwise incapable of consenting to treatment himself the response of the hospital staff is to consult, when possible, with the patient's relatives or friends. What legal validity has a consent given by the relatives of an adult? The answer is none at all. The crucial factor when surgery is performed on an unconscious patient is whether what was done was immediately necessary.[39] We have seen that further surgery in the course of an authorized operation was not justified when it was not immediately necessary to save the patient's life, albeit it was objectively in her long-term interest. Similarly, treatment carried out on a patient brought unconscious into hospital must be shown to be medically necessary before the patient can be expected to regain his senses. Consulting relatives is courteous, but is legally significant solely in that as a matter of evidence it establishes that the doctor's attitude was reasonable, and may indicate the patient's own attitude. Only if the patient dies and his dependants seek to sue the doctor for performing the operation do their views become directly relevant.

One difficult problem arises in this sort of case. A patient is wheeled in unconscious and needs an immediate blood transfusion. His wife

38. See P. D. G. Skegg, 'Justification for Medical Procedure Performed without Consent' (1974) 90 LQR 512; S. A. M. McLean and A. J. McKay, 'Consent in Medical Practice', in S. A. M. MacLean (ed.), *Legal Issues in Medicine*, Gower, Aldershot, 1981; *Wilson* v. *Pringle*, above, note 5.
39. See *F.* v. *West Berkshire HA* [1989] 2 All ER HL.

says, truthfully, that he is a Jehovah's Witness and would thus refuse a transfusion. Can the doctor lawfully give a transfusion? The procedure is necessary but the doctor knows the patient would be likely to refuse it. The doctor's defence would have to be that in the absence of knowledge of the patient's own wishes in the actual predicament he found himself in, it was not for the doctor to assume that he would refuse immediately necessary treatment. When it came to the crunch the patient might prefer to be saved. By contrast, if a Jehovah's Witness agrees to operation X and expressly instructs the surgeon that he will not accept a blood transfusion if one is called for, the surgeon cannot justify administering a transfusion. The patient has anticipated the emergency and refused the treatment. In *Malette* v. *Shulman*,[40] a Canadian case, a young woman was brought unconscious into Casualty. She carried with her a card clearly stating that she was a Jehovah's Witness and that she would in no circumstances consent to a blood transfusion even if her life was in danger. The Canadian court held that the doctor who none the less administered a transfusion committed a battery. There was in that case no room for doubt that the patient had taken pains to ensure that no doctor should be in doubt of her refusal of blood in any contingency. Attempts to argue that a refusal of treatment must be 'informed' by knowledge of the actual circumstances of treatment were rejected by the court.[41]

Conclusions

The law relating to consent to treatment pays little more than lip service to patient autonomy. The patient has the right to reject any treatment at all, and to demand that she be injected in the right, not the left arm. Gross interventions without any consent are penalized, as are gross errors such as removing the right eye instead of the left. Beyond this, the English courts seem to say that patients must accept and acquiesce in a degree of medical paternalism many enlightened doctors now reject. That is not good for patients, and it is not good for doctors.

Doctors justifiably complain that to the lawyer, and the academic lawyer in particular, the issues discussed in this chapter are simply

40. (1988) 63 OR (2d) 243 (Ontario High Court).
41. Discussed in (1990) 5 *Professional Negligence* 118.

fascinating points of debate. For the doctor they are his daily diet. The influence the law can ever have is minimal. The law cannot improve the conditions in which doctors meet patients. It cannot and should not lay down a code of detailed guidance for pre-treatment counselling. What it should do is create a framework in which patients' rights and doctors' duties are defined with clarity, and on the basis of an informed understanding of patients' needs and wants. The current state of the law does medicine a disservice. Encouragement of further litigation will not help the growth of public confidence in the medical profession or doctors' confidence in the law. Patients, doctors and lawyers meet in court as adversaries. They need to meet as colleagues. The issue of informed consent needs investigation by a body combining legal, medical and lay experience. The case for a Commission to examine medicolegal and ethical issues is made out in part by the unsatisfactory approach the law on its own has shown to the matter of consent to treatment.

CHAPTER 5

Competence, Consent and Compulsion

In Chapter 4, the principles relating to consent to treatment by mentally competent adults were examined. This chapter looks at two further dimensions of consent to medical treatment. When an adult is incapable of deciding for herself whether or not to agree to treatment, how can treatment be lawfully authorized on her behalf? If an adult refuses to agree to treatment, can that refusal ever be overruled, either on the grounds that the patient 'irrationally' refused treatment which was in her best interests, or perhaps because, untreated, her physical or mental condition threatens the safety of other people?

The law relating to medical treatment of mentally handicapped patients is currently under review by the Law Commission. The Commission issued a fairly tentative consultation paper in April 1991. With luck, some of the uncertainties and difficulties in the law may be resolved by legislation resulting from the Commission's final recommendations some time in 1992 or 1993.

Doctors and nurses caring for a mentally handicapped patient confront an awkward dilemma. What does the law allow and require them to do when a patient who is chronologically 30 has a 'mental age' of 3? Once a person reaches 18, the age of majority, no one else, be he next of kin or a professional carer such as a social worker, can consent to treatment on his behalf. So the doctor may be faced with a patient who cannot himself give the consent required to make treatment lawful and so not a battery, and yet there is no one else who *can* lawfully act as the patient's proxy. Not to treat the patient at all would be inhumane and a breach of the duty of care owed to each and every patient. If a patient's physical condition threatens her life, or grave injury to her health, a defence of emergency might well justify necessary treatment, just as it does when an otherwise competent patient is wheeled unconscious into Casualty.[1] But what if there is no grave emergency? Consider these examples. An elderly demented lady suffers from cataracts. A middle-aged patient with severe mental impairment has a hernia. A 19-year-old mentally handicapped girl is found to be pregnant. None of these cases are true life-threatening emergencies, yet both the patients' families and their doctors will agree that the patients would be 'better off' for treatment.

A legal limbo

Those caring for and treating incompetent patients operate in a legal limbo. The patient himself is not capable of authorizing his own treatment, and no one else has the legal authority to act for him. How has this state of affairs come about? Contrast the position of adult patients whose mental condition disables them from deciding on treatment for themselves with that of young children whose immaturity similarly disables them. Parents are able to authorize treatment in the best interests of their child. If there is doubt or some dispute about whether a particular treatment is in the best interests of the child, the Family Division of the High Court can intervene via the wardship jurisdiction.[2] Before 1983, section 34(1)[3] of the Mental Health Act 1959 allowed a guardian, appointed to care for a mentally handicapped adult, to consent to treatment on behalf of a patient just as a parent does on behalf of her child. Section 8 of the Mental Health Act 1983, which replaces the provisions of the 1959 Act, however, restricted the powers of guardians substantially, so that a guardian can no longer consent to treatment of his 'adult ward' for any physical ill. Adult guardianship in any case has been little used in this country.[4]

---

1. *Wilson* v. *Pringle* [1986] 2 All ER 440, 447.
2. See further Chapter 15.
3. Section 34 provided that the guardian enjoyed all the powers of the parent of a child under 14.
4. See B. M. Hoggett, *Mental Health Law*, 3rd edn, Sweet & Maxwell, London, 1990, p. 280.

What of the powers of the court? Can adults with mental handicap be made wards of court as children can? Again, no. The Mental Health Act 1983 makes provision for applications to court and for a judge to manage the property and affairs of a patient.[5] But that power has been interpreted as restricted to the management of the patient's financial affairs and to exclude the management of his person or his everyday care.[6]

The wardship jurisdiction over children is not statutory alone. The courts enjoy an inherent jurisdiction derived from the prerogative powers of the Crown as *parens patriae*. An analogous, though *not* identical, *parens patriae* jurisdiction over adults fell into disuse long ago, but survived in theory until 1960.[7] The Mental Health Act 1959 was considered to be a comprehensive code for the proper care of mentally handicapped and mentally ill patients. Consequently the Royal Warrant under which *parens patriae* powers could be exercised was revoked in 1960.[8] Perhaps that did not matter too much in 1960 because under section 34(1) of the 1959 Act the patient's guardian, if he had one, could authorize treatment for him. Then, the 1983 Act destroyed that power.

The Mental Health Act 1983 does, of course, contain a whole part, Part IV, devoted to consent to treatment. Section 63 dispenses with any requirement for consent to treatment for mental disorder on the part of patients detained under the Act. Section 63 is of limited use. Very few patients are in fact detained under the Act. The majority of mentally handicapped or ill patients live in the community or are voluntary patients in hospital. And even when a patient is detained under the Act, section 63 authorizes non-consensual treatment only for mental disorder. It authorizes psychiatric treatment only, not treatment for any physical injury or disease.[9] Doctors may require a detained patient to accept medication for schizophrenia. They have no power to authorize surgery for a hernia, or an abortion or sterilization of a mentally handicapped young woman.

5. Part VII; see sections 92–6.
6. *F.* v. *West Berkshire HA* [1989] 2 All ER 545, 554, HL.
7. For a history and evaluation of the *parens patriae* jurisdiction see B. M. Hoggett, 'The Royal Prerogative in Relation to the Mentally Disordered: Resurrection, Resuscitation or Rejection', in M. D. A. Freeman (ed.), *Medicine, Ethics and Law*, Stevens, London, 1988.
8. See *F.* v. *West Berkshire HA* [1989] 2 All ER 545, 552, HL.
9. See *T.* v. *T.* [1988] 1 All ER 613.

The mentally handicapped patient thus finds herself in a legal limbo, created by a series of unthinking legislative blunders. I suspect that until recently no one gave much thought to the law governing treatment of such patients – they just went ahead on the paternalistic theory that 'doctor knows best'. The rise in medical litigation and increased concern for patients' rights in the 1980s caused health care professionals understandable concern. Doctors and nurses feared litigation if they went ahead with unauthorized treatment. And they feared litigation if a patient suffered because they did nothing.

F. v. West Berkshire Health Authority[10]

The trigger for judicial action to clarify the legality of treatment of mentally handicapped patients came from 1987 onwards with a series of cases relating to the sterilization of mentally handicapped women over 18.[11] If the girl was under 18, she could be made a ward of court and the court, if it agreed with her parents and her doctors that sterilization was in her best interests, could authorize that radical surgery.[12] Whether or not they should do so is discussed further in Chapter 17. T. was 19 years old. Somehow despite her mother's care she became pregnant. She had a 'mental age' of $2\frac{1}{2}$, she could barely communicate and she was doubly incontinent. Her mother and her doctors applied to Wood J. for a declaration that to terminate T.'s pregnancy and then to sterilize her would not be unlawful. He granted that declaration, finding that where a patient was suffering from such mental abnormality as *never* to be able to consent to proposed treatment a doctor was justified in 'taking such steps as good medical practice demands'.[13]

In 1989 the problem reached the House of Lords. F. was a 36-year-old woman with a mental age of 5 to 6. She was a voluntary patient in a mental hospital and had entered into a sexual relationship with a male fellow patient. The House of Lords in *F. v. West Berkshire HA*[14]

10. [1989] 2 All ER 545, HL.
11. *Re T.* (14 May 1987, unreported); *Re X, The Times*, 4 June 1987; *T.* v. *T.* [1988] 1 All ER 613.
12. See *Re B. (A Minor) (Wardship: Sterilization)* [1987] 2 All ER 206, HL, discussed further in Chapters 15 and 17.
13. *T.* v. *T.* [1988] 1 All ER 613, p. 625.
14. [1989] 2 All ER 545, HL.

granted a declaration stating that F. might lawfully be sterilized. Lord Brandon declared:[15]

... a doctor can lawfully operate on, or give other treatment to, adult patients who are incapable, for one reason or another, of consenting to his doing so, provided that the operation or other treatment concerned is in the best interests of the patient.

Doctors, lawyers and, of course, patients had mixed reactions to the judgement in F. On the one hand, their Lordships had made it clear that incompetent adults can lawfully receive medical care and treatment. The elderly confused lady with cataracts can have those cataracts removed. But F. in effect empowers doctors to decide on what treatment a patient receives with no restriction imposed on the exercise of that power. Operating on an old lady with cataracts is one thing, sterilizing a mentally handicapped girl is an intervention of a rather different order of magnitude. The Court of Appeal in F.[16] had tried to meet that problem. If some radical, irreversible intervention such as sterilization or use of the patient as an organ donor was proposed, the Appeal Court said that doctors *must* apply to the High Court for a declaration that the intervention truly was in the patient's best interests. The House of Lords concluded by a majority of four to one[17] that they had no jurisdiction to require doctors to apply for a declaration before any form of surgery or treatment on mentally incompetent patients. However, they said that as a matter of practice a doctor contemplating radical and/or irreversible treatment should normally *choose* to make an application to the court.

Protecting doctors: protecting patients?

Disquiet about the decision in F. v. *West Berkshire HA* arises, at least in part, from a suspicion that the judgement protects doctors rather

15. p. 551.
16. [1989] 1 All ER 764, CA.
17. Lord Griffiths dissented. He argued that a grave decision such as sterilization with all its implications should not be left to doctors alone. He believed that it was open to the House of Lords to develop a common law rule that prior judicial approval was required before an operation as radical as sterilization could be performed (pp. 561–2).

more than patients. There are three primary sources for such suspicion.

First, if doctors are not *required* to seek a declaration, however radical the proposed intervention, when will they choose to do so? Obviously a gynaecologist concerned about the propriety of sterilizing a young woman is very likely to seek a declaration that he acts lawfully in so doing. If he 'gets it wrong' acting on his own initiative, he might subsequently face an action for battery. A declaration from a High Court judge protects him from any such subsequent litigation. Particularly if there is some dispute between the woman's relatives, or relatives and carers, the *doctor* benefits from the court's intervention.

Second, how is the propriety of the proposed intervention to be evaluated? The judgement in *F*. directs that the *Bolam*[18] test is to be applied. Treatment will be lawful if it conforms with a reasonable and competent body of professional opinion, albeit there may be another reasonable and competent body of professional opinion which would take a contrary view. The *Bolam* test is the traditional test for professional negligence. A doctor should not perhaps be found negligent because he conforms to one professional school of thought in a disputed area of treatment. But is this test appropriate when judging what is in effect the compulsory treatment of incompetent patients?[19] Gynaecologists have sharply differing views about the circumstances in which involuntary sterilization is justified. The application of the *Bolam* test to determine whether a doctor acts lawfully in the patient's 'best interests' may mean that young women afflicted with exactly the same degree of mental handicap will be sterilized in Brighton but not in Manchester or vice versa. Moreover, whose professional opinion is to be evaluated? Do we look to the views of the doctors carrying out treatment or of those whose expertise lies in assessing the patient's mental capacity? Using the example of sterilization again, is it responsible opinion in gynaecology or psychiatry which is the touchstone? Lord Goff in *F*. stresses the need for an inter-disciplinary approach.[20] Of course, he is right to do so. But applying the *Bolam* test

18. See *Bolam* v. *Friern Hospital Management Committee* [1957] 1 WLR 582 discussed fully in Chapter 6, pp. 119ff.
19. See M. A. Jones, 'Justifying Medical Treatment without Consent' (1989) 5 *Professional Negligence* 178.
20. p. 567.

across disciplines will not be easy. In effect the judgement in *F.* entrusts decisions on the treatment of mentally handicapped patients to the medical profession. If a doctor conforms to that profession's standards he conforms to the law. The courts will not, it appears from *F.*, take an active role in investigating the propriety of treatment.

A third reason for disquiet about *F.* is rather different. The judgement lays down no criteria for deciding *when* a patient is incompetent. In *F.*, as in all the other judgements relating to sterilization of adult women and girls save the very first, *Re D.* in 1976,[21] the woman's incompetence is assumed. Yet that is perhaps the key question in the debate on when treatment may lawfully be given without the patient's own consent.

Criteria for competence[22]

On the facts of a case like *T.* v. *T.*,[23] it is hardly surprising that the judge did not even address the issue of competence. The young woman was said to have a 'mental age' of 2½ and could hardly communicate with others at all. *F.* communicated at the level of a 2-year-old and was said to have a 'mental age' of 4 or 5. Much is made in the judgements of 'mental age'. That concept triggers a picture of a real child. Were I to propose, for example, that a child of 7 should be allowed to consent on her own authority to sterilization or organ donation, I should be laughed out of court. Hence perhaps a proper analysis of what is entailed in competence has been overlooked because of the use of child analogies.

What is clear is that in English law competence depends on the particular transaction in issue. There are no rigid criteria which decide that X is competent or incompetent for all legal purposes. The relevant question is rather whether X enjoys the necessary degree of understanding to embark on that particular enterprise, be it entering into a contract, or getting married, or making a will. The illuminating case of *In the Estate of Park*[24] highlights the flexible nature of the concept of

21. [1976] 1 All ER 326.
22. See generally, M. Brazier, 'Competence, Consent and Proxy Consents', in M. Brazier and M. Lobjoit (eds.), *Autonomy and Consent: Protecting the Vulnerable*, Routledge & Kegan Paul, London, 1991.
23. [1988] 1 All ER 613.
24. [1954] P. 112.

competence in English law. Mr Park, an elderly man who had previously suffered a severe stroke, married his second wife one morning and that afternoon he executed a new will. He died soon afterward. His family challenged the validity of the marriage. His widow challenged the will. He was found to be mentally competent to marry, but to lack the necessary mental capacity to make a will. His impaired understanding and reasoning power was sufficient for him to grasp what was entailed in marriage, but his confusion and loss of memory disabled him from having the necessary recollection of his properties and his obligations to make a will.

What then must a patient be capable of understanding to give a valid consent to medical treatment? In *Chatterton* v. *Gerson*[25] Bristow J. held that for consent to be valid the patient need only be informed in broad terms about the nature and purpose of proposed treatment. If that is all the patient needs to be told about treatment to give a valid consent, then that is all he needs to be able to understand about treatment to have the competence to give such a consent. The level of understanding at which a patient is legally competent to give her own consent to treatment is thus relatively low.

Consider these examples. An elderly demented patient needs dental treatment for an abscessed tooth. He has little concept of time, sometimes does not recognize his wife and engages on occasion in bizarre behaviour. But is he incompetent to consent to dental treatment? What does he need to be told and to understand? (1) His tooth hurts. (2) The tooth can be removed so the hurt will be 'cured'. Despite his dementia, he is almost certainly competent to authorize for himself that simple procedure. A woman of 21 has a 'mental age' of 7. She cannot care for herself. She plays with dolls and if she could choose her companions she would choose 'real' children. Yet is she without doubt incompetent to consent to sterilization? What does she have to understand? (1) It is not a good idea for you to have a baby. (2) An operation on your tummy can stop you having a baby. Most 7-year-olds today understand enough about how babies are born to comprehend that information. And the woman of 21, while she may enjoy only the limited reasoning capacity of the 7-year-old, has the experience of a woman. She has experienced puberty and menstruation and hopefully has been trained to understand and care for her body.

A minimal level of competence enables many patients with some

25. [1981] QB 432.

degree of mental handicap to remain competent to authorize their own treatment. But it also entails the risk that although the patient understands enough to authorize their own treatment, they may none the less refuse to do so. The elderly patient with toothache may, like a child, allow his fear of the dentist to overrule his desire to be rid of the toothache. The 21-year-old woman may decide that she would quite like a baby to 'play with'. Both outcomes will be seen by others as undesirable. They provoke another question as yet undebated in the English courts. When may a refusal of treatment by a patient whose competence is disputed or borderline be overruled? Care should be taken before rushing to enforce treatment in the patient's 'best interests'. Several thousand indubitably competent people damage their dental health by staying away from the dentist. Just because a patient is labelled demented or mentally handicapped, can we enforce his visit to the dentist? Many, many women have babies when they are not fitted to be mothers. If we decide that, whatever she wants, the 21-year-old with a mental age of 7 must be sterilized, are we really acting in *her* interests alone, or to protect the interests of her child, and safeguard society from yet another child whose mother cannot care for it herself?

Parens patriae and proxy consents

Whatever legal rules govern the treatment of incompetent patients, criteria for competence need to be defined. Where the patient is incompetent, are there better means of authorizing treatment for him than the current rules in *F.* v. *West Berkshire HA*? The practical impact of *F.* is that the health care professionals carrying out treatment authorize that treatment. The *doctor* acts as the patient's proxy. He proposes and disposes. This 'medical practice model' of treatment is easy to criticize, but what are the alternatives?

In *T.* v. *T.*, Wood J. made an eloquent plea for the restoration of the *parens patriae* jurisdiction.[26] Just as a child can be made a ward of court, so that any disputed or sensitive treatment can be authorized by a High Court judge in the Family Division, so should mentally handicapped patients be able to be made wards of the court. Doctors would then be obliged to seek judicial authorization for any radical procedure, not just be free to do so to protect themselves. Restoration of

26. [1988] 1 All ER 613, p. 625.

parens patriae would have beneficial effects. It would signal the import-ance attached to protecting the interests, and where possible the auton-omy, of patients with mental handicap. But its effect would be limited. Only the most serious or unusual cases could go to the court. There would still need to be a general rule for authorizing routine health care procedures, with the Family Division acting, as it does in the case of children, as a forum of last resort. And consideration should also be given as to whether a Family Court judge sitting alone is the most appropriate arbiter of such cases. Should he sit with assessors with qualifications and experience in the care of patients with mental handicap?

Restoration of *parens patriae* leaves open the question whether routine treatment should be subject to the rules in *F.* or some alterna-tive model for consent. The obvious alternative is to provide for some form of adult guardianship, so that a relative or carer could act as the patient's proxy.[27] After all, in practice, doctors will consult the patient's family before deciding on treatment. If a 19-year-old with mental handicap is still living at home with her parents, it seems sensible to give the parents legal power to authorize treatment on her behalf. Her mother will have a better understanding of what is of value to her daughter, what she enjoys and what she fears, than will any doctor. Proxy consent via adult guardianship appears an attractive proposition. Yet it has pitfalls. At present the law requires a decision taken on behalf of a mentally handicapped patient to be based on her 'best interests'. There is a risk that a proxy who is also a carer will allow her interests to override the patient's. A mother of 60 caring for an adult mentally handicapped daughter naturally dreads the thought of adding to her current burdens a mentally handicapped grandchild. Separating the interests of patients and carers may be simply unrealistic. A further difficulty with proxy consent is that with older patients it may be hard to find a suitable proxy. The simple fact that X is Y's next of kin is not enough. If X has not set eyes on Y, her brother, for twenty years she is in no position now to act for him. Elderly patients may have no immediate family. Social workers or residential home managers may come into consideration as appropriate guardians. But once in effect we are looking to a 'professional' proxy rather than an intimate friend or relation, we need to be sure that 'professional' proxy is a more appropriate decision-maker than the doctor actually treating the patient.

27. See the legislation in Alberta.

Criticizing the current 'medical practice model' for authorizing treatment of mentally handicapped patients is a tempting pastime. Yet the alternatives are not problem-free. Maybe what is needed if we retain the 'medical practice model' is an effective system for reviewing medical judgements. A model for such a system already exists in respect of psychiatric disorder in the Mental Health Act 1983.

Mental Health Act 1983[28]

Part II of the Act makes provision for the detention in hospital of certain mentally disordered patients. Only a tiny minority of patients with mental disorder are in fact detained in hospital under the Act. An application for admission for assessment (observation and tests) must be based on the written recommendations of two medical practitioners who testify that the patient (1) is suffering from mental disorder of a nature warranting his detention in hospital, at least for a limited period, and (2) ought to be so detained in the interests of his own health or safety, or to protect others.[29] Admission for the assessment authorizes the patient's detention for twenty-eight days. If he is to be detained longer an application for admission for treatment must be made.[30] Such an application made under section 3 of the Act must be founded on grounds that the patient:

(a) ... is suffering from mental illness, severe mental impairment, psychopathic disorder or mental impairment and his mental disorder is of a nature or degree which makes it appropriate for him to receive treatment in a mental hospital; *and*

(b) in the case of psychopathic disorder or mental impairment, such treatment is likely to alleviate or prevent a deterioration in his condition; *and*

(c) it is necessary for the health and safety of the patient or for the protection of other persons that he should receive such treatment and it cannot be provided unless he is detained under this section.

'Severe mental impairment' is defined as 'a state of arrested or incomplete development of mind which includes severe impairment of

28. For full discussion of the 1983 Act see Hoggett, op. cit.
29. See s. 2. An emergency application founded on the recommendation of a medical practitioner may be made under s. 4 and authorizes detention for up to seventy-two hours.
30. A successful application for admission for treatment authorizes detention for an initial period of six months.

intelligence and social functioning'. 'Mental impairment' is similarly defined, save that impairment need not be severe. Where the grounds for detention are based either on degree of mental impairment or on psychopathic disorder there must additionally be evidence of 'abnormally aggressive or seriously irresponsible conduct'.

The number of mentally handicapped individuals eligible to be detained under the Act is thus small. (1) In the case of mental impairment, whether existing since birth or as a result of accident or disease, condition (b) (treatability) is unlikely to be met. Being shut up in hospital will not do them any good. Their condition is not treatable. (2) A mentally handicapped person is unlikely to be a danger to others and can be protected from herself by means other than detention, so condition (c) will not be met. (3) Government policy is now to promote care in the community, and all over the country long-stay mental hospitals are being closed down. Only the most dangerously disordered and profoundly handicapped patients will be detained in hospital under the Act.

Compulsory treatment under the 1983 Act

Part IV of the Mental Health Act provides for the compulsory treatment of that minority of patients detained under the Act, and provides a model for treatment decisions which might be made more widely applicable. Section 63 provides that:

The consent of a patient shall not be required for any medical treatment given to him for the mental disorder from which he is suffering, not being treatment given within section 57 or 58 [of the Act].

Section 63 applies to detained patients only. It cannot be used on voluntary patients, or on an out-patient basis. At one hospital doctors admitted patients under section 3, gave them long-term medication, then released them on licence until their next dose of medication was due. That practice was found to be unlawful.[31] Section 63 could be used to dispense with a patient's consent to treatment only where that patient actually needed to be detained in hospital. If he did not need to be so detained, the conditions laid down in section 3 for admission for treatment were not met, and the use of section 3 to enforce treatment was an unlawful fiction.

31. *R.* v. *Hallstrom ex p. W. (No. 2)* [1986] QB 824.

105

Section 63 thus authorizes routine psychiatric treatment. As I said earlier, it cannot be used to authorize treatment for physical illness; it applies only to treatment for mental disorder. Sections 57 and 58 provide safeguards for patients.

Section 57 is unusual in that it applies to *all* patients and not just those detained in hospital. Any form of psychosurgery,[32] such as lobotomy, and any surgical implantation of hormones to reduce male sexual drive will be unlawful[33] unless (1) the patient consents *and* (2) an independent doctor (appointed by the Mental Health Commission) certifies that (a) the patient is capable of understanding the nature and purpose of the treatment proposed and its likely effects; and (b) the treatment is likely to benefit the patient. The role of the Mental Health Act Commission is crucial. The Commission was created by the 1983 Act to act as a watchdog for patients' interests. It has a lay Chair and a mixed professional/lay membership. The Commission[34] has had its teething troubles but represents a laudable effort to provide informed, independent scrutiny of professional decisions.

Section 58 applies to detained patients only. Electro-convulsive therapy[35] and any long-term medication (administered for longer than three months[36]) are authorized only if either (a) the patient consents and a doctor certifies that he is competent to do so or (b) an independent doctor certifies that the patient is incapable of giving consent or has refused to do so but that none the less '. . . having regard to the likelihood of [the treatment] alleviating or preventing a deterioration of his condition the treatment should be given'.

The Mental Health Act offers a relatively simple model for non-consensual treatment of incompetent patients. The decision on routine treatment is entrusted to their doctors. The more serious the proposed treatment, the greater are the safeguards provided for the patient by

32. See s. 57(1).
33. See s. 57(2); and the Mental Health (Hospital Guardianship and Consent to Treatment) Regulations 1983 (SI 1983 No. 893) reg. 16(2). S 57(2) empowers the Secretary of State to bring other treatments within the ambit of s. 57(2).
34. See Part VIII of the Mental Health Act 1983 and note the Code of Practice promulgated by the Commission in 1989.
35. See s. 58(1) and SI 1983 No. 893 reg. 16(2). Again the Secretary of State is empowered to bring further treatments within the ambit of s. 58(1).
36. See s. 58(2).

way of independent review of the doctor's judgement. Following this model it would be possible to provide that the current principle in *F.* v. *West Berkshire HA* should apply to everyday care decisions, for example drug therapy for 'normal' illnesses, dental treatment and minor surgery such as cataract operations or hernia repairs. Long-term medication and major surgery would require review and authorization by an independent medical practitioner. Irreversible or controversial surgery would be lawful only if authorized by a doctor appointed by the Mental Health Act Commission, or, if so desired, by a judge acting under a restored *parens patriae* jurisdiction.

Compulsory treatment beyond the 1983 Act

Whatever principles are adopted to govern the treatment of incompetent patients, the question remains whether compulsory treatment of a competent patient can ever be legally justifiable. Can an elderly, demented yet still competent patient be required to submit to dental treatment In his own 'interests'? Can a patient who refuses to bathe, yet remains competent, be compelled to do so in the interests of those who share the ward with him?

In England, unlike in the USA,[37] legislation has never enforced sterilization on those seen as mentally or physically unfit to reproduce. In England, unlike in many countries in Europe, childhood vaccination has never been compulsory. Compulsory treatment outside the sphere of mental health has been confined to the treatment of virulently infectious disease. The Public Health (Control of Disease) Act 1984 provided that patients suffering from 'notifiable diseases', for example cholera or typhus,[38] lose not only their right to confidential treatment, but also their right to decide on whether to accept treatment at all. Magistrates may order such a patient to be removed to hospital,[39] and they may order suspected carriers of the disease, or a patient thought to be incubating the disease, to submit to medical examination.[40] AIDS is not a notifiable disease under the 1984 Act. However, the

---

37. For discussion of compulsory sterilization laws in the USA see M. D. A. Freeman, 'Sterilizing the Mentally Handicapped', in *Medicine, Ethics and Law*, Stevens, London, 1988.
38. See ss. 10, 11, 16.
39. See s. 38.
40. See s. 35.

Public Health (Infectious Diseases) Regulations 1985 apply the provisions of the Act giving magistrates powers to order compulsory treatment and examination to people who have, or are suspected of having AIDS, or to be HIV positive. To my knowledge these powers have only once been invoked in the case of a patient with AIDS.

The basis of enforced treatment under public health legislation is quite simply the protection of the public. A person can be removed to hospital if precautions to prevent the infection spreading can be taken, are not being taken, and a 'serious risk of infection is thereby caused to other people'. There is no pretence that the compulsory powers are exercised solely in the 'best interests' of the patient. Where the patient albeit through no fault of his own poses a threat to the health of others, his interest in autonomy cedes to others' interest in health and safety.

At common law an individual enjoys a right to self-defence. This is a common-law right which almost certainly survives the enactment of a public right to use force to prevent crime in section 3 of the Criminal Law Act 1967. If I am attacked by a person so mentally disordered that he could not be found guilty of any crime, I am still lawfully entitled to fend off my attacker using whatever degree of force is necessary.[41]

Might there then be circumstances in which treatment of a competent but confused or disturbed patient could be justified because of the harm his untreated condition poses to others? Can a patient who refuses to bathe be washed to prevent him becoming a hazard to hygiene? Such a suggestion sounds like heresy. Apart from the provisions in the Mental Health Act (discussed earlier) and special provisions in the National Assistance Act 1948 concerning elderly patients,[42] treatment of patients whose competence is disputed is lawful only if in the patient's 'best interests'.

---

41. See *Clerk and Lindsell on Torts* (16th edn), paras. 8-02–8-04.
42. Section 47 of that Act (as amended the National Assistance (Amendment) Act 1951) empowers community health physicians to remove from their homes and place in a suitable hospital a person 'suffering from chronic disease or being aged, infirm or physically incapacitated' and unable to care for themselves. The CHP may apply to a magistrates' court for an order removing such a person to hospital either in his own interests or to 'prevent injury to the health of, or serious nuisances to, other persons'. Section 47 is highly controversial and many geriatricians refuse to invoke such powers.

'Best interests': a pious fiction

There can be little doubt that health care professionals are imposing 'treatment' on patients which cannot be shown to be exclusively in the patients' interests. I am not suggesting for one moment that gynaecologists are sterilizing women for eugenic reasons, or that surgeons are experimenting on unfortunate patients. But patients are washed against their will. Patients are sometimes given medication they would rather not have, perhaps disguised in their food! Without such stratagems nurses struggling to care for wards catering for confused geriatric patients, or long-stay institutions for voluntary mental patients, might give up the struggle. Should such miscreants be tracked down and prosecuted for assault? Or should we look carefully at the 'best interests' test?

It is very dubious whether it is ever possible to divorce the interests of the individual entirely from the interests of the carer. The example that follows is unpleasant but is an instance of a dilemma that doctors have to face and parents may have to live with. A young woman lives at home with her father. She is physically adult and normal but has the mind of a 2-year-old. She is sexually provocative and fertile. She is incontinent and it is her father who every month has to cope with her periods. None of this distresses her any more than it would a 2-year-old child. Sterilization by hysterectomy could never be said to be in her best interests even if sterilization *per se* could. Yet her father may find that he cannot cope much longer. Dealing with menstruation is the straw that breaks the camel's back. Is that young woman better off without a uterus but with her father, or with her uterus in an institution? Her interests and her father's are inextricably intertwined.

The interests of the patient must be the predominant interest to be considered. But perhaps other interests should also be taken into account. Individuals live as part of society. Society has obligations to the individual, especially the vulnerable individual. Individuals, though, have reciprocal obligations to society. Moreover, a careful review of all the decided cases on non-consensual treatment may suggest that courts do in fact take note of interests other than the patient's. If 19-year-old T. would never have been properly aware of her pregnancy, or the birth and removal of a child, that experience may at any rate not have harmed her. Her mother and the child would certainly suffer. Would it be wrong to consider their interests? But if the interests of others will inevitably be considered, would it not be better to do so openly and not hide behind a pious fiction of best interests?

Best interests/substituted judgement

In judgements on the treatment of mentally incompetent patients the trend in the USA is to reject a 'best interests' test in favour of 'substituted judgement'. The court seeks to ascertain what the patient himself, had he been competent, would have desired. So in the famous *Quinlan*[43] judgement, it was held that Karen Quinlan's father could authorize doctors to switch off the ventilator keeping his unconscious daughter alive because that is what Karen would have wanted herself. 'Substituted judgement' is attractive, but dangerous. 'Best interests', what the reasonable patient would want or need, is often a fiction. Individuals differ so much in their needs and desires that the reasonable patient is a myth. What would be intolerable to me may be quite bearable to you. Where a patient has once been competent, with known preferences and idiosyncrasies, having told family and friends of what he would and would not want done if terminally ill or grossly disabled, 'substituted judgement' is a useful criterion on which to make treatment decisions. In Chapter 21 I look at means by which patients using advance directives can make their wishes known in advance of any incompetence. But if a patient is afflicted by mental handicap from birth, 'substituted judgement' is unworkable. The poor young woman in *T*. v. *T*. was never capable of communicating to others her choices – she was never capable of making any choices.

Conclusions

The Law Commission's preliminary consultation paper,[44] published in 1991, reviews the issues discussed in this chapter. The Commission addresses the fundamental problem of defining competence and goes on to examine several alternative models for decision-making on behalf of incompetent patients. In particular, views are sought on the desirability of introducing into English law some form of adult guardianship. The consultation paper also seeks advice on how far it would be possible and beneficial to equate decision-making procedures relating to the financial and property affairs of an incompetent patient with procedures for taking decisions concerned with his personal welfare.

43. *In re Quinlan* (1976) 355 A. 2d. 647.
44. See Law Commission Consultation Paper No. 119, 'Mentally Incapacitated Adults and Decision-Making: An Overview'.

For example, if X is authorized to act on the patient's behalf to deal with his money and property, would it be sensible for X also to enjoy the power to make decisions relating to that patient's everyday life and medical care? The Commission argues that the two cannot be separated. If the patient needs long-term medical care and nursing, selling his house to fund that care may be a necessary first step to safeguarding his welfare. The consultation paper is lucid and comprehensive. It poses crucial questions for the development of the law. How swiftly those questions will be answered remains to be seen.

Meanwhile the courts and the doctors have to work out together the implications of *F.* v. *West Berkshire H A*. Procedural rules have been promulgated to standardize the form in which applications for a declaration that treatment is lawful should be made.[45] The more difficult question has been when should the doctor seek a declaration and when may he properly rely on his own and his colleagues' judgement of the patient's 'best interests'? It has been held that where two doctors have certified that the abortion of a mentally handicapped woman is lawful under the Abortion Act 1967, there is no need to seek judicial sanction for that operation.[46] Nor is judicial approval needed for a proposed hysterectomy to be carried out to protect an incompetent woman's physical health and approved by two consultant gynaecologists.[47] These recent judgements reinforce the point that, as it stands, the doctor acts as proxy for his incompetent patient in authorizing treatment.

---

45. See *J.*v.*C.* (*Note*) [1990] 3 All E R 735; *Practice Note* (*Sterilization: Official Solicitor*) [1989] 2 F L R 447.
46. *Re G.*, *The Times*, 31 January 1991.
47. *Re E.*, *The Times*, 22 February 1991.

CHAPTER 6

Medical Negligence

The civil law of negligence is designed to provide compensation for one individual injured by another's negligence. Gross negligence may occasionally also be punished by the criminal courts. I will consider any possible criminal liability incurred by doctors later. A person seeking compensation for negligence has to establish (1) that the defendant owed him a duty to take care, (2) that he was in breach of that duty, that he was careless, and (3) that the harm of which the victim complains was caused by that carelessness. He must satisfy all these tests to succeed. A widow succeeded in establishing that a hospital doctor was careless in not coming down to Casualty to examine her husband. He was admitted to hospital in an appalling state which eventually proved to be caused by arsenical poisoning. He died within hours. She failed to recover any compensation from the hospital in respect of her husband's death because the evidence was that even had he been properly attended he would still have died.[1]

The bare bones of the law of negligence outlined above are general to everyone, in the conduct of their everyday activities and in carrying out their job. They are not special to doctors. But certain special factors about medical negligence claims need to be introduced here. I have already mentioned the factual difficulty of proving negligence where there is a clash of medical opinion, and the effect that the need to prove fault has on the medical profession's reaction to claims against them. They become, not unnaturally, highly defensive. For a long time

1. *Barnett* v. *Chelsea and Kensington HMC* [1969] 1 QB 428.

112

the judges too were most unwilling to find against a medical man. A brotherly solidarity bound the ancient professions of law and medicine together. Judicial attitudes are changing somewhat, but that process of change is neither radical nor swift. None the less the medical profession is increasingly haunted by the spectre of a medical malpractice crisis. And fears of such a crisis are deployed in court in attempts to deter judges from too ready findings of medical negligence.

Malpractice crisis: reality or illusion?

Those who contend that the United Kingdom faces a medical malpractice crisis put forward several arguments. (1) The numbers of claims made are escalating dramatically and, increasingly, doctors are found to be negligent on 'unfair' grounds. (2) The cost of compensation awards to patients is rapidly becoming prohibitive. (3) Consequently doctors will opt for 'defensive medicine'. That is to say, a doctor will choose the treatment for the patient which is most likely to be 'legally safe', to ensure that he will not be sued by the patient. That treatment may not necessarily be medically best for the patient, and may be unnecessarily expensive and time-consuming. A common example of alleged defensive medicine is a decision to carry out a Caesarean section as soon as there is any sign of difficulty in the course of labour, rather than to run the risk of continuing to attempt a natural delivery. (4) The rising tide of medical negligence actions is destroying good doctor/patient relationships and driving promising young doctors away from specialties such as obstetrics, which have become 'high-risk' specialties for negligence claims.

In fact, such evidence as there is tends to dispute the existence of any crisis. Much of the brouhaha about a malpractice crisis derives from fears that experiences in the USA are likely very soon to be repeated on this side of the Atlantic. There is little doubt that in the USA medical malpractice claims are big business. The USA is a litigious nation. Despite talk of an English malpractice crisis, patients leaving NHS hospitals are still more likely to return with a box of chocolates for the staff than with a writ! Moreover, there are significant differences in the organization of both health care and legal services in the USA which should make us wary of relying too heavily on experiences in that country.

Research undertaken by the King's Fund Institute and the Centre for Socio-Legal Studies, Oxford,[2] indicate that suggestions of an imminent malpractice crisis in the United Kingdom are not well founded.

(1) It is true that the numbers of medical malpractice suits brought rose sharply in the decade 1977–87.[3] The medical defence organizations reported that the numbers of claims notified to them doubled between 1983 and 1987. And it is also true that the average cost of compensation awards more than doubled, with the highest award moving from just over £132,000 in 1977 to over a million pounds in 1987. In December 1990 the parents of a child suffering brain injuries at birth won an award of £1.2 million.[4] Seven months later £1.7 million was awarded in a similar case. But the proportion of successful claims has not apparently risen significantly in that period. A doctor is not at greater risk of being found negligent now than he was in 1977, though he is more likely to be sued. As for allegations that doctors are 'unfairly' found negligent by lawyers, this allegation just does not stand up to scrutiny. For in deciding whether a doctor is negligent the court relies on expert *professional opinion*.[5] A doctor can only be found to be negligent, not if lawyers say so, but if his peers testify to his negligence.

(2) The cost of medical negligence claims is a cause for concern. The spectre of a medical malpractice crisis had substance for doctors until the end of 1989 mainly because of its impact on their pockets. In 1978 a doctor's annual subscription to his medical defence organization cost him £40. In 1989 that subscription had risen to nearly £1,400. The rising cost of medical indemnity prompted the government to alter the provision made for indemnifying hospital doctors. Under the NHS indemnity scheme (discussed fully in the next chapter) hospital doctors no longer have to belong to a medical defence organization. Their employer, the health authority or NHS trust, indemnifies them directly against liability for professional negligence. Cynics claim that now doctors no longer need fear ever-rising costs of medical indemnity, less may be heard of a medical malpractice crisis. But someone has to pay for medical litigation and for compensation awards. Where a claim

2. C. Ham, R. Dingwall, P. Fenn and D. Harris, *Medical Negligence: Compensation and Accountability*, King's Fund Institute/Centre for Socio-legal Studies, Oxford, 1988.
3. ibid., pp. 11–12.
4. ibid.; see Figs. 1–3, p. 11. For the £1.2 m. award to Hugo Cassel see the *Guardian*, 22 December 1990.
5. *Bolam* v. *Friern HMC* [1957] 1 WLR 582.

is made by an NHS patient, that money comes off the NHS budget. Money to compensate an injured patient and money to defend claims brought in respect of alleged negligence must come out of funds which might otherwise have been used to employ an extra surgeon, or pay for a new neo-natal unit, or support a programme of preventive medicine.

(3) The prospect that doctors will base decisions concerning treatment not on their professional judgement of what is ultimately best for the patient, but on what is 'legally safest' for the doctor, does sound appalling. But is there hard evidence that doctors are being forced to practise defensive medicine? So far the answer seems to be that there is probably not.[6] The classic example given of defensive medicine – the rise in the rate of Caesarean sections – has been found to be explicable by many other factors. Caesarean rates are rising in several countries, not all of which have experienced rising litigation rates.[7] And then there is the question of what is meant by defensive medicine. In the House of Lords, Lord Pitt eloquently argued that the rising tide of litigation meant that doctors ordered unnecessary and sometimes painful tests, and he predicted '. . . an increase in defensive medicine with an alarming waste of resources'.[8] The difficulty is to decide when further tests and cross-checks cease to be a sensible precaution in the interests of the patient and become a 'waste of resources'.[9]

(4) What is undoubtedly true is that many doctors have become so frightened by the spectre of a malpractice crisis that doctor/patient relationships have been damaged. Evidence of defensive medicine may be disputable, defensiveness in medicine is a sad fact.[10] And doctors in 'high-risk' specialties such as obstetrics and anaesthetics are the worst affected among the profession. Doctors, and indeed all health care professionals, in the United Kingdom need to be aware of the reality

6. See M. A. Jones and A. E. Morris, 'Defensive Medicine: Myths and Facts' (1989) 5 *Journal of the Medical Defence Union* 40.
7. See Ham *et al.*, op. cit., pp. 14–15, and note in particular Fig. 6.
8. HL Official Report, 10 November 1987, cols. 1350–51.
9. See generally P. Danzon, *Medical Malpractice*, Harvard University Press, Cambridge, Mass., 1985.
10. Hence Ian Kennedy argues eloquently that what is required to defuse any 'crisis' is better information about the law for doctors so that they will not feel constrained to practise 'defensive medicine': see 'Review of the Year 2. Confidentiality, Competence and Malpractice', in P. Byrne (ed.), *Medicine in Contemporary Society*, King's Fund, London, 1987.

of the current state of medical litigation here. Claim rates here remain in general less than a third of the rate in the USA and awards of compensation are minimal compared to the highest US awards. Nor are we likely to repeat US patterns. There are three main reasons why this is so unlikely.[11]

(1) In the USA virtually all medical care is provided by the private sector. Thus if your original treatment goes wrong and you suffer as a result of some medical accident, you will have to pay out more money for whatever corrective treatment is required. Naturally an aggrieved patient is going to be looking to the doctor whom he perceives as responsible for the accident for the money to pay for the necessary corrective treatment. Most patients will, of course, carry private health insurance, but their insurers will be as keen as the patient to ensure that any costs, possibly arising from medical negligence, are recovered from the doctor and his insurers. In a private health system such as that of the USA, health care is charged on a fee-for-service basis. The more tests a doctor carries out the more money he makes. Perhaps some of the apparent evidence for 'defensive medicine' is really explained as 'expensive medicine'? Finally, it may be the case that patients who pay directly for treatment will tend to be more aggrieved by medical accidents than those treated within a public health system. Doctors who charge their patients may lose some of their professional aura and become just businessmen to be sued if their 'goods' fall short of the customers' expectations.

(2) Legal services in the USA are organized on a different basis from those in the UK. A patient who is contemplating a medical negligence action in England will have substantial difficulties funding such an action. Unless he qualifies for legal aid, he will have to be sufficiently rich, not just to pay his own legal fees, but to risk having to pay the defendants' legal costs if his action fails! Lawyers acting for the clients in medical negligence actions in the USA act on a contingency fee basis. If the case fails, the client pays nothing; if the claim succeeds the lawyer takes a percentage of the damages, normally about one third. Such a system makes it much easier for patients to litigate,

---

11. See generally Ham *et al.*, op cit., pp. 19–20. And note too suggestions that any US malpractice crisis is at least in part a creation of the medical insurers seeking to protect their profits. See N. Terry, 'The Malpractice Crisis in the United States: A Dispatch from the Trenches' (1986) 2 *Professional Negligence* 145.

and gives lawyers a direct interest in the levels of damages awarded.

Contingency fees on the American pattern have been rejected in England. However, the Courts and Legal Services Act 1990[12] does provide for conditional fee agreements. The Lord Chancellor has been given the power to make regulations allowing English lawyers to agree to provide legal services on a basis whereby either no fee is charged at all unless the case succeeds or the amount of the fee may be increased if the litigant is successful. What effect such conditional fee agreements may have on medical litigation remains to be seen. A similar arrangement in Scotland, the speculative action, does not seem to have prompted any rise in the rate of litigation in that jurisdiction.

(3) Awards of damages in the USA are decided not by the judge, as is the case in England, but by the jury. Compensation for pain and suffering is infinitely more generous in the USA than it is here. Moreover, damages in this country are awarded solely for the purpose of compensating the patient for what he has lost as a result of the defendant doctor's negligence. A US jury is empowered in certain circumstances to double the compensatory damages by making a further award of punitive damages, to punish the defendant for negligence.

A medical malpractice crisis in England is a spectre with little substance. Propaganda advertising such a crisis damages proper evaluation of the legal rules governing medical litigation. There is, as we shall see, a great deal wrong with our current system for medical litigation. Neither doctors nor patients do well out of that system. But the King's Fund research paper concluded: '. . . [I]nsofar as there is a malpractice crisis, it concerns the difficulties facing patients and their relatives bringing a claim against doctors.'[13]

With that assertion in mind I go on to review the principles relating to medical negligence and then, in the next chapter, I outline the practical problems of litigation. What will emerge is that much of the justifiable criticism of medical negligence actions derives not from the substantive principles of law but from the clumsy, inequitable and horrendously expensive process of litigation.

Duty of care

A patient claiming against his doctor or a hospital usually has little

12. See s. 58.
13. See Ham *et al.*, op. cit., p. 5.

difficulty in establishing that the defendant owes him a duty of care. A general practitioner accepting a patient on to his list undertakes a duty to him. A hospital and all its staff owe a duty to patients admitted for treatment. If the patient is an NHS patient the duty derives from the law of tort, which imposes a duty wherever one person can reasonably foresee that his conduct may cause harm to another. Where the patient is a private patient the duty arises from his contract with the doctor or the hospital. It is the same duty regardless of its origins. I will look later at the circumstances in which the private patient is owed duties other than that of care.

Difficulty arises where a person has not been accepted as a patient. The law of negligence does not oblige anyone to be a Good Samaritan. If a man has a coronary attack on an Inter-City express, and a doctor fails to respond to the guard's call 'Is there a doctor on the train?', the doctor incurs no liability to the victim who dies for lack of medical treatment. Indeed, the law almost discourages the Good Samaritan. For if the doctor comes to the sick man's aid he undertakes a duty to him and will be liable if his skill fails him.

A practical problem today arises from the increasing practice of health authorities to centralize casualty facilities in the larger hospitals. More and more hospitals have notices on their gates stating that they do not accept emergencies and accident victims. The notice refers the injured to another named hospital. An accident victim whose injuries worsened because of the delay in reaching a casualty department is unlikely to succeed in a claim against the hospital which refused him admission. It never assumed any duty to him. A hospital which operates a casualty department, by contrast, is responsible for the patients who come within its doors regardless of whether they have been formally admitted to hospital. By running a casualty department an NHS hospital undertakes to treat those who present themselves and will be liable in negligence if any failure on the part of their staff causes the patient to be sent away untreated.[14] Similarly a GP owes a duty to emergency patients as well as to those on his own list. His contract with the NHS provides that he will treat visitors to his district falling suddenly ill. Like the hospital with the casualty ward he undertakes to treat the genuine emergency as much as his regular patients.

One sadly common scenario does however pose a tricky question relating to a hospital's or health authority's duty to a patient. A

14. *Barnett* v. *Chelsea and Kensington HMC* (above).

patient is referred by her GP to an Out-Patients clinic at the local hospital. The consultant who examines her decides that she needs surgery as soon as possible. Lengthy waiting lists mean that surgery is delayed and the patient's condition deteriorates. Could she sue the hospital for negligence, arguing that she was owed a duty as a patient from the time she was first given an appointment to attend the hospital clinic? The courts have refused to order hospitals to operate on patients, refused to review waiting-list priorities,[15] but if she can prove actual damage from delay might she have a claim in negligence? Determining what constitutes negligence would be awkward.[16]

The medical standard of care

The second matter that any claimant in negligence has to prove is that the defendant was careless. The onus of proof is on the plaintiff. He must show that the defendant fell below the required standard of care. The basic standard is that of the reasonable man in the circumstances of the defendant. So a professional man must meet the standard of competence of the reasonable man doing his job. A woman who went to a jeweller to have her ears pierced developed an abscess because the jeweller's instruments were not aseptically sterile. The jeweller had taken all the precautions that any jeweller could be expected to take. The woman's claim failed. The defendant had done all a jeweller could reasonably be expected to do.[17] If she wanted the standard of care a surgeon could offer she should have consulted a surgeon.

The standard of care demanded of the doctor, then, is the standard of the reasonably skilled and experienced doctor. In *Bolam* v. *Friern HMC*[18] the judge said:

The test is the standard of the ordinary skilled man exercising and professing to have that special skill. A man need not possess the highest expert skill; it is well established law that it is sufficient if he exercises the ordinary skill of an ordinary competent man exercising that particular art.

15. See *R.* v. *Central Birmingham HA ex P. Collier*, *The Times*, 6 January 1988, CA, above, p. 22.
16. For a thorough survey of problems *re* duties to patients see I. Kennedy and A. Grubb, *Medical Law: Text and Materials*, Butterworths, London, 1989, Chapter 2.
17. *Phillips* v. *William Whiteley Ltd* [1938] 1 All ER 566.
18. [1957] 1 WLR 582, 586, 118.

The defendant doctor will be tested against the standard of the doctor in his particular field of medicine. The general practitioner must meet the standard of the competent general practitioner; the consultant gynaecologist the standard of the competent consultant in that specialty. As Lord Scarman put it: '. . . a doctor who professes to exercise a special skill must exercise the ordinary skill of his speciality'.[19]

So a patient who attends his general practitioner complaining of an eye disorder cannot require him to have the skill of a consultant ophthalmologist. But he can complain if the GP fails to refer him on to a consultant when his condition should have alerted the reasonable GP to the need for further advice or treatment.

No allowance is made for inexperience. The Court of Appeal has consistently rejected the idea that standards of care should vary to allow for the degree of experience possessed by the defendant. They held an L-driver liable where, although she had done the best that could be expected of a learner, she fell short of the standard of the reasonably competent and experienced motorist.[20] In *Wilsher* v. *Essex AHA*[21] the appeal court considered the liability of junior hospital staff. Martin Wilsher was born nearly three months prematurely. He was admitted to a neo-natal unit managed by the defendant health authority where skilled treatment probably saved his life. He needed extra oxygen to survive. Sadly, junior doctors made an error in monitoring the oxygen levels in Martin's blood, and on two occasions he received an excess of oxygen. It was argued by Martin's lawyers that excess oxygen caused him to develop retrolental fibroplasia (RLF), a retinal condition which left Martin nearly blind. Ultimately the House of Lords held that the plaintiff had failed to prove that excess oxygen caused RLF in Martin and ordered a retrial.[22] The importance of the Court of Appeal's judgement lies in their exposition of the rules on negligence by junior staff. Argument by the defendants that staff concerned did their best in view of their inexperience was rejected. The law requires all medical staff in such a unit to meet the standard of competence and experience society expects from those filling such demanding posts. Their Lordships recognized the need for medical staff to train

19. *Maynard* v. *West Midlands RHA* [1984] 1 WLR 634, 638.
20. *Nettleship* v. *Weston* [1971] 2 QB 691, CA.
21. [1986] 3 All ER 801, CA.
22. [1988] 1 All ER 891; see below, p. 132.

'on the job'. They stressed that the judgement of negligence on one occasion did not imply incompetence. The court canvassed two further ideas for future cases. (1) Should patients' recourse be not against individual junior staff but directly against any health authority using junior staff for tasks for which they were not yet experienced? (2) Would a junior doctor who, recognizing his inexperience, sought advice from his consultant have discharged his duty? Responsibility in law might then move to the consultant.[23] Just as no allowance is made for youth so none will be made for age. The 80-year-old GP, continuing his private practice, must meet the same standard of alertness and dexterity as his 30-year-old colleague.

Ascertaining the standard of care

How does a court ascertain the standard of skill which the doctor should have met? As I have said earlier, they have to ask the doctors. Let us consider the case of Mr Bolam again. He was given electro-convulsive therapy and sustained fractures. He argued that the doctor was negligent (1) in not giving him relaxant drugs, (2) as drugs were not given, in failing to provide adequate physical restraints, (3) in not warning him of the risks involved in the treatment. We have seen that he failed in his argument that he should have been warned. As to the absence of relaxant drugs or restraints, the evidence was that while some doctors would have thought them necessary many did not. The judge found the doctor not guilty of negligence for he acted:

... in accordance with a practice accepted as proper by a responsible body of medical men skilled in that particular area ... a man is not negligent, if he is acting in accordance with such a practice, merely because there is a body of opinion who would take a contrary view.[24]

The test of 'accepted medical practice' is firmly entrenched in English law. It applies to all stages of medical treatment. In *Whitehouse* v. *Jordan* a woman of 4 ft 10 ins was in great difficulty in labour with her first child. The doctor attending her summoned the senior registrar, Mr Jordan. He attempted to deliver the baby by forceps. He pulled six times. He then abandoned the attempt and moved swiftly to deliver

23. See *Jones* v. *Manchester Corporation* [1952] 2 QB 852, 871. Note that in *Wilsher*, above, Dr Wyeth, the house officer, was found not negligent.
24. *Bolam* v. *Friern HMC* [1957] 1 WLR 582, 587–8.

the child by Caesarean section. The baby was severely brain-damaged. The mother claimed that the excessive force in using forceps caused the damage. He should have pulled less often. Lord Denning in the Court of Appeal said that if Mr Jordan was at fault it was at most an error of clinical judgement for which a doctor could not be held liable.[25] The House of Lords too found that Mr Jordan was not liable. They found that the original trial judge's inferences from the expert evidence that Mr Jordan was negligent were wrong. (I will return to this aspect of the case in a later chapter.) But their Lordships were scathing about Lord Denning's suggestion that errors in clinical judgement were immune from question. Lord Edmund-Davies said, quoting the *Bolam* case:

'The test is the standard of the ordinary skilled man exercising or professing to have that special skill.' If a surgeon fails to measure up to that standard in *any* respect ('clinical judgement' or otherwise), he has been negligent . . .[26]

The case of Staff Nurse Maynard illustrates the strength of the accepted medical practice test. She consulted a consultant physician and a surgeon with symptoms both thought might well be tuberculosis, but she also displayed symptoms which might indicate Hodgkin's disease. The doctors decided on a diagnostic operation, mediastinoscopy. It carried a risk of damage to the vocal cords and Mrs Maynard's vocal cords were in fact damaged. And in fact she proved to have tuberculosis. She alleged that the doctors were negligent in subjecting her to the operation. The plaintiff's expert witness, Dr Hugh-Jones, argued that the operation should never have been done. He would have regarded her condition as almost certainly a case of tuberculosis. The defendants called a formidable number of experts who testified that the fatality rate for Hodgkin's disease if treatment was delayed justified the defendants in exposing Mrs Maynard to the risk of the mediastinoscopy. The original judge preferred Dr Hugh-Jones's evidence. The Court of Appeal and the House of Lords overruled him. Lord Scarman said:

. . . a judge's 'preference' for one body of distinguished professional opinion to another also professionally distinguished is not sufficient to establish negligence in a practitioner . . .[27]

25. [1980] 1 All ER 650, 658, CA.
26. *Whitehouse* v. *Jordan* [1981] 1 WLR 246, 258, HL.
27. *Maynard* v. *West Midlands RHA* [1984] 1 WLR 634, 639, HL.

Accepted professional practice is not a test uniquely applied to doctors. It is applied to all skilled men. The judge is no more an expert in plumbing, or carpentry, or accounting practice than he is in medicine. But in relation to other professions the courts are ready to challenge accepted practice as unsatisfactory.[28] We have seen Lord Scarman's attitude to Mrs Maynard's claim. He would not adjudicate between the two schools of opinion. The Court of Appeal recently asserted that there could be cases where the courts would think it appropriate to intervene. The Master of the Rolls, Sir John Donaldson, has said that a practice must be '. . . *rightly* accepted as proper by a body of skilled and experienced medical men'.[29]

In an appropriate case a judge may reject a medical view shown to be manifestly wrong. But this has very rarely happened in England. In one case a patient attended a physiotherapist for a course of treatment. He was severely burned in the course of that treatment. The defendant had warned him of the danger in the manner approved by the Chartered Society of Physiotherapists. The judge held the warning to be inadequate to safeguard the patient.[30] There is, as far as I know, no case where a medical practitioner conforming to accepted professional practice has none the less been found to be negligent. It is worth noting, too, that Sir John Donaldson's statement was made in the light of a claim relating to the amount of information a surgeon gives his patient. The judges may be readier to intervene in such cases, as opposed to claims relating to such matters as diagnosis or choice of treatment.

'Accepted practice' means current practice

It is, of course, no defence for a practitioner to say that a practice was widely accepted when he was at medical school and is therefore accepted once informed medical opinion has rejected the practice.[31] The practitioner must keep up to date with new developments and incorporate them in his practice. But there is an inevitable 'time-lag'

28. See Kennedy and Grubb, op. cit., pp. 408–20.
29. *Sidaway* v. *Board of Governors of the Bethlem Royal and the Maudsley Hospital* [1984] 2 WLR 778, 792, CA. Lord Bridge endorsed this view in the House of Lords [1985] 2 WLR 480, 505.
30. *Clarke* v. *Adams* (1950) 94 Sol. J. 599.
31. *Hunter* v. *Hanley* (1955) SC 200.

between the making of new findings by researchers and the percolation of their ideas through to doctors in the field. The doctor will be judged by the standard of awareness and sophistication to be expected of a doctor in his sort of practice. Great emphasis is placed on the professional position and the specialty of the defendant.[32] A patient who suffered from brachial palsy as a result of his arm being extended in a certain position while he was given a blood transfusion in the course of a bladder operation brought a claim against the anaesthetist. Six months before the operation an article had appeared in the *Lancet* condemning this practice because of the risk of brachial palsy. The claim failed. Failure to read one recent article was not negligent.[33] Another doctor made a mistaken diagnosis of cancer of the bladder. If he had used a cystoscope he would not have made such a mistake. But at that time cystoscopes were not freely available. The defendant did not have one. Few doctors outside the major teaching hospitals did. He was not negligent.[34]

All doctors are not expected to have the level of awareness or sophisticated equipment available to a professor in London. They must be judged on what is to be expected of a doctor in regular everyday practice. The Department of Health in London issues a flow of circulars to hospitals updating doctors on new developments. One, for example, outlined procedures to protect against surgical accidents.[35] Failure to take a precaution outlined in the circular would be strong evidence of negligence. This is material readily available to all hospital doctors of which they might reasonably be expected to take note and advantage. Being unaware of materials made available by the medical defence unions might similarly be negligent.

It must be stressed that the relevant date to judge current practice must be the date of the operation or treatment and not the date the claim comes to trial. In *Roe* v. *Ministry of Health* a patient had become permanently paralysed after an injection of the spinal anaesthetic Nupercaine, administered in 1947. His claim against the doctors and the hospital came to trial in 1954. Before the operation

32. See A. J. Gamble, 'Professional Liability', in S. A. M. McLean (ed.), *Legal Issues in Medicine*, Gower, Aldershot, 1981, p. 89.
33. *Crawford* v. *Board of Governors of Charing Cross Hospital, The Times*, 8 December 1953, CA.
34. *Whiteford* v.*Hunter* (1950) 94 Sol. J. 758, HL.
35. HM (72) 37.

the drug had been kept in glass ampoules in a solution of phenol. The accident to the patient occurred because phenol percolated through invisible cracks in the ampoules and contaminated the Nupercaine. No one had ever known this to happen. The claim in negligence failed. Lord Denning said: 'We must not look at the 1947 accident with 1954 spectacles.'[36]

Once a tragic incident of this nature has occurred and has been attended by publicity then of course a further incident would easily be proved to be negligence. Current practice would have been shown to be wanting.

Departing from 'accepted practice'

A doctor is legally 'safe' when he conforms with existing practice. Does he put himself 'at risk' if he departs from that practice? If liability in negligence automatically followed once harm resulted from the adoption of a novel method of treatment, medical progress in England would be stultified. Doctors would be fearful to challenge orthodox views, which might be mistaken, and they could be wary of any innovation. It would be a brave man who would risk the blow of a finding in negligence to his career and reputation. This does not mean that I think that the patient should go uncompensated. I shall discuss in Chapter 10 schemes that would provide compensation more readily and effectively in this sort of case than the present law of tort.

In *Clark* v. *MacLennan*[37] Peter Pain J. suggested a compromise. The plaintiff suffered from stress incontinence after the delivery of her first child. Early attempts at conservative treatment made her no better. One month and eleven days after the birth, the defendant operated to repair the weakness in her bladder and muscles. The plaintiff haemorrhaged and the repair broke down. Two further operations failed to repair the damage. The plaintiff was left permanently affected by stress incontinence. The operation performed on the plaintiff was a common procedure. But most gynaecologists delayed such an operation for at least three months after the birth to minimize the risk of haemorrhage and breakdown. The plaintiff's experts satisfied the judge that this was the orthodox view of treatment, the general practice. The judge held

36. *Roe* v. *Ministry of Health* [1954] 2 KB 66, p. 84.
37. [1983] 1 All ER 416.

125

that while it was for the plaintiff to prove negligence, once she had shown a departure from an accepted practice, designed to guard her from the very sort of harm which she suffered, the burden moved to the defendants to justify their departure from accepted practice. Alas, the House of Lords in *Wilsher* v. *Essex AHA*[38] rejected and condemned this compromise. As a matter of law the burden of proving negligence remains with the plaintiff. It cannot now be argued that where the defendant doctor has deviated from accepted practice he must disprove negligence. None the less, where such a deviation has occurred and no explanation consistent with the exercise of proper skill and care on the part of the doctor is forthcoming, the plaintiff patient should have little difficulty in satisfying the burden on him of proving negligence.

A doctor who departs from orthodox views is not automatically branded as negligent. But he will have to justify his course of action either by indicating features of the individual case which call for a different mode of treatment or by showing his novel method to be superior or at least equal to the general practice. I look now at some examples of decided and settled cases to see how the accepted practice test actually works.

Diagnosis

A wrong diagnosis is by itself no evidence of negligence on the part of the doctor. As a Scottish judge has said:

In the realm of diagnosis and treatment there is ample scope for a genuine difference of opinion and one man is clearly not negligent merely because his conclusion differs from that of other professional men . . .[39]

A patient alleging that a wrong diagnosis was negligent must establish either that the doctor failed to carry out an examination or a test which the patient's symptoms called for, or that his eventual conclusion was one that no competent doctor would have arrived at. While the myth of total infallibility of 'clinical judgement' has been exploded, a patient who relies solely on an allegation that the doctor's conclusions were mistaken will rarely succeed. Not surprisingly a doctor who failed to diagnose a broken knee-cap in a man who had fallen 12 ft on to a

---

38. *Wilsher* v.*Essex AHA* [1988] 1 All ER 891; see below, p. 132.
39. *Hunter* v. *Hanley* 1955 SLT 213, 217.

concrete floor was found to be negligent.[40] Other examples are hard to find.

The courts are readier to find negligence when a patient and his experts can point to a specific failure on the part of the doctor. A casualty doctor, who failed to examine or X-ray a drunken patient admitted with the information that he had been seen under a moving lorry, was found to be negligent when after his death next day he was discovered to have eighteen fractured ribs and extensive damage to his lungs. It was no defence that the patient never complained of pain. The doctor should have known that alcohol would dull the patient's reaction to pain.[41] The doctor must be alert to the patient's background. A GP who failed to test for and diagnose malaria in a patient who had recently returned from East Africa was held liable for the patient's death. The doctor was consulted nine days after the patient's return to this country, and a relative suggested malaria but the doctor diagnosed flu. Six days later malaria was diagnosed in hospital, where the patient died that day.[42] Failure to diagnose diabetes where the symptoms complained of by the patient should have alerted the doctor to this possibility may lead to liability.[43] Too hasty a diagnosis of hysteria will often be negligent.[44] By dismissing the patient as 'neurotic', physical symptoms go uninvestigated.

In all the above examples the doctor was negligent because he failed to act on information available to him and/or to perform routine tests. Where a diagnostic procedure is not routine, is costly, or painful, or risky, an additional factor has to be considered. Do the symptoms displayed by the patient justify subjecting him to the procedure? The doctor faces a legal as well as a medical dilemma. If he does not arrange for the test and the patient does suffer from some condition which the test would have revealed, the doctor may be sued for that failure. If he does arrange the test and an inherent risk of the test harms the patient, the patient may sue if the test reveals that the

40. *Newton* v. *Newton's New Model Laundry*, *The Times*, 3 November 1959.
41. *Wood* v. *Thurston*, *The Times*, 25 May 1951.
42. *Langley* v. *Campbell*, *The Times*, 6 November 1975; and see *Tuffil* v. *East Surrey Area HA*, *The Times*, 15 March 1978, p. 4. (Failure to diagnose amoebic dysentery in a patient who had spent many years in the tropics.)
43. Annual Report of the MDU, 1990, pp. 26–7.
44. *Serre* v. *De Filly* (1975) OR (2d) 490; and see Annual Report of the MDU, 1982, pp. 22–3; and 1983, p. 24.

doctor's suspicions were groundless. We saw that that is what happened with Staff Nurse Maynard.[45] The defendants were found not to be liable to her because they had followed accepted practice in going ahead with the test despite its dangers. Doctors argue forcefully that alacrity to pin liability on them for every diagnostic error may cause patients to be submitted to more expensive and potentially risky procedures than may be strictly medically desirable.

Treatment

A claim in respect of negligent treatment may be based on an allegation that the treatment chosen was inappropriate, or that while the treatment embarked on was correct it was negligently carried out. In the case of the first sort of allegation, nothing more can be said than that the test will be whether the chosen method of treatment conformed with accepted practice. It is examples of the latter sort of case which I will now examine.

First, all doctors involved must act on adequate information and supply each other with adequate information. A GP prescribing drugs must check what other medication the patient is on. So in 1982 the Medical Defence Union settled a case where a prescription of a powerful pain-killer for pain in the wrist and fingers of an elderly patient reacted with long-term anti-coagulants also prescribed for the patient and caused neurological problems.[46] Doctors must be alert to common drug reactions and actively seek relevant information from patients. A clinic which injected a woman with penicillin was held liable for her death an hour later.[47] Had they inquired of her, or examined her records, they would have been aware of her allergy to penicillin. A GP arranging for the admission of a pregnant patient to hospital while he was treating her for a septic finger was found negligent in not so informing the hospital. She contracted septicaemia. Had the hospital known of the state of her finger they would have put her on antibiotics straight away.[48] But doctors must be wary of relying entirely on information supplied by their colleagues. In 1984 the Medical Defence Union settled this claim. A patient was admitted for a gynaecological

45. *Maynard* v. *West Midlands RHA* [1984] 1 WLR 634; see p. 122.
46. Annual Report of the MDU, 1982, p. 24.
47. *Chin Keow* v. *Govt of Malaysia* [1967] 1 WLR 813.
48. *Hucks* v. *Cole* (1968) 12 Sol. J. 483.

operation. The gynaecologist asked a general surgeon to remove what he said was a ganglion from the patient's wrist. Thus the patient would be spared two separate operations. It was not a ganglion. Surgery of that sort was inappropriate and the patient's hand was permanently paralysed. The MDU settled because the general surgeon should have made his own pre-operative assessment and not relied on a colleague from another specialty.[49]

Once the doctor is properly informed and has selected his course of treatment he must ensure that he carries it out properly. He must check the dosage of any drug. Prescribing an overdose will readily be found to be negligent.[50] He must be sure that his handwriting is legible. In *Prendergast* v. *Sam and Dee*[51] the defendant doctor's handwriting was so appalling that the pharmacist dispensed the wrong drug to the plaintiff-patient. Doctor and pharmacist were both held liable for the ensuing injury to the unfortunate Mr Prendergast. Care must also be taken always to read drug labelling properly. In a tragic case settled by the Medical Defence Union in 1989,[52] a senior house officer misread a label and administered potassium chloride instead of saline to a newborn infant. The baby died.

Where surgery is called for, the risk of injury is increased. Especially risky for any patient is the administration of the anaesthetic. Nearly 3 million Britons undergo an anaesthetic every year. Between 250 and 300 will die. The anaesthetist will be found to be negligent if he failed to make a proper pre-operative assessment of the patient, failed to check his equipment, failed to monitor the patient's blood pressure and/or heartbeat in the course of surgery or if, an inevitable accident having occurred, the anaesthetist fails to invoke adequate resuscitation measures. Some specific failure on the defendant's part must be pinpointed. A disturbing number of claims settled by the Medical Defence Union arise from failure to intubate the patient properly (putting the tube in the wrong place) or attaching tubes to the wrong gas so that the patient fails to receive essential oxygen.[53] A recent cause of much

49. Annual Report of the MDU 1984, p. 18.
50. *Dwyer* v. *Roderick* (1983) 127 SJ 806, and see J. Finch, 'A Costly Oversight for Pharmacists' (1982) 132 NLJ 176.
51. *The Times*, 19 March 1989, CA. And see Annual Report of the MDU, 1982, pp. 14–16, 1988, p. 40.
52. Annual Report of the MDU, 1989, p. 32.
53. See Annual Report of the MDU, 1988, pp. 28–9, 1989, pp. 20–21.

litigation has arisen from failure to anaesthetize the patient completely. Patients are paralysed and unable to communicate, but remain awake and feel pain throughout surgery![54]

An anaesthetic tragedy of itself is generally not evidence of negligence. An anaesthetist who failed to check equipment and ended up administering carbon dioxide instead of oxygen was put on trial for manslaughter in New Zealand.[55] An anaesthetist who injected cocaine instead of procaine was found negligent in this country,[56] as was the junior doctor who injected pentothal into an anaesthetized patient, causing his death.[57] If the wrong drug, or the wrong dosage, or a contaminated drug, is used, the patient's claim will generally be made good. The exception will be where the error cannot be laid at the anaesthetist's door. So, as we saw in *Roe* v. *Ministry of Health*[58] a patient who was paralysed because a then unknown risk of phenol percolating into the ampoules of local anaesthetic materialized, recovered no compensation.

Surgery itself must be performed with the utmost care. One judge has suggested that the more skilled the surgeon the higher the standard of care.[59] Some errors advertise their negligence. Leaving swabs and equipment inside the patient is a good example. And the surgeon must accept responsibility for such matters and not rely on nursing staff.[60] Nor does the surgeon's responsibility end with the careful completion of surgery. He must give his patient proper post-operative care and advice. A surgeon performed a cosmetic operation just below the eye. He told his patient to inform him if bleeding occurred within forty-eight hours. It did and the patient tried to telephone the surgeon and got no reply. The surgeon was held to be negligent.[61]

I have done no more here than to outline a few examples of decided and settled claims. I go on in the next chapter to the practical problems of medical litigation. In a claim for negligence it helps to pinpoint some specific failure by the doctor. In the next chapter we will see how that may be done.

54. ibid.
55. Annual Report of the MDU, 1984, pp. 34–5.
56. *Collins* v. *Hertfordshire CC* [1947] K B 598.
57. *Jones* v. *Manchester Corporation* [1952] 2 QB 852.
58. [1954] 2 QB 66, CA.
59. *Ashcroft* v. *Mersey AHA* [1983] 2 All E R 245, 247.
60. *Urry* v. *Biere, The Times*, 19 July 1955.
61. *Corder* v. *Banks, The Times*, 9 April 1960.

Relating the injury to medical negligence

So far the majority of the cases examined involved something going wrong as a result of a medical mistake. The patient's problem has been to prove that what was done, or not done, amounted to actionable negligence. But, as I said at the beginning of the chapter, proving negligence by the doctor does not conclude the case in the patient's favour. He must also show that his injury, his worsened or unimproved condition, was caused by the doctor's negligence. He must prove causation. In practice, proving causation is often the most problematic aspect of a patient's claim. The difficulties of causation in medical malpractice cases fall into two main categories. (1) Can the patient convince the court that it was the relevant medical negligence which caused his injury, rather than the progress of his original disease or condition? (2) How should the courts proceed when the essence of a claim is, not that medical negligence caused any fresh or additional injury to the patient, but that negligence deprived him of a chance of full recovery from his original disease or condition? A number of attempts by trial judges to ease the burden of causation for patients have been firmly quashed and condemned by the House of Lords. In each and every case the patient must advance evidence showing that it is more likely than not that the defendants' negligence caused the injury of which he complains.

Two judgements of the House of Lords illustrate the difficulty of proving that negligence, and not the pre-existing condition of the patient, caused his injuries. In *Kay* v. *Ayrshire and Arran Health Board*,[62] a 2-year-old boy, Andrew Kay, was rushed into hospital suffering from pneumococcal meningitis. He was negligently given a massive overdose of penicillin and nearly died as a result. Intensive efforts by hospital staff saved Andrew's life and he recovered from both the toxic overdose and from meningitis. But he was found to be profoundly deaf. His parents on his behalf sued the Scottish health board responsible for the hospital where Andrew had been treated. The board admitted negligence, but denied that Andrew's deafness resulted from that negligence. Deafness is often a complication of meningitis even where the disease has been correctly treated. Massive overdoses of penicillin of the sort that Andrew was given are mercifully rare, so there was little available evidence of whether such an overdose

62. [1987] 2 All ER 417.

materially increased the risk that Andrew would become deaf as a result of his disease. The House of Lords quashed the trial judge's finding in Andrew's favour. Lord Keith commented that the lack of recorded cases demonstrating the effect of overdose of penicillin '. . . cannot in itself make good the lack of appropriate evidence'.[63]

As we have seen in *Wilsher* v. *Essex AHA*[64] junior doctors were found to be negligent in administering excess oxygen to a very premature baby, Martin Wilsher. Martin succumbed to retrolental fibroplasia (RLF), an incurable condition of the retina causing gradual blindness. The question that went to the House of Lords was whether Martin's lawyers could prove that RLF resulted from that negligent administration of excess oxygen. The scientific evidence suggested that RLF *may* result from excess oxygen, but there were five other possible causes of RLF in very sick, very premature infants. The trial judge had held that as negligence had been proved the burden of disproving that that negligence caused Martin's injuries moved to the defendants. He said that as the evidence showed that the doctors were in breach of their duty to Martin and failed to take a precaution expressly designed to safeguard Martin from RLF, it was then up to them to prove that Martin's condition resulted from one of the other possible causes. The House of Lords roundly condemned such an approach, and ordered a retrial. The burden of proving causation rests on the plaintiff alone, and does not move to the defendant even though negligence has been proved or admitted.

What is crucial for the plaintiff is thus the quality of the expert scientific evidence presented on his behalf. That evidence must at the very least demonstrate that it is more likely than not that the defendants' negligence either materially contributed to the plaintiff's condition or materially increased the risk that the plaintiff would succumb to such a condition.[65] Where the scientific evidence is ambivalent or suggests a variety of competing causes for the plaintiff's state, the action for negligence will fail.

When the poor plaintiff complains not of some new injury inflicted by the defendants, but of a lost chance of recovery, his claim is, if

63. ibid., p. 421.
64. [1988] 1 All ER 871, HL.
65. See *per* Lord Bridge, pp. 882–3. For discussion of the application of the complex judgement in *McGhee* v. *NCB* [1973] 1 WLR 1 HL to medical negligence claims see *Clerk and Lindsell on Torts* (16th edn), paras. 11–25.

anything, even more difficult to prove. In *Hotson* v. *East Berkshire HA*[66] the plaintiff, a schoolboy of 13, fell heavily from a rope on which he had been swinging to the ground 12 ft below. He was taken to hospital. His knee was X-rayed and revealed no injury. No further examination was made and the plaintiff was sent home. Five days later the boy was taken back to the same hospital and an injury to his hipjoint was diagnosed and subsequently swiftly and correctly treated. But the injury had traumatic consequences. The boy suffered a condition known as avascular necrosis. This condition, caused by a restriction of the blood supply in the region of the original injury, leads to misshapenness of the joint, disability and pain, and later in life almost certainly brings on osteoarthritis in the joint. The plaintiff's disability might have ensued from the accident in any case. But there was a 25 per cent chance that given the correct treatment immediately the plaintiff might have avoided disability and made a nearly full recovery.

The defendant hospital admitted negligence in failing to diagnose and treat the plaintiff's injury on his first visit. Both parties agreed that prompt treatment would have offered a 25 per cent chance of avoiding permanent disability. The trial judge awarded the boy 25 per cent of full compensation for his condition, that is a sum of money to compensate him for a 25 per cent lost chance of full recovery.[67] The House of Lords quashed his judgement.[68] Their Lordships held that the plaintiff had failed to prove that it was more likely than not that avascular necrosis resulted from the negligent delay in treatment, because there was a 75 per cent chance he would have suffered from avascular necrosis even if treatment had been given promptly. To recover damages for the avascular necrosis the plaintiff needed to establish at least a 51:49 likelihood that 'but for' the negligent delay in treatment he would have made an uncomplicated recovery from his original injury. Had he succeeded in so doing he would have been entitled to 100 per cent compensation for his disability. But their Lordships declined to say that loss of a less than 50 per cent chance of full recovery was never recoverable in a medical negligence claim. They left that question open.

A patient who seeks compensation for loss of a less than 50 per cent chance of recovery will only be able to do so, if at all, in the following

66. [1987] 2 All ER 909, HL.
67. [1985] 3 All ER 167.
68. [1987] 2 All ER 909, HL.

sort of circumstances. He would have to be able to produce compelling expert evidence to the effect that the relevant negligent mismanagement of, or delay in, treatment diminished his statistical prospects of recovery by an ascertainable percentage. For example, if a doctor negligently failed to diagnose cancer and a further period elapsed before a proper diagnosis was made and treatment begun, the patient might be allowed to recover damages for diminished prospects of survival and recovery.[69] Perhaps at the time when the diagnosis should have been made the patient would have had a 75 per cent chance of recovery, but by the time it was in fact made that chance had diminished to 50 per cent. Difficult though it would be to assess in monetary terms that loss should be recoverable. Such a case differs from *Hotson* in this way. On the evidence available in *Hotson* no one could say whether or not but for the relevant negligence the plaintiff would or would not have suffered avascular necrosis. In the example of the unfortunate cancer patient scientific and statistical evidence strongly indicates that 'but for' the relevant negligence the patient would have enjoyed a much greater chance of prolonged survival.

Overtired, overworked doctors

Any account that lists the claims which succeed against, or are settled by, doctors distorts the true picture and appears unfair. The proportion of claims in relation to visits to GPs, hospital admissions and successful surgery is low. And no account is taken of the hours some doctors work. Many junior hospital doctors work more than eighty hours a week. Some are forced to put in a hundred hours. Who would not occasionally make a mistake faced with such pressure? If such a doctor makes a mistaken diagnosis because he is intolerably weary, or makes a surgical error because his dexterity fails him, will the patient's rights be in any way affected? No. The courts rightly will not accept any argument that the doctor's duty is fulfilled if he provides an adequate service generally and only occasionally falls below the required standard of competence.[70] Judges sympathize with hard-pressed doctors. But a doctor who carries on beyond the point when fatigue and over-

69. For an example of a successful claim of this type, see *Sutton* v. *Population Services Family Planning Ltd*, *The Times*, 7 November 1981, and see M. Brazier (1990) Vol. 6 *Journal of the MDU* 7.
70. *Wilsher* v. *Essex AHA* [1986] 3 All ER 801, CA.

work impair his judgement remains liable to an injured patient. The fact that the doctor was required by his employer to work such hours will not affect the patient. The patient might, though, more appropriately proceed too against the doctor's employers, the hospital authority. He would allege that the hospital undertook to provide him with adequate care.[71] Requiring their doctors to work to the point of utter exhaustion is a breach of that duty. The essence of the patient's claim would become not that the hospital or health authority was vicariously liable for an individual doctor's negligence, but that there was a breach of a primary duty to ensure an adequate and competent service. In the Court of Appeal's judgement in *Wilsher* v. *Essex AHA*[72] Browne-Wilkinson VC suggested that in many cases this was a more appropriate analysis of medical negligence claims, avoiding stigmatizing overworked doctors for understandable errors. But there is a risk that even fewer patients may obtain compensation if this analysis were accepted. The defendant hospital or health authority might then seek to plead in its own defence the problems it faces arising from lack of resources. If patient A suffers an injury because the surgeon who operated on him was too tired to perform the surgery properly and no other surgeon was available, the authority may argue that it could not afford to employ more, or more senior, surgeons. It will be contended that although far from ideal the level of service was reasonable in the light of the defendants' limited budget. And in one judgement already a judge has said that lack of resources must be taken into account in medical negligence claims.[73] The 'wrong' inflicted on the overworked junior doctor should not be remedied at the expense of the patient. The doctor should have a remedy against the employer who demands that he work impossible hours. The decision of the Court of Appeal that young doctors whose health is threatened by the impossible demands made on them may bring their own action in negligence against the health authority is much to be welcomed.[74]

71. See *Cassidy* v. *Ministry of Health* [1951] 2 KB 14; see Chapter 7.
72. [1986] 2 All ER 801, pp. 833–4.
73. *Knight* v. *Home Office* [1990] 3 All ER 237.
74. *Johnstone* v. *Bloomsbury HA* [1991] 2 All ER 293.

Liability of nursing staff [75]

Nurses, as well as doctors, may sometimes make mistakes. All that has been said in relation to doctors applies equally to them. A nurse will be judged in accordance with the standard of skill and carefulness to be expected of a nurse in this position and specialty with this seniority. A midwife must show a midwife's skill. It is not enough, for example, to display only the standard of an SRN who has done thirteen weeks' obstetrics. The midwife holds herself out as a specialist. There are a few decided cases relating to nurses. A nurse who either failed to note or act on evidence of a lump in a patient's breast when she examined her at a Family Planning Clinic was held to be negligent. She should have taken steps to ensure that the patient's incipient cancer was properly investigated.[76] The more independent the nurse's function, the greater the risk of a finding of liability. Where she is in the front line with some responsibility for diagnosis and choice of treatment, her responsibility equates with that of her doctor colleagues.

Within hospitals nurses may find themselves liable for negligence if they fail to take careful note of instructions given to them, or if they fail to provide adequate nursing care or attention. A patient was prescribed thirty injections of streptomycin for boils. The sister failed to note on the treatment sheet when the prescribed course was completed. An additional four injections were given before the error was discovered. Damage to a cranial nerve resulted. The sister was found to be negligent.[77] Failure to make or record routine tests required by medical staff or failure to ensure that these are properly carried out can result in liability resting on the nurse. Where nurses and doctors work together, as in the operating theatre, liability for an accident may be shared. The theatre sister should check that all swabs are removed; so should the surgeon. They are jointly liable. A swab marker was inadvertently not removed from an elderly lady after exploratory surgery. The patient developed complications. An X-ray was taken. A consultant radiologist missed the swab marker on the X-ray. Fifteen months later the lady was admitted to hospital with an intestinal obstruction. The error was discovered. A settlement was reached.

75. For a specific text on nursing and law see B. Dimond, *Legal Aspects of Nursing*, 1990.
76. *Sutton* v. *Population Services*, *The Times*, 7 November 1981.
77. *Smith* v. *Brighton and Lewes HMC*, *The Times*, 21 June 1955.

Liability was shared in equal proportion between the surgeon, the consultant radiologist and the hospital on behalf of the theatre sister.[78]

Private patients

A patient who pays for his treatment enters into a contract with his doctor. They are free to set the terms of that contract, save that the doctor cannot exempt himself from liability for any injury to his patient arising from his negligence.[79] There is rarely a written contract between them. The terms will be implied from their relationship. This usually means that the doctor undertakes a duty of care to the patient. His duty of care to his private patient is indistinguishable from his duty to his NHS patient.

In private practice could a doctor be found to have contracted to *guarantee* the desired result of treatment? This can never happen in the NHS. The doctor can only be liable in tort for a failure in care. Only rarely however will a private doctor be found to have guaranteed a result in contract either. Where a patient is ill and seeks a cure, unless the doctor foolishly and expressly promises success in his treatment, no court will infer any term other than that the doctor will exercise skill and care. And, so far, claims by patients who have undergone private sterilization have ultimately failed in attempts to argue that the surgeon guaranteed permanent sterility.[80]

Criminal liability

Negligence is normally a matter for the civil, not the criminal, law. However gross, however culpable an act of negligence, it will generally not be criminal in England unless made so by an Act of Parliament, as in the case of careless driving. The picture changes if the victim dies. Gross negligence causing death can lead to a conviction for manslaughter. Much more than ordinary negligence, of the sort which would found a civil action for negligence, must be proved. Convictions are rare to say the least. Usually the negligence will be seen to derive from some morally disgraceful conduct – say, a doctor operating while

78. Annual Report of the MDU, 1984, pp. 24–5.
79. Unfair Contract Terms Act 1977, s. 2.
80. *Eyre* v. *Measday* [1986] 1 All ER 488; *Thake* v. *Maurice* [1986] 1 All ER 497, CA.

drunk or under the influence of drugs. In *R.* v. *Bateman*[81] the Court of Appeal overruled a conviction for manslaughter of a doctor whose ignorance and failure to send a woman to hospital resulted in his patient's death. The judge at the trial had failed to direct the jury properly. Criminal liability required more than the degree of negligence needed to establish civil liability. The doctor must be shown to have shown '. . . such disregard for the life and safety of others as to amount to a crime against the State and conduct deserving of punishment'.

Hence convictions for manslaughter will fortunately be few and far between in the absence of some personally disgraceful conduct on the part of a doctor. But recklessly unwise courses of action widely condemned in the profession may engage criminal censure. A dentist was convicted of manslaughter when a patient died in the dental chair.[82] He had extracted a tooth and administered a general anaesthetic entirely alone. This dual role of surgeon and anaesthetist had led to perhaps 100 deaths in the UK over the past twenty years. The General Dental Council had campaigned vigorously against it. The unfortunate dentist was the first to be convicted of manslaughter. But he did not go to prison. He was fined £1,000 and given a suspended sentence. His more unfortunate patient was dead. An anaesthetist whose patient suffered a fatal cardiac arrest when he had left the operating theatre to get himself a drink was similarly convicted of manslaughter.[83] He too avoided prison, unlike the unfortunate train driver whose failure to stop at a red signal caused a fatal rail accident.[84] The criminal law is rightly reserved for the most culpable cases of carelessness. No one would wish to see doctors who make mistakes go to gaol. But there is a feeling abroad that professionals receive preferential treatment from the courts.

Conclusions

The principles of the law of negligence applicable to the medical profession have been criticized as leaning too far in favour of rubber-

---

81. (1925) 41 TLR 557.
82. Annual Report of the MDU, 1982, p. 64.
83. See generally D. Tribe and G. Korgaankar, 'Medical Manslaughter' (1991) 7 *Journal of the Medical Defence Union* 10.
84. He was originally sentenced to eighteen months' imprisonment reduced to four months by the Court of Appeal.

stamping professional practice. Yet in the last fifteen years judicial attitudes have changed. Courts are more ready, albeit reluctantly, to find against the doctor on occasion. Two problems bedevil medical litigation. First, the medical profession becomes increasingly resentful of what they see as judicial interference and the damage done to medical careers. While compensation for injured patients depends on proof of fault on the part of medical staff, judicial 'interference' is inevitable and likely to increase. A judgement that a doctor on one day was liable for actionable negligence is not a finding that that doctor is a bad or incompetent doctor. It is merely a decision that in one isolated instance his conduct was such as to give a fellow citizen a claim for compensation. But that is not how the doctors see it. Second, the issue of judging when a doctor falls below an acceptable standard remains a thorny problem. If it is not to be judged by responsible medical opinion, how is it to be decided? The real problem is ascertaining the content of responsible medical opinion. The rules of litigation in England allow each side to call its own experts. The trial becomes a trial of strength between opposing experts. Investigation of what actually happened to the patient becomes nigh on impossible. In the next chapter I go on to examine this issue and to see how in practice the rules on negligence are applied in the courtroom and outside. As we shall see, the Department of Health is proposing an arbitration scheme as an alternative to litigation. Some means of ensuring patients have confidence in the civil law relating to medical negligence is crucial. As this book was in press two junior doctors were convicted of manslaughter after a patient died when they mistakenly injected a drug in the spine rather than intravenously. The doctors had failed to read the instructions for the drug sufficiently carefully. The judge said they were guilty of momentary recklessness and sentenced them to suspended terms of imprisonment. Resort to the criminal law will be called for more and more often if other grievance procedures fail to satisfy patients.

CHAPTER 7

Medical Litigation

In Chapters 4 to 6 I examined the principles governing liability for medical malpractice. Now I look at the actual process of litigation. Formidable practical problems confront the patient plaintiff.[1] Whom should he sue? How quickly must he act? How do you prove negligence? What level of compensation is available? Is it worth it? These are some of the issues this chapter attempts to cover.

Whom should the patient sue?

One of the first practical matters which the patient and his legal advisers must consider is whom they should sue. The legal doctrine of vicarious liability is important here. This provides that when a person who is an employee commits a tort in the course of his employment, his employer too is responsible to the victim. The employer will often be better able to pay compensation than an individual employee.

Let us look first at a claim by a patient who alleges that he suffered injury in the course of treatment as an NHS patient in an NHS hospital. If he can identify a particular individual as negligent he may, of course, proceed against him, be he consultant, anaesthetist, houseman, nurse, physiotherapist or hospital porter. And he may also sue that person's employer, the district health authority responsible for the

---

1. For practical advice see C. J. Lewis, *Medical Negligence – A Plaintiff's Guide*, Frank Cass, 1988; C. J. Lewis and N. Staite, 'How to Start a Medical Negligence Action' (1984) 81 Law Soc. Gaz. 3432; and see Diana M. Kloss (1984) 289 BMJ 66.

hospital or, in the case of an NHS trust hospital, the NHS trust itself.

Where a hospital doctor is a defendant in the action, payment of any award of compensation made against him is guaranteed. Until January 1990 hospital doctors were required as a term of their contract of employment to be fully insured against professional liability. Traditionally British doctors did not insure themselves with commercial insurers. They subscribed to medical defence organizations, preeminent among which are the Medical Defence Union and the Medical Protection Society. The doctor's defence organization agreed to indemnify him against any professional liability to patients and to advise and assist him if he became a party to any relevant litigation. But the rising number of medical negligence claims and the rising cost of settling such claims led first to the government agreeing to re-imburse to all NHS hospital doctors two thirds of the cost of their subscriptions to a defence organization. Then in 1989 the government decided that as they were paying much of the cost of medical indemnity they might as well take it over completely. NHS indemnity, introduced in January 1990,[2] provides that any liability incurred by an NHS hospital doctor will be met by his employer. District health authorities and NHS trusts will indemnify doctors directly just as they have always done for nurses and other hospital employees. How far the introduction of NHS indemnity will help patients making medical negligence claims will be discussed at the end of the chapter. One implication of the change must be mentioned immediately. Patients who bring a claim based on the alleged negligence of a nurse rarely bother to name the nurse personally as a defendant in the action. Patients and their lawyers should ponder the wisdom of suing a doctor personally. As his employer will in any case meet in full any award of compensation there may be little to gain from naming the doctor in the claim. Although membership of a defence organization is no longer compulsory, many doctors will retain membership so as to have access to individual legal advice. A doctor who sees his reputation on the line may seek to pressure his employer to fight the case tooth and nail. Health authorities may be more prepared to settle swiftly. However, suing a doctor individually may be a course of action designed not to obtain compensation but to ensure accountability. As long as complaints and review procedures in health care are perceived by patients as inadequate,

2. See HC (89) 34 and M. Brazier, 'NHS Indemnity: The Implications for Medical Litigation' (1990) 6 *Professional Negligence* 88.

patients may go on using medical negligence claims as a means to ensure accountability.

The employer to sue, as vicariously liable, in the case of NHS treatment will normally be the district health authority or NHS trust.[3] But as privatization creeps into the health service this must be examined carefully. Take this example: an elderly, confused patient slips and falls on a highly polished floor. Who, if anyone, is responsible? The relevant negligence may be that a nurse failed to supervise the patient, or it may be that cleaners were careless. The nurse will be employed by the health authority. The cleaner these days may be the employee of a private contractor. If the patient can rely only on the doctrine of vicarious liability to make someone other than the individual nurse or cleaner liable, he may have difficulty in selecting the correct defendant. Health authority and contractor may each blame the other's employee.[4] And what too of the case where an NHS patient is treated in a private hospital by virtue of an arrangement between the health authority and the private hospital? Who then, other than the responsible individual, may the patient sue if things go wrong?

What we need now to examine is the direct, primary liability of the health authority to an NHS patient. First, the authority will be liable for any failure of its own. A patient may suffer injury not because any particular doctor or nurse is careless but because the system provided by the authority is inadequate. There may be insufficient medical staff to cope swiftly enough with injured patients admitted to the casualty ward. Lack of experienced staff on night duty may cause injury to a patient whose condition deteriorates rapidly, and whom the staff on duty cannot, with the best will in the world, treat sufficiently promptly. For such faults an action may lie directly against the health authority.[5]

---

3. National Health Service Act 1977, Sched. 5 para. 15, as amended by the Health Services Act 1980 and the National Health Service and Community Care Act 1990.
4. Consider also the problem of agency nurses. Increasingly health service cuts force NHS hospitals to rely on nurses casually engaged from nursing agencies. Inadequate nursing care may be proved, but it may be impossible to determine whether the fault was that of an agency or a full-time NHS nurse. Agency and authority may each try to shift the blame to the other. Nor in many cases is the agency an employer of its nurses. In that case the only remedy lies against the nurse herself.
5. See *Wilsher* v. *Essex AHA* in Chapter 6, p. 135.

Lord Denning, however, would take the direct responsibility of health authority to NHS patients an important step further. He has argued thus.[6] When a patient is admitted for treatment under the NHS the health authority undertakes to provide him with reasonably careful, competent and skilled care and treatment. Should any aspect of his care and treatment fall below that standard, the authority is directly, and not just vicariously, responsible to the patient. So if an elderly patient falls on a slippery floor, and had proper care been taken that would not have happened, the authority is liable. It matters not whether a nurse employed by the authority or a cleaner employed by a contractor was the individual personally at fault. The authority undertook to care for the patient. It failed and it is directly liable. A patient offered a hip-replacement on the NHS need not be concerned if the operation is contracted out to a private hospital. The health authority undertook to provide the care and treatment. If anything goes wrong through negligence the authority is liable. The patient can lie back and enjoy the trimmings of the private hospital.

The importance of Lord Denning's view of direct liability in today's health care conditions can clearly be seen. It has received some, but not universal, academic approval.[7] It has not been tested because until recently it hardly ever mattered whether the authority was sued vicariously or directly. Practically everyone working in NHS health care was an NHS employee. Now that is no longer the case, Lord Denning's view should prevail.

Our next concern is the private patient. A private patient who engages a pay-bed in an NHS hospital generally contracts individually with his surgeon and anaesthetist for the surgery and the administration of the anaesthetic, and contracts separately with the health authority for nursing and ancillary care. Even if the surgeon and the anaesthetist are employed by the health authority when caring for NHS patients,

---

6. See *Cassidy* v. *Ministry of Health* [1951] 2 KB 343, pp. 359–60; and *Roe* v. *Ministry of Health* [1954] 2 QB 66, 82.

7. *Street on Torts* (8th edn), Butterworths, London, 1988, pp. 453–4, *Winfield and Jolowicz on Tort* (12th edn), Sweet & Maxwell, London, 1984, p. 577. But note the doubts expressed in A. M. Dugdale and K. S. Stanton, *Professional Negligence*, 2nd edn, Butterworths, 1989, p. 398, and the judgement in *Yepremian* v. *Scarborough General Hospital* (1980) 110 DLR (3d) 513 (Ontario). Note also the possibility of an action for breach of statutory duty; see *Razzel* v. *Snowball* [1954] 3 All ER 429.

when they act for a private patient they are acting on their own behalf and not in the course of their NHS employment. So if an error by surgeon or anaesthetist causes the patient injury he can sue only the responsible individual. If the carelessness is that of nursing or other medical staff he may sue the health authority. As we shall see, this may cause problems of proof of negligence.[8] Identifying who was the responsible individual may be nigh on impossible, leaving surgeon and authority to blame each other and the patient to go uncompensated.

A patient entering a private hospital needs to consider carefully the exact nature and scope of his contract. The usual arrangement is similar to that entered into by a private patient taking a pay-bed within the NHS. The patient engages his own surgeon and anaesthetist who will not be employees of the hospital. The hospital contracts to provide other medical and nursing care. Like the private patient within the NHS, the patient must proceed against the surgeon for any error of his, and against the hospital for error by their staff. But some private hospitals and clinics will contract to provide a whole 'package' of care and treatment. When the hospital undertakes to provide total care, the operation, anaesthetic, post-operative care, etc., then it is liable for any failure to meet the required standard of care. They are in breach of contract.[9] It is irrelevant that the surgeon, anaesthetist, or anyone else is not an employee of the hospital. The hospital is not vicariously liable for any fault of a particular person. It is directly responsible for its own breach of contract.

What, now, of claims against general practitioners? First of all, general practitioners are not employees of the health authority. A claim relating to negligence by a GP operating a single-doctor practice lies against that GP alone. And general practitioners are not obliged to belong to a medical defence organization. The vast majority, of course, do, but a slight risk remains that a GP sued may be personally impecunious and professionally uninsured. Where a GP is a member of a partnership his partners may be sued as jointly responsible for any negligence. If it is not the doctor himself who is at fault but a receptionist

---

8. See below, pp. 156–8.
9. Note the Supply of Goods and Services Act 1982, s. 13 (implied term that service will be carried out with care and skill); and Part I of that Act imposing conditions as to goods supplied in the course of a contract for services; see A. P. Bell, 'The Doctor and the Supply of Goods and Services Act 1982' (1984) 4 LS 175.

or nurse employed by the practice, then the GP and his partners are vicariously liable as employers. So if a receptionist refuses to allow a home visit, refuses to allow the patient to speak to a doctor, and fails to pass any information on to the doctor with the result that a seriously ill patient becomes sicker or even dies, the doctor, while he may be personally blameless, will be vicariously at fault and liable to the patient or his family.

The thorny question of whom to sue in relation to general practice arises out of the use of locums and deputizing services. Locums and deputies are not employed by the regular general practitioner as a hospital doctor is employed by the health service. Therefore the general practitioner is not vicariously liable for any and every act of negligence on their part.[10] Of course, he may be liable for any personal carelessness of his in selecting a locum or deputizing service. Failing to check the qualifications of a locum, engaging a deputizing service notorious locally for its incompetent doctors, will be negligence on the part of the GP. It is arguable too that engaging a locum or deputy without checking whether he carries professional indemnity insurance may equally be a breach of duty to the patient. It would be an extension of the present law. But I would suggest that a GP selecting another to care for his patients must consider not only the stand-in's medical skill but his ability to meet any claim against him. Doctors know all too well that such a claim can arise out of the occasional error made by even the most skilled practitioner.

But once again we must return to Lord Denning's view of direct responsibility for health care to see if the patient is inevitably to be left to sue the locum or deputy alone. When a GP accepts a patient on to his list he undertakes to provide for that patient health care of a standard and nature to be expected of a competent GP. If the health care provided falls below that standard, the patient's own GP should be liable regardless of whether he or a locum or deputy is the one at fault. By analogy with Denning's view of the obligation of the health authority to an NHS patient in hospital, the GP is directly responsible to the patient for his general health care. The arrangements the GP makes to provide care at night or when he is on holiday are beyond the patient's control and not his concern. Such a solution is fairer to

10. If the deputizing service actually employs the doctor working for it, the service may be sued. This is unlikely; deputies are usually engaged on a 'casual labour only' basis.

patients and not unfair to the GP, who is free and able to arrange appropriate insurance cover and whose subscription to a medical defence organization will be reimbursed as expenses by the Family Health Services Authority.

When must proceedings be started?[11]

A patient contemplating an action for medical negligence must act relatively promptly. The general rule is that all actions for personal injuries must be brought within three years of the infliction of the relevant injury. This is known as the limitation period and is laid down in the Limitation Act 1980. A writ must be served on the doctor or hospital authority no later than three years from the date of the alleged negligence. But sections 11 and 14 of the 1980 Act provide that where the patient originally either (1) was unaware that he had suffered significant injury, or (2) did not know about the negligence which could have caused his injury, the three-year period begins to run only from the time when he did discover, or reasonably should have discovered, the relevant facts. Where the patient knew all the relevant facts, but was ignorant of his legal remedy, the three-year limitation period runs from the time when he was or should have been aware of the facts.

All is not quite lost for the patient who delays beyond three years or who is ignorant of the law. A judge may still allow him to start an action later. Section 33 of the 1980 Act gives to the court a discretion to override the three-year limitation period where in all the circumstances it is fair to all parties to do so. The courts will examine the effect of allowing the action to go forward on both parties, taking into account, among other things, the effect of delay on the cogency of the evidence, the conduct of the parties, and the advice sought by and given to the patient by his lawyers and medical advisers. The three-year (or longer) limitation period applies only to *starting* legal proceedings. Once started, an action may drag on for years before it is settled or finally decided.

One further aspect of the rules on limitation must be noted. Where the injured patient is under a legal disability at the time he suffers injury, that is to say he is under age (under 18) or mentally incompetent, the limitation period does not begin to run until he reaches the age of

11. See Lewis, op. cit., Chapter 27.

majority or ceases to be mentally incompetent. This means that, for example, a baby might be injured at birth and the obstetrician could face an action in respect of the injury eighteen or nineteen years after the event! Or course, the child's parents were free to bring the action earlier on their child's behalf. But until 1990 Legal Aid rules provided that if they did so their income would be taken into account in assessing their child's eligibility for legal aid. Now the child's income alone (if any) is relevant. Parents no longer face a financial deterrent to taking action at the earliest possible stage to obtain compensation for their child.

Access to records

When considering whether he has a claim in respect of negligence and whom he should sue, the patient and his legal advisers will clearly benefit by gaining access to the patient's notes, reports and X-ray and other test records. Disclosure of records benefits the public interest too. A claim may be seen to be fruitless or a particular individual exonerated. Money and effort will be saved. Before 1970 the patient usually had to go ahead in the dark and ask at the trial for a subpoena ordering the health authority and the doctor to produce their records. Legislation in 1970 introduced a right to pre-trial access to records.[12] That original legislation has now been replaced by the Supreme Court Act 1981.

The effect of section 33 of the 1981 Act is this. A patient may apply for a court order requiring the doctor or the authority whom he plans to sue to disclose any records or notes likely to be relevant in forthcoming proceedings. Section 34 goes further. The court may order a person *not* a party to proceedings to produce relevant documents. So if the patient has started proceedings against the doctor but believes that the hospital authority or clinic holds notes of value to his claim, the authority or clinic can be made to hand over the notes. This will help the private patient in a dilemma as to whether he should properly proceed against doctor or hospital. And it may of course lead to the hospital being brought into the proceedings.

Once legislation compelling disclosure of documents was enacted, hospitals and medical defence organizations reluctantly became

12. Administration of Justice Act 1970, ss. 32–5 (the legislation was based on recommendations of the Winn Committee, Cmnd 3691 (1968)).

prepared to hand over documents voluntarily. They feared a spate of fishing expeditions by aggrieved patients. But they preferred to disclose records to the patient's medical adviser alone, and not to the patient or his lawyers. Indeed, they sought to argue that this was the limit of their obligation. The House of Lords disagreed.[13] Under the 1970 statute, they said, the patient himself was entitled to see the documents produced. Pleas that patients would be unduly distressed and fail to understand medical data cut little ice with their Lordships. The 1981 Act is less favourable to patients. A court may limit disclosure to (a) the patient's legal advisers, or (b) the patient's legal and medical advisers, or (c) if the patient has no legal adviser, to his 'medical or other professional adviser'. It is up to the court to decide whether the patient sees the records. But as long as he has retained a lawyer, his lawyer must be permitted to examine the documents. Hospitals and medical protection societies offering voluntary disclosure often still try to keep records even from the patient's lawyers. Lawyers in the medico-legal field advise against accepting such an offer: a lawyer may spot relevant material in support of a claim which even the most experienced medical advisers could miss.

Three important matters on disclosure need a mention. First, the intention to bring proceedings and the likelihood that they will go ahead must be real before the court will order disclosure. The patient must have some solid ground for thinking he has a claim. He cannot use an application for disclosure as a 'fishing expedition' on the off-chance that some evidence of negligence will come to light.[14] Medical defence organizations used to advise doctors to say nothing and disclose no records without first consulting them. The Medical Defence Union and the Medical Protection Society always refuted allegations that they then attempted to obstruct disclosure of records in all cases. And indeed, if a claim by a patient on its face suggested obvious negligence the defence organization representing the doctor's interests had good reason to co-operate with the patient's lawyers and settle quickly and quietly. Whatever the truth of allegations that the defence organizations sought to prevent disclosure of records, in many cases now their views are marginal. Where the claim arises out of alleged

13. *MacIvor* v. *Southern Health and Social Services Board, Northern Ireland* [1978] 2 All ER 625.
14. *Dunning* v. *United Liverpool Hospitals' Board of Governors* [1973] 2 All ER 454.

mistreatment in an NHS hospital, NHS indemnity means that the health authority or NHS trust controls defence of the action and *their* lawyers decide whether to disclose records voluntarily or force the patient to seek a court order. Problems with health authorities in the past have tended to relate not to any deliberately obstructive attitude but to difficulties in locating the right records. How far regional health authority legal departments have the resources to cope with claims may determine how efficiently those claims are dealt with. It remains to be seen too how far if at all the enactment of the Access to Health Records Act 1990[15] will change the atmosphere for disclosure of records. That Act gives patients a qualified right to see their records even where no litigation is contemplated. It would be odd if patients with a legal grievance were offered less generous disclosure. And may it be that a knowledgeable patient, believing she has a grievance, might resort first to the 1990 Act?

Second, will the patient be able to see notes of any inquiry ordered by the health authority into his misadventure? The position is complex. If the inquiry was held mainly to provide the basis of information on which legal advice as to the authority's legal liability is based, then the records are protected by legal professional privilege. But if the dominant purpose of the inquiry was otherwise, for example to improve hospital procedures or to provide the basis of disciplinary proceedings against staff, then the patient may be allowed access to the notes of the inquiry.[16] That is the legal position. The Court of Appeal has expressed its disquiet about the effect such claims of legal professional privilege may have on the patient's claim. Claims of privilege can be and are used to frustrate the patient's attempt to find out what happened, what went wrong. In *Lee* v. *South West Thames RHA*[17] a little boy, Marlon Lee, suffered a severe scald at home but he should have recovered completely. He was taken to a hospital run by health authority A and then transferred to a burns unit controlled by health authority B. The next day he developed breathing problems, was put on a respirator, and still on the respirator was sent back to A in an ambulance provided by health authority C, the South West Thames RHA. When three days later the boy was taken off the respirator he

15. See above, p. 64.
16. *Waugh* v. *BRB* [1980] AC 521; and see Diana M. Kloss (1984) 289 BMJ 66.
17. *Lee* v. *South West Thames RHA* [1985] 2 All ER 385.

was found to have suffered severe brain damage, probably due to lack of oxygen. In her attempts to find out what went wrong, the child's mother sought disclosure of records and notes on her son prepared by staff of all three authorities. Health authority A asked South West Thames RHA to obtain a report from their ambulance crew. South West Thames RHA complied and forwarded the report to A. It was this report which the plaintiffs went to court to obtain access to. South West Thames RHA had revealed its existence but refused to hand it over to the family. They claimed it had been prepared in contemplation of litigation and to enable legal advice to be given in connection with that litigation. So it had, but it had been prepared on the request of health authority A to obtain advice as to A's liability to the child. Reluctantly the Court of Appeal held that the privilege attaching to the document was enjoyed by health authority A. South West Thames could not be ordered to disclose the report. Even had they been prepared to do so they could not have handed over the report without A's agreement. The principle was that defendants or potential defendants should be '. . . free to seek evidence without being obliged to disclose the result of his researches to his opponent'.

So a child was damaged for life in circumstances pointing to negligence on someone's part, and the law was powerless to help his mother find out what exactly caused his brain damage. The Court of Appeal expressed their disquiet and called for reform of the law. Within the doctor/patient relationship Sir John Donaldson MR said there was a duty to answer questions put before treatment was agreed to.[18] Why should the duty to be frank with the patient be different once treatment was completed? And in 1987[19] he again emphasized the importance he placed on what he termed a duty of candour. How such a duty should be enforced is less clear. In Lee[20] the president of the Court of Appeal had suggested that some new remedy based on breach of a duty to inform might evolve. Such a remedy came too late for Marlon Lee. What seems to have happened since though is that judges now recognize that patients have a right to see their records. Access to records is not a concession kindly granted or withheld at the discretion of the health authority. Health authorities or other defendants who drag

18. See *Sidaway* v. *Board of Governors of the Bethlem Royal and the Maudsley Hospital* [1985] 2 WLR 480; see Chapter 4.
19. *Naylor* v. *Preston AHA* [1987] 2 All ER 353.
20. pp. 389–90.

their feet may ultimately be punished by an order of costs against them.[21]

Third, the court retains the power to refuse to order disclosure where to do so would be injurious to the public interest.[22] This is unlikely to be the case where what is asked for is the plaintiff's own medical notes. An attempt by the Secretary of State for Health to plead public interest immunity to avoid disclosure of records in the actions brought by several haemophiliac patients who had contracted HIV and AIDS from contaminated blood products failed.[23]

Pre-trial medical examinations

One distressing but inevitable feature of a claim of medical malpractice is that the patient, who is presumably already unwell, has to submit to several further medical examinations and sometimes to painful diagnostic tests. I stressed at the beginning of this chapter the importance of expert testimony on the patient's behalf. What is so often at issue is whether the patient's present condition results from the normal progression of disease, or an inherent risk of surgery, or carelessness. The patient's own expert cannot advise him and testify for him without examining him. So first the patient must be examined by his own expert witness, or witnesses. But he must also agree to be examined by the defendant's experts. If he refuses, the defendant may apply to stay the action, to have it stopped from proceeding any further. The ability to call his own expert witnesses is a fundamental right of the defendant. The patient will not be allowed to frustrate that right by refusing an examination.

The courts in the past showed scant sympathy for patients unhappy about such 'compulsory' medical examinations. A patient sought to insist on the presence of her own doctor as a condition of agreeing to examination by the defendant's doctor. The court refused.[24] They did suggest that had she been confused or elderly, or the defendants' expert been known to be fierce or intimidating, then exceptionally a patient might be allowed the support of her own doctor. And of course a woman will be allowed to insist on the presence of another woman

21. See Lewis, op. cit., pp. 58–9.
22. Supreme Court Act 1981, s. 35.
23. *HIV: Haemophiliac Litigation, Guardian*, 28 September 1990, CA.
24. *Hall* v. *Avon AHA* [1980] 1 All ER 516, CA.

before undergoing examination by a male expert. Another patient sought to make disclosure of the defendant's expert's report to him a condition of agreeing to examination. He failed.[25]

That last example raises again the question of disclosure of reports. We saw above that disclosure will be ordered of notes and records contemporaneous to the treatment complained of. It used to be the case that the courts would not order disclosure of reports of examinations of the patient by expert witnesses.[26] The defendants were in effect permitted to keep the essence of their defence secret until the day of the trial. In *Wilsher* v. *Essex AHA*[27] that resulted in total misunderstanding by the parties as to what matters were disputed between them. A trial scheduled to take five days took four weeks. The judges in the Court of Appeal were understandably furious. So in *Naylor* v. *Preston AHA*[28] Sir John Donaldson MR signalled a radical change in attitude to disclosure of records. He distinguished between the parties' right to keep confidential evidence which they gather to prepare their case which was protected by privilege, as in the case of Marlon Lee, and their duty to disclose the affirmative case they intend to argue at the trial. Parties were entitled to privacy in seeking out the cards for their hands, but once those cards were together they must put them on the table! Each side was entitled to know in advance the substance of the case to be argued by his opponent. 'Forensic blind man's buff' was a game the courts would no longer allow the parties to play. Since *Naylor*, the relevant Rule of the Supreme Court, Ord. 38 r. 37(1), has been amended to make it crystal clear that mutual disclosure of expert evidence should be the normal procedure.

Mutual disclosure of expert evidence has several benefits. First, court time is saved, as the issues actually in dispute are clearly identified in advance of the trial. Second, it will encourage attempts to settle claims and avoid the trauma of a court hearing.[29] But the patient still has to submit himself to two sets of examinations. A joint examination by his and the defendants' experts might be preferable for the patient, but the court cannot require the defendants to agree to such a strategy.

---

25. *Megarity* v. *Ryan (D.J.) & Sons* [1980] 1 WLR 1237, CA.
26. *Rahman* v. *Kirklees AHA* [1980] 3 All ER 610.
27. [1986] 3 All ER 801.
28. [1987] 2 All ER 353, CA.
29. And see RSC Ord. 38 r. 38 encouraging 'without prejudice' meetings of experts.

An adversarial system of justice takes its toll in terms of patients' distress and discomfort.

Proving negligence

I come now to the very heart of the problem. How does the patient prove negligence? The onus lies on him. He must demonstrate that it is more likely than not that his deterioration in health or his injury resulted from the negligence of the defendant. Mrs Ashcroft underwent an operation on her left ear. In the course of the operation she suffered damage to the facial nerve and her face was left permanently partly paralysed. The judge found the evidence finely balanced. There was formidable evidence that this should not have happened if proper care was taken. There was equally formidable evidence that in such delicate surgery damage to the nerve might occur even where the utmost skill and care were used. The judge held that the plaintiff must fail.[30] There were, he said, 'no winners in such circumstances'.

How does the plaintiff discharge the onus of proof laid on him? In the majority of cases he will be heavily reliant on expert testimony. He will need to put forward medical evidence to demonstrate (1) that there was negligence on the part of the defendant, or a person for whom the defendant was responsible, and (2) that the relevant negligence caused the harm of which the plaintiff complains. Finding an expert to testify may not be easy. Doctors are unhappy about voicing public criticism of a colleague. Knowing that all men and women make mistakes, helping to condemn a fellow doctor who is unlucky enough to make a mistake with disastrous consequences is not a popular task. In practice the patient's expert witness will have to be found from a different area of the country. Colleagues in the same health authority simply refuse to testify against each other. To their credit, the Royal Colleges will offer assistance in finding expert witnesses, and AVMA (Action for Victims of Medical Accidents) maintains a comprehensive list of helpful and reliable medical experts. Not only must the doctor chosen be impeccably qualified and substantially experienced, he must also be able to stand up to cross-examination by the defendant's counsel.

Once an eminent and helpful expert is found, the problems for the patient are only partly solved. For the defendant too will be free to call

30. *Ashcroft* v. *Mersey AHA* [1983] 2 All ER 245.

his own experts and will usually find it far easier to obtain supporters. The court will be faced with conflicting accounts of what the proper standard of care in the procedure in issue is, and whether the harm caused did result from anything done or not done by the defendant. A glance at a leading case highlights the court's dilemma. In *Whitehouse* v. *Jordan*[31] (which we have already looked at in the context of principles of liability) a claim was brought on behalf of a baby born disastrously and irretrievably brain-damaged. His mother, who was aged 30 and 4ft 10ins, had refused to submit to any internal examination or to an X-ray of her pelvis. The consultant in charge of her pregnancy put on her notes that 'trial of forceps delivery' should be attempted. But when Mrs Whitehouse went into labour he was not there. He was ill with flu. The difficulty of the case caused the young doctor on duty to summon help. Mr Jordan, a senior registrar, came to his aid. He had never seen the plaintiff before. Mr Jordan had five or six attempts to deliver the baby by forceps. He then discontinued the attempt and proceeded swiftly and efficiently to deliver the baby by Caesarean section. The baby was born damaged. The mother alleged that this resulted from Mr Jordan's continued attempts to deliver by forceps and that he had persevered in those attempts beyond the point where a competent obstetrician would have desisted. He had pulled too hard and for too long. He was negligent, she said, in not proceeding sooner to delivery by Caesarean section. On the central issue of the extent to which it is correct practice to pursue an attempt to deliver by forceps, the trial judge was faced with a galaxy of 'stars' from the field of gynaecology and obstetrics. For the child, there appeared Professor Sir John Stallworthy (past president of the Royal College of Obstetricians and Gynaecologists) and Professor Sir John Peel (former gynaecologist to Her Majesty). For Mr Jordan, there lined up Professor Sir John Dewhurst (past president of the RCOG), Professor L. B. Strang, Professor J. P. M. Tizard, and Dame Josephine Barnes (past president of the RCOG). The plaintiff's witnesses put in a joint report, originally prepared by them but 'settled' by counsel, that is, her lawyers prepared the final draft! Lord Denning in the Court of Appeal criticized the report as wearing 'the colour of a special pleading rather than an impartial report'.[32] Not surprisingly then, the opinions of the experts as to how far an attempt at forceps delivery could be pursued were

31. [1981] 1 All ER 287, H L.
32. [1980] 1 All ER 650, p. 655.

miles apart. It is disturbing for the lay person to discover how large a gap can exist as to what constitutes proper obstetric practice.

Faced with the contradictions offered by the experts, the trial judge based his decision on a report by Professor Maclaren, the head of the unit, that the child's head had become impacted. The judge interpreted this as meaning that the head was in the pelvis and that Mr Jordan continued to pull with the forceps, thus subjecting the head to undue pressure. Professor Maclaren subsequently said that 'impacted' did not carry this meaning, and the defence experts supported him. And at the end of the day so did the House of Lords.

The claim in *Whitehouse* v. *Jordan* dragged on for eight years from the issue of the writ. The child was nearly 11 before his claim was finally dismissed. The cost of three Queen's Counsel, two junior counsel, the solicitors' and experts' fees must have been astronomic. Two questions in particular raise concern. Six experts appeared. Why are the numbers not limited? The courts seem adamant that parties be allowed to choose as many experts as they like, rather like football teams.[33] And is it right that lawyers should 'doctor' the doctors' reports? Finally, the curious laywoman will wonder why the original decision to go for trial of labour rather than an elective Caesarean was never questioned. After all, the mother was exceptionally small and her refusal to be examined meant that her doctors had no idea of her internal pelvic size. The answer is that although an action was started against Professor Maclaren, who had been in charge of her pregnancy, this was discontinued early on. Thus that issue was closed to the courts.

Let no one be misled. The function of an English court is not invariably to investigate the claim, to uncover the truth, and do abstract justice. The judge is too often the referee in a game whose rules are loaded against the plaintiff. But in few cases do the rules of the game in the long run do much for the defendant's peace of mind and reputation.

Furthermore, difficult though it may be to credit, the central issue of *Whitehouse* v. *Jordan*, the question of what is or what is not proper practice, may not be the most difficult matter on which conflicting expert evidence may be put to a judge. In *Whitehouse* v. *Jordan* the trial judge's finding that the brain damage was caused in the course of delivery was not questioned. Where whether the harm did actually

33. See *Hall* v. *Avon AHA* (above).

result from the alleged negligence is in issue, the task of the courts is even more difficult. They will be deluged by technical data, submerged by medical debate. Two possible reforms need urgent consideration. First, on the issue of the factual cause of the harm suffered, has not the Continental practice of the court appointing one eminent and important expert much to commend it? And second, should the case for a judge occasionally sitting with medically qualified assessors to advise him be considered?

Where the burden of proof shifts to the doctor

While in the majority of cases the patient must prove negligence and the doctor is not called on to prove his 'innocence', we should now look at those occasions when that burden shifts to the doctor. There is a general rule of the law of negligence that where the defendant is in complete control of the relevant events, and an accident happens which does not ordinarily happen if proper care is taken, then the accident itself affords reasonable evidence of negligence. The defendant will be held liable unless he can advance an explanation of the accident consistent with the exercise of proper care by him. This rule is known as *res ipsa loquitur* (the thing speaks for itself).[34]

Res ipsa loquitur can be applied in medical negligence cases. At first it was argued that *res ipsa loquitur* applied only where everyone of reasonable intelligence would know that that sort of accident did not ordinarily happen without negligence. As most people are not medically qualified, how could they know whether the accident to the patient was one which could or could not happen if proper care was taken? The Court of Appeal said that expert medical evidence was admissible to establish what should and should not occur if ordinary care was exercised.[35] *Res ipsa* has proved to be a boon in straightforward cases. A typical example is where sometimes after an abdominal operation a swab or even a pair of forceps is discovered in the patient's body. *Res ipsa* is also of value to the NHS patient who has clearly suffered because someone was negligent either in the theatre or in the course of post-operative care, but he cannot identify that someone. If every member of the staff who might be responsible is employed by the health authority then an inference of negligence is raised against the

---

34. See *Street on Torts*, pp. 215–22.
35. *Mahon* v. *Osborne* [1939] 2 KB 14.

authority, who are necessarily vicariously liable for whoever may be the culprit.[36] So in *Cassidy* v. *Ministry of Health*[37] a patient was operated on for Dupuytren's contraction affecting two of his fingers. After the operation the patient's hand and lower arm had to be kept rigid in a splint for up to fourteen days. When the splints were removed the plaintiff's whole hand was paralysed. Upon finding that all the staff involved in Mr Cassidy's care were NHS employees, the court held that there was evidence of negligence against their common employer. The onus shifted to the authority to explain how this disaster might have struck without *any* of its employees being negligent. In many operations the source of greatest danger for the patient lies not in the surgery itself, but in the anaesthetic. An anaesthetic mishap will not usually be of itself evidence of negligence, but the *res ipsa* principle was applied in *Saunders* v. *Leeds Western HA*.[38] The patient was a 4-year-old girl in otherwise perfect health who was undergoing surgery to correct a congenitally displaced hip. She suffered a cardiac arrest and consequent brain damage. Mann J said:

It is plain from evidence called on her [the child's] behalf that the heart of a fit child does not arrest under anaesthesia if proper care is taken in the anaesthetic and surgical processes.

But what if one of the staff caring for the patient is not an employee of the health authority? For example, the theatre sister may be an agency nurse. Can the authority say, 'No inference of negligence is raised against *us* because the negligent actor may well have been that nurse for whom we are not responsible'? Once again it depends on whether the hospital's liability is solely vicarious, or whether Lord Denning is right and the hospital is directly liable for any failure to measure up to the required standard of skill and care.[39] As long as the Denning view is correct, which I maintain it is, it matters not to the patient who actually employs the negligent individual.

The private patient may be less fortunate. As we have seen, whether he enters an NHS or a private hospital he will usually contract separately with the surgeon and the anaesthetist for surgery and anaesthetic. The surgeon and the anaesthetist will not be acting as employees of the

36. *Roe* v. *Ministry of Health* [1954] 2 QB 66.
37. *Cassidy* v. *Ministry of Health* [1951] 2 KB 343.
38. (1985) 82 Law Soc. Gaz. 1491.
39. See pp. 143ff.

hospital. If something goes wrong in the operating theatre or post-operatively and it is not clear who is to blame, *res ipsa loquitur* probably cannot be invoked. The hospital is not liable for any negligence on the part of the surgeon or anaesthetist. He can raise an inference of negligence against the hospital only if he can trace the relevant negligence to one of their staff. He can raise an inference of negligence against the surgeon or anaesthetist only if he can pin the relevant act on one of them personally. If surgeon and hospital are both sued, neither can be compelled to testify against the other. And in many cases they may refuse to give evidence. The patient's task is made even harder because of an agreement between hospital authorities and medical protection societies that generally neither will join the other as co-defendant. They will not engage in mutual accusations of blame which might offer evidence which could assist the patient. They will simply remain silent, leaving the patient in the dark.

Once again Lord Denning offers some hope to the patient who can show there has been negligence but cannot identify the negligent actor. He has said this:

... I do not think that the hospital authorities and [the doctor] can both avoid giving an explanation by the simple expedient of throwing responsibility on to the other. If an injured person shows that one or other or both of two persons injured him, but cannot say which of them it was, then he is not defeated altogether. He can call on each of them for an explanation.[40]

Thus robust common sense would force open any 'conspiracy of silence'.

Nevertheless, the value of *res ipsa loquitur* in a medical negligence claim must not be overstated. Very often expert medical evidence is needed to establish that what happened does not ordinarily occur if proper care is taken. Conflicting expert evidence on that issue can be just as confusing and just as contradictory as on any other issue related to proving medical negligence.

Awards of compensation.

Once a patient has overcome all the formidable hurdles in his path and has satisfied the court that there has been malpractice by the defendant as a result of which he suffered harm, what damages will he receive?

40. *Roe* v. *Ministry of Health* [1954] 2 QB 66, p. 82.

There are no special rules governing medical malpractice awards. The patient's damages will be assessed to compensate him for any actual or prospective loss of earnings and for the pain, suffering and disability which he has endured and will endure. His compensation for loss of earnings will include a sum representing any period in which he would have expected to be alive and earning but because of his injuries he will be prematurely dead.[41] Additionally to these sums to represent what he has lost, the patient will be awarded an amount to cover extra expenses which he and his family will incur. So if he requires intensive nursing care, or his house needs adapting to his invalid needs, or he requires constant attendance so that his wife gives up her job, all these expenses will be reflected in the award of damages. If the patient himself is dead, the damages awarded to his family will reflect the loss to them of the moneys he regularly expended on them. They recover for their loss of dependency.[42] It takes little imagination to see that if the patient dies the burden of compensation will be reduced. Dead he suffers no pain. Dead he incurs no expenses

Returning now to the living patient, certain thorny problems do bedevil the question of damages. The first is this. The patient must usually sue within three years.[43] At that stage a prognosis of his future health is very much speculative. All his medical advisers may be able to say is something like this. The patient has a degree of brain damage. He is mildly handicapped now. There is a 20 per cent chance he may deteriorate to a vegetable condition in ten years' time. Until 1985 the process of assessing damages for such a patient was ludicrous. The courts would work out what he should receive if he did deteriorate and award him 20 per cent of that sum! If the prospect of deterioration materialized, the patient was grossly under-compensated. If it never did, the doctor had paid out a sum to compensate for damage that had never happened. Section 32A of the Supreme Court Act 1981[44] offers a remedy for this absurdity. The court now has power to make an award of provisional damages based on the assumption that the

41. This is known as compensation for the 'lost years'; see *Pickett* v. *BRB* [1980] AC 136.
42. Fatal Accidents Act 1976 as amended by the Administration of Justice Act 1982.
43. See p. 146.
44. Inserted by the Administration of Justice Act 1985, s. 6. For the procedure relating to a claim for provisional damages, see RSC Ord. 37 rr. 8–10.

prospect of further damage or deterioration will not materialize. Should it do so at some later date, the patient may return to court to ask for a further award to compensate him for the consequences of that damage or deterioration.

Save for that provision in section 32A of the Supreme Court Act damages have to be assessed on a once and forever basis as a lump sum. The court cannot order periodic payments which could be varied to suit the plaintiff's changing circumstances. There are mechanisms by which settlements can achieve this end.[45]

The need to award a lump sum poses a particular difficulty in estimating claims for future expenses. This is especially acute where the patient is so damaged as to be unable to manage his own affairs.[46] Large sums of money can be claimed to cover the cost of his future care in expensive nursing homes. But there is no guarantee that that money will be so spent. The patient may be consigned to the NHS and the money deposited to grow with interest and eventually when the patient dies to form a windfall for relatives. The courts are alert to this danger. They will seek to ensure that the sum awarded is such as will be wholly exhausted by care of the patient, leaving no surplus as a bonus for relatives. Plans for care must be realistic. And one further change has recently been made. Section 5 of the Administration of Justice Act 1982 provides that 'any saving to the injured person which is attributable to his maintenance at public expense . . . in a hospital . . . or other institution shall be set off against any income lost . . .'

One final quirk in the law is that the plaintiff may be able to claim for the full cost of any private medical care he selects regardless of whether such facilities are available free on the NHS.[47] Even where exactly identical surgery to alleviate the patient's condition could have been performed without charge, the plaintiff may claim the full cost of the private care for which he opted.

Yet all the above issues are mere pinpricks compared to the main anxiety of doctors and health authorities, the escalating costs of personal injuries awards. As more malpractice actions are begun, lawyers become more astute at establishing the highest possible quantum of

45. D. Allen, 'Structured Settlements' (1988) 104 LQR 448.
46. Where the plaintiff is completely incapable of managing his own affairs the award may be managed by the Court of Protection.
47. Law Reform (Personal Injuries) Act 1948, s. 2(4).

damages. Inflation pushes the costs spiral higher. The kind of injury suffered in medical accidents is often of the most dire, brain damage or paralysis. And the skill and dedication of doctors themselves have played their part. New medical techniques keep alive many damaged patients who would have died a decade earlier. Many now live but need constant and expensive care. And as I have said, the living gain and need much higher levels of compensation than the dead.

The highest award so far made in a medical negligence claim in England is the £1.7 million in July 1991, beating the £1.2 million pounds awarded to Hugo Cassel, who suffered devastating brain injuries at birth.[48] In 1987 £1,032,000 had been awarded in the *Aboul-Hosn*[49] case. That plaintiff was a brilliant young engineering student whose life was blighted by a bungled operation on his brain. He was reduced to a mental age of 2 and rendered incapable of ever earning or caring for himself. The award of damages comprised substantial sums to compensate him for his future loss of earnings and to provide for his care for the next forty years. For despite his grievous injuries, the plaintiff's lifespan was not affected by accident. Less than 10 per cent of the award represented damages for pain and suffering. Awards of a million pounds plus are not likely to be common. Awards of between half a million and a million may be more so in those sad cases where, for example, a baby is brain-damaged at birth or a relatively young person is drastically brain-injured in an anaesthetic tragedy. Chance will however play a large part in the award. Hugo Cassel came from a wealthy family. The judge assumed he would have had a glittering and prosperous future and made a commensurate award for Hugo's lost earning capacity. Aboul-Hosn was a promising student who lost a highly paid professional future. Were Hugo the child of unemployed parents, or Aboul-Hosn a poorly paid labourer, the awards would never have topped £1 million. Delay in settling claims, sometimes for as long as eight years,[50] add to the total cost of litigation for defendant health authorities.

As the *Aboul-Hosn* award illustrates, damages for pain and suffering remain relatively low in England. In 1986 the Court of Appeal set a tariff of £75,000 as proper compensation for tetraplegia (paralysis

48. *Guardian*, 22 December 1990.
49. *Aboul-Hosn* v. *Trustees of the Italian Hospital*, July 1987 (unreported).
50. See, for example, *Thomas* v. *Wignall* [1987] 1 All ER 1185.

from the neck down).[51] Non-physical pain is compensated even more stingily. The normal rule is that no compensation is awarded for grief. If your mother dies in agony as a result of even a grossly negligent operation, your compensation is zero. Damages for bereavement will be awarded only where the relevant death is that of a spouse or a child under 18. And the amount is fixed at £7,500.[52]

The fact that currently damages in England are designed mainly to recompense pecuniary losses, that is loss of earnings and/or earning capacity and cost of care, means that awards of damages are highly unlikely to escalate to American proportions. But there is pressure to introduce much more generous compensation for pain and suffering and bereavement. The Citizens' Compensation Campaign (CITCOM),[53] under the patronage of Lord Scarman, has called for damages of at least £10,000 for bereavement, and radically higher awards for pain and suffering. It is easy to see that a parent offered £7,500 for the loss of a child feels devalued and insulted. But can any sum of money truly recompense the loss of a child, or compensate a girl of 16 for spending the rest of her life in a wheelchair? And in medical negligence claims every extra £1 awarded to those few patients who succeed in litigation is £1 taken from patient care and *not* spent on measures to protect future patients from medical accidents.

A litigation lottery?[54]

Only a tiny minority of patients who suffer a medical accident ever actually obtain any compensation. Of those who start legal action about eight in ten are doomed to fail. A survey of a hundred claims taken at random from the files of West Midlands RHA in 1987 showed that after three years seventy-three claims had been withdrawn, twelve had settled out of court, fourteen were still pending and one

51. *Housecroft* v. *Burnett* [1986] 1 All ER 332, CA. Allowance must be made for inflation.
52. See s. 1A of the Fatal Accidents Act 1976 inserted by the Administration of Justice Act 1982.
53. CITCOM seeks to establish a Compensation Board to recommend higher levels of damages.
54. See C. Ham, R. Dingwall, P. Fenn and D. Harris, *Medical Negligence: Compensation and Accountability*, King's Fund Institute/Centre for Socio-Legal Studies, Oxford, 1988.

patient had won in court.[55] It would be comforting to think that so few patients win compensation because medical care is so good. But it is dubious if this is so, and the scores of patients who fail in attempts to obtain compensation remain convinced that first medicine and then the law has failed them. Patients seeking compensation through the tort system face a series of obstacles. Have they the money to fund an action? They may have to re-mortgage their home to go ahead. Can they find a good lawyer? Case after case appears in the press where a patient has seen his claim drag on for years because his lawyers have bungled their job. Can a reliable expert be instructed who will be more convincing to the judge than the defendants' experts? And so it goes on. Meanwhile the cost of litigation escalates. Martin Wilsher's claim was, as we saw, sent for a retrial. Agreed damages totalled just under £117,000. Litigation costs before any retrial already exceeded £200,000.

Perhaps unbelievably though, for patient–plaintiffs the past few years have seen some improvements in the litigation lottery. Given a strong lead by Sir John Donaldson MR[56] judges now see access to records as the patient's right in the majority of cases. Action for Victims of Medical Accidents (AVMA),[57] founded in 1981, has helped to co-ordinate the development of expertise among solicitors in medical negligence claims and offers a free, accessible advisory service to all patients. AVMA conferences keep lawyers up to date with developments in law and medicine, and educate lawyers in medicine. Choosing your expert is all-important. Choosing an expert from the right specialty is crucial. For example, a common error in brain damage at birth injury cases is to go only to an obstetrician for expert evidence, whereas you may also need a neurologist to testify to the causes of brain injury *and* a paediatrician to assess what care the child will need.

As lawyers begin to do their job properly the percentage of patients who succeed in legal action should increase. But 'winners' in the tort system will always be in a minority, and in Chapter 10 I consider whether the tort system itself should be scrapped. For the adversarial nature of the tort system of itself does great damage to patients and doctors. If patients are seen (albeit rarely) as 'winners', doctors see

55. C. Hawkins and J. Paterson, 'Medico-Legal Audit in the West Midlands Region: Analysis of 100 Cases' (1987) 295 BMJ 1533.6.
56. See above p. 150.
57. AVMA operates in London only now and is seriously under-funded.

themselves as 'losers', pilloried for an unfortunate error. All professionals make mistakes. Doctors' mistakes can turn into tragedies. The young solicitor who makes a mistake drawing up a contract can check the document and correct his error. The young surgeon gets no such second chance. That may not be fair, but is an inescapable fact. But so long as patients must sue in the tort of negligence for medical accidents, efforts must be made to make the system work.

A significant government intervention to 'make the system work' was, as we have seen, the introduction of NHS indemnity.[58] Will sidelining the medical defence organizations help patients? It seems unlikely. The government circular implicitly admits that regional health authority legal departments may be unable to cope with the influx of work by expressly permitting them to contract out defence work to independent firms of solicitors and to the defence organizations! Moreover, it is dubious whether health authorities will or should be more ready to meet patients' claims than were the defence organizations. Health authorities are public bodies dealing with taxpayers' money. An authority will rightly need to be satisfied that a claim is very likely to succeed in court before agreeing to settle out of court. As for hospital doctors, they have some cause for concern that, in deciding how to deal with claims, authorities will not consult the individual doctors', especially junior doctors', interests adequately.

The most recent proposed reform from the Department of Health concerns proposals to introduce a system of arbitration as an alternative to litigation in medical claims. The arbitration tribunal would comprise a lawyer in the chair and two doctors, one nominated by each party. The tribunal would review written evidence and records only. Legal representation before the tribunal would not be allowed, although patients could seek legal advice in preparing their case. Without doubt such arbitration procedures would be infinitely cheaper than litigation. Whether they would command patients' and doctors' confidence is most difficult to predict.

58. See M. Brazier, 'N H S Indemnity: The Implications for Medical Litigation' (1990) 6 *Professional Negligence* 88.

CHAPTER 8

Drug-induced Injuries

Not so long ago the pharmaceutical industry basked in the warm glow of public acclaim. The development of antibiotics, of drugs to combat high blood pressure and heart disease, to alleviate the pain of rheumatism, and later the invention of the contraceptive Pill, brought benefits to many and bought life itself for some.[1] The sixties were to change the drug companies' image. Starting with the thalidomide tragedy, a series of disasters taught us all the painful lesson that drugs can be dangerous and their use must be paid for. The list of drugs enthusiastically promoted in the first place and withdrawn from the market a few years later, amid bitter allegations that the drug in question caused injury and even death, is long. Debendox, Opren, junior aspirin and, most recently, Halcion are but a random sample of the better-known cases. Meanwhile allegations of gross profit-making by the multinational drug companies have proliferated.[2]

Thalidomide had been developed originally by West German manufacturers, Chemie Grunenthal. A British company, Distillers, bought the formula and manufactured and marketed the drug here under

1. But see H. Teff and C. Munro, *Thalidomide: The Legal Aftermath*, Saxon House, London, 1976, pp. 101–4, discussing the doubts expressed about the 'pharmaceutical miracle' and suggesting that eradication of disease had as much to do with improved standards of living and hygiene as with the invention of new drugs.
2. See J. Braithwaite, *Corporate Crime in the Pharmaceutical Industry*, Routledge & Kegan Paul, London, 1984; S. Adams, *Roche versus Adams*, Jonathan Cape, London, 1984.

licence from Chemie Grunenthal. The drug was promoted as a safer alternative to existing sedatives and was expressly claimed to be suitable for pregnant and nursing mothers. Thalidomide was alleged to be the cause of gross foetal deformity. All over Europe, wherever thalidomide had been available, babies began to be born suffering from startlingly similar deformities, notably phocomelia (flipper limbs). After a long and bitter campaign, Distillers and the children's parents reached a settlement to provide compensation for children recognized as damaged by thalidomide.[3] Debendox, prescribed to alleviate morning sickness, is similarly charged with causing foetal deformities. Actions in the USA failed, parents of British children fight on for compensation. They claim that the drug marketed in Britain had a component not present in the drug available in the USA. The anti-rheumatic drug Opren, withdrawn here in 1982, is alleged to have caused kidney and liver damage, and even death, in some of its elderly users.

Patients who suffered injury as a result of taking Opren took legal action on both sides of the Atlantic. American Opren sufferers secured substantial compensation payments. British victims found themselves entangled in lengthy and complex litigation. They won some pre-liminary skirmishes,[4] but ultimately the cost of litigation forced many of them to accept an out-of-court settlement offering in general only meagre compensation.[5] Other Opren victims fought on in the courts. The defendant drug company successfully contended that they took legal action too late and so are barred from either benefiting from the settlement or pursuing their case further in the courts.[6] Lengthy and costly litigation ending in minimal compensation payments has been the pattern for virtually all claims for drug-induced injury in England.[7] Among the claims currently being pursued are thousands by patients

---

3. For a full and lively history of the events surrounding the thalidomide tragedy, see Teff and Munro, op. cit.
4. See, for example, *Davies* v. *Eli Lilly and Co*. [1987] 1 All ER 801, CA.
5. In *Davies* v. *Eli Lilly and Co* [1987] 2 All ER 94, CA it was held that the costs of litigation must be borne proportionately by all claimants. Legally aided claims could not be used to provide 'lead' cases so that the costs would be borne by the legal aid fund.
6. *Nash* v. *Eli Lilly and Co*., *The Times*, 13 February 1991.
7. Indeed no reported English case of an award of damages for personal injury for drug-induced injury can be discovered: see H. Teff, 'Regulation under Medicines Act 1968' (1984) 47 MLR 303, 320–22.

who became addicted to tranquillizers. They argue that the drug companies and prescribing doctors failed to give adequate warnings and advice on the dangers of these drugs said by some to be more addictive than heroin or cocaine. Another group of patients are suing over a dye, Myodil, used in X-rays of the spine and allegedly triggering chronic back pain and damage. The prospects of success for either group of plaintiffs are pretty dismal.

In 1987 Parliament enacted the Consumer Protection Act imposing on all producers of goods strict liability for unsafe products. This Act was based on a European Community Directive which had required all Member States to introduce such strict liability for products. In part the intention of the Directive was to ensure fair competition between businesses in the Community. If France required French producers to meet more stringent safety laws than other Member States, French businesses competed at a disadvantage to their rivals. But much of the impetus for strict liability for unsafe goods in Europe and the United Kingdom arose from a desire to give more effective protection and remedies to people who suffered injury as a result of defects in goods. The public horror provoked by the thalidomide disaster was perhaps the trigger for reform of the law.

The Consumer Protection Act might be thought to make the law on drug-induced injury straightforward. Alas, that has not proved to be the case. Victims of drug-induced injury may well complain that the Act itself is 'defective'. A drug which causes kidney damage or foetal abnormality would be perceived by most lay observers as 'unsafe'. Defining 'defective' under the Act will be seen to be more problematical. The damage caused by some drugs takes years to manifest itself. No action under the Act is allowed more than ten years after the drug in question was put on the market. Nor is a drug company's liability under the Act truly strict, for the Act permits producers to plead a 'development risks' defence and so escape liability. Such a defence might well have availed the producers of thalidomide itself. Victims of drug-induced injury must thus on occasion still resort to prior common-law remedies in contract and the tort of negligence. And negligence liability for drug-induced injury needs to be understood to evaluate whether the much vaunted strict liability under the Act is actually much of an advance on the bad old rules thalidomide and Opren victims had to play under.

Product liability and drugs

First, though, it must be acknowledged that whatever scheme for compensation is in operation there are problems relating to drug-induced injury which will not go away. The law, here and in the USA, purports to treat drugs as just another product.[8] For legal purposes a defective drug is little different from a defective electric blanket or kettle. In practice there are vital distinctions affecting both user and manufacturer if litigation is even started. Defects in products can be of two sorts: in design, which means that every example of the product will prove defective, or in construction, which means that some but not all of the eventual products will be faulty simply because they have not been put together properly. Faults in electric blankets, kettles, and even aircraft are often construction faults. Defects in drugs are almost invariably design defects. That means that when a drug company faces a claim alleging their product to be defective they are facing a disaster. There are going to be not just one or two claimants but a whole host of embittered and injured users. The cost to the company may put it out of business. So the company fights back with equal vigour.

From the user's viewpoint, his greatest difficulty in any claim against the drug company is going to be proving that the drug caused his injury. Should a new brand of electric blanket suffer a design defect and within a week of purchase 5 per cent of users suffer an electric shock, the link between cause and effect will be clear. With a new drug the process may be nothing like so swift or sure. Consider the case of diethylstilboestrol, a drug prescribed over twenty years ago to women threatening to miscarry. Now evidence has emerged that young women, *in utero* when their mothers took the drug, are affected in disproportionate numbers by vaginal and cervical cancer.[9] Delay in effect is only one of the problems. There may be very real uncertainty as to whether injury resulted from the drug taken, the original disease, or some other natural cause. When a drug is alleged to cause foetal deformity this is

8. In contrast to West Germany, which after the thalidomide disaster enacted a special regime of liability for injury caused by drugs.
9. A particular difficulty here has been establishing which manufacturer made the actual drug taken by the mother. There were several brands of the same drug on the market; see *Sindell* v. *Abbott Laboratories* (1980) 26 Cal. 3d. 588, and on this and other problems of liability for defective drugs see Newdick, 'Liability for Defective Drugs' (1985) 101 LQR 405.

a particular difficulty. Was the child's disability the result of the drug, or of some inherited disorder or disease in the mother, or one of a number of other possible causes? Then in all claims there is the problem of proving that the drug was taken by the patient in the proper dosage, and as very often the same drug is manufactured under different brand names it must be shown which brand the patient actually used.[10] Medical records are too often far from perfect, and memory is fallible. Finally, there is the intractable difficulty of personal idiosyncrasy. A drug beneficial to 99.9 per cent of us may be lethal to 0.1 per cent. Is that drug defective? Should the company, or anyone else, compensate the 0.1 per cent who suffer injury?

The drug companies rightly refuse to let government and legislators forget these special problems. They press other claims for special treatment too. Drugs are intrinsically dangerous. Patients should accept that there is a balance of benefit and risk. And the pharmaceutical industry argues too that laws which weighed too onerously on it would inhibit research. Medicine would be held back and British companies would suffer loss of competitiveness. Some view this claim sceptically. Today much of the competition appears aimed at producing new brands of the same basic drugs. The pace of innovation has slowed down.[11] Doctors are moving away from prescribing as freely as in the past. Any decline in the pharmaceutical industry is as likely to be due to these factors as it is to be the result of law reforms to help drug-injured patients.

Consumer-buyers: most favoured plaintiffs

There can be no doubt that any victim of drug-induced injury who actually bought the offending drug himself, or acquired the drug in the course of a contract, has a more effective remedy than any of his fellow sufferers. Despite the Consumer Protection Act, consumer buyers remain the most favoured plaintiffs in England. The 1987 Act merely adds an additional alternative remedy for injured consumers. It does not remove or alter existing legal remedies in contract and tort.

Two conditions are implied in every contract for the sale of goods.

10. See *Sindell* v. *Abbott Laboratories* (above).
11. See Teff, 'Regulation under the Medicines Act 1968' (1984) 47 MLR 303; Stewart and Wibberley, 'Drug Innovation – What Is Slowing It Down?' (1980) 284 *Nature* 118–20.

The goods must be merchantable.[12] This means they must be in a reasonable state to be sold at the sort of price charged. And the goods must be reasonably fit for the purpose for which they are sold.[13] When drugs are bought over the counter they must meet these conditions just like any other goods. To take a simple example, a patient buying a bottle of cough mixture suffers internal injury because the medicine is contaminated by powdered glass. That patient may recover full compensation for his injuries from the pharmacist who sold him the medicine. The pharmacist may be entirely without fault. The medicine may have been supplied by the manufacturer in a sealed, opaque container. That does not matter; the medicine was not fit to be sold and the pharmacist is in breach of his contract with the patient. This simple and effective remedy, from the patient's viewpoint, has a defect, however. It is available only when the person suffering injury from the defective drug bought it himself. Had the contaminated medicine of our example been purchased by a husband and taken by his wife, she would have had no remedy in contract. She cannot benefit from a contract to which she is not a party.

How useful then is the contractual remedy in practice? Medicines sold without prescription are, after all, the least likely to cause harm. Drugs prescribed within the NHS will not attract any conditions of merchantability and fitness for purpose, because there is no contract between the pharmacist and the patient into which such conditions can be implied, even though the patient will often have to pay for his prescription.[14] The pharmacist dispenses the drug as part of his obligation under his contract with the local Family Health Services Authority to provide pharmaceutical services in the area. The patient pays a statutory charge. He does not buy the drug; he in effect pays a tax for NHS services.

By contrast, when drugs are dispensed under a private prescription a contract does exist between the pharmacist and the patient. The patient pays the full cost of the drug directly to the pharmacist. It matters not whether the contract is one of simple sale or a contract of service under which the pharmacist provides a skilled service and incidentally supplies the drug. Now conditions of fitness are imposed in identical

12. Sale of Goods Act 1979, s. 14(2)(b).
13. ibid., s. 14(3).
14. *Pfizer* v. *Ministry of Health* [1965] AC 512; *Appleby* v. *Sleep* [1968] 1 WLR 948.

terms regardless of whether goods are supplied in the course of a service or in a straight sale transaction.[15] With the introduction of the 'limited list' of prescribable NHS drugs the number of private prescriptions may well rise. The pharmacist is exposed on the front line of liability for defective drugs.

Once prescription drugs become the subject of conditions of fitness, certain problems of applying those conditions are likely. The question may arise as to whether a drug perfectly safe for all but pregnant women is fit to be supplied. First, if it is specifically aimed at pregnant women, for example a morning sickness preparation, then clearly if it damages the woman or her baby it is not fit for the purpose for which it is supplied. Second, if it is a general medicine, such as a hay-fever remedy, it could be argued that if it carries risk to a substantial section of the community, pregnant women, then it is not merchantable, not fit to be on general sale. This immediately raises further issues. Did the manufacturer warn of the risk to pregnant women? Should the doctor have prescribed that drug? Should the woman herself be aware of the dangers of taking drugs and avoid drugs while pregnant?

These are the sorts of problem which inevitably plague questions of liability for defective drugs. But where a remedy lies in contract, once a court finds the drug unsafe, the plaintiff's claim for compensation is established. It is no defence for the retailer of the drug, or the pharmacist dispensing the drug, to argue that he personally was blameless. Nor is it any answer to the patient's claim that the state of scientific and technical knowledge at the time when the drug was produced was such that the defect could not have been discovered. There is no 'development risks' defence against a claim in contract. The liability imposed on the retailer or supplier is truly strict. In 1991 an attempt to impose similar strict conditions for all NHS prescriptions in Rosie Barnes MP's National Health Service (Compensation) Bill failed at its Second Reading in the House of Commons.

The remedy in negligence

Patients who suffer injury as a result of drugs prescribed within the NHS must look outside the law of contract for a remedy. Prior to the Consumer Protection Act 1987 that remedy would have to be found in

15. See the Supply of Goods and Services Act 1982; A. P. Bell, 'The Doctor and the Supply of Goods and Services Act' [1984] *Legal Studies* 175.

the tort of negligence. The 1987 Act applies only to products marketed *after* 1 March 1988, so that any claim arising out of a drug put on the market *before* that date (albeit taken by the patient at some later date) will still lie exclusively in negligence. And, as will become apparent, gaps in the Consumer Protection Act mean that even now victims of drug-induced injury cannot ignore the tort of negligence. An action in negligence arises where one person suffers injury as a result of the breach of a duty of care owed him by another. Such a duty, as we have seen, is owed by the doctor to his patient. The doctor may well be the first person too to whom the patient turns for a remedy when he believes a drug prescribed by that doctor has harmed him. The doctor will be liable for drug-induced injury if the drug caused damage because he prescribed an incorrect dosage, or because he ought to have appreciated that that drug posed a risk to a particular patient in the light of his medical history, or where drugs have been prescribed in inappropriate and harmful combination. Similarly if the injury to the patient results from a negligent error by the pharmacist in, for example, dispensing the wrong drug, or indicating the wrong dosage, an action in negligence lies against the pharmacist. In a number of cases it may be the cumulative result of negligence by both doctor and pharmacist which causes injury, as where a doctor's atrocious handwriting misled the pharmacist into dispensing entirely the wrong drug.[16] The problem for the patient is that all he knows is that he is ill and he believes the drug to be the cause. He will initially have no means of knowing whether an inherently 'safe' drug was prescribed for him in an unsafe and careless fashion, or whether the drug is inherently defective and harmful however careful the doctor may be. Hence patients contemplating litigation for drug-induced injury probably have to start by considering suing the doctor, the pharmacist *and* the manufacturer, and must hope that evidence of who was actually to blame will emerge in the course of the litigation.

Turning now to the liability in negligence of drug companies manufacturing drugs, the manufacturer of any product

> ... which he sells in such a form as to show that he intends them to reach the ultimate consumer in the form in which they left him with no reasonable possibility of intermediate examination, and with the knowledge that the absence of care in the preparation or putting up of the products will result in

16. *Prendergast* v. *Sam and Dee*, *The Times*, 14 March 1989, CA.

injury to the consumer's life or property, owes a duty to the consumer to take that reasonable care.[17]

There is no doubt that this duty to take care attaches as much to the manufacturer of drugs as to the manufacturer of ginger beer or any other product. The duty covers the design and formulation of the drug as well as its construction. Nor is the duty limited to the original manufacturer. We saw that thalidomide was initially developed by a West German company and manufactured under licence here by Distillers. Distillers still owed a duty to test and monitor the formula before putting the finished product on the UK market. Even if they had imported the drug ready-made, if they had then sold it under their brand name they would have owed a duty to English patients to take steps to check on the safety of the drug.[18]

Establishing a duty to avoid negligence is not then the problem. Determining what amounts to negligence is a formidable task. The potential harm caused by a defective drug is such that a very high standard of care will be imposed on the manufacturer. This is generally acknowledged. However, in England no action for personal injuries against a drug company has yet resulted in an award of damages by a court. What are the obstacles confronting claimants, then? First, the drug company must be judged by the standards for drug safety and consumer protection pertaining at the date when the drug was put on the market, not at the date proceedings are taken against them. Drug companies, like doctors, must not be judged negligent on hindsight alone. Today the risk to the developing foetus of drugs taken by the mother is well known to all lay women. When thalidomide was first on the market it is far from clear that the dangers of drugs to the foetus were widely appreciated even by gynaecologists and scientists.

Consideration of the history of the thalidomide claim[19] leads us into the second area of difficulty for litigants. How does a claimant get hold of the hard evidence he will need to prove the company careless? The thalidomide story is instructive, albeit depressing. The charge against Distillers was that they should have foreseen that the drug

17. *Donoghue* v. *Stevenson* [1932] AC 562, 599.
18. *Watson* v. *Buckley and Osborne, Garrett & Co. Ltd* [1940] 1 All ER 174 (duty imposed on distributors of hair dye).
19. Teff and Munro, op. cit., Chapters 1 and 2.

might harm the foetus and therefore should have conducted adequate tests on it before promoting it as safe for use in pregnancy and/or that once adverse reports on the drug reached them they should have withdrawn it at once. In retrospect, the available evidence that Distillers were negligent falls into three categories. First, there was material available from 1934 onwards to suggest that drugs did pass through the placenta and could damage the foetus. Second, in the 1950s a number of drug companies marketing new products had carried out tests to check the effect on the foetus mainly by way of animal experiments. Such evidence would need to have been given by experts and might not have been conclusive. The burden of proof lies on the claimant. The defendant's experts would have argued that when thalidomide was developed it was by no means universally accepted that drugs could damage the foetus, the efficacy of animal tests would have been disputed, and it would have been strongly submitted that in any case such tests were not then current general practice.

The third and final category of evidence might have been more damning if the claimants could have got hold of it. Reports of the original testing of thalidomide in West Germany by Chemie Grunenthal suggest that it may have been a pretty hit and miss affair. Fairly early on, adverse reports on the drug and concern over risk to the foetus were in the hands of Chemie Grunenthal. Some considerable time elapsed before they withdrew the drug there. Distillers seems to have acted faster, taking the drug out of circulation soon after adverse reactions were reported to them. The contents of adverse reports on a drug, the sequence and exact dates on which those reports are received, are of crucial importance to a claimant. No drug company is going to hand the reports over voluntarily. The process of discovery, of compelling a defendant to hand over documents, was seen to be complex enough in a malpractice claim against an individual doctor. In a claim against a drug company the process may become an insuperable obstacle race.

One last general point on the law of negligence as it affects drug claims can be made by way of illustration from the thalidomide case. It may at the end of the day prove to be the case that there is insufficient evidence that the company were negligent when they originally marketed the drug. But there may be evidence, however hard to come by, that they were negligent in failing to act on adverse reports and recall the drug. Is that a breach of the manufacturer's duty? Two separate situations must be examined. Had it been proved that a child was injured by thalidomide when the drug taken was put on the market by Distillers after a date by which they should have known it to be dangerous, there is no problem. The drug that injured that child was negligently put into circulation. Difficulty would arise where the drug taken by the mother had been put into circulation before Distillers should have known it was dangerous but was actually prescribed to her and taken by her after that date. Although it is not as clearly established as the duty to manufacture a product carefully,[20] I believe that a court would hold that the manufacturer owes a further duty to monitor his product and to take reasonable steps to withdraw it if it proves unsafe. Proving breach of the duty could be a nightmare. Stories of doctors continuing to prescribe, and pharmacists retaining stocks of withdrawn drugs, recur. The patient suing in such a claim could falter and sink in a sea of allegation and counter-allegation between drug company, doctor and pharmacist.

The inadequacy of the tort of negligence as an effective means of compensating victims of drug-induced injury has been demonstrated time and time again. Successive reviews of negligence as a means of remedying personal injuries resulting from any defective, unsafe product concluded that the reform of product liability laws was essential.[21] What must now be evaluated is how effective reform by way of the Consumer Protection Act 1987 has proved to be.

Strict liability: the Consumer Protection Act[22]

The concept of strict liability for products is simple. A plaintiff making

20. *Wright* v. *Dunlop Rubber Co. Ltd* [1972] 13 KIR 255; and see Forte, 'Medical Products Liability', in S. A. M. McLean (ed.), *Legal Issues in Medicine*, Gower, Aldershot, 1981, p. 67.
21. Notably the Law Commission in their report 'Liability for Defective Products' (1977) Law Com. No. 82, Cmnd 6831, and the Royal Commission on Civil Liability and Compensation for Personal Injury (1978) Cmnd 7054 (the Pearson Report).
22. The pharmaceutical industry repeatedly argued that drugs should remain exempt from any regime of strict liability, mainly on the grounds that (1) scientific research and innovation would be adversely affected; (2) the nature of drug disasters meant that strict liability could have catastrophic results for the industry; (3) the difficulty of defining defect in a drug: these arguments have been consistently rejected; see Law Com. No. 82 (above), pp. 19–21; Pearson Report, para. 1274.

a claim for compensation against the manufacturer of a product need prove only (1) that the product was defective *and* (2) that the defect in the product caused his injury. Strict liability is seen as fairer to claimants because it establishes that responsibility for an injury caused by a defective product is borne by the person creating the risk and benefiting financially from the product, that is the manufacturer. The manufacturer too is in the best position to exercise control over the safety and quality of the product, and can more conveniently insure against the risk of injury posed by the product than may individual users. Proponents of strict liability for products also argued that prolonged, expensive and complex litigation was likely to be less common with a strict liability regime than has been the case with the tort of negligence. The arguments for strict liability are impressive. But does the Consumer Protection Act achieve the aims of strict liability for patients injured by defective drugs?

The Act imposes liability for personal injury arising from defective products on all *producers* of goods. 'Producers' embraces a wider category of businesses involved in the marketing of drugs than simply the companies manufacturing the finished products.[23] Manufacturers of components are liable for any defect in the components. Companies importing drugs into the European Community will be liable under the Act as if they manufactured the drug in England. So if the drug in issue was actually manufactured in Japan or Switzerland, the aggrieved patient need not concern himself with the potential difficulties of suing the Japanese or Swiss drug company abroad, he can bring his claim here in England[24] against the European Community company who brought the drug into the Community. A company that brand-names a drug is a producer within the Act. Companies cannot use their name to claim the credit and the profit for a drug and then when something goes badly wrong disclaim any responsibility for that drug. Finally, any supplier[25] of a drug will be deemed to be a producer unless he identifies the source of his supply. This provision is crucial for patients. The patient may well receive his prescription or injection in a form

---

23. See ss. 1–2.
24. Even if the importer is not an English company, but a company based in another EC state, the victim will be able to sue here in England if he suffered injury here; see the Civil Jurisdiction and Judgments Act 1982.
25. This includes pharmacists dispensing NHS drugs even though they do not sell NHS drugs to patients.

such that he cannot possibly identify the original producer of the drug. The community pharmacist or hospital pharmacy supplying the drug must assist him to trace the producer or bear liability for the patient's injuries themselves. The intention of the European Directive,[26] on which the Act is based, and of the Act itself is that there should, as far as humanly possible, always be an identifiable producer on whom liability must rest. No company should be able to hide behind a smokescreen as to its identity.

So far so good, but having identified a defendant the next stage of a claim under the Act for drug-induced injury becomes more problematical. How do you establish that the drug is defective? Section 3(1) provides that

... there is a defect in a product ... if the safety of the product is not such as persons generally are entitled to expect;

Section 3(2) goes on to direct the judge to take into account all the relevant circumstances pertaining to the safety of a product including

(a) the manner in which, and purposes for which, the product has been marketed, its get-up, the use of any mark in relation to the product and any instructions for, or warnings with respect to, the doing of anything with or in relation to the product;

(b) what might reasonably be expected to be done with or in relation to the product; and

(c) the time when the product was supplied by its producer to another;

and nothing in this section shall require a defect to be inferred from the fact alone that the safety of a product which is supplied after that time is greater than the safety of the product in question.

Determining when a drug falls within that definition will be far from easy.[27] Drugs are by their nature dangerous. They are designed to do damage to the bacteria or diseased cell or whatever caused the original disease. How much safety are persons generally entitled to expect? Side-effects are often unavoidable. The court will have to try to balance the potential benefit against the risk when deciding if an unwanted ·

26. Council Directive of 25 July 1985.
27. See the thorough and excellent discussion of this problem in Newdick, op. cit., pp. 409–20.

side-effect renders a drug defective. Distinctions may be drawn based on the condition that the drug was designed to combat. A minor tranquillizer which carried an unforeseen 5 per cent risk of liver damage could be deemed defective when an anti-cancer drug carrying identical risk probably will not. Relief of moderate anxiety may be seen as insufficient to warrant the risk, whereas the battle against cancer may justify that degree of inherent danger. Anticipated risks raise different issues. Clearly an anticipated risk must be warned against. Will the tranquillizer be deemed not defective if its potential danger is outlined to doctors and patients, leaving this choice to them? Clearly the warning must be taken into account. An antibiotic harmful only to the foetus will almost certainly not be defective if a warning of its risk is clearly given. Less essential drugs may remain defective even if risks are detailed in the literature supplied to doctors. The patient may never have the warning passed on to him after all. In such a case, though, a heavy share of liability would rest with the doctor prescribing the drug in contravention or ignorance of warnings from the producer.

Other problems in applying this definition of defective can easily be predicted. What of the patient who suffers injury because of an allergic reaction to the drug? The drug is perfectly safe and effective for you, but lethal to me. So might it be argued that the drug is safe for 'persons generally'? Such an argument will fail. Society, 'persons generally', demands that regard be had to the safety of all of us where, as in the case of drugs, allergic and idiosyncratic reactions are a well-known risk of the product. If risk to an individual or group is foreseeable and *not* warned of in the presentation of the product it is defective. Clearly an individual is entitled to expect that the manufacturer will not simply ignore an identified danger to however small a group. When the risk is not foreseeable, the size and predictability of the affected group will be crucial. A sedative which causes damage to the foetus or liver damage in 10 per cent of the over-seventies will be defective. Pregnant women and the elderly are large groups of potential consumers known to be vulnerable to drug-induced injury. But what if the sedative injured only a handful of users out of millions?

The difficulties that may arise in applying definition of defective in the Act could be detailed at much greater length. For potential claimants the disturbing news is this. The 'new' test of defectiveness offers as much of a prospect of prolonged litigation as the 'old' test of negligence. And proving defectiveness is only the start of the claimant's difficulties. Causation remains as thorny a problem as ever. The onus remains on the claimant to prove 'the causal relationship between defect and damage'.[28] Liability comes entirely to an end ten years after the product is put into circulation. Drugs such as the anti-miscarriage drug which caused cancer up to twenty years later in some of the daughters *in utero* thus escape the regime of strict liability.

Finally, the effect of the development risks defence adopted in the UK must be examined.[29] A 'development risks' defence amounts to this. The manufacturer will not be liable if he can prove that the state of scientific and technical knowledge at the time when he put the product into circulation was not such as to enable the existence of the defect to be discovered.[30] This means that if a drug manufactured in 1988 is in 1991 shown to be defective, but applying 1988 standards for the manufacture and testing of drugs the drug company did all it could be expected to, the company will not be liable for any damage done by their defective product. It will remain the case that the company can no more be judged by hindsight than it could under the previous law of negligence. Of great value to the defendant will be the irrefutable evidence that the Committee on Safety of Medicines (CSM) saw fit to grant him a product licence. Unless there is evidence that the defendant misled or was not frank with the CSM, a court may be reluctant to say that in their opinion the manufacturer failed to comply with the standards of the time when the experts, the CSM, had found he did.[31]

What benefits then, if any, will the Act afford? A great deal will depend on how the judges interpret defectiveness. Otherwise the

28. See Article 4 of the EC Directive.
29. See s. 4 (1)(e). The remainder of s. 4 outlines a number of other defences which will only rarely be relevant in claims for drug-induced injuries.
30. The European Directive Article 7(e) permitted states to incorporate a development risks defence. Article 7(e) framed such a permitted defence in terms of the state of scientific and technical knowledge generally available. Section 4(1)(e) of the Consumer Protection Act provides '. . . the state of scientific and technical knowledge was not such that a producer of products of the same description as the product in question might be expected to have discovered the defect . . .', i.e. knowledge and practice in the pharmaceutical industry. The EC Commission has referred s. 4(1)(e) to the European Court of Justice, alleging that the UK government has in fact adopted a broader development risks defence than the Directive allows.
31. The Pearson Commission considered and rejected arguments that in the case of drugs the grant of a product licence should be a complete defence; Pearson Report (above), para. 1260.

greatest material change will be this. While a producer able to raise the development risks defence will still be able to plead that according to the current practice he could have done no more than he did, the onus will lie on him to prove this. Once a claimant has shown that the product was defective and that it injured him, the ball moves into the defendant's court. Distillers, if sued over thalidomide under the current regime of strict liability, would have had to prove that current practice did *not* involve tests for effect on the foetus, and to reveal what tests were conducted. They would have been forced to disclose all the material available to them to support their case. The greatest potential benefit of the reforms proposed at present is that defendants will lose the advantage of trying to keep as much as possible of the scientific and expert evidence available to them out of the hands of the plaintiff.

What must now be asked is why the British government was so insistent on the development risks defence. All the bodies which have previously investigated product liability reform have come out against such a defence. The Pearson Commission, which reviewed the whole of the law relating to personal injuries, said:

... to exclude development risks from a regime of strict liability would be to leave a gap in the compensation cover, through which, for example, the victims of another thalidomide disaster might slip.[32]

The government allowed itself to be swayed by counter-arguments from industry. They claim that innovation would be discouraged and that the cost of insurance against development risks would be crippling.[33] Their case has convinced only the government and was expressly rejected in all earlier inquiries. There is another disquieting feature of the acceptance of a development risks defence too. West Germany, which boasts a thriving pharmaceutical industry, has rejected the development risks defence specifically with regard to drugs while adopting it in relation to other products. West Germany does not want to become a testing ground for risky drugs. Does Britain? The government should think again.

32. Pearson Report, para. 1259; and see Law Com. No. 82 (above).
33. See HC Deb. Vol. 1357 Col. 808.

Prevention: better than cure?

The horror of the thalidomide tragedy provided the impetus for one change unrelated to compensation for injury. Measures were taken to improve the monitoring of drugs before they were permitted to be marketed in the UK. This was first effected by way of a voluntary scheme. The government set up a Committee on Safety of Drugs to examine and approve new drugs and to monitor those already on the market. Drug companies were not compelled to accept the scheme, but the majority complied.[34] In 1968 the Medicines Act 1968 introduced statutory compulsory vetting of new drugs. It is this statute which still largely provides for the licensing and monitoring of drugs in the UK today. I deal only briefly with its provisions simply to show that mechanisms do exist which are designed to protect patients from injury caused by unsafe pharmaceutical products.

The 1968 Act entrusts the licensing of new drugs and the scrutiny of drugs already on the market to the Health Minister.[35] No medicine may be manufactured, imported or marketed without a licence from the Minister. When a new product is developed, a clinical trial certificate must be obtained before it can be tested on patients, and a product licence is required before the drug can be marketed.[36] The Minister acts on the advice of a body known as the Medicines Commission and its specialist committees. The Commission's powers are general in nature. It is directed to advise the Minister on (*inter alia*) the practice of medicine and pharmacy, and the operation of the pharmaceutical industry.[37] The Committee on Safety of Medicines (CSM), one of three committees established by the Medicines Commission, has the more specific, central role in licensing new drugs. The CSM is empowered to advise on the safety, quality and efficacy of drugs, and to promote the collection of information on adverse reactions and advise on action to be taken as a consequence thereof.[38] It is to the CSM that applications for clinical trial certificates and product licences are

34. For details see Teff and Munro, op. cit., pp. 111–18.
35. Medicines Act 1968, s. 6.
36. ss. 7 and 35; for limited exemptions to the requirement for a clinical trial certificate see Medicines (Exemption and Licences)(Clinical Trials) Order 1981 SI No. 164.
37. s. 2.
38. s. 4.

first referred. The Minister cannot refuse a licence without first consulting the CSM.[39] In practice if not in law, in the overwhelming majority of cases the CSM is the licensing authority.

When deciding whether to grant a licence the Minister and the CSM are directed to consider:

(1) the safety of the drug to which the application relates;
(2) the efficacy of the drug for the purpose for which it is to be administered; and
(3) the quality of the drug, having particular regard to its method of manufacture, and arrangements proposed for its distribution.[40]

The CSM is expressly *excluded* from taking into account any question of whether other existing drugs are equally or more efficacious for the purpose proposed.[41] So the CSM cannot reject an application for a product licence for a new tranquillizer simply because it considers there are already sufficient effective drugs of that sort available. The CSM's remit is to protect the consumer from injury, and not from a plethora of expensive close-copy drugs. When the CSM advises and the Minister agrees that a licence be granted, a product licence is operative for five years[42] and a clinical trial certificate for two.[43] At the end of those periods the manufacturer must apply again for renewal of his licence. The CSM is also responsible for monitoring adverse reaction to drugs in use. Section 28 of the Medicines Act 1968 empowers the Minister, on the advice of the CSM, to revoke an existing licence. Several grounds for revocation are established, of which the most important is where:

... medicinal products of any description to which the licence relates can no longer be regarded as products which can safely be administered for the purposes indicated in the licence, or can no longer be regarded as efficacious for those purposes ...

The decision to withdraw a drug from the market is no longer solely a matter for the manufacturer.

A manufacturer aggrieved by the advice of the CSM that a licence be refused, or an existing licence be revoked, may seek to have the

39. s. 20(3).
40. s. 19(1).
41. s. 19(2).
42. s. 24.
43. s. 38.

advice of the CSM reviewed by the Medicines Commission. A manufacturer whose product has been approved by the CSM and/or the Commission but who is refused a licence by the Minister has a right to a further hearing. The Minister, the licensing authority in law, is obliged to consult the CSM. If he chooses, as he may, to reject their advice, he must set up an independent inquiry before which the manufacturer may state his case.[44] This has happened only once since the Medicines Act 1968 came into force. The Minister rejected the advice of the CSM to license the injectable contraceptive Depo-Provera for long-term use. After receiving a report from the independent inquiry panel set up, the Minister licensed the drug under strict conditions.

It can be seen then that an elaborate framework for licensing drugs in the UK exists. I have only skimmed the surface of the scheme. Detailed provision is made for the submission of applications, and a great deal of work and manpower is expended both by the companies and by Health Ministry and CSM staff. The pharmaceutical industry has attacked the procedure. They claim that it is over-burdensome and bureaucratic. Drug companies in the UK are suffering. They dare not innovate. They cannot compete. The drug companies' well-orchestrated self-pleading has been vigorously resisted. Consumer groups counter-attack. In particular, concern has been voiced over the close links between many members of the CSM, and the pharmaceutical industry. And with the spectre of several drug disasters hanging over us, today does not seem to be the time to weaken existing consumer protection laws which have not in themselves proved entirely adequate.[45]

Claims against the Minister and the CSM

The possibility of governmental liability for drug-induced injury was aired even in the thalidomide days. The then Health Minister, Sir Keith Joseph, dismissed suggestions that the government could be liable. He argued further that even when the elaborate licensing provisions of the 1968 Act were in force, the legal liability for any defect in the drug rested on the manufacturers alone.[46] The patients injured by the anti-arthritic drug, Opren, sought compensation from the Health

44. s. 21(5).
45. Discussed fully in Teff, 'Regulation under the Medicines Act 1968' (above).
46. HC Deb. Vol. 847 Col. 440–41, 29 November 1972.

Minister and the CSM as well as from the drug company.[47] They contended that the government and the CSM had been negligent both in originally licensing the drug and for continuing to allow it to be marketed after its dangers should have become apparent to the Ministry and the CSM. The Opren case against the government was ultimately abandoned. Claims by haemophiliac patients who contracted HIV and AIDS from contaminated blood products raised legal issues similar to those entailed when a victim of drug-induced injury seeks to sue the government. The essence of the claim by haemophiliac patients was this. The Department of Health continued to import blood products (Factor 8) from abroad which are essential to the treatment of haemophilia after they should have been aware that such products might well be contaminated by infection, including hepatitis B and HIV. The government resolutely denied liability but ultimately succumbed to political pressure and offered haemophiliac patients an *ex gratia* settlement.[48]

Could a claim against the government, in effect for negligently monitoring drugs and/or blood products, succeed? The aggrieved patients would have to convince the court that the Department of Health and/or the CSM owed a duty of care to individual patients in the exercise of their public powers. The inherent problem for the patients is that the defendants would argue that, yes, the powers entrusted to them by Parliament imposed a duty to exercise those powers properly, but that this was a duty owed to the public at large and not to individuals.[49] In *Anns* v. *Merton LBC*[50] the plaintiff's maisonette was found to be severely defective because the block of flats had been built on inadequate foundations. He sued the builder and the local authority. His claim against the local authority was that they had been negligent in the exercise of their statutory powers to inspect and approve building works. In 1978 the House of Lords found the local authority liable. Their Lordships held though that a public authority could be liable for a negligent exercise of statutory powers only if it could be said that the authority had misused its powers, that it had failed to consider

47. The claim against the CSM was dropped.
48. The amounts awarded proved to be significantly less than the plaintiffs would have won had the case proceeded to trial.
49. See *R.* v. *Secretary of State for Social Services ex p. Hincks* (1979) 123 SJ 436, above, p. 21.
50. [1978] AC 728.

adequately the relevant considerations which it should have weighed up in making the decision or decisions under attack. So the victim of a drug disaster or a haemophiliac patient afflicted by HIV would have to advance evidence suggesting a flaw in the relevant defendant's decision-making process.

Alas, even should he be able to do so and so 'pass' the *Anns* test, he will then confront the other problems. The actual decision in *Anns* that the local authority were liable to the plaintiff for his *economic* loss, the cost of repairing his maisonette, was overruled by the House of Lords in 1990.[51] It was left open whether the authority would still be held liable should a plaintiff in similar circumstances to Mr Anns suffer actual personal injuries. But the climate of judicial opinion seems to be turning against holding public authorities liable in tort to individual members of the public.

Claims brought abroad

The majority of drug companies are multinationals. Drugs are not clearly confined within national borders. British women who suffered injury as a result of using the Dalkon Shield IUD sued the manufacturers in the USA and are now claiming compensation from a settlement fund set up when the company went bankrupt. When can an injured patient resort to a foreign court and why should he want to?

Whenever a claim has a foreign element a set of rules known as the rules of private international law, or conflict of laws, comes into play. These are excessively complex and I shall give only the barest outline of the relevant law. Essentially, when a claim for negligence is brought the claimant can sue in any country where a relevant act of negligence occurred.[52] There may be more than one such country. So in the case of a defective drug, negligence may have occurred both in the country where it was carelessly manufactured and in the country where it was carelessly marketed as safe[53] and injured the claimant. It is on the

---

51. *Murphy* v. *Brentwood DC* [1990] 3 WLR 414.
52. RSC Ord. 11, r.l(f); Civil Jurisdiction and Judgments Act 1982 enacting the European Convention on jurisdiction and judgements; Art. 5(3).
53. *Distillers Co.* [*Biochemicals*] *Ltd* v. *Thompson* [1971] AC 458 (New Zealand mother allowed to sue the British company Distillers in New Zealand over thalidomide manufactured here; essence of the negligence alleged was failure to warn her, in New Zealand, of the danger to her baby).

basis of the careless manufacture of the device in the USA that the women suing over the Dalkon Shield were able to go to Court in America. Where there is a dispute over whether an action should be allowed to go ahead, the law of the country where the claimant is trying to sue determines whether it should do so. British women claiming in the USA that US formulated contraceptive Pills caused heart attacks and strokes won a substantial settlement.

Why should anyone want to sue abroad? After all, if they took the drug here and were injured here they can bring their action in their homeland on the basis of negligent distribution in the UK. There are two main reasons why claimants may opt for the hassle of a foreign lawsuit. First, the procedural rules in the foreign courts may be more favourable to claimants. They may be able to conduct a 'class action' more effectively than in England. That is to say, the group of claimants will be able to bring their action co-operatively, sharing expenses and expertise. The Opren and haemophiliac claims have seen moves to facilitate class actions here, but such claims may still be easier abroad, especially in the USA. Second, there are powerful financial incentives to sue in the USA if you can. Not only is liability for drugs strict, but awards of damages are made by juries still, and are generally much higher than English judge-made awards. Most important, though, is the contingency fee system. To start off with, the claimant need pay his American lawyer nothing. If the case is won, the lawyer takes a share of the damages. Should the claimant lose, the lawyer may not get a penny. Claimants can afford to start an action unhampered by fears of the expense of their case. And finally just a threat to sue in the USA may prompt the defendants into offering a more generous settlement than would otherwise have been the case!

A possible solution: no-fault 'liability'?

The pharmaceutical industry itself remains apprehensive of strict liability despite the view of many commentators that its position regarding liability for injury will in practice be little changed. The Association of British Pharmaceutical Industries (ABPI) appears to favour more radical reform, a move to a scheme of no-fault compensation. This would differ from strict liability in this way. Under strict liability the claimant has to show that he was injured by a drug and that that drug was defective. A no-fault scheme would simply require proof that the drug caused harm. Claimants would recover compensation from a state fund for injury without anyone having to be shown to be at fault in any way. No-fault compensation raises several questions. Who will pay for it? Is ABPI support for a compensation scheme which appears so much more generous to patients just a device to evade the spectre of a massive compensation award consequent on a drug disaster? Why separate out drug-induced injury for special treatment? Will such a scheme encourage irresponsibility by companies freed from the threat of court action? These are questions raised in relation to medical malpractice as well as drug injuries. I examine them in Chapter 10. I look now at the one example of a very limited no-fault scheme in operation today, the Vaccine Damage Payments Act 1979. How successful has this well-meant scheme been?

Vaccine damage: a special case

Vaccine damage is a candidate for special treatment because of the distinction in social effect between vaccines and other drugs.[54] Generally the benefit and risk of taking a drug rests with the individual patient alone. No one else suffers directly if he does not take the drug. No one else benefits directly if he does. With a vaccine the position is different. If a child is immunized against contagious disease, the child himself benefits from the immunity conferred and his friends and schoolfellows benefit from the elimination of the risk that he will pass that disease on to them. Consequently vaccination of young children against tetanus, diptheria, polio, measles and whooping cough is actively promoted by the Department of Health. It is the whooping cough vaccine that has caused the greatest outcry and distress. A number of children healthy before vaccination have, their parents claim, suffered severe and lasting brain damage as a consequence of receiving the vaccine.

What remedies have the parents of a vaccine-damaged child? First they may, as a number of parents of children allegedly damaged by whooping cough vaccine have done, seek to use the tort of negligence to obtain compensation. The advantage of this course is that if the claim was successful their children would receive full compensation for any handicap caused by the vaccine. The problem for the parents is whom to sue. The present vaccine is controversial. Doctors argue vehemently whether the risk of the vaccine to a child is greater than the

54. See in particular the Pearson Report, Chapter 25.

risks posed by contracting the disease itself. An action against a doctor for negligently using the vaccine is likely to fail because although some doctors and experts condemn its use, a substantial body of informed opinion still backs the vaccine. A malpractice action is really viable only if some special feature of the child's history should have ruled out routine vaccination, or if symptoms at a first vaccination, indicating that further vaccination was unwise, were missed. Suing the manufacturers will run into the problem of the risk/benefit ratio of the product. The manufacturers dispute the level of risk from the vaccine and will argue that the overwhelming benefit to the community of vaccination outweighs any risk to a very few. And they deny that the vaccine does indeed cause brain damage.

One parent of a brain-damaged child attempted to sue the Department of Health.[55] The Department argued that the case against them was totally untenable and should be struck out without a full hearing. The judge held that in so far as the claimants challenged the *policy* decision by the Department to promote vaccination their action would be stopped. But allegations that Department advice as to the circumstances and manner of vaccination was inadequate would be allowed to go forward. The attempt by the Department to have the claimants' case against them entirely blocked as untenable failed.

However, although the parents of brain-damaged children succeeded in some preliminary battles to win full compensation for their children, their hopes received a near-fatal blow in 1988. For in *Loveday* v. *Renton*[56] a High Court judge held that the plaintiffs had failed to prove causation. They had failed to demonstrate that it was more likely than not that the whooping cough vaccine caused brain damage. Reviewing the extensive expert evidence in a lengthy judgement the judge concluded that that evidence suggested that some other cause, congenital damage or concurrent infection, might well have triggered the damage that the parents attributed to the vaccine.

The enormous problems of litigation for negligence deter many parents from going to court. Successive reviews of the issue of compensation for vaccine damage recognized that it is an example of injury where compensation via the tort of negligence may be totally inappropriate. There may at the end of the day prove to be no negligence on anyone's part because the benefit to the majority is held to

55. *DHSS* v. *Kinnear*, The Times, 7 July 1984.
56. *The Times*, 31 March 1988.

justify the risk to a small minority. Yet it is scarcely fair that those who suffer damage should bear the whole burden of their handicap alone. On the recommendation of the Pearson Commission, Parliament enacted the Vaccine Damage Payments Act 1979 to provide for a no-fault compensation scheme for vaccine-damaged individuals. The scheme is far from generous. It provided originally for an award of £10,000 only where a person suffers 80 per cent disablement as a result of vaccination against a disease to which the Act applies. In July 1985 the amount payable was raised to £20,000 but only for claims made after that date. Claims for payments under the Act are made initially to the Department of Health. If the Department official responsible is not satisfied that the claim is made out, the claimant may ask for the decision to be reviewed by an independent medical tribunal. The decision of the tribunal is final. The making of a payment under the 1979 Act does not debar a claimant from also suing for negligence in respect of the vaccination.

The most bitter criticism of the Act is that even the increased payment of £20,000 is woefully inadequate. The Act, it is said, is no more than a sop to public opinion. It has not replaced the tort of negligence with an adequate compensation mechanism. Other critics complain that the ever-present problem of causation of drug-induced injury is simply ignored in the Act. The claimant must establish on the balance of probability that his disablement resulted from the vaccine. Disputed cases go to the independent tribunals. Statistics seem to show that establishing cause and effect is not a precise science. It is difficult to see what factors account for a 39 per cent success rate in disputed cases before the Manchester tribunal in contrast to only a 12 per cent success rate in Belfast.[57] The judgement in *Loveday* v. *Renton* that whooping cough vaccine does not cause brain damage has plunged the vaccine damage scheme into even greater disarray.

What of the future?

The difficulties of establishing that a drug is defective within the new strict-liability regime introduced by the Consumer Protection Act do not appear to offer much comfort to victims of drug-induced injuries or other medical products. The problems of proving causation remain formidable. The glimmer of hope for patients seeking compensation in

57. See Newdick, op. cit., p. 429.

future is to be found in changes not in the substantive law governing liability but in improved procedures. For a start, solicitors acting for patients are now much better at their job. They act together and coordinate their work for their separate clients. The example of the Opren Action Campaign provides a model for solicitors acting in later claims. As we saw in Chapter 7, judges are today much more willing to order disclosure of evidence, be it the patient's medical records or expert advice given to drug companies. The cards are not stacked so heavily against the patient. None the less, drugs will always be dangerous substances and perhaps society should not forget to put as much effort into preventing injury as it does into dealing with the consequences of injury.

CHAPTER 9

Hospital Complaints Procedures

The bravest patient may well quail at embarking on litigation for medical malpractice. For litigation to be economically worthwhile it must offer some hope of substantial compensation. Moreover, money may not be the aggrieved patient's primary concern. Many simply want an explanation of what went wrong and perhaps an apology. Despite the clumsy and inadequate nature of a lawsuit as a means of investigating medical error, some patients sue just to try to find out what really happened. One such patient, a mother whose delivery of twins at a private hospital went disastrously wrong (one baby died), won £31,000 in damages. The money, she said, was much less important than finding out why her child died.[1] Going to court was her only remedy. Interestingly, private hospital organizations are considering setting up complaints procedures.[2]

Within the National Health Service there is an assortment of complaints mechanisms. The Health Service Commissioner, district and regional health authorities and the Health Minister all have a role to play. Many of the procedures had no statutory basis until 1985. The number of complaints to the Commissioner has risen over the years. Handling of critical complaints will be seen to be poor and sometimes to aggravate patients' original grievances. In 1985 Parliament acted to initiate a review of complaints procedures.

1. *The Times*, 28 June 1985; and see *Kralj* v. *McGrath* [1986] 1 All ER 54.
2. See the *Sunday Times*, 21 July 1985, p. 3.

Hospital Complaints Procedures Act 1985

This Act derives from the personal experience of Michael McNair Wilson MP while he lay in a series of NHS hospitals acutely ill with renal failure. He was on the whole grateful for and impressed with the care he received. One or two things did go badly wrong though. For example, a stitch left in his leg went septic and he got septicaemia. Like many other patients, he asked himself: '... to whom do I complain? Who will offer me compensation? Who will listen to my problem?'[3]

When he returned to the House of Commons he introduced the Private Member's Bill which became the Hospital Complaints Procedures Act 1985. The Act is brief. The Health Minister already had power to give directions to health authorities.[4] Section 1 of the 1985 Act imposes a duty on the Minister to give directions to health authorities to ensure that in each hospital for which the authority is responsible arrangements are made for dealing with patients' complaints and that adequate publicity is given to those arrangements. The scheme to be followed by the authority must comply with the directions of the Minister. The Act did not become law immediately. For three years, extensive consultations took place with the health authorities and health care professions. Not until 1988 did the Minister issue the directions required by the 1985 Act.[5]

The central feature of the 1988 directions is the requirement that there must be in each hospital for which a health authority has responsibility a designated officer, often the Unit General Manager, whose duty it is to receive and handle complaints. He is intended to be in effect a hospital 'Ombudsman'.[6] All complaints will go first to him. Where the complainant so wishes, the designated officer should attempt informal conciliation. The Department of Health rightly stresses the importance of good communications between patients and hospital staff. Problems often arise from mutual misunderstandings which can be resolved informally. In cases where conciliation is opposed by the patient or proves fruitless, the subsequent procedures depend on the nature and seriousness of the complaint. 'Minor' complaints are to be

3. HC Deb. Vol. 1337 Col. 1377 (1985).
4. National Health Service Act 1977, s. 17.
5. HC (88) 37 replacing HN (78) 39, HC (81) 5, HN (83) 31, DA (86) 14.
6. See HC Deb. Vol. 1337 Col. 1379 (1985).

investigated and reported on by the designated officer himself. If a patient is dissatisfied with the designated officer's report he should be advised to refer the matter to the Health Service Commissioner, providing it is a complaint within that official's jurisdiction. More serious complaints are beyond the jurisdiction of the designated officer alone. These comprise any complaint (1) that raises any question of *clinical judgement* which cannot be resolved by discussion with the consultant concerned, (2) that the authority is satisfied constitutes a *serious untoward incident* involving harm to a patient, (3) that involves conduct which ought to be the subject of *disciplinary proceedings*, (4) that concerns a *possible criminal offence*, and (5) that involves the designated officer himself. On receiving such a complaint the designated officer must bring it to the attention of senior officers of the authority (e.g. the District General Manager), including where appropriate the Regional Medical Officer. A complaint concerning clinical judgement will then be dealt with by the special procedures expressly provided for such complaints, which may ultimately lead to an *independent professional review* of that judgement. In other cases the authority must itself conduct further inquiries and decide on appropriate action, which may include establishing a health authority inquiry, instituting disciplinary proceedings and, of course, in any case of suspected crime, calling in the police.

There is no requirement that complaints must be in writing, and where a patient is incapable of acting for himself a relative or friend may act on his behalf. Normally, complaints should be submitted within three months of the alleged incident. Complaints should be dealt with speedily and the complainant must be informed of progress at all stages. Health authorities are mandated to publicize complaints procedures effectively, and to monitor complaints regularly. I understand that when a hospital becomes an NHS trust the contract with the health authority purchasing services from the hospital will require the trust to implement all the above procedures, and give the authority the right to see and monitor all complaints against the trust.

It cannot be said that the procedures implemented as a result of the 1985 Act are radically different from those obtaining under the previous non-statutory code of practice.[7] There are some minor amendments, such as providing that a complaint need not always be in

7. See HC (81) 5 and the Report of the Davies Committee on Hospital Complaints Procedures, HMSO, 1973.

writing. The most important change is the requirement that a particular, identifiable individual should be responsible for dealing initially with all complaints. The designated officer becomes, as I said earlier, a quasi-Ombudsman rather than an anonymous officer of the authority, as under previous practice. Moreover the enactment of a statute expressly dealing with hospital complaints gives formal recognition and greater force to the crucial role effective complaints procedures play in the NHS. The impact of the Hospital Complaints Procedures Act is as much psychological as substantive. One word of warning from the earlier non-statutory code remains as relevant today as it ever was. As the DHSS then warned and as the rest of this chapter amply illustrates, '. . . unsatisfactory handling of a complaint may become the cause of further complaint'.

The Health Service Commissioner

Patients and ex-patients unhappy with the initial response to their complaint may next take the matter to the Health Service Commissioner. The office of Commissioner was created in 1973 and his powers are now set out in Part V of the National Health Service Act 1977.[8] The Commissioner is empowered to investigate any complaint where it is alleged that a failure in the health service or maladministration in the service resulted in injustice or hardship. His jurisdiction does not extend to all areas of the NHS. He may not, for example, investigate complaints about general practitioners.[9] Hospitals, ambulance services, clinics and district nursing services are among the bodies which he may review.[10] Even then important restrictions are placed on him. The two most central restrictions on his powers are these. The Commissioner may not pursue a complaint where the person concerned may have a remedy in the courts unless he is satisfied that it is not reasonable to expect the complainant to invoke that remedy. And he may not investigate any action taken as a result of the exercise of the professional, clinical judgement of doctors or nurses. What then is the extent of the Commissioner's power and influence?

8. There are separate Commissioners for England, Wales and Scotland; see s. 110 of the National Health Service Act 1977.
9. For complaints procedures re GPs, see Chapter 16.
10. The relevant bodies within the Commissioner's jurisdiction are set out in National Health Service Act 1977, s. 109.

Investigating a complaint

Complaints to the Commissioner must be made in writing, normally within one year of the incident giving rise to the complaint.[11] The complaint may be made by a patient personally or by some responsible person acting on his behalf.[12] The Commissioner has an unreviewable discretion as to whether to pursue a complaint.[13] His powers of inquiry are extensive. He and his staff investigate in private. They will contact all hospital staff involved with a complaint and seek their comments. The Commissioner has complete control of the investigation. If co-operation from hospital staff or administrators is not forthcoming, the production of records and documents may be ordered and staff may be compelled to testify to the Commissioner.[14] Exceptionally evidence can be taken on oath, but this has happened only once so far to my knowledge.[15] In that case the preliminary evidence from the parties had been totally irreconcilable. The Commissioner regretted this occasion. Successive Commissioners pride themselves on good relations with health service staff, rendering resort to powers of compulsion unnecessary.

On completion of an investigation the Commissioner reports to the complainant, the health authority, and any individual against whom allegations were made. The report will contain a decision as to whether the complaint was justified and recommend a remedy. In 1989–90[16] 42.7 per cent of complaints investigated were found to be justified. The most common remedy is an apology from the authority and the staff member involved. Increasingly he recommends too that the Department of Health and health authorities make changes in practice to avoid a recurrence of similar complaints. For example, in 1984–5[17] on the initiative of the Commissioner steps were taken to review

11. National Health Service Act, s. 114.
12. ibid., s. 111.
13. ibid., s. 113.
14. See ibid., Part I, Sched. 13.
15. Report of the Select Committee on the Parliamentary Commissioner for Administration, HC 53 (1981–2).
16. Annual Report of the Health Service Commissioner 1989–90, HC 538 (1989–90).
17. Annual Report of the Health Service Commissioner 1984–5, HC 445 (1984–5), pp. 39–45.

procedures for writing to GPs on the patient's discharge, to improve communication with relatives and to improve monitoring of complaints procedures. Very occasionally the Commissioner may additionally recommend the making of an *ex gratia* cash payment to a patient by way of compensation. These are usually small sums, arising from cases where maladministration has resulted in loss of patients' property or unnecessary expenses. The Commissioner does not regard it as his function to grant monetary compensation for pain and hardship suffered by patients.[18]

Each year the Commissioner makes an Annual Report to Parliament published by HMSO and available to the public. Additionally in the course of each year he publishes two or three reports of the details of selected investigations with all the parties involved kept anonymous. His activities are monitored by a Select Committee of MPs who have, as we shall see, encouraged him in his work and spurred him on to greater efforts on behalf of patients. The issue of maladministration in the NHS is thus brought firmly into the public eye. From 1977 to 1985 the number of complaints submitted to the Commissioner rose steadily. Then for four years a downward trend was welcomed by the then Commissioner, Sir Anthony Barrowclough QC. In 1989–90 the incoming Commissioner noted a reversal of that downward trend. The number of complaints received rose by 5.4 per cent to 794.[19] This may seem a relatively trivial number, but remember that the Commissioner enjoys only a limited jurisdiction and is designed to be the complainant's last resort.

The work of the Commissioner

The reports of the Commissioner from 1974 onwards make interesting, if somewhat depressing, reading. Certain sorts of complaints recur. Waiting lists, lack of communication by medical staff, inadequate liaison with GPs, delay in attendance by doctors, and unsatisfactory supervision of the elderly and vulnerable appear again and again. Maternity and geriatric care seem to generate a disproportionate number of complaints. Rudeness, lack of sympathy and even in extreme cases allegations of assault by staff cause the Commissioner much concern.

18. Annual Report for 1981–2, HC 419 (1981–2) p. 36.
19. See the analysis of complaints submitted to and dealt with by the Commissioner in the Annual Report for 1989–90.

The Annual Report for 1984–5 identifies six topics which have caused the Commissioner particular concern. They are (1) care and supervision of the elderly and handicapped, (2) contents and use of medical records, (3) delay in doctors attending patients, (4) arrangements made for discharge from hospital, (5) recording and investigation of alleged assaults, and (6) the initial handling of complaints by hospitals. Five years later, in 1989–90, the main topics of concern were listed as (1) observation and management of patients, especially elderly or handicapped patients, (2) arrangements for discharge, (3) procedures and management, in particular delayed operations, (4) patients being led to believe they would have to opt for private treatment, as they were unlikely to receive NHS treatment promptly, (5) the handling of complaints by hospitals, (6) the procedures for independent professional review, and (7) the operation of Family Practitioner Committees. It is a profoundly depressing list. It is depressing because three of the main concerns expressed in 1984–5 recur again five years later. There seems no evidence of improvements in these areas. Two of the 'new' causes for concern, delayed operations and patients being misled into thinking that they must resort to the private sector, indicate a deep malaise in our public health service.

What can the Commissioner do to allay such disquiets? Often his role can be no more than to advise and admonish. In cases relating to care and management of vulnerable patients, he has made it clear that rudeness and dictatorial behaviour are unacceptable. Two cases upheld in 1989 illustrate just such unpleasant attitudes. In one[20] a nurse was found to have bossed an elderly patient around as though he were a recalcitrant child and had failed to help him to the bathroom in time. The ward stank of urine and the elderly patient developed sores. In another, lax and callous arrangements for dealing with the body of a deceased transplant patient[21] caused great distress to the patient's family. The Commissioner is constantly vigilant to ensure that patients and families are treated with kindness and respect.

Failures relating to discharge arrangements require revised procedures and better communications between hospitals and patients and hospitals and community medical services. In one sadly typical case in 1984–5 an elderly woman was discharged from hospital after nine

20. Case W 12 88–9, HC 199, pp. 107–41.
21. Case W 241 88–9, HC 199, pp. 172–88 (the body was decomposing when collected by the undertaker).

weeks' hospitalization for chest trouble.[22] Earlier that week she had scalded herself and on the day of discharge she fell in the ward. The Commissioner found that inadequate arrangements were made to inform the GP of her condition and that her husband was given insufficient information to care for her at home. Successive Commissioners have been highly critical of poor communications within the NHS, alas to little avail.

The depressing theme of mishandled complaints generating further complaints to the Commissioners goes on and on. In his Annual Report for 1989–90 the new Commissioner, W. K. Reid, commented sadly:[23]

Sometimes an indifferent or careless local investigation or even the lack of an apology for an obvious mistake are all that is needed to send the complainant along a stressful – and perhaps increasingly exasperating – path to my door. Fear of litigation may at times lie behind defensiveness on the part of the person complained against, but that is quite possibly the last thing that the complainant had in mind when looking for an explanation.

Five years earlier his predecessor had lamented, '. . . a very large number of complaints would never reach me if they were dealt with more thoroughly, accurately, promptly and sympathetically in the first instance'.[24]

The Commissioner's remarks are well illustrated by the following complaint. The complainant's daughter was referred by the GP to a consultant psychiatrist. She was admitted to hospital twice and diagnosed as suffering from manic depression. Her parents thought that her symptoms seemed to be related to her menstrual cycle. The consultant arranged for tests to be made by a gynaecologist colleague. The parents were not given the results of the tests until some seven months after they were available to the hospital. In the meantime they removed the girl to the care of a private doctor and complained to the health authority about the delay. The response was a letter from the consultant's solicitors threatening a libel action. At every further stage to which they pursued the complaint the parents were obstructed until the Commissioner found for them.[25]

22. Case W 24 84–5; HC 418 (1984–5) p. 141.
23. Constant changes in health service management structures cannot help.
24. Annual Report for 1984–5.
25. Case W 696 83–4; HC 418 (1984–5), p. 110.

No one would deny that a number of complaints are trivial and that distressing allegations are sometimes made against doctors and nurses with absolutely no basis. But complainants do not go away if they are ignored or even threatened. Very often a simple explanation is all that is called for. If that is not forthcoming, the complainant will simply progress to the next stage of the procedure. Investigation by the Health Service Commissioner wastes more valuable medical time, causes more anxiety and is more likely to damage the doctor's or nurse's reputation than a thorough prompt internal inquiry. For this reason it is to be hoped that the Hospital Complaints Procedures Act leads, as was intended, to an effective and uniform scheme based on the individual hospital Ombudsman.

The concerns of the Commissioner in 1989–90 echo familiar themes from the previous fourteen years. Other areas which have generated complaints of particular importance include failing to tell patients of their right to object to the presence of medical students,[26] inadequate explanations when obtaining consent to surgery,[27] failing to listen to the patient, and many others in a catalogue illustrating the importance to the patient of being treated as an intelligent individual. Other complaints arise from sheer mismanagement. Dentures get lost. Special diets are ignored, and so on. A number of disquiets arise from the lack of resources. Waiting lists for hip replacements, and delays in surgery generally, have been investigated by the Commissioner several times. He cannot wave a magic wand and end the waiting. He can ensure that maladministration does not extend the waiting time, that the lists are properly organized, and once again that patients are kept fully informed.

The Commissioner and the courts

Many of the complaints dealt with by the Commissioner would not be the subject of court action for a variety of reasons. In one disgraceful case an elderly gentleman left to suffer from acute pain and dying of terminal cancer died the next day.[28] Claiming damages would not have been worthwhile for his widow. Imposing the presence of medical students or publishing photographs of a naked patient give rise to

26. e.g. Case W 309 77–8; HC 1 (1979–80), p. 67.
27. e.g. Case W 61 77–8; HC 98 (1978–9), p. 224.
28. Case W 309 83–4; HC 33 (1984–5), p. 99.

no legal remedy in England, where privacy is poorly protected by the law.[29] Other investigations undertaken by the Commissioner are more likely subjects of a claim for malpractice, for example those cases where the Commissioner finds a lack of complete or voluntary consent to treatment. One notorious example concerned a woman of 23. She sought an abortion in 1970 and attended the hospital with her mother. The woman held a job but suffered from temporal lobe epilepsy and a degree of personality disorder. After discussion with the parents the consultant sterilized the woman with their consent. The first she learned of the operation was when some years later and married she was trying to have a baby. DHSS guidelines stated that sterilization of persons suffering from mental disorder should never be carried out without that person's consent unless the patient was unable to understand the nature and consequences of that operation. The Commissioner found no evidence that sterilization was necessary for the woman's health. He judged that acting in breach of DHSS guidance, which he had never read, the consultant was at fault.[30]

This example is by no means the only case where the Commissioner has inquired into lack of full consent, an issue which as we saw in Chapter 4 can give rise to litigation. The restriction on the Commissioner's power to investigate cases which might go to court is mitigated in two ways. He alone decides the matter, and he is directed to consider not whether a court case is technically possible but whether in all the circumstances it is reasonable to expect that complainant to go to court. Informed consent is a legal hot potato. Litigation could have been contested all the way to the House of Lords and resulted in relatively low compensation even if successful. The Commissioner rightly took on the complaint.

Other cases where a court remedy looks more straightforward sometimes come before the Commissioner. A Caesarean section resulted in injury to a patient who had had problems with anaesthesia in earlier surgery. The complainant alleged that records of her previous difficulties were not transferred to her obstetric records, that her own warnings were ignored, and that her complaint was badly and unsympathetically dealt with. Her first two allegations are of simple negligence. The Commissioner nevertheless agreed to investigate the case in return for an undertaking that the complainant would not take

29. See Case W 415 83–4; HC 418 (1984–5), p. 39.
30. Case W 236/75–6; HC 160 (1976–7), p. 23.

legal proceedings.[31] This has become a common practice.[32] The undertaking is not legally binding and there is nothing to stop a complainant assuring the Commissioner he will not sue and then launching proceedings on the basis of evidence uncovered by the Commissioner. Apparently this has happened only twice. Of course, if it was a regular occurrence the Commissioner might feel bound to reject all cases where there was any possibility, however remote, of court action.

Is the restriction on dual access to the Commissioner and the courts justifiable? The Commissioner seems to think so. In 1980 he expressed his concern that he might be used to provide a free investigation service to enable potential litigants to decide whether or not to sue.[33] Is there anything wrong with that? We have seen the tremendous difficulties faced by patients in litigation. If negligence has resulted in injury, and investigation as opposed to adversary litigation discovers that negligence, the patient ought to get compensation. His only crime is that he has not played the game by the old English rules. The rules are wrong.

The Commissioner and clinical judgement

It is generally accepted, except by the medical profession, that the exclusion of clinical judgement from review by the Commissioner is the most serious limitation on his effectiveness. Public concern about errors of clinical judgement is illustrated by the fact that out of 470 complaints rejected as outside the Commissioner's jurisdiction, 204 related to clinical judgement.[34] The 1977 Act provides that the Commissioner may not investigate any '. . . action taken in connection with the diagnosis of illness or the care or treatment of a patient being action which, in the opinion of the Commissioner in question, was taken solely in consequence of the exercise of clinical judgement . . .'[35]

Narrowly and literally interpreted, this limitation could have put senior doctors at least beyond the Commissioner's reach. Successive

---

31. Case W 241/79–80; HC 51 (1982–3).
32. In 1984–5, forty-two complaints were rejected because a legal remedy was open to the complainant. Annual Report, p. 46. In 1989–90 seventy complaints were rejected on that ground. Annual Report, p. 23.
33. Annual Report for 1979–80, HC 650 (1979–80).
34. See tables at p. 23, Annual Report for 1989–90.
35. Sched. 13, part II, National Health Service Act 1977.

Commissioners have declined to follow that path. In the case discussed earlier, of the woman with epilepsy sterilized without her consent, the consultant first raised the 'defence' of clinical judgement. The Commissioner's finding that the consultant's decision was not founded on any decision that sterilization was necessary for her health enabled him to continue his investigation. In 1979–80 a complaint by a woman who had undergone mastectomy and was refused a breast prosthetic on the NHS was investigated. The consultant argued that he never authorized prosthetics, that they were unnecessary and purely cosmetic. The Commissioner rejected his claim that the decision was arrived at in the exercise of clinical judgement. It had nothing to do with treating the complainant's illness; it was not a medical decision. The Commissioner condemned the refusal.[36] One final example: a consultant genuinely concerned with the accessibility of records and X-rays refused to honour an appointment with a patient when the X-rays and records failed to be delivered. He would not even remove the plaster on his leg. The Commissioner found the doctor at fault. His concern for proper access to records was commendable. He may have been in the right in his dispute with the administration but he did not treat that patient properly. Nor could he claim that he acted in the exercise of clinical judgement. His course of action was not related to the care of the patient before him.[37]

Despite the Commissioner's activism in restricting clinical judgement to its proper sphere, strictly medical decisions on the treatment of the individual patient, the exemption of clinical judgement still causes concern. Drawing the line is very difficult. The Commissioner is, as we saw, unhappy about discharge arrangements. He cannot, however, question the original medical decision that the patient is fit for discharge. The case of the elderly lady discharged after having been scalded and after a fall exemplifies his problem. The essence of that complaint seems to be whether she should have been discharged at all.

The Select Committee on the Health Service Commissioner has urged since 1978 that the Commissioner's jurisdiction be extended to cover clinical judgement.[38] Commissioners have seemed less keen. The in-

36. Case W 439/79–80; HC 9 (1981–2), p. 105.
37. Case W 342/76–7; HC 130 (1977–8), p. 73; and see Annual Report for 1977–8; HC 417. p. 13.
38. Report of the Select Committee on the Parliamentary Commissioner for Administration HC 45 (1977–8).

troduction of review of clinical judgement is seen as bringing radical change to the office. More senior medical staff would need to be attracted to the Commissioner's staff.[39] And the Commissioner has expressed fears of complainants using the investigation as a pre-litigation service. The Commissioner felt that investigation should only be allowed if a choice between the Commissioner and the courts could be made binding. If you went to the Commissioner, you would be barred from court.[40] At present the debate on clinical judgement and the Commissioner is at stalemate. In 1981 the DHSS introduced a new procedure for examining clinical judgement.[41] The Select Committee on the Health Service Commissioner gave it a cautious welcome.[42] The Commissioner when he rejects a complaint because it concerns clinical judgement will advise the complainant of this new procedure which I go on to examine. The number of complaints reaching the Commissioner about the operation of this procedure does not bode well for its success.

Independent professional review of clinical judgement

The procedure providing for a review of clinical judgement is laid down in a circular from the Department of Health addressed to all health authorities.[43] Complaints relating to clinical judgement are dealt with in three stages. The complaint may be addressed either to the consultant in charge of the patient or to an officer of the authority. If such a complaint is addressed to the designated officer he must seek the advice of senior colleagues. The first stage of the complaint requires that the consultant in charge should examine the clinical aspects of the complaint. The consultant should see the complainant and attempt to resolve the problem. After further consultations the district general manager will reply to the complainant on behalf of the authority. Any reference to clinical matters in the reply, whether interim or final, should be agreed by the consultant concerned. If the complainant remains dissatisfied, the second stage of the procedure is to refer the complaint to the Regional Medical Officer, who will attempt to resolve

39. Annual Report for 1977–8; HC 417 (1977–8).
40. Annual Report for 1979–80; HC 650 (1979–80).
41. HM 81(5).
42. Report for 1981–2; HC 53 (1981–2).
43. Originally issued as HC 81(5). See now HC (88) 37 Annex B.

the complaint in discussions with the consultant and his professional colleagues. Should the complaint remain unresolved the RMO may then set in motion the third stage – independent professional review. The complainant has no right to demand an independent professional review.

Independent professional review is intended to deal with substantial complaints not likely to give rise to court action and not suitable for the formal inquiry procedures available to the health authority. For professional review two independent consultants in active practice in the specialty will be appointed. They will be nominated by the Joint Consultants' Committee, which represents the Royal Colleges and the BMA. One should be a doctor from a comparable hospital working in another region. These 'second opinions', as the circular calls them, are to have access to all clinical records, and to meet with the complainant, the consultant, and any other medical staff involved. Their meeting with the complainant is to explore his medical problems, and if they find the complaint unjustified they attempt to allay his anxieties and explain to him what happened. At the end of their investigation the 'second opinions' report to the regional health authority advising on any action to be taken. The complainant will not see the report. He will be told of any action to be taken. Action contemplated seems generally directed at preventing the recurrence of similar incidents. The 'second opinions' have no coercive powers and cannot award compensation. They can presumably recommend invocation of formal inquiry procedures.

The record of independent professional review so far is not good. The procedure is long drawn out and to the cynic appears designed to offer the doctor every opportunity of avoiding any systematic investigation of his conduct. In 1989–90 the Health Service Commissioner, as we have seen, mentioned the procedure as one of his main causes of disquiet in his Annual Report. Two specific complaints upheld by the Commissioner illustrate patients' dissatisfaction with independent professional review. In the first[44] the complainant's wife gave birth to a stillborn son in 1985. He made a formal complaint about her treatment. The ensuing independent professional review did not take place until 1988 and no one actually present at the birth gave evidence. A second complaint[45] concerned lack of action subsequent to an independent

44. Case W 496/88–9, and W 379/89–90; HC 33 (90–91).
45. Case SW 64, 89–90; HC 33 (90–91).

professional review of the circumstances surrounding the death of the complainant's mother. The Health Board failed to inform her of any changes in procedure resulting from the review, in effect claiming that it was none of her business. The Commissioner saw reassurance to the complainant that action had been taken to prevent that type of complaint recurring as of the essence of independent professional review.

The very nature of independent professional review is ambiguous. The meeting between the 'second opinions' and the complainant should, it is said, be 'in the nature of a medical consultation'. The complainant has few, if any, rights. In 1986 consultants conducting an independent review refused to allow an elderly couple complaining about the circumstances of their son's death the assistance of a community health council official to present their case.[46] For many patients, facing eminent consultants alone in order to pursue a complaint about one of their brethren is an awesome task.

Health authority inquiries

Where at any stage in an investigation of a complaint further action is found to be necessary, the matter may be referred on to the regional health authority. The authority may appoint one or more of its own members to look into the complaint, or in serious cases may set up an independent inquiry.[47] The inquiry will be conducted by a small committee consisting usually of a legally qualified chairman and two medical practitioners, one from the same specialty as the person whose competence is in issue. All inquiring members will be unconnected with the hospital where the complaint originated. Copies of all documents are circulated to all parties. The complainant and the subjects of the complaint may be legally represented, and cross-examination of witnesses is allowed. Legal aid is not available, and no one can be compelled to attend the inquiry. The committee's findings of fact are then submitted to the staff concerned for further comment. Finally the committee reports its findings and recommendations to the authority.

The inquiry procedure can be effective. We shall see later that it can also be cumbersome and unfair. And if hospital staff refuse cooperation the procedure may break down altogether. In 1976

46. See the *Guardian*, 6 March 1986.
47. HC 66(15).

Elizabeth Shewin entered hospital for a gall-bladder operation. In the course of the operation she suffered irreversible brain damage. On the advice of their medical defence organization, all ten doctors involved with Miss Shewin refused to give evidence to the inquiry. They finally agreed to appear on condition that the authority met any costs and award that might result if court action were later taken. The inquiry discovered that Miss Shewin's injury resulted from her being given nitrous oxide instead of oxygen because of an improvised and inadequate repair to anaesthetic equipment in the operating theatre. Miss Shewin's relatives sued the authority for negligence and won damages of £262,500. The authority in turn sued the manufacturers of the anaesthetic equipment.[48] The doctors were virtually exonerated.

In a second example, a 26-year-old man, David Woodhouse, entered hospital in 1981 for an appendectomy. He never regained consciousness and ten months later still lay in a coma. Pressure from MPs led the health authority to set up an inquiry. Again, on the advice of their defence organization the doctors refused to testify. The inquiry was abandoned. The authority then asked three independent experts to examine the case. They reported on a series of disasters. For example, the anaesthetist's command of English was poor, he could not spell the names of basic drugs, and neither he nor the duty registrar knew how to use the ventilator. Mr Woodhouse was left without oxygen for twenty minutes. The health authority promised to tighten up procedures. An out-of-court settlement was reached to pay compensation to David Woodhouse and his family.

Inquiries by the Health Minister

The National Health Service Act 1977 section 89 empowers the Health Minister to '. . . cause an inquiry to be held in any case where he deems it advisable to do so in connection with any matter arising under this Act'. At such an inquiry all those involved may be compelled to attend and to produce documents, and if the person appointed to hold the inquiry sees fit all evidence may have to be given on oath. The Health Minister rarely uses his coercive power. MPs pressed him to do so in the David Woodhouse case. He refused. Inquiries by the Health Minister are at present limited to cases of national scandal, such as ill-treatment of mental patients or the conditions at Stanley Royde Hos-

48. Reported [1979] BMJ 1232.

pital which led to an outbreak of salmonella food poisoning. Successive Ministers have argued that their power to order an inquiry was not intended for use in cases of individual error or even gross incompetence. His powers are to be invoked only to protect the public at large. Yet serious cases of accidents involving individuals may reveal dangers to the public. The Minister refused to order an inquiry in the Woodhouse case despite tremendous pressure in Parliament.[49] The authority's own endeavours revealed grave risks to anyone accepting anaesthesia in the area. Was it not in the public interest that this be revealed? Are prospective patients not entitled to know that their health authority may be employing doctors whose knowledge of English and resuscitation procedures may be lamentably and dangerously inadequate?

Evaluating inquiry procedures

At first sight the trouble with inquiry procedures is that the Health Minister's powers are reserved for national *causes célèbres* and that health authority inquiries have no teeth. Look more deeply at the problem and the cause lies partly in the defensive attitude of the doctors. Too often they have not co-operated. Advised by his defence organization, if there is the slightest chance of litigation the doctor stays silent. Yet the Shewin case shows that an inquiry may exonerate the doctor and remove the taint of suspicion which might impede his career. What can be done?

Patients might well answer that doctors should be forced to co-operate. After all, within the NHS they are the employees of the health authority. It is a strange situation where an employer cannot require his employee to explain conduct that has resulted in injury to the 'clients of the business'. Other people whose error may result in injury to persons are made to co-operate. After every rail accident involving casualties, an inquiry is held and every British Rail employee involved is required to give evidence. The inspector holding the inquiry then publishes a report giving his findings of fact and the name of anyone found to be negligent and responsible for the accident. Very often the inquiry report reveals not individual incompetence but some defect in the system or unforeseeable event.

Are doctors to be treated differently from railmen? An objection

49. See the *Sunday Times*, 7 March 1982; and see HC Deb. Vol. 14 Cols. 965–9 (1981–2).

based solely on the distinction between an ancient profession and the artisan cuts little ice today. Real objections are three-fold: fear of baseless complaints, fear of litigation and fear of publicity. Baseless complaints do not evaporate. Refusal to attend an inquiry may generate more attention than co-operation with the inquiry. The Woodhouse case did. Any sensible person knows full well that doctors are vulnerable to unjustified attack. In grief, pain and bereavement some people will always turn on the doctor. Refusing to help in the investigation of complaints just makes matters worse. Where a doctor will not explain his action and help in discovering what went wrong, the general reaction may be that there is no smoke without fire. For the sake of every 'guilty' doctor protected by medical defensiveness from the consequences of an error, an 'innocent' and competent doctor is left tainted by suspicion.

Fear of litigation is a constant theme. Why should the doctor assist a patient to find evidence against him? Every hospital doctor, at least, is indemnified against personal liability. Any compensation will not come out of his own pocket. He will now be automatically indemnified by his employing authority or NHS trust. But what doctors fear is perhaps rather the damage to their reputation. Is it right to expose the doctor to double jeopardy, to the inquiry and then to a suit for malpractice? The patient, some say, should choose. He should shut up or sue. More moderate voices urge a compromise: allow investigations but make access to investigations conditional on forfeiting the right to go to court for compensation. This compromise has had the backing of the Health Service Commissioner himself. I reject it. The root cause of disquiet is that in England we are just not accustomed to doing justice by way of investigation. The adversary game rules. The lawyers devise the rules. Doctors cannot be blamed for playing by them. Some doctors are beginning to reject them.[50]

What about the fear of publicity which is closely allied to fear of litigation? We have already said that refusing co-operation may not make publicity go away. Co-operation may clear the doctor. Perhaps that is a little naïve. The press may well latch on to the start of an inquiry. A story may appear on the front page detailing the complainant's allegation that Dr X amputated his left leg unnecessarily, while drunk and flirting with the nurses in the theatre. Two days later a

50. See the address by Dr Havard, Secretary of the BMA, to the American Bar Association; *The Times*, 19 July 1985.

sentence hidden away in the middle of the paper reports the doctor's exoneration. Doctors are vulnerable to bad publicity. Statistically they must be at far, far greater risk of baseless complaint after a medical accident than the railman after a rail accident. Their career can be put at risk. Their private practice will be threatened. Surely it is not beyond the wit of the lawyers and politicians to devise procedures with which all staff must co-operate but which protects their privacy up until the stage that findings and recommendations are made?

Who should judge clinical judgements?

Any proposal for change must tackle this thorny problem. In the crucial area of clinical judgement can the medical profession be allowed to continue to police itself? Is independent professional review working? The omens, as we saw, are disturbing. The Health Service Commissioner deals with matters of great import to individual patients, but sometimes, reading his reports, with their several accounts of lost property, petty autocracy and bungled complaints procedures, you can fear that issues of greater general concern remain buried beneath the surface. What of the doctor who does not really know his job? What of the infant born damaged as a result of mismanaged labour? These questions of judgement are beyond the Commissioner's reach. Yet they require independent investigation for the benefit not just of the complainant but of future patients. The fact that the complainant never receives the 'second opinions' report after independent professional review and that no one other than a doctor is involved in the process may detract from the scheme's independence in the public eye. The ultimate answer lies in co-operation between the profession and independent opinion. The Select Committee continues to press for the Health Service Commissioner to be free to look into clinical judgement. He would need more qualified medical staff. A formal post of Deputy Commissioner (Medical) could perhaps be created.

Any reform needs the goodwill of the medical profession. To call for reform is not to doubt the concern of the profession for their patients or their commitment to the highest standards of health care. Doctors must be persuaded to shed certain misconceptions and to abandon defensive attitudes to patients. Accountability for error cannot be avoided for ever. Thorough investigation is better than a strategic campaign to avoid inquiries. Avoiding inquiry may create damaging publicity for the profession as a whole. Co-operating with the inquiry may, as the Shewin case did, prove the doctors to be innocent of blame. Doctors must be more open to inquiry when things go wrong. Patients must learn that medical accidents, like any other accident, can happen without anyone being to blame. Above all, though, there must be a political will for change. The Hospital Complaints Procedures Act offered an unparalleled opportunity to act.

Ensuring that complaints are initially dealt with swiftly in the hospital where the patient received treatment is a valuable first step. It does not go far enough. The whole maze of assorted complaints procedures should be reviewed and rationalized.

The Wendy Savage affair: a doctor's perspective[51] and a warning

I have examined so far inadequacies of NHS complaints procedures as perceived by patients. Events in 1985 highlighted aspects of health authority inquiry procedures profoundly disturbing to doctors. Tower Hamlets Health Authority suspended Wendy Savage, a consultant obstetrician and senior lecturer at the London Hospital. Allegations of incompetence were laid against her by her colleagues, and a health authority inquiry was launched. Charges against her focused on her handling of five maternity cases, accusing Mrs Savage of allowing sympathy for women wanting a natural birth to override her professional judgement and endangering mother and child. In only one of the cases cited against Mrs Savage had a patient complained. Two patients were outraged that their treatment was being used as evidence against a doctor whom they trusted and backed implicitly. They were also horrified when their confidential medical records were made public at the inquiry. The Savage inquiry was, in essence, not an inquiry into complaints of unsatisfactory treatment by patients, but a public ventilation of professional disagreements.

The procedure at the inquiry left much to be desired. The initiation of the complaint by colleagues of a doctor, rather than patients, cannot be faulted in principle. Protection of patients requires that procedures exist to allow practitioners to air their concern about the practices or competence of a colleague. Fundamentally there are three flaws in the inquiry procedure revealed by the highly publicized Savage inquiry. (1) Before the start of an inquiry immense power rests in the hands of the

51. For Mrs Savage's own account of the 'affair', see *The Savage Inquiry*, Virago, London, 1986.

health authority chairman. The decision to suspend a doctor is his. Allegations have been made that health authority chairmen are over-free with the use of this power to suspend, hoping that, unlike Mrs Savage, the suspended doctors will simply resign quietly.[52] (2) The inquiry is not an *investigation*. The procedure at the Savage inquiry resembled a criminal trial. A QC engaged by the authority 'prosecuted' Wendy Savage. He called medical experts who saw her practices as unsound and leapt on any error they could discern. Mrs Savage's counsel 'defended' her. Experts favourable to her had their say. At no stage did an observer feel that a difficult problem of correct obstetric practice was being objectively investigated. (3) Mrs Savage was effectively 'on trial'. Yet she had no automatic claim to the support of her defence organization as would have been the case had she faced a civil suit for negligence. The MDU at first refused to fund Mrs Savage's 'defence' by the lawyers of her choice. They did eventually agree and assist her.

The Savage inquiry demonstrated once again that English legislators and lawyers seem incapable of devising a genuinely investigatory procedure. It showed too that a procedure designed to consider complaints by patients is ill-equipped for use either as a forum for debate on what constitutes good medical practice or to resolve difficulties between colleagues antipathetic to each other. Wendy Savage was acquitted of all charges of incompetence. Getting her back in her post against the continued hostility of some other doctors proved, alas, a tougher battle for her and for the health authority obliged to reinstate her.

More disturbing still though is the fact that the Savage 'affair' looks set to be repeated in a number of instances across the country. Doctors have been suspended pending a Savage-style inquiry not because their patients have complained, but because they are in dispute with their employers. Speaking out against inadequate and unsafe conditions in our hospitals, failure to conform to the majority view of your specialty, seems more likely to result in disciplinary proceedings against a hospital doctor than failing to meet patients' needs.

52. See *The Times*, 9 July 1986.

CHAPTER 10

Radical Reform: An End to Fault Liability

In earlier chapters in this Part, I examined the present system for compensating injured patients and investigating patients' complaints and found both to be less than satisfactory. The medical profession perceives an action for negligence against a doctor as an attack on his professional integrity and a potential blight on his career. Not unnaturally, lawyers acting for defendant doctors and health authorities will seek to exploit every opportunity provided by our adversary system of litigation to defeat the patient's claim. Furthermore, the defensive attitude engendered by the law relating to malpractice actions carries over into the way in which the profession and health authorities react to any form of complaint. I have suggested that to some extent the doctors' fears are misplaced. The function of the tort of negligence is to compensate an individual injured by another's errors, not to adjudicate on a defendant doctor's general competence. I have further sought to explain that complaints procedures as often exonerate the doctor as condemn him. Very often all a patient wants is an explanation of what went wrong; he is not gunning for the doctor. Better communication between lawyers and doctors might alter such medical attitudes. But what must be recognized is that there is reasonable cause for the doctors' concern. It is all very well to say that the action for negligence has little to do with blame. To the non-lawyer the term negligence itself connotes blame, neglect, carelessness and so on. The conduct of litigation creates an atmosphere of conflict. The patient may not start out with any intention of harassing the doctor. The rules of 'the game' of litigation ensure that at the end a 'me against him' mentality exists. The spectre of a malpractice action hangs over complaints procedures too. There the doctor is haunted by the risk that by co-operating fully he may provide incriminating evidence against himself.

The rules of the game cry out for reform. What I consider now is whether the time has come to change the game. Should the action for medical malpractice be replaced by an entirely new scheme to compensate for injuries arising out of medical misadventure? What is proposed, and now receives support from many doctors, is a system of no-fault compensation. Under such a system a patient who suffers injury in the course of medical treatment would receive compensation without any need to prove that the medical staff involved were at fault. I shall look at the arguments advanced in favour of such a scheme, consider how similar schemes operate abroad, and begin to examine the problems of implementing a no-fault compensation scheme.

An attack on tort

Criticism of the tort of negligence as a means of compensating for personal injury however caused, whether by medical error or in a road accident or any other area of human activity, is far from new.[1] The tort system has been condemned as unpredictable, expensive and unfair.[2] These criticisms are as valid today as they ever were.

The nature of the tort system is unpredictable. The injured person, on whom the burden of proving negligence falls, cannot know in advance whether he will receive any monetary compensation. This has damaging consequences. The claimant cannot plan his personal finances and put his life in order. For example, a person rendered paraplegic in an accident cannot know whether he will be able to afford to convert his house to meet the limitations imposed by his new disability. The uncertainty and delay as he fights his claim through the courts may even impede his recovery to health.

The tort system is expensive because of the enormous cost of protracted litigation. A part of the cost is already borne by the state.

1. See in particular P. S. Atiyah, *Accidents, Compensation and the Law*, 4th edn, Weidenfeld & Nicolson, London, 1987; T. C. Ison, *The Forensic Lottery*, Staples Press, London, 1967.
2. The Pearson Report (Report of the Royal Commission on Civil Liability and Compensation for Personal Injury), Cmnd 7054 Vol. 1 paras. 246–63.

Where the claimant is legally aided the state funds his claim, perhaps with nothing to show for it in the end. The cost of courts and officials to man the system comes again from the state. The prohibitive price of litigation may deter some claimants with a genuine case from pursuing it if they are not wealthy but are sufficiently well off to fall outside provision for legal aid. The expense of any no-fault scheme, often given as an argument against its introduction, must be measured against the existing total cost of the tort system. The National Consumer Council claims that for every £1 awarded as compensation 85p is eaten up by the costs.[3] In *Wilsher* v. *Essex AHA*[4] we saw that the costs of that action (£200,000 +) exceeded the agreed damages of just over £116,000 even before any retrial!

Most of all the tort system is not fair. First, the difficulties and cost of litigation place enormous pressure on a claimant to settle for less than full compensation. Second, the dividing line between negligence and no-negligence is paper thin. Think back to the controversial case of *Whitehouse* v. *Jordan*[5] discussed at length in earlier chapters. The experts were divided on whether Mr Jordan acted wrongly when delivering the child. The judges were divided. At the end of the day Mrs Whitehouse went away without a penny. Yet the opposite outcome would have been equally unfair to Mr Jordan. He came into the case late at night for the first time. He pursued a course many distinguished experts backed. Others disagreed. To condemn him on that basis would have been inappropriate. This feature of the law of tort, the need to apportion blame for medical accidents and the difficulty of doing so, has attracted criticism from the judiciary as well as from doctors and academics. In *Ashcroft* v. *Mersey AHA*[6] Kilner Brown J. reluctantly dismissed the plaintiff's claim for compensation after an operation on her ear left her with a degree of facial paralysis. He found the expert evidence on whether such damage could occur without negligence equally balanced and so the plaintiff failed to discharge the burden of proof. He commented:

Where an injury is caused which never should have been caused common

3. In evidence to the Lord Chancellor's review of civil justice, *The Times*, 5 August 1986.
4. [1988] 1 All ER 871, HL.
5. [1981] 1 All ER 287, HL; see pp. 153–6.
6. [1983] 2 All ER 245.

sense and natural justice indicate that some degree of compensation ought to be paid by someone.[7]

Finally, the tort system has been attacked as unfair on the grounds that it lacks any proper moral basis. What is the justification for giving X, who can attribute his injury to human error, full compensation, and leaving Y, whose injury has some other cause, to struggle along on state benefits?

The Pearson Report[8]

Criticism of the operation of the law of tort and the introduction of alternative compensation schemes elsewhere in the world led to the creation in 1973 of the Royal Commission on Civil Liability and Compensation for Personal Injury chaired by a Law Lord, Lord Pearson. The Pearson Commission was set up to consider to what extent, in what circumstances and by what means, compensation should be payable in respect of death and personal injury. They were specifically instructed to examine the tort system in the light of other provision made for compensation, whether via insurance or social security benefits.

The Pearson Commission reported in 1978. They advised against wholesale abolition of the tort of negligence as a means of compensating personal injuries. They made a number of specific proposals for more limited reforms. I concentrate on the proposals which relate to medical and drug-induced injuries. The Commission decided against recommending a no-fault scheme for all medical injuries.[9] They did propose a scheme whereby the government would become strictly liable to victims of vaccine damage[10] and those conducting medical research would be strictly liable for injury caused to volunteers in the course of clinical trials.[11] The Report further recommended the introduction of strict liability against producers of defective

---

7. p. 246. And see *Wilsher* v. *Essex AHA* (1986) 3 All ER 801 *per* Mustill LJ, p. 810.
8. Pearson Report, Vols. 1–3.
9. ibid., paras. 1304–71.
10. ibid., paras. 1372–1413; and see Chapter 8.
11. ibid., paras. 1340–41 (opinion among the medical profession and the drug industries has moved towards favouring a centrally funded no-fault scheme

drugs.[12] And they urged, too, the creation of new disability allowances for all severely handicapped children irrespective of whether their handicap resulted from anyone else's fault.[13] The Commission further said that although in 1978 they had decided against an overall no-fault scheme for medical accidents, some Commission members found the question difficult and saw the arguments for and against as finely balanced.[14] All agreed that circumstances might change, calling for review of the Commission's decision, and accordingly the progress of no-fault schemes elsewhere, particularly in Sweden and New Zealand, should be studied and assessed.

The Commission's Report has gathered dust ever since. Their major proposals in all fields have gone largely unheeded. In the medical field we have seen that a half-hearted attempt to create a compensation scheme for vaccine damage was made. No change has been made in the law on clinical trials, although we shall see that in practice drug companies are largely operating a no-fault scheme voluntarily. Strict liability for defective drugs was introduced by the Consumer Protection Act 1987, but will, in practice, help few victims of drug-induced injury. The reform came not as a result of the Pearson Report but because of pressure from Europe. And the 1987 Act is clearly flawed by the development risks defence expressly condemned by Pearson. Review of foreign no-fault schemes is under way under the aegis of the British Medical Association and other doctors' groups, and by a Labour Party working group. In 1990 Harriet Harman, a Labour spokesperson on health matters, sought to introduce a Bill into Parliament enacting a no-fault scheme for medical accidents. No government action has yet been taken.

The case for a medical no-fault scheme

The case for a no-fault scheme is made out in part by the manifest defects of the present tort-based system. It is beyond the scope of this book to consider whether a comprehensive no-fault scheme for all types

---

for injury sustained by volunteers in clinical trials; see CIBA Foundation Study Paper (1980) BMJ 1172).

12. ibid., paras. 1193–278. The Commission's proposals related to all defective products and not drugs alone. And see Chapter 8.
13. ibid., paras. 1488–535.
14. ibid., paras. 1370–71.

of accidents should be introduced. In an ideal society any person suffering from disability from whatever cause would receive appropriate financial aid. The person paralysed by a stroke has identical needs to the person paralysed by a fall from a ladder or a bungled operation. That ideal would require not an accident compensation scheme but provision of a general disability income.[15] Even in New Zealand compensation for disability continues to exclude disability arising from disease or other non-accidental cause. Such a radical reform can never be expected to happen instantly. It must be approached incrementally. A medical scheme can operate as a model, and a pilot project for a general accidents scheme. Experience of an accidents scheme may lay the foundation for a general disability income.

So what are the arguments for and against a medical accidents scheme? One of the grounds on which the Pearson Commission rejected a scheme for all medical accidents must be taken note of by subsequent champions of such a scheme. The Commission argued that the tort, fault-based system served a valuable purpose in emphasizing the accountability and responsibility of *individual* medical staff. They could not hide behind a bureaucratic smokescreen. However, the major reason for the Commission's rejection of a general scheme was the problem of causation. The Commission felt that distinguishing between an injury arising from treatment given and the natural progression of disease or inescapable side-effects of treatment was just too difficult. They were anxious too about the overall cost of any no-fault scheme and about the way in which it could be designed to cover public and private medicine. Moreover, the Commission seemed to be unimpressed by what they had seen of the no-fault scheme already operating in New Zealand.

The objections of the only official body to investigate a change to no-fault provision must be answered if the case for change is to stand up. I consider that although the Commission's concern about causation is valid the problem of causation is insufficient reason to rule out a change to no-fault compensation. Causation presents just as much of a problem within the present system. Reform of the law introducing the no-fault principle would have the following benefits. A greater number

15. See C. Ham, R. Dingwall, P. Fenn and D. Harris, *Medical Negligence: Compensation and Accountability*, King's Fund Institute/Centre for Socio-legal Studies, Oxford, 1988.

of claimants would obtain compensation to help them adapt their lives to their disabilities or to meet the financial loss resulting from death of a breadwinner. The damage done to relations between the medical profession and the public by bitter and protracted litigation would be removed. The link between compensation for the patient and blame for the doctor would be broken. The patient would obtain compensation because he suffered as a result of treatment going wrong. The issue of *why* it went wrong and the doctor's competence as a doctor would be for completely separate investigatory procedures. The problem of causation would still be there. Nevertheless, distinguishing between injury and the progression of disease or whatever would be made easier in one sense. The issue of causation would be *investigated*. It would not be part of a battle between the patient and the doctor, with the doctor having a vested interest in finding experts to deny that the patient's condition was caused by the treatment. Consideration could be given to whether the burden of proof of causation might be alleviated by either requiring only proof of a reasonable possibility of causation, or demanding that if negligence is proved the doctor should disprove causation.

The overall cost of a no-fault scheme is difficult to judge. The Commission did not go into this in detail, and before any new scheme could be finally agreed detailed costings and projections would be necessary. The Working Party set up by the King's Fund Institute and the Centre for Socio-Legal Studies, Oxford, suggested that a no-fault system might cost £117 million per year as against £75 million for the current tort system.[16] No-fault compensation will not be cheap but will, with luck, be far more cost-effective. In New Zealand 93p in every £1 spent by the Accident Compensation Corporation is paid out to victims. The cost of administering the scheme is thus a mere 7p in the £1. Any cost-benefit analysis must take into account the costs, human and financial, of the present system. The Commission's concerns about the operation of a scheme to cover public and private medicine and the difficulties they had noted in New Zealand are important points to which I attempt later to provide some response.

The Pearson Commission recognized that the case for a no-fault scheme for medical injury was sufficiently strong for it to be likely that at some later stage the issue might be reviewed again. Since 1978 when their Report was published and shelved, medical litigation has in-

16. See Ham *et al.*, pp. 30–32.

creased markedly. The courts are being pushed to extend the boundaries of the existing fault-based system. In general judges refuse to do so, backing, as the patient sees it, the doctor against the patient. This does nothing to improve public confidence in the courts or the medical profession. A marked change in judicial attitude, a willingness to extend the concept of negligence to embrace a greater number of medical errors, has equal if different dangers. The risk of the practice of defensive medicine as happens in the USA is real if often much exaggerated. Take once again the example of *Whitehouse* v. *Jordan*. Had Mr Jordan been found liable, what would have been the likely reaction of his colleagues? The legally 'safe' option would become to resort to Caesarean section at the least hint of a problem. Thousands of women who since 1981 have enjoyed normal if difficult deliveries might have been subjected to surgery.

As litigation increased, so did the dissatisfaction of the medical profession with the present state of the law. This is scarcely to be wondered at. The immediate consequence was a sharp rise in the doctors' insurance premiums, although doctors' premiums remained lower than those paid by many other professionals. But from January 1990 NHS hospital doctors have been indemnified directly by their employer,[17] and the cost of indemnity cover for general practitioners has fallen dramatically. Only doctors with substantial private practices can today have any cause to complain about the cost of insurance cover. The same cynics who say that now medical litigation no longer hits doctors in their pockets we shall hear less about malpractice crises also predict that we shall hear fewer calls from doctors for no-fault compensation. None the less the BMA remain committed to campaign for no-fault compensation, as do many senior and distinguished members of the medical profession.[18] The financial cost of litigation may have been eased, the emotional impact on the individual remains as traumatic as ever. And, of course, reducing the cost of litigation for individual doctors has raised the cost for the NHS

Deterrence and accountability

If doctors back no-fault compensation how do patients' organizations feel? Action for Victims of Medical Accidents (AVMA) remains some-

17. See above, p. 141.
18. Notably the Royal College of Physicians.

what sceptical about doctors' motives for backing no-fault compensation. AVMA focuses on the Pearson Report's concerns about accountability. One of the functions of the tort system after all is to make the defendant accountable for what he has done, and to deter negligent conduct. The tort system may be costly and inefficient, may be inequitable in whom it compensates, but if it deters medical malpractice, can we afford to abandon it? I do not believe that the tort system has much systematic deterrent effect in health care. And I believe that the alleged deterrent impact of tort often obscures the crucial question of accountability.

(1) The tort system is capricious in its operation. Obstetricians are at high risk of a law suit. Geriatricians are hardly ever sued. This is not because obstetricians are more likely to be negligent than their colleagues in geriatrics. It is because if Granny dies as a result of a negligent overdose so little could be claimed by way of damages that it is not worth suing the responsible doctor.

(2) Even where doctors are sued, the deterrent effect of tort will not be great. The damages will not come out of the doctor's pocket nor will his 'premiums' be increased. The deterrent functions of tort generally operates via the insurance system. Poor drivers are deterred from carelessness and encouraged to improve because 'carelessness costs money'. Of course, as I said a little earlier, there is always the emotional impact of litigation. Does the worry of being sued deter the incompetent doctor? I doubt it. Where negligence is gross and obvious, claims are settled swiftly to avoid adverse publicity. It is the cases where there truly is doubt about whether an error is negligent that drag on in the public eye. I suspect 'good' doctors worry about litigation and 'bad' doctors rarely give the possibility much thought.

(3) Finally, there are a number of cases where, albeit there was actionable negligence, there is no moral culpability. Doctors who make mistakes after hours without sleep in under-resourced hospitals cannot be blamed for their error. The tort system could operate to deter such 'negligence' only by encouraging such a doctor to refuse to treat patients at all, once he suspected he could not do so entirely competently. Such a result would prompt more not less patient suffering.

However, one caveat must be issued before dismissing the impact of deterrence via the tort system. The combination of the move to NHS indemnity and the reforms in the National Health Service and Community Care Act 1990 have a potentially disturbing effect. Health authorities and NHS trusts will be in control of medical litigation and at the same time are encouraged to become competitive and cost-conscious. Is there a risk that an authority anxious to offer the lowest-cost appendectomy will cut corners and offer less than safe appendectomies? The fear of litigation might operate on the collective mind of the health authority or trust to deter economy measures that prejudice patients' safety. The impact on authorities and trusts must not be overlooked in the no-fault debate.

Returning to accountability, does the tort system ensure that individuals in the health care professions are made to account for their conduct? Again it would seem that tort's role in ensuring accountability is minimal. The very nature of adversarial litigation militates against such an outcome. If an operation goes wrong and a patient is injured, what went wrong and why it went wrong needs investigation. The professional or professionals involved should be required to explain all they can to the patient and their conduct should be evaluated to discover whether it fell below a standard of good practice and to consider what measures might be taken to avoid such an accident in future. It may well be that even though there is no negligence in the tort sense, doctors and nurses can learn from the accident and amend standard procedures in the light of that knowledge. Adversarial litigation does not allow such an investigation of the incident. The parties line their experts up for 'trial by battle'. Little opportunity exists to evaluate disputed practices. Doctors and nurses in the shadow of litigation clam up; they are naturally wary of admitting any doubts they may have as to what they did or did not do. And of course if the patient fails to prove negligence, within the tort system that is the end of the matter. Accountability is crucial. The tort system provides only token accountability.

Experience abroad[19]

A growing number of no-fault compensation schemes operate abroad. I outline only two, the New Zealand accident compensation scheme, which covers medical injury within comprehensive provision for compensation for personal injury from all causes, and the Swedish Patients' Insurance Scheme, designed specifically for medical injuries. Review of New Zealand's and Sweden's experience will highlight certain problems

19. For detailed studies of the New Zealand and Swedish schemes in the 1970s see the Pearson Report, Vol. 3.

of no-fault liability. They are problems which should be taken as instruction in mistakes to avoid rather than as indication that the whole idea of no-fault liability should be avoided. In this brief review of both schemes I concentrate on how the basic principle of no-fault liability works. Space does not allow me to consider in detail the funding and administration of either scheme. I believe that what must be accepted initially is the principle of change. How it is to be effected can then be investigated in a positive spirit lacking in earlier reviews.

The New Zealand scheme[20] is administered by the Accident Compensation Corporation. About 130,000 claims a year are made to the Corporation, whose remit is to award compensation to anyone who has suffered 'personal injury by accident'. Personal injury by accident is defined as including 'medical, surgical, dental or first aid misadventure'. Damage caused exclusively by disease, infection or the ageing process is specifically excluded. The distinction between damage caused by medical misadventure and that resulting from disease poses the Commission its first problem *re* medical injuries. The distinction has also been criticized as unfair. There may be two elderly women side by side in a hospital ward. One has suffered a stroke in the course of minor surgery and is awarded compensation for medical misadventure. The other suffered hers by Act of God and gets nothing. The New Zealand Commission, whose report led to the implementation of the accident compensation scheme, hoped that eventually the scheme would embrace disease as well as accident.

The second difficulty for the Commission in claims for medical injury lies in applying the concept of accident and the term 'misadventure' to damage suffered when something goes wrong with medical treatment. Failure to give treatment at all has not generally been classified as misadventure. The birth of a child after a failed sterilization has not led to compensation unless the claimant can point to some specific error in the surgery itself. Misadventure has been defined,

20. For a favourable account of the operation of the New Zealand scheme, see Richard Smith (1982) 284 BMJ 1243–5, 1323–5, 1457–9; for a highly critical analysis of the scheme as it affects medical accidents, see S. A. McLean, 'No Fault Liability and Medical Responsibility', in M. D. A. Freeman (ed.), *Medicine, Ethics and Law*, Stevens, London, 1988, p. 147; and for a detailed survey, G. Palmer, *Compensation for Incapacity: A Study of Law and Social Change in New Zealand and Australia*, OUP, Wellington, 1979. And see Vennell (1989) 5 *Professional Negligence* 141.

in the course of a report rejecting a claim for compensation for failure to arrange adequate treatment, as:

... injury or damage ... caused by mischance or accident, unexpected and undesigned in the nature of medical error or medical mishap.

Applying this definition to three cases in England where the plaintiff failed to win compensation, it is clear that one at least of the claimants would have failed also in New Zealand. In *Ashcroft* v. *Mersey AHA*[21] the surgeon accidentally cut into a nerve in the course of delicate facial surgery. He was acquitted of any negligence. A claim in New Zealand would have succeeded because, although the surgeon could not be blamed, the patient's injury was unexpected and undesigned, an unfortunate mischance. In New Zealand Mrs Ashcroft would be classified as a victim of a medical mishap, '... an intervention or intrusion into the administration of medical aid, care or attention of some unexpected or undesigned incident, event or circumstances of a medical nature which has harmful consequences for the patient'.[13] Mrs Whitehouse,[23] had she claimed in New Zealand in respect of the brain damage suffered by her son, would have faced no less acute difficulty in establishing that his injuries resulted from Mr Jordan's use of forceps. Moreover, as everything Mr Jordan did was by design, the issue of whether the baby's injury resulted from misadventure might again turn on whether Mr Jordan's course of action was medically proper or not. She might well have been forced to argue that what was in issue was a medical error. Error in New Zealand has been defined as a failure to observe '... a standard of care and skill reasonably to be expected of ...' a practitioner.[24] That sounds like a return to negligence.[25] Faced with catastrophic injury the Corporation has tended to be generous, and might have found that although Mr Jordan's attempt at normal delivery was in no way erroneous, the ultimate outcome was beyond what was expected and designed and qualified as medical mishap. The third of our trio of unsuccessful English plaintiffs, Mrs

21. [1983] 2 All ER 245.
22. *Review No. 77 (R 1352); Accident Compensation Commission* v. *Auckland Hospital Board* [1981] NZ ACR 9.
23. [1981] 1 WLR 246 HL.
24. *Review No. 77 (R 1352); Re Munday* [1984] NZ ACR 339; *Re Stopford* [1984] NZ ACR 783.
25. See S. A. McLean, op. cit., pp. 154–6.

Sidaway,[26] would have failed in New Zealand as she failed here. She complained of her surgeon's failure to warn her of a well-known, albeit slight, inherent risk of the surgery to which she consented. The risk materialized and she suffered injury but there had been no accident, no misadventure. Everything went as the surgeon planned.

Medical misadventure has proved a difficult concept to apply in New Zealand. It has excluded from compensation some claimants, for example patients suffering from a failure to treat, who might succeed in the tort of negligence. The tort of negligence is not entirely dead in New Zealand. If his claim falls outside the accident compensation scheme, making him ineligible for an award, he is still free to pursue a claim in the court, for common-law negligence. Experience of the restrictive interpretation of medical misadventure may in future prompt more claimants to elect for the old common law remedy.

The Swedish Patients' Insurance Scheme[27] is expressly designed to provide compensation for medical injuries. How does the basis of no-fault liability then differ in Sweden from the New Zealand scheme? Compensation is payable in respect of any injury or illness resulting from any procedure related to health care. Injury arising from any diagnostic procedure, inappropriate medication, medical treatment or surgery thus falls within the ambit of the Swedish scheme. But compensation for such injury is subject to three important provisos. As in New Zealand, the injury must be proved to result from the procedure in issue, and not from the original disease. Injury resulting from a risk taken by the doctor to save life or prevent permanent disability is excluded. Most crucially, the claimant has to show that the procedure causing his injury was *not medically justified*. The test of whether the procedure was medically justified often re-introduces the question of negligence. Had Mrs Whitehouse claimed in Sweden, the central issue would have been whether Mr Jordan's delay in proceeding to Caesarean surgery was justified. Faced with balancing the risk of surgery against the risk of vaginal delivery, did he take the correct medical decision?[28] Certain claimants who lose in England will obtain com-

---

26. [1985] 2 WLR 480 HL.
27. See C. Oldertz, 'The Swedish Patient Insurance Scheme: Eight Years of Experience' (1984) 52 *Medico-Legal Journal* 43–59; C. Oldertz, 'Security Insurance, Patient Insurance and Pharmaceutical Insurance in Sweden' (1986) 34 Am. J. Comp. Law 635.
28. See Brahams, op. cit.

pensation in Sweden. Mrs Ashcroft, who suffered injury to a facial nerve when the surgeon accidentally cut the nerve, would recover. The surgeon was not to blame, but cutting the nerve was not medically indicated.[29] Mrs Sidaway once again would probably lose in Sweden as she would in New Zealand and did in England.[30] The limitation in the Swedish scheme to injury arising from acts not medically justified is as restrictive as, if not more so than, the term 'medical misadventure' in New Zealand. What the Swedish scheme does embrace where New Zealand's does not is injury arising from failure to treat if the failure is not medically justified.

Examination of the deficiencies of the schemes operative in New Zealand and Sweden must not obscure their advantage. Patients uncompensated by a tort-based system benefit in those countries. The investigation of the cause of a medical mishap may still involve issues as to the doctor's negligence. But it is an investigation. The patient will discover what happened. The opportunities for scoring points, seeking to disclose as little as possible about what went wrong, and the advantages to be gained from having the best advocate rather than the best case, just do not exist in New Zealand or Sweden.

The way ahead for the UK

The experience of New Zealand and Sweden must be considered carefully and learned from. The basic structure of any scheme would be to redirect claims for compensation for medical injury away from the courts and towards an independent tribunal. Tribunal staff would initially investigate each claim. They would have access to all relevant records. Provision for hearings and appeal against an unfavourable initial decision would have to be made. Care would need to be taken to prevent the lawyers taking over the process and adding to its expense, formality and technicality. The underlying problems confronted in Sweden and New Zealand of defining the criteria for compensation would have to be faced. The basic premise of any British scheme would be the same. Compensation claims for personal injury would be made not in the courts against the doctor but to an administrative tribunal. Tribunal staff would examine medical notes and see the parties involved. There would be no adversarial hearing. Provision

29. ibid.
30. ibid.

would need to be made for the grant of a hearing to the claimant where appropriate and for appeals by claimants dissatisfied by the initial decision. The distinction between injury resulting from disease and injury resulting from medical treatment is a problem we must probably live with. Ideally a system would be devised whereby the healthy provided funds to alleviate the discomfort and disadvantage of disability and disease, however caused. This is at present an ideal unlikely to be realized, and reform must have a more limited aim by replacing the tort of negligence by a fairer and less destructive system of compensation for medical injury.

The scheme proposed should embrace two categories of medical injury. (1) Injury or illness arising from an absence of, or delay in, appropriate medical treatment[31] provided that (i) treatment would have prevented that injury or illness, and (ii) a reasonable request for medical care from a person or authority under an obligation to provide care has been made by the patient or some other person acting on his behalf. (2) Injury or illness resulting from medical treatment provided that (i) the injury or illness is not caused by the natural progression of disease or the ageing process, and (ii) the injury or illness is not the consequence of an unavoidable risk inherent in the treatment of which the patient has received proper warning.

Category 1 would cover injury arising from failure to treat, both in circumstances where the present tort of negligence would operate and where it would not. For example, a request for treatment might be made and not acted on by the GP because at the time he acted reasonably in thinking an immediate visit was not necessary. Events prove him wrong. They do not render him negligent. Under this proposed no-fault scheme the patient would recover because he did in fact suffer as a result of lack of treatment, albeit no one was to blame.

Category 2 is more difficult to define. Very careful drafting of any legislation will be called for, and I do not attempt that formidable task. The intention of category 2 is that it should extend to any damage to the patient which is neither the result of the natural progression of his original disease or condition nor a consequence inherent

31. Treatment would be defined to include treatment given to the mother and injuring the child. Consideration of the implications of ante-natal treatment would be required, e.g. (1) would treatment necessary for the mother but injuring the child be excluded? (2) what about pre-conception injury to either parent?

in that treatment and unavoidable if that treatment is to be successful. Under that last limitation the side-effects of certain surgery and therapy would be excluded. At one level the patient could obviously not recover compensation for pain and suffering ordinarily attendant on surgery. At another level unpleasant and dangerous side-effects, for example the patient's hair falling out during chemotherapy or the risk of a stroke in some forms of brain surgery, would have to be excluded if they were inescapable in the pursuit of proper treatment. One important proviso is attached to the exclusion of unavoidable side-effects from compensation. The patient must have been properly warned. Failure to give proper warning, which results in injury unexpected and unconsidered by the patient, would remain a ground for compensation. What amounts to proper warning may remain a ground for controversy.

Ways and means

My emphasis on principle rather than detail does not mean I am blind to the problems inherent in setting up a no-fault scheme or to its potential cost. But until the impetus for reform is sufficiently cogent, any examination of ways and means may be an exercise in attempting to find insuperable problems.

The means adopted in Sweden to provide finance and to administer the scheme, however, recommend themselves. An insurance-based scheme would draw on resources already employed in making compensation payments and fighting compensation claims. Funds in Sweden are drawn from the authorities maintaining public health facilities and from doctors and clinics operating in the private sector. Similar provision could be made here for levying premiums on the health authorities and private care organizations. The need for resources here is likely to be greater than in Sweden. Benefits paid in Sweden are limited to what is needed to 'top up' their already generous social security system.[32] A levy on individual practitioners would almost certainly be required. The governing principle in determining the funding of the scheme should be that those organizations and individuals who provide health care should contribute to the funds needed to compensate those injured in the provision of that care. In the light of the finding in the King's Fund Institute report that a no-fault scheme

32. See Ham et al., op. cit., pp. 31–2.

will cost perhaps just over one and a half times as much as the current tort scheme, additional funds will be required from general taxation, but presumably this will be offset to some extent by reduction in social security payments now made to claimants outside the tort system.

The ultimate cost of a no-fault scheme would depend very much on the level of payments made to victims. Several hard questions would have to be addressed. It would seem obvious that the payment of compensation for loss of income and cost of care should generally be by way of periodical payments rather than as a lump sum. Payments can then be adjusted to meet the claimant's current needs. But should there be a ceiling on payments? Under the tort system a high-earning solicitor rendered unable to work obtains money to make up for her actual loss of income. Should no-fault compensation be limited to sufficient to provide for the claimant's needs arising from her disability up to 'average' standard of living?[33] What about compensation for pain and suffering? The harder a no-fault scheme tries to offer generous compensation, the harder it is to fund a scheme to meet the needs of the widest possible range of claimants.

Drugs and medical injuries[34]

What about the relationship between drug-induced injury and medical injury? We have seen how the distinction operates at present, often denying a patient any remedy because he cannot establish whether he was damaged because the doctor prescribed negligently or because there was some inherent defect in the drug. The Consumer Protection Act introducing strict liability for defective drugs has been shown to be somewhat defective itself. How would a no-fault scheme for drugs operate and how would it relate to the medical injury scheme?

Under a no-fault scheme for drugs, the first benefit to ensue would be an end to the kind of unproductive expensive lawsuits discussed in Chapter 8. A patient injured by a drug would receive compensation without need to prove the company negligent, or the drug defective. It would be no answer to a claim that the damage to the patient resulted

33. In New Zealand a maximum limit of 80 per cent of actual earnings is now placed on compensation for loss of income.
34. For detailed discussion of proposals for a no-fault scheme for drugs see A. L. Diamond and D. R. Lawrence, 'Product Liability in Respect of Drugs' (1985) 290 BMJ 365–8.

from some condition peculiar to him. Question of whether risk to a particular group was sufficiently great to be taken into account would cease to be relevant. The drug companies could save a great deal of money which they now spend on lawyers. Compensation would be paid even where the manufacturer cannot be identified, for example where the patient took a general drug and records to trace the manufacturer are unavailable. Issues of the balance of risk versus benefit of a drug would be removed from the courts. A dilemma posed by some drugs is this. They benefit 99.9 per cent of us and damage 0.1 per cent. Under no-fault the 0.1 per cent would get proper compensation. And the issue of whether they should ever have been exposed to that risk is properly and impartially investigated, not submitted to the adversary atmosphere of a court. Causation remains an inescapable problem. But as with medical injury, I believe that investigation of a claim for no-fault compensation is more likely to reveal the truth than a battle in court with the drug company having a vested interest in disclosing as little as possible.

The central problem to be tackled in implementing a no-fault scheme will be whether it should be separate from or incorporated within a medical injuries scheme. My preference would be for incorporation and a definition of medical treatment including drug-induced damage. That way, resources for the unified scheme could be maximized, with the drug companies contributing. Against unification lies the argument that inclusion of drug-induced damage, and so potentially another thalidomide disaster, would impose too great a strain and imbalance on the scheme's resources. But some relationship between medical and drug-induced injury must be worked out to ensure that no future patient falls between the two stools, ending up admittedly injured but unable to get himself into the right scheme to obtain compensation.

The Harman/Barnes Bills

In 1990 and 1991 first Harriet Harman, a Labour spokesperson on health, and then Rosie Barnes, SDP MP for Greenwich, sought to introduce Private Member's Bills into Parliament which aimed at implementing a no-fault compensation scheme for medical accidents. Both Bills were doomed to fail, as the government opposed any such proposal. More surprisingly, neither Bill received unqualified support from patients' organizations or AVMA. Alas, both Bills were flawed. Neither proposal adequately tackled the task of defining medical accident, and so patient eligibility for compensation. For example, Harriet Harman's Compensation for Medical Injury Bill contained this phrase in its definition provision, Clause 3: a medical mishap does not occur if resulting from 'reasonable diagnostic error, having regard to the state of medical knowledge and best medical practice'. The risk would be that within a purported no-fault scheme negligence-centred criteria would continue to apply. Rosie Barnes's National Health Service (Compensation) Bill left the definition of 'mishap' open: ' "Mishap" includes, but is not restricted to, any act or omission which gives rise to an action at common law . . .'

However, the most cogent criticism of the two Bills lay in the absence of effective procedures to ensure professional accountability. One of the prime aims of a no-fault compensation scheme is to separate compensation and blame. One of the fears expressed by opponents of no-fault is that the removal of the element of blame will lead to a decline in standards of competence and care. This must not happen. Any reform of the compensation system for medical and drug-induced injuries must be matched by a thorough review of complaints procedures. Detaching fault from compensation is necessary because, in the medical field at least, the finding of fault in a negligence action has little to do with ascertaining the doctor's real competence. The fault system damages medical care and doctors' relationships with patients. Doctors must accept though that freeing them from a fault-based compensation system must be paid for by the establishment of thorough *investigatory* procedures to deal with allegations of incompetence or want of care. And the introduction of such procedures should precede any introduction of no-fault compensation.[35]

35. For an overview of the debate on no-fault compensation see R. D. Mann, and J. Havard (eds.), *No Fault Compensation in Medicine*, Royal Society of Medicine, 1989.

PART III

Matters of Life and Death

CHAPTER 11

Pregnancy and Childbirth

CONCEPTION TO BIRTH

Today medical care begins long before a baby is born. Research into the growth of the foetus in the womb has established the crucial importance of good ante-natal care. The thalidomide tragedy highlighted the vulnerability of the developing foetus. The drug thalidomide was prescribed to a number of pregnant women to help them sleep. It was described as non-toxic and safe for use by pregnant and nursing mothers. It was not safe. Many children were born without limbs and with other awful disabilities. The drug company denied negligence. A settlement was eventually reached, but not all the children received compensation because of dispute as to whether their disabilities did relate to the mothers' taking the drug.[1] A further difficulty for the children was that at the time of the birth of children deformed by the drug thalidomide, the courts had never decided whether doctors, or drug companies, or anyone at all, could be sued by children for injuries suffered by them before their birth.[2] So Parliament enacted the Congenital Disabilities (Civil Liability) Act 1976. The Act governs the child's rights only.

---

1. For a thorough discussion of the legal implications of the thalidomide tragedy see H. Teff and C. Munro, *Thalidomide: The Legal Aftermath*, Saxon House, London, 1976. And see Chapter 8.
2. In *B.* v *Islington HA* Potts J. held a duty was owed at common law to a child born in 1967: *The Times*, 15 November 1990. Liability at common law was conceded in *Williams* v. *Luff*, *The Times*, 14 February 1978; and see *McKay* v *Essex AHA* [1982] 2 All ER 771.

Can parents sue?

The parents of damaged children may be able to recover for their loss at common law. The doctor caring for the mother in pregnancy owes her a duty not only in relation to her own health but also to care for the health of the developing embryo. The damage which she will suffer if she bears a disabled child, the emotional trauma[3] *and* the financial burden of the extra expenses such a child brings with him are readily foreseeable and recoverable. But will she be able (1) to prove negligence, and (2) to prove that the child's disability resulted from that negligence? Proving negligence is, as we have seen, no easy task in any malpractice claim. A claim in relation to the birth of a damaged child has two special problems of its own. First, if the claim lies against the doctor, it has to be established that he should have been aware of the risk posed to the embryo by drugs he prescribed or treatment he gave. Second, where a mother becomes ill in pregnancy or the pregnancy itself is complicated, the interests of mother and child may conflict. An ill or injured pregnant woman may need drugs or surgery known to carry some risk to the child. For example, a woman injured in an accident may need surgery which can only be carried out under general anaesthetic. The anaesthetic may harm the baby. The doctor's duty to the mother, his patient, is this. (1) He must consult and advise her, giving her sufficient information as to her needs and the risk to her baby. If she chooses to reject a particular course of treatment for the sake of her baby he cannot impose it. (2) He must in any case aim at a course of action which will benefit the mother with minimum risk to the child. Even if it can be shown that the doctor has failed in his duty to the mother, that he was negligent, establishing that the infant's disability resulted from that negligence is likely to be even more difficult.[4] Despite immense advances in knowledge concerning the development of the embryo, pinpointing the exact cause of a birth defect is extremely difficult. Success in a claim for negligence depends on proof that it is more likely than not that the relevant negligence caused the injury. All

3. *S.* v. *Distillers Co.* [1970] 1 WLR 114.
4. On the difficulties in proving causation of birth defects see the Report of the Royal Commission on Civil Liability and Personal Injury (Pearson Report) Cmmd 7054 (1978) paras. 1441–52, and see the essay 'Ante-Natal Injuries' by S. A. M. McLean in S. A. M. McLean (ed.), *Legal Issues in Medicine*, Gower, Aldershot, 1981.

a claimant with a damaged child is likely to be able to prove is that a drug she took or treatment she received may have caused the defect in the baby. But equally it may be some inherited disease, some problem that she suffered in pregnancy, or some other unknown cause. So she may well fail to satisfy the burden of proof.

Congenital Disabilities (Civil Liability) Act 1976

This Act, passed to give rights and a remedy to children born disabled as a result of some human fault, is ambitious, complex, and now largely irrelevant. It is ambitious in that it sought to provide a scheme to protect children not just against negligence, such as drugs wrongly prescribed to mothers in pregnancy, but against any act at any stage of either parent's life which might lead ultimately to a disability affecting a child. Its complexity I will outline in succeeding sections. It is irrelevant because it fails to address the central problem in this type of claim. How do you prove that the disability resulted from an identifiable act of negligence? Just as his mother's claim is likely to founder for lack of proof of the cause of the disability so is the child's. If Parliament intends and desires to give children disabled by human act a remedy, it must consider whether retaining the normal burden of proof in actions by mother and child is possible and workable.

The Act applies to all births after 1976, and purports to provide a comprehensive code of liability for disabled children in respect of damage caused to them before birth. Under the Act the child's mother[5] is generally exempt from any liability to her child. The father is offered no such immunity. The Act entirely replaces the common law and it would not be possible for a child unable to recover under the Act to argue that liability exists at common law. So, for example, a child seeking to sue his mother, exempt under the Act, must fail, however

---

5. She is liable for injuries caused through negligent driving of a vehicle on the road; s. 2. A claim against the mother was in general seen as (a) not likely to be pursued by the child within a happy family relationship. The child would have to act through a 'next friend'. The mother would not proceed against herself. The father would do so only where the marriage had broken down, and (b) women are subject to such contradictory advice as to the management of pregnancy that establishing negligence would be extremely difficult. Negligence while driving a car, by contrast, is easy to prove, and in reality the claim would be against the mother's insurers.

reckless her conduct in pregnancy and however clear it might be that she caused him to be born disabled.

The scheme of the Act is this. The child must be born alive.[6] He must establish that his disabilities resulted from an 'occurrence' which either (1) affected the mother or father in her or his ability to have a normal healthy child (pre-conception event), or (2) affected the mother during her pregnancy, or (3) affected mother or child in the course of its birth. At this first hurdle, proving the cause of the disability, many claims will fail. Where proof of cause is forthcoming the child faces further formidable obstacles. It is not enough to show that the person responsible for the occurrence was negligent. The child must prove that the person responsible for the occurrence was liable to the affected parent. The child's rights are derivative only. Of course the likelihood is that the occurrence at the time caused the parent no harm. Thalidomide's original effect was to sedate anxious mothers-to-be. So the Act provides that it is no answer that the parent affected suffered no visible injury at the time of the occurrence providing there was '. . . a breach of legal duty which, accompanied by injury, would have given rise to the liability'. The breach of duty is the negligence of the defendant in relation to the affected parent's reproductive capacity. Sandra Roberts recovered £334,769 in compensation for catastrophic damage she suffered during her mother's pregnancy.[7] A blood transfusion administered to her mother seven years before her birth rendered her parents rhesus incompatible, creating danger for any child of theirs. The hospital knew of Mrs Roberts's condition. They failed to act to prevent or minimize the risk to Sandra. This was negligent care for the mother and thus created a right to compensation for mother and via her for Sandra. Other cases are less straightforward.[8]

Drugs[9] and damage to the embryo

Let us take first what appears to be a simple case, the sort of case the Act was intended to remedy. A pregnant woman takes a drug which damages her baby and he is born disabled.

6. The mother may be able to claim for the pain and suffering of miscarriage or stillbirth.
7. *The Times*, 26 July 1986; the hospital conceded liability.
8. See the defences provided by s. 1(4) and s. 1(7) below, pp. 244–5.
9. On drug-related damage generally, see Chapter 8.

The drug was prescribed for her by her doctor. The child can prove that his disability results from the effect of the drug on the foetus. He will have to show that the doctor was negligent towards his mother. It must be proved that (1) the doctor knew or ought to have known that she was pregnant, and therefore was in breach of duty to her in prescribing a drug which might damage her baby, and (2) that he ought to have been aware of the risk posed by the drug. It will be no defence for the doctor to answer that far from injuring the mother the primary effect of the drug benefited her by, for example, ameliorating the symptoms of some common ailment, or helping her to relax or sleep. The doctor's responsibility to her embraces taking care to avoid harm to the child she carries. Two real difficulties arise. First, a general practitioner is judged by the standard of the reasonable, average GP. He is not expected to be an expert on embryology or drug-related damage. Proving that he ought to have been aware of the risk of the drug may be awkward. Second, the doctor may be aware of the risk to the baby but argue that the risk to mother and child of not prescribing the drug is greater. This was the case, many English doctors suggested, with the controversial drug Debendox, once commonly prescribed for morning sickness. Now it is alleged that it caused deformities in children whose mothers took the drug. A number of doctors (a) are still not entirely convinced by the available evidence that it caused deformities, and (b) argue that any slight risk was justifiable because of the danger and acute distress caused by continuing severe morning sickness. The drug has now been withdrawn in this country, but an action against a GP for prescribing it earlier would seem doomed to failure.

The doctor, of course, is not the only potential source of compensation for a drug-damaged child. Could the child sue the drug company? Providing the relevant drug was marketed after 1 March 1988, the defendant company's liability would be governed by the Consumer Protection Act 1987. Is the drug defective, and did it cause the relevant injury to the foetus? There can be little doubt that if the company can be shown to be aware of a risk of foetal damage, yet still marketed the drug with *no* warning of that risk, the drug is defective. But few cases are likely to be as straightforward as that. First, the unborn baby is most vulnerable to harm in the earliest embryonic stages of pregnancy. The mother may not know that she is pregnant. Warnings about the use of many non-prescription medicines in pregnancy are now routine, but futile if a woman is unaware of her pregnancy. Is a drug defective simply because it poses a risk of foetal harm? Clearly that cannot generally be the case with prescription drugs. The benefit such drugs offer when properly prescribed outweighs the fairly remote chance of unwitting foetal harm. Over the counter, non-prescription medicines might be looked at differently. If a cough remedy poses a substantial risk of harm, greater than other similar products, for relatively small benefit, that product might be found to be defective. A second difficulty in establishing liability under the 1987 Act arises where the company can show that it was unaware of any risk of foetal harm. The Act allows the defendant to rely on the development risks defence, and it is at least arguable that such a defence would have enabled the manufacturers of thalidomide to escape liability.[10]

Finally, there remains, as always, the hurdle of proving causation. When actions were brought in the USA concerning Debendox (named Benedictin in the USA), those actions failed because patients failed to prove that the drug caused the relevant birth defects.

Suing a doctor

I have already briefly mentioned the potential liability of the mother's GP in prescribing drugs for her. She will no doubt meet other doctors during ante-natal visits. One special feature of suing a doctor under the Act needs note: section 1(5) of the 1976 Act, 'the doctors' defence'.

The dilemma posed by drugs like Debendox and the differences of opinion that exist in the medical profession as to the management of pregnancy and childbirth are responsible for the inclusion of section 1(5). Inserted after pressure from the doctors, this sub-section says:

The defendant is not answerable to the child, for anything he did or omitted to do when responsible in a professional capacity for treating or advising the parent, if he took reasonable care having due regard to the then received professional opinion applicable to the particular class of case; but this does not mean that he is answerable only because he departed from received opinion.

The aims of those who sought the inclusion of those words 'then received professional opinion' were probably twofold. First, they quite reasonably wanted it made clear that hindsight as to the effect of a drug or course of treatment should not prejudice a doctor, and second, less reasonably, they did not want the courts to adjudicate on the

10. See above, p. 180.

adequacy of received opinion. As the defendant's standard of care will always be tested by what was expected of the competent practitioner at the time of the alleged breach of duty, that first objective was met at common law and, as to the second, we have earlier seen that no court as yet has challenged in any medical negligence claim the received opinion of the profession. The final phrase of section 1(5), that the doctor is not to be answerable 'only because he departed from received opinion', might appear to the cynical to be an attempt by the medical profession to have their cake and eat it. Its practical importance is limited to this. In *Clark* v. *MacLennan*[11] (a claim relating to negligent treatment of a post-natal complication), Peter Pain J. said that where there is but one orthodox course of treatment and the doctor chooses to depart from that he must justify that departure. Could a doctor defending a claim by a disabled child under the Act maintain that that approach is outlawed by the Act in such claims? One hopes not. All that is said is that the doctor cannot be answerable *only* because he departs from received opinion. The words of the Act are satisfied so long as the doctor is offered an opportunity to explain and justify his conduct.

Ante-natal screening

Brief mention must be made at this point of the use of ante-natal screening to diagnose foetal abnormalities. In amniocentesis a needle is inserted through the mother's abdomen and the uterine wall into the sac surrounding the foetus. A small amount of the amniotic fluid surrounding the baby is removed. Tests on the fluid will indicate whether a number of abnormalities are present, including spina bifida and Down's syndrome (mongolism). Cultures from the fluid may be grown which will disclose the child's sex. A mother who underwent amniocentesis and was told that she carried a spina bifida or Down's syndrome baby could then opt for an abortion. A mother who knew she was a carrier of haemophilia and learned that she carried a male child might similarly seek a termination. But there are medical problems with amniocentesis. It cannot be performed before the fourteenth week of pregnancy and is usually delayed until the sixteenth week. It carries about a 1 per cent risk of causing a miscarriage. It sometimes

---

11. [1983] 1 All ER 416. Note that in no circumstances is the burden of proof on the plaintiff reversed; *Wilsher* v. *Essex AHA* [1988] 1 All ER 891, HL.

causes the mother an acute if short period of discomfort. And it is an expensive procedure, reserved largely at present for mothers at special risk of producing a disabled infant, in particular those over 35 or women whose routine blood tests suggest some abnormality in the baby. Chorionic villus testing, whereby early placental cells are removed and analysed, is possible much earlier in pregnancy, at about eight to ten weeks. So far, though, chorionic villus testing can be used only for a more limited group of genetic defects than amniocentesis and carries a higher risk of precipitating miscarriage. Increasingly doctors are seeking to limit the number of women who need to undergo invasive tests of this sort by using simple blood tests to identify high-risk pregnancies. A blood test to discover raised alpha-protein levels, an indication of possible spina bifida, has been available for some time. Now a blood test identifying possible cases of Down's syndrome is under trial. Only women whose blood tests indicate some possible genetic problem will then have to undergo the invasive procedures of amniocentesis or chorionic villus testing. Finally, ultra-sound scans are now routinely used to check on the growth and development of the foetus, and will in certain cases reveal the presence of such deformities as spina bifida without the need to submit the pregnant woman to any risky or invasive tests.

What are the legal implications of amniocentesis and chorionic villus testing? First, they involve an invasion of the mother's body. Her consent is essential and should be obtained expressly and in writing. Second, the risk that a healthy baby may be lost should be communicated to the parents. The duty of the gynaecologist caring for the mother must embrace offering her the information on which to make such a crucial decision. And obviously all tests must be carried out and analysed with due care. Negligent ante-natal screening will result in a legal remedy for the parents if a disabled child is born and if, of course, they can prove that, had they known of the relevant disability, the mother would have elected to terminate the pregnancy. The parents' claim in *Rance* v. *Mid-Downs HA*[12] failed because by the time an abortion could have been performed the foetus was found to be 'capable of being born alive' under the Infant Life (Preservation) Act 1929 and so in 1983 abortion was no longer lawful at that stage in pregnancy. The ultra-sound scan which the parents alleged should have indicated to doctors that the foetus had spina bifida was not carried out until

12. [1991] 1 All ER 801.

Mrs Rance was twenty-five and a half weeks pregnant. Now[13] that in cases of foetal handicap there is no time limit on legal abortion, a negligent failure to detect handicap and offer the parents the option of abortion may be actionable at whatever stage in pregnancy that negligence occurred. But what of the rights of the child himself? If tests are indicated and not carried out, or if tests on the amniotic fluid are carelessly conducted so that a mother continues her pregnancy and gives birth to a disabled child, can the child sue the doctors who negligently allowed him to be born? If a mother refuses amniocentesis when it is indicated, or rejects an abortion after amniocentesis, or any other indicated ante-natal test, has revealed abnormalities, will the child's rights when born against any person whose negligence caused the abnormality be affected?

Wrongful life, wrongful birth and wrongful disability

The example I considered earlier arose where the defendant's negligence caused a foetus normal at conception to be affected by disabilities in the course of its mother's pregnancy. What of the case where the baby was damaged from conception by, for example, genetic disease, and tests that should have revealed the disease failed to do so? Or where German measles damages the baby but is not detected? *McKay* v. *Essex AHA*[14] recounts such a tragedy. Such claims are often called claims for 'wrongful life'. The plaintiffs in *McKay* were a little girl, born disabled as a result of the effect of German measles suffered by her mother early in pregnancy, and her mother. When Mrs McKay suspected that she had contracted German measles in the early weeks of her pregnancy, her doctor arranged for blood tests to establish whether she had been infected. As a result of negligence by either her doctor or the laboratory staff employed by the Area Health Authority, Mrs McKay was wrongly informed that she had not been infected by German measles. So she continued with the pregnancy. Had she known the true position she would, as her doctor was well aware, have requested an abortion under the Abortion Act 1967. The little girl was born in 1975 before the Congenital Disabilities Act was passed. The Court of Appeal had to decide the position at common law. They said that no action lay where the essence of the plaintiff's claim was that

13. See below, pp. 302–4.
14. [1982] 2 All ER 771.

but for the negligence of the defendant she would never have been born at all. The child's claim was thrown out, although her mother's claim was allowed to proceed. But the case is not solely of historical interest. The judges further said that under the Act no child born after its passing could pursue such a claim.

In the view of the Court of Appeal, the Act[15] can never give rise to a claim for 'wrongful life'. Ackner L. J., considering section 1(2)(b) of the Act, said that the relevant 'occurrence' has to be one that affected the mother in pregnancy 'so that the child *is born* with disabilities which would not otherwise have been present'. Clearly under the Act, then, where the breach of duty consists of carelessness in the conduct of the pregnancy or the birth the claim must relate to disabilities inflicted as a result of the breach of duty by the defendants. Where the essence of the claim is that the child should never have been born at all, it lies outside the scope of section 1(2)(b). Thus a claim by the child that amniocentesis should have been performed, or that subsequent tests were negligently conducted so that the pregnancy continued and he was born disabled, will fail.

The effect of the judgement in *McKay* is that in England a child injured before birth may claim compensation only for *wrongful disability*, that is against a defendant whose conduct actually caused his disability. He cannot sue for *wrongful life*. The Court of Appeal gave three main reasons for ruling out such claims. (1) It was not possible to arrive at a proper measure of damages representing the difference between the child's disabled existence and non-existence.[16] (2) The law should not impose a duty on doctors to abort, to terminate life *in utero*.[17] (3) To impose any duty to abort would be to violate the sanctity of life and to devalue the life of handicapped persons.[18] The second and third reasons are difficult to sustain in the light of the fact

15. It has been argued that the Act does not apply to a 'wrongful life' claim. The Act provides a scheme to compensate for disability inflicted by human error, not to a claim for allowing a disabled foetus to be born at all. The argument is of academic interest only. For the Court of Appeal were adamant that at common law no such action lay either.

16. pp. 782, 787 and 790. See the American judgements in I. Kennedy and A. Grubb, *Medical Law: Text and Materials*, Butterworths, London, 1989, pp. 826–39, for possible solutions to this dilemma.

17. p. 787.

18. p. 781.

that the court did allow Mrs McKay to pursue her *wrongful birth* action. Parents who allege that negligence caused the birth of a handicapped child who 'but for' that negligence would have been aborted do have a valid claim in England. In *Scuriaga* v. *Powell*[19] a young woman underwent a legal abortion early in pregnancy. Through negligence only one of twin foetuses was aborted. She was awarded damages in respect of the birth of the surviving child. Allowing wrongful birth actions by parents means that doctors are subjected to a duty to abort, albeit to the parents not the child. Inroads have already been made into the sanctity of life, and the rationale of the Abortion Act does necessarily accord the disabled foetus a lesser value than his healthy sibling. The justification for the judgement in *McKay* must rest on the claimed impossibility of arriving at a proper measure of damages.

Children damaged by pre-conception events

Let us move on now to look at claims by children born disabled as a result of events affecting a parent before conception. This could happen, for example, where the father or mother is affected by radiation or drugs so that the sperm or ovum carries a serious defect. Or the child may be damaged if doctors mismanage a previous pregnancy, for example if they fail to take note of and treat Rhesus incompatibility in the mother and the second child is born brain-damaged.[20] The Act obviously intended to cover such cases, providing as it does that the relevant occurrence may be one which affected either parent in his or her ability to have a healthy child. But it may be argued that if the claim is that the child was born disabled because one of his parents is incapable of creating a healthy infant, his claim is essentially that he should never have been born at all, and that it is an action for 'wrongful life' and is barred under the Act. I think this is a mistaken view of the Act. The child's claim in the case of a pre-conception occurrence rests on the hypothesis that *but for* that occurrence he would have been born normal and healthy, and that his actionable injury is therefore the difference between the life he might have had and the life he must now perforce endure. In *McKay* the infant plaintiff sought to maintain that her actionable injury was life itself, and as such her claim was not

19. (1979) 123 SJ 486.
20. See *Lazenvnick* v. *General Hospital of Munro City Inc. Civ. Act* 78–1259 Cmnd Pa., 13 August 1980.

and would not be sustainable. What *McKay* does clarify in cases of *pre-conception* injury is that a doctor, not responsible for that original injury, cannot be liable under the Act if he fails to diagnose the child's deformities in pregnancy and so fails to perform an abortion in such circumstances.

What if a parent realizes the risk?

Further problems confront the child plaintiff whose claim is based on pre-conception injury. Section 1(4) of the Act provides that in such cases if the affected parent is aware of the risk of the child being born disabled the defendant is not answerable to that child. Responsibility for knowingly running the risk of creating a disabled baby is placed with his parents, and whatever the degree of his fault, the original creator of the risk is relieved of any liability to the child. There is one exception to this rule. Where the child sues his father, the fact that the father is aware of the risk of begetting an abnormal child will not defeat the child's action as long as his mother is ignorant of the danger. This raises a nice question. A young man suffers contamination by some chemical at work through the negligence of his employers. He is warned that his reproductive capacity has been damaged, that he is likely to beget abnormal offspring, and is strongly advised never to have children. He ignores the warning, marries and tells his wife nothing. A disabled child is born to them. The child cannot sue his father's original employers. Even if they were in breach of duty to his father, 'the affected parent', the father's knowledge of the risk is a complete defence. But can the child sue his father? The answer has to be no. The child, like the infant plaintiff in *McKay*, can only claim against his father that he should never have been born at all. His father's condition at the time of the relevant 'negligence', begetting the child, was such that he could not beget a normal child. The father's 'negligence' was in creating him, not in inflicting a disability which but for some act or omission on his part would not have been present.

The question that arises now is whether a father can ever be liable to his child under the Act? Unlike the mother he is not granted any express immunity. If he assaults the mother during her pregnancy and damages the child in the womb, he will be liable in battery to her and through her to the child for its injuries. But it is difficult to envisage any other example of paternal liability. Other examples, such as the one we discussed above, or the father who knows he has syphilis, all fail to result in liability because the father's essential negligence is in creating a child at all, not in inflicting disabilities which the child could have been born without.

Must a mother consider abortion?

The partial defence that the affected parent shared responsibility for the child being born disabled, which may result in the child's damages being reduced, raises the final difficulty where the child sues in respect of pre-conception injuries. The child's disabilities may be diagnosed, perhaps when the mother has an ultra-sound scan, or through amniocentesis, well before his birth. Blood tests may cause the doctor to recommend amniocentesis but the mother refuses. This may also happen with a child damaged in the course of its mother's pregnancy. Once the mother knows of the damage or potential damage to her child, she will under the 1967 Abortion Act be entitled to an abortion on the grounds that there is substantial risk that the child if born would be seriously handicapped. Assuming that it is the mother who is the affected parent, does she 'share responsibility for the child being born disabled' if she refuses an abortion? No court has yet had to face that unhappy dilemma. But in *McKay* v. *Essex AHA*, refusing to allow the infant plaintiff's claim that she should have been aborted, Ackner LJ said that he could not accept:

. . . that the common law duty of care to a person can involve, without specific legislation to achieve this end, the legal obligation to that person, whether or not in utero, to terminate his existence. Such a proposition runs wholly contrary to the concept of the sanctity of human life.[21]

Applying Ackner LJ's proposition to a submission that the mother should have accepted abortion advanced by the defendant responsible for inflicting the disabilities suffered by the child, such a submission must fail. To impose an *obligation* on a mother to undergo an abortion would appear if anything even more repugnant to the concept of the sanctity of human life than to impose an obligation to abort on a doctor.

However, at least one High Court judge has exhibited an attitude to abortion dramatically different from that of Ackner LJ. In *Emeh* v. *Kensington, Chelsea and Fulham AHA*, the plaintiff underwent ster-

21. p. 787.

ilization.[22] The operation was carried out negligently by the first defendant and she became pregnant again. She claimed damages for the cost of bringing up the child. In the course of this unexpected and unwanted pregnancy the plaintiff had been offered but had refused an abortion. She said she was afraid of putting herself in the hands of the doctors again. The judge held that once she elected to continue the pregnancy the pregnancy ceased to be unwanted, and that the birth of the child was the result of her own actions and not a consequence of the defendant's negligence. He said that in the circumstances the plaintiff's refusal to consider an abortion was so unreasonable as to eclipse the defendant's wrongdoing.

The Court of Appeal overruled him.[23] Mrs Emeh did not become aware of her pregnancy until it was about seventeen to eighteen weeks advanced. Refusing an abortion at that stage in pregnancy could not be considered unreasonable. Whether the Court would have taken a different view had the pregnancy been less advanced remains open to question. Waller LJ laid great stress on the increased risk, discomfort and hospitalization entailed in abortion at twelve weeks plus.[24] Slade LJ was emphatic that abortion should generally never be forced upon a woman. He said:[25]

Save in the most exceptional circumstances, I cannot think it right that the court should ever declare it unreasonable for a woman to decline to have an abortion in a case where there is no evidence that there were any medical or psychiatric grounds for terminating the particular pregnancy.

Three further matters must be weighed in deciding whether a mother who refuses abortion once her baby's disabilities are diagnosed shares responsibility for him being born disabled. (1) There is, of course, a difference between such a mother and Mrs Emeh. The defendant may argue that foetal abnormality presents a medical ground for termination, and Slade LJ's dictum condemning 'forced' abortion excluded cases where medical grounds for termination were present. On the other hand, the Court of Appeal in *McKay* pronounced against obliging the doctor to abort where medical grounds should, had care been taken, have been diagnosed. Why should a mother be less favourably

22. *The Times*, 3 January 1983.
23. [1984] 3 All ER 1044.
24. See p. 1048.
25. p. 1053.

treated? (2) The issue in a child's claim under the Act is rather different from a mother's claim for a failed sterilization. The child's damages are to be reduced if a parent 'shares responsibility for the child being born disabled'. The mother who refused an abortion may share responsibility for the birth but she does not share responsibility for the disability. The original purpose of this partial defence appears to have been the sort of case where a mother ignores medical advice and worsens her child's condition by drinking, smoking or failing to take precautions advised by her doctors. She contributes to the disability. That is very different from refusing abortion. (3) Even where a court is prepared to entertain the defence, how will they assess the mother's decision? Is it to be what the hypothetical reasonable woman in 1992 would do, a totally objective test? Or are the mother-to-be's own moral views and religious affiliation to be considered? Whatever a court decides, controversy will follow.

PRE-PREGNANCY ADVICE AND GENETIC COUNSELLING

It is becoming increasingly common for women planning a child to seek medical advice before allowing themselves to conceive. For a healthy woman this may be simply a check that she is immune from German measles, a disease which if contracted in early pregnancy can damage the nervous system, causing the child to be born with severe disabilities. Another may seek reassurance that pregnancy will not damage her own health, for example if she has a history of cardiac or kidney disease. Finally, couples in whose family hereditary disease or defects have appeared, or couples who already have a damaged child, may need specialized genetic counselling.

In all these cases, the doctor counselling the woman undertakes a duty to her in relation not only to her own health and welfare as it may be affected by the course of pregnancy and childbirth but also in relation to the birth of a healthy child. If she is given the green light to go ahead with a pregnancy and suffers at the end of it the trauma and financial burden of a damaged child, she may have an action in negligence. Once again, proving negligence may not be easy. Not only must she show that the doctor failed to take into account factors relating to her medical history or genetic background, or failed to conduct tests that would have alerted him to the danger, but she must show that a reasonably competent doctor would have discovered the risk. If a woman today requests a test for immunity from German measles, is brushed aside, and subsequently contracts the disease in pregnancy, her claim will succeed. The enormous publicity given to the Department of Health campaign to eradicate the risk to the unborn child posed by German measles is such that any GP must be aware of and guard against that risk. If the sister of a haemophiliac consults her doctor and explains her brother's condition, and he fails to refer her for counselling with the result that she bears a haemophiliac son, she too should succeed. But beyond these obvious examples of want of competence the medical profession is much divided on the value of pre-conception advice. Some doctors run special clinics and advise special diets and total abstinence from alcohol when attempting to conceive. Greater evidence of the relationship of such regimes to the reduction of risk to the child, and their acceptance by the profession at large, will be needed before a claim based on the lack of such detailed guidance could succeed.

A woman claiming damages for the birth of a disabled child may face two further obstacles. (1) She will have to establish that had she received proper advice she would not have allowed herself to become pregnant when she did. (2) If the defect in the child is diagnosed in pregnancy and she is offered and refuses an abortion, she may face the argument that in refusing an abortion she becomes the author of her own damage. I have already expressed my view that such an argument should never prevail. However, should the woman elect to undergo abortion then she should receive compensation for the suffering, physical and emotional, that that operation entails.

Has the damaged child himself a remedy? We must distinguish three types of cases where negligent pre-pregnancy advice results in the birth of a disabled child. (1) The relevant negligence may be that the woman was encouraged to become pregnant when, had proper care been taken, she could have been advised never to contemplate pregnancy because of the risk to any child she might bear. The child's action in such a case will fail because the essence of his claim is that he should never have been born at all. It is once again a claim for 'wrongful life' and excluded by the Court of Appeal in *McKay*. (2) The negligence may have been in failing to counsel the mother properly on precautions to take, or the timing of pregnancy. Such a claim may raise an awkward problem. For example, a woman is not tested for immunity to German measles or the test is negligently conducted. She is wrongly told that she has immunity. She becomes pregnant, contracts the disease and the child is damaged. Had she been properly advised, she would have been vaccinated against the disease and advised in the strongest of terms to delay pregnancy for three months after the vaccination. The actual child born would thus never have been born. The particular set of genes in the egg and sperm that went to create him would never have met. A literal interpretation of *McKay* would deny the child a remedy on the grounds that that unique individual would never have been born had the mother had proper advice. It would seem a harsh result, but the conclusion that it follows from the interpretation of the Act by the Court of Appeal in *McKay* is difficult to resist. Examples of this sort could be multiplied endlessly. There could be a parent who is undergoing treatment for venereal disease. He or she is carelessly advised that pregnancy is now safe. It is not. Treatment was not complete. The child born disabled would not have been born had proper advice been given. A woman knows a little of a family history of genetic disease affecting the males in her family. She seeks counselling. She should have been advised of the risks to male children and been offered amniocentesis in pregnancy, so that she could if she wished have terminated a pregnancy had the tests shown that she carried a male child. A male child born disabled cannot sue under the Act, for had amniocentesis been offered and accepted that male child would not exist. A similar analysis would apply where the mother argues that she should have been offered IVF and pre-implantation diagnosis to avoid the birth of a genetically handicapped child. That embryo, the disabled child, would have been screened out and never born at all. (3) And so there is only one very limited class of case where the child's action based on allegedly careless pre-pregnancy advice may succeed. That is where the advice omitted, or inadequate in content, would have enabled that very child to be born hale and hearty. Realistic examples are difficult to think of. Perhaps one topical example concerns the relationship between the maternal diet before conception and spina bifida. There is some evidence that a special treatment with multi-vitamins may reduce the likelihood of that terrible disability. A child might argue that had his mother been advised to follow that regime his disability would not have developed. He would have been born but not disabled. Such a child claims for his disabilities, not wrongful life. He overcomes the first problem in his claim against medical staff, but will he be able to prove that the treatment if given would have prevented his disability? It is a matter for controversy among doctors. We shall see in Chapter 19 that the question of how to test the theory has aroused other controversy.

What I should make clear is that in the first two classes of case, while the child's claim may fail as a 'wrongful life' claim, the parents' claim will still succeed. The distinction between 'wrongful life' claims by the child and 'wrongful birth' claims by the parents may not be very logical but seems at present to be entrenched in English law. Public policy arguments against allowing a parental claim seem to have been largely rejected.[26] What will be interesting to observe is whether the judges will be prepared to apply the doctrine in *McKay* strictly to cases likely to arise from the burgeoning discipline and science of genetics.

Genetic counselling and confidentiality

The genetic counsellor's legal problems are not confined to his obligations to the woman seeking his advice. If he discovers that she is, or is likely to be, the carrier of congenital disease, then he will be well aware that any sisters of hers are also at risk as carriers, and so to a lesser degree are other female relatives. Obviously he will ask her permission to inform her sister or her sister's doctor. What if the woman refuses permission? She will argue that the counsellor owes her an obligation of confidence. But if the sister later bears a damaged child, the consequences to her are dreadful and she might sue the counsellor. The sister could contend that the risk to her was readily foreseeable and the counsellor had a duty to warn her. I would suggest that in such circumstances the counsellor exceptionally may be justified in breaking his obligation of confidence. The Court of Appeal[27] have held that information obtained in a confidential relationship may be disclosed if disclosure is in the public interest. The interest in preventing the birth of damaged children is sufficient to merit disclosure.

26. See the first edition of this book, pp. 171–2.
27. *W.* v. *Egdell* [1990] 1 All ER 835; *Lion Laboratories Ltd* v. *Evans* [1984] 2 All ER 417.

CHILDBIRTH

How much choice?

Our grandmothers gave heartfelt thanks if they survived the perils of childbirth. Our mothers were the first generation to have general access to hospital confinement and skilled attention if things went wrong. Today medical technology offers a whole range of sophisticated devices to monitor mother and baby and ensure safe delivery. But increasingly groups of women reject the panoply of machinery found in many hospital labour wards. Accepting that necessity of 'high-tech' birth for a minority of difficult cases, the natural childbirth movement has campaigned for the medical profession to be more willing to let nature take its course. For a number of women the ideal would be delivery of their baby at home in the comfort of familiar surroundings. The debate is largely medical and social. Gynaecologists in many areas of the country have accepted the ideas propounded. Hospital birth in 1992 is probably substantially less interventionist and impersonal than in 1977. But home delivery is more difficult to obtain. Few general practitioners will now deliver babies at home. There are insufficient NHS community midwives to meet demand. Progress is being made, but the overall impression which a laywoman is left with is that while doctors will make considerable efforts to meet women's demands for more natural childbirth in hospital, all but a few in the profession are opposed to home delivery.

What role does the law play in this debate? Childbirth is a medical monopoly. The law effectively denies a woman, unable to persuade a doctor or midwife to attend her at home or a hospital to comply with her wishes concerning the birth, the choice of seeking alternative help.[28] She may either give birth alone or fall in with medical requirements and accept medical help. For it is a criminal offence for a person other than a registered midwife or a registered medical practitioner to attend

28. Nurses, Midwives and Health Visitors Act 1979, s. 17. An exception is made for emergencies to protect family, policemen and ambulance crew from liability for helping in emergencies. For thorough discussion of the monopoly on childbirth see J. M. Eekelaar and R. W. J. Dingwall, 'Some Legal Issues of Obstetric Practice' [1984] JSWL p. 258, and J. Finch, 'Paternalism and Professionalism in Childbirth' (1982) 132 NLJ pp. 995 and 1011.

a woman in childbirth. An offender faces a maximum fine of £2,500. And any person means any person. On 6 August 1982 a husband was convicted of delivering his own wife and fined £100.[29] Nor is the unqualified attendant the only potential 'criminal'. The mother herself, if she procures the other's services – in ordinary English, if she asks for their help – may be guilty of counselling and procuring a criminal offence. So her choice as delimited by the law is to accept the medical help available or give birth alone. Giving birth alone is not a very encouraging option and is itself not free of legal hazard, not to speak of medical risk. For if the baby dies the mother may face prosecution for manslaughter. Gross negligence by attendants in the delivery of a baby has resulted in criminal conviction where the baby died.[30] The issue where an unattended mother was on trial would be whether refusing medical attendance was sufficiently culpable negligence in relation to the safety of her child.

The rationale for the legislation which makes medical attendance at childbirth compulsory appears self-evident. If a person refuses to seek medical help for any other life-threatening condition he physically harms himself alone. A woman refusing medical attention in childbirth puts her baby at risk. Yet she can lawfully refuse attention for the nine months up to delivery. Proposals that maternity grants and benefits should be made dependent on ante-natal visits have been made. Nobody has yet suggested that it should be a criminal offence to fail to attend the ante-natal clinic. The truth is that there is no express and considered policy on the respective rights and liberties of mother and baby. The legislation originally enacted to require professional attendance at childbirth was intended to outlaw the 'Sarah Gamps', the elderly and often not entirely clean local women who made their living as unqualified midwives.[31] Today's legislation has moved a long way from that point. It may by chance be correct, but it needs proper consideration whether a husband delivering his wife, or a mother her daughter, should be branded as criminal when all goes well and mother and baby thrive.

29. For further discussion of this case see Finch, op cit.
30. *R.* v. *Senior* (1832) 1 Mood. C.C. 346; and see *R.* v. *Bateman* (1925) 19 Cr. App. R. 8.
31. See Finch, op. cit., pp. 995–6.

Hospital birth

Entering hospital, the mother puts herself into the hands of the doctors and the midwives. She consents to all the inevitable invasions of her body that delivery of her child must normally entail. So such acts will not be a battery. The extent of the mother's consent to treatment in childbirth has been put in this way.

Apart from any express prohibition she might make, if she receives substantially that form of treatment, a lack of explicit consent to particular details will not make it unlawful, providing that those details relate reasonably to the treatment according to the prevailing professional standards.[32]

Let us apply and test this statement of the law. One of the most controversial issues of hospital birth is the use of episiotomy. Episiotomy is the procedure whereby a small cut is made in the vagina to assist delivery and prevent tearing. One of its advantages is said to be that the deliberate cut will heal better than a random tear. But it has been alleged that episiotomy became routine. It was performed regardless of any necessity for it. And since those allegations were discussed in the press the number of episiotomies has fallen. The law, as the statement quoted makes clear, will render such a procedure unlawful if the woman *expressly* bans it. Many women will enter the labour ward confused and a little overwhelmed. They will give no express instructions. On the statement quoted, episiotomy on them is lawful without express consent, providing the procedure conforms to 'prevailing professional standards' in obstetrics. The Wendy Savage inquiry showed that obstetricians do not agree on what constitutes 'prevailing professional standards'.[33] I would regard episiotomy without express consent as unlawful. For it is not an inevitably necessary invasion of the mother's body, as are for example the contacts by the midwife as she feels the abdomen and assists the baby's exit. Episiotomy is a greater invasion of the body than the contacts implicitly authorized simply by seeking professional aid. The skin is cut. A wound, however small, is made. The law should uphold the mother's right to control what happens to her. The controversy over whether the law should compel medical attendance in childbirth would be much less substantial if the woman's rights in hospital were fully protected.

32. Eekelaar and Dingwall, op. cit.
33. See pp. 210–11.

It goes without saying that a mother suffering injury as a result of carelessness in the management of childbirth is entitled to compensation for negligence. She will recover compensation for her pain and suffering and for the shock and grief consequent on the death of a baby, or the birth of a disabled child. Damages may also include any effect of the mismanaged delivery on her prospects of future childbearing.[34] Two sorts of cases pose special difficulty. Since 1985 a number of women have brought claims against the hospitals where they were delivered based on evidence that they remained awake throughout Caesarean sections. The general anaesthetic administered to them rendered them paralysed and unable to speak but still conscious and so in appalling pain and terror. At first such claims were dismissed as hysterical imaginings. Many have proved well-founded and women have been awarded substantial damages where they were able to prove that the anaesthetist was negligent in failing to anaesthetize them adequately. Proof of negligence may sometimes be awkward.[35] For in Caesarean surgery a delicate balance must be struck between providing sufficient anaesthetic to render the mother fully unconscious and risking any harm to the baby. The second difficult type of case is a claim based on an allegation that the baby was born brain-damaged as a result of lack of oxygen in the course of delivery. A simple example of such a claim is this. The parents allege that the obstetric team carelessly failed to note or act on signs of foetal distress and did not therefore carry out a necessary Caesarean delivery at all or as swiftly as the infant's condition demanded. The problem in this sort of claim is not so often proving negligence as proving causation. A highly charged debate is in progress as to how far oxygen deprivation at delivery can be proved to be a cause of brain damage and in particular of cerebral palsy.[36]

The child's rights

So far in this section I have concentrated on the mother's choices. What of the child's rights? Has he a remedy if the doctors or midwives are incompetent and he suffers injury? What are his rights if his mother

34. *Kralj* v. *McGrath* [1986] 1 All ER 54.
35. See, for example, *Ludlow* v. *Swindon Health Authority* [1990] 1 Med. LR 104.
36. Plaintiffs' experts argue 'Yes'; defendants' experts argue 'No'!

refuses a course of action that will benefit him and thus causes him injury?

The child's rights are now governed by the Congenital Disabilities (Civil Liability) Act 1976, albeit the Act appears to go unnoticed in the relevant case-law. For that Act covers not only injury to the child in the womb but also any occurrence which affected mother or child in the course of its birth. It is quite clear that the common law recognized a duty to a child in the course of delivery.[37] It has been argued that the 1976 Act, which replaces the common law, reduces the child's rights.[38] For liability under the Act arises only where the defendant would have been liable in tort to the affected parent. Where the failure by the defendant attending the mother, failure to proceed quickly enough to Caesarean section or whatever, is in no way the responsibility of the mother, no problem is caused to the child. I have argued before that the duty to the mother embraces care of her child. A breach of duty to her which injures the child creates rights for both her and her child.

The thrust of the argument that the Act reduces the child's rights lies in these sorts of circumstances. The child is believed to be at risk. Doctors recommended Caesarean section. The mother refuses and the child is born suffering brain damage. The child will not be able to sue the doctor. The doctor is clearly not liable to the mother. The child cannot sue his mother, for the Act grants immunity to mothers.[39] More seriously than that, it is argued[40] that if there is no duty directly to the child a doctor cannot after the 1976 Act advance his duty to the child as a defence to acts done to the mother. Were there still a direct duty to the child, the doctor might contend that in exceptional circumstances he could, for example, proceed to Caesarean section without consent in order to save the baby.

Two points should be made on this argument. First, as the authors of the argument themselves say, a doctor who can establish the necessity of a battery against the mother to save the child may still have a defence of necessity to an action by her, regardless of the absence of a *direct* duty to the child. Second, it may perhaps be doubted whether in relation to damage done in the course of delivery the 1976 Act does

37. *Whitehouse* v. *Jordan* [1981] 1 WLR 246, HL
38. Eekelaar and Dingwall, op. cit., pp. 264–6.
39. s. 1(2).
40. Eekelaar and Dingwall, op. cit., p. 265.

negate a direct duty to her child. Section 1(1) of the Acts speaks of an occurrence affecting 'mother *or child* in the course of its birth'. The later provision in section 1(3) that the defendant must be liable in tort to the affected parent does not make sense if the occurrence is one which the Act applies to because it has affected the child. It is another example of the inadequacy of that Act. But interpreting the Act to give a limited direct duty to the child in the course of its birth would not solve the basic problem of conflict between rights of the mother and duties to the child. When does the 'course of its birth' begin? The position could be reached where a direct duty to perform a Caesarean was owed under the 1976 Act to the child in distress whose mother was already in labour, but *not* to the child whose mother's condition indicated that an immediate Caesarean was called for but who had not yet gone into labour.

In the United States two strategies have been pursued to protect the unborn child against its own mother. First, in a number of states foetuses have been made wards of court, enabling the court to order the mother to submit to Caesarean section or other medical intervention.[41] Second, where a child has died, allegedly as a result of maternal neglect, mothers have been prosecuted for manslaughter.[42] To attain the goal of safeguarding an unborn child when its mother's refusal of medical intervention appears to threaten its well-being, even its life, by making that unborn child a ward of court might appear a superficially attractive option. It is an option that the Court of Appeal in England rightly rejected in *In Re F. (In Utero)*.[43] The mother was a 36-year-old woman who suffered from severe mental disturbance, but she was not 'sectionable' under the Mental Health Act 1983. She refused ante-natal care and had disappeared by the time the local authority started proceedings to make the foetus a ward of court. There was understandable concern for the child's welfare. Refusing to extend the wardship jurisdiction to unborn children, the court advanced the following reasons for

41. See *Jefferson* v. *Griffin Spalding Country Hospital Authority* (1981) 274 SE 2d 457 (Jehovah's Witness ordered to submit to blood transfusions and Caesarean surgery); and see generally Kennedy and Grubb, op. cit., pp. 358–63.
42. Though, as far as I know, no such prosecution has ultimately yet succeeded. See generally, J. Gallagher, 'Fetus as Patient', in *Reproductive Laws for the 1990s*, ed. S. Cohen and N. Tubb, Humana Press, New Jersey, 1989, p. 185.
43. [1989] 2 All ER 193.

their decision. (1) In English law the foetus has no legal personality until it is born, and has an existence independent of the mother. (2) To extend the wardship jurisdiction to the foetus with its predominant principle that the interests of the ward are paramount would create inevitable conflict between the existing legal interests of the mother and her child. Is the mother to be 'sacrificed' for the child? (3) There are immense practical difficulties in enforcing any order against the mother. If she is, for example, refusing to consent to an elective Caesarean and is not already in hospital, will the police be called on to go and arrest her? (4) There would be problems with the limit of such a jurisdiction. Mothers can do most harm to their unborn children early in pregnancy by, for example, alcohol and drug abuse. Yet up to twenty-four weeks in pregnancy a mother may well be able to obtain a legal abortion. Would a woman who wants her baby be subject to coercive measures in the baby's interests, yet free to destroy it should she change her mind? May LJ concluded that in the light of these problems any such radical extension of the wardship jurisdiction was a matter for Parliament and not for the courts themselves. In the event, and unbeknownst to the court, while they were hearing the action the mother had already safely given birth to a healthy child.

Parliament should, like the Court of Appeal, firmly reject any proposal to extend the wardship jurisdiction to unborn children. Over and above those reasons given by the Court of Appeal, such a proposal should be thrown out on the grounds of the damage it would do to ante-natal care generally. Obstetricians, knowing that they could in the end coerce their patients, would become less willing to inform and persuade, to rely on patience rather than compulsion. Women, knowing that ultimately they could be forced against their will to submit to blood transfusion or surgery, may opt out of formal obstetric care and far more babies could be born damaged as a result. The law must continue to recognize the pregnant woman's autonomy and *her* sovereignty over *her* own body.

Instinctive support for such a principle gains further credence from the evidence of how forced Caesareans actually work in the USA. Of the women subjected to forced obstetric intervention 81 per cent belonged to an ethnic minority, 44 per cent were unmarried and none were private patients.[44] Moreover in a startling number of cases where

44. See L. Nsiah-Jefferson, 'Reproductive Laws, Women of Color and Low-Income Women', in Cohen and Tubb, op. cit., p. 39.

a court ordered a 'necessary' intervention, the woman, having evaded the court officials seeking to enforce the order, went on to give birth to a healthy child without that intervention.[45] Very, very few pregnant women do refuse to follow their doctors' advice. Giving the courts legal powers to enforce medical orders would do far more harm than good to the principles and practice of obstetric care.

45. See J. Gallagher, op. cit.

CHAPTER 12

Assisted Conception

I move on now to examine the legal problems affecting procedures to relieve infertility.[1] It is estimated that as many as one in ten couples, and maybe more, have difficulty conceiving naturally and seek medical help. The technical ability of the doctors to give that help has made incredible progress in the last decade. The development of *in vitro* fertilization (IVF) and the birth of the first 'test-tube' baby, Louise Brown, in 1978 gave hope to thousands of childless couples. The advent of surrogacy offered the chance of a child even to the woman who had undergone hysterectomy. Yet for every man or woman who rejoiced at what the doctors could now do, there were as many who condemned the technical advances as unnatural and contrary to the will of God. And much publicized though these new techniques have been, they have brought heartbreak too, for the success rates are still low. Such was the furore created that the government established a Committee under Dame Mary Warnock (now Baroness Warnock) to consider:

. . . recent and potential developments in medicine and science related to human fertilization and embryology; to consider what policies and safeguards should be applied, including consideration of the social, ethical and legal implications of these developments; and to make recommendations.

1. See generally, P. Singer and D. Wells, *The Reproduction Revolution*, OUP, 1984; D. Cusine, *New Reproductive Techniques: A Legal Perspective*, Dartmouth, 1990; and for an international survey J. Gunning, *Human IVF. Embryo Research, Fetal Tissue for Research and Treatment and Abortion: International Information*, HMSO, 1990.

The Warnock Report was published in the summer of 1984.[2] It fuelled rather than stilled the controversy. Media attention focused on the Report's recommendation to permit research on embryos of up to fourteen days' development. That was a proposal from which three members of the committee dissented. The status to be accorded to the human embryo cannot help but be an emotive and complex question. Alas, the publicity accorded to that one part of the Warnock Report distorted debate on the Report as a whole, and contributed to the shameful delay in implementing *any* of Warnock's proposals. The central plank of the Report was its insistence that the burgeoning business of reproductive medicine should be regulated and the status of children born as a result of *all* the new and various forms of assisted conception should be clarified. Infertile patients needed protection against charlatans. Medical practitioners needed a framework within which to practise legally and ethically. And children were entitled to a proper family structure, above all to know who in law were their mother and father. Warnock's sensible recommendations on all these matters remained in abeyance until enacted in a modified form in the Human Fertilisation and Embryology Act 1990. The Act reached the statute book only after vitriolic debate in Parliament and the publication of two further reports by the government, a general consultation document early in 1987[3] and a White Paper[4] later that year. Both were designed, I suspect, as well-meaning attempts to secure an impossible consensus.

The Human Fertilization and Embryology Authority

The delay in implementing Warnock from 1984 to 1990 prompted the medical profession to take unilateral action. In 1985 the Medical Research Council and the Royal College of Obstetricians and Gynaecologists (RCOG) agreed to set up a Voluntary Licensing Authority (VLA) to monitor and license all embryo research and IVF treatment. In 1989, in a heavy hint to the government, the authority changed its

2. Report of the Committee of Inquiry into Human Fertilization and Embryology, Cmnd 9314 (1984) (The Warnock Report).
3. *Legislation on Human Infertility Services and Embryology* Cm 46 HMSO, 1987.
4. *Human Fertilization and Embryology: A Framework for Legislation* Cm 259 HMSO, 1987.

name to the Interim Licensing Authority (ILA). At no stage in its life did the authority have any legal powers. Chaired by Dame Mary Donaldson, the VLA gained the confidence of medical practitioners. It had some notable successes,[5] especially in limiting the number of embryos which should be replaced in a woman undergoing IVF so as to minimize the risks of a multiple pregnancy.[6] Critics argued that the ILA was too much the creature of the profession and took it upon itself to become an ardent partisan of the pro-research lobby. But at a time when government sat on its hands, the ILA attempted to police reproductive medicine and to safeguard patients' interests.

The ILA is replaced by the Human Fertilisation and Embryology Authority (HFEA), a statutory licensing authority, established by section 5 of the Human Fertilisation and Embryology Act. Schedule 1 of the Act prescribes the authority's membership. Neither the chairman nor the deputy chairman may be a medical practitioner or anyone else professionally involved in embryo research or assisted conception. At least one third, but fewer than half, of the members shall be persons so involved in research or infertility treatment. Interestingly the Secretary of State for Health, who appoints members of the HFEA, is directed to '. . . have regard to the desirability of ensuring that the proceedings of the Authority, and the discharge of its functions, are informed by the views of both men and women'. This has resulted in a substantial number of female members of the HFEA.

The HFEA is endowed with impressive powers. Section 3 of the Act makes it a criminal offence to bring about the creation of an embryo outside the human body except in pursuance of a licence granted by the HFEA. Any infertility treatment requiring the creation of an embryo by means of *in vitro* fertilization (IVF), that is the creation of a 'test-tube' embryo, *must* be licensed. Section 4 prohibits any storage of gametes (sperm or eggs), and the use of donor sperm or eggs, without a licence from the HFEA. Any infertility treatment involving artificial insemination by donor (AI) or egg donation is thus unlawful unless licensed by the HFEA. Sections 3 and 4 also outlaw a number of specific procedures, for example creating human/animal hybrids. Those issues will be dealt with further in the next chapter. This chapter

5. The Reports of the VLA and ILA are invaluable sources of information about the development of assisted conception from 1985 to 1991.
6. ILA guidelines (12) provide that no more than three or exceptionally four eggs or embryos should be replaced in GIFT or IVF treatment.

concentrates on the role of the HFEA in relation to, and the legal principles governing, assisted conception.

Any clinic that offers IVF or AI is subject to the control of the HFEA. It cannot operate lawfully without a licence and its staff and procedures will be strictly monitored and controlled. Failure to comply with HFEA guidelines as to, for example, safety procedures, numbers of embryos to be implanted, selection of donors or assessment of patients may lead to forfeiture of that licence. However, one area of reproductive medicine seems to be beyond the ambit of the Act and the control of the HFEA. Gametes Intra-Fallopian Transfer (GIFT) is a procedure whereby eggs are taken from an infertile woman and sperm from her partner. Eggs and sperm are mixed together in the laboratory and returned to the woman's body before the process of fertilization begins. Thus there is no creation of an embryo outside the body of a woman which would require to be licensed. There are arguments that a provision in section 1, the section defining embryo (section 1(2)(a)), which provides that the Act does apply to an embryo created partly *in vitro* and partly in the body, may 'catch' GIFT. But this is unlikely as, in GIFT, fertilization does not even begin until the eggs and sperm are returned to the woman's body. Section 1(2)(a) is probably designed to cover a procedure whereby if a woman undergoes IVF at a clinic with no facilities to store embryos, the 'surplus' embryos are collected in a minute glass tube which is then placed in the woman's vagina. She thus acts as an 'incubator', and goes to a clinic with storage facilities. There 'her' embryos are removed and frozen. Every attempt in Parliament to include GIFT expressly and unequivocally in the Act failed. This is a disgraceful state of affairs. One specific method of assisted conception remains unpoliced, an open invitation to those who may know their expertise would not be sufficient to win a HFEA licence to concentrate on GIFT. And there is another area of concern about GIFT. There seems to be growing evidence that GIFT is more likely than IVF to result in multiple pregnancies, with attendant risk to mother and children, and to overstretched neo-natal facilities.

How will the HFEA be financed? By enacting the Human Fertilisation and Embryology Act the government appears to be giving official blessing to IVF and other means of assisted conception. It is a pretty empty blessing. For the Authority is to be financed by the clinics it licenses. Its budget will derive primarily from licence fees. Nor is there any indication that extra money will be allocated from the NHS budget to fund assisted conception. The money it will cost a clinic to get a licence may mean that assisted conception will continue to be offered mainly in the private sector, with few NHS clinics offering a full service. Private fees will have to rise. The cost of paying for a licence will be yet another incentive for poorer clinics to offer only GIFT, which does not require a licence.

Whatever its demerits however, the Human Fertilisation and Embryology Act 1990 does make significant changes in the law governing the various forms of assisted conception. The Code of Practice issued by HFEA in August 1991 supplements the general principles laid down in the Act.

Artificial insemination by donor (AI)[7]

Where it is the man who is infertile, a couple may be offered the opportunity to have a child by another man, by artificial insemination by donor (AI). As a procedure, AI is far from new and is so simple that it can be, and has been, performed without medical assistance. The problems are legal and ethical, not medical. Let us look first at AI in its most favourable setting. A couple are happily married. They are carefully counselled. The husband fully and freely consents. Up to 1987 a child born as a result of AI was born into a legal limbo. Even if his mother was a married woman whose husband, the 'social' father, had agreed to AI, the child was in law the illegitimate child of his mother and the donor. He had no legal relation with his 'social' father. Should the 'social' father leave the child's mother before the birth, the child had no claim to maintenance against him. If his 'social' father died intestate, 'his' child had no claim on his estate. Moreover, should the 'social' father seek to assert parentage by registering the child as his, he committed perjury! No wonder AI developed as a procedure shrouded in secrecy. The first attempt to clarify the status of AI children came in the Family Law Reform Act 1987. Section 27 of that Act provided that where a married woman received AI, with her husband's consent, the child was in law the child of the woman and her husband. Sections 28 and 29 of the Human Fertilisation and Embryology Act go a stage further than that. Section 28(2) re-enacts the provision relating to AI children born within marriage, deeming the child to be the husband's child.[8] Section 28(3) extends that

7. The abbreviation AI seems to have replaced AID in general use.
8. In cases where the husband's consent is disputed it would be for him to prove that he did not consent.

263

provision to children born to unmarried couples seeking AI together because the male partner is infertile. Whenever AI is provided for a woman and a man together by a person to whom a licence applies, the man is to be treated as the father of the child. That means he is subject to the same rights and obligations as any other natural father not married to the mother of his child.[9]

Section 28(4) provides that wherever the woman's husband or partner is to be treated as the child's legal father, no other person is in any sense the legal father of the child, that is all links between the donor and the child are severed. Even when no husband or partner is to be deemed to be the child's father, where a donor donates sperm and gives the appropriate consent to donation required by the Act in Schedule 3, he is not to be treated as the child's father.[10] Thus, whenever AI is provided in a licensed clinic, in accordance with the rules laid down in the Act, the donor has no legal relationship to the child. The child has no claim on the donor. He can never assert any parental rights. The effect of severing the link between donor and child will be seen to be significant.

AI and single mothers

An increasing number of women who have no regular male partner want to have a child of their own. Such a woman may well reject as distasteful the prospect of a 'one-night stand' to get pregnant, and may not in any case want a transient partner to have any legal claim on 'her' child. If she is a lesbian, sexual intercourse with a man will be repugnant to her. Up to 1990 there have been a number of clinics prepared to offer AI to a woman alone. RCOG guidelines sought to limit AI to heterosexual couples who were either married or in a 'stable heterosexual relationship'. Some doctors were willing to help single women. Attempts were made in Parliament to outlaw AI for women without a male partner altogether. They were very nearly successful. A compromise is embodied in section 13(5) of the Act. Section

9. He does not automatically share parental responsibilities with the mother. Section 4 of the Children Act 1989 enables him to apply to the court for full parental rights, or he and the mother may expressly agree to share parental responsibilities. The child enjoys the same rights of inheritance as a child born within marriage.

10. See s. 28(6).

13(5) provides, apparently innocuously, that a licence holder treating a woman must take into account the welfare of any child who may be born as a result of treatment, *including the need of that child for a father*. This is to be a mandatory condition of any licence granted by the HFEA, who may elaborate on that condition. A number of MPs and peers hoped that the HFEA would ban AI, and other forms of assisted conception, for all single women save in the most exceptional circumstances. The Code of Practice paras. 3.10–18 will disappoint them.

Should a woman be helped to have a child who will have no father? The effect of section 28(6) severing all links between an AI donor and his child is that a child born to a woman with no partner is quite literally fatherless. It is argued that society cannot allow fatherless children to be born by AI. Children need a parent of either sex to develop properly. Yet countless children are born by natural means to women alone, and countless more lose contact with their 'legal' father. If it is asserted that a woman unable to have children by the usual means must be denied help via assisted conception, unless she has a male partner, a case must be made out that her child's welfare is likely to be imperilled by fatherlessness. Perhaps never having a Dad is less traumatic than losing one. A woman who sets out to have a child alone is not misled into thinking she can always rely on a man for support. Finally, whenever arguments are advanced to ban AI for women without a male partner, those arguments should be analysed carefully. Is the essence of the argument that *any* woman without a male partner should not be helped, or that lesbians must not be allowed to use AI to have children? I suspect that it is often the latter.

Artificial insemination by husband (AIH)

There are some rare cases where although the husband is fertile he cannot beget a child because he is incapable of normal intercourse. His sperm may be used to impregnate his wife by artificial means. The child will be just as much the legitimate child of the couple as if it were conceived naturally. If the marriage has never been consummated, the acceptance of AIH will not prevent the wife from petitioning the court to annul the marriage,[11] although on policy grounds the court may refuse a decree if they consider that in having the child the wife

11. *L. v. L.* [1949] P. 211.

approbated the marriage. The child will in any case remain legitimate even if his parents' marriage is later annulled, for they were married when he was conceived and non-consummation only renders a marriage voidable by the court. It does not mean that the marriage was never valid at all.

The facility to store sperm by freezing may cause further problems if a husband banks sperm for later insemination of his wife. He may choose to do so before undergoing vasectomy or treatment that might damage his fertility, or that might pose a risk to children later conceived. To whom do the sperm belong when the husband dies? May the wife ask for insemination then, and if so, what is the child's status? In France a court ordered a sperm bank to release her deceased husband's sperm to his widow.[12] Alas, the attempt at AIH failed and she did not conceive. Addressing the problem of AIH after the husband's death, Warnock expressed disquiet about allowing such a procedure to go ahead at all. Indeed the Warnock report recommended posthumous AIH should be actively discouraged.[13] No express provision limiting posthumous AIH is to be found in the Human Fertilisation and Embryology Act, but Warnock's other proposal relating to posthumous AIH has been enacted. Section 28(6)(b) provides that where the sperm of any man or an embryo created from his sperm is used after his death, he (the deceased man) is not to be treated as the father of the child. So if a widow is inseminated with her dead husband's sperm, a child resulting from that AIH has no claim on his natural father's estate. Again he is a child who is legally fatherless.

The Act does not prohibit posthumous AIH. Could an English widow demand AIH like her French counterpart? Schedule 3 of the Act requires any consent to donate sperm to a sperm bank to specify what is to be done with the sperm should the donor die. So a husband storing sperm prior to chemotherapy might stipulate that, should he die, his wife should be allowed to use his sperm for an attempt at AIH. This does not give her a right to demand sperm. The ultimate decision remains, it seems, with the clinician.[14] In the context of private treatment a widow might seek to argue that she has a contractual right to AIH. The possibility remains of attempts to contend that the frozen

---

12. *Parpalaix* v. *CECOS*. See Kennedy and Grubb, op. cit., p. 621.
13. p. 55.
14. Who must presumably take into account 'the need of the child for a father' as required by s. 13(5).

sperm form part of the deceased husband's estate. Should a court accept that sperm can be classified as 'property' and 'inherited' by the wife, it would logically follow that she could demand 'her' sperm, but she could not require the AI clinic to inseminate her.[15] In the light of the underlying philosophy of the 1990 Act, it seems unlikely such a 'property' argument would succeed.

Female infertility

Female infertility has always posed a much greater medical problem. Test-tube babies and the potential for surrogacy are just two of the many recent advances of medical science in this area. I go on now to look at these and other techniques. All were primarily designed to overcome female infertility, but some have also proved useful where it is the man who is sub-fertile.

Test-tube babies (IVF)

A woman who ovulates normally, but whose Fallopian tubes are absent or damaged, will never conceive naturally because the ova (eggs) that she produces cannot travel to meet sperm and be fertilized. The test-tube baby procedure (*in vitro* fertilization or IVF) offers such women the chance of their own child. Ova are removed from the woman and fertilized in the laboratory with sperm taken from the woman's husband or partner. The embryo, or embryos, thus created are carefully tested and then implanted in the mother's womb. This technique may also be used where the woman is fertile but her partner has a very low sperm count. Fertilization in the laboratory in such cases appears to be more successful than fertilization by normal means. No issue of family law arises. The child has the same status and relationship to its parents as if it were naturally conceived. If the parents are married at the time of fertilization or marry before the birth, the child is a marital child and both parents share full parental rights. When the parents are unmarried, the father is in the same position as any unmarried father, that is he may apply to the court to share parental responsibilities with his partner. It is the possible variations of IVF, where eggs or sperm (or both) are provided by a third party, which raise the question of the

15. See the discussion in I. Kennedy and A. Grubb, *Medical Law: Text and Materials*, Butterworths, London, 1989, pp. 618–24.

child's legal status and family law. A woman may be infertile because of blocked Fallopian tubes *and* have an infertile male partner. Donor sperm can then be used to fertilize her eggs, again returning the resulting embryo or embryos to her womb. A child born as a result of this combination of IVF and AI is to be treated in law just like any other AI child. If the woman is married, and her husband consents to IVF and AI, the child is a child of the marriage. The husband, not the donor, is the legal father. If the couple are unmarried but seek treatment together, again the male partner, the 'social' father, is the legal father of the child.[16]

Egg donation and embryo transplants

Some women, by reason of congenital defect or as a result of disease, do not ovulate at all. And so they can never conceive naturally. Intensive hormone treatment helps many such women to start or re-start ovulation, but for a number that treatment proves fruitless. They can never have a child genetically theirs. They can be helped by egg donation. Egg donation may also be used where the woman carries a genetic disease to avoid transmitting that disease to her children. Eggs can be taken from a fertile woman (the donor), fertilized in the laboratory with the infertile woman's partner's sperm, and the resulting embryo or embryos implanted in the infertile woman's (the recipient's) womb. Should both partners be infertile, or both be carriers of genetic disease, egg and sperm donors may be used, and an embryo created and implanted in the woman's womb which is genetically unrelated to either partner.

The first question arising from egg donation is: who is the legal mother of the child? Is it the donor, or the woman who carries and bears the child? At common law this was disputable.[17] Section 27(1) of the Human Fertilisation and Embryology Act gives a clear answer:

> The woman who is carrying or has carried a child as a result of the placing in her of an embryo or of sperm and eggs, *and no other woman* [my italics], is to be treated as the mother of the child.

The woman who gives birth to the child is its mother. The genetic 'mother' has no legal claim on the child, nor has he any claim on her.

16. See s. 28, discussed above.
17. See the first edition of this book, pp. 192–5.

When the infertile woman's partner provides the sperm, the legal status of the child is thus identical to a child naturally conceived by that woman. If donor sperm are used, the same rules deeming the male partner to be the legal father apply as apply to any use of AI in a licensed clinic.

If the Human Fertilisation and Embryology Act clarifies the legal status of a child born as a result of egg donation or embryo transplant, are there any remaining legal or ethical problems related to the procedure? Warnock saw no ethical objection to egg donation as such. They regarded it as the female counterpart of AI. Clearly anyone objecting to the separation of sexual intercourse and procreation, or to the use of third parties for reproductive purposes, will object to egg donation as they oppose AI. But such objections are confined to a relatively small sector of society.

One general concern about egg donation focuses on the collection of eggs from the donor. Unlike AI, egg donation requires a surgical procedure, an invasion of the donor's body. Her consent is therefore essential if the doctor is to avoid liability for battery. Two problems exist with consent to egg donation. First, to collect only one egg at a time is a pretty futile exercise. Standard IVF practice is to give a woman drugs to induce her to super-ovulate, to produce several eggs at once. A number of eggs are then fertilized, the best embryos are implanted, defective embryos are disposed of, and 'spare' embryos are frozen for possible future use. Super-ovulation carries certain risks to the health and in a very, very few cases to the life of the woman.[18] A woman undergoing IVF runs identical risks, but she does so to have 'her' baby. Egg donors are asked to be a means to an end. They are asked to risk harm with no prospect of benefit to themselves. Healthy volunteers who agree to participate in medical research are invited to act in a similarly altruistic manner. It could not be right to prohibit altruism, but what is quite clear is that there must be no doubt that the donor has given full and free consent. She should be given as much information as possible about the risks of egg collection. The *Sidaway*[19] standard of requiring only such disclosure of information as responsible professional opinion requires is as inappropriate in this context as it is in relation to research on volunteers.[20]

18. See Morgan and Lee, op. cit., pp. 120–21.
19. See above, pp. 82–5.
20. See below, pp. 417–18.

A further difficulty about consent to egg donation lies in the recruitment of donors. In its submission to Warnock the RCOG suggested that eggs might 'conveniently' be collected from patients undergoing sterilization or hysterectomy. Such action might be seen as avoiding unnecessary surgical interference by using women already scheduled for surgery. However, the procedure for actually collecting eggs is itself now relatively simple and risk-free. The risks centre on super-ovulation. So a woman asked to donate eggs concurrently with other surgery is in effect asked to agree to a further risky and, for her, unnecessary procedure. Will she be in a proper state of mind to give a full and free consent? Will she feel constrained to 'help out' the doctor treating her? Of particular concern has been the practice of some private clinics in offering free sterilization to women who agree to be donors. Waiting lists for NHS sterilizations can be lengthy. For a woman to be offered a private sterilization free of charge may be a powerful inducement to agree to donate eggs. The Human Fertilisation and Embryology Act prohibits payments, of money or other benefits, for eggs and sperm (gametes), unless authorized by directions from the HFEA.[21] The ILA condemned inducements to persuade women to be egg donors by offering free sterilizations, or, in the NHS, promotion up the waiting list, to donors.[22] The risks of super-ovulation and the implications of the decision to donate eggs, to give another woman 'your' child, are such that egg donation should be independent of other medical treatment of the donor. It should be allowed and recognized as an act of pure and properly informed altruism.

The need for surgical intervention, however minor, and, perhaps, differences in attitude to eggs and sperm mean that egg donors tend to be thinner on the ground than sperm donors. Men have millions of sperm. Women have far, far fewer eggs, and seem less happy about donating their genetic material. A number of women appeared to be prepared to donate eggs to an infertile sister or close friend, but not to the world at large. The ILA expressed strong doubts about the ethics of sister-to-sister donation. Their guidelines prohibit the use of known donors, including close relatives. There was concern about problems of identity for the child, and potential conflicts between its 'mothers'.[23] No prohibition on such donations is made by the Human Fertilisation

21. See s. 12(e).
22. See ILA Report.
23. See ILA guideline 13(j).

and Embryology Act, but it seems likely that the HFEA will continue to discourage such donations.

Freezing gametes and embryos

It is now possible to freeze and store eggs, sperm and embryos. Freezing eggs has so far had limited success. Only a tiny minority of eggs when thawed will fertilize successfully. Freezing sperm has been routine for several years now. The sperm can be thawed and retain its potency. Freezing embryos is relatively new but appears to be successful. The first British baby to 'start life' as a frozen embryo was born in Manchester in 1985.

Storage of gametes and eggs is lawful only if licensed by the HFEA,[24] and the Act prescribes a maximum statutory storage period of ten years for gametes and five years for embryos.[25] The technology to freeze gametes and embryos has advanced techniques of assisted conception. A man undergoing chemotherapy and fearing that treatment may damage his sperm can have sperm stored for later use. A couple undergoing IVF can have several embryos created, and the 'surplus' stored for later attempts at pregnancy if the first effort fails, or for a second child if all goes well. Several sets of IVF 'twins', actually born years apart, have now been delivered.

The problems arising from freezing embryos are these. Is the process safe and, if so, for how long can gametes and embryos safely be stored? Is the process acceptable to society? And who decides the ultimate fate of stored gametes and embryos? Experience appears now to have established that healthy babies can be born from frozen sperm and embryos. How long such material can safely be stored remains in dispute. In opting for maximum storage periods of ten years for gametes and five years for embryos the Act has sought to impose limits recognized as safe today. The long-term implications of the freezing process cannot be known until children born from stored gametes and embryos become adults and have children of their own. As to the acceptability of freezing, it is difficult to see why, if AI and IVF are acceptable, freezing should not be, with one *caveat*. It would be just about possible to practise IVF creating one embryo at a time

24. s. 4.
25. See s. 14(4)(5). Section 14(5) allows for reduction or extension of these periods by regulations.

and implanting that embryo. Success rates would drop dramatically, but there would be no 'surplus' embryos. Freezing is designed to deal with that surplus. The process inevitably means that at the end of the storage period there will be embryos left unused. The Act requires that such embryos be 'allowed to perish'.[26] Those who regard the embryo as having from fertilization the same rights as a born human person must necessarily oppose a process that inevitably means the destruction of some embryos.

As to the fate of embryos in storage, we shall see that the Act requires anyone storing gametes or embryos to decide what may or may not be done with those embryos before any treatment begins. The donors of the genetic material decide its fate in foreseeable circumstances. Not all problems can ever be eliminated altogether. In Texas a couple separated while they still had several frozen embryos in storage. The wife sought to have embryos implanted in her womb. Her husband opposed such a move and sought destruction of the embryos. A judge awarded the 'mother' custody of 'her' embryos. The policy of the Human Fertilisation and Embryology Act is to attempt to avoid such conflict by requiring couples to take decisions about what may happen to 'their' embryos before such embryos are created.

Regulating assisted conception

The Human Fertilisation and Embryology Act provides no more than a basic framework of the rules governing assisted conception in the United Kingdom. The Act entrusts to the Human Fertilisation and Embryology Authority (HFEA) powers to fill in the details of those rules and to regulate the practical and ethical problems of assisted conception. Two crucial ground rules are however to be found in the Act and deserve special mention here.

First, section 12(e) prohibits payment for gametes (eggs or sperm) or embryos unless payment is authorized by directions from the HFEA. It has never been the practice in this country to make direct payments for eggs or embryos, although, as we saw, indirect inducements have been offered to potential egg donors. Payments for sperm have been routine. Advertisements appear in local and student newspapers in teaching hospital areas, and private AI clinics offering £10 and £25 per donation. That may seem a small sum but represents several visits to

26. s. 14(1)(c).

the pub for an impecunious student. AI clinics hope that the HFEA will be generous in its attitude to continuing payments. They fear that without payments sperm donors will become a scarce commodity. But is it right to pay sperm donors? In the UK the governing philosophy for donation of all other products has rested on the 'gift relationship'.[27] Blood is given freely. It is a criminal offence to buy or sell a kidney.[28] It can scarcely be ethical to pay for sperm but not eggs, when egg donors face greater risk and trauma. Donation of eggs or sperm should be allowed only as a considered act of altruism. There may be no physical risk in donating sperm, but have the young donors considered the implications of their act? How might they feel if later in life they are unable to have children of their own?

The main argument *for* paying for sperm is the problem of supply. Perhaps British clinics should look to a wider source of donors than, as at present, students, and mainly medical students at that. In France all donations are made without payment. The donor must be a mature man who has proved his paternity. Normally the consent of his partner will also be obtained. Donation becomes a 'couple-to-couple' donation and there seem to be no problems with finding suitable donors.

The second ground rule to be found in the Act focuses on consent to treatment and donation. The Act expressly recognizes in Schedule 3 the crucial importance of free and informed consent in assisted conception. Before a valid consent can be given, be it to IVF treatment, or the storage of gametes (eggs or sperm) or embryos, or donation of gametes, the potential patient or donor must be '. . . given a suitable opportunity to receive proper counselling about the implications of taking the proposed steps'.[29] And he or she must be provided with such relevant information as is proper.[30] Consent to the use of any embryo must specify whether it is for the use only of the couple seeking treatment, or may be used to treat another couple, or may be used for research purposes.[31] The capacity to fertilize several embryos and freeze 'surplus' embryos means that once a couple seeking IVF

---

27. See Richard Titmuss's seminal book *The Gift Relationship: From Human Blood to Social Policy*, Allen & Unwin, London, 1971.
28. See the Human Organs Transplant Act 1989, discussed fully in Chapter 18.
29. Sched, 3, para. 3.
30. Whether 'proper' is defined by reference to professional opinion (the *Sidaway* standard) or a patient/donor-centred standard remains undecided.
31. Sched, 3, para 2.

have completed their family, those 'surplus' embryos will not be needed by them. 'Their' embryos cannot be given to another couple or used for research purposes without their consent. Similar rules apply to the storage of gametes.[32] Consent given to the storage of gametes must specify what is to be done with the gametes if the donor dies. The rules detailing the matters consent under the Act must cover serve two purposes. (1) They assign to the people providing embryos or gametes the right to decide what is done with their genetic material, allaying fears that by agreeing to IVF treatment they give up any right to control the fate of 'their' embryos. (2) They ensure that provision is made to decide on the fate of embryos and gametes should the donors meet with death or disaster.[33] In Australia just such a dilemma arose. A wealthy couple sought IVF treatment. They died in an air crash, leaving several embryos in storage in the state of Victoria. The husband's children by his first marriage vehemently opposed use of the embryos, fearing any resultant child might claim a share in their inheritance. No child now born in England could claim from his dead 'parents'' estate. Whether he should ever have the chance to be born at all is a decision his genetic parents are required to take before any attempt at his creation is begun.

The HFEA will have to operate within the framework set by the Act, but many decisions will be left to them. We have seen some examples already – should sister-to-sister egg donation be banned, should egg collection concurrent with sterilization be allowed? The developments in the techniques of assisted conception will all pose new problems for the HFEA. One matter which concerned Warnock may also concern the HFEA. How often should gametes from one donor be used? The more often sperm from one donor is used the higher the risk grows of unwitting incest. Warnock proposed that no single donor be used for more than ten inseminations.[34] Some of the problems that will confront the HFEA will lie on the borderline between assisted conception and embryo research. Techniques developed in the late 1980s allow scientists to discover the sex of the embryo. In 1990 pre-implantation diagnosis was used to enable women who were carriers

32. Sched. 3, para 3.
33. The HFEA may give further directions as to what additional matters must be covered in the patients' consent. The fate of embryos on divorce for example is not required to be dealt with by the Act.
34. p. 27 in the Report. See HFEA Code of Practice, para. 7.10.

of congenital disease affecting only males to have female embryos implanted. Should the HFEA place limits on pre-implantation diagnoses? Or should parents be left free to choose the sex of the embryo?

Grand ethical issues will certainly face the members of the HFEA. Their everyday difficulties may be more mundane. The overwhelming problem will be to decide whether to license clinics with poor success rates. IVF is not a very successful treatment as yet. Pregnancy rates in the best centres remain less than 20 per cent with actual births running at less than 15 per cent a treatment cycle. Small, less well-equipped centres achieve less than 5 per cent success, some centres having virtually nil births to their credit. The HFEA must decide whether to refuse to license the unsuccessful clinics. It should certainly publish its data identifying the 'poor' clinics. Patients embarking on the trauma and, in the private sector, the expense of IVF treatment deserve to know what prospects of success they enjoy.[35]

What should the child be told?

Should a child born as a result of assisted conception be told the manner of his conception? A child born as a result of IVF treatment in which his parents provided the egg and sperm is little different from the child born by Caesarean section. The actual manner of conception and birth may be of some interest to him but is unlikely to affect his sense of identity and family relationships. But if donor sperm or eggs are used, has the child the right to know the identity of his genetic parents? An adopted child has at 18 a right of access to his original birth certificate and so has the opportunity to trace his natural parents.[36] AI has tended to be shrouded in secrets. The provisions of the Human Fertilisation and Embryology Act deem a child to be the child of the woman who carries him and her husband or partner, whatever his true genetic origins. Yet if an adopted child may trace his birth mother and genetic father, why should children born from gamete donation be denied a similar right?

Warnock recommended that donors should retain their anonymity for two reasons. First, infertile couples seek to have 'their' child, not to adopt someone else's. Treatment and the legal rules governing treatment should respect their wishes. Second, considerable fears are

---

35. The ILA never identified the success rates of actual clinics.
36. Adoption Act 1976, s. 51.

expressed that donors will not come forward if they may face the prospect of years later being confronted by their 'children', with consequent disruption to any family they may by then have founded. None the less Warnock saw that children might have a need for basic genetic information to protect their health or that of their own offspring. And steps had to be taken against siblings unwittingly marrying each other.[37] Hence the Human Fertilisation and Embryology Act adopts a compromise. Section 31 provides that the HFEA shall keep a register detailing the provision of treatment services and the use of gametes. At the age of 18 a person may, after proper counselling, request information from that register. Section 31(4)(b) provides that information *will* include information about whether or not the applicant and a person whom he proposes to marry are related. And section 31(4)(a) provides that such other information relating to the applicant 'as the Authority is required by regulations to give' shall be made available to him. Thus, the HFEA will decide later exactly how much information children born from gamete or embryo donation may be entitled to. The wording of section 31(4)(a) is such that HFEA would be free to decide that the information should include the *identity* of the child's genetic parents, the gamete donors.

Section 31(4)(a) caused uproar in AI circles. Prohibiting payments to sperm donors was bad enough, destroying anonymity was regarded as a near fatal blow for AI. Hence at a late stage in the Act's passage through Parliament, section 31(5) was inserted, ensuring that the removal of anonymity cannot be retrospective. If anonymity prevailed when sperm was donated, a later change in the rules will not give children access to the identity of the donor. The debate about whether anonymity should be preserved for all time goes on. Now that donors can never be legally liable to maintain any child born as a result of donation, the case for preserving anonymity seems weak. If donation is seen as an ethical, altruistic act why must it be kept secret? Above all it must be recognized that what should be paramount are the rights and interests of the child, not those of the parents or the donors. If adopted children need to know the identity of their genetic parents, why are the needs of children born from gamete or embryo donation less pressing?

37. See the Report, pp. 24–5.

Access to assisted conception

Does the law play any role in determining who has access to assisted conception? We saw that the Human Fertilisation and Embryology Act seeks to discourage the provision of any form of assisted conception to single women. But even for couples access may be hard to obtain. IVF treatment is largely provided in the private sector, with very limited NHS facilities for those who cannot pay for treatment. NHS clinics have to make hard choices and many operate criteria based on the likelihood that patients will be good parents. Some follow adoption guidelines used by local social services departments. Most will offer treatment only where neither partner has any existing children.

One disappointed patient took an IVF clinic to court.[38] Mrs Harriott was a patient at St Mary's Hospital, Manchester. She was ultimately refused IVF because of a criminal record for prostitution offences and because she and her husband had been rejected as prospective adoptive or foster parents by Manchester social services department. The clinicians referred her case to the hospital's informal ethical advisory committee, who endorsed their decision. She sought judicial review of that decision, alleging that the grounds for refusing her treatment were unreasonable and unlawful. The judge held that decisions on IVF treatment could be reviewed by a court. If a patient was refused treatment on grounds, say, of religion or ethnic origin, that would be clearly unlawful. Public bodies and officials, including clinicians taking decisions within the NHS, must act reasonably and not on the basis of irrational prejudices. But in Mrs Harriott's case the judge found that the grounds for regarding her to be an unsuitable parent were reasonable. That suitability for parenthood is a valid consideration in determining who should receive treatment is reinforced by section 13(5) of the Act directing those providing treatment services to take into account the welfare of the child. It would seem clear that for the moment at least English law rejects any rights to be assisted to reproduce.

38. R. v. *Ethical Advisory Committee of St Mary's Hospital ex p. Harriott.* [1988] IFLR 512

Liability for disability

What if an attempt to help a patient overcome infertility results not in the birth of a healthy child but in the birth of a disabled infant? This could happen for several reasons. In AI the donor may turn out to be the carrier of some disease or congenital defect. Babies have already been born abroad suffering from HIV contracted from donor sperm. An error may be made in the laboratory, damaging an IVF embryo. Or perhaps there is negligence in the process of screening embryos and a defective embryo is returned to the womb. Finally, the very process of IVF and freezing might in years to come be shown to produce abnormalities manifesting themselves only when the children reach maturity or try to have children themselves.

The legal questions are these. (1) Can the parents and/or the child bring an action against the doctors and the clinic concerned? (2) Will they be able to prove negligence? (3) Are there any specific defences available to the defendants?

The parents' right to sue is unproblematic. Parents will be able to maintain an action against the doctors and the clinic if mother or child is injured by negligence. Clearly if the mother herself suffers any injury, for example in the course of collecting eggs, she may recover compensation for that injury. The hospital or clinic will be in breach of its duty of care to her. But that duty of care extends beyond the mother's immediate physical health to the safety of her child. The woman accepted for treatment expects care, not only in relation to herself, but also in the 'production' of a healthy infant. If, by negligence, the child is born disabled, damage to the parents is readily foreseeable. Both mother and father will suffer emotional trauma and face the added expense of bringing up a disabled child. Is there a problem if the parents cannot pinpoint exactly who was negligent? It may be impossible for them to know if the embryo was damaged by the gynaecologist removing the eggs and implanting the embryo, or by the scientists in the laboratory. In NHS clinics, the health authority or NHS trust owes a direct duty to the parents and is responsible for negligently failing to discharge that duty. In the private sector patients should ensure that the clinic similarly undertakes a contractual duty to provide and underwrite the whole course of treatment.[39] One final point relating to actions by parents is that while they may have legal redress if a

39. See above, pp. 157–8.

damaged baby is born, there will be no legal remedy if no baby is born. Success rates for IVF remain low, less than 20 per cent at best, neither NHS nor private clinics undertaking more than to attempt to assist conception using all due skill and care.

What of an action by the child itself? He will need to rely on the right of action in respect of pre-birth injuries enacted in the Congenital Disabilities (Civil Liability) Act 1976. On the original wording of the 1976 Act it was dubious whether negligence in assisted conception fell within the ambit of the Act. The Act covered cases where injury resulted from a parent being harmed in his or her reproductive capacity, or the child suffering injury in the womb or course of its birth. Damage in the actual process of conception was hard to fit into either category. The Human Fertilisation and Embryology Act expressly amends the 1976 Act to allow for an action arising out of negligence in the process of assisted conception. Section 44 inserts into the 1976 Act a new section 1A which provides for an action if a child carried by a woman as a result of the placing in her of an embryo, or sperm and eggs, or AI, is born disabled, and the disability results from negligence in the selection, or keeping or use outside the body, of the relevant embryo or gametes. Providing the defendant is answerable in tort to one or both of the parents, he is liable too to the child. The sorts of cases envisaged by this new section 1A are thus just the examples I mentioned earlier – the child born HIV positive because doctors failed to screen donors adequately, the child born damaged by some technical error in his creation, and the child born disabled because a defective embryo was negligently returned to the mother. A further extension to the rights of the child is made in section 35(4) of the 1990 Act, again amending the 1976 Act, to provide that injury to the reproductive capacity of the genetic parent gives rise to a derivative action under the 1976 Act for the child. Sections 34 and 35 of the 1990 Act make extensive provision for disclosure of information necessary to any action by parent or child for damages occasioned by assisted conception.

None the less, one difficulty facing an action by the child remains. If the essence of his action is for 'wrongful life', not 'wrongful disability', then, as we have seen from the Court of Appeal's judgement in *McKay* v. *Essex AHA*,[40] no action can lie. Much will then turn on *how* it is alleged the child came to suffer injury. If it is claimed that gametes and

40. [1982] 2 All ER 771, CA, discussed above, pp. 241–3.

embryo were originally healthy, but damaged by some act of the doctors or scientists treating the mother, the claim is for 'wrongful disability'. It is in effect on a par with a claim that a healthy foetus was damaged *in utero* by drugs given to the mother or surgery on her. But what if the alleged negligence is that infected sperm was used to inseminate the mother or a defective embryo implanted in her? Such a claim must logically be classified as a 'wrongful life' claim. Assume these facts. An AI clinic negligently fails to check donors for HIV. Baby X is born with HIV from contaminated sperm. Had the clinic exercised due care in the collection of sperm, that individual, Baby X, would never had been born at all. Similarly if a defective embryo is not screened and discarded in the laboratory, any action the child brings is for 'wrongful life'. His parents could, 'but for' the relevant negligence, have had a healthy child. It would not have been that child.

Both parents and children seeking compensation for disability may face acute problems actually proving negligence where it is difficult to isolate the cause of the damage to the child. A baby resulting from AI born HIV positive or clearly afflicted by a genetic disease carried by the father poses no legal problem in an action by his parents. Competent screening should have discovered the disease or defect and that sperm should never have been used to inseminate the mother. Linking a defect to an error in the laboratory will be far from easy. An action based on abnormalities manifesting themselves later in life is almost bound to fail. If say in 2005 it is shown that freezing embryos produces cancer in the late teens and early twenties, the defence to any claim in negligence will be that responsible professional opinion, endorsed by countless official reports, believed freezing to be safe in 1990.

Finally, if parent or child has a right to sue and proves negligence, are there defences open to the doctor based on the parents having agreed to run the risk of a damaged child or the mother's refusal to terminate the pregnancy when the defect was diagnosed *in utero*? Section 44(3) provides that an action by the child shall fail if either or both parents knew of the risk of their child being born disabled '. . . that is to say, the particular risk created by the act of omission'. So if the mother is known to carry a genetic disease herself and is counselled that it would be better to use donor eggs for an IVF pregnancy yet insists on a child that is genetically hers, she cannot turn round and sue the doctors who carried out her wishes, if that genetic problem is inherited by her child. However, it would be no defence for a defendant simply to say, 'Well, parents know that this is a relatively new and risky process, so I am not liable.' The parents must be aware of the particular risk of harming their child. Quite often the risk of harm to an IVF or GIFT baby arises from the increased danger of a multiple pregnancy. A parent who was not fully counselled on this risk might argue that not warning of that particular risk was negligent. Of course, to succeed in an action she would then have to prove that had she been warned she would not have gone ahead with the treatment.

IVF pregnancies are carefully monitored, so that any abnormality in the foetus is likely to be discovered well before birth. The mother will be offered an abortion. The Court of Appeal in *Emeh* v. *Kensington, Chelsea and Fulham AHA*[41] has held that a refusal to terminate a pregnancy did not constitute either a *novus actus* or contributory negligence where the mother sued for the birth of a child subsequent to a negligently performed sterilization. In the context of IVF it might be contended that: (1) *Emeh* is distinguishable because abortion in this case is to prevent the birth of a damaged child – Slade LJ in *Emeh* did after all leave open the question of whether it might be unreasonable to refuse an abortion for which there were 'medical' grounds;[42] (2) doctors might further argue that before treatment mothers will have been told of the extensive screening and monitoring programme in IVF pregnancies and have in effect agreed to the whole package. It remains my view that an argument that a mother can be held contributorily negligent, or responsible for the birth of her disabled child, because she refuses to abort is neither good law nor good ethics.

Surrogate mothers

I have left until last what is for many people the most emotive issue of all, surrogacy. Surrogacy may take a number of forms. The most common arrangement so far is this. A surrogate agrees to artificial insemination with the male partner's sperm. She agrees to carry any resulting child and to hand the child over to the father and his wife, or partner, immediately it is born. But IVF offers a couple where the woman does ovulate, but cannot safely carry a child to term, the chance of a baby who is genetically theirs. Eggs are taken from the woman, fertilized in the laboratory with sperm from the man, and the embryo implanted in the surrogate. The surrogate once again carries

41. [1984] 3 All ER 1044, discussed above, pp. 245–7.
42. p. 1053.

the child and agrees to hand it over at birth. The surrogate is in effect merely a 'hostess' for the couple's embryo. Surrogacy in all its forms has attracted vociferous condemnation in Britain. The greatest outcry is against commercial surrogacy, where the couple approach and pay an agency who find the surrogate and make all the necessary arrangements. 'Buying babies' is seen as repugnant and distasteful. After the Warnock Report the one swift response from the government was to ban commercial surrogacy.[43] Warnock went further, and would have prohibited any third party, commercial agency or doctor, from assisting a couple to arrange a surrogate pregnancy. Warnock proposed to ban both forms of surrogacy, whether the child is genetically the child of the surrogate or of the couple.[44]

What are the legal issues arising out of surrogacy? There are three. Can it ever amount to a crime to arrange a surrogate pregnancy? What happens if the surrogate changes her mind and refuses to hand the baby over? Where the baby is genetically that of the wife and implanted in the surrogate via IVF, what are the rights of the genetic parents?

Surrogacy where no money changes hands is perfectly lawful in the sense that no crime is committed. Once payment is made to the surrogate or an agency, however, an offence is committed. The Surrogacy Arrangements Act 1985 makes it a criminal offence for anyone to play any part in setting up a surrogacy arrangement on a commercial basis. Advertising or compiling information to promote or assist surrogacy arrangements are also made criminal. Offenders face a punishment of a fine and/or up to three months in prison. Under the Act, no offence is committed by a woman herself seeking to become, or becoming, a surrogate, nor is any offence committed by the man or the couple who persuade her to carry the child. The Act is limited to banning the activities of any commercial agencies or individuals aiming to make a profit out of surrogate motherhood. Under the Act, a gynaecologist who helps an infertile couple choose a suitable surrogate to carry a child for them incurs no criminal liability so long as he does not charge for his services. The Warnock proposal that *any* third-party intervention, including professional help from a doctor, which was intended to set up a surrogacy arrangement should be made illegal has not been acted on. The 1985 Act does, however, embrace all forms of surrogacy regardless of whether the surrogate is the genetic mother or

43. Surrogacy Arrangements Act 1985.
44. p. 46.

merely the 'hostess' for an embryo created from the ova and sperm of the infertile couple.[45]

Although the surrogate and the couple engaging her services do not commit any offence under the 1985 Act even if she is paid for what she does, all three involved may be guilty of an offence under the Adoption Act 1976.[46] For it is a criminal offence, punishable by a fine or up to six months in prison, to give or receive any payment in relation to the adoption of a child, the grant of consent to adoption, or the handing over of a child with a view to its adoption, unless that payment is authorized by a court. In order to make the baby born to the surrogate certainly and legally theirs, where the surrogate is the child's genetic mother, the infertile couple must ultimately adopt the child. If the fee paid to the surrogate is found to include a sum in payment for her agreement to the adoption and handing over the child, the surrogate and the prospective adopters may face prosecution. Moreover, the Adoption Act further provides that the court may order the infant to be removed to a place of safety 'until ho can be restored to his parents or guardians or until other arrangements can be made for him'. So the child could in theory be removed from all those involved in the surrogacy arrangements and given in the end to fresh adopters. But would such drastic action make any sort of sense if that surrogate was happy to hand over the baby, and there was no reason to believe that the commissioning couple were unfit to care for the child? How to respond to such a surrogacy case was a dilemma which confronted Barnet Social Services in 1985. A baby girl was born in their area amid great publicity. Her mother had agreed to carry her for a childless couple from abroad. She was artificially inseminated with the husband's sperm. The arrangements were made through an agency who were paid £13,000 by the father, of which the surrogate received £6,500. At the relevant time the Surrogacy Arrangements Act had not yet been enacted. The baby was born and the mother prepared to hand her over. Barnet Social Services stepped in. Eventually the little girl was made a ward of court. Latey J.[47] had to decide on her fate. He said that the crucial issue before him was what was best for this baby. The

45. The 1985 Act will apply however the embryo came to be created, be it by GIFT or IVF; see s. 36 of the Human Fertilisation and Embryology Act 1990.
46. s. 57.
47. *In re a Baby, The Times*, 15 January 1985.

methods used to create the child and the commercial aspects of the case raised delicate problems of ethics, morality and social desirability. They were not for him to decide. Careful inquiries showed that the father and his wife were eminently suitable to be parents. The judge granted them custody of the baby and permission to take her abroad with them to their home. The question of adoption and so the illegality of any payments under the Adoption Act did not arise in that case.

Barnet Social Services were criticized for intervening at all. But what else could they do? Had the child later figured in a child abuse case, opprobrium would have been heaped on Barnet. At a time when surrogacy was neither effectively prohibited nor properly regulated, making any baby so born a ward of court was probably the only option.

Two years after the Barnet case, Latey J. was called on again to adjudicate on the consequences of a surrogacy arrangement where all the parties desired to abide by that arrangement.[48] Mr and Mrs A arranged for Mrs B to carry a child for them. The child was conceived by natural sexual intercourse between Mr A and Mrs B. Mrs B was to be paid £10,000.[49] A baby was born and handed over to Mr and Mrs A after birth. They sought to adopt the child, as they had to do to acquire parental rights. Were they in breach of the Adoption Act and so at risk of losing their child? Latey J. found they were not. He held that the payments were *not* to procure Mrs B's consent to adoption. At the time of the agreement this was not in the parties' minds. The payments were, if anything, in the nature of expenses for Mrs B, some recompense for her time and inconvenience. Furthermore, the judge held that, even if he were wrong and the payments *were* illegal payments, he had power to ratify those payments retrospectively. Payments authorized by the court are not unlawful. As a matter of pure legal reasoning Latey J.'s grounds for finding the payments made by Mr and Mrs A to Mrs B were lawful may well be faulty. What is clear is that Latey J. saw no reason to upset an arrangement which had worked, or to remove the child, now 2, from the only parents it had known. What else could he do? If Parliament wanted to ban surrogacy, it should have done so outright.

So it looks as though if the surrogate is happy to hand the baby

48. *Re an Adoption Application (Surrogacy)* [1987] 2 All ER 826.
49. In the event Mrs B. accepted only £5,000 of the agreed fee, having co-authored a book on her experience of surrogacy.

over, the courts will help the commissioning couple to keep the baby. But what if she changes her mind? First, it is absolutely clear in England that surrogacy agreements are not enforceable as contracts. The commissioning couple cannot sue the surrogate for breach of contract, or ask a court to order performance of a contract. Nor, of course, could the surrogate sue if she did not receive any agreed payments. If there were any doubt[50] on the unenforceability of surrogacy 'contracts', that doubt is eliminated by section 36(a) of the Human Fertilisation and Embryology Act. Section 36(1) inserts a new section 1A in the Surrogacy Arrangements Act 1985, providing quite simply that:

> No surrogacy arrangement is enforceable by or against any of the persons making it.

It does not matter by what means the child was created, be it sexual intercourse, AI or IVF, the arrangement is not an enforceable contract.

That still leaves open the question of what happens if the surrogate wants to keep the baby. In the *Baby M.* case in New Jersey, USA, a surrogate mother Mary Beth Whitehead fought a long, bitter and public battle with her child's genetic father William Stern and his wife Betsy. The Supreme Court of New Jersey[51] quashed the first-instance finding that Mary Beth was bound by her contract with Mr and Mrs Stern. But she still lost her baby. It was found to be in the child's 'best interests' that she be brought up by the Sterns.

In England it seems that if the surrogate changes her mind she will be allowed to keep the child. In *A* v. *C.*[52] as long ago as 1978, a young woman agreed to have a baby by AI and hand over the child to the wealthy father and his partner. She was to be paid £3,000. When the child was born she refused to give him up. The father sought care and control. The first instance judge found that the mother should be allowed to keep the child, but granted the father limited access. The Court of Appeal removed his rights of access, condemning the whole arrangement as 'irresponsible, bizarre and unnatural'. Nor does it

---

50. See the first edition of this book, pp. 197–8.
51. *Baby M.* (1988) 537 A 2d 1227, extracted in Kennedy and Grubb, op. cit., p. 717, and see on p. 719 the detailed 'contract' agreed between Mary Beth Whitehead and the Sterns.
52. [1985] FLR 445 (FD and CA).

seem that greater tolerance of surrogacy, as evidenced in Latey J.'s judgements above, has changed judicial policy where surrogates change their minds. In *Re P. (Minors) (Wardship: Surrogacy)*[53] Sir John Arnold P. refused to order a surrogate mother to hand over twins born as a result of her artificial insemination by the father. It would seem that in England a surrogate would be deprived of her baby only if she were an unfit mother who would not be allowed to keep the child however it had come to be conceived. Surrogacy is an arrangement couples enter into at their peril. If all goes to plan, they will get 'their' baby. If the arrangement breaks down, the law will not assist them in a battle with the surrogate.[54]

Is the position any different where the surrogate is *not* the genetic mother, where the child was created by IVF from the eggs and sperm of the commissioning couple? Prior to the Human Fertilisation and Embryology Act the genetic mother might have argued thus. I am this baby's mother. I do not need to adopt my own child. She (the surrogate) has no right to keep my child from me. That argument is killed stone dead by section 27 of the Act. Section 27 provides, as we have seen, that the woman who carries the child *and no other woman* is to be treated as the mother of the child. However, late in its passage through Parliament a new section, section 30, was inserted in the Act to help some commissioning couples in their surrogacy arrangements. It provides for a procedure, other than adoption, by which some couples will be able to acquire parental rights over 'their' child. The section was introduced by a Cumbrian MP after representations from a couple in his constituency who objected to having to adopt 'their' IVF child.

Section 30 gives the court power to order that the commissioning couple be treated in law as the parents of the child, but *only* in a limited number of circumstances. (1) The couple must be married. So the unmarried couple in *A. v. C.* could not have used this procedure, even had it been available. (2) The child must have been conceived from either the placing of the embryo (IVF) or sperm and eggs (GIFT) in the woman, or by AI. And the eggs or sperm or both must come from the couple. Children conceived by natural intercourse between the surrogate and the husband are not within the ambit of section

53. *Re P. (Minors)(Wardship: Surrogacy)* [1987] 2 FLR 421.
54. For a thorough analysis of the American experience of surrogacy see Martha Field, *Surrogate Motherhood*, Harvard University Press, 1988.

30.[55] (3) At the time of the making of the order the child must be living with the couple, and the surrogate must have given full and free consent not less than six weeks after the birth. Section 30 is of no relevance if the surrogate changes her mind and is not willing to hand over the child. Nor is it a backdoor route to enforcing a surrogacy contract. (4) No payments (other than for expenses reasonably incurred) must have been made to the surrogate unless authorized by the court.

In effect, section 30 is a statutory embodiment of what might be called the Latey approach to surrogacy. If it has worked out and a child is settled with 'its parents', the law should give legal effect to the actual family circumstances prevailing.

The attitude to surrogacy in England now is pragmatic. Keep commercial agencies at bay and otherwise treat each case as it arises. Difficult questions remain unanswered. What happens if the baby is born disabled and no one wants it? What if the commissioning couple split up? Surrogacy is fraught with risk. Experience, particularly in the USA, shows that surrogates tend to be relatively poor and not well-educated, while commissioning couples are better off. So is there a risk of exploitation of young, poor women by wealthy, infertile couples? But could surrogacy be banned effectively? Assisted conception offers new ways of achieving surrogacy but is not essential to surrogacy. As we have seen, it can just as easily be achieved by normal sexual intercourse between the father and the surrogate. Cases where couples resort to surrogacy are often among the saddest of infertility cases. The woman cannot conceive because she has lost her uterus through surgery or premature menopause. Some of the opposition to surrogacy seems to rest on a belief that it will lead to hordes of healthy career women using surrogates to avoid the inconvenience of pregnancy. I doubt that will happen more than once in a blue moon.

Conclusion

The Human Fertilisation and Embryology Act has succeeded in providing answers to the awkward questions of the family status and relationships of children born as a result of assisted conception. The fears of conflict between competing sets of 'parents' have been stilled. The

55. As was the case in *Re an Adoption Application (Surrogacy)* (above, note 48).

287

tenor of the Act as it emerged from Parliament is to attempt to limit assisted conception to couples living in a traditional family structure. Whether that will result in a refusal of treatment to all single women will depend very much on the HFEA. The Act does nothing to make assisted conception more accessible to infertile couples of limited means. NHS clinics will still have to make hard choices as to who deserves a baby. Finally IVF is inextricably linked to embryo research. The battle to ban or limit such research will not be abandoned after one defeat. If research is banned IVF and so much of assisted conception will go with it.

Addendum: the Code of Practice

The practical working of the Human Fertilisation and Embryology Act can only be fully understood if read together with the HFEA Code of Practice and, where relevant, HFEA directions issued to implement the Act. Only the briefest summary of these matters is possible. The distinguishing feature of the Code of Practice is the priority given to protecting patients and ensuring that donors are fully informed and properly counselled. The HFEA has not sought to place more difficulties in the path of single women seeking AI or IVF. It has affirmed the ILA prohibition on implanting more than three embryos in IVF. Payment for sperm has not yet been outlawed, but payment levels are frozen and the ultimate intent is to move to a genuine donation system. On research the HFEA has as yet given little concrete guidance. Sorting out the practicalities of implementing the Act has been a hard enough task for the first year's work.

CHAPTER 13

Abortion and Embryo Research

Few medico-legal issues provoke as much bitter public controversy as the legal status of the human embryo. For, if a life given by God begins at conception, the deliberate destruction of any embryo, be it in the course of embryo research, or by abortion, is the equivalent of murder. The killing of the embryo can only be justifiable, if at all, where the mother's life is at risk. But if the human embryo has, as others contend, no greater moral status than a mouse embryo, neither research nor abortion is morally wrong. And for many feminists a right to abortion is part and parcel of the woman's rights over her own body. The present law on abortion represents in many respects an attempt to reach a compromise in a debate in which there is no consensus. In 1990 Parliament enacted the Human Fertilisation and Embryology Act permitting embryo research up to fourteen days, and also sanctioning abortion in certain cases up to the moment of birth. 'Pro-life' campaigners have vowed to go on fighting to ban research and to restrict abortion. The law is controversial and complex. There is little hope that the legal and ethical problems surrounding the human embryo will ever be satisfactorily resolved. I shall examine the law relating to early abortion first, and then return to the vexed question of embryo research.

Criminal abortion

The present law relating to criminal abortion is to be found in section 58 of the Offences Against the Person Act 1861. This statute makes it a criminal offence punishable by a maximum of life imprisonment (1) for any woman, being with child, unlawfully to do any act with intent to procure a miscarriage, and (2) for any other person unlawfully to do an act with intent to procure the miscarriage of any woman. Self-induced abortion by the woman herself is therefore criminal only if the woman is in fact pregnant. Any act by a third party is criminal regardless of whether or not the woman can be proved to be pregnant. This limited protection afforded to the woman extends only to cases where she acts entirely alone. If she seeks help from a doctor, or any other person, she may be charged with aiding and abetting that person to commit the offence of criminal abortion[1] or of conspiracy with him to commit that offence.[2] The law embodied in the 1861 Act was applied rigorously up to 1967. In one case in 1927, a girl of 13 was prosecuted for attempting to induce an abortion on herself by taking laxative tablets and sitting in a hot bath. The rigour of the law was tempered by a defence to a charge of criminal abortion by a doctor, that he acted to preserve the life or health of the mother.[3] At no time in England was abortion absolutely prohibited so as to require the mother to be sacrificed for her unborn child. Indeed, in *R.* v. *Bourne*,[4] acquitting a doctor of a charge of criminal abortion, the judge suggested that there might be a *duty* to abort to save the 'yet more precious' life of the mother. But the extent of the defence available to doctors was unclear. Some doctors interpreted this defence liberally as including the mother's mental health and even happiness. Others would intervene only to prevent a life-threatening complication of pregnancy endangering the woman. Illegal abortion flourished. And several thousand women were admitted to hospital for treatment after back-street abortions. The Abortion Act 1967 was introduced to bring uniformity into the law, to clarify the law for the doctors, and to stem the misery and injury resulting from unhygienic, risky illegal abortions.

The Abortion Act 1967

This Act provides that abortion may be lawfully performed under certain conditions. A pregnancy may be terminated by a registered medical practitioner if *two* registered medical practitioners are of the opinion, formed in good faith, that grounds specified in the Act are met. These grounds are (1) that the continuance of the pregnancy

1. *R.* v. *Sockett* (1908) 72 JP 428.
2. *R.* v. *Whitchurch* (1890) 24 QBD 420.
3. *R.* v. *Bourne* [1939] 1 KB 687.
4. ibid., p. 693.

would involve risk to the life of the pregnant woman, or of injury to her physical or mental health, or that of the existing children of her family, greater than if the pregnancy were terminated, and (2) that there is a substantial risk that if the child were born it would suffer from such physical or mental abnormalities as to be seriously handicapped. In assessing any risk to the health of the woman or her children, account may be taken of the woman's actual or reasonably foreseeable environment. Exceptionally one registered medical practitioner may act alone when he is of the opinion that an abortion is immediately necessary to save the life of the woman or to prevent grave permanent injury to her physical or mental health. Section 4 of the Act provides that no person shall be under any duty to participate in the performance of an abortion if he has a conscientious objection to abortion, save where immediate treatment is necessary to save the life of the woman or to prevent grave permanent damage to her health.[5]

The furore surrounding the 1967 Act intensified rather than abated after the Act became law. Clinics offering abortions proliferated, and there was suspicion that some clinics were scrupulous neither about observing the conditions laid down by the Act, nor in their care of their patients. A committee was set up, headed by a woman judge, Dame Elizabeth Lane. She reported in 1974,[6] and certain changes were made relating to the approval of clinics operating outside the NHS. Critics of the Act were not satisfied. Clear evidence was emerging that women could obtain an abortion on request from some gynaecologists. On the other hand claims were made that there were also, and still are, areas of the country where the Act is so restrictively interpreted that abortions are not much easier to obtain than before the Act was passed. In the latter case the only legal remedy would be for a woman to sue if she did suffer damage to her health as a result of the continuance of a pregnancy, or gave birth to a handicapped child, and successfully persuaded a court that the refusal of the abortion was negligent and unreasonable.[7] Unless her request for abortion was on the ground of manifest damage to her health or perhaps of foetal handicap, her hopes of success in legal action might be slim.

5. See *Janaway* v. *Salford AHA* [1988] 3 All ER 1051, HL, discussed below, p. 307.
6. Report of the Committee on the Working of the Abortion Act (Cmnd 5579).
7. In *McKay* v. *Essex AHA* [1982] 2 WLR 890 (see above, p. 241), a mother claimed that had tests for German measles been properly conducted, she

Abortion on demand or request?

Gynaecologists who admit that they are prepared to perform an abortion simply on the request of the pregnant woman rely on statistics which appear to show that statistically the risk of abortion in the first twelve weeks of pregnancy is always less than the risk of childbirth. Therefore any abortion performed in that period meets the requirement of the Act that the continuance of the pregnancy poses a greater risk to the health of the woman than does termination. The medical profession itself is divided on the validity of the statistics. The issue has never been tested in court. Doctors performing abortions have to make a return to the Department of Health stating the grounds for the operation. Some returns simply stated 'pregnancy' as the grounds. The Department changed its forms in 1982 in an attempt to tighten up on rules for legal abortions. The new form demanded to know the main *medical* condition justifying abortion. Pro-choice doctors continued to return 'pregnancy' as the grounds justifying an operation. No prosecutions have been brought in these cases. A successful prosecution against a doctor performing an abortion on demand would have to establish (a) that the statistics indicating that abortion posed less risk than childbirth were invalid, and (b) that the doctor on trial did not believe them to be valid and so failed to act in good faith. In view of the fact that only one successful prosecution has ever been brought against a doctor for performing an abortion purportedly under the 1967 Act in bad faith,[8] such a course would appear a clumsy means of regulating or eliminating abortion on demand or request. Frequent attempts by Private Members' Bills to amend the Act to require the risk of pregnancy to be *substantially* greater than that of abortion have also failed. The Abortion Act confers on women no right to abortion. By making doctors the 'gatekeepers' for the Act, abortion in England is a privilege granted or withheld at the doctors' discretion.[9]

---

would have known that she had the disease, and had an abortion. Her claim for negligence resulting in the birth of her handicapped daughter is still proceeding. And note *Rance* v. *Mid-Downs HA* [1991] 1 All ER 801, where the parents' claim failed only because by the date termination was feasible the child was 'capable of being born alive'.

8. *R.* v. *Smith (John)* [1974] 1 WLR 1510 CA.

9. Indeed, the history of abortion in England from well before the 1967 Act is

Post-coital birth control and the 'abortion pill'

The 1967 Act envisaged that once a diagnosis of pregnancy had been made, the doctor faced with a request for an abortion would then consider and weigh any risk to the woman or the child. But there is a drug approved for general use which will, if taken by a woman within seventy-two hours of intercourse, ensure that any fertilized ovum will not implant in the womb. This, inaptly named, 'morning-after' pill is not the only means by which a fertilized ovum (egg) may be disposed of at a stage before pregnancy can be confirmed. An intra-uterine device (IUD) fitted within a similar time after intercourse will have the same effect.[10] And finally, if more than seventy-two hours elapse after unprotected intercourse before the woman seeks help, menstrual extraction can be used at or just after the due date of her next period. By this technique, an instrument attached to a vacuum is used to remove the whole of a woman's monthly period within a few minutes, including, if it exists, the product of any unwanted conception.

Are such methods lawful? They raise the question of where the line is to be drawn between contraception and abortion. A distinction must be made between the 'morning-after' pill and the IUD on the one hand, and menstrual extraction on the other. The first two operate at a time before the fertilized ovum can implant in the womb. By the time menstrual extraction is utilized, the ovum will have become an implanted embryo. The action taken to remove that embryo by the vacuum clearly constitutes an induced abortion. The crucial legal issue then, in relation to the use of the 'morning-after' pill and the IUD, is whether a procedure which prevents implantation is an act done to procure a miscarriage so as to make the doctor liable for criminal abortion. The woman herself will not be able to be proved to be with child. She will thus not be guilty of an offence herself, but could, as we have seen, be prosecuted for conspiracy with her doctor. The argument that prevention of implantation is no offence runs thus. There is no carriage of a child by a woman before implantation takes place, and so

---

marked by 'medicalization'; see J. Keown, *Abortion, Doctors and the Law*, CUP, 1988.

10. In *R.* v. *Price* [1969] 1 QB 541, a prosecution for criminal abortion was brought against a doctor who inserted an IUD into a woman who was some months pregnant. The prosecution failed because it was not proved that he knew her to be pregnant.

to prevent that event even occurring cannot be an act done to procure a miscarriage. Many fertilized ova fail to implant naturally and no one then suggests that a miscarriage has occurred. The opponents of post-coital birth control reply that the fertilized ovum is present within the body of the woman; she carries it within her. Therefore there is carriage of a child, and any act removing that child from her womb is an act done to procure a miscarriage. Up to 40 per cent of *implanted* embryos also abort spontaneously. Thus arguments based on spontaneous loss of fertilized ova are irrelevant.

No successful prosecution has ever been brought in respect of either the 'morning-after' pill, or the use of an IUD, as means of post-coital birth control. In 1983[11] the Attorney-General expressed his opinion that prior to implantation there is no pregnancy and so means used to prevent implantation do *not* constitute procuring miscarriage. In 1991 a judge dismissed a prosecution for criminal abortion based on the insertion of an IUD agreeing with the Attorney-General that until implantation there is no pregnancy. The Attorney-General's ruling is persuasive,[12] but not binding on his successors. The matter remains unresolved by higher judicial authority. In practice, however, doctors are prescribing the 'morning-after' pill without any pretence of applying the criteria laid down in the Abortion Act.[13]

Menstrual extraction appears now to be a procedure little used. It was once lauded by feminists as a means of self-abortion, albeit a dangerous one.[14] The development of mifepristone (RU-486), the 'abortion pill', may render menstrual extraction obsolete. Mifepristone is a drug which is administered orally in the first twelve weeks of pregnancy, and will, in most women, induce a complete miscarriage within

11. HC Official Report, 10 May 1983, Col. 238–9.
12. A prosecution under the Abortion Act requires the consent of the DPP. The DPP is answerable to the Attorney-General, so as long as that officer concurs with the opinion given by Sir Michael Havers a prosecution is unlikely to get off the ground: see the Prosecution of Qffences Regulations 1985; and see *R. v. Dhingry* (unreported) (1991).
13. For a stout defence of the legality of the use of the 'morning-after pill' see J. K. Mason, *Human Life and Medical Practice*, Edinburgh University Press, 1988, pp. 90–92. For a contrary view see J. Keown, 'Miscarriage: A Medico-Legal Analysis' [1984] Crim. L.R. 604.
14. For further discussion on menstrual extraction, see the first edition of this book, p. 203.

forty-eight hours or so. A small percentage of women will require a surgical abortion to complete the evacuation of the embryo.[15] Clearly the use of mifepristone is lawful only within the conditions laid down in the 1967 Act. The development of the drug does not in any way change or liberalize the law on abortion. 'Pro-life' campaigners fear, though, that by making abortion 'easier', mifepristone will contribute to the rise in the number of abortions. In France anti-abortion campaigners forced the manufacturers to withdraw the drug. The French government responded by ordering the drug company to resume sales of mifepristone. The drug has been the subject of clinical trials in England and section 37(3) of the Human Fertilisation and Embryology Act clears the way for its routine use in England by authorizing the Secretary of State for Health to approve clinics prescribing the drug. 'Pro-life' campaigners will no doubt continue to believe that the 'abortion pill' is the ultimate development of an abortion, 'anti-life', mentality. What mifepristone does do is to place responsibility for ending her pregnancy on the woman taking the drug. She cannot evade responsibility by seeing the abortion as something done to her. The procedure involves experiencing the pain and distress of a miscarriage. The loss of the embryo will be very evident to her. It is no more likely to be used lightly than recourse to surgical abortion.

Embryo research: the debate[16]

It cannot '. . . be morally preferable to end the life of an embryo *in vivo* than it is to do so *in vitro*'.[17] The law regulating abortion in England now sanctions the killing of thousands of embryos every year.

15. The woman will be asked to agree to undergo surgical abortion should the drug fail to work before being given mifepristone. She cannot of course be forced to go through with the surgical procedure should she later change her mind. But, providing she has been properly warned of the risk of failure and possible adverse effect on the embryo, neither she nor any child damaged by the drug could sue in respect of their injuries. See 'Unfinished Feticide' (1990) 16 J. Med. Ethics 61–70.
16. See generally A. Dyson and J. Harris (eds.), *Experiments on Embryos*, Routledge, London, 1989.
17. J. M. Harris, *The Value of Life*, Routledge & Kegan Paul, London, 1985, p. 117.

Advocates of embryo research ask how society can logically accept abortion yet ban research. If the embryo can be destroyed at its mother's request, how can it be unethical to destroy it in the course of beneficial scientific research? Both camps in the debate on embryo experiment sought to link the questions of abortion and research.[18] But were they right to do so? Does it follow that if we retain laws permitting abortion, we must also allow embryo research?

At the heart of the debate lies the question of the moral status of the developing embryo. When does it acquire the same right to protection as you and I enjoy? Is it at fertilization, when a new unique genetic entity comes into being? Or is it at some later stage in embryonic development? This might be at fourteen days, when the primitive streak forms,[19] or when brain activity, brain life, is first discernible at eight to ten weeks.[20] Or is it much, much later, indeed after birth? One school of philosophy[21] argues thus. Humanity is just another species of animal and as such has no greater moral status than any other animal. What gives rise to moral rights is not being a human animal, but being a person. It is the capacity to value your own existence which gives a person rights, including the right to life. Embryos, and newborn infants, lack that capacity and so are *not* persons.

Each ethical school of thought marshals impressive arguments in support of its thesis. To some extent any argument that the embryo enjoys full human status from fertilization is an argument often resting on theological grounds. If you believe that human life is divinely created in the image of God, and that human beings possess an immortal, immaterial soul, you are unlikely to find any argument based on personhood acceptable. The crucial moment when the embryo acquires humanity becomes ensoulment. Traditionally that moment might be seen as fertilization, but a number of eminent Christian theologians have argued for a later date – either the appearance of the primitive streak as marking clear individuality, or the beginning of

---

18. See M. Brazier, 'Embryos' "Rights": Abortion and Research', in *Medicine, Ethics and Law*, ed. M. D. A. Freeman, Stevens, 1988, pp. 9–23.
19. See the Warnock Report, pp. 63–4.
20. See in particular M. Lockwood, 'When does a life begin?', in M. Lockwood (ed.), *Moral Dilemmas in Medicine*, OUP, 1988.
21. See J. M. Harris, op. cit., pp. 18–25; and 'Embryos and Hedgehogs', in Dyson and Harris (eds.), op. cit., p. 65; and see Jonathan Glover, *Causing Death and Saving Lives*, Penguin, Harmondsworth, 1977.

brain life.[22] Any concept of human life as special *per se* is irrelevant to those who support the personhood thesis.

How does the law respond to such a divergence of moral opinion? Consensus is impossible to attain. Proponents of embryo research argue that no one is compelled to participate in research. A liberal democracy should respect divergent moral views. But that is anathema to 'pro-life' groups. It is rather like saying that if a sufficient number of people decide redheads are not human and have no moral claim on society, anyone who holds that belief may kill off any redhead he meets. Of course, no 'pro-redhead' will be *required* to join in the slaughter! So what is the difference between redheaded adults and embryos? On any analysis the redhead enjoys moral and legal rights. She is without doubt a person. The embryo's true nature is unprovable. I happen to believe that from fertilization the embryo is *very probably* of the same moral value as myself. It is a unique being created in the image of God, in whom I believe. I cannot prove that belief. But then nor can those who maintain that humanity is just another animal species prove their contention. The verdict on the nature of the embryo must be 'not proven'.

What consequences should the 'not-proven' nature of the embryo have for its legal status? It must be accorded recognition and respect. But if its claims to rights conflict with the claims of an entity whose status is beyond doubt, its claims may be subordinated to that entity's. Thus if there is a conflict between the rights of the embryo and the rights of the mother, an indubitably legal person, the mother's rights must take precedence. My belief that the embryo must be respected as fully human from fertilization requires that I reject abortion as an option for myself. As that belief is unprovable, I cannot legitimately enforce it on other women.[23] Embryo research, by contrast, gives rise to no such direct conflict of rights. The question becomes whether society can legitimately destroy an entity which *may* be fully human in

22. See G. R. Dunstan, 'The Moral Status of the Human Embryo: A Tradition Recalled' (1984) 10 J. Med. Ethics, 38; Keith Ward, 'An Irresolvable Debate?', in Dyson and Harris, op. cit., p. 106.
23. For a powerful argument that even if the embryo is presumed to enjoy full human status abortion remains defensible, see J. Jarvis Thompson, 'A Defence of Abortion', in R. M. Dworkin (ed.), *The Philosophy of Law*, 1977, p. 112. But note the response by J. M. Finnis, 'The Rights and Wrongs of Abortion', in the same book, p. 129.

nature and status. The embryo must be given the benefit of the doubt. Of course, justifications have always been advanced for permitting the killing of indubitably human persons in certain cases. It might be argued that the public 'good' expected from embryo research justifies destruction of these 'maybe' human persons. But at the very least the onus of proof lies on those who advocate research.

What are the goods which, it is argued, will flow from research? They include improvements in infertility treatments, particularly IVF, the development of more effective means of contraception, the detection and 'cure' of genetic defects and disease, and, perhaps, the use of early embryonic tissue to transplant into sick adults and children. How realistic the prospect of such advances are, and whether certain of them could be achieved without research on live human embryos, is hotly disputed. It is difficult for a layperson to evaluate the scientific debate, mainly because scientific opinion on the merits of research seems to depend on what stance the scientist takes on the ethics of research. However, if the 'pro-research' camp faces some difficulty establishing that the manifest benefit of research justifies the destruction of arguably human embryos, the 'anti-research' camp has a fundamental problem of its own. If an embryo is arguably human, it is wrong to destroy it, to experiment on it for a purpose not designed to benefit it, so that it must ultimately perish. If it is wrong to destroy embryos for research purposes, it must also be wrong to destroy them in the course of infertility treatments using IVF. As long as 'spare' embryos are created, the surplus are doomed to die. To return to a practice of harvesting only one egg from the woman, and so creating and implanting just one embryo, would probably deal a fatal blow to IVF. But it is difficult to argue that it is ethical to destroy embryos to alleviate infertility and yet unethical to destroy embryos in order to improve our knowledge and treatment of genetic disease. Those who oppose research must logically also oppose IVF.[24]

Embryo research: the Human Fertilisation and Embryology Act

The debate on embryo research will go on for the present. Parliament has legislated to enact, with some modification, the proposal made by

24. See M. Brazier, 'The Challenge for Parliament: A Critique of the White Paper on Human Fertilization and Embryology', in Dyson and Harris (eds.), op. cit., p. 142.

a majority of the Warnock Committee to permit licensed research up to fourteen days. It is a criminal offence punishable by up to two years' imprisonment to bring about the creation of an embryo (outside the human body) or to keep or use an embryo except in pursuance of a licence.[25] No embryo may be kept or used after the appearance of the primitive streak, that is fourteen days from the day the gametes were mixed, '... not counting any time during which the embryo was stored'.[26] Certain activities are expressly prohibited. Human embryos or gametes may not be implanted in animals, nor may animal embryos be inserted in humans.[27] Replacing the nucleus of a cell taken from any person or embryo (cloning) is outlawed.[28] Trans-species fertilization, the attempt to create human/animal hybrids, is forbidden save for the 'hamster' test to establish the fertility or normality of sperm, when any resulting embryo must be destroyed at the two-cell stage.[29] The genetic structure of an embryo may not be altered '... except in such circumstances (if any) as may be specified in ...' regulations to be made by the HFEA.[30]

The rules governing embryo research in the Act rest on two principles. (1) The Act implicitly accepts that respect is due to the embryo from fertilization, but that up until the development of the primitive streak, the 'goods' to be expected from research outweigh the interests of the embryo. The Act grants full protection to the embryo only from fourteen days. This attitude continues the stance taken by the ILA, who permitted research up to fourteen days on what that Authority insisted should be termed 'pre-embryos'.[31] (2) The Act seeks to allay fears of a science-fiction nightmare in which scientists freely create all sorts of clones, hybrids and other monsters. It should be noted that until the enactment of the Human Fertilisation and Embryology Act embryos *in vitro* enjoyed no legal protection at all. The wording of abortion legislation prohibiting 'procurement of miscarriage' meant that in theory 'test-tube' embryos could then be grown and destroyed at will.

25. See s. 3(1). Any prosecution under the Act will require the consent of the DPP; s. 42.
26. s. 3(3)(a).
27. See s. 3(2) and s. 3(3)(b).
28. s. 3(3)(d).
29. s. 4(1)(c); Sched. 2 para. 3(5).
30. Sched. 2 para. 3(4).
31. See the Third Report of the ILA, p. 22.

Subject to the express prohibitions above, however, researchers are given a remarkably free hand by the Act. Schedule 2 outlines what a research licence may authorize. Five specific purposes are outlined:[32] (1) promoting advances in the treatment of infertility; (2) increasing knowledge about the causes of congenital disease; (3) increasing knowledge about the causes of miscarriage; (4) developing more effective techniques of contraception; (5) developing methods for detecting the presence of gene or chromosomal abnormalities in embryos before implantation. Those five specific purposes may be seen, perhaps, as justification for the destruction of embryos, aimed at improving medicine and increasing human happiness, designed to re-assure those who are doubtful about but not adamantly opposed to research. But to those named purposes is added an apparently innocuous phrase 'or for such other purposes as may be specified in regulations'. The HFEA can therefore by its regulations extend the permitted ambit of research within only the limits set by the Act itself.

The HFEA will indeed possess powers of life and death. And it will be able to influence the very future and nature of human society. How far, for example, will the HFEA sanction pre-implantation diagnosis? If it is acceptable to avoid implantation of a male embryo into a haemophilia carrier, is it acceptable to avoid implantation of a healthy female embryo into a woman who does not want a daughter? What degree of genetic defect justifies resort to pre-implantation diagnosis? If it becomes possible to identify the gene carrying colour blindness, may colour-blind embryos be screened out?[33]

Embryo to foetus: foetus to baby

For the present, then, the embryo *in vitro* may not be allowed to develop beyond fourteen days from fertilization. What of the embryo *in vivo* growing and developing in his mother's womb? By twelve weeks the embryo will, if seen on an ultra-sound scan, bear a distinct resemblance to a baby and from then on will be termed a foetus. In many legal systems the protection given to the embryo/foetus is extended as the pregnancy progresses, and the foetus develops. Thus, in France, abortion is allowed on demand up to ten weeks' gestation, and from

32. Sched. 2 para 2.
33. See D. Morgan and R. G. Lee, *The Human Fertilisation and Embryology Act 1990*, Blackstone, 1991.

then on is permissible only on the ground of risk to the mother's health. In the USA the Supreme Court in *Roe* v. *Wade*[34] declared that *any* restriction on abortion in the first twelve weeks of pregnancy was unconstitutional. States may regulate abortion to protect maternal health from twelve to twenty-four weeks, and from viability (between twenty-four and twenty-eight weeks) the interests of the foetus take precedence over the interests of the mother. The law thus adopts a gradualist approach to the conflict of rights between the mother and her unborn child.

In England, the Abortion Act 1967 originally set no limit to the time when an abortion might lawfully be performed. Section 5(1) provided instead that nothing in the Act should affect the provisions of the Infant Life (Preservation) Act 1929 protecting the viable foetus. Under that Act any person who with intent to destroy the life of a child capable of being born alive causes the child to die before it has an existence independent of the mother is guilty of child destruction. The foetus was deemed to be capable of being born alive at twenty-eight weeks. The objective of the 1929 law was to protect the foetus in the course of delivery,[35] and to safeguard any foetus who but for improper intervention could have been born alive. The 1929 Act placed an outside limit of twenty-eight weeks on abortions in England and Wales.[36] But that did not mean any earlier abortion at twenty-four or twenty-six weeks was necessarily lawful. If the prosecution could prove that the foetus was 'capable of being born alive', the doctors carrying out any abortion were guilty of child destruction. Developments in neo-natal medicine resulted in premature babies surviving at ever earlier dates. In the best-resourced units some babies of twenty-four weeks, and even younger, survived. Controversy thus reigned over when a baby is 'capable of being born alive'.[37] David Alton MP introduced an Abortion (Amendment) Bill seeking to impose an eighteen-week limit on abortions, save in exceptional cases.[38] In *C.* v. *S.*[39] a young man,

---

34. (1973) 93 S Ct. 705; currently several attempts are being mounted by anti-abortion campaigners to reverse *Roe* v. *Wade*.
35. Thus closing a lacuna in the abortion laws.
36. The 1929 Act never applied in Scotland.
37. See Glanville Williams, *Textbook on Criminal Law*, 2nd edn, p. 304.
38. For example where the woman had been raped or the baby was incapable of independent life.
39. [1987] 1 All ER 1230.

seeking to stop his girlfriend aborting their child at eighteen weeks, argued that at eighteen weeks a foetus is 'capable of being born alive'. It is fully formed and its heart may beat for a second or so after expulsion from the mother. But at eighteen weeks there is no prospect of a baby breathing independently of its mother even with the aid of a respirator. The Court of Appeal found that to be 'capable of being born alive' a foetus must be able, on delivery, to breathe either naturally or with mechanical aid. The fight to limit late abortions returned to Parliament. Anti-abortion campaigners persuaded the government to agree to the introduction of an amendment to the Human Fertilisation and Embryology Bill designed to reduce the time-limit for abortions. Their attempt misfired, and after a night of confusion, section 37 of the Human Fertilisation and Embryology Act emerged. Section 37 is in fact a liberalization, rather than a restriction, of abortion laws in England.

Section 37 amends the Abortion Act 1967 to provide that the time-limit for lawful abortions carried out on grounds of risk to the physical or mental health of the woman of her existing children shall be *twenty-four* weeks. But in three cases, section 37 further provides that there shall be *no* time-limit, i.e. an abortion may be performed right up to the end of the pregnancy. Abortion up to birth is lawful when (1) termination is necessary to prevent grave permanent injury to the physical or mental health of the mother or (2) continuance of the pregnancy threatens the life of the mother or (3) there is a substantial risk that if the child is born it would suffer from such physical or mental abnormalities as to be seriously handicapped. It is the third of these cases which is controversial. The Infant Life (Preservation) Act always permitted any action necessary to save the life of the mother, even if doing so inevitably entailed the destruction of the child. Moreover, preventing grave permanent injury to her health was also almost certainly permissible.[40] Such cases of a stark choice between mother and child are few and far between in modern medicine. The third case permitting abortion up to forty weeks on grounds of foetal handicap is novel and controversial. In debate in Parliament that provision seemed to be regarded as covering only the most grave and horrifying of handicaps, perhaps where a woman was found late in pregnancy to be carrying an anencephalic child who would be incapable of surviving more than a few hours after birth. However, the wording of section 37

40. See *R.* v. *Bourne* [1939] 1 K B 687.

is identical to the general foetal handicap ground provided for in the 1967 Act. Hence, if Down's syndrome or spina bifida are diagnosed, however late into pregnancy, the foetus may lawfully be destroyed. The impact of section 37 of the Human Fertilisation and Embryology Act is that in the United Kingdom children capable of being born alive may be killed providing they are handicapped. The protection afforded to the viable foetus by the Infant Life (Preservation) Act is withdrawn from the handicapped foetus.[41] A medical practitioner acting within the provisions of the amended and extended Abortion Act cannot be convicted of child destruction. The 1929 Act remains in force, but applicable only to unlawful late abortions, and those cases where a violent attack on a pregnant woman kills the child within her.[42]

There is one crucial practical consequence of the new legal regime on abortion. Doctors aborting handicapped foetuses late on in pregnancy must ensure that they use means that will destroy the foetus before it emerges from the mother. For if a child is born alive nothing in the Abortion Act or the Human Fertilisation and Embryology Act authorizes its destruction. And on occasions, whatever the foetus is subjected to, a living child is born. Horror stories abound of premature infants left to die in the sluice room adjacent to the operating theatre where an abortion was attempted. What are the legal rules applicable when an attempted abortion results not in a dead foetus but a living albeit sick infant? The child once born alive is protected by the law of murder. Any positive act to destroy it is murder. Failure to offer the child proper care *with the intention that it shall die* on the part of persons with an obligation to care for the child is once again murder. In 1983 a consultant gynaecologist was charged with attempted murder. The prosecution was brought after pressure from anti-abortion campaigners. Police had been informed that a baby had been left on a slab to die for some time before being transferred to a paediatric unit. The allegation against the doctor was that he performed an abortion on the basis of an estimate of twenty-three weeks' pregnancy and, when the baby proved to be of thirty-four weeks' gestation, left it without attention intending it to die. The prosecution was dismissed by magistrates for lack of evidence. Failure to offer the child proper care out of incompetence or carelessness is manslaughter. The theory is clear.

41. See Chapter 14.
42. For analysis of the parliamentary votes on section 37 see Morgan and Lee, op. cit., p. 49.

Reality is more problematical. A doctor who embarks on an abortion undertakes the care of the mother and undertakes to relieve her of her unwanted child. Yet the criminal law imposes on him an obligation to the child. His position none the less is clearly distinct from that of the doctor undertaking safely to deliver a mother of a desired child. And what of the child born handicapped? The doctor sets out to abort on the grounds of the substantial handicap to the child, but if it survives must he then use all his efforts to save it? This leads us into the whole issue of medical care of the defective newborn baby, its rights and those of its parents, a minefield I enter in the next chapter.

Selective reduction: selective feticide

So far, discussion of the legality of abortion has proceeded on the basis that the procedure used terminates the woman's pregnancy completely. But there are now cases where only selected foetuses in a multiple pregnancy are destroyed, and the woman's pregnancy continues to term when she delivers her surviving children. Selective reduction, or selective feticide, may be advised either when the woman has a multiple pregnancy and is unlikely to carry all the foetuses safely to term, or when one of two or more foetuses is handicapped. The 'surplus' or handicapped foetuses will, using fetoscopically directed procedures, be killed. The dead foetuses are not expelled from the uterus, but become 'foetus papyraceous', and emerge on delivery of its healthy brothers and sisters. Selective reduction to destroy a handicapped twin has been quietly practised for some time. The development of IVF and consequent increase in multiple pregnancies brought the procedure to public attention. In a number of clinics, to maximize the woman's chances of pregnancy, several embryos were implanted. If she conceived quadruplets or more, the risk was that the several infants would be delivered prematurely and in the worst case scenario *all* might fail to survive. Selective reduction offered the prospect of one or two healthy children being safely born.

However, the deliberate destruction of selected foetuses raised ethical and legal problems. The ILA sought to discourage the implantation of the number of embryos likely to make selective reduction necessary. No more than three embryos should normally be returned to the woman.[43] Legal debate focused on whether selective reduction could

43. See above, p. 261.

ever be lawful.[44] Some doctors tried to argue that as the dead foetus was not expelled from the mother's body, selective reduction was outside the ambit of the abortion laws altogether, for what the Offences Against the Person Act prohibits is 'procuring a miscarriage'. Other commentators contended that selective reduction was within the Offences Against the Person Act and so prima facie a crime, but beyond the ambit of the Abortion Act 1967. The 1967 Act provided lawful grounds for 'terminating a pregnancy'. Selective reduction did not terminate the pregnancy. Section 37(5)[45] of the Human Fertilisation and Embryology Act provides a relatively clear legal regime for selective reduction. Selective reduction is unlawful unless performed for one of the grounds on which termination of the whole pregnancy is lawful. Thus, if foetuses are destroyed on grounds of foetal handicap, or because a multiple pregnancy poses a risk to the mother's health, selective reduction of the chosen foetal victims is as lawful as ending the pregnancy altogether would be. The anomalous situation is this. In the IVF multiple pregnancy the underlying reason for wanting to destroy foetus A and B is to maximize the prospects of a healthy birth for foetuses C and D. The ground that would need to be invoked is that permitting abortion to safeguard the health of any 'existing children' of the pregnant woman. But can foetuses be regarded as 'existing children'? The whole philosophy of English law relating to the status of the foetus is that a foetus is *not* for legal purposes a child!

What section 37(5) does do is to give legal recognition to a much disputed procedure.[46] If foetuses can be selected and destroyed in

---

44. See J. Keown, 'Selective Reduction of Multiple Pregnancy' (1987) 137 NLJ 1165; D. P. T. Price, 'Selective Reduction and Feticide: The Parameters of Abortion' [1988] Crim. L.R. 199.

45. Section 37(5) amends s. 5(2) of the Abortion Act 1967 which now reads:
    for the purposes of the law relating to abortion, anything done with intent to procure a woman's miscarriage (or, in the case of a woman carrying more than one foetus, her miscarriage of any foetus) is unlawfully done unless authorized by section 1 of this Act and, in the case of a woman carrying more than one foetus, anything done with intent to procure her miscarriage of any foetus is authorized by that section if:
    (a) the ground for termination of the pregnancy specified in subsection (1)(d) of that section applies in relation to any foetus and the thing is done for the purpose of procuring the miscarriage of that foetus (foetal handicap ground).
    (b) any of the other grounds for termination of the pregnancy specified in that section applies.

46. See Morgan and Lee, op. cit., pp. 55–60.

effect as part and parcel of infertility treatment, the message from Parliament seems to be that unborn life is little more than a means to an end. The foetus itself counts for nothing. The parents' desire for children justifies its destruction. Selective killing of handicapped foetuses with legal blessing reinforces the second-class status of the handicapped foetus.

Nurses and abortion

Many nurses naturally find abortion distasteful and distressing. Many have exercised their right of conscientious objection to refuse to participate in abortions. Some complain that doing so has prejudiced their career. And some doctors have complained of 'disloyalty' by nurses reporting irregularities in performing abortions, particularly late abortions. But the nurses' greatest concern relates to a change in the manner of performing abortions in the middle months of pregnancy. The Abortion Act provides for circumstances when a pregnancy may lawfully be terminated by a registered medical practitioner, a doctor. In 1967 all lawful abortions were carried out by surgical means. The surgeons removed the foetus and ended the pregnancy. By 1972 medical induction of abortion was introduced as the standard method of terminating pregnancies in the middle months of pregnancy. Nurses play the leading role in this treatment. A doctor inserts a catheter into the woman's womb. Later, a nurse attaches the catheter via a flexible tube to a pump, which feeds the hormone prostaglandin through the catheter and induces premature labour. The nurse administers another drug via a drip in the woman's arm to stimulate her contractions. The immature foetus is born dead. The substances that cause the abortion are administered by the nurse. She in effect terminates the pregnancy.

The Royal College of Nursing became concerned about the legality of medical inductions of abortion. They argued that a pregnancy terminated by a nurse was not lawfully terminated. Nurses might face prosecution for conducting criminal abortions. The Department of Health and Social Security issued a circular upholding the legality of medical inductions of abortion. The Royal College of Nursing went to court for a declaration that the circular was wrong in law. The College lost in the High Court, won in the Court of Appeal and finally lost by three to two in the House of Lords.[47] A total of five judges out of nine

47. *Royal College of Nursing* v. *DHSS* [1981] AC 800.

agreed with the College. But it is the House of Lords' judgement that counts. The majority of their Lordships held that the Act must be construed in the light of its social purposes, first, to broaden the ground on which abortions may lawfully be obtained, and second, to secure safe and hygienic conditions for women undergoing abortion. The Act contemplated the participation of a team of hospital staff involved in the overall treatment of the woman, and exonerated them all from criminal liability if the abortion was carried out within the terms of the Act. It was not necessary for a doctor to perform every physical act leading to the termination of the pregnancy. Provided a doctor accepts full responsibility for every stage in the treatment, a nurse acting under his instructions and in conformity with accepted medical practice does not act unlawfully when she administers the drugs which terminate the pregnancy in an induced abortion.

Conscientious objection

A vital component of the compromise on which the Abortion Act 1967 was based is the right of conscientious objection. Section 4 provides that no person shall be under any duty 'to participate in any treatment authorized by this Act to which he has a conscientious objection'. Section 38 of the Human Fertilisation and Embryology Act confers a similar right to refuse to participate in embryo research or any of the infertility treatments regulated by that Act. It is for the person objecting to prove that their objection rests on grounds of conscience. And, in the case of abortion, the professional's conscience does not relieve him of any duty to intervene to save the life of the mother or to prevent grave permanent injury to her health.

In *Janaway* v. *Salford AHA*[48] the House of Lords was asked to determine *who* was entitled to rely on the right of conscientious objection. Mrs Janaway was a devout Roman Catholic employed as a secretary. She refused to type abortion referral letters and the authority dismissed her. She challenged her dismissal as unlawful because, she argued, she was entitled to rely on the right of conscientious objection provided for by section 4. Her action failed. The Law Lords ruled that the term 'participate' in section 4 meant actually taking part in treatment designed to terminate a pregnancy. Mrs Janaway was not asked to do anything that involved her personally in the process of abortion.

48. [1988] 3 All ER 1051, HL.

Yet she was an essential cog in the wheel. Abortion was as repugnant to her as murder. For Mrs Janaway, however irrational others might perceive her views to be, asking her to type abortion referral letters was the equivalent of asking her to type out a death warrant.

The House of Lords' restrictive interpretation of the right to conscientious objection has other consequences too. A health care professional may legitimately refuse to carry out, or assist at, an abortion. He cannot withdraw from any contact with abortion advice. Consider this example. A woman of over 35 receives her ante-natal care from an obstetrician adamantly opposed to abortion. He never discusses with her whether in view of her age she should undergo amniocentesis to test for Down's syndrome. The prevalence of Down's syndrome increases in mothers over 35. If she gives birth to a Down's baby, the mother may sue the obstetrician for negligence. If, as I strongly suspect, the overwhelming body of responsible professional opinion regards amniocentesis (or other available tests for Down's) as routine for pregnant women over 35, the obstetrician's right to conscientious objection will be of no avail to him. If his duty of care (as defined by his peers) extends to advice on amniocentesis, then even though that advice on amniocentesis is almost inevitably an act preparatory to abortion, he must fulfil that duty, for it involves no active participation in the process of ending a pregnancy.

The right to conscientious objection is limited in scope and in practice difficult to exercise. Hospitals are not unnaturally somewhat wary of staff who will not participate in what has become a fairly common operation. It is said to be near impossible in most hospitals to gain a post in midwifery or gynaecology if you declare your conscientious objection to abortion. Yet there remain areas of England where abortion within the NHS is nigh on unattainable. Is that a violation of women's rights caused by giving undue precedence to the professional's right to his conscience? The irony is that consultants and general practitioners can avoid involvement in abortion without having to invoke the right to conscientious objection. The doctor simply refuses to certify that a ground specified in the Act is made out. The woman can only try then to find another more sympathetically inclined doctor. Her only remedy against the first practitioner would lie if she could prove that to refuse her an abortion was a breach of the duty of care owed to her. If the doctor is a consultant or a GP, no one can order him to participate in an abortion.

Fathers and abortion

Has the father of the unborn child any say in whether or not the child be aborted? In 1978 in *Paton* v. *British Pregnancy Advisory Service*,[49] a husband tried to prevent his wife having an abortion. She had been concerned about her pregnancy and consulted her doctor, but did not consult her husband. She obtained a certificate from two registered medical practitioners that the continuance of the pregnancy would involve risk to her health. So an abortion could lawfully proceed. Her husband intervened. He went to court to ask for an injunction (an order) to prevent the abortion from being carried out without his consent. The court refused an injunction. The judge said that the 1967 Act gave no right to the husband to be consulted. In the absence of such a right under the Act, the husband had 'no legal right enforceable at law or in equity to stop his wife having this abortion or to stop the doctors from carrying out the abortion'.

The abortion went ahead. The husband went to the European Commission on Human Rights, arguing that the Act and the judge's decision infringed the European Convention on Human Rights. He argued that his right to family life and the unborn child's right to life had been infringed. The Commission dismissed his claim.[50] They said that where an abortion was carried out on medical grounds, the husband's right to family life must necessarily be subordinated to the need to protect the rights and health of the mother. The unborn child's right to life was similarly subordinate to the rights of its mother, at least in the initial months of pregnancy. The Commission's decision suggests that a rather different view might be taken of abortions performed later in pregnancy and of abortions performed other than to protect the mother's health. However, in *C.* v. *S.*[51] the Court of Appeal, having held that the abortion of a foetus at eighteen weeks did not contravene the Infant Life (Preservation) Act 1929, refused the father any right *qua* father or as guardian of the unborn child to challenge the proposed abortion. It is clear that in England husbands have no standing to oppose an abortion agreed to by the wife, nor has a father any right to intervene to 'save' the foetus, nor can anyone argue that the foetus itself has legal personality so enabling him to act as its

49. [1979] QB 276.
50. [1980] 3 EHRR 408.
51. [1987] All ER 1230.

'guardian' and stop an abortion. The legality of an abortion depends exclusively on whether or not it conforms to the 1967 Act.

Just one issue remains open. The father in *Paton* reluctantly accepted that the doctors' certificate as to the need for the abortion was issued in good faith. Had he challenged the certificate, could he have asked for an injunction to prevent an unlawful abortion taking place? The judge in *Paton* did not have to decide this point. He expressed the view that an injunction would not be granted. The supervision of abortion and the issue of the doctors' good faith is left to the criminal law and a jury. The Court of Appeal in *C*. v. *S*.[52] endorsed that opinion. A remedy that consists of the prosecution of the doctor after the event is not one to bring much comfort to fathers.

Girls under 16

The Abortion Act makes no special provision for abortion on girls under 16. Must her parents consent to such an abortion? In 1981 a sad case was reported.[53] A 15-year-old girl who already had one child became pregnant again while in local authority care. She wanted an abortion. Her doctors believed that the birth of a second child would damage her mental health and endanger her existing child. The girl's father objected. Abortion was contrary to his religion. The local authority applied to have the girl made a ward of court and thereby seek the consent of the court to the operation. Butler-Sloss J. authorized the abortion. She said that while she took into account the feelings of the parents she was satisfied that the girl's best interests required that her pregnancy be ended. Her decision was approved by the House of Lords in *Gillick* v. *West Norfolk and Wisbech AHA*.[54] Indeed, the result of that notable case would appear to be that as long as the girl is old enough to understand what abortion entails physically and emotionally, the doctor may go ahead on the basis of her consent alone. If the girl is insufficiently mature to make a decision for herself, the doctor must act in her best interests. Should her parents refuse consent to abortion, then, like the local authority in the case discussed above, the doctors should seek to make the girl a ward of court[55] and ask a

52. p. 1243.
53. *Re P. (A Minor)* (1981) 80 LGR 301.
54. [1985] 3 All ER 402, HL.
55. See *Re B*, *Guardian*, 21 May 1991 (Hollis J. authorized abortion for 12-year-old girl).

judge to decide on the conflict between medical and parental opinion. A doctor who ignores parental views will not be guilty of an offence of criminal abortion though. He may face legal action by the girl's parents in the civil courts, or, in an extreme case, prosecution for an assault on her.[56]

Mentally handicapped women

In *T*. v. *T*.[57] a woman of 19 became pregnant. She was said to have a mental age of 2, was doubly incontinent and incapable of any comprehensible speech. The problem for her mother and her doctors was that T. was quite incapable of giving her consent to the proposed abortion and, as she was an adult, no one else could authorize treatment on her behalf. Wood J. granted a declaration that performing an abortion on T. was not unlawful if that operation was considered to be in her best interests and in conformity with good medical practice. Wood J.'s judgement was confirmed in *F*. v. *West Berkshire HA*.[58] The general questions of treatment of mentally handicapped patients is fully dealt with in Chapter 5. In cases of disputed abortions one crucial factor may be whether the woman understands that she is pregnant and what the proposed abortion entails. If she has that degree of understanding, she is almost certainly competent to make the decision on whether or not to end the pregnancy for herself.

Conclusions

The debate on the morality of abortion continues. Pro-and anti-abortion campaigners shift ground from issue to issue. Consensus on the moral claims of the human embryo is unattainable. The law in England is none the less clear on one matter: the embryo/foetus has no legal personality or rights of its own until birth. It is recognized as an entity whose status deserves protection but not as a legal person with rights equal to yours and mine. The question thus becomes how much protection should the embryo/foetus be afforded and at what cost to maternal rights and interests? And should that protection increase with gestational age? Today the law recognizes two classes of foetus. Handicapped foetuses are denied any protection from destruction even

56. See Chapter 15.
57. [1988] 1 All ER 613.
58. [1989] 2 All ER 545, HL.

once capable of surviving birth. 'Normal' foetuses acquire a qualified right to birth at twenty-four weeks dependent on their survival posing no grave risk to the mother. Up to twenty-four weeks the fate of the 'normal' foetus rests in the hands of its mother's doctors. Whatever the intentions of the 1967 Act, in practice it has conferred the authority to grant or withhold abortion to the medical profession. If the fate of the embryo/foetus cannot in our community be decided on the basis of consensus as to its moral status, would it not be better to leave women to make the decision on abortion? Can it be right on any analysis that a woman's entitlement to abortion and her child's claim to life should depend on where in the country the woman happens to live?

CHAPTER 14

The Handicapped Infant: Whose Rights? Whose Decision?

The birth of a severely handicapped baby is a human tragedy that most of us prefer to imagine will never happen to our family. The joy of normal childbirth is replaced by fear for the infant's and the family's future. Until relatively recently, two factors to some extent mitigated the parents' dilemma. Very little could be done for such a baby. Many handicapped babies survived only a few weeks or months from birth. Their parents suffered the pain of their loss, but they were spared anxiety as to the child's future. In any case, whether the child lived or died, the decision was made by 'God or nature'. The parents could do nothing about it. Advances in the care of the newborn and in neo-natal surgery have changed the picture. Doctors are now able to prolong the lives of the majority of handicapped infants. At first they applied their skills to the maximum possible number of damaged babies. Today some paediatricians voice publicly their doubts as to the wisdom of that original policy. It is even argued by some authors that in extreme cases the most gravely handicapped babies should be actively put to death. The parents of a badly handicapped baby today may be faced with agonizing decisions as to the treatment of their baby within hours of the trauma of birth.

Euthanasia and neonaticide

It is not only in relation to the handicapped newborn that doctors have begun to question the wisdom of *always* applying the full range of available modern treatment to prolong life. The problem arises equally acutely in relation to the terminally or chronically ill adult, or an adult or older child desperately and irreversibly injured in an accident. I deal with these topics in Chapter 21. I treat the subject of the handicapped newborn separately from the general question of adult euthanasia for the following reasons. First, the conscious adult patient can speak for himself. The decision as to any continuation of treatment may be his. Even if unconscious, he may earlier have expressed his wishes should the question arise. The baby cannot express any preference. His parents may give their views. The issue is then joined as to whether society and the law should regard those views as paramount. The *British Medical Journal* sees the parents as the instrument through which the baby accepts or rejects treatment.[1] Their wishes are therefore decisive. Parents' views are crucial, but children have rights too. Second, the baby's plight is very different from that of a newly handicapped adult. He does not move from full health to handicap. He does not endure a dramatic drop in his expectations of life. A life of handicap is all he can know. Third, a clear body of opinion has developed among doctors, philosophers and lawyers that the problems of the treatment of damaged or sick adults and the handicapped newborn raise separate if related issues. The term neonaticide[2] has been coined to cover the latter. Somehow the life of a newborn infant has come to be regarded in certain circles as having a lesser value. Proposals have been made for specific legislation on neonaticide. One feature of the debate and the proposals, though, is a distinct lack of agreement as to when the period after birth when neonaticide might be seen as permissible should end.

All in all, a tremendous shift in the climate of opinion has occurred among the professions. It may be doubted whether their views command wide popular support. What has brought about this shift? (1) For paediatricians one major factor must be that the universal application of sophisticated medicine and surgery to all damaged babies has had disappointing long-term results. This is best illustrated by the example of babies born suffering from spina bifida. The development of surgery to effect external repairs, and of 'shunts' to drain water from the brain where the frequent complication of hydrocephaly was present, was hailed as a landmark in the treatment of spina bifida. Virtually all affected babies were operated on within hours of birth.

1. Medical News (1981) 283 BMJ 567.
2. See, in particular, J. K. Mason and R. A. McCall Smith, *Law and Medical Ethics*, Butterworths, London, 1991, Chapter 7.

Research has shown[3] that barely 41 per cent of the children treated reach their tenth birthday. Of the survivors, only about 7 per cent can hope to lead something approximating to a normal, adult life. All the children underwent repeated painful surgery and long stays in hospital. (2) The Abortion Act permits the termination of pregnancy when there is a substantial risk that the child, if born, will be severely handicapped. Amniocentesis is increasingly used to test mothers at risk for spina bifida or Down's syndrome. At present it is normally carried out at sixteen weeks into pregnancy, and if the results are positive the pregnancy is ended at about twenty weeks. The amendment of the Abortion Act by section 37 of the Human Fertilisation and Embryology Act will, however, allow the abortion of such a child right up to the end of the pregnancy. Parents may find it difficult to understand why a child who could have been actively destroyed if his handicap had been diagnosed in pregnancy must be the subject of intensive life-saving measures if his handicap goes unnoticed until his birth. (3) The concept of the sanctity of each and every human life is under attack. Forceful arguments are advanced[4] that the value of life lies in its quality and the contribution possible to society, rather than in any intrinsic merit in life itself. The newborn infant is no more a 'person' than the embryo or the foetus. Such arguments are equally forcefully rebutted,[5] but seem to have commanded a measure of support among the medical profession as far as severely damaged babies are concerned.

1981: Baby Alexandra

The debate on the treatment of the handicapped newborn reached the English courts in 1981 in a blaze of publicity. First, there occurred the case of Baby Alexandra; this little girl was born in 1981 suffering from Down's syndrome and an intestinal obstruction. In a normal child, simple surgery would have been carried out swiftly with minimal risk to the baby. Without surgery the baby would die within a few days.

3. J. Lorber, 'Results of the Treatment of Myelomengole', *Developmental Medicine and Child Neurology*, 1971; and 'Spina Bifida Cystica', *Archives of Disease in Childhood*, 1972.
4. See Jonathan Glover, *Causing Death and Saving Lives*, Penguin, Harmondsworth, 1977, Chapter 12. And see earlier in Chapter 2 of this book.
5. See, in particular J. K. Mason, *Human Life and Medical Practice*, Edinburgh University Press, 1988, Chapter 6.

The baby's parents refused to authorize the operation. They agreed that God or nature had given their child a way out. The doctors contacted the local authority and the child was made a ward of court. A judge was asked to authorize the operation. He refused to do so. The authority appealed, and the Court of Appeal[6] ordered that the operation go ahead. Counsel for the parents submitted that in this kind of decision the views of responsible and caring parents must be respected and that their decision should decide the issue. The Court of Appeal rejected the submission, holding that the decision must be made in the best interests of the child.

Templeman LJ said:

It is a decision which of course must be made in the light of the evidence and views expressed by the parents and the doctors, but at the end of the day it devolves on this court in this particular instance to decide whether the life of this child is demonstrably going to be so awful that in effect the child must be condemned to die, or whether the life of this child is still so imponderable that it would be wrong for her to be condemned to die. There may be cases, I know not, of severe proved damage where the future is so certain and where the life of the child is so bound to be full of pain and suffering that the court might be driven to a different conclusion, but in the present case the choice which lies before the court is this: whether to allow an operation to take place which may result in the child living for 20 or 30 years as a mongoloid or whether (and I think this brutally must be the result) to terminate the life of a mongoloid child because she also has an intestinal complaint. Faced with that choice I have no doubt that it is the duty of this court to decide that the child must live.

The case of Stephen Quinn and the trial of Dr Arthur

In October of 1981 the Director of Public Prosecutions announced that he would not proceed against a doctor who had been reported as taking no action to preserve the life of a spina bifida baby, Stephen Quinn.[7] Then, in November, Dr Leonard Arthur, a distinguished paediatrician from Derby, faced trial for murder.[8] A baby boy was born in the hospital where Dr Arthur was consultant paediatrician. He suffered from Down's syndrome. His parents did not wish him to

6. *Re B.* [1981] 1 WLR 1421.
7. *The Times*, 6 October 1981.
8. See 'Dr Leonard Arthur: His Trial and its Implications' (1981) 283 BMJ 1340; H. Beynon, 'Doctors as Murderers' [1982] Crim. L. R. 17; M. Gunn and J. C. Smith, 'Arthur's Case and the Right to Life of a Down's Syndrome Child' [1985] Crim. L. R. 705.

survive. He died sixty-nine hours after his birth. The prosecution alleged that Dr Arthur ordered nursing care only and prescribed a drug which would suppress the baby's appetite and so starve him to death. They claimed that apart from being a Down's baby the baby was otherwise healthy, and that his death resulted from lack of sustenance and the effect of the drug causing him to succumb to bronchopneumonia. Defence evidence established that (1) the baby suffered from severe brain and lung damage, (2) Dr Arthur followed established practice in the management of such an infant, (3) that in the first three days of life normal babies take in little or no sustenance and usually lose weight (which the dead baby had not done). The baby patently did not starve to death. The judge directed that the charge be altered to attempted murder. Summing up on the law for the jury, the judge stressed that there is '... no special law in this country that places doctors in a separate category and gives them special protection over the rest of us ...' He emphasized that however severely handicapped a child may be, if the doctor gives it drugs in an excessive amount so that the drugs will cause death then the doctor commits murder. He highlighted the distinction between doing something active to kill the child and electing not to follow a particular course of treatment which might have saved the infant. Considering the ethical arguments on terminating newborn life, the judge reminded the jury that if ethics and the law conflict, the law must prevail. But his lordship concluded:

... I imagine that you [the jury] will think long and hard before deciding that doctors of the eminence we have heard in representing to you what medical ethics are and apparently have been over a period of time, you would think long and hard before concluding that they in that great profession have evolved standards which amount to committing crime.

The jury acquitted Dr Arthur.

A confused picture emerges from 1981. The baby girl with Down's syndrome was ordered to be saved. The DPP implied that no crime was committed in withholding treatment from a spina bifida baby. Dr Arthur was not guilty of a crime in relation to his treatment of a severely damaged Down's infant. In attempting to rationalize and reconcile these three decisions, the starting point must be that the jury's acquittal of Dr Arthur tells us very little about the law. The confusion over the pathological evidence may well have irretrievably prejudiced the jury against the prosecution's case. The baby's multiple abnormalities should have been irrelevant to the reduced charge of attempted murder. When Dr Arthur ordered nursing care only, he thought that he was dealing with a 'normal' Down's baby. But did the jury see it that way? Above all a charge of murder, with its emotional baggage and a mandatory life sentence, was always going to be difficult to sustain against a defendant renowned as a dedicated and caring paediatrician. As J. K. Mason puts it: 'Murder, in the popular sense of the word, was the one thing of which Dr Arthur was certainly innocent.'[9] So what can be deduced from the legal events of 1981? Two later judgements, *Re C*.[10] in 1989 and *Re J*.[11] in 1990, make it clear that it is *Re B*. (Baby Alexandra) that forms the key to judicial decision-making on handicapped infants. In the light of those two judgements a tentative attempt can then be made to outline the guiding principles of law in these sad and difficult cases.

Deliberate killing

Neither doctor, nor parents, nor any other person may do any *act* intended *solely* to hasten the death of the handicapped baby. The deliberate killing of any human being is murder. The moment that the child has an existence separate from his mother,[12] the moment he has independent circulation, even though the afterbirth may not yet fully have been expelled from the mother's body, he is protected by the law of murder. It has on occasion been faintly argued that a grossly malformed child, 'a monstrous birth', should not be regarded in law as human.[13] No court is likely to accede to such a view. Defining humanity, other than by virtue of human parentage, would be an impossible and unacceptable task. Does 'monstrous' refer to appearance, in which case an intelligent infant of appalling mien could legitimately be destroyed? Does it cover lack of intelligence, lack of a brain? Both are almost impossible to measure at birth.

One area of doubt does exist. What of the doctor who administers

9. *Human Life and Medical Practice*, Edinburgh University Press, 1988, p. 63.
10. [1989] 2 All ER 782, CA.
11. [1990] 3 All ER 930, CA.
12. Some dispute exists as to the moment in childbirth when this occurs. The child need not have breathed apparently. See *R*. v. *Poulton* (1832) 5 C. & P. 329, and *R*. v. *Brain* (1834) 6 C. & P. 349; and see J. C. Smith and B. Hogan, *Criminal Law*, 5th edn, p. 274.
13. See (1981) 283 BMJ 1340, 1341.

drugs, or large quantities of a drug, with the primary intention of relieving a baby's suffering but in the knowledge that the drugs may shorten the baby's life or weaken his capacity to survive? In *R*. v. *Adams*[14] a doctor was charged with the murder of an elderly patient by means of excessive quantities of pain-relieving drugs. He was acquitted. Directing the jury, Devlin J. said:

> If life were cut short by weeks or months it was just as much murder as if it were cut short by years.

He went on to say

> But that does not mean that a doctor aiding the sick or the dying has to calculate in minutes or hours, or perhaps in days or weeks, the effect on a patient's life of the medicines which he administers. If the first purpose of medicine – the restoration of health – can no longer be achieved, there is still much for the doctor to do, and he is entitled to do all that is proper and necessary to relieve pain and suffering even if measures he takes may incidentally shorten life.

Two conditions, then, limit the administration to a baby of medicines that may in themselves, or in the quantities administered, as a secondary effect shorten his lifespan. (1) His handicap or congenital defect must be of a kind that will in the course of nature lead to his death early in infancy. If he is handicapped but has a lifespan measurable in years, even though significantly less than that of a healthy child, the use of such drugs must be avoided. This proposition then begs the question as to the case of a child suffering from a defect that could kill him swiftly but whose life could be prolonged by active treatment. I consider this in the next section, taking the view that if the doctor may lawfully withhold treatment then he may lawfully do all he can to mitigate the suffering of the untreated baby. (2) The drugs must be shown to be necessary to relieve suffering in the baby. It may be that the main threat of the charge of murder against Dr Arthur was blunted once the defence showed that the drug he prescribed was given not to an uncomplicated Down's baby but to a severely damaged and probably suffering infant. The jury may have reasoned thus. The child's condition killed him in the end. His doctor was entitled to make his hours on earth comfortable.

14. *R*. v. *Adams* [1957] Crim. L. R. 365, discussed more fully in Chapter 21. See also Lord Devlin's account of the trial, *Easing the Passing* (1985).

Withholding treatment

To what extent, then, does the law require parents and doctors to provide treatment to prolong the baby's life? The bare bones of the law can be stated quite simply. Before any failure to treat a child can engage criminal liability, it must be established that a duty to act was imposed on the accused. Parents are under a duty to care and provide for their dependent children. Failing to provide proper care, including medical aid where necessary, will result in a conviction for wilful neglect of the child, provided that the parent was aware of the risk to the child's health.[15] Should the child die, the parents may be convicted of manslaughter.[16] Parents who are well aware of the danger to a child's health but who do not seek medical aid because of religious or other conscientious objection to conventional medicine have no defence to criminal prosecutions for neglect or manslaughter.[17] Parents who deliberately withhold sustenance and care from a child intending him to die may be guilty of murder.[18] Finally, a range of other legal remedies is available to local authority social services departments. Failure to provide medical aid may be a ground for taking a child into care,[19] or the child may be made a ward of court.[20] What of the doctor? If he is under a duty to treat a baby then, like the parent, should the child die, he may be prosecuted for manslaughter if his omission resulted from neglect, or for murder if he intended the infant to die. Once the doctor accepts the baby as a patient he assumes a duty to that baby to give him proper medical care. Nor is it likely that a paediatrician could, should anyone ever want to, evade responsibility by refusing to accept the child as a patient after his birth. His contract with the NHS imposes on him an obligation towards the children born in his hospital or area, giving rise to a duty to the individual infant.[21]

Parents and doctors, then, have a duty to provide medical aid, but what is the scope of that duty? Where a baby is born suffering from

15. Children and Young Persons Act 1933, s. 1(1).
16. *R.* v. *Lowe* [1973] QB 702.
17. *R.* v. *Senior* [1899] 1 QB, 823.
18. *R.* v. *Gibbins and Proctor* (1918) 13 Cr. App. Rep. 134.
19. Children Act 1989 s. 31.
20. As happened in *Re B.* (the Baby Alexandra case).
21. See Beynon, op. cit., pp. 27–8.

gross handicap, may proper medical care be defined as keeping the baby comfortable but deliberately withholding life-prolonging treatment? Two factors play a vital role in the decision as to whether to treat a handicapped newborn infant. What do his parents desire? What is the practice of the medical profession in the management of this kind of handicap? The answer to the second question is that in a number of cases doctors will explain the treatment available, give a prognosis as to the child's future, and then abide by the decision taken by the parents. That practice does not accord with the view of the Court of Appeal in the case of Baby Alexandra, when they ordered that a Down's baby undergo surgery to remove an intestinal blockage against the wishes of the child's parents. But, say some, it is supported by the decision not to prosecute doctors who omitted to operate on a spina bifida baby, and by the acquittal of Dr Arthur. The conditions of the children in issue were somewhat different. Baby Alexandra suffered from the mental and physical handicaps attendant on Down's syndrome. If treated, she could expect the same quality of life as any one of the other many, many Down's babies born each year. She would suffer no pain from her handicap, and the evidence suggests that if properly cared for such children are within themselves reasonably happy. The surgery needed to save her was simple and without risk. The spina bifida baby faced an operation leading to a series of further operations with a less than 50 per cent chance of his survival beyond ten years old. His life would be one of pain and lived mostly in hospital. Dr Arthur's infant patient was severely damaged over and above his condition as a Down's baby. The issue of whether Dr Arthur should have actively intervened to save him once he developed broncho-pneumonia was never properly examined at his trial.

Is the legality of withholding treatment then dependent on the degree of the infant's handicap and the degree of suffering prolonged life may cause him? A grossly handicapped infant whose existence appears to give him no pleasures of any sort and to cause him pain need not be treated? That some sort of balance between the pain of prolonged life and the finality of death has to be struck seems to emerge from the post-1981 case-law. And it is also beyond doubt that parental views, while always to be considered, are never in law conclusive as to their child's fate.

At the centre of any judgement of what may be done or not done for a handicapped infant must be the interests of that infant. In Canada the parents of Stephen Dawson, a 6-year-old boy with hydrocephalus, refused consent to the replacement of a shunt. The little boy was grossly handicapped, but medical evidence suggested that without the shunt he would not die swiftly and painlessly. He would endure increasing disability and pain. The Supreme Court of British Columbia[22] ordered the replacement of the shunt. Treatment needed to avoid suffering cannot be refused by the parents.

In *Re C.*[23] a baby girl had been made a ward of court shortly after birth on ground of her parents' inability to care for her. She was later to be found grossly handicapped. She suffered from an exceptionally severe degree of hydrocephalus, and the brain structure itself was poorly formed. She appeared to be blind and virtually deaf. At 16 weeks she was, apart from her enlarged head, the size of a 4-week baby. It was said to be inevitable that she would die in a matter of months at most. The issues put before the court were these. If it became impossible to go on feeding her by syringe, must she be fed naso-gastrically or intravenously? If she developed an infection, must she be treated by antibiotics? The judge, at first instance, asked the Official Solicitor to intervene and he sought the advice of an eminent professor of paediatrics, who examined C. He advised that those caring for C. should not be *obliged* to resort to artificial feeding, or treat C. with antibiotics, simply to prolong her life. The judgement on how to treat C. should depend primarily on relieving her suffering. The judge therefore made an order that leave be given to 'treat the ward to die'. This infelicitous phrase caused an outcry, being wrongly interpreted by some of the media as sanction for active euthanasia. The Court of Appeal none the less affirmed the judgement, deleting the unfortunate phrase. Lord Donaldson MR saw C.'s case as very different from that of Baby Alexandra in *Re B*. C. was inevitably dying. Her life appeared to offer her no pleasures. The court ordered: 'The hospital authority be at liberty to treat the minor to allow her life to come to an end peacefully and with dignity . . .'

A year later in *Re J.*[24] the Court of Appeal confronted a rather more difficult issue. J. had been born thirteen weeks premature and with a birth weight of 1.1 kg. He nearly died several times but was saved by medical skill. He was found to have very severe brain damage: 'A large area of fluid filled cavities where there ought to have been brain tissue.' J. was said to be likely to develop paralysis, blindness

22. (1983) 145 DLR (3d) 610.
23. [1989] 2 All ER 782, CA.
24. [1990] 3 All ER 930, CA.

and probable deafness. But, unlike C., he was not imminently dying and his life expectancy might extend to his late teens. If he developed an infection, must he be treated? If he suffered, as he had before, a further episode of cyanosis and collapse, must he be resuscitated? The Court of Appeal found he need not. Lord Donaldson regarded *Re B.* as near to binding authority that a balancing exercise should be performed in assessing the course to be adopted in the best interests of the child. The exercise must seek to reflect the 'assumed' view of the child. In deciding whether the prolonged life of the child will be 'demonstrably awful', the child's perspective on life is the crucial test. He will know no other life, and the amazing adaptability and courage of handicapped people must be considered.

But in the end there will be cases in which the answer must be that it is not in the interests of the child to subject it to treatment which will cause increased suffering and produce no commensurate benefit, giving the fullest possible weight to the child's, and mankind's, desire to survive.[25]

The principles that emerge from the English case-law thus appear to be: (1) Any decision relating to the treatment, or non-treatment, of a handicapped infant is to be based on the best interests of the child, and the child alone. He is accorded no lesser value by the law if he is newborn than if he was 5, 15 or 50. And indeed, as we have seen, the court applies similar principles to tiny babies a few days old, such as Alexandra, infants a few months old, such as C. and J., and children of 6, such as Stephen Dawson in Canada. (2) The wishes of the parents are not conclusive. Parental judgements that a child be left to die do not of themselves authorize doctors to act lawfully in withholding treatment. (3) When the infant is dying, treatment to prolong the process of dying is not mandatory. The object of treatment must be to allow the child to die with minimum suffering. The child need not be given antibiotics to achieve some short prolongation of life, nor *need* he be artificially fed. (4) Where a child is terribly handicapped, *albeit not imminently dying*, treatment (antibiotics to cure infection or further surgery) to prolong his life may be withheld providing (a) his continued life is from his perspective 'demonstrably awful' and (b) withholding treatment will *not* expose the child to additional suffering. It remains unclear whether a child judged to be in such a state may lawfully be denied nutrition. I would suggest not. Clearly, if he can feed normally, he may no more be starved to death than his

25. p. 938.

non-handicapped sister. If the child cannot be fed save naso-gastrically or intravenously,[26] only in the most extreme cases should food be withheld from a non-dying infant. And it must be clear beyond peradventure that withholding artificial feeding will not cause the child to suffer.

Two features predominate if this analysis of the law is correct. First, the interests of the child are assessed on the basis of an assumption that he receives proper care in his future life. It has been argued that handicapped children rejected by their parents enjoy such a low quality of life in institutions and foster-homes that death must be in their best interests. If this is so, it is an indictment of our society and not of the state of the law. Second, to put it brutally, the result of the application of the points outlined above represents the present law as this. The child with gross spina bifida or hydrocephalus must be afforded general nursing care, and fed if he demands food. A considered decision by doctors and parents conforming to proper paediatric practice that no other steps be taken to prolong his life, not to resort to surgery or not to treat an infection with antibiotics, will not expose the doctor to criminal liability. The baby suffering from Down's syndrome, or other mental handicap, plus some other defect requiring surgery, must be operated on. If he contracts an infection, he must be treated. Mental handicap is more horrifying to some than physical defect. A mentally handicapped child creates a heavy burden for his family. But no one would, I hope, deny that careful thought must be given before judges or society decide that the mentally handicapped should deliberately be left to die for want of routine treatment.

The law as it stands revolves very largely around the degree of suffering likely to be endured by the child. And quality of life is judged very much in terms of such suffering. The question that remains open is whether the balancing exercise referred to by Lord Donaldson in *Re J.* has to be undertaken by a court. If a case such as J. recurs, must the child be made a ward of court, or if parents and doctors agree that treatment should be withheld, is it lawful to act on·that consensus? *Re J.*, at least to some extent, clarifies the principles relating to treatment or non-treatment. It seems clear that if on the basis of those principles a parental decision to refuse further treatment is in the 'best interests' of the child, there is no need to make the child a ward of court. Wardship should be used only if there is a dispute over the fate of the

---

26. In a number of American cases however artificial feeding has been regarded as just another form of treatment. See below, p. 454

child, or if some other feature of the case distinguishing it from *Re J.* makes it desirable to seek judicial guidance. Doctors will be understandably wary of going out on a limb in such cases. After all, if they get it 'wrong', they like Dr Arthur might be faced with a trial for murder!

Proposals for legislation

Legislation on neonaticide has been proposed on three grounds. (1) The law should be clarified. No other doctor ought to face, as Dr Arthur did, a test case in an uncharted area charged with the offence of murder. (2) The law should more readily permit doctors to withhold treatment, where parents concur, from children whose objective quality of life is low. (3) In extreme cases the law should sanction active measures to end the child's life. This is seen by some as more humane than leaving the child to a lingering death.[27] Proposals for legislation met with a lukewarm to hostile reaction from the medical profession. I will examine two such proposals

The first is a detailed draft 'Limitation of Treatment Bill' proposed by two lawyers, Diana and Malcolm Brahams.[28] Their Bill proposes that no criminal offence would be committed where a doctor refused or ceased treatment of an infant under twenty-eight days, provided that (1) the parents gave their written consent, and (2) two doctors, both of at least seven years' standing and one of them being a paediatrician, certified in writing that the infant suffered from severe physical or mental handicap which was either irreversible or of such gravity that after receiving all reasonably available treatment the child would enjoy no worthwhile quality of life. The Bill directs the doctors to consider a number of factors in assessing the child's likely quality of life. They must consider (*inter alia*) the degree of pain and suffering likely to be endured, the child's potential to communicate, and also the willingness of the parents to care for him and the effect that that may have on *their* physical and mental health.

A doctor/lawyer team, Professor Mason and Dr McCall Smith of Edinburgh University, suggest a much shorter, single-clause piece of legislation. Their first draft Bill, in the first edition of their book *Law and Medical Ethics*, reads:[29]

27. See Rachels (1975) 292 New Eng. J. Med. 78.
28. (1981) 78 Law Soc. Gaz. 1342.
29. At p. 89.

It will not be an offence if two doctors, one of whom is a consultant paediatrician, acting in good faith and with the consent of both parents, if available, arrange within the first 72 hours of life for the termination of the life of an infant because further life would be intolerable by virtue of pain and suffering or because of severe cerebral incompetence; and the underlying condition is not amenable to reasonable medical treatment.

Both proposals apply only to the more severely damaged of babies. The baby must have 'no worthwhile quality of life' under the first; his prospect of life must be 'intolerable' under the second. Thus neither would seem to excuse non-treatment of a Down's baby with no additional defect or deformity likely to lower his quality of life. The term 'severe cerebral incompetence' in the second proposal suggests a total inability to appreciate one's surroundings or communicate with others. As it stands, it is a phrase which could cause endless difficulties of interpretation. The differences between the two proposals highlight the difficulties in the path of any legislator. The Brahams' proposal is the wider, in that the latitude offered to doctors lasts for up to twenty-eight days. It allows time for tests and diagnosis, and time for parents to recover from the trauma of birth and make a considered decision. It takes into account the interests of the parents and the family, thus permitting a greater degree of parental control over the final decision. It stops short of sanction for any active measures to end the baby's life. The original Mason/McCall Smith proposal allowed only seventy-two[30] hours for any decision to be made, and essentially the decision will be that of the doctors. The parents must consent. They may require the doctor to treat the child but they cannot oblige him to withhold treatment. It is in this sense a much more child-centred proposal. The child's life may be terminated if and only if his life is medically likely to be intolerable. The parents' ability and willingness to care for him are not to be a factor in the decision. The controversy inherent in the original Mason/McCall Smith Bill is that it seemed to sanction active measures to kill the baby. Their revised draft quite clearly does not, simply stating 'it will not be an offence to withhold [positive] treatment'.[31] Yet actively ending such babies' lives is an issue that ought to be faced, however distressing it is. For the argument

30. In the revised draft proposal in the second edition (p. 167) the seventy-two hour limit is abandoned.
31. *Law and Medical Ethics*, Butterworths, 1991, p. 167.

goes: if it is permissible to stand by and watch the baby die slowly, why is it impermissible to end his life swiftly and painlessly? The intention in both cases is the same, that the baby should die. It is an issue which must be faced again in relation to euthanasia and adults, and I can suggest no solution to it that will not be deeply disturbing to many members of society.

Neither proposal has met with much favourable response from the medical profession. The Brahams 'Bill' was vigorously criticized by Dr Havard of the BMA.[32] He saw it as an attempt to confine and define medical discretion to an unacceptable degree. He also, and with some justification, feared a situation where the interpretation of such a statute could be argued through the courts at length. Dr Havard would prefer a statement by the Attorney-General to the effect that no doctor taking a decision relating to a severely handicapped baby would face prosecution if he made the decision in a suitable paediatric unit. If necessary he would support legislation to that effect. Such a course will not commend itself to lawyers. It would be in effect an abdication by the law and society from all decision-making in this sensitive area.

If legislation is to be enacted in this field, society must take a series of deeply difficult and divisive decisions. Do we accept some distinction in the value of the life of the newborn, and the older child or adult? If so, where is the line to be drawn? Is it seventy-two hours, or twenty-eight days, or later still? C. and J. were both about 4 months old. The Abortion Act has altered our perception of the sanctity of life. But debate has ebbed and flowed for centuries as to the status and humanity of the unborn. Abortion, although severely punished, was never equated with murder. Birth is a clear dividing line. No other distinction can be as clear. Do we regard the parents as standing proxy for their child in any decision as to treatment? If so, why draw the line at twenty-eight days? Older children develop chronic disease, are disabled in accidents, are discovered to suffer from gross handicap later in childhood.

The enormity of the moral and legal problems facing an intending legislator makes the prospect of legislation remote. The experience of attempts to legislate on the related area of voluntary euthanasia does not make encouraging reading for intending legislators.[33] Before giving up on any attempt to introduce reform, one question needs answering.

---

32. 'Legislation is Likely to Create More Difficulties than it Resolves' (1983) 9 J. Med. Ethics 18.
33. See Chapter 21.

The doctor attending a handicapped baby has an awesome responsibility. If, with entirely honest motives, he makes a decision out of line with a law which is far from clear, he may be punished as a murderer. It may be that the decisions taken by the doctors, the responsibility we entrust to them, are of such importance that the awfulness of the penalty for misjudgement is justified. But we must be satisfied that this is so before engaging too readily in criticism of the profession for attempts to protect its members.

CHAPTER 15

Doctors and Child Patients

In this chapter I examine generally the impact of the law on the doctor's relationship with his child patients and their parents. Victoria Gillick's campaign to prevent girls under 16 being prescribed the Pill without their parents' knowledge thrust the issue of parental rights into the limelight. At the end of the day the House of Lords ruled against her. But the Gillick saga illustrates the many legal problems concerning parents, children and doctors.

I look at the decision in *Gillick*,[1] and the recent judgement of the Court of Appeal in *Re R*, and consider their impact on the medical treatment of children generally, not just on the question of contraception for teenage girls. Where does the law stand on the question of blood transfusions for the children of Jehovah's Witnesses? May a doctor insist on administering a transfusion against the parents' wishes? Are there limits to treatment to which a parent may agree on behalf of the child? For instance, may a mother, learning that her 4-year-old daughter is a likely carrier of haemophilia, have the child sterilized at 4? What role does the law play in limiting damaging or mutilating surgery on children, for example the ghastly practice of female circumcision? These are just some of the issues addressed now.

Family Law Reform Act 1969

The Family Law Reform Act 1969 reduced the age of majority from

1. *Gillick* v. *West Norfolk and Wisbech AHA* [1985] 3 All ER 402 HL; *Re R (A Miner)* [1991] 4 All ER 177.

21 to 18. For the purposes of medical treatment, however, children attain adult status at 16. When the 1969 Act was before Parliament it was unclear as to what effect, if any, a consent to medical treatment given by a minor, a person under the age of majority, might have. Numbers of 16- and 17-year-olds live, or spend considerable periods of time, away from their parents. Some are married and parents themselves. Section 8 of the 1969 Act clarified the law concerning 16- to 18-year-olds and empowered them to consent to their own medical treatment. Sub-sections (1) and (2) of section 8 are clear. They provide:

(1) The consent of a minor who has attained the age of 16 years to any surgical, medical or dental treatment which, in the absence of consent, would constitute a trespass to his person shall be as effective as it would be if he were of full age: and where a minor has by virtue of this section given an effective consent it shall not be necessary to obtain any consent for it from his parent or guardian.

(2) In this section 'surgical, medical or dental treatment' includes any procedure undertaken for the purposes of diagnosis, and this section applies to any procedure (including, in particular, the administration of an anaesthetic) which is ancillary to any treatment as it applies to that treatment.

So far, so good; once a person is 16, providing he is mentally competent, he can decide for himself on matters of medicine and surgery. That does not mean that any parental consent relating to their children under 18 is always ineffective. If the child of 16 or 17 is incapable of giving consent, for example, because of mental handicap, his parents may still act on his behalf until he comes of age. Section 8 went on in sub-section (3) to provide:

(3) Nothing in this section shall be construed as making ineffective any consent which would have been effective if this section had not been enacted.

The majority of lawyers and doctors interpreted section 8(3) in this way. The common law had never directly determined the issue of when, if at all, a child could give effective consent to medical treatment. The assumption acted on was that the law gave effect to consent by a minor provided she or he was sufficiently mature to understand the proposed treatment or surgery.[2] Sixteen was the *average* age at which doctors judged patients to be old enough to give consent without consulting parents on every occasion. At 16, too, a person may choose

2. See P. D. G. Skegg, 'Consent to Medical Procedures on Minors' (1973) 36 MLR 370, pp. 370–75.

his own doctor,[3] and at 16 a person may without reference to his parents seek voluntary treatment in a mental hospital.[4] Nevertheless, many doctors regarded themselves free to treat children *under* 16 without parental approval if the individual child appeared sufficiently intelligent and grown up to take the decision on treatment alone. The issue before 1969 in *every* case turned on the doctor's assessment of the particular minor in his surgery. The 1969 Act freed the doctor from doubt and risk where the patient was over 16. He no longer had to consider the maturity of a patient over 16. He could assume adult status and capability. Sub-section (3), then, it was argued, simply preserved the status quo for the under-16s. Doctors could continue to treat a child under 16 as long as the child was mature enough to make his own judgement. This assumption, that there had always been a limited freedom to treat children under 16 without parental consent, and that what sub-section (3) did was preserve that freedom, was the issue at the heart of the Gillick saga.

The Gillick case

The Gillick saga has its origins in a circular issued by the DHSS in 1974, outlining arrangements for a comprehensive family planning service within the NHS. Section G dealt with provision for the young. Statistics on the number of births and induced abortions among girls under 16 led the DHSS to conclude that contraceptive services should be made more readily available to that age group. The essence of the DHSS advice was that the decision to provide contraception to a girl under 16 was one for the doctor. He might lawfully treat, and prescribe for, the girl without contacting her parents. Indeed, he should not contact parents without the girl's agreement. In 1980 the DHSS revised its advice. The revised version stressed that every effort should be made to involve parents. But if the girl was adamant that her parents should not know of her request for contraception, the principle of confidentiality between doctor and patient should be preserved. The parents must not be told.

This amended advice from the DHSS did not satisfy critics appalled

3. NHS (General Medical and Pharmaceutical Services) Regulations 1974, SI 1974/160 as amended by SI 1975/719. As to persons under 16 away from the parental home, see Lord Fraser in *Gillick* (above), p. 408.
4. Mental Health Act 1983 s. 131(2).

at the prospect of young girls being put on the Pill in their parents' ignorance. Victoria Gillick, then the mother of four daughters under 16, wrote to her local health authority seeking an assurance that none of her daughters would be given contraceptive or abortion advice or treatment without her prior knowledge and consent until they were 16. The assurance was refused, and after further fruitless correspondence Mrs Gillick went to court in August 1982. She sought declarations (1) against her health authority and the DHSS to the effect that their advice that children under 16 could be treated without parental consent was unlawful and wrong, and (2) against her health authority to the effect that medical personnel employed by them should not give contraceptive and/or abortion advice and/or treatment to any child of Mrs Gillick's under 16 without her prior knowledge and consent.

Mrs Gillick's concern was with contraceptive and abortion advice and treatment for under-16s. She had no axe to grind in respect of other forms of medical treatment of children. The trouble was that this issue could not that easily be isolated from more general problems. And there was another legal problem to bedevil the debate. Mrs Gillick's counsel pursued a two-pronged attack. They challenged the assumption that the common law had ever permitted medical treatment of children under 16 in the absence of parental consent. And they argued in relation to contraception specifically that as it is a crime for a man to have sexual intercourse with a girl under 16, providing her with contraception amounts to the crime of causing or encouraging sexual intercourse with a girl under 16.

Children under 16 and consent to treatment

The first judge[5] to consider Mrs Gillick's claim rejected emphatically her contention that a doctor may never treat a child under 16 without parental agreement. He saw that issue as a straightforward question of whether the consent of a child prevented a contact with the child from constituting a battery. If the doctor examined a girl physically before prescribing the Pill, did he run the risk of committing a civil battery or even a criminal assault on the girl? No, said Woolf J., provided the girl had the maturity and understanding to appreciate the nature of the consent she gave, the doctor could safely go ahead with treatment on the basis of her consent alone. The finding was not limited to contracep-

5. [1984] 1 All ER 365 (Woolf J.).

tion but applied to all forms of medical treatment. The nearer the child was to 16, and the more minor the nature of the treatment, the more likely it was that the child would be considered capable of giving the necessary consent. Where treatment with long-term implications was proposed, and the judge gave the example of sterilization, he warned that he doubted whether the consent of the child would ever be sufficient to justify the doctor's action. Woolf J. upheld the assumption as to how the common law approached the issue of consent given by children. Section 8(3) of the Family Law Reform Act, he found, simply preserved the common law position.

Mrs Gillick took her case on to the Court of Appeal and scored a famous victory in that arena.[6] The judgement of Woolf J. and the majority opinion among medical practitioners that the validity of a child's consent depended upon the individual child's maturity and capacity to understand the proposed treatment was rejected by the Court of Appeal as '. . . singularly unattractive and impracticable particularly in the context of medical treatment'.[7]

For the Court of Appeal the issue centred not on whether a child might be sufficiently mature to give consent to any particular contact with another, but on parental rights to control what happened to their children. They held that the common law gave to parents rights of custody and control over their children until either a child reached the age of majority, or common law or statute expressly set a lower age for emancipation from parental control in respect of a specified activity. So the Family Law Reform Act had empowered children to consent to medical treatment at 16. But below 16, at any rate where girls were concerned,[8] the parents' rights were paramount and the consent of a child was irrelevant and of no effect.

Not only treatment was unlawful without parental agreement. Any information or advice on contraception or abortion was unlawful in the absence of parental knowledge and agreement. After the Court of Appeal judgement a doctor could not safely see a child under 16 in his surgery or clinic without a parent's presence. And the legality of sex education in schools was thrown into doubt.

Arguments that the doctor was entitled to override parental rights

6. [1985] 1 All ER 533, CA.
7. p. 540.
8. The Court of Appeal invoked the ancient common law concept of the age of discretion as relevant to determine parental rights to physical control of their children. This was set at 16 for girls and 14 for boys.

Arguments that the doctor was entitled to override parental rights to promote the best interests of a child patient were dismissed unequivocally. A doctor could intervene only in an emergency or with the backing of a court order. What amounted to an emergency, whether it referred to general medical treatment to save a child rushed to a casualty ward, or envisaged emergency contraceptive treatment, was not defined by the Appeal Court.

The end of the story?

The DHSS appealed to the House of Lords. By a majority of three to two the House of Lords held that the original advice circulated by the DHSS was not unlawful and that a child under 16 could in certain circumstances give a valid consent to contraception or abortion treatment without parental knowledge or agreement.[9] To consider the implications of their decision for doctors, parents and children, the Law Lords' judgement will be dissected into three parts: (1) the general issue of consent by children to medical treatment, (2) the special problems of contraception and abortion and consent thereto, and (3) the criminal law as it affects contraception.

The general problem of consent

The majority of their Lordships rejected the Court of Appeal's finding that consent given by a child under 16 was of no effect. They accepted the view that the Family Law Reform Act had left the question open. The matter was for the common law to determine. But the common law was not static, fossilized in eighteenth-century notions of the inviolable rights of the paterfamilias. Judge-made law must meet the needs of the times. Parental rights derived from parental duties to protect the person and property of the child. Modern legislation qualified and limited parental rights by placing the welfare of the child as its first priority. Parental rights being dependent on the duty to care for and maintain the child, they endured only so long as necessary to achieve their end. As Lord Scarman put it: '. . . the parental right yields to the child's right to make his own decisions when he reaches a sufficient understanding and intelligence to be capable of making up his own mind on the matter requiring decision'.[10]

9. [1985] 3 All ER 402.
10. p. 422.

Parental rights were thus not absolute. Furthermore, the court found that the common law had never regarded the consent of a child as complete nullity. Were that the case, sexual intercourse with a girl under 16 would inevitably be the crime of rape. That is not so. Provided the girl is old enough to understand what she is agreeing to, intercourse with her with her consent will not be rape. Parliament, to protect girls under 16 from the consequences of their own folly, enacted a separate offence of unlawful sexual intercourse with girls under 16 in the commission of which the girl's consent is irrelevant. And if the girl validly consented, that is the only offence committed, and not the more serious crime of rape. In another context, just a year before the *Gillick* hearing, the House of Lords had considered the crime of kidnapping as it related to children under 16. They held that the central issue was the agreement of the child, not either parent, to being taken away by the accused.[11] In the case of a young child absence of consent could be presumed. With an older child the question was whether he or she had sufficient understanding and intelligence to give consent.

Moving from the general issue of consent by children to the problem of consent to medical treatment, the House of Lords saw no reason to depart from the general rule. Lord Fraser thought it would be ludicrous to say that a boy or girl of 15 could not agree to examination or treatment for a trivial injury. Importantly, Lord Templeman, who dissented on the specific issue of contraceptive treatment, agreed with his colleagues that there were circumstances where a doctor could properly treat a child under 16 without parental agreement. He concurred that the effect of the consent of the child depended on the nature of the treatment and the age and understanding of the child. A doctor, he thought, could safely remove tonsils or a troublesome appendix from a boy or girl of 15 without express parental agreement. With some confidence, then, it may be predicted that in relation to general problems of medical treatment, the *Gillick* case concludes that a child below 16 may lawfully be given medical advice and treatment without parental agreement, provided that child has achieved sufficient maturity to understand fully what is proposed. The doctor treating such a child will not be at risk of either a civil action for battery or criminal prosecution. One could go further and say that on this general issue *Gillick* is the end of the story.

11. *R.* v. *D.* [1984] 2 All ER 449.

The special problems of contraception and abortion

Lord Templeman, as we have seen, departed from his brethren's views on the specific issue of contraception. The core of his disagreement with them is this. He did not accept that a girl under 16 has sufficient maturity and understanding of the emotional and physical consequences of sexual intercourse to consent to contraceptive treatment. His Lordship put it thus:

> I doubt whether a girl under the age of 16 is capable of a balanced judgement to embark on frequent, regular or casual sexual intercourse fortified by the illusion that medical science can protect her in mind and body and ignoring the danger of leaping from childhood to adulthood without the difficult formative transitional experiences of adolescence. There are many things a girl under 16 needs to practise but sex is not one of them.[12]

The majority of his colleagues disagreed with Lord Templeman. They conceded that a request by a girl under 16 for contraception coupled with an insistence that parents not be told posed a problem for the doctor. Assessing whether she is mature enough to consider the emotional and physical consequences of the course she has embarked on will not be easy. But that question is to be left to the clinical judgement of the doctor. Lord Fraser set out five matters the doctor should satisfy himself on before giving contraceptive treatment to a girl below 16 without parental agreement. They are:

> ... (1) that the girl ... will understand his advice; (2) that he cannot persuade her to inform her parents ...; (3) that she is very likely to begin or continue having sexual intercourse with or without contraceptive treatment; (4) that unless she receives contraceptive advice or treatment her physical or mental health or both are likely to suffer; (5) that her best interests require him to give her contraceptive advice or treatment or both without the parental consent.[13]

Lord Fraser's carefully devised formula failed to satisfy Mrs Gillick and her many supporters. They regard it as inadequate in two respects. First, in a busy surgery or clinic has any doctor sufficient time to embark on the investigation and counselling of the girl necessary to fulfil the criteria laid down? Second, underlying the judgements of the majority is acceptance of the view that, as significant numbers of

12. p. 432.
13. p. 413.

young girls under 16 today are going to continue having sexual intercourse regardless of whether they have lawful access to contraception, it may be in their best interests to protect them from pregnancy by contraceptive treatment. Mrs Gillick disagreed. She contended that if access to contraception without parental agreement were stopped, at least the majority of young girls would (a) be deterred from starting to have intercourse so young by fear of pregnancy and/or parental disapproval, and (b) would have a defence against pressure from their peers to 'grow up' and sleep with someone. Both sides in the debate on 'under-age' contraception agree that early sexual intercourse increases the danger of disease to the child, be it cervical cancer or venereal disease. Most agree as to the emotional damage the child risks. They are no nearer agreement as to how girls under 16 may best be protected than on the day Mrs Gillick first went to court.

The divide between Mrs Gillick and her opponents is too wide and their disagreement too bitter for the Law Lords' judgement to be regarded as definitely marking the conclusion of legal manoeuvres to ban or restrict contraception for children under 16. Two courses of action are open to those who support Mrs Gillick. First, they may be able to persuade an MP to promote legislation specifically on contraception for children under 16. The debate could then move to Parliament. Argument would be just as vitriolic, but at least the issue would be clearer for being dealt with independently and apart from the general issue of medical treatment for children. Second, individual parents could pursue legal action against a doctor who had prescribed for their daughter in circumstances which they allege contravene the guidelines put forward by the Law Lords. Such actions would be highly speculative. They would raise the issue of whether Lord Fraser's guidelines are legally enforceable. For if the girl understood what was entailed in the physical examination conducted by the doctor preparatory to prescribing contraception and any physical invasion of her body if mechanical means of contraception were to be fitted, it is difficult to see how a civil suit for battery or a criminal prosecution for assault could lie.[14] The guidelines may represent the pious hopes of their Lordships rather than a statement of law. In the end the Lords' judgement may be seen to have left scope for further bitter litigation. Doctors are not yet free from the threat of legal action by angry

14. See Glanville Williams, 'The Gillick Saga I and II' (1985) 135 NLJ 1116 and 1180.

parents discovering that their child has been given contraception.

Finally, express mention must be made of abortion. The greater part of the Law Lords' judgement concentrated on contraception. It is clear that the rules for abortions on girls under 16 are the same. If a girl is intelligent and mature enough to understand what is involved in the operation, the doctor, if the girl insists on not telling her parents or if they refuse to agree to an abortion, may go ahead on the basis of the girl's consent alone. The House of Lords endorsed the approach of Butler-Sloss J. in an earlier case.[15] A 15-year-old girl, with one child already, became pregnant again while in the care of the local authority. She wanted an abortion. Doctors considered that the birth of a second child would endanger the mental health of the girl and her existing child. Her father objected. Abortion was contrary to his religion. The local authority applied to have the girl made a ward of court and so seek the court's consent to the operation. The judge authorized the operation. She said the decision must be made in the light of the girl's best interests. She took into account the parents' feelings but held that they could not outweigh the needs of the girl.

The criminal law, sexual intercourse and contraception

So far I have examined only the issues relating to a child's capacity to consent to treatment. The second prong of Mrs Gillick's argument related to the criminal law, which renders it a crime to have sexual intercourse with a girl under 16 regardless of her consent or encouragement. Section 28 of the Sexual Offences Act 1956 provides further that it is an offence '... to cause or encourage ... the commission of unlawful sexual intercourse with ... a girl for whom [the] accused is responsible'. The majority of the Law Lords found that a doctor who *bona fide* provided a girl with contraception in the interests of her health, to protect her from the further risks of pregnancy and consequently abortion or childbirth, committed no crime. He was not encouraging the continuance of sexual intercourse and implicitly the crime of unlawful sexual intercourse, but offering '... a palliative against the consequences of crime'. Doctors should, however, tread carefully. For while in general a doctor commits no crime by giving a young girl contraceptive treatment, the judgement makes it clear that any doctor who fails to assess his patient carefully and make a judge-

15. *In Re P. (A Minor)* (1982) 80 LGR 301.

ment based on medical indications as to her health may face prosecution. Lord Scarman said:

> Clearly a doctor who gives a brief contraceptive advice or treatment not because in his clinical judgement the treatment is medically indicated ... but with the intention of facilitating her having unlawful sexual intercourse may well be guilty of a criminal offence.[16]

This limb of the judgement, too, failed to satisfy Mrs Gillick. For her, contraception for young girls cannot be medically indicated. Once again the judgement may leave room for further legal disputes. Opponents of 'under-age' contraception will be on the look-out for doctors who appear to prescribe contraceptives too freely to young girls or who express views that intercourse is intrinsically acceptable at such a young age. Such doctors will risk prosecution. Additionally, both Lord Fraser and Lord Scarman stressed the role of the General Medical Council in ensuring that doctors adhered to strict guidelines in providing contraceptive treatment for young girls. Mrs Gillick expressed her intention to gather dossiers on doctors who appear over-liberal in their provision of contraception to children under 16.

Confidentiality and children under 16

A young girl, embarking on a sexual relationship and considering seeking contraception, probably does not contemplate her capacity to give consent to treatment, but the more immediate issue of 'Will the doctor tell my mum?' The thought that a doctor may be free to give contraceptive advice to a child without the parents even knowing of what is proposed was perhaps at the heart of Mrs Gillick's campaign. The disruption of family life, and the danger that the girl herself might omit to give the doctor information on other drugs she might be taking, horrified many caring parents. The courts paid surprisingly little attention to the issue of confidentiality. The House of Lords held that in exceptional cases the doctor was free to treat the girl without parental knowledge. The question which remains is whether a doctor *must* preserve confidentiality in his dealings with his young patient. By implication the House of Lords endorsed the view that the doctor owed a duty of confidentiality to his patient under 16. They upheld the DHSS guidelines, laying down the rule that if the girl was adamant

16. p. 425. For trenchant criticism see Glanville Williams, op. cit.

that her parents must not be contacted, confidentiality must be preserved. Will a doctor, faced with a girl of 15 who tells him she has started an affair, be at risk of an action for breach of confidence by the girl if he refuses her contraception and telephones her mother?

For a number of reasons an action for breach of confidence is likely to run into difficulties. The major obstacle will be that the doctor may invoke in his defence arguments that disclosure is in the patient's interest and in the public interest. The public interest defence to an action for breach of confidence justifies disclosure of iniquity.[17] The doctor may contend that he is acting to disclose to those most closely concerned with the girl's welfare the commission of a crime, unlawful sexual intercourse, upon her. We saw that the extent to which a doctor may lawfully breach his patient's confidence, to disclose crime, is uncertain. The Court of Appeal judgement in *W*. v. *Egdell*[18] does, though, suggest that a court should take into account too the public interest in young girls seeking protection against pregnancy.

It is not the courts but the medical profession itself which is most likely to safeguard the child patient's confidences. Breach of confidentiality normally constitutes serious professional misconduct, an offence for which a doctor may be struck off the medical register by the General Medical Council. Before Mrs Gillick first challenged DHSS guidance on contraception for the under-16s in the courts, the GMC required that, while doctors should always try to persuade girls requesting contraception to involve their parents, if the girl refused to permit her parents to be contacted '. . . the doctor must observe the rule of professional secrecy in his management of the case'.[19] When Mrs Gillick won in the Court of Appeal the GMC had no choice but to amend this rule to comply with the law laid down by the court.[20] To the dismay of many doctors involved in family planning, the GMC, after the Lords' ruling, has not returned to its previous stance[21] of *guaranteed* confidentiality for young patients. Whether a doctor informs a girl patient's parents is to depend on *his* judgement of the girl's maturity, welfare and best interests, though if he elects to do so

17. See Chapter 3, pp. 51–7.
18. [1990] 1 All ER 855, CA.
19. GMC 'Bluebook' *Professional Conduct: Fitness to Practise*, August 1983; p. 20.
20. *Professional Conduct: Fitness to Practise*, April 1985, p. 21.
21. *Professional Conduct and Discipline: Fitness to Practise*, February 1991,

he must inform the girl and his 'judgement concerning disclosure must always reflect both the patient's best medical interests and the trust the patient places in the doctor'. The ultimate result of the judgement of the House of Lords and the consequent ruling on ethics by the GMC is this. Parents have no 'right to know' if their daughter seeks contraceptive or abortion advice or treatment. Daughters have no unequivocal 'right' to confidentiality.

Parents and younger children

We must consider now the rights and obligations of parents and doctors in relation to children who have not achieved the degree of intelligence and understanding enabling them to give their consent to treatment. The absence of any arbitrary age limit as to when this stage of development is attained is the doctor's first difficulty. One can perhaps safely say that the child under 12 has virtually never reached sufficient maturity; that the 12- to 14-year-old can rarely be said to be at that stage, and that the grey area revolves largely around the 14+ age group. Nevertheless, in each case it is the maturity of the individual child which the doctor must assess. Once he judges the child to be too immature to decide for himself on treatment, what legal principles determine the doctor's duty to the child and its parents? Do the parents enjoy an unfettered right to approve or reject treatment proposed for the child?

In the straightforward case of a sick child and caring parents, parental consent to treatment required for the benefit of the child authorizes the doctor's actions. The doctor will be safe from an action for battery. Problems surface when either (a) a parent is not available or is simply uninterested, or (b) a parent expressly refuses consent to treatment. The first case is relatively easy to resolve. A casualty officer, faced with a young child injured in a road accident or rushed in from school with an acutely inflamed appendix, may safely go ahead with

---

p. 20. But has anything really changed? In 1971 Dr Browne was acquitted of professional misconduct after he informed the parents of a girl of 16 of her request for contraception. The GMC found he acted 'in the girl's best interests'. *GMC* v. *Browne, The Times*, 6 and 8 March 1971. See J. K. Mason and R. A. McCall Smith, *Law and Medical Ethics*, Butterworths, London, 1991, p. 187; BMA, *Philosophy and Practice of Medical Ethics*, 1988, p. 31.

whatever treatment is immediately required. His legal justification derives either from the defence of necessity or from the reasonable assumption that just as the unconscious adult may be presumed to agree to treatment needed to safeguard his life or health, so may the absent parent be presumed to agree to similar treatment for his child. When a parent is physically present but displays no interest in the care of his child or fails to turn up to meet medical staff, again the doctor must do as he sees fit. It is the parents' duty to obtain adequate medical care for their children. Rights to determine the content of that care are dependent on fulfilling that duty.[22]

It is in the second example, when a caring parent expressly refuses consent to treatment of the child, that an acute legal problem for the doctor is posed. Take the examples of a Christian Scientist refusing to allow any medical treatment of his child, and the Jehovah's Witness refusing to authorize a blood transfusion for his critically injured and haemorrhaging child. What may the doctor lawfully do next? I suggest that where treatment is *immediately* necessary to preserve the child's life or health the doctor may simply proceed with treatment. He does not need first to involve the local authority or make the child a ward of court. The essence of the House of Lords' decision in *Gillick* was that parental rights over children derive from parental duties to children.[23] Parents have a duty to provide adequate medical care for their children. That duty has so far usually been interpreted objectively. What would the average parent do to aid his sick child? A parent who fails to obtain adequate medical care for his child commits the offence of wilful neglect.[24] Should the child die, he may face a charge of manslaughter. The courts have held that it is no defence for a parent who appreciated the gravity of his child's condition that he refrained from seeking conventional medical help out of sincere religious conviction.[25]

Faced by a parent rejecting any medical help, for example a parent

---

22. 'Emergency, parental neglect, abandonment of the child or inability to find the parent are examples of exceptional situations justifying the doctor proceeding to treat the child without parental knowledge and consent . . .' *per* Lord Scarman in *Gillick* v. *West Norfolk and Wisbech AHA* (above), p. 424.
23. *Per* Lord Fraser, p. 410 in *Gillick*.
24. Children and Young Persons Act 1933, s. 1(1).
25. *R.* v. *Senior* [1899] 1 QB 283.

seeking to remove his child from Casualty after the child arrives there from school, the doctor's course of action is clear. The parent has no right to refuse *all* treatment for his child. Indeed, he commits a criminal offence if he does so. The case of the Jehovah's Witness parent is rather more problematical. Earlier decisions by courts on when refusal of treatment amounts to the crime of child neglect concern parents refusing any form of medical aid. The Jehovah's Witness, by contrast, accepts any treatment save for the administration of blood. Is his refusal of that form of treatment when the child's life is thereby endangered a sufficient deviation from reasonable standards of parenting to render his conduct criminal? The advent of AIDS and the fear of contaminated blood engendered by that disease has been called on by Jehovah's Witnesses to support their religious objections to transfusion. There may well be some doubt as to whether a jury would convict a parent of neglect for refusing to sanction a transfusion.

Nevertheless I believe that the civil law will still protect the doctor who administers a transfusion despite parental opposition. The doctor, too, has a duty to the child, his patient. The criminal law on child neglect serves to illustrate that the content of that duty is to be determined by what is objectively considered medically necessary, and not by sole reference to the parents' individual and idiosyncratic viewpoint. The doctor must act in the best interests of his patient. In 99.9 per cent of cases the best interests of the child are represented by his parents. When doctor and parents disagree, parents' views may not be lightly disregarded. On any form of optional or disputed treatment, such as vaccination for whooping cough, parental views must prevail. When treatment is considered necessary but is not immediately called for, the court must be the arbiter of the dispute between parents and the child's doctors. But if there is no time to seek judicial advice the doctor may go ahead with immediately required treatment such as a blood transfusion. As Lord Templeman put it in *Gillick* v. *West Norfolk and Wisbech AHA*:[26]

Where the patient is an infant, the medical profession accepts that a parent having custody and being responsible for the infant is entitled on behalf of the infant to consent to or reject treatment if the parent considers that the best interests of the infant so require. Where doctor and parent disagree, the court can decide and is not slow to act. I accept that if there is no time to obtain a decision from the court, a doctor may safely carry out treatment in an

26. p. 432.

emergency if the doctor believes the treatment to be vital to the survival or health of the infant and notwithstanding the opposition of a parent or the impossibility of alerting the parent before the treatment is carried out.

The role of the court

The doctor's freedom to act on his judgement alone in defiance of parental views is strictly limited to emergency treatment. An essential transfusion can be performed at once. But take another example of religious objections to treatment: what if a Roman Catholic parent objects to an abortion for an 11-year-old daughter? The doctor must delay and refer the issue to the courts via wardship proceedings. A few days' delay will not usually prejudice the child's health.

What happens then? An application will be made to make the child a ward of court, and judicial approval sought for treatment proposed. The formula then is that the court decides the issue 'in the best interests of the child'. The child's interests include the effect on the family relationship of authorizing the disputed treatment. The family's religious beliefs will be a factor for consideration. There seems little if any doubt that where a normal child's life is at stake, saving that life will prevail over parental religion. In the case of a disputed abortion, if the girl appears to want an abortion or is too immature to form a view on the question, the court will probably authorize the operation.

Religious convictions on abortion and any other form of medical treatment are not the only arena for potential dispute between parents and doctors. What of the parent who after agonized consideration refuses further 'heroic' surgery on her child? For example, should a parent refuse a heart and lung transplant for a sick infant, would a court order that surgery proceed? No definite answer is possible. The court will be guided, as it was in *Re B.*, the 'Baby Alexandra' case,[27] by the prospects of success for the operation, the pain entailed for the child and his future quality of life. The views of the child, if he is old enough to understand anything of his condition, may be sought. The judge takes from the doctor the power of life or death. For the overwhelming majority of Her Majesty's judges the call to exercise this power will never come. Whether a trained lawyer sitting on his own is the appropriate forum to answer these agonizing questions may be open to doubt.

27. [1981] 1 WLR 1421, discussed above, pp. 315–16.

A second example of proposed treatment which might end up before a court concerns brain-damaged children. An American court refused to make a 12-year-old Down's syndrome boy a dependent child, a ward of the court, in order to authorize surgery to repair a congenital heart defect.[28] The court regarded the burden of displacing the parents' loving decision as not met. In England the principles derived from the case-law relating to handicapped infants discussed in the previous chapter would be applied, and would, I think, produce a contrary result. Only if the suffering produced by the proposed treatment and consequent prolongation of life outweighs *any* benefit the child might gain from continued life may his parents lawfully refuse life-saving treatment. Brain damage itself is no lawful cause for denying the child life, for 'pulling the plug'. One factor may in certain circumstances distinguish the older child from the infant. Consider this scenario. An intelligent, athletic 11-year-old is grievously injured in a road accident. He can no longer walk or see. His speech is impaired. His misery is evident. That child's appreciation of his own dilemma distinguishes him from the handicapped baby. In attempting the 'balancing exercise'[29] between life and suffering, his parents may properly take into account the child's dreadful knowledge of his happy past and unhappy future.

When the child objects to treatment

What legal effect, if any, does a child's objection to medical treatment entail? So long as the parents retain exclusive rights to authorize treatment on behalf of a child too immature to make his own decision on treatment, the child's objection may safely be overruled. The 5-year-old's vociferous objections to vaccination or to dental treatment have no legal effect. The older the child the more regard should be given to explaining treatment and seeking to obtain his assent and co-operation. But if he has not reached sufficient maturity to comprehend the proposed treatment and give his own consent to that treatment nor can he veto treatment. He is not, as Lord Donaldson MR has pithily styled the test, '*Gillick* competent'.

More problematical is the case of the older child who is '*Gillick* competent' and could give an effective consent to treatment. If she is

28. *Re Phillip B.* App. 156 Cal. Rptr 48 (1979).
29. Mandated by Lord Donaldson, MR in *Re J.*, discussed above, p. 322.

345

capable of authorizing treatment, it would seem to follow that she is equally capable of refusing treatment. Lord Donaldson MR in *Re R*.[30] has suggested that this is not so. R. was a 15-year-old girl suffering from severe psychiatric problems. She refused to continue taking her prescribed medication. The local authority responsible for R. made her a ward of court and sought judicial guidance. The trial judge held that because R. was not '*Gillick* competent' her parents or guardians could still authorize treatment against her will. '*Gillick* competence' enabled a child to consent to treatment but not to veto it. Consent was akin to a key which 'unlocked the door to treatment' making the doctor's action lawful but not obligatory. Once a child became '*Gillick* competent', or attained the age of 16 giving her competence under the Family Law Reform Act, she becomes a keyholder. Her parents remained keyholders able to authorize treatment right up to the minor's 18th birthday. Doctors faced with willing parents and unwilling children were not obliged to treat the child, indeed might well choose not to, but they could lawfully elect to act on the basis of the parental consent alone.

Lord Scarman in *Gillick* spoke of parental right 'yielding' to the child's right when that child was capable of authorizing her own treatment. It seems a strange right which entitles a child to say 'yes' but not 'no'. In practical terms legal principles which result in a mother having no say as to whether her teenage daughter agrees to an abortion, no right even to know of the operation, but being able to require that same daughter to undergo abortion against her will, are odd in the extreme.

The limits of parental consent

Parental rights to determine medical treatment of their children derive from the parental duty to obtain adequate medical care for them. Their rights over their children are not unfettered. As with all other parental rights, they are to be exercised in the child's best interests. A parent may give '. . . a legally effective consent to a procedure which is likely to be for the benefit of the child, in the sense of being in the child's best interests'.[31] Routine treatment or surgery for an existing

---

30. *Re R*. [1991] 4 All ER 177 CA. (This section was inserted at proof and only attempts a brief introduction to the complex issue raised by *Re R*.)
31. See Skegg, op. cit., p. 377.

physical condition, diagnostic procedures, preventive measures such as vaccination, pose no problem here. The likely benefit is there for all to see. More intricate and even risky procedures cause little difficulty. Not all parents might agree to complex heart surgery on a tiny baby, but if doctors and parents weigh risk and benefit and conclude in favour of going ahead, they have exercised their respective duties properly.

Where problems do surface is in relation to medical or surgical procedures which are not immediately called for to treat or prevent ill-health. Two classic issues are dealt with later – whether a child can donate organs or tissue,[32] and when children can be used for medical research purposes.[33] The issue that has engaged the direct attention of the English courts is the sterilization of children.

In 1976 the case of *Re D*.[34] came before Heilbron J. It concerned a handicapped girl aged 11. She suffered from Soto's syndrome and was afflicted by epilepsy and a number of other physical problems. The girl was also to some extent emotionally and mentally retarded. Her mother was anxious as to her future and considered that she would never be capable of caring for a child, that having a child would damage her, that she might all too easily be seduced and would be incapable of practising any form of contraception. Accordingly she sought to have her sterilized before these risks should materialize. The girl's paediatrician agreed, and a gynaecologist was found who was ready to perform the operation. An educational psychologist involved with the child disagreed and applied to have the child made a ward of court. Heilbron J. ordered that proposals for the operation be abandoned. Her function, she said, was to act as the 'judicial reasonable parent', with the welfare of the child as her paramount consideration. She found that medical opinion was overwhelmingly against sterilization of such a child of 11. The irrevocable nature of sterilization, the potential emotional impact on the girl when she discovered what had been done to her, her present inability to understand what was proposed, coupled with evidence that her mental development was such that she would one day be able to make an informed choice for herself on childbearing, all these factors led the judge to conclude that the operation was '. . . neither medically indicated nor necessary, and

32. See Chapter 19, pp. 397–8.
33. See Chapter 20, pp. 420–23.
34. [1976] 1 All ER 326.

that it would not be in [the girl's] best interests for it to be performed'.[35]

Eleven years later in *Re B*.[36] (1987) the House of Lords sanctioned the sterilization of 17-year-old Jeanette. Jeanette was much more profoundly handicapped than D. She was said to have a mental age of 5 or 6, with a much more limited capacity to communicate. She had no understanding of the link between sexual intercourse and pregnancy. Those caring for her testified that, apart from sterilization, no means of reliable contraception would be suitable for Jeanette. If she became pregnant, delivery might well have to be by Caesarean section, and the girl had an unbreakable habit of picking and tearing at any wounds. Despite her profound handicap, Jeanette was sexually mature and provocative. The Law Lords held that the legality of the proposal to sterilize Jeanette must depend only on whether sterilization would '. . . promote the welfare and serve the best interests of the ward'.[37] Consideration of eugenics, and whether sterilizing Jeanette would ease the burden on those caring for her, were irrelevant.[38] However, the House of Lords rejected any distinction between 'therapeutic' and 'non-therapeutic' interventions. It was argued before them that the 'reasonable' parent, and the courts acting in a quasi-parental capacity, could only authorize procedures designed to promote the health of the minor, to cure or prevent disease. 'Non-therapeutic' sterilization, an operation not called for to deal with some existing health problem in the minor, should not be allowed. The Canadian Supreme Court in *Re Eve*[39] had earlier outlawed such 'non-therapeutic' procedures. Lord Hailsham found the distinction '. . . totally meaningless, and if meaningful, quite irrelevant to the correct application of the welfare principle'.[40] Their Lordships concluded that as Jeanette (1) would never be capable of making any choice for herself on whether to have a child, (2) would never even appreciate what was happening to her, and (3) would suffer damage to her health if she ever became pregnant, she could lawfully be sterilized by occlusion of her Fallopian tubes (not hysterectomy). Lord Templeman, however, suggested that the radical nature of steril-

35. p. 335.
36. [1987] 2 All ER 206.
37. *Per* Lord Bridge, p. 213.
38. See *per* Lord Oliver, p. 219.
39. (1986) 31 DLR (4th) 1.
40. p. 213.

ization was such that a girl of 18 should never be sterilized without the consent of a High Court judge.[41]

A doctor performing a sterilization operation with the consent of the parents might still be liable in criminal, civil or professional proceedings. A court exercising the wardship jurisdiction emanating from the Crown is the only authority which is empowered to authorize such a drastic step as sterilization after a full and informed investigation.

However, the requirement for judicial authorization of sterilization of girls under 18 applies only to sterilization for contraceptive purposes. If the girl requires surgery to treat some separate health problem, her parents' consent is sufficient to authorize that surgery albeit an inevitable result of the operation will be to render her sterile.

The judgement in Re B. that sterilization was in Jeanette's best interests was trenchantly criticized by Professor Michael Freeman.[42] Subsequent judgements on sterilizing young girls[43] confirm Professor Freeman's fears and are explored further in Chapter 17. What the judgement clearly demonstrates in the context of children's treatment generally is that parental powers are strictly limited. Albeit the parent honestly believes she is acting in her child's interests, if she proposes to authorize some irreversible or drastic measure, her authorization alone will not make that measure lawful. It must be shown to be in the child's interests. No mother could, for example, authorize the sterilization of her 4-year-old daughter because that daughter was a haemophilia carrier. She has no right to deprive her child of the right to take that decision for herself. The child's best interests include her potential right to autonomy. It seems unlikely that parents could authorize a vasectomy on even the most grossly handicapped son. For such an operation would never be in his interests, albeit it benefited society. Similarly no parent, however strong or genuine his commitment to medical research might be, could lawfully authorize the entry of his healthy child into a research trial posing real and substantial risk to that child's health.

Other examples could be proliferated and debated endlessly. Just

41. p. 214.
42. 'Sterilizing the Mentally Handicapped', in *Medicine, Ethics and Law*, ed. M. D. A. Freeman, Stevens, London, 1988.
43. *Re M (A Minor) (Wardship: Sterilization)* [1988] 2 FLR 997; *Re P (A Minor) (Wardship: Sterilization)* [1989] 1 FLR 182.

two will be considered here. What is the position *re* cosmetic surgery? May a mother put her son through painful surgery to advance his career as a male model? Certainly not. That cannot be said to be in the interests of the child, rather than the mother's vicarious ambition. But surgery on boys with 'bat ears' is common and lawful. The pain of surgery is balanced by the child's misery at being taunted for his deformity. Parents are allowed to judge the outcome of the 'balancing exercise'. Difficult questions are posed by cosmetic surgery on Down's children. Cosmetic surgery may make the child more socially acceptable. Is that in the interests of the child?

What of circumcision of male infants and girl children; can those procedures be lawful? Medical opinion on male circumcision is divided. Until recently many doctors regarded it as rarely medically indicated. Now it seems circumcision provides some protection against venereal disease, at any rate for the circumcised man's partner! Male circumcision is a matter of medical debate. For Jewish and Muslim parents it is an article of faith. The child suffers momentary pain. Although medical opinion may not necessarily regard it as positively beneficial, it is in no way medically harmful if properly performed. The community as a whole regards it as a decision for the infant's parents. Female circumcision carried out on girls at, or before, puberty is regarded by most with revulsion in all its forms. Medical opinion condemns the pain and trauma for the girl and warns of serious risks to her when she comes to bear a child. No English judge would be even remotely likely to regard female circumcision of a girl under 16 as in her best interests. Yet for the practice to be effectively banned here, Parliament had to enact the Prohibition of Female Circumcision Act 1985.

Procedures to protect children

Re D. and the Prohibition of Female Circumcision Act illustrated how random and inadequate the machinery to protect children from inappropriate 'treatment' may be. In the course of the judgement in *Re D*., it emerged that two similar sterilization operations on mentally subnormal girls had already been performed in Sheffield. D. was lucky. Her psychologist was persistent. Chance took D.'s dilemma to the High Court. And this must often be the case when parents and doctors agree. Despite judicial pronouncements that sterilization of girls under 18 must always be a matter for the courts, some gynaecologists still sterilize girls by hysterectomy for 'hygienic' reasons without seeking judicial approval. These cases involve girls who cannot in any sense cope with menstruation. They may refuse to wear or, in extreme cases, eat their sanitary towels. It is not clear beyond doubt that such an operation is in the girl's interests, though it is certainly in her carers' interests. The problem of protecting such girls is: who will ever know what happened? Only if some interested third party intervenes will the matter reach the light of day in time to prevent the procedure going ahead. Nor is the law much of a deterrent to doctors or parents. Technically if a procedure is not medically indicated and/or in the child's best interests it amounts to a civil battery against the child and may be a criminal assault. In debates on prohibition of female circumcision Lord Hailsham argued that it was already a crime, assault occasioning actual bodily harm. But who will tell the authorities; who will prosecute? Besides which, had the common law been faced with the question of female circumcision, difficult questions would have been set in answering the question of the girl's best interests. What if she agreed, wishing to fall in with the customs of her community? What of arguments that the girl's mental well-being required that she meet the customs of her people? And if ritual male circumcision is permissible, why not female circumcision if carried out by surgeons in aseptic conditions? Litigation, if it started, would have been protracted.

Child abuse

The complexities of the law relating to child abuse is beyond the scope of this book, but one or two issues of especial concern to doctors and nurses working with children should be mentioned.

A general practitioner or paediatrician treating a child whom he suspects may have been abused faces a difficult dilemma. He may wish to examine the child in such a way as to confirm or dispel his suspicions, and he will know that the accompanying parent is likely to veto any such examination and whisk the child away out of the surgery. The dilemma is particularly acute if sexual abuse is suspected. In Cleveland,[44] several children were removed from their families after paediatricians diagnosed sexual abuse on the basis of an intimate examination of the child's vagina and/or anus (the anal dilation test). Legal proceedings against the doctors were settled without judicial

44. See Report of the Inquiry into Child Abuse in Cleveland 1987, Cm. 412 (1988).

resolution of the many legal issues at stake. In what circumstances may a child be so examined without parental consent? The doctor cannot rely on implicit consent based on the parent presenting the child for examination of some other, as far as the parent is concerned, unrelated medical condition. If a mother takes her asthmatic son to the doctor to have his chest examined, it cannot be implied that she also consents to an anal examination. However, if the doctor has reasonable grounds to believe (1) that the child's asthma and failure to thrive result from abuse, (2) that if he alerts the mother to his suspicions, she will refuse to co-operate and the child may be abused again, he may do what is immediately necessary to safeguard the child. It will not be unlawful to examine the child, even against the mother's will, so that the doctor can decide what further steps to take. The onus of proving reasonable grounds for his suspicions, and the necessity of acting immediately, falls on the doctor. Where there is no immediate risk of the child being further abused, or disappearing, the doctor should look to the Children Act 1989[45] for remedies to protect the child. These will include contacting social workers, who may seek an emergency protection order[46] or a child assessment order. Child assessment orders, introduced for the first time by section 43 of the 1989 Act, may prove especially useful in cases of suspected abuse and neglect. Prior to that Act there was no power to require parents to present their child for a medical examination. If a doctor or health visitor had some, but no compelling, grounds to suspect that a child's failure to thrive related to neglect or abuse, she faced a cruel choice. Do nothing and the child might suffer. Activate the social services department and the child might be taken away from his parents on a place of safety order,[47] with all the trauma of separation, and on examination the doctor's suspicions might be proved incorrect. The child assessment order enables health care and social services professionals to require parents to co-operate in assessing the cause of the child's mental or physical condition without at that stage breaking up the family. Clearly in making a decision on how to act in cases of suspected abuse the doctor owes a duty of care to the child. Damage to

45. The Children Act 1989 will not be fully in force until 1992. For an account of previous procedures to deal with child abuse see C. Lyon and P. de Cruz, *Child Abuse*, Jordan, Bristol, 1990.
46. See s. 44 of the Children Act 1989.
47. The predecessor to the emergency protection order.

the child is readily foreseeable, as is damage to a parent wrongfully accused of abuse and deprived of his child. But is there a duty of care to the parent? Would imposition of such a duty conflict with the primary duty owed to the patient, the child? Courts are wary of imposing a duty to a third party conflicting with an established duty owed to a professional's client or patient. In the case of child abuse though, any conflict may well be resolved in this manner. A doctor mistakenly diagnosing abuse is liable only if negligent, if he has acted in a way out of line with any responsible body of professional opinion. A doctor proved to be so negligent in acting to initiate the separation of child and parent will have damaged his patient, the child, as much as the third party, the parent. The perceived conflict of interest is illusory.

One final legal question affects doctors dealing with suspected child abuse. Do they risk action for breach of confidence by the parents if they disclose information to the police or social workers? First, where that information relates to the child, there is no breach of any confidential relationship with the parent. And even where information derived from the relationship with the parent is disclosed, if it is done to prevent imminent danger to the child that disclosure is justified on the principles discussed in Chapter 3.

Conclusions

This chapter serves to illustrate not that fundamental legal reform is called for, not that official busybodies should monitor every consultation between doctors, parents and children, but rather to show the limitations of the law, however well intentioned. The question of parental rights to refuse to consent to treatment occupied the courts for over three years. *Gillick* produced only a partial answer and posed more questions. *Re R.* has further muddied the waters. The issues of consent, confidentiality and compulsion in relation to children will never go away. There is no simplistic solution. Recognition of the problems of law, ethics and medicine and co-operation in striving to solve them may make them more manageable.

CHAPTER 16

General Practice

At first sight legal problems concerning patients and their general practitioners appear few and far between. Patients visit their GP on average four or five times a year and make one or two hospital visits in a lifetime. Yet malpractice actions against GPs are rare and barely more than a handful of reported cases exist. There are several reasons for this state of affairs. First, the NHS arrangements for general practice and the quality of consistent care offered by the vast majority of GPs are such that family doctors still occupy a high measure of esteem. Second, patients have traditionally enjoyed a longstanding personal relationship with their GP. A mistake is more likely to be forgiven and forgotten in the context of a GP's continuing care than in the impersonal hospital atmosphere. The patient is less likely to want to put a man or woman he knows well 'into the dock'. But there are other reasons too. Proving negligence, and that the patient's injury resulted from that negligence, is always difficult. Against a GP the problems multiply. How do you prove that the child's sudden deterioration resulted from the GP not visiting at once? Would immediate treatment have arrested the condition? Added to these difficulties, the common run of complaints about general practice do not tend to be the sort that make litigation with its expense, pomp and ceremony worthwhile. Patients object to unhelpful receptionists, difficulty in getting home visits, and often simply sense a lack of sympathy. Rarely do these irritations cause injury serious enough to merit litigation. I shall look at what the law, in particular the NHS regulations, has to offer. I shall see how the medical profession seeks to enforce standards. And finally I shall examine how far, if at all, government reforms have undermined the GP's freedom to practise as he or she thinks fit.

Terms of service

While it remains the case that general practice generates relatively few legal issues as between the doctor and his patient, the increasingly complex regulation of general practice by the government merits a legal text of its own. The health care reforms introduced in 1990 resulted in many alterations to the general practitioner's terms of service and to the very nature of general practice in some instances. No more than the briefest summary of these changes as they affect patients is attempted in this chapter.

The National Health Service Act 1977[1] imposes a duty on district health authorities to make arrangements for general practice in their district. They are required '. . . to provide personal medical services for all persons in the district who wish to take advantage of the arrangements'. The actual administration of such medical services is a matter for the local Family Health Services Authority (FHSA). The FHSA is crucial to general practice. It administers arrangements for general practice, maintains the medical list of GPs in the area, administers pharmaceutical and other ancillary medical services, and acts as a grievance body for dissatisfied patients. And it is the FHSA with whom the general practitioner 'contracts'. The composition of the FHSA is designed to ensure a balance of doctors, representatives of other medical professions and lay people.[2]

Family Health Service Authorities take over from Family Practitioner Committees responsibility for arrangements for the provision of primary health care.[3] This responsibility includes dental, ophthalmic and pharmaceutical services as well as general practice.[4]

A doctor seeking to enter general practice must apply to have his name entered on the medical list in the area where he wishes to practise. The district health authority will refer his application to a central Medical Practices Committee, who will examine his qualifications and

1. s. 29(1). And see the Health Services Act 1980, s. 1(7) and Sched. I.
2. Sched. I, Part II, National Health Service and Community Care Act 1990.
3. See s. 2 of the National Health Service and Community Care Act 1990.
4. See s. 15 of the National Health Service Act 1977 as amended by s. 12 of the National Health Service and Community Care Act.

experience.[5] If 'passed' by that Committee[6] then, save where there is already an excess of doctors in a particular neighbourhood, the doctor's name must be entered on the list. Once on the list the GP enters into a 'contract' with the local FHSA to provide general medical services. He may additionally apply to be entered on the obstetric list and provide care for his own maternity patients. The terms of his 'contract' with the FHSA are laid down in lengthy and detailed Regulations.[7] The original Regulations made in 1974 have been heavily amended, most notably by amending regulations made in 1989 which came into force in 1990.[8] Unlike the 1974 Regulations, which resulted from a negotiated agreement between the government and the medical professions, the new 1990 'contract' was imposed on general practitioners. The 1990 Regulations set out in detail, far more than used to be the case, the services a GP must offer his patients. The discretion enjoyed prior to 1989 as to how a GP fulfilled his duty to his patients has been significantly reduced. For example, a GP *must* now offer a consultation and medical examination to all new patients, he must contact and offer a consultation to any patient whom he has not seen for three years, and he must provide domiciliary visits and assessments to all patients over 75 years. Targets for vaccination and cervical smear tests have to be met at risk of financial penalties. Many GPs object to this loss of autonomy. They regard some of the 'compulsory' consultations as

5. National Health Service Act 1977, s. 30(1); Health Services Act 1980, s. 1(7) and Sched. I; as amended by ss. 22–3 of the National Health Service and Community Care Act 1990.
6. As to experience and qualifications demanded of GPs, they must complete a course of training and apply for a certificate from the Joint Committee on Postgraduate Training for General Practice. Between 1981 and 1985 fewer than fifteen out of 7,000 applications were refused; see NHS Vocational Training Regulations 1979, SI 1979 No.1644; 1980 No. 1900; 1981 No. 1790; 1984 No. 215.
7. See the NHS (General Medical and Pharmaceutical Services) Regulations 1974 SI No. 160 Sched. I as amended by amending regulations SI 1975 No. 719; 1976 No. 690, No. 1407; 1980 No. 288; 1982 No. 1283; 1983 No. 313; 1985 No. 290, No. 540, No. 863, No. 955, No. 1053, No. 1712; 1986 No. 381, No. 916, No. 1480; 1987 No. 5, No. 407, No. 1425; 1988 No. 1106; 1989 No. 1360, No. 1987; 1990 No. 801.
8. For a good practical account of the new contract as it affects GPs, and particularly its financial implications, see J. Chisholm (ed.), *Making Sense of the New Contract*, Radcliffe Medical Press, Oxford, 1990.

pointless. Why spend time on healthy new patients or patients who have not seen the need of their services? The target for certain forms of treatment are even less popular. Doctors with high proportions of middle-class, middle-aged female patients will find it relatively easy to meet the cervical smear target. The GP in a rundown area with a floating population has a less happy task. Stories have abounded in the press of women being pressured into 'agreeing' to tests and recalcitrant patients being struck off GPs' lists.

The crucial question for patients though is what is the nature of the GP's 'contract'? What is absolutely clear is that it is in no sense a contract with the patient. A new patient cannot sue the GP for failing to offer him a consultation as mandated by the 1989 amending regulations. He cannot have in any circumstances a contractual remedy against his GP. His remedy, if any, lies in the tort of negligence. But the Court of Appeal confirmed in 1990[9] that there is a contract between the GP and FHSA. The GP offers to provide medical services for the FHSA when he applies to be entered on the local medical list. The offer is accepted by the FHSA and the 1974 Regulations, as amended, constitute the terms of the contract. It would appear that section 4 of the National Health Service and Community Care Act 1990, declaring that 'contracts' entered into by one health service body with another are *not* in law contracts, does not affect the Court of Appeal's analysis of the legal relationship of the GP and the FHSA. Recognition that GPs do have a legal contract for services with the FHSA is crucially important for the legal rights of GPs. The existence of the contract and its detailed terms is not irrelevant to patients. It is very likely that in any action for negligence by a patient a court will look at the obligations undertaken by the doctor as part of his contract with the FHSA in deciding the scope of the obligations owed to the patient.

By contrast with the NHS patient, the private patient paying for his personal physician's services does have a contract with his doctor. The terms of that contract are up to the parties themselves. Two special features of private general practice need noting. First, a GP may *not* concurrently provide private services for his NHS patients. He may have an NHS list and a private list but the two must not overlap. Second, the grievance procedures open to the NHS patient have no counterpart in private practice. One may wonder whether the growth

9. *Roy* v. *Kensington and Chelsea and Westminster FPC* [1990] 1 Med. L.R. 328

of private GP care may lead to an equal growth in malpractice suits against GPs. Without an obvious avenue to channel complaints and having paid directly for the service, will private patients more readily resort to the courts?

GPs and negligence

Having as we have seen no contract with his GP, an aggrieved patient seeking compensation from a GP must sue in negligence. I look now at a few of the cases where GPs have been taken to court, and I examine too some common complaints about general practice to see how likely it is that a claim would succeed if litigation were started.

Every GP must attain that standard of skill and competence to be expected of the reasonably skilled and experienced GP. It is no defence that he has just entered practice or that he is elderly and infirm.[10] But nor can he be expected to have the skill or qualifications of a consultant specialist. His terms of service with the FHSA put the matter in a nutshell: the doctor is not to '. . . be expected to exercise a higher degree of skill, knowledge and care than general practitioners as a class may reasonably be expected to exercise'.[11] Should he offer additional services to his patients, for example, if he is on the obstetric list and is prepared to attend home confinements, then he must show the skill that he holds himself out as possessing. He must attain the standard not of the consultant obstetrician but of the specially qualified and experienced GP.[12]

In reported cases where negligence has been proved against GPs, certain danger areas stand out. The maintenance of proper records and ensuring adequate communication with hospitals and other doctors sharing the care of a patient is one. A failure to record and pass on to a hospital information on patients' allergy to certain drugs is a clear case of negligence.[13] Similarly, a failure to check exactly what treatment has been given by the hospital may result in liability. A GP was found liable for a young man's death in this case.[14] The man

10. See, for example, *Nickolls* v. *Ministry of Health*, *The Times*, 4 February 1955 (surgeon working on while fatally ill).
11. SI 1974 No. 160 Sched. I. para. 3 as amended.
12. See *Hucks* v. *Cole*, *The Times*, 9 May 1968.
13. *Chin Keow* v. *Government of Malaysia* [1967] 1 WLR 813.
14. *Coles* v. *Reading and District HMC*, *The Times*, 30 January 1963.

had gone to a cottage hospital after a lump of coal had fallen on him and crushed his finger. A nurse dressed the wound and instructed him to go to another larger hospital. Either because this was not properly explained to him or because he was in shock he did not go. He went later to his own doctor, who did not inquire as to his earlier treatment and simply put on a new dressing. At no stage did the patient receive an anti-tetanus injection and he died of toxaemia. The cottage hospital and the GP were both found to be negligent and responsible for the youth's death. The judge made his views emphatically clear: 'the National Health Service had been developed on the basis that a patient might well be transferred for treatment from one person to another so that the responsibility for the patient shifted ... Any system which failed to provide for effective communication was wrong and negligently wrong.'

The careful prescription of drugs is another area where GPs must be ultra-cautious, not just out of professional concern for the patient but also in order to safeguard themselves. In 1982 a GP prescribed Migril for a Mrs Dwyer. Carelessly he in fact wrote down a prescription for a massive overdose of the drug. A pharmacist dispensed the drug as prescribed. Mrs Dwyer became acutely ill. A partner in the same practice attended her at home. The Migril was on a table in her bedroom but the second doctor did not notice the bottle. Mrs Dwyer suffered gangrene as a result of the overdose. She sued both doctors and the pharmacist. All were originally found liable.[15] Mrs Dwyer received £100,000 in damages. Eventually the second doctor was exculpated on appeal. At the end of the day, the GP whose slip caused the over-prescription paid 45 per cent of the damages and the pharmacist 55 per cent. In *Prendergast* v. *Sam and Dee Ltd*[16] a general practitioner prescribed Amoxil, a common antibiotic, for the plaintiff who was suffering from a chest infection. The doctor's handwriting was so atrocious that the pharmacist read the prescription as an instruction to dispense Daonil, an anti-diabetic drug. The plaintiff succumbed to hypoglycaemia and brain damage. The Court of Appeal upheld Auld J.'s finding that both the doctor and the pharmacist were negligent. The doctor was liable because he should have foreseen that his careless writing of the prescription might mislead the pharmacist into

---

15. *Dwyer* v. *Roderick* (1983) 127 SJ 806. Recounted in 'A Costly Oversight for Pharmacists' (1982) 132 NLJ 176.
16. [1990] 1 Med. L.R. 36.

a dangerous error. The pharmacist was liable because the dosage prescribed and other indications on the prescription should have alerted him to the fact that the doctor did not intend to prescribe Daonil. Both judgements operate as timely warnings against sloppy practice. Doctors must exercise great care in writing out prescriptions. Pharmacists must exercise even greater care in checking on the doctors.

Other reported cases relating to GPs exhibit no consistent pattern. Certain common features with other malpractice suits can be identified. Courts will be unwilling to question the doctor's judgement. In *Hucks* v. *Cole*[17] a GP was consulted by a maternity patient with a septic spot on her finger. He put her on a five-day course of antibiotics. At the end of the five days, when he saw her in the maternity home where he had delivered her baby, the lesion was not completely healed but the doctor did not prescribe any further treatment. The patient contracted acute septicaemia. In her claim against the doctor she alleged that (1) a different antibiotic should have been prescribed, and (2) a further course of antibiotics should have been prescribed as the sepsis remained unhealed. The trial judge refused to condemn the doctor's choice of drug but held him negligent for failing to take further measures when he could clearly see that the sepsis persisted. The Court of Appeal upheld his judgement. A clear and definite risk to the woman's health had been proved, and the absence of treatment led directly to her contracting an acute and dangerous disease. Sachs LJ held that the essence of the doctor's defence was that the patient had been 'just unlucky'. But when grave danger should have been noted by the doctor, however small the risk was of that danger materializing, the doctor must act. Failure to act will lead more swiftly to liability than taking steps which prove with hindsight to be wrong.

One final case may interest those patients who complain that 'the doctor never listens'. In *Langley* v. *Campbell*[18] a patient visited his GP with symptoms of fever nine days after his return from East Africa. The GP diagnosed flu. Six days later the patient died of malaria in hospital. The GP was found liable for failing to consider and test for malaria, having been told by the patient of his recent return from the tropics, where such disease is rife.

17. *The Times*, 9 May 1968.
18. *The Times*, 6 November 1985.

Duty to attend

One frequent complaint about GPs is that patients have difficulty getting swift appointments or home visits and that receptionists take it upon themselves to decide when and if someone can see the doctor. What exactly is the GP's duty to attend his patients and who in law are his patients?

The doctor's contract with the FHSA provides that his patients are firstly those who are accepted on his list.[19] Provision is made for the FHSA to assign various patients to him to ensure that no one is ever without a GP. And most importantly, the doctor's patients include persons accepted as 'temporary residents' and 'persons to whom he may be requested to give treatment which is immediately required owing to an accident or other emergency at any place in his practice area',[20] providing that *inter alia* the doctor is available and the patient's own doctor is not able to give immediate treatment. The doctor's obligation to the health service then is to provide an umbrella of cover. Wherever an NHS patient goes he should be able to see a doctor. If he falls ill on holiday and can get to a doctor himself, he can go temporarily on to the local doctor's list. In dire emergency he or his friends can call on and count on any GP practising in the area to come to his aid. Failure to meet this obligation could lead to the doctor being disciplined by the FHSA.

But is there any obligation directly to the patient? Could a patient sue if denied treatment so that his condition deteriorated? After all, we saw in Chapter 6 that a doctor on an express train could sit by and watch a fellow passenger die of a coronary. There is no legal duty to be a Good Samaritan. The GP's position is quite different. As far as the patients on his list are concerned, he has a continuing duty to them. A failure to attend such a patient where a competent GP would recognize the need for attendance is as much a breach of duty as giving wrong and careless treatment. Patients accepted as 'temporary residents' by a GP are in the same position for as long as they are registered with that GP.

The class of patients whose rights are hotly debated are the 'emergency cases'. The doctor's obligation to the FHSA is to treat such

19. The patients the doctor undertakes to treat within the NHS are defined in SI 1974 No. 160 Sched. I. para. 4.
20. ibid., para. 4(h).

cases *in his practice area* when he is available to provide medical care. The GP on the Inter-City express is therefore as immune from responsibility for fellow passengers as his consultant colleague. Within his practice area, when he is 'on duty' in surgery or on call at home, does he have a legal responsibility to emergency patients? In 1955 lawyers acting for a doctor being sued by a patient on his NHS list conceded that the creation of the National Health Service had created a legal duty on a doctor to treat any patient in an emergency, whether or not the patient was on his list.[21] A commentator has doubted the correctness of this concession, stating such a state of affairs to reflect '. . . the standards by which the medical profession regards itself as bound and would wish to be judged [but] from the strictly legal point of view too wide'.[22] I cannot see why it is 'too wide'. The doctor has undertaken to provide an emergency service. The area and circumstances in which he must act are closely defined. The obligation on him is not unbearably onerous. Emergency patients within his practice area when he is on duty are a foreseeable class of persons to whom, by accepting the position of GP within the health service, he has undertaken a duty, and a duty which should be legal and not merely moral.

Failure to attend and treat

Establishing a duty to treat will rarely be a cause of difficulty, except towards emergency cases. A patient suing a GP will find that his problems start when he seeks to prove, as he must, that the GP's failure to treat him was negligent. Some patients make intolerable demands on their doctors. The doctor is not obliged to respond immediately to every call. He may indeed be in breach of duty to his more patient patients if he always responds to the most insistent call on his services. He has to exercise his judgement. In 1953 a GP was sued when he failed to visit a child whose mother reported (a) that the child had abdominal pains, and (b) that she had previously been examined by a hospital casualty officer who had sent her home. The child proved to have a burst appendix. The judge found that the

21. *Barnes* v. *Crabtree*, *The Times*, 1 and 2 November 1955.
22. P. C. Nathan and A. R. Barrowclough, *Medical Negligence*, Butterworths, London, 1957, p. 38.

casualty doctor was negligent and the GP was not. He had acted reasonably on the information available to him.[23]

The information available to the doctor is vital in assessing his obligation to the patient. When a patient changed his address without telling his doctor and then summoned the doctor, the doctor was found not negligent when after an attempt to visit the old address he left to complete other calls. The judge found that he acted reasonably in assuming that if urgent treatment was needed he would be contacted again. The doctor could not be expected to mount a search for his missing patient.[24] Similarly, information as to the patient's condition must be full and accurate. A patient may fail in any action for failure to treat if all he said to the doctor was that he felt sick and had a headache, when in fact he was feverish, vomiting and had severe abdominal pains. The courts will condemn the doctor who fails to act on information from his patient. The patient must give the doctor the information to act on.

Often, information about requests for visits and appointments is not given directly to the doctor. It is channelled via the receptionist. This makes not a jot of difference to the doctor's legal obligation. His terms of service with the FHSA require that he provide treatment during approved hours or, if he operates an appointments scheme, that the patient be offered an appointment within a reasonable time. And if the patient's condition so requires, he must be visited at home. The doctor is obliged to 'take all reasonable steps to ensure that a consultation is not deferred without his knowledge'.[25] He is responsible for his staff and must ensure that their service as well as his is efficient. His liability for them is absolute. Let us imagine a perfect GP whose receptionist in a burst of temper totally out of character abuses the mother of a seriously ill toddler and refuses to ask the doctor for a visit. The child has peritonitis and dies for lack of immediate treatment. The receptionist, not the doctor, was negligent, but as her employer he is legally responsible for her negligence.[26]

23. *Edler* v. *Greenwich and Deptford HMC, The Times*, 7 March 1953.
24. *Kavanagh* v. *Abrahamson* (1964) 108 Sol. J. 320.
25. See SI 1974 No. 160 paras. 16, 17, 25 and 26. The 1989 amending regulations prescribe minimum 'contact' hours with patients.
26. Because of the doctrine of vicarious liability discussed earlier in Chapter 7.

Deputies and locums

The increasing use of deputizing services at night and at weekends has caused major public concern. Steps have been taken to improve the control exercisable by the FHSA over the use of such services, and to limit the hours during which a GP may use deputies. From a strictly legal point of view, I have argued earlier that the intervention of a deputy or locum is irrelevant to the patient. His GP owes him a duty to provide appropriate medical care. If inadequate or incompetent treatment is given, the GP is in breach of that duty, and if that breach results in injury to the patient, he is entitled to compensation.[27]

An intolerable burden of liability?

I have taken a view of the potential liability of the GP somewhat wider than may commend itself to the BMA. In particular, I maintain that there is a legal obligation to treat emergencies and an absolute responsibility for the negligent actions of deputies. This attitude does not result in any way from a belief that general practice on the whole meets a low standard of health care. Nor do I believe that an increase in malpractice actions against GPs is desirable or would promote higher standards. The action for negligence remains in this country the main scheme for providing adequate compensation for personal injury. It requires proof of fault. Fault does not mean moral culpability. Every doctor makes mistakes. They are unlucky when their mistakes cause injury. But so are the patients. The doctor can insure against his mistakes, as does the lawyer, the architect and the lorry driver. GPs are not obliged to carry professional insurance. Most do. They all should. Until and unless the law changes to bring about a more adequate system of compensating injury, a patient should be entitled to compensation when he is denied adequate treatment.

Freedom to choose: the patient

Fortunately for the majority of patients, the law relating to responsibility for negligence is relevant only in that it creates a framework within which they enter into a relationship with their GP. They will

27. See Chapter 7, pp. 144–5; and see the GP's terms of service SI 1974 No. 160 para. 17 as amended by SI 1982 No. 1283.

never have cause to test it in court. More important to that majority is their ability to select the doctor of their choice. The well-off can always opt for private care. For most people, general practice remains a NHS preserve. The NHS seeks to embody in the system the principle of choice of doctor. Some limitation on freedom of choice is necessarily imposed by the need to limit the numbers on doctors' lists,[28] and by the number of doctors in the neighbourhood. Patients in a leafy suburb will in practice have a greater degree of choice of doctor than patients in run-down inner-city areas. The Department of Health has sought to counter that problem by providing financial incentives, designated area practice allowances, to doctors willing to set up practice in 'under-doctored' localities. As elderly patients have greater health needs, a higher capitation fee is paid to the doctor for each patient on his list over 65. The aim is to try to ensure that doctors do not refuse to have 'unprofitable' patients on their lists. But the need to meet targets for certain sorts of treatment, for example cervical smear tests, may work to the contrary effect. Patients likely to be un-cooperative may be rejected. However, perhaps the most important element of patient choice in general practice is the freedom to change your GP. Many patients are on the list of a particular GP only because their parents put them on that list. On moving to a new neighbourhood the initial choice of GP is often pretty random. Until 1990 changing GPs was not easy. The GP could apply to have a patient removed from his list without giving any reason. The patient wanting to change his GP, without actually moving from the latter's practice area, had first to seek either the written consent of his GP or the FPC. He had a right to change, but having to tell your GP you want to change was a strong inhibition on exercising that right. Now the patient simply finds a new GP who will accept him on his list and notifies his former doctor and the FHSA. Patients have the same right to choose doctors as doctors have to choose patients.[29]

Patient choice is one of the main planks of government health service reforms. To exercise choice patients need information. Hence, under pressure from the government, the medical profession's attitude to advertising is changing. Touting for patients once ranked as one of the

28. SI 1974 No. 160 Reg. 17 (3,500 for single doctor, 4,500 for doctor in partnership subject to an average of 3,500 per partner).
29. SI 1974 No. 160 Reg. 18 as amended by SI 1974 No. 907; SI 1987 No. 445; SI 1989 No. 1630; SI 1990 No. 538.

profession's most serious crimes. Now the GMC[30] encourages doctors to 'provide factual information about their qualifications and their services'. They may distribute leaflets giving such information and may publish such information in the media. They must not disparage other doctors and glossy advertising remains discouraged. It is laudable that patients have access to more information. But there are limits on the effect patient choice will have on the quality of general practice. The first-class public relations specialist may be a poor doctor. And however wide the patient's choice, if general practitioners in the NHS have insufficient cash to do their job properly, the quality of the service to patients will decline.

Complaints

Litigation is uncertain and expensive. A complainant may not want financial compensation. Money cannot replace a dead relative. And in many cases where a patient is understandably aggrieved there may be no cause of action. The patient's condition might have deteriorated in any case, even if his doctor had treated him promptly and properly. Yet he still has cause to complain if his doctor did not attend him or gave inappropriate treatment. What are the avenues open to complainants unhappy about their treatment by a health service GP?

The Family Health Services Authority

The FHSA, which administers general practice and with whom the GP contracts to offer his services, also investigates any failure by the GP to comply with those terms of service. An aggrieved patient makes his complaint to the FHSA. On receiving a complaint, the FHSA may attempt to solve the difficulty by informal means. A 'negotiator' is appointed to mediate between doctor and patient. He will usually be a lay member of the full FHSA, but may ask that one of the doctors on the medical service committee advise him on the complaint. The 'negotiator' has no power to impose any sanctions on the doctor. If informal conciliation is not resorted to or fails, the full complaints procedure comes into play.[31] The FHSA is required to set up service

30. *Guidance for Doctors on Advertising*, GMC 1990.
31. For a GP's perspective on the procedure, see J. Oldroyd, 'Any Complaints' (1981) 282 BMJ 29, 117, 193.

committees for the various services they administer, for example a medical service committee for GPs, a dental service committee for dentists, and a pharmaceutical service committee for pharmacists.[32] It is the medical service committee with which we are concerned. The service committee is obliged to investigate any complaint made against a doctor. Complaints must normally be made within thirteen weeks of the event giving rise to the complaint. The committee can hear complaints outside this thirteen-week period if good cause for the delay is shown, as long as the doctor consents. If he disagrees, the committee can seek approval from the Department of Health to go ahead.

Once the service committee has notice of the complaint, the chairman will make a preliminary decision as to whether it discloses any evidence of failure by the doctor. If after a further opportunity for the complainant to substantiate his complaint nothing further is disclosed, the matter will go forward to the committee without a formal hearing being required. Where a formal hearing takes place, the patient may ask someone else to assist him to present his case. There is no legal aid in such cases. Even where the patient pays for advice from a lawyer, the lawyer is not entitled to act as an advocate or to speak at all at the hearing. The patient himself may speak and put questions to the doctor. The hearing is private and the press are therefore excluded from such hearings.

The procedure before service committees has aroused much disquiet. The patient is dependent to a large extent on his own articulacy in presenting a case. So is the doctor. He too is denied an advocate. The likelihood is, though, that the doctor will be better educated than the patient and will be advised throughout by lawyers and other experts from his defence organization.

Once a hearing is complete, the service committee reports to the main FHSA. The FHSA must decide what action to take if breach of the terms of service is shown. They have no power to award compensation as such to the patient. The FHSA may (*inter alia*)[33] limit the number of patients for whom the doctor may provide treatment, recommend to the Department of Health withholding of remuneration, or recommend to the Department of Health that the doctor be warned to

---

32. See National Health Service (Service Committees and Tribunals) Regulations 1974 SI 1974 No. 455, as amended by SI 1974 No. 907; SI 1987 No. 445; SI 1989 No. 1630; SI 1990 No. 538.

33. Reg. 10.

comply with his terms of service more closely in future. Finally, the ultimate sanction available to the FHSA is to recommend to a special tribunal specially established for the purpose that the doctor be removed from the medical list.[34]

From any decision of the FHSA, either party may appeal if the decision is adverse to him. The appeal lies to the Health Minister.[35] No oral hearing is required to be held. Where an oral hearing is held, proceedings again take place in private. Where a recommendation to exclude a doctor from the medical list is made, that recommendation is only the first step in a lengthy process. The tribunal of three members must be chaired by a lawyer of no less than ten years' standing, appointed by the Lord Chancellor. At least one of the other two members will be a doctor.[36] Proceedings are yet again in private, and the doctor is entitled to legal representation. If the decision goes against the doctor he may appeal to the Secretary of State, or if he challenges a point of law in the tribunal's decision he may go to the High Court.

Reforms of the system for complaints in 1990 have gone a little way to meet disquiet about its operation.[37] The time-limit for submitting complaints was extended from eight to thirteen weeks. Equal numbers of lay and professional members must be present at service committee hearings. It is made clear that patients are entitled to be represented by a trade-union official or representative of the local community health council. The Council on Tribunals,[38] which supervises the operation of all tribunals in England and Wales, is still unhappy about service committee procedures. The Council believes that patients should be entitled to legal representation and that service committees need greater powers to compel the attendance of witnesses and production of documents. Delays in the system remain too great. The Health Service Ombudsman[39] who has jurisdiction over FHSAs has equal concerns over the informal conciliation procedures. He considers the informal

---

34. See National Health Service Act 1977, s. 46 and Sched. 9.
35. Reg. 11.
36. National Health Service Act 1977, Sched. 9.
37. Recommended in *Primary Health Care: An Agenda for Discussion* (Cmnd 9771), HMSO, and implemented by the National Health Service (Service Committee and Tribunal) Regulations SI 1990 No. 538.
38. Annual Report of the Council on Tribunals for 1988/89, p. 5.
39. Annual Report of the Health Service Commissioner (1987–8), HC 534, pp. 15–16.

procedures are too often used inappropriately when a formal investigation is called for.

General Medical Council

The role of the GMC in regulating the medical profession was discussed fully in Chapter 1 of this book. But the function of the GMC in disciplining doctors deserves mention again. The Professional Conduct Committee of the GMC investigates complaints by patients of serious professional misconduct. Adultery with a patient remains the most notorious example of misconduct, and may still often lead to the doctor being struck off the register.[40] Advertising, drug addiction and alcoholism will also bring about the doctor's downfall. Growing public concern has focused on the moral, sober but incompetent doctor. When will the GMC act? An isolated mistake is not the concern of the GMC. Nor is incompetence as such. Failure to attend and treat a patient may be. The case of a doctor in 1982[41] illustrates that the Council can take a tough line. The doctor refused to visit two sick little girls on separate occasions. One died. One suffered brain damage when an appendectomy went wrong. The child who died could not have been saved by the doctor. The brain damage to the other was not his fault. So the parents could not have sued for negligence. Their complaint was of the lack of treatment and the distress caused to them. The Council found against the doctor and he was struck off. This was the first time in fifteen years that a doctor had been struck off for failing to visit a patient rather than being merely suspended for a year. One wonders why it took them so long. In recent years, however, the GMC has begun to show the will to tackle the problem of 'inadequate' doctors. They are just beginning to take a tougher line with the 'bad' doctor in disciplinary proceedings, and the GMC itself has proposed the introduction of performance review procedures to check on the incompetent doctor.[42] General practitioners work far more on their own than their hospital colleagues. Effective review of general practice by the GMC is thus all the more important.

40. *Evans* v. *GMC*, reported in (1985) 1 *Professional Negligence* 114.
41. *Rodgers* v. *GMC*, reported in (1985) 1 *Professional Negligence* 111.
42. See above, pp. 15–17. Note that the GMC is already informed of any withholding of money from a GP by the FHSA where the sum withheld exceeds £100.

The NHS Ombudsman

The Health Service Ombudsman, discussed in Chapter 9, has no jurisdiction to investigate general practitioners or the deliberations of medical service committees. He can investigate maladministration by health service employees who administer FHSAs. And he may examine complaints relating to informal procedures.[43] In one case a woman complained that her doctor had told her not to waste his time when she asked for a blood test for German measles. She was planning to have a baby and wanted to check that she was immune from that disease. The administrator to whom she handed in her complaint told her to change doctors if she was not satisfied with her treatment. He never passed the complaint on to the FHSA. The Ombudsman found that to be maladministration.

Doctors: freedom to care

General practitioners are not salaried employees of the NHS. They are independent contractors who by virtue of their contracts with FHSAs provide services for the NHS and the community. At the inception of the NHS the professional autonomy of the GP was regarded as fundamental. The arrangements for general practice were designed to safeguard the doctor's independence to give treatment as he saw fit to the best of his professional ability. Today some general practitioners claim that that independence has been unacceptably eroded to the detriment of patient care.

Certain restrictions on freedom to practise have existed for some time and are generally, if not universally, accepted. Legislation to control drug abuse precludes most GPs from prescribing drugs like heroin or cocaine to addicts. Only specially designated doctors may prescribe for addicts. Legislation relating to contagious diseases requires GPs in some cases to breach confidentiality and notify the disease to community medical officers. These sorts of limits on clinical freedom have been worked out between the profession and the government and remain relatively uncontroversial.

What are controversial are the limits placed on GPs' autonomy designed primarily to ensure that the NHS gets what the government

43. See above, note 39, and see Annual Report of the Health Service Commissioner 1979–80, HC 650, pp. 65–7.

perceives as value for money from general practice. The first move came in 1985 when the Department of Health in an attempt to cut down the NHS drugs bill introduced a limited list of drugs which may be prescribed on the NHS.[44] Drugs not on that list may be prescribed only privately. The limited list is designed to include all drugs deemed to be effective by the Department of Health and to exclude drugs designated as unnecessarily costly or of dubious effect. But many doctors disagreed with the judgements made and found themselves obliged to ask patients to pay for the drug they deemed clinically appropriate. Next, as we have seen,[45] the new GP 'contract' laid down far more specifically the duties GPs owe to their patients. But the greatest concern and outcry was generated by the provisions in the National Health Service and Community Care Act 1990 for GP 'budgets' and the introduction of 'fund-holding' practices. Section 18 of the Act provides that the FHSA shall indicate to every general practice an amount which in the opinion of the FHSA it is reasonable to expect that practice to spend on prescribing drugs. This 'budget' is not, as was originally feared, fixed and immutable.[46] If the general practitioner finds that by March he is running out of cash, he may exceed the 'indicative' amount with the consent of the FHSA. What is obvious is that financial management will have to become a priority for every GP. For 'fund-holding' practices finance will be even more pre-eminent. Section 14[47] provides that a practice may apply to the Regional Health Authority for recognition as a 'fund-holding' practice. Briefly, such a practice will not only undertake the primary care of its patients, but be responsible for the patient's total health care. Out of funds allocated to the practice by the Regional Health Authority, the general practitioner will arrange any necessary surgery or hospital treatment, shopping around for the best 'buy' from local district health authorities and NHS trusts. He will then 'contract' for the patient's treatment. Section 4 provides that such 'contracts' are not legally enforceable contracts in the normal sense of the word.

44. See NHS (General Medical and Pharmaceutical Services) Amendment Regulations 1985, SI No. 290 and No. 803. Moves to cut down drug bills by introducing generic prescribing failed largely owing to pressure from the pharmaceutical industry. On possible legal implications of the limited list, see the first edition of this book, pp. 254–8.
45. See above, p. 356.
46. Budgets are said to be indicative only.
47. Will the GP be directly liable for any failure in that treatment?

The ramifications of indicative budgets and the establishment of fund-holding practices are beyond the scope of this book and the expertise of the author. The risk is that both will trigger an increase in litigation against general practitioners. Patients will on occasion perceive, maybe wrongly, that clinical misjudgements have been based on financial motives. Take a simple example. A child is brought into the surgery with a sore throat and a rash. The doctor fails to diagnose scarlet fever, now a rare childhood disease. He follows his usual practice with children's sore throats and does not prescribe antibiotics. The child becomes very ill and perhaps suffers complications. The parents may well believe that the misdiagnosis was not just an error, maybe even a non-negligent error, but that their child was sacrificed for the doctor's budget.

Conclusion: the role of the law

It is only too easy to carp at the GP, only too easy to say that the law ought to do this and that. The limited role the law can play in promoting good general practice needs clear recognition from doctors and patients. The law can provide a scheme for compensating the victims of medical error. The present scheme, based on the law of negligence, will work more effectively if doctors recognize that error does not automatically equal incompetence. The law can and should ensure a better and simpler scheme for the thorough investigation of complaints. It can do little else. The maintenance and raising of standards is for the profession and the government. Proposals by the BMA of greater incentives for the good GP ought to arouse the sympathy of this government. Moves by the Royal College of General Practitioners to fix higher entrance standards should be listened to carefully. The impact of NHS reforms on general practice or medical litigation should be carefully monitored.

CHAPTER 17

Family Planning

Just over 100 years ago Charles Bradlaugh was convicted of, and imprisoned for, publishing an obscene libel when he issued a pamphlet advocating and explaining methods of birth control. In 1924 Marie Stopes sued for libel after her books and work in slum clinics had been described as a 'monstrous campaign of birth control', with the rider that 'Bradlaugh was condemned to jail for a less serious crime'. In the House of Lords, Viscount Finlay said of the practice of birth control:

... it is impossible to hold that the bounds of fair comment are exceeded by the expression of an opinion that such practices are revolting to the healthy instincts of human nature. There is an old and widespread aversion to such methods on this ground.[1]

And as late as 1954 Lord Denning MR said of vasectomy:

Take a case where a sterilization operation is done so as to enable a man to have the pleasure of sexual intercourse without shouldering the responsibilities attached to it. The operation is plainly injurious to the public interest. It is degrading to the man himself. It is injurious to his wife and any woman who he may marry, to say nothing of the way it opens to licentiousness, and unlike other contraceptives, it allows no room for a change of mind on either side. It is illegal, even though the man consents to it . . .[2]

Attitudes have certainly changed, but how much? And where does the law stand now?

1. *Sutherland* v. *Stopes* [1925] AC 47, p. 68.
2. *Bravery* v. *Bravery* [1954] 3 All ER 59, pp. 67–8.

Can family planning be criminal?

Contraceptives have never been totally banned in England, as they still partially are in Eire, and were in France until 1967, although not until 1967 was formal provision made for contraceptive advice and treatment to be offered within the NHS.[3] And still the criminal law cannot be totally divorced from family planning. The fine line between prevention of pregnancy and early abortion, seen most dramatically in relation to the use of the 'morning-after' pill, has been examined earlier.[4] And prescribing contraceptives to girls under 16 was unsuccessfully argued to be aiding and abetting unlawful sexual intercourse.[5] The campaign moved to Parliament to create a specific statutory offence. The diversity of opinion in our society concerning sexual morality, and a range of views, from a position that the use of contraception is always morally wrong, through the view that contraceptives should be solely a means of spacing a family within marriage, to the point where contraception is seen as a right for all regardless of age or status, ensures that occasionally acrimonious debate will continue.

But what of sterilization? Is there any substance in Lord Denning's argument that there are circumstances now in which performing a sterilization could entail criminal liability for the surgeon? That cannot now be the law. His argument was based on the principle that a victim's agreement cannot make lawful an inherently criminal act. So a man who sadistically beat a 17-year-old girl was convicted of a criminal assault upon her despite her consent to be beaten.[6] Inflicting violence on another person for sexual gratification is unacceptable to society. Lord Denning argued that sterilization without medical cause was mutilation of the patient, and unacceptable to society because of its potential for risk-free immorality. Several thousands of Britons every year undergo sterilization. It has become an acceptable option for birth control.[7] It seems most unlikely that any judge would now categor-

---

3. See National Health Service (Family Planning) Act 1967 as amended by the National Health Service (Family Planning) Amendment Act 1972.
4. See Chapter 13, pp. 293–5.
5. See Chapter 14.
6. *R.* v. *Donovan* [1934] 2 K B 498.
7. See the discussion on this matter in the essay on 'Sterilization' by S. A. M. McLean and T. D. Campbell in S. A. M. McLean (ed.), *Legal Issues in Medicine*, Gower, Aldershot, 1981.

ize sterilization as inherently unlawful and put the surgeon on a par with the sadist! The issue today is rather how readily the law will *impose* sterilization on young women with mental handicap.

Contraception, sterilization and marriage

Two questions arise in this context. Can the use of contraception by, or the prior sterilization of, one of the spouses affect the initial validity of a marriage? Does a refusal to have children give rise to grounds for divorce?

English law provides that a marriage which remains unconsummated because of the incapacity or wilful refusal of one party to consummate the marriage is voidable and may be set aside as a nullity. The earlier sterilization of one of the spouses, or the use of mechanical or chemical contraception, will not prevent consummation taking place.[8] Consummation means full sexual intercourse regardless of whether or not the act is open to the procreation of children. So a husband who had unwillingly used a contraceptive sheath when engaging in intercourse with his wife failed in his attempt to argue that therefore the marriage had never been consummated. Neither will refusal by one spouse to have intercourse unless contraceptives are used amount to wilful refusal to consummate.[9] This can create a knotty problem. If one party is entirely prepared to engage in normal sexual intercourse only if contraceptives are used and the other, for religious reasons perhaps, only if they are not, the marriage remains unconsummated, but neither spouse is guilty of wilful refusal to consummate and the marriage cannot be set aside.[10] Their remedy lies in divorce. Any hardship in having to await a divorce is alleviated by the Matrimonial and Family Proceedings Act 1984, which now permits divorce in normal circumstances after one year of marriage only.

A divorce will be granted if the petitioner can establish that the marriage has irretrievably broken down. One means of establishing the breakdown is to show that the respondent has behaved in such a way that the petitioner cannot reasonably be expected to live with him or her. This test of 'unreasonable behaviour' has replaced the previous

8. *Baxter* v. *Baxter* [1948] AC 274.
9. ibid.
10. See P. M. Bromley, *Family Law*, 7th edn, Butterworths, London, 1987, p. 87.

test of cruelty as a ground for divorce and is more liberally interpreted by the courts. Undergoing a vasectomy after the marriage,[11] or insisting on using contraceptives,[12] was held in the past to be cruelty on the part of the husband if the effect was damaging to the wife's health. Today a wife would probably succeed in establishing unreasonable behaviour without having to show evidence of damage to her health. Equally, a husband could prima facie show it to be unreasonable for his wife to refuse, without good reason, to have children. But one difficulty can be outlined. In *Archard* v. *Archard*[13] the parties were both Roman Catholics. The wife was advised on medical grounds not to conceive for a while, and refused to have intercourse without the use of contraceptives. Her devout husband refused to have intercourse if contraceptives were used. She failed to establish that his behaviour was unreasonable, as she was aware of his faith and his views. Equally, he would have failed to establish her behaviour to be unreasonable on the grounds of her medical condition. The reasons for one party's refusal to have children must be examined in determining whether this conduct is such that the petitioner can no longer be expected to go on with the marriage, and today may well not be limited to cases where the wife (or the husband) is medically advised against contraception but may embrace the whole of the parties' lifestyle and aspirations.

Finally, there is one anomaly in the law. What if one spouse has been sterilized before the marriage and never tells the other? We have seen that that is no ground for nullity. Nor is it evidence of unreasonable behaviour so as to support a petition for divorce. For the conduct, undergoing sterilization, takes place before the marriage. A divorce can be granted only on the basis of conduct *after* the marriage.[14] The unhappy spouse will have to establish the breakdown of the marriage on other grounds. A divorce may be granted after two years' separation where the other party consents. Should the contesting party be obdurate, a divorce can be granted without consent after five years' separation. Five years may be enough to end an older woman's hope of children within a future marriage. The Law Commission's proposals[15]

---

11. *Bravery* v. *Bravery* (above), p. 62.
12. *Baxter* v. *Baxter* (above).
13. *The Times*, 19 April 1972; see Bromley, op. cit., p. 186.
14. *Sullivan* v. *Sullivan* [1970] 2 All ER 168, CA.
15. Law Com. No. 192, *Family Law: The Ground for Divorce*, Cm. 636, HMSO, 1990.

for 'no-fault' divorce after a waiting period of one year will bring to an end the law's role in disputes over a spouse's 'right' to a child. If the other party's refusal to have children in effect destroys a marriage, no longer will that refusal have to be fitted uncomfortably into the straitjacket of unreasonable behaviour.

Contraceptives: patients' rights

An infallible contraceptive has yet to be invented. The more sophisticated and convenient contraceptives, such as the Pill and the IUD, have carried a price-tag. They all pose some risk to women's health. Contraception has become very much a medical as well as a social issue. And it largely concerns women, for except for the still experimental male 'Pill', all the more sophisticated contraceptives which pose some medical risk are used by women. Women seek two sorts of protection from the law. First, they require definition of the doctor's obligation to assist them to avoid pregnancy at the least possible risk to health. And second, they increasingly demand greater information, and consequently greater control of their own bodies and lives. The law is pretty well equipped for the first task, and almost entirely a futile weapon in the second.

A doctor advising a woman on contraception owes her the same duties as in any other area of medicine. He must offer her competent and careful advice. He must perform any mechanical procedure, for example inserting an IUD, skilfully. And he must obtain her consent to any invasive procedure. When a woman consults her GP his obligation to her is part and parcel of his ordinary care of her. He will be aware of her medical history, prescribe in the light of that history, and take note of any symptoms of general ill-health that are revealed by any examination he undertakes. But many women prefer to consult specialist Family Planning Clinics. They feel the clinics have greater experience, and some may prefer not to discuss their sexual lives with the family doctor. Clinics must beware. Their obligation is not limited to providing competent advice on how to avoid conception. Contraception cannot be divorced from general health and medical care. The clinic must act on any indication that the woman's general health is at risk, whether from the prescription of a particular contraceptive, or independently. In *Sutton* v. *Population Services Family Planning Ltd*,[16]

16. *The Times*, 7 November 1981.

Mrs Sutton visited the defendant's clinic and was examined by a nurse preparatory to being given contraceptive advice. The nurse either failed to note, or failed to act on, evidence of early signs of cancer. The cancer was diagnosed much later, with the result that far more drastic treatment was called for and the disease was likely to recur at least four years earlier than would have been the case had it been promptly treated. Mrs Sutton was awarded damages for her additional suffering. So clinics must act to ensure that women receive treatment when signs of disease are present. This will usually be done by advising the patient to contact her GP. While the clinic staff may not wish to alarm a patient with what may be a very tentative diagnosis, she must be given sufficient information on which to act, and if she agrees, her GP will be directly notified. Of course, the clinic must respect her confidence, and should a woman refuse permission to contact her GP, say where a sexually transmitted disease is suspected, they must not breach her confidence. In such a case a clinic must take steps to advise the woman on alternative sources of treatment.

Problems with the Pill

Scare stories about the Pill and the risk it poses of cancer, heart disease or thrombosis hit the headlines about once a year. Research into side-effects has had two main medical consequences. A number of brands of Pill once popular have been withdrawn. Women over 35 have been advised to think carefully about its long-term use. Socially, a growing awareness of the potential risks has led many women to demand more information about a substance that so many of them swallow every day. What can the law do for them? First, a doctor prescribing the Pill must be properly informed about the current stage of research and knowledge as to brands of Pill and their risks to particular patients. A GP is not required to have the experience of a consultant gynaecologist specializing and himself researching into the control of fertility. But he must be adequately informed if he elects to offer advice personally rather than referring women to a specialist clinic. His terms of service do not oblige him to offer contraceptive services. Second, what degree of information is the woman entitled to? The leaflets accompanying prescriptions of the Pill have lengthened considerably in recent years in their description of side-effects to which women should be alert, and of contra-indications to taking that brand. Clearly both her doctor and the drug company manufacturing the Pill are required to give the woman sufficient information to enable her to make an informed choice as to whether to use, or continue to use, that method of contraception. What the doctor must tell her is judged by the *Sidaway*[17] test. Has he acted in accordance with a body of responsible medical opinion in formulating the advice he gave her about the risks and benefits of the Pill as against other forms of contraception? An attempt by the judge at first instance in *Gold* v. *Haringey HA*[18] to apply a 'reasonable patient' rather than the 'reasonable doctor' test to contraceptive advice was firmly quashed by the Court of Appeal. The doctor's duty to warn his patient about the risks of the Pill does not, however, relieve the drug company of its own responsibility to provide adequate information and warning about its product to both the prescribing doctor and the patient. A Canadian court expressed the manufacturer's duty in this way:[19]

... the manufacturer's duty is to provide to the consumer written warnings conveying reasonable notice of the nature, gravity and likellhood of known or knowable side-effects and advising the consumer to seek fuller explanation from the prescribing physician or other doctor of any such information of concern to the consumer.

In respect of any product put on the market after 1 March 1988, the drug company will be subject to strict liability under the Consumer Protection Act 1987 for injury arising from a defect in that product. Unfortunately the introduction of strict liability is, as we have seen, unlikely to make the task of suing in respect of drug-induced injury much easier for any victim. This is especially the case with the Pill – and what is said about the Pill applies too to certain mechanical methods of contraception such as the IUD. The problem is this. Risks associated with the Pill are well known, particularly the risk of a woman succumbing to a stroke. Hence all manufacturers do expressly warn patients of those risks, and seek to ensure that women specially vulnerable to that risk, for example older women or women who smoke, avoid the Pill. None the less 'at-risk' women continue to take the Pill. The Pill is a lesser evil than unwanted pregnancy. And

17. [1985] 2 All ER 643; see above, p. 83.
18. [1987] 1 All ER 888; see above, p. 86.
19. *Buchan* v. *Ortho-Pharmaceuticals (Canada) Ltd* (1986) 54 OR (2d) 92, 100; and see generally I. Kennedy and A. Grubb, *Medical Law: Text and Materials*, Butterworths, London, 1989, pp. 558–72.

occasionally a woman with no identifiable risk factor falls seriously ill. The legal questions become: (1) Were the manufacturers' warnings adequate? (2) Bearing in mind the innate risk posed by the Pill balanced against its benefit as an effective contraceptive, is the Pill defective? (3) Can the woman prove that her injury was predominantly caused by taking the Pill? The analysis of these questions and their ultimate answers are unlikely to be different whether the woman's action is framed in negligence or under the Consumer Protection Act 1987. Strict liability under the 1987 Act may help a patient injured by some construction defect in a contraceptive, such as a condom which splits, or a negligently constructed IUD which damages the cervix. It will do little for the patient claiming that the inherent design of a contraceptive drug or mechanism is defective.[20] For such an action to succeed there will need to be overwhelming evidence that the manufacturer failed to note and act on evidence of clear risk to women's health which could not be justified by the contraceptive benefit of the product. It should be stressed that the manufacturer's duty is a continuing duty. It is no answer for the manufacturer to contend that his product was safe by 1988 standards, if evidence of its dangers has emerged from its use, and that same product is still being marketed in 1992.

The Depo-Provera affair

An injectable, long-acting contraceptive sounds ideal. No messy devices, no need to remember to take a pill every day, what more could be desired? Depo-Provera is such a drug and yet has been the source of acute controversy. Depo-Provera is a synthetic form of a natural hormone, which acts like most brands of the Pill to prevent eggs developing and, further, makes the womb hostile to any fertilized embryo which makes it that far. One injection is effective for at least three months. Doctors favour the use of the drug for women for whom the Pill is a health risk, women who are considered too unreliable to be trusted to use other means of contraception and where pregnancy should be completely ruled out, for example when a woman has just been vaccinated against German measles. But Depo-Provera can produce unpredictable and unpleasant side-effects, the most notable of which is severe and irregular bleeding. Long-term fertility may also be affected by the drug. Complaints have been made that (1) some women

20. See Kennedy and Grubb, op. cit., pp. 563–72.

were injected with the drug without ever being told of its nature, and (2) even where Depo-Provera was expressly prescribed and described as a contraceptive, inadequate explanation of its potential side-effects was given. Fears were voiced that Depo-Provera might be forced on the inarticulate or not particularly intelligent woman.

A woman who is injected with Depo-Provera without being told what is in the syringe or without being asked for her agreement may claim in battery against the doctor. She will get compensation for the unlawful violation of her body, and for any unpleasant side-effects which flow from the injection. She will get some compensation even if the drug does her no harm, for the doctor acted unlawfully in acting without her consent. A Salford woman, Mrs Potts, won £3,000 damages[21] after she was injected with Depo-Provera concurrently with a vaccination against German measles. She later suffered severe bleeding. The injection was given days after the delivery of her third child, and she thought that it was a routine post-natal 'jab'. The aim of her doctor was laudable, to protect her from pregnancy while the vaccine might harm any unborn child, but he had no right to deprive her of her choice of whether or not to accept or decline a controversial drug. Women must be told the nature of the drug offered to them, and if their right to choose is to be effective they must have its advantages and disadvantages explained to them. The judge awarding Mrs Potts's compensation said: 'She should have been given the choice, and she was entitled to know beforehand what the decision entailed.'

The controversy over Depo-Provera and fears that it could be forced on unwilling, uninformed patients led the Minister of Health to take an unusual measure in 1983. The Committee on Safety of Medicines advised the Minister to grant Depo-Provera a full licence for general long-term use. The Minister's concern was such that he established an independent panel to inquire into the use and abuse of the drug[22] and to take evidence from interested parties. As a result of the inquiry's findings, Depo-Provera was granted a licence for long-term use but strict conditions were attached to that licence.

21. See the *Guardian*, 23 July 1983, p. 24.
22. See the discussion in *The Times* of 13 April 1983, p. 8. And see Chapter 8, p. 181.

Voluntary sterilization

When a further pregnancy or the burden of caring for more children may endanger a woman's physical or mental health, therapeutic sterilization may be suggested by doctors. Non-therapeutic sterilization is increasingly sought as a method of permanent birth control, both by older couples who feel that their family is complete and by some younger childless women who are adamant that they never wish to reproduce. Both sorts of prospective patients express some disquiet about present practice. Too many doctors within the NHS, it is claimed, regard the decision to sterilize as theirs and not their patients'.[23] They are over-inclined to sterilize women whom they regard as physically or mentally unfit for childbearing or childrearing. They are disinclined to help the fit but unwilling. The latter class will find no legal remedy. A plethora of private clinics has grown up offering female sterilization and vasectomy at a price. To those clinics men and women refused sterilization within the NHS must resort if they can meet the cost. By contrast, any woman alleging that she was hustled into sterilization without her full consent may usefully look to the law for assistance.

A doctor undertaking sterilization of a patient must ensure that the patient understands and agrees to what is to be done. Operating without any consent to the physical invasion of the patient's body would be a battery. Nor can sterilization be automatically performed concurrently with some other gynaecological operation to which the patient has consented. The doctor may correctly adjudge in the course of some other form of surgery that a woman should not risk pregnancy again. He cannot go ahead and act 'in her best interests' without her agreement. In *Devi* v. *West Midlands AHA*,[24] a married woman of 33 who already had four children entered hospital for a minor gynaecological operation. Her religion outlawed sterilization or contraception. In the course of the operation the surgeon discovered her womb to be ruptured and sterilized her there and then. She received £4,000 damages for the loss of her ability to conceive again and £2,750 damages for the neurosis caused by the knowledge of what had been done to her. The choice as to whether to accept sterilization is the patient's. It may be

23. See H. Draper, 'Women and Sterilisation Abuse', in M. Brazier and M. Lobjoit (eds.), *Protecting the Vulnerable*, Routledge, 1991, Chapter 6.
24. [1980] 7 Current Law S. 4.

more convenient to sterilize the patient on the spot but, again, it is never so *immediately* necessary as to justify acting in an emergency without consent.

A doctor who has obtained the patient's consent to the operation may still be liable for negligence if he fails to discuss properly with the patient the implications of the operation in a manner consistent with good medical practice. The doctor must not only give the patient sufficient information on which to make up her mind, but also do so at a time when she is in a fit state to take a reasoned decision. A Roman Catholic woman of 35 was awarded £3,000 damages in negligence when she was sterilized in the course of a Caesarean operation to deliver her second child. She signed the consent form just as she was about to be wheeled into the operating theatre. The judge said that, although she consented to the additional surgery and understood what would physically be done to her, she had been inadequately counselled as to its implications for her.[25] Sterilizing a woman in the course of an abortion or Caesarean saves time and money for the NHS and cuts down on pain and suffering for the patient. It is a course of action rightly fraught with legal hazard unless the patient has been properly advised as to the physical and emotional consequences of electing to be sterilized. The doctor must assess not just his patient's physical condition but also her religious and moral attitudes to enable him and her to take into account the possible emotional effect of the decision. Moreover, where sterilization is proposed on therapeutic grounds the patient's consent must necessarily be based on adequate and careful advice as to the medical need for sterilization. In *Biles* v. *Barking HA*[26] the plaintiff was advised to undergo sterilization on the grounds that she was suffering from a severe, and probably fatal, kidney complaint. That diagnosis was proved later to be mistaken and negligent. Mrs Biles recovered damages of £45,000, which included the cost of a failed attempt to reverse the sterilization and the cost of IVF treatment to try to enable her to have a child of her own, despite her surgically blocked Fallopian tubes.

Many doctors still believe that they should seek the consent of one spouse for the sterilization of the other. There is no legal obligation to do so. Indeed, if one spouse objected to consultation with the other the surgeon would be obliged to respect his patient's confidence. The

25. *Wells* v. *Surrey Area Health Authority, The Times*, 29 July 1978.
26. See M. Puxon and A. Buchan 'Damages for Sterility' (1988) 138 NLJ 80.

surgeon cannot be obliged to operate, but he does not, in law, owe any duty to the patient's spouse. Nor, providing he has advised his patient properly, can he be liable to a patient whose spouse repudiates the marriage on learning of the sterilization.

Who pays for the unplanned child?

Contraception is known to be fallible. No doctor guarantees avoidance of conception. He undertakes to use his skill only to maximize a couple's chances of preventing pregnancy. Sterilization is expected and intended to be final. What if it fails? This can happen if the surgeon is negligent. But there is also a minute but real risk inherent in both vasectomy and some forms of female sterilization that tissues will rejoin naturally and conception once again be possible. Who foots the bill for the unexpected infant?

When the surgeon admits that sterilization failed because he was negligent the only issue is the amount of damages he should pay. At first judges limited damages to compensation for the mother's pain and discomfort arising from the useless operation and from the subsequent pregnancy. In *Emeh* v. *Kensington, Chelsea and Fulham AHA*,[27] Mrs Emeh discovered that she had become pregnant again when her pregnancy was about seventeen to twenty weeks advanced. She was offered and refused an abortion. Park J. found that the birth of the child resulted from her unreasonable act in refusing to terminate her pregnancy. That decision, he said, eclipsed the doctor's original and admitted negligence. She was responsible for the child's birth. Mrs Udale, who similarly discovered herself pregnant after a negligent sterilization, was refused compensation for her fifth and unexpected infant on the grounds of public policy. Jupp J. held[28] that the birth of a healthy child could not be allowed to create a claim in damages. He argued that the child, when he came to know of the award, might feel unwanted and the family's relationship be disrupted. Doctors might put pressure on women to have abortions. Children were a blessing, and any financial loss was offset by the joy of their birth. One judge did not agree with his brethren. In 1984 Peter Pain J. saw no reason to refuse damages for the birth of a child born after a failed vasectomy.[29]

27. *The Times*, 3 January 1983.
28. *Udale* v. *Bloomsbury AHA* [1983] 2 All ER 522.
29. *Thake* v. *Maurice* [1984] 2 All ER 513.

Fortunately Mrs Emeh was persistent and went to the Court of Appeal. That Court unanimously held[30] that (1) her decision not to abort was not such an unreasonable act as to eclipse the defendant's negligence, and (2) there is no reason of public policy to debar a claim for damages in respect of the unplanned child's upbringing.

What are the rules now? The Court of Appeal said forcefully that a court should never declare that a woman in the position of Mrs Emeh ought to have an abortion. Mrs Emeh was over seventeen weeks' pregnant. Abortion then would have involved considerable physical pain, emotional trauma and some real risk to her health. What of a woman who discovers her pregnancy early enough to take advantage of the relatively simple procedure for abortion available in the first twelve weeks of pregnancy? She would not be an identical case to Mrs Emeh, and counsel might seek to argue that the Court of Appeal's decision related only to late abortions. So it did. But whenever pregnancy is discovered, refusal of an abortion should not excuse the defendant's original failure. He undertook to exercise care to avoid the necessity for further pregnancies and consequently painful decisions as to whether to continue a pregnancy. Abortion early in pregnancy may be physically risk-free. The emotional impact of the decision to abort takes it totally beyond the realm of routine medical treatment which an injured plaintiff might reasonably be expected to accept to mitigate her loss. The defendant should well foresee that it is an option many women would refuse.

As to public policy, the Court of Appeal warned of the dangers of laying down lines of policy to refuse claims that were on the ordinary principles of negligence clearly sustainable. They were right to do so. Jupp J.'s well-intentioned reasons for refusing Mrs Udale damages do not hold water. Children are a blessing to most parents. They are invariably an expense. A family is far more likely to be disrupted by increased poverty caused by an extra child than by the child discovering it was a 'mistake'. Several thousand 'mistakes' have comfortably survived that experience. Yet despite the Court of Appeal's judgement in *Emeh* it is clear that individual judges still regard compensation for the birth of a healthy unplanned child distasteful.[31]

30. [1985] 3 All ER 1044.
31. See the remarks of Ognall J. in *Jones* v. *Berkshire HA*: (unreported) quoted by Lloyd LJ in *Gold* v. *Haringey HA* [1987] 2 All ER 888 at 890, CA.

What of the case where conception occurs because tissues heal naturally? The operation has been performed impeccably. An act of God or nature reverses the operation. At first sight it appears that the surgeon is in no way responsible. What could he have done? The practice of most surgeons for some time has been to warn patients of the risk when discussing the proposed operation with them. Can a failure to warn give rise to a claim against the surgeon? This happened in *Thake* v. *Maurice*. Mr and Mrs Thake had five children and little money. They wanted no more children. Mr Thake decided to have a vasectomy and paid the defendant £20 for the operation. The judge found that the defendant never warned Mr and Mrs Thake of the small but real risk that nature would reverse the surgery. Mrs Thake became pregnant again. She did not discover her pregnancy until it was nearly five months advanced. The couple sought compensation from the defendant surgeon.

As Mr Thake had paid for his vasectomy, unlike an NHS patient, he had a contract with the surgeon. The trial judge held[32] that Mr Thake had agreed to an operation that he understood would render him irreversibly infertile. That is what he contracted for. The defendant was in breach of contract if he failed to achieve that aim. By failing to warn Mr Thake of the risk of natural reversal of the vasectomy, he guaranteed to make him sterile. He was responsible for the financial loss to the family occasioned by the birth of the unplanned infant.

The Court of Appeal[33] held by a majority that the surgeon never guaranteed to make Mr Thake sterile. Neill LJ found that no reasonable person would have understood the defendant as giving a binding promise that the operation would achieve its purpose. They nevertheless unanimously found for Mr Thake on grounds which will enable private, and NHS, patients to sue if they are not warned of the risk of nature reversing sterilization of either sex. They held that failure to warn of this risk was negligent. That negligence resulted in Mrs Thake being unaware of her pregnancy until abortion was no longer a safe option. The defendant was responsible for that state of affairs and thus for the birth of the child. He was liable in contract to his private patient. He would have been liable in negligence to an NHS patient.

In *Thake* v. *Maurice* counsel for the defendant had conceded that failure to warn the patient of the risk of reversal in vasectomy was

32. [1984] 2 All ER 513.
33. [1986] 1 All ER 497, and see *Eyre* v. *Measday* [1986] 1 All ER 488.

negligent. In later actions the crux of the dispute became the question of when such a failure could be proved to be negligent. Advising a patient on the pros and cons of sterilization is tricky. The doctor will want the patient to perceive the surgery as irreversible. Reversal of both female sterilization and vasectomy is possible but success cannot be guaranteed, and success rates are disputed. Yet at the same time as stressing the irreversibility of sterilization, must the doctor warn the patient of the risk of the natural reversal? Practice among gynaecologists differed. In *Gold* v. *Haringey HA*[34] Mrs Gold was sterilized immediately after the birth of her third child. She conceived again and sued on the grounds that she was never advised of the risk of failure, nor that vasectomy for her husband would have carried a much lower risk of failure. Her claim failed, despite evidence that very many gynaecologists would have given her just that information. There remained a responsible body of medical opinion in 1979, when Mrs Gold was sterilized, which held that patients should *not* be warned of the risk of failure. And the Court of Appeal affirmed the test to be applied was again the 'reasonable doctor', the *Sidaway*, test and not a test based on what the 'reasonable patient' might want to know. Today, even applying the *Sidaway* test, an action based on failure to warn of the failure rate for sterilization would be almost bound to succeed in proving negligence. The formal advice given by the Department of Health[35] on consent to sterilization, male and female, stresses that such information should routinely be given. The model consent form contains a clause: 'that sterilization/vasectomy can sometimes fail and that there is a very small chance that I may become fertile again after some time'. The Department's advice, based on expert gynaecological opinion, should be enough to render any failure to warn now a maverick, not a responsible, opinion.

A patient suing for compensation for the birth of an unplanned child on the grounds of a failure to warn of the risks of reversal would none the less still confront problems of causation. She would have to prove either that, had she been properly advised, she and her partner would have opted for a 'safer' means of sterilization or, more usually, that had she been warned of the risk her pregnancy would have been diagnosed much earlier, enabling her to have a safe, early

---

34. [1987] 2 All ER 888.
35. See *A Guide to Consent for Examination or Treatment*, NHS Management Executive.

abortion. So if the woman has a religious or other objection to abortion, she may have no remedy at all in respect of the failed surgery.
For she cannot prove any loss arising from the failure to warn her that
she might conceive again. The relevant loss is the 'lost' option to
abort. If she could not have countenanced abortion, she has not suffered such a loss.

Where the plaintiffs are able to establish both negligence and causation, they will be able to claim substantial damages to compensate
them for the cost to them of raising the child. In *Benarr* v. *Kettering
HA*[36] damages included the cost of private school fees to a family able
to show they were very likely to send the child to a public school!

Involuntary sterilization

Unlike in a number of American states, no statute in England has ever
provided for the compulsory sterilization of mentally handicapped
patients or of criminals. But in 1987, as we have seen, the House of
Lords in *Re B*.[37] authorized the involuntary sterilization of a girl
under 18. And two years later, in 1989, in *F.* v. *West Berkshire HA*,[38]
their Lordships ruled that sterilization of an adult woman with mental
handicap was not unlawful if that operation was in her 'best interests'.
A woman may not be sterilized in the interests of society, of her
potential children, or on eugenic grounds. She may be sterilized only
where she is incapable of making any decisions on childbearing for
herself and to protect her health and welfare. In *Re B*. (1987) Lord
Oliver said of the argument that sterilizing Jeanette violated her right
to reproduce: '[A] right to reproduce is of value only if accompanied
by the ability to make a choice . . .'[39]

Where a woman lacks the ability to choose, and pregnancy may be
harmful to her, any right to reproduce may thus be taken from her.
But does it logically follow that just because the woman is incapable of
making a rational decision on whether to embark on childbearing, it is
in her interest to be sterilized?[40] A number of questions arise.

36. [1988] NLJR 179.
37. [1987] 2 All ER 266.
38. [1989] 2 All ER 545, HL.
39. p. 219.
40. See M. D. A. Freeman, 'Sterilizing the Mentally Handicapped', in M. D. A.
    Freeman (ed.), *Medicine, Ethics and Law*, Stevens, London, 1988.

(1) Sterilizing a mentally handicapped woman 'protects' her from one evil which might befall her if she is enticed or coerced into sexual intercourse. It in no way safeguards her from exploitation by men taking advantage of her handicap, from perversion or from sexually transmitted disease. Indeed it is quite likely that, knowing she cannot become pregnant, those caring for her will be less vigilant in any attempt to prevent her being enticed into exploitative sexual relations.

(2) Of course, one reason advanced for sterilizing severely mentally handicapped women is precisely that they can then be allowed more freedom and mixed-sex units in hospitals become more viable. Free from the risk of pregnancy, the woman although deprived of a right to reproduce can exercise a 'right' to sexuality. Two difficulties confront this superficially attractive proposition. First, has the woman capacity to consent to sexual intercourse at all? T.[41] was said to have a mental age of 2. Sexual intercourse with T. would constitute rape by her partner. It may well be that Jeanette[42] understood enough of what was entailed in sexual intimacy to give consent to intercourse and certainly seemed to invite such contact. Yet intercourse with her would still be a criminal offence. Sexual intercourse with a mentally defective woman is an offence contrary to section 7 of the Sexual Offences Act 1956. In effect women are being sterilized to facilitate crime! Second, if the rationale for sterilizing mentally handicapped women is to enable them to enjoy sexual pleasure, sterilization on its own is not enough. For a right to sexuality to have any meaning, positive steps would need to be taken to ensure circumstances where such women could enjoy such pleasure safely and without risk of harm or disease.

(3) Perhaps the most troubling question of all remains how to decide who should be sterilized. Does Re B. represent the first step on a slippery slope to wholesale sterilization of those whom society regards as unfit to bear children? Sir Brian Rix of MENCAP greeted Re B. with horror, claiming that sterilizing mentally handicapped girls was to reduce them to the status of pets to be neutered at will. Lord Hailsham condemned Sir Brian's remarks as intemperate. Two judgements subsequent to Re B. provide some post facto justification for Sir Brian's outrage. In Re M.[43] Bush J. authorized the sterilization of a girl whose limited mental capacity was similar to Jeanette's in Re B. The

41. See T. v. T. [1988] 1 All ER 613.
42. See Re B. [1987] 2 All ER 206.
43. [1988] 2 FLR 997.

additional factor in *Re M*. though was that there was said to be a 50 per cent chance that if M. did conceive her child too would suffer from some degree of mental handicap. Bush J. affirmed that eugenic considerations are irrelevant to the decision of whether or not M. should be sterilized. Then he went on to say that none the less it was relevant that, if M. did become pregnant, an abortion on the grounds of foetal handicap would be likely to ensue. Repeated abortions would harm M.'s health, thus strengthening the case for sterilizing her. Eugenics forbidden to enter the debate by the front door appear to have slipped in through the back entrance.

Another novel feature in *Re M*. was evidence given by the expert gynaecologist to the effect that, with improvements in tubal surgery, sterilization operations had a 50–75 per cent chance of reversibility. Evidence of reversibility was crucial in *Re P*.[44] P. was a much less severely handicapped girl than M. or Jeanette. At 17 she was said to have a mental age of 6, but unlike M. and Jeanette she had good communication skills and could cope with her own bodily needs. She seemed to have some maternal feelings, she understood what was involved in sexual intercourse and said that she thought it sounded horrid and painful. Her mother feared that as she was of an attractive 'normal' appearance she would be vulnerable to seduction, and that if she became pregnant she might well refuse to have an abortion. The judge acknowledged that P. was a borderline case and even accepted that she might well have the necessary capacity to marry, yet he still authorized her sterilization. In *Re B*. Lord Oliver had agreed with Dillon LJ in the Court of Appeal that '. . . jurisdiction in Wardship proceedings to authorize such an operation is one which should be exercised only in the last resort . . .'[45] Was P. really a case of this magnitude? The judge said that it no longer need be proved that sterilization was the 'last resort'. Professor Robert Winston had testified that reversal of sterilization carried out by clips on the Fallopian tubes now achieved a 95 per cent success rate. The House of Lords in *Re B*. had perceived sterilization as irreversible. If that is no longer the case, judges could properly accept less draconian criteria for authorizing that 'reversible' surgery. Unfortunately not many gynaecologists do think that they could attain a 95 per cent success rate for reversal

44. [1989] 1 FLR 182; see M. Brazier, 'Sterilization: Down the Slippery Slope' (1990) 6 *Professional Negligence* 25.

45. p. 218.

of sterilization – and how realistic is it to expect even a mildly handicapped woman to be offered reversal surgery? P. understood enough about childbearing for her mother to fear that she would oppose any proposal for an abortion if she became pregnant. True, pregnancy might well be a disaster for P. and her child, but if that is the criterion for involuntary sterilization we are a long way down that slippery slope!

La Forest J. in the Canadian Supreme Court declared in *Re Eve*:[46]

> The importance of maintaining the physical integrity of a human being ranks high in our scale of values, particularly as it affects the privilege of giving life. I cannot agree that a court can deprive a woman of that privilege for purely social or other non-therapeutic purposes without her consent. The fact that others may suffer inconvenience or hardship from failure to do so cannot be taken into account.

Are English judges in effect authorizing the sterilization of young women for the benefit of others under disguise of the patient's 'best interests' test?

Disquiet about involuntary sterilization in England must be even greater where the woman concerned is over 18, for as we saw in Chapter 5 the House of Lords in *F.* v. *West Berkshire HA*[47] found that there was no jurisdiction enabling them to *require* doctors to seek a declaration before sterilizing an adult incompetent woman. As a matter of good practice their Lordships declared that doctors contemplating such radical surgery should choose to seek a declaration confirming that sterilization was in the woman's interests and in conformity with responsible medical opinion. A Practice Direction of the High Court confirms this advice and sets out the procedure for such a declaration. None the less it remains the case that it is not unlawful in England to sterilize an adult woman with no judicial sanction. More worryingly though, for the vast majority of doctors will seek a declaration for their own protection, is the decision in *F.* to apply the *Bolam* test to determine the legality of a proposed operation. Sterilization will be lawful if the decision to sterilize that particular woman is in conformity with a responsible body of medical opinion. *Re P.* illustrates that the, in practice, hypothetical reversibility of sterilization has convinced some responsible gynaecologists that it is now appropriate for a much

46. (1986) 31 DLR (4th) 1.
47. [1989] 2 All ER 545, HL; see above, pp. 97–100.

broader category of women. Sterilization need no longer be the last resort, merely perhaps the most 'convenient' means of contraception. Other doctors are much more dubious about accepting any proposition that the reversibility of sterilization should affect the initial decision about whether to sterilize a mentally handicapped woman. Applying the *Bolam* test could lead to this result. Women living in City A may lawfully be subjected to involuntary sterilization, when had they resided thirty miles away in City B they would not have been considered proper subjects for such radical non-consensual treatment. So long as the criteria operated in City A conform to a responsible body of medical opinion, it matters not that in City B a directly contrary opinion is taken. Whether or not a mentally handicapped adult woman retains any right to reproduce may be determined by geography.

Conclusions

The law's role in controlling fertility can be seen to be confused and uncertain. Perhaps one reason for this uncertainty is the lack of any explicit recognition of a right to reproduce. Article 12 of the European Convention on Human Rights confers on men and women of marriageable age the right to marry and to found a family. Article 12 itself is imprecise. For example, is the right to found a family dependent on, and consequent on, the right to marry and so confined to married couples? But were we in England to recognize expressly a right to reproduce, would that clarify our thinking on legal issues relating to contraception and family planning? In the context of involuntary sterilization it would at least seem to require the formulation of much more precise grounds on which that right could lawfully be abrogated by others. In other contexts recognition of a right to reproduce would unearth new problems. If X has a right to reproduce does his/her spouse have an obligation to reproduce? Nor does recognition of a right to reproduce assist those who seek exactly the opposite end, to ensure they do not conceive or beget a child. What is really at stake is once again the patient's right to autonomy and self-determination. Issues arising out of family planning and sterilization are simply yet a further illustration of how relatively undeveloped legal principles relating to autonomy remain.

CHAPTER 18

Organ and Tissue Transplantation[1]

Despite the number of lives saved by transplantation, organ donation has had a stormy history. Controversial debates involving clinical, ethical, scientific, financial and resource considerations have raged on for more than a generation. Public acceptance of, and attitudes towards, what are relatively standard procedures, such as kidney transplants, has been affected from time to time by more controversial matters relating to heart transplantation, and recent controversy concerning the use of foetal tissue. Public response to transplantation has been erratic, influenced by publicity given to dramatic success and failures. For example, in the early days of heart transplantation the major media publicity given to declarations which described transplant surgeons as 'human vultures', and the headline stories of organs which have been removed from bodies before 'real death' had occurred, all contributed to excite public concern and hostility. On the other hand, the media can be effective in publicizing the benefit of transplantation and creating maximum favourable public awareness on the subject. In 1984 the television programme *That's Life* campaigned on behalf of Ben Hardwick, a 2-year-old baby who needed a liver transplant: a suitable donor was found and the transplant was carried out. Opinion polls revealed that the programme's publicity had swung public opinion significantly in favour of transplantation procedures generally. In 1989 media coverage of disciplinary proceedings against four doctors charged with involvement in the sale of kidneys had, unsurprisingly, the opposite effect.

1. See generally G. Dworkin, 'The Law Relating to Organ Transplantation in England' (1970) 33 MLR 353.

Today, it is not uncommon for surgeons to remove the liver, heart, pancreas, kidneys and eyes from, for example, road accident casualties who have suffered irreversible brain damage. But it will take some time yet before the public accepts as a matter of course such multi-organ harvesting.

The benefits of, and problems associated with, transplantation procedures are best illustrated by looking at kidney disease. Thirty years ago, permanent cessation of kidney function was a sentence of death within a few days. But the development of the 'artificial kidney' and kidney transplantation has changed the situation dramatically, and patients now have the opportunity, in theory at least, of lasting relief. Yet the waiting list for kidneys at present in this country is about at least 3,500; and patients still die each year for lack of effective kidney treatment. Indeed, it is alleged that more people are allowed to die of chronic renal failure in the UK than in any comparable European country. Renal dialysis is very expensive: the cost of keeping a patient alive on a kidney machine over, say, a five-year-period is far higher than the cost of a kidney transplant and the continuing cost of drugs, even were the supply of kidneys sufficient to meet all demands.[2]

Such a situation obviously poses many social and ethical problems. Should more financial resources be channelled into this specialty to meet the demand for kidney treatment? If the capability of providing treatment is inadequate, then what considerations determine which patients should be treated and which may be left to die? Improvements in the dialysis service over the past five years have meant that fewer patients are now rejected for dialysis than used to be the case. Patients with renal failure are no longer condemned to die simply because they are over 50 or diabetic. Yet demand continues to outstrip supply, and patients still die unnecessarily. Moreover, dialysis itself is no more than a partial answer to kidney disease. Patients on dialysis enjoy a much poorer quality of life than their luckier brethren who achieve a transplant.

Thus the major need today with kidney transplantation is to obtain an adequate supply of kidneys to meet the demand. There is a social need to persuade healthy people to think ahead and be prepared to agree to donate their kidneys for use after their death. If it were possible, for example, to have available for use the healthy kidneys of

2. See the Report of the Working Party on the Supply of Donors for Transplantation, 1987.

all the victims of road traffic accidents, the problem would be solved.[3]
Is the law as it is effective to meet current social needs or should it be
changed?

The success of the heart transplantation programme in the UK over
the past few years has largely dispelled public doubt about the ethics
of such operations. The cost remains problematic. Some maintain that
NHS funds poured into the transplant programme to benefit the few
would better be used in the prevention of heart disease. Heroic transplant surgery on tiny infants arouses mixed emotions. Is the pain and
trauma justifiable when the infant fails to survive? Increasingly though
there is evidence that babies, whose immune systems are not fully
developed, are actually less likely to reject donor organs than their
adult counterparts. The problem, as ever, is finding a suitable donor.
For every baby saved by 'miracle' heart surgery another baby must
die. Ethical problems focus on the permissibility of using anencephalic
babies as donors.

Live donor transplantation

For one person to subject himself to an unnecessary procedure for the
benefit of someone else is a commendable act of altruism. A distinction
must be made between donation of regenerative and non-regenerative
organs. The blood donor undergoes some temporary discomfort, but
his body replaces the blood he has lost. The bone-marrow donor
suffers more pain but again no irrevocable loss. Blood and bone
marrow are regenerative tissue. Many non-regenerative organs such as
the heart and lungs are, of course, impossible for a living donor to
donate in normal circumstances![4] The major non-regenerative organ
which is a candidate for live donation remains the kidney. The donor
agrees to major surgery and accepts a significant risk to his own
health. The law should be designed to ensure that such a donation is
truly voluntary and not the result of any coercion. The question then
arises about whether payment for donation should be permitted. The
British tradition has been that the donation of body products should

---

3. It is suggested, however, that the change in the law making the wearing of
   seat belts compulsory has reduced considerably the number of car accident
   donors.
4. Although 'swaps' of hearts and lungs have taken place with the recipient of
   a double heart/lung transplant donating her heart to another patient.

be just that, not a sale.[5] No part of a person's body should be treated as a commodity subject to the pressures of the market.[6] Now the Human Organs Transplant Act 1989 has given legal effect to that tradition, outlawing payments for non-regenerative organs.

Is donation lawful?

We have examined elsewhere the fact that there is no specific legal ruling which determines what limits, if any, are set to permissible surgical operations. It has always been assumed that surgical operations are lawful, where a patient properly consents, because the intrusive procedures are for the medical benefit of the patient. It also seems clear that the law will not permit a person to consent to any intrusive procedures simply because he is willing, or indeed anxious, to submit to them. The courts have, on a number of occasions, disregarded the consent of people to mutilating procedures upon themselves in a non-medical context.

Accordingly, an immediate question which must be asked in connection with transplantation from live donors is whether a potential donor can, in law, give consent to, for example, a kidney being taken from his body; the transplant is of no physical therapeutic benefit to the donor, and in some cases loss of a kidney could prove to be harmful. Almost certainly, the courts will regard this as a public policy issue. In the very early days of transplantation it is conceivable that the courts might have hesitated to approve of the removal of a healthy organ; and it might have been held that consent to such procedures was not permitted; but we have proceeded too far along the transplantation road for that argument to be of any avail today. Thus, Lord Edmund-Davies has said extra-judicially that he would be surprised if a surgeon were successfully sued for trespass to the person or convicted of causing bodily harm to one of full age and intelligence who freely consented to act as donor. But he then added the proviso that the operation should not present unreasonable risks to the donor's life or health. That proviso was important for 'a man may declare himself ready

5. For the arguments in favour of the sale of organs, see I. Kennedy and A. Grubb, *Medical Law: Text and Materials*, Butterworths, London, 1989, pp. 1007–18.
6. See R. M. Titmuss, *The Gift Relationship: From Human Blood to Social Policy*, Allen & Unwin, London, 1971.

to die for another, but the surgeon must not take him at his word'.[7]

How voluntary is consent?

Thus a person is permitted to consent to surgeons taking an organ from his body in certain circumstances. There is, of course, the problem of the genuineness of consent. Live donors are usually related closely to the potential donee, and it is often the case that the potential donor is the only person whose compatibility is such that the relative's life can be saved.[8] In such circumstances the psychological pressure which exists on a person can be enormous, and if the consent is not really free the surgeon may well be exposed to moral and legal censure. Full discussion and counselling are essential before a donor is asked to sign an appropriate consent form.

Children as donors

More difficult are those cases where organs or tissue are to be taken from young children. Can they be organ donors? If they are under 16 they may not have the capacity to give consent themselves for serious medical treatment, or other medical procedures, which are for their benefit. This must be given by a parent or guardian. Can they go further and consent to 'non-therapeutic' procedures upon their charges?

This is a problem which in fact arose in the USA in the early days of kidney transplantation. The first kidney transplants took place in 1956. Because of the importance of compatibility, the operations were between sets of minor twins aged 19, 14 and 14 respectively. In each case the healthy twin was willing to donate a kidney to his dying brother, but it was not clear whether the law permitted this. Applications were thereupon made to the court for guidance. The court fastened on the psychiatric evidence which was given to show that each donor had been fully informed about the nature of the procedure and also that, if it were not possible to perform the operation and the sick twin were to die, there would be a resulting grave emotional

7. (1969) 62 Proc. Roy. Soc. Med. 633, 634.
8. In one American case a court, not surprisingly, refused to *order* the only possible donor to submit to a bone-marrow transplant; *McFall* v. *Shimp* (1978).

impact on the surviving twin. This enabled the court to be satisfied in each case that the operation was for the benefit not only of the donee but also of the donor, and that accordingly a parent was capable of giving consent to such a 'therapeutic' procedure.[9]

Would an English court be similarly prepared to sanction a kidney donation from a child? It seems unlikely.[10] And in any case renal transplant surgeons in this country appear of their own volition to have ruled out kidney donations by minors. But bone-marrow donations by children, including very young children, to help treat siblings suffering from leukaemia are routine. Nor is judicial authorization sought for such procedures. Parental consent is assumed to authorize the removal of bone marrow from one child to benefit the other. The legality of bone-marrow donations by young children can depend only on reasoning analogous to that used to authorize twin-to-twin kidney transplants in the USA. The healthy child 'benefits' by the survival of her sibling. Perhaps in this context too the American reasoning is more persuasive. Taking bone marrow from the healthy sibling is a relatively minor procedure attended by very little risk or pain to the donor. Removing a kidney is major surgery and so it is that much harder to argue that the presumed psychological benefit outweighs the manifest physical risk. Doubt must be cast too on the role of parents as decision-makers in this context. Can a parent be expected to make an impartial evaluation of the interests of one child when the life of another of their children is at stake?

The lengths to which American courts have gone in authority 'donations' by incompetent patients is further illustrated in *Strunk* v. *Strunk*.[11] A 28-year-old married man who was dying of a fatal kidney disease sought the permission of the court for a kidney donation from his 27-year-old brother, who had a mental age of 6 and who was detained in a mental institution. The court emphasized the emotional

9. Curran, 'A Problem of Consent: Kidney Transplantation in Minors' (1959) 34 N.Y. Univ. L. Rev. 891.
10. Though note that the Council of Europe Resolution on the Harmonization of Transplantational Legislation contemplates the removal of organs from minors or otherwise legally incapacitated persons providing the donor and his legal representative are given appropriate information about the possible consequences, in particular medical, social and psychological consequences: resolution (78) 29 Art. 6.
11. (1969) 35 ALR (3d) 683.

and psychological dependence of the mentally handicapped person on his brother, and that his well-being would be jeopardized more severely by the loss of his brother than by the removal of a kidney. Accordingly, it applied a doctrine of 'substituted judgement', whereby the court was able to act in the same manner as the incompetent would have acted had he possessed all his faculties, and in these circumstances it gave consent on behalf of the donor. In a more recent decision in Texas the court applied the same principles, emphasizing first that nothing should be construed as being applicable to a situation where the proposed donee is not a parent or sibling of the incompetent and, second, that it would be preferable for legislation to provide a proper system of rules in these cases.[12]

Strunk v. *Strunk* has by no means been universally endorsed in the USA.[13] In this country the question of authorizing a 'donation' from a mentally incompetent adult is complicated by the lack of any *parens patriae* jurisdiction over adults. An adult donor could not be made a ward of court so that a judge could authorize the procedure, nor is there anyone else who could 'consent' on the patient's behalf. Following the House of Lords judgement in *F.* v. *West Berkshire HA*,[14] all that could be done would be to seek a declaration that the 'donation' was not unlawful, or go ahead with surgery and risk a subsequent action for battery! It is interesting to note that in the Court of Appeal Neill LJ at least implied that organ 'donation' by a mentally incompetent patient was not inevitably unlawful. He argued that such radical surgery should require judicial sanction but seemed to accept that there might be circumstances where such sanction would be forthcoming.[15] Justification for enforced 'donations' by mentally incompetent donors none the less seems dubious. Any argument based on psychological benefit is even more strained than is the case with child siblings. As to 'substituted judgement', if the donor has suffered from mental handicap since birth applying such a doctrine is no more than a legal fiction.

12. *Little* v. *Little* (1979) 576 SW 2d 493.
13. See *In Re Pescinski* (1975) 226 HE 2d 180; *In Re Richardson* (1973) 284 So 2d 185.
14. [1989] 2 All ER 945; discussed above, in Chapter 5.
15. [1989] 2 WLR 1025 at 1051–3.

The Human Organs Transplant Act 1989

In 1989 scandal relating to the sale of kidneys and a private London hospital prompted Parliament to enact the Human Organs Transplant Act in record time. Four medical practitioners were found guilty of serious professional misconduct by the GMC. Evidence was presented which established that money had been paid to poor Turkish citizens in return for their agreement to come to London, where a kidney was removed from each of them for transplantation into wealthy private patients. Allegations were made by one of the Turkish 'donors' that he was not even aware that he had agreed to the removal of a kidney. He believed that he had consented to an operation for his own benefit. If those allegations were true, clearly the doctors involved acted without consent and were guilty of the crime of causing grievous bodily harm and the tort of battery. It may even be the case that *any* purchase of organs amounts to an assault. The public policy reasons justifying altruistic donation may not necessarily apply to trafficking in organs, if a court were to find such traffic unethical. Complex arguments that the sale of organs may be illegal as an assault on the donor are rendered largely otiose by the Human Organs Transplant Act. Section 1 of the Act makes it clear beyond peradventure that making or receiving any payment for the supply or offer of an organ is illegal and punishable by a substantial fine or up to three months' imprisonment. The Act prohibits the sale of organs regardless of whether the 'donor' is living or dead. Any commerce in any non-regenerative organ is illegal. The Act applies to kidneys, hearts, pancreas, lungs and livers, to '. . . any part of a human body consisting of structured arrangement of tissues which, if wholly removed, cannot be replicated by the human body'.[16] It does not ban payments for regenerative body products such as blood or bone marrow. Payments for gametes, semen or eggs, are, as we have seen,[17] prohibited by the Human Fertilisation and Embryology Act except with the authorization of the Human Fertilisation and Embryology Authority.

However, the Human Organs Transplant Act goes much further than its original purpose of prohibiting commerce in organs. Section 2 makes it a criminal offence to remove a non-regenerative organ from a living person intended for transplantation into another person, or to

16. s. 7(2).
17. Discussed above, pp. 272–3.

transplant such an organ removed from a living person into someone else, unless the donor and the recipient are closely genetically related. For the purposes of the Act[18] you are closely genetically related to (1) your natural parents or children, (2) your siblings of the whole or half blood and (3) your nephews and nieces, and your uncles and aunts, again of the whole or half blood. Regulations made under the Act specify how such a relationship must be proved.[19] In the absence of such close genetic relationship, removal of a non-regenerative organ from a donor and its transplant into the recipient is lawful only with the permission of the Unrelated Live Transplant Regulatory Authority (ULTRA). Such permission for the use of unrelated living donors will be granted only if ULTRA is satisfied (1) that no payment has been made in contravention of section 1 of the Human Organs Transplant Act 1989[20] and (2) that a full and informed consent has been given by the donor.[21]

The need to ensure tissue-matching between donor and recipient means that the doctor will normally prefer a living donor to be closely related to the recipient. Such genetic relationship maximizes the prospect of a successful transplant. But why ban unrelated donations save with the permission of ULTRA? The primary reason may well be to enforce the ban on commerce in organs. If section 1 of the Act, prohibiting sale of organs, stood alone, 'donors' and desperate recipients might seek to mislead health care professionals, claiming to be siblings or close friends involved in an altruistic donation when in fact the recipient is buying a kidney. The Act requires proof of the sibling relationship, and outlaws the friend's donation except where ULTRA is prepared to give its blessing.[22] By allowing unrelated live transplants only with the sanction of ULTRA, the Act seeks too to protect donors from coercion or exploitation. Donating a kidney is no trivial matter in terms of the pain of surgery or its risks. ULTRA is created

18. See s. 2(2).
19. See the Human Organs Transplant (Establishment of Relationship) Regulations SI 1989 No. 2107.
20. See s. 2(3).
21. See the Human Organs Transplant (Unrelated Persons) Regulations SI 1989 No. 2480.
22. Section 3 of the Act also requires detailed information to be supplied to the Department of Health about *all* transplant operations. See the Human Organs Transplant (Supply of Information) Regulations SI 1989 No. 2108.

to ensure that donors fully appreciate what they are doing and cannot be made use of save of their own informed volition. The anomaly is that coercion, at any rate emotional coercion, is most likely where donor and recipient are closely related. Imagine the pressure a family could put on one brother to save the life of another when the latter is dying from renal failure. Having decided to create an unprecedented system of regulation for live organ transplants, should Parliament have required all live donations to be authorized by ULTRA?

Cadaver transplantation – the Human Tissue Act 1961

Most organs for transplantation today are taken from persons who have died rather than from living donors. Interestingly, a person has no legal right at common law to determine what shall happen to his body after his death. A body, or part of it, cannot ordinarily be the subject matter of ownership, and normally it is the legal duty of the close relatives of a deceased or those who are in 'lawful possession' of the body to arrange for its burial at the earliest opportunity. Thus, it is not legally possible for a person to impose a duty upon others that he be cremated after death. All he can do is indicate that he desires to be cremated, and those concerned with burial are free to comply with or ignore such a wish as they see fit. It follows, technically, that a person has no legal power to donate organs from his body after his death under the ordinary law; equally nobody has any right to interfere with a corpse, and any such interference would be a criminal act.[23]

However, the law relating to cadaver transplantation is now governed by statute. In 1952, the Corneal Grafting Act, recently amended by the Corneal Tissue Act 1986, authorized the use of eyes for therapeutic purposes in some circumstances. This statute attracted little publicity at the time; nor was there much more public interest when, in 1961, the Human Tissue Act widened the law to cover any other parts of the body. It is this Act which today governs the use of organs for transplantation purposes and, although at one time it served as a model for similar legislation in many other countries, it is now

23. In *R.* v. *Lennox-Wright* (1973) Crim. L.R. an unqualified person removed eyes from a cadaver for further use in another hospital. He was successfully prosecuted for contravening s. 1(4) Human Tissue Act 1961, which prohibits removal save 'by a fully registered medical practitioner'. But see Kennedy [1976] 16 Med. Sci. Law 49.

widely· regarded as being unsatisfactory both in connection with its wording and also, in some respects, in its narrowness of approach.

Authority for the removal of parts of the body may be obtained in two ways. Any form of payment for organs is, of course, prohibited by the Human Organs Transplant Act 1989.

At the express request of the donor

First, there is a 'contracting-in' provision whereby any person may in writing at any time, or by word of mouth in the presence of two or more witnesses during his last illness, express a request that his body be used after his death for therapeutic purposes (or for purposes of medical education or research). If such a request is made, then the person lawfully in possession of his body after his death has the power (though not the duty), unless he has reason to believe that the request was subsequently withdrawn, to authorize the removal from the body of any part or, as the case may be, a specified part, for use in accordance with the request.[24] The problems arising from this provision are mainly practical. The usual way in which a person determines what should happen after his death is by will. Relying upon a will would rarely be of much use in a transplantation situation. It is essential, in order to make use of organs which are taken from a body after death, to remove them within a very short time of death taking place. By the time the will was obtained and read, the relevant organs would be useless for transplantation purposes. Hence, since 1981 the medical profession and the government have sought to encourage people to carry donor cards. The card, signed by the holder, will specify which organs may be removed, or may state that 'any part of my body be used for the treatment of others'. The holder's signature and the telephone number of the next of kin are required. Two problems afflict the use of donor cards. First, the number of people carrying donor cards remains disappointingly low. Second, even if someone has signed a donor card there is a significant risk that it will not be on his person when needed, that is when he is found brain-stem dead after a traffic accident. Most women carry their cards in their handbag. The handbag will not necessarily be united with the potential donor in the Casualty unit of the hospital proposing to remove her organs.

24. Human Tissue Act 1961, s. 1(1).

With the consent of relatives

The second method provided for in the Act, and which does not depend upon the express consent of the deceased, enables a person 'lawfully in possession' of the body of a deceased person to give permission for organs to be removed if, 'having made such reasonable inquiry as may be practicable', he has no reason to believe either that the deceased had expressed an objection to his body being so dealt with after his death, and had not withdrawn it; or that the surviving spouse or any surviving relative of the deceased objects to the body being so dealt with.[25]

This particular provision bristles with difficulties and ambiguities. It is also capable of causing serious distress to close relatives unless its exercise is handled with care.

For example, it has not yet been determined authoritatively who is regarded in law as the person 'lawfully in possession of the body'. Take an example, by no means unusual, where a young man who has been killed, or fatally injured, in a motorcycle accident is brought into hospital and there is delay in connection with his identification. In those circumstances, it would appear that it is the hospital which is lawfully in possession of his body until such time as the relatives can be traced and can carry out their normal duties in connection with its disposal.[26] The hospital authorities may wish to use the organs of that person, and the law provides that they may do so if 'having made such reasonable inquiry as may be practicable' they have no reason to believe that the deceased or close relatives object. It is not clear whether the practicability of such inquiry relates to the interests of the relatives or the interest of the hospital. For example, in order to trace relatives and establish their views, it would not be unreasonable to take days or even weeks; the family of the deceased may be on holiday and may not be traceable for some time. If the requirement is concerned primarily with the need to establish their views, it would be unlawful for the hospital to act before those relatives were contacted; and so the body would be 'wasted' for transplantation purposes. Alternatively, it is possible to interpret the need to make such reasonable inquiry as may be practicable as relating to the particular use for which the parts of

25. ibid., s. 1(2).
26. This was the view of the DHSS, who require the NHS hospitals to designate one of their officers to exercise the function. DHSS 1975 HSC 15 (156).

the body are required, bearing in mind the very short time in which it is possible to make effective use of a deceased's organs. Thus, it can be argued that if the hospital is unable to trace the relative within a few hours then it has made such reasonable inquiries as it could and is free to act. Those who regard the Human Tissue Act as being far too restrictive in any event would naturally regard the latter interpretation as the better one. One may doubt, though, whether that is the correct interpretation.

But even then, there is a technical problem in connection with which relatives should be consulted to establish whether or not they object. The Act specifies the surviving spouse *or any* surviving relative of the deceased. If there is a surviving spouse, does that mean that it is not necessary to consult any other relatives should that spouse agree to the body being used? If there is no surviving spouse, *any* relative suggests, on a literal reading, that the person lawfully in possession of the body must make inquiries of *all or any* of the relatives, so that even a very distant second cousin would have the power to object. In most cases the hospital authorities would act sensibly and so also would close relatives; and it may be, therefore, that some of the technical difficulties created by the rather wide wording of the section would not raise problems in practice. However, difficulties have arisen from time to time. One woman, who had been separated from her husband for more than six years and who had not been consulted before his kidneys had been removed upon death, afterwards maintained that he had indicated a very strong objection during his life to any organs being transplanted from his body.[27] In other cases, serious distress has been caused to parents upon discovering that children who were crash victims have had organs removed from their bodies and they have not been approached. In all these cases, the hospital authorities maintained that all reasonable inquiries had been made!

The role of the coroner

Where there is reason to believe that an inquest may have to be held on a body, or a post-mortem examination may be required by the coroner, it is necessary to obtain the authority of the coroner to the removal of any part of the body. This, too, could have the effect of delaying for an unacceptably long period the opportunity to remove

27. *The Times*, 8 September 1976.

organs. This may be the case particularly where a coroner regards his duty to act as coroner as being of greater importance than the secondary power which he has to authorize the use of organs before his coroner's duties are complete. In a controversial case in Leicester in 1980, the father of a girl who had died in a road accident had given surgeons permission to use any of her organs, including her heart, which had been removed by surgeons. At a subsequent inquest, the coroner complained that he had not given permission for the heart to be removed since permission had been sought from him only for the removal of a kidney. He therefore directed that in future written permission would have to be obtained from him and countersigned by a pathologist. This incident highlighted the problem that coroners, acting in pursuance of what they regarded as their legal duties, could adversely restrict the use of organs even where parents or other relatives had consented. It was for such reasons that the Home Secretary circularized coroners, stressing that it was not part of a coroner's function to place obstacles in the way of the development of medical science or to take moral or ethical decisions in this matter, and that the coroners should assist rather than hinder the procedure for organ removal. A coroner should refuse his consent only where there might be later criminal proceedings in which the organ might be required as evidence, or if the organ itself might be the cause or partial cause of death, or where its removal might impede further inquiries.[28]

Life must be extinct

The Human Tissue Act 1961 does not deal at all with live donor transplantation; it is concerned solely with the removal of parts of a body *after death*. What is death? The Act simply states that 'no ... removal shall be effected except by a fully registered medical practitioner, who must have satisfied himself by a personal examination of the body that life is extinct'. Largely as a result of the need, for transplantation purposes, to act as soon as possible after death has occurred[29] the traditional medical definition of death has been reformulated, and the implications of this generally will be examined in

28. HC (77) 28 August 1975.
29. A kidney which is removed from the body and 'cooled' may be kept for at least 12 hours and may function satisfactorily for as long as 2 days, but the longer the delay the greater the damage to the kidney.

a later chapter. However, it must be emphasized here that the difficulty of establishing an acceptable criterion of death has operated as the most powerful factor to sustain transplantation issues at the centre of media interest as a matter of high emotional and public concern. Public concern was voiced, for example, at the suggestion that a doctor and his medical team might have conflicting interests in that, on the one hand, their duty would be to act in the best interests of the ill or dying patient to keep him alive and yet, on the other, there might be pressures to certify a potential donor's death at the earliest possible moment to enable organs to be removed for the benefit of other donees. Some suggested that there might be two types of death: one for medical purposes and one for legal! Thus, in one of the early heart transplant cases, a surgeon at the National Heart Hospital was reported as saying that the donor was 'clinically dead but legally alive by some criteria'. Such confusion was more confounded by the need in some cases to maintain a person who was dead, clinically and legally, on what was confusingly described as a 'life-support' machine to ensure that the kidneys to be removed were kept in good condition. The fact that the media and the public may often have been misled and were ill-informed about the correct situation did not affect the major unease about the whole question of certification of death. To this I shall return in a later chapter.

Prospects for reform

It is widely believed that the law is in an unsatisfactory state. The blame, though, lies not at the feet of the draftsmen or the judges but rather with a society which is still unable to make up its mind about changes in the law to meet its demand.

The British Transplantation Society has attributed the shortage of organs for transplantation purposes to several factors. First, and most important, was thought to be apathy in the medical profession. It is taking a very long time to persuade doctors to assist positively in the search for organs and the needs of transplantation. The second factor, which perhaps is now beginning to change, was thought to be ignorance among the public and the medical profession as to how serious the shortage is. Kidney transplantation has been carried out for so long that perhaps many people feel that the state of affairs at present is satisfactory, and that patients who need kidneys can always receive them. But perhaps of greatest importance is the fear among doctors that by being involved in organ donation they may in some way be contravening the law, with its present uncertainty of interpretation, or that they may meet with hostility from relatives by asking permission for kidneys to be removed after death, or that they may be accused of hastening the death of a potential donor.

In 1975 the British Transplantation Society recommended that a Code of Practice for Organ Transplantation Surgery be adopted to provide safeguards (beyond those contained in the Human Tissue Act) for those who needed reassurance about possible abuses of practice by over-zealous transplant teams. Thus, (1) before organs are removed from a body for transplantation purposes, death should be certified by two doctors, one of whom has been qualified for at least five years; and neither of these doctors should be members of a transplantation team. (2) In cases of irreversible and total brain death, where respiration is dependent on mechanical ventilation, the decision to stop ventilation must have no connection with transplantation considerations. Brain death would be established using agreed criteria (as discussed later). Two sets of tests should be carried out, separated by a twenty-four-hour interval. (3) Where it has been decided that death of the brain has occurred and mechanical ventilation is to be stopped, the question of organ removal should be discussed fully and sympathetically with available relatives so that their informed consent is obtained for the removal of organs either before or after mechanical ventilation is finally stopped. (4) If available relatives objected to the use of the deceased's organs for grafting, even if it were established that the deceased himself has not objected, the relatives' wishes would be followed. This Code was agreed in 1979.

Contracting in or out?

But by far the most important consideration from a legal point of view is the question whether or not the present system, which is essentially a 'contracting-in' provision, should be changed to a 'contracting-out' system. This means in effect that the law would allow surgeons to assume that a dead person had not objected to his organs being removed for transplantation purposes unless he had expressly put on record, for example on a public register, that he had objected to such use. In most cases this would mean, in law at least, that relatives would lose the right of veto. Such a law, which now exists in Austria, Denmark, Belgium and France, should, in theory, enable surgeons to acquire all the organs they need, unless there happened to be a dramatic change in public attitude so that large numbers of people went to the trouble of registering their objections. Alas, in France[30] the change in the law has made little difference in practice. Doctors remain unwilling to remove organs without the consent of the deceased's family. In England a Renal Transplantation Bill which sought to amend the Human Tissue Act to introduce a 'contracting-out' system failed in 1968. It was felt that such a radical amendment of the Human Tissue Act would be too controversial, bearing in mind the strong objections which members of the public and politicians have expressed over recent years to such ideas. To introduce a contracting-out system, it has been suggested, would be to pay too little respect to minority feelings which may be both strong and inarticulate. Nevertheless, such a change may well come. Thus in 1984 a television poll was commissioned (at a particularly propitious time) which showed that 71 per cent of the public supported an 'opting-out' system.[31]

A further option for reform of the Human Tissue Act is to introduce a system of 'required request'. It is suggested that one of the main reasons for the shortfall in donor organs is the failure by doctors to ask relatives to agree to cadaver organ donations. A number of American states[32] have thus enacted legislation requiring hospital staff to request permission from the deceased's family to remove suitable organs. So far there is no sign that the British government is keen to enact such legislation here. The Department of Health prefers to rely on encouraging more individuals to carry donor cards and educating health care professionals to request organs as a matter of course. Plans are also well advanced for computerizing records of potential donors.

Foetal tissue transplants

The potential for the use of foetal tissue for transplantation has aroused much ethical debate. Already foetal brain cells have been taken from aborted foetuses and transplanted into the brains of patients with

30. See Redmond-Cooper, 'Transplants Opting-Out or In – the Implications' (1984) 134 NLJ 648.
31. For fuller discussion of the debate on 'contracting-out' and arguments that the law should sanction removal of cadaver organs regardless of objections, see Kennedy and Grubb, op. cit., pp. 1042–57.
32. See Kennedy and Grubb, op. cit., pp. 1048–57.

Parkinson's disease, considerably improving the recipient's condition. In 1989 a committee chaired by the Rev. Dr Polkinghorne reported and recommendèd a Code of Practice for the use of foetuses and foetal material in research and treatment.[33] Many of the fears about the use of foetal tissue focus on concern that women with relatives suffering from Parkinson's disease may deliberately become pregnant, intending to abort the foetus to provide the needed brain cells. The ethical implications of in effect breeding a human 'medicine' are frightening. The law is relatively simple. Any abortion must conform to the provisions of the 1967 Act. The Code of Practice mandates that any question of the use of foetal tissue must be independent of decisions relating to the management of the pregnancy. The only remaining question is whether the mother's consent is needed before doctors may make use of the aborted foetus. BMA guidelines require such consent, as does the Code of Practice, but whether consent is mandatory in law is less clear. Does the mother own the foetus, so that 'misuse' of it is an interference with her property? Even if the foetus is 'property', which I doubt, has she in making the decision to abort abandoned her property?

Liability for mishaps[34]

A number of questions about potential liability if organ transplantation goes awry are now increasingly relevant. A failed transplant does not of itself give rise to any legal claim by the recipient. The renal surgeon does not guarantee success any more than any other medical practitioner. But what if, for example, donated blood or kidneys prove to be infected, perhaps with HIV? May the donor or the transplant team be liable in tort? It would seem unchallengeable that donors owe a duty of care to recipients which is breached by a donor knowingly donating organs or tissue when he is aware that he is infected by, say, hepatitis or HIV. The recipient's problem will be tracing the donor. Public policy grounds for protecting the anonymity of donors may be found to outweigh the recipient's individual right of action.

33. *Review of the Guidance on the Research Uses of Fetuses and Fetal Material*, Cm 672, HMSO, 1989, and see R. Gillon (1988) 296 BMJ.
34. Note the interesting case of *Urbanski* v. *Patel* (1978) 84 DLR (3d) 850, where the donor claimed that the defendant's negligence in removing his daughter's only kidney caused injury (the loss of his kidney) to him!

Realistically any claim in respect of contaminated body products will lie against the hospital supplying those products. Actions in negligence against the Department of Health by haemophiliacs who contracted HIV from contaminated Factor 8 were settled out of court.[35] The recipient's problem will be proving negligence. The Pearson Commission recommended that strict liability should be imposed on authorities responsible for the supply of human blood and organs. It is unclear whether the Consumer Protection Act 1987, which introduces strict liability for defective products, includes human tissue in its definition of a product.

Should donors and suppliers of organs be granted immunity from liability to the recipient? It is argued that immunity along the lines of that proposed in the American Uniform Anatomical Gift Act will encourage donation. It would do so at an unacceptable cost to the rights of injured recipients.

Transplantation: the future

The most important single issue in the context of organ and tissue transplantation is to find means of ensuring an adequate supply of cadaver organs. Fascinating as the legal issues relating to live donor transplantation may be, they should be irrelevant. If there were an adequate supply of cadaver kidneys, live donations would be unnecessary. Bone-marrow donations from live donors would continue to be required. The law relating to donations by children should be clarified. And sooner or later, as the number of conditions suitable for foetal tissue transplants grows, society will have to decide if foetuses can be allowed to be means to an end.

35. See above, p.184.

CHAPTER 19

Medical Research

In 1981 an elderly widow, Mrs Wigley, died from the effects of an experimental drug she had been given subsequent to an operation for bowel cancer. She died not from bowel cancer but from bone-marrow depression induced by the drug. Without her knowledge or consent she had been entered in a clinical trial of the new drug. At the inquest into her death the coroner thought the matter to be one deserving of public notice.[1] In 1984 and 1985 two apparently healthy young medical students died in the course of clinical trials of new drugs. In 1989 the media carried several stories about students being paid to participate in risky trials of new drugs and procedures. Such incidents arouse great public concern. Yet every time any one of us receives a prescription for antibiotics we benefit from research performed on others in the past. It is becoming a human guinea pig oneself that is at first sight unattractive. But if medicine is to progress to combat cancer and continue the battle against diseases such as diabetes and multiple sclerosis, new drugs and procedures must be subject to trials.

In this chapter[2] I examine the role the law does and should play in the control of medical research involving human subjects. There are three fundamental legal issues. (1) How far, if at all, should there be

1. On the debate as to the ethics of the case among doctors, see M. Phillips and J. Dawson, *Doctors' Dilemmas*, Harvester Press, London, 1984, pp. 63–74.
2. On the general background to the debate on research see I. Kennedy and A. Grubb, *Medical Law: Text and Materials*, Butterworths, London, 1989, pp. 846–69.

statutory regulation of clinical research? Anyone wishing to undertake a research project using animals may do so only under a licence from the Home Secretary.[3] An embryologist experimenting on a human embryo of up to fourteen days' development may do so only with the sanction of the Human Fertilisation and Embryology Authority.[4] Yet a doctor may lawfully carry out research on a human adult or child with no such equivalent authority. (2) The authority to carry out research on the human adult derives from that person's consent. The second crucial legal issue thus becomes: how satisfactory are the principles governing consent to participation in clinical research? (3) And, finally, what provision does the law make for an individual suffering injury in the course of his participation in such clinical research?

Clinical research may be classified in a number of ways. Non-intrusive research involves no direct interference with the subject, for example research into medical records, epidemiological research. Intrusive research may be non-invasive, for example psychological inquiries, or invasive, involving actual contact with the patient's body, for example taking blood, administering drugs, testing new surgical techniques. Therapeutic research involves research on patients in the hope that it will benefit those patients. Non-therapeutic research involves volunteers who agree to participate in a research project not likely to confer any personal benefit to themselves. The boundaries between these categories are difficult to draw. The more invasive the research the greater are the ethical problems. And non-therapeutic research generates particular difficulties.

Research ethics committees

In the absence of formal statutory regulation of medical research on humans, akin to the detailed control exercised over animal research, the responsibility for regulating medical research is entrusted largely to local research ethics committees. Within the NHS Department of Health policy has since 1975 required each district health authority to '... appoint a properly constituted local research ethics committee, which meets regularly, to register, review and approve (or not approve) the research conducted by its staff or using its premises and facilities ... and research undertaken by general practitioners within its

3. See the Animals (Scientific Procedures) Act 1986.
4. See above, pp. 298–300.

413

boundaries'.[5] The NHS local research ethics committee is formally a sub-committee of the health authority. There can be no doubt that as such the authority is legally responsible for the decisions of the committee. The authority *and* each individual member of the committee owe a duty of care to all those who participate in research approved by the ethics committee. Although there has as yet been no case in England where an ethics committee has been sued by a research subject, it is important to recognize that ethics committees have direct legal responsibilities to research subjects.[6] In addition to local research ethics committees established within the NHS, a number of informal ethics committees exist. These include ethical review committees set up by universities, private hospitals and the pharmaceutical companies.

The practices and effectiveness of ethics committees have been much disputed.[7] Criticisms have been many and diverse. The number of members on committees has varied from four to forty. Some committees never met, conducting all their business by mail. Committees were dominated by the doctors, and in a few cases had no lay members at all. If the success of an institution is to be judged by its results, the case of Mrs Wigley constitutes a damning indictment of ethics committees. For the trial in which she died of a drug she never knew had been given to her was approved by no less than *eleven* of them.

There is, however, now a strong will to reform ethics committees and improve their working practices and effectiveness. New guidelines for research ethics committees have been issued in 1991 by the Department of Health[8] and in 1989 by the Royal College of Physicians.[9] Both sets of guidelines emphasize the constitution of the committee. A committee 'should command technical competence and judgement' and 'accommodate respected lay opinion'.[10] The Department of Health

5. See *Local Research Ethics Committees*, Department of Health (1991) replacing HSC (15) 153 (1975).
6. On liability of ethics committees, see M. Brazier, 'Liability of Ethics Committees' (1990) 6 *Professional Negligence* 186.
7. For vigorous criticism of ethics committees and professional attitudes see Carolyn Faulder, *Whose Body Is It?*, Virago, London, 1985, pp. 95–100; and see the periodical literature cited by her.
8. See above, note 5.
9. *Guidelines on the Practice of Ethics Committees in Research Involving Human Subjects*, 2nd edn, Royal College of Physicians, 1989.
10. ibid.

guidelines prescribe that each committee should be drawn from both sexes and a range of age groups. Members should include hospital medical staff, nursing staff, general practitioners and at least *two* lay members in a committee of no more than eight to twelve members. Committees should (*inter alia*) meet regularly, and *not* conduct business by mail or telephone. They should use specialist referees to advise on any aspect of a research proposal where the committee itself lacks sufficient expertise in the area concerned. In reviewing each research proposal submitted to them the ethics committee must consider:

(1) The scientific merit of the proposal.
(2) Whether the subject's health may benefit from, or be affected by, the research.
(3) Hazards to the subject and facilities to deal with hazards.
(4) The degree of discomfort and distress to the subject.
(5) Whether the investigator is adequately qualified and experienced.
(6) Any financial or other rewards to the authority, doctors, researchers or subjects.
(7) The need to ensure an adequate consent has been obtained from the subject.
(8) Whether an appropriate information sheet for the subjects has been prepared.

If research ethics committees comply with these guidelines and prove able to meet the aims embodied in them, it may then be the case that there is no need for formal statutory regulation. Although a researcher contravenes no law in carrying out research without ethics committee approval, in practical terms that is unlikely. An NHS employee failing to seek approval from his local research ethics committee could be disciplined by his employing authority. Outside the NHS, conducting research without ethical review may well constitute 'serious professional misconduct'. The RCP guidelines state unequivocally:

All medical research involving human subjects should undergo ethical review before it commences, in accordance with the principle that investigators should not be the sole judge of whether their research raises significant ethical issues.

But *will* the guidelines operate effectively? Success depends on the wholehearted co-operation of ethics committee members and of researchers. Lay participation in ethical review is crucial. It is not enough to have a lay presence. Lay members must be sufficiently informed and vocal to challenge medical assumptions. Medical members must be prepared to give up precious time to ethical review. Their contribution to assessing the scientific merit of proposals and potential hazards to subjects is irreplaceable. A committee dominated by lay members because medical members have too little time to attend would be as bad as a committee dominated by the doctors. For there could be little as unethical as unwittingly sanctioning a proposal with no scientific merit. Perhaps statutory regulation of ethical review is called for simply to confirm the importance society places on the protection of research subjects who risk their health and comfort for the benefit of the community.

Consent to participation in trials

Outrage over Mrs Wigley's death centred on the revelation that a patient should be the subject of a risky trial without her knowledge or consent. To criticism that this should ever have been allowed to happen, the chairman of one of the ethical committees which had approved the trial responded that consent to the surgery embraced consent to related drugs, albeit the drug was experimental. Furthermore, ethical codes of conduct promulgated by the medical profession accept that in certain limited circumstances consent need not be sought. Let us look first then at the international ethical code on research on humans, the Declaration of Helsinki. Within the Declaration a distinction is made between therapeutic and non-therapeutic research. This distinction, we shall see later, may have vital legal consequences too. Therapeutic research concerns procedures experimental in nature but which it is hoped will benefit the subject of the research, the patient. The medical staff engaged in therapeutic research will be combining care of the patient with the conduct of the experiment. Non-therapeutic research involves generally healthy volunteers to test the efficacy, side-effects, and general operation on the human body of a novel procedure. Patients may become volunteers for non-therapeutic research into conditions unrelated to their illness.[11] The basic principle promulgated by the Helsinki Declaration provides that every subject '... must be adequately informed of the aims, methods, anticipated benefits and potential hazards of the study and the discomfort it may entail ... The doctor should ... obtain the subject's freely given informed consent,

11. See again the Declaration of Helsinki, reproduced in full in appendices to Phillips and Dawson, op. cit., and Faulder, op. cit.

416

preferably in writing.' In relation to therapeutic research an exception to an absolute requirement for the patient's consent is made.[12] If the doctor considers it essential *not* to obtain informed consent, he must give detailed reasons to an independent scrutiny committee (research ethics committee). This was done in Mrs Wigley's case and the ethics committees had approved the trial. No exception to the rule on consent is made in relation to non-therapeutic research.

How far does the ethical code conform with the law? I have dealt earlier with the issue of consent in general medical care.[13] The English courts demand that the doctor explain the general nature of the procedure to the patient.[14] In the absence of such explanation any contact with the patient may be a battery. His consent is invalid because he does not know what he consents to. When the patient understands what is to be done to him, but receives no information, or what he sees as inadequate information, on the risks and side-effects of treatment, the *Sidaway*[15] judgement held that he may have an action in negligence if risks or side-effects materialize *and proper medical practice would have required that he be warned of that possibility.*

Apply these principles to Mrs Wigley and the Helsinki Declaration. To perform a procedure whose nature and purpose are not communicated to the patient at all is to commit a battery. The exception to the need for any consent embodied in the Helsinki Declaration is not recognized as such by the law. Had Mrs Wigley's relatives gone to court, their claim would have turned on whether the experimental procedure could truly have been considered part and parcel of the surgery to which she agreed. Medical opinion appears deeply divided on that issue. On the other hand, the Declaration, and the ethical guidelines promulgated by the Department of Health and the Royal College of Physicians, may go further than English law at present in defining in their basic principles the degree of information on risks,

---

12. The Department of Health draft guidelines (1991) originally incorporated a similar exception to the requirement for consent: 'In some cases of therapeutic research there may be times when it is inappropriate to explain all the details of the treatment to gain consent.' This exception is omitted from the final version.
13. See Chapter 4.
14. *Chatterton* v. *Gerson* [1981] QB 432.
15. *Sidaway* v. *Board of Governors of the Bethlem Royal and the Maudsley Hospital* [1985] 1 All ER 643, HL.

side-effects and discomfort the patient should be given. The question to be resolved is whether the *Sidaway* test of judging what information a doctor must volunteer by reference to current medical practice will be adopted in the context of research. Will doctors engaged in research effectively determine what research subjects are entitled to be told?

No case involving consent to participation in clinical research has yet reached the English courts. So far the courts have adamantly refused to allow any departure from the *Sidaway* principle that a doctor who conforms to a responsible body of medical opinion discharges his duty of disclosure to his patient. The attempt at first instance in *Gold* v. *Haringey HA*[16] to distinguish between *therapeutic* and *non-therapeutic* procedures was firmly quashed by the Court of Appeal. None the less, consent to participation in research is likely to be subject to a more stringent, research-subject centred, test than *Sidaway*. First, Lord Bridge in *Sidaway* asserts '. . . the judge might in certain circumstances come to the conclusion that the disclosure of a particular risk was so obviously necessary to an informed choice on the part of the patient that no reasonable prudent medical man would fail to make it'.[17] Failure to disclose risks inherent in research would seem to fall within that category. Not to be advised of a known or suspected danger of a trial negates any realistic choice on the part of the research subject. He can in no way make a judgement about whether to risk entry into the trial.

Second, in assessing responsible professional practice in clinical research, it would be iniquitous for a court simply to proceed in the usual manner of hearing expert medical witnesses and deciding whether the defendant's witnesses are sufficiently eloquent and eminent to constitute a responsible body of medical opinion. Recourse would have to be had to the Department of Health and Royal College of Physicians guidelines and the practice of local research ethics committees. They require that patients and volunteers be given full and sufficient information, and detailed, frank explanatory information sheets are becoming the order of the day. Responsible professional practice must conform to the ethical standards set by the profession collectively. There is no room in the field of clinical research for equally acceptable but divergent responsible bodies of opinion.

There may be a temptation for the courts to distinguish between the

16. [1987] 3 WLR 649.
17. p. 663.

duty of disclosure owed to volunteers agreeing to participate in non-therapeutic research, and that owed to patients consenting to take part in therapeutic research. It is a temptation that should be resisted. Setting a stringent test for disclosure in the context of clinical research in Canada in *Halushka* v. *University of Saskatchewan*[18] Hall JA declared:

There can be no exceptions to the ordinary requirements of disclosure in the case of research as there may well be in ordinary medical practice. The researcher does not have to balance the probable effect of lack of treatment against the risk involved in treatment itself. The example of risks being properly hidden from a patient when it is important that he should not worry can have no application in the field of research. The subject of medical experimentation is entitled to a full and frank disclosure of all the facts, probabilities and opinions which a reasonable man might be expected to consider before giving his consent.

Self-evidently Hall JA's principle must be applied to volunteers No one but the volunteer can be allowed to assess what risk he is prepared to accept for the community's welfare. They apply equally to patients who agree to become research subjects. Of course, the doctor in such cases hopes that the patient may benefit from the experimental treatment. But that treatment remains experimental. The patient is exposed to additional, unquantifiable risk at least in part to benefit others not himself. If the doctor fears that the patient is unable to cope with assessing and judging for himself the risks and benefits of agreeing to take part in the trial, that patient should never have been entered in the trial.

In the case of non-therapeutic research a further problem is whether the volunteers are truly volunteers. Do medical students feel under compulsion to assist in trials mounted by their teachers? Do patients feel obliged to 'help' their doctor if he asks them to participate in non-therapeutic research?[19] Where resort is had to volunteers outside the medical schools and hospital patients, payment is still often made in this country. Amounts paid are relatively modest but may still constitute an inducement to impoverished students and the

18. (1965) 52 WWR 608.
19. Department of Health and Royal College of Physicians guidelines both require patient consent forms to state expressly that whether or not the patient agrees to take part in the trial will not affect his medical care and that the patient is free to withdraw from the trial at any time.

unemployed. The principles of law are clear. Any degree of compulsion renders any written consent given invalid. Proving compulsion would be the difficulty for a medical student. And for an unemployed 'volunteer', economic compulsion arising from his circumstances rather than any action by the research team is as yet unrecognized in English law.

The issue of free and full consent is central to the propriety and legality of clinical trials. Should the public, and patients in particular, come to believe that there is a real likelihood of being involved in a trial unknowingly, or, having agreed to participate, discovering that they have been given inadequate or inaccurate information, the supply of volunteers for research will dry up and patients' confidence in general health care will be seriously undermined. But the issue of what constitutes a proper consent is, as we have seen, far from easy. The line between experimenting on a patient and doing your utmost for him is blurred.[20] For example, if a doctor caring for patients with AIDS attempts as a last resort a novel treatment, knowing that there is no conventional treatment which will prolong the patient's life, has he crossed that line and made the patient a research-subject? The thorny problem of consent and medical research should not be left for a *cause célèbre* to be fought through the courts. Attempts should be made to work out in advance a statutory code of practice which (a) safeguards the rights of, and protects the interests of, patients and research subjects, and (b) ensures that properly regulated research can continue and flourish.

Children in medical research programmes

Very real difficulties beset the question of consent to clinical trials by adults. The problems are even greater where children are concerned. When can a child give his own consent to participation in a trial? If the child is incapable of giving an effective consent, may a parent give consent on his behalf?

The House of Lords' ruling in *Gillick*[21] empowers a minor to consent to medical treatment when he or she has reached an age and individual

---

20. On the problems of the development of a doctrine of 'informed consent' in the research context see J. K. Mason and R. A. McCall Smith, *Law and Medical Ethics*, Butterworths, London, 1991, pp. 358–62.
21. *Gillick* v. *West Norfolk and Wisbech AHA* [1985] 3 All ER 392; see Chapter 15.

maturity to judge what the treatment entails and assess its benefits and disadvantages. In the case of therapeutic research where the child may expect benefit from the procedure, the test might be the same. And if the child is over 16, the Family Law Reform Act 1969 statutorily empowering minors over 16 to consent to medical treatment will offer absolute protection to the medical team. Non-therapeutic research poses a more awkward problem. Does the *Gillick* ruling apply to a procedure of no immediate benefit to the minor? There is no reason why it should not. The basis of the judgement is not limited to medical treatment alone but concerns the general capacity of older children to make decisions for themselves. Provided the child or young person truly appreciates what he is agreeing to, provided he is sufficiently mature to make the judgement on whether the benefit to the community justifies any risk to himself, he may give consent as an adult may to participation in a research project. What the medical team must assess is the maturity and understanding of that individual. They must do this with any research subject under 18. The Family Law Reform Act empowers 16- to 18-year-olds to consent to their own medical treatment only. It has no application to non-therapeutic research.

What then of younger children? Therapeutic research poses little difficulty. The agreement of the parents to a procedure, albeit novel, which it is hoped will benefit the child will authorize the doctors' action. Parental consent is legally effective to authorize any treatment of the child aimed at promoting the best interests of that child. Non-therapeutic research on a child offers no immediate benefit to the child. On the present state of authority in England, it is unclear whether parental consent to such research on a child is of any effect.

The arguments on the present law can be put in this way. The test of the legality of procedures performed on children centres on the individual child. What will benefit him? What are the pros and cons as far as he is concerned? So in *Re D.*,[22] sterilization of an 11-year-old girl was prohibited because it was an invasion of her right to choose for herself on reproduction, and because of the emotional damage early sterilization might cause her. Social questions, for example the risk that any baby she had might be a burden on the community or be disabled itself, were barely touched on. And, although the House of Lords authorized the sterilization of 17-year-old Jeanette

22. *Re D.* [1976] 1 All ER 326; and see Chapter 15, pp. 388–92.

in *Re B.*,[23] their Lordships stressed that that operation was lawful only on the grounds that it benefited Jeanette. The benefit to her carers or society in general was to be totally disregarded. By analogy then, is one forced to say that non-therapeutic research on any child must be barred because the risk to the child, however slight, cannot be justified in the absence of some immediate benefit to him? In 1962 that was the advice given to doctors by the Medical Research Council.[24]

Paediatricians emphasize the need for some degree of carefully controlled research on children. Children respond differently to drugs, they suffer from illnesses not afflicting adults and, above all, their suffering when afflicted is particularly poignant. The British Paediatric Association considers non-therapeutic research on children to be neither unethical nor illegal. They have laid down guidelines centring on the principles that research should never be done on children which could adequately be done on adults and that the benefit/risk ratio must be carefully assessed.[25]

The Association's belief that experimentation on children is legal can generally only be right if the courts were prepared to accede to the following argument. Parental rights to consent to procedures involving their young children are generally said to be dependent on the procedure being in the child's best interests. That embraces any procedure, not just strictly medical matters; for example taking blood to ascertain paternity is allowed.[26] The best interests of the child include the interests of the community. The child benefits from serving the community and may in the long term benefit himself. For example, a 3-year-old from whom blood is taken as part of a control group and compared with blood from a group of diabetic children may develop diabetes himself or his child may. Hence may he be said to benefit indirectly from research into the disease? A further argument may be advanced to this effect. The case-law from which the 'in the best interests' of the child test derives concerns radical and major treatment decisions. Should a young girl be sterilized? May parents withhold consent from surgery necessary to prolong their newborn infant's life?[27] Such de-

23. [1987] 2 All ER 506.
24. 'Responsibility in Investigation on Human Subjects' (1964) 2 BMJ 178.
25. See generally Kennedy and Grubb, op. cit., pp. 890–95.
26. See P. D. G. Skegg, 'Consent to Medical Procedures on Minors' (1973) 36 MLR 370, pp. 379–80.
27. As in *Re B. (A Minor) (Wardship: Medical Treatment)* [1981] 1 WLR 1421.

cisions touch on matters which may be seen as involving acts and omissions positively 'against the interests' of the child. The House of Lords in *S. v. S.*[28] were asked to authorize a blood test on a child to determine his paternity. Lord Reid described a parent power to authorize such a test in this way:

> Surely a reasonable parent would have some regard for the general public interest and would not refuse a blood test unless he thought that would clearly be *against the interests of the child* [my italics].

In other words, where any risk to the child is minimal, parents may authorize any procedure which is not perceived as against the interests of the child. It is by no means certain that in all cases such an argument will succeed. Of crucial importance will be the extent to which the parents genuinely participated in the decision. Did they have the information and understanding to weigh the benefit of the programme against the risk to the child? The slighter the risk to the child, though, the more likely a court will accept parental judgement as the arbiter of their child's interests and welfare. The law does not require that children be mollycoddled from every conceivable physical risk.[29]

This matter is too vital to be left to the unpredictability of the common law. Statutory force should be given to a code of practice which (1) determines when consent may be given, and who may give effective consent, to research on children, and (2) provides for independent expert scrutiny of research proposals involving young children.[30]

Incompetent adults

Perhaps more problematic than the question of research involving children is the question of the research involving mentally ill, mentally handicapped or unconscious patients. The law is clear on one issue.

28. [1972] AC 24.
29. R. H. Nicholson (ed.), *Medical Research with Children: Ethics, Law and Practice*, OUP, Oxford, 1986.
30. On experimentation and children generally, see P. D. G. Skegg, 'English Law Relating to Experimentation on Children' (1977) 2 *Lancet* 754–5; G. Dworkin, 'Legality of Consent to Non-Therapeutic Medical Research on Infants and Young Children' (1978) Vol. 53, *Archives of Disease in Childhood*, pp. 443–6.

No other person can give a proxy consent to authorize the use of an incompetent adult in a research project.[31] The legality of treatment of such patients depends on proof that the doctor acted in the patient's best interests and in conformity with responsible professional opinion. A similar test might be applied to therapeutic research but cannot of itself legitimate non-therapeutic interventions. Ethical guidance sanctions non-therapeutic research with the agreement of the patient's family where risk is minimal and the research offers the prospect of substantial benefit to patients suffering from the same illness or handicap as the subject.[32] Incompetent patients should never be involved in research which could equally well be carried out using competent subjects. Whether English law would confirm that ethical guidance as representing the law of the land is unclear. It seems anomalous in effect to allow the researcher to authorize the subject's participation in the trial without carefully designed legal safeguards for that subject.[33]

Randomized clinical trials[34]

At the heart of much modern medical research lies the randomized clinical trial (RCT). Patients suffering from the same illness are divided into two groups and subjected to different treatments. Most commonly, either (a) one group will receive the conventional treatment, and another be given the experimental and hopefully more effective treatment, or (b) one group will be given a new drug, and the other a placebo. For an outsider there are a number of worrying features to RCTs. First, there is again the question of consent. Second, there is concern that the control group is denied a chance of superior treatment. In particular, public anxiety was highlighted by a trial involving 3,000 women at risk of conceiving a spina bifida baby. Studies had shown that similar women appeared to suffer a reduced incidence of carrying a spina bifida baby if treated with special vitamin supplements. The trial involved randomizing the women into four groups. One group

31. See *F.* v. *West Berkshire HA* [1989] 2 All ER 645, HL.
32. See Department of Health guidelines, above.
33. See 'Competence, Consent and Proxy Consents', in M. Brazier and M. Lobjoit (eds.), *Protecting the Vulnerable: Autonomy and Consent in Health Care*, Routledge, London, 1991.
34. For trenchant criticism on ethical and legal grounds of randomized clinical trials, see Faulder, op. cit., in particular Chapters 5–7.

received the full treatment under trial, another part only of the supplement, a third the other element of the supplement, and the fourth a placebo. Why should any woman at risk be denied a treatment which *might* help her avoid a spina bifida conception? Further criticism of randomized trials includes this point, that while the control group in a test may be denied a benefit, laymen are also concerned at the risk in some tests to the experimental group. And finally, who controls and monitors RCTs?

The law's involvement in the control of RCTs can only be peripheral unless specific legislation were to be introduced. The role the law plays now is largely restricted to the need to obtain, and the difficulty of obtaining, consent to an RCT. There are doctors and researchers who believe that the RCT is most effective if conducted 'blind', that is the patient is told nothing at all. The issue then is whether consent to treatment given generally is negated by unwitting participation in the RCT. The law will decide the issue on how closely related the RCT is to the condition under treatment and whether consent to treatment impliedly includes consent to what was done in the trial. At best, a patient asked to take part in an RCT will be told just that. The nature of the trial and the purpose of random allocation may be explained. Exactly what will be done to the patient cannot be explained, by virtue of the very nature of an RCT. Consent on the strength of a proper explanation of the trial and free acceptance by the patient of its random basis would appear both sufficient and necessary. Entering the patient in a random test with no explanation and no consent places the doctor at risk of an action for battery if the patient finds out. Fears that patients if properly informed will refuse to participate are natural. The erosion of personal freedom resulting from allowing 'blind' trials is not justified by those fears. A patient who will not agree to, or cannot understand the implications of, a trial should not be entered in that trial.[35]

Apart from questions of consent, the other means by which the courts may be invoked to consider the RCT arise when something goes wrong, and a subject suffers injury. Will the law enable him to obtain compensation? I move on to this next, and later consider general procedures to monitor clinical trials.

---

35. See the useful discussion in Phillips and Dawson, op. cit., pp. 61–71.

Compensation for mishap

At present, compensation for personal injury suffered as a subject in a clinical trial is available only either to a subject who can prove negligence on the part of the operator of the trial, or on an *ex gratia* basis. A claim in negligence may arise in two contexts in an RCT. A subject from the control group may complain that he was denied an improved prospect of cure. Subjects from the experimental group may allege that unjustifiable risks were taken. Neither is likely to succeed. As long as conventional treatment of the control group remained proper medical practice, the control has no claim in negligence. As long as the novel procedure was a properly conducted piece of research, carried out in conformity with a well-founded and responsible body of medical opinion, the subject of that procedure is likely to fail. One interesting speculation may be made. In the spina bifida trial, might a court be prepared to consider whether if there was a realistic hope of benefit the trial was really necessary? Could a mother denied the full vitamin supplement allege that her doctor treated her negligently? Or would the issue return full circle to the question of whether she freely consented to take part in the trial?

Next, what about the case where something goes disastrously and unexpectedly wrong? The subject will not know why. It may be an inherent risk in the trial, it may be that the staff conducting the trial were negligent. In principle, carelessness by the research team, be it in selecting subjects on the basis of their previous medical history, or in conduct of the trial or in their monitoring of the effects of the trial, creates a remedy for the patient. Moreover, he has in theory a possible remedy too against the ethics committee which approved the trial. Did that committee act negligently in approving a hazardous trial and fail in its duty to safeguard the interests of patients and volunteers? His problems lie in proof of negligence, just as any other patient-plaintiff's do.[36] And they are more acute. If proving negligence in the operation of standard procedures is difficult, how much more difficult it is to prove negligence in embarking on novel procedures.

No-fault compensation again!

One issue on which lawyers, doctors and drug companies do agree is

36. See Chapter 7 on the problems of litigation.

that the present law is inadequate as a means to provide compensation for injury suffered as a subject of medical research. The Pearson Commission,[37] which inclined towards retaining the law of negligence for medical accidents generally, nevertheless favoured strict liability in the context of medical research. The person who put himself at risk for the community was entitled to compensation from the community. The Commission recommended that 'Any volunteer for medical research or clinical trials who suffers severe damage as a result should have a cause of action, on the basis of strict liability, against the authority to whom he has consented to make himself available.'[38]

No change in the law has yet been effected. The Department of Health and the pharmaceutical industry operate *ex gratia* compensation schemes. The injured subject's legal rights remain, in general, dependent on the vagaries of the law of negligence. When a research subject suffers injury in a drug trial he may, of course, gain some slight advantage from the regime of strict liability imposed on drug companies by the Consumer Protection Act 1987. But he still has to prove that his injury resulted from a defect in the drug, and that it was that defect which caused his injury. If the drug company chooses to dispute liability, once again the matter is clumsily resolved by adversarial proceedings.[39] An individual, volunteer or patient, who agrees to subject himself to risk in the cause of medical science and the better health of the community deserves better than this.

Extra-legally, drug companies in the United Kingdom have begun to recognize the research subject's moral right to compensation independent of proof of fault. The Association of British Pharmaceutical Companies (ABPI) operates an *ex gratia* scheme whereby any healthy volunteer in a drug trial mounted by an ABPI member will receive compensation for any injury arising from that trial. However, many drug trials in British hospitals relate to drugs manufactured by foreign companies. Such companies may well not be ready to accept the ABPI guidelines. The Royal College of Physicians advises research ethics committees that they should require from such companies a written agreement to provide for research subjects 'at the least the same

37. See Chapter 10.
38. Royal Commission on Civil Liability and Compensation for Personal Injury, Cmnd 7054 HMSO 1978 paras. 1340–41.
39. For the problems of establishing strict liability under the 1987 Act, see Chapter 8.

protection' as that offered by the ABPI. Such advice raises the interesting question whether a failure by a research ethics committee to obtain such assurances to safeguard research subjects might constitute negligence on the part of the committee.

Patients agreeing to participate in research, and volunteers involved in non-drug trials, remain outside this informal no-fault provision. And the *ex gratia* nature of the ABPI scheme means that compensation remains dependent on the drug companies' generosity and is in no sense a right enjoyed by research subjects.

The case for no-fault compensation of persons injured in the course of research now receives wide support among doctors too.[40] It is patently fairer to doctor and subject than the present law. The Pearson proposal for reform via strict liability against the authority to whom the subject made himself available is seen as causing immense practical difficulties. The problem of insurance is one. The inequity in landing blame on one institution where the risk inherent in a trial happens to materialize is another. And the term 'authority to whom the volunteer made himself available' is hopelessly vague. The burden of compensating those injured in the course of research to benefit us all should have a wide base. A fund could be financed from all bodies promoting research, from the profession, the pharmaceutical industry and the Department of Health. The prospects for introduction of a scheme to compensate medical research victims along these lines appear brighter than prospects for a general no-fault scheme for all victims of medical accidents. Practical problems of definition, administration and finance will be faced, but with a will most difficulties could be overcome.

However, a scheme limited to injury suffered as a research subject will confront one very real problem. Exactly who would be entitled to benefit under the scheme? Would eligibility be confined to volunteers for non-therapeutic research? The moral case for automatic compensation for that group is overwhelming. Volunteers put their health on the line with no hope of personal benefit. Yet as patients may be used as subjects in non-therapeutic research into conditions unrelated to their illness, the line between therapeutic and non-therapeutic research may be blurred. If the compensation scheme is to extend to all research subjects, the problem of deciding eligibility moves to determining when a patient suffers injury as a result of a research enterprise, as opposed

40. See the deliberations and recommendations of the CIBA Foundation Study Group [1980] BMJ 1172–5.

to in the course of general health care which may include resorting to some novel procedure. Neither of these potential problems is insuperable. They illustrate perhaps that a general scheme of compensation embracing all victims of medical mishaps is to be preferred.

Monitoring research programmes

In the absence of specific legislation, the law's role in the control of medical research is limited to intervention when disaster has struck. At present it is only in relation to new drugs that legislation provides machinery which seeks to prevent disasters.[41] New drugs must be licensed in most cases before being granted a limited clinical trial certificate. The company seeking a licence must disclose results of preliminary research and animal tests. Only if the Committee on Safety of Medicines (CSM), established under the Medicines Act 1968, is satisfied with the information submitted by the company may clinical trials on patients begin. Provision is made for reporting back of adverse reactions to the CSM via the 'yellow card' system. It is this aspect of the process which has been much criticized. The evidence is that the wider the trial, the more doctors and patients involved in the trial, the less reliable is the reporting system. The continuing list of anti-rheumatic drugs withdrawn only after several patients have suffered serious reactions and even death is a poignant instance of the partial failure of the system to monitor drugs. The persistent allegations of high-pressure marketing to persuade doctors to enter their patients for trials of new products cause further disquiet. Review of the Medicines Act is clearly called for. But it does at least seek to regulate experimentation.

What should now be asked is whether central legal control of research programmes concerning new procedures should be imposed. A possible pattern for legislation is provided for by the Medicines Act in its regulation of clinical trials of new drugs. All research procedures could be made subject to approval by a body responsible to the Health Minister. Research would be permitted only under licence from the government. Such a proposal would be anathema to the medical profession. It would be seen as undermining their clinical freedom. And it would. The definition between doing your best to provide optimum care for a patient and experimenting would cause endless dispute. The additional burden in terms of money and time spent obtaining licences

41. See Chapter 8, p. 181.

would eat into the public purse and valuable professional time. The case is not made out yet. Local research ethics committees play a valuable role in representing the public's and the patient's views. Bodies within the medical profession, especially the Medical Research Council, act as central brakes on individual over-enthusiasm.

There are two areas of danger. The first is that a series of incidents in which research victims die or suffer serious injury may lead to litigation. As we have seen, the law, be it on consent or compensation, is unclear and unsatisfactory. Litigation may be bitter. If the reaction of the medical staff involved is to go on the defensive, saying nothing and defending the claim to the bitter end, the probity of medical research in general may be questioned. The second is, paradoxically, that pressure for the introduction of no-fault compensation is successful, and the threat of litigation is removed without the introduction of stringent measures to ensure accountability. In New Zealand in 1988 a public inquiry revealed a horrific tale. An individual gynaecologist was convinced that orthodox opinion on cervical smear tests was wrong. A positive smear, he believed, was not a precursor of cervical cancer. No action should be taken until an actual malignancy was apparent. He recruited thousands of women into his trial using manifestly inadequate consent procedures. Many, many women suffered dreadfully when cancer did develop and by that stage of the disease they had to undergo painful, invasive surgery. For years no other doctor dared speak out and challenge the investigator. New Zealand operates a no-fault system of compensation. The cervical smear trial started before that system was introduced. It will never be possible to know whether the knowledge that no patient could sue for their injuries either reinforced the investigator in his blind faith in his misguided theory, or deterred his colleagues from taking action earlier if only out of self-protection. Recourse to court is a clumsy weapon, but it must not be taken from the research subject without affording him other safeguards. Litigation may provoke distrust, leading to public demand for all-embracing and stringent statutory controls on research. Abolishing legal liability in clinical research may provoke a scandal that will have the same effect unless existing controls are seen to operate effectively.

There is an increasingly popular compromise between leaving things much as they are and moving to a statutory licensing scheme. One of the problems with local research ethics committees as the guardians of patients' interests is that they operate unevenly. Some are good, some are bad, some are diabolical. The new Department of Health guidelines seek in part to address that problem. But there will still be well over a hundred diverse committees, and inevitably on occasion those committees may reach different decisions as to the ethics of a trial. It can then be the case that investigators plan a multi-centre trial which is found to be ethical in London and unethical in Manchester. That does not necessarily mean Manchester is right and London is wrong. There may be local factors justifying the contradictory decisions. None the less, multi-centre trials pose a problem. A suggested solution is the creation of a National Ethics Committee. That Committee would have two primary functions. (1) It would review multi-centre trials and examine any trials raising issues of especial controversy. (2) It would monitor the work of the several local research ethics committees. A National Ethics Committee would thus seek to ensure consistency in ethical review and maintain standards in ethical decision-making. Much would ultimately depend on the constitution and composition of such a committee. If it is to be effective as a means of ensuring accountability in clinical research, it must have teeth, and it must not be dominated by the medical profession itself.

Confidentiality and medical research

To advance the development of medicine and to enable research when completed to benefit other patients, the results of research must be published. Does publication of research findings amount to a breach of confidence to the patient? First, the patient, if he has given full and free consent to his participation in a trial, may at the same time agree to information about him being disclosed once the trial is completed and a report is prepared. This must be the preferable course of action. In setting the ethical standard of confidentiality, the General Medical Council recognizes medical research as an example of an exception to the general rule on confidentiality. Information may be disclosed if necessary for the purpose of a medical research project which has been approved by a recognized ethical committee. The NHS draft code on confidentiality recognizes a similar exception to its general rule. Whether in law disclosure in the course of a research project of confidential information about a patient without his consent amounts to an actionable breach of confidence depends yet again on the nebulous test of whether that disclosure can be justified by the public interest in the advancement of the relevant research.

What is clear, though, is that disclosure should be limited to information strictly necessary to the project and that the anonymity of the patient must be protected. The NHS Ombudsman upheld a complaint from a young man who discovered in a medical textbook a full-face frontal picture of his naked body!

The way forward

Three criteria should determine the future of law reform pertaining to medical research. The fundamental principles governing consent to participation in research must be defined and enforced. The option of leaving it hazy until and unless the courts intervene is not good enough. The case for automatic compensation for injury suffered in forwarding the public good must be met. And most vitally, the debate on control of experiments must continue. It cannot be left to the doctors alone. Their interests are too heavily involved in the projects they monitor. Ethical committees in individual hospitals and areas provide for lay involvement in individual projects. Greater lay involvement in central control and debate on principle is necessary if control of experimentation is not to pass entirely from the hands of the doctors and to be replaced by rules and regulations allowing no room for individual initiative and individual brilliance.

CHAPTER 20

Defining Death

The traditional definition

Biologically, death is a process and not an event. Different organs and systems supporting the continuation of life cease to function successively and at different times.

Traditionally, the key factors in that process which were used to determine whether death had occurred were the cessation of breathing and the cessation of heartbeat, matters which could be verified with simplicity. Thus, the irreversible cessation of heartbeat and respiration implied death of a patient *as a whole*; but that did not necessarily imply the immediate death of every cell in the body.

The need to determine an exact or, at best, approximate time of death may be important for many reasons. The law not infrequently requires such a finding. If a person is to be charged with murder, his victim must have died within a year and a day of the unlawful act; thus he may escape a murder charge if his victim survives beyond that period. Establishing the date of death may be important for property purposes: until death is established, steps cannot be taken to obtain probate or letters of administration to that person's estate; the interest of a beneficiary under a will is usually dependent upon the beneficiary surviving the testator; in some cases, where the testator and the beneficiary die at around the same time, it may be important, certainly for their heirs, to know when each death took place; thus, where parties die in a common accident, there may be a presumption that the elder died before the younger, unless evidence can be established as to the precise time of death of either; and the property consequences of this decision can be significant.[1] There may also be tax factors: if a person gives away property before his death, that property may be free from tax, or be subject to less tax, if he survives the gift for a specified period.[2] There have been many stories written involving relatives of such donors going to great lengths to postpone or conceal the 'true moment' of death so that he 'survives' beyond the relevant statutory period for tax purposes! Another possibility may be that the spouse of a person who is either dead or dying may wish to remarry and, in the absence of clear evidence as to whether death has occurred, there may be a potential risk of bigamy. Finally, if the victim has a claim for damages for the injuries sustained, the amount of damages may differ substantially between cases where the victim is comatose yet living, or dead.[3]

Until twenty years ago, determining whether a person was dead rarely posed any difficulty in practice. The medical profession accepted and used the traditional methods of establishing death: when a person's heart stopped beating and he stopped breathing, he was dead. Advances in medicine and in medical technology, however, gradually began to reveal that this was not a valid test for all purposes: elective cardiac arrest of open-heart surgery, for example, or cases of spontaneous cardiac arrest followed by successful resuscitation. Machines such as mechanical ventilators or respirators have effected major improvements in techniques of resuscitation and life support for those who are desperately ill or injured. Where these efforts are successful and the patient recovers satisfactorily, one may praise the advances in medical techniques. But sometimes such measures do not provide any satisfactory outcome, for example where the person's heart continues to beat on the machine long after breathing has stopped but his brain is irreversibly damaged.

In such circumstances, keeping a person going on a machine can be as undesirable as it is pointless. It is distressing to relatives. It can have an adverse effect on nursing staff morale; the cost of maintaining the patient in such intensive care can be very high and, indeed, the use of machines in these cases can mean that other patients, better able to benefit from them, may be denied access to them. The major back-

1. See Law of Property Act 1925, s. 184
2. Inheritance Tax Act 1984; Finance Act 1986, s. 101, Sched. 19.
3. e.g. *Lim Poh Choo* v. *Camden and Islington AHA* [1980] AC 174.

ground reason for dissatisfaction, of course, was the rapid development of transplantation programmes, which highlighted the need for speed in diagnosing death and taking organs from the body.

Thus, pressures developed to produce a redefinition of death based upon a new concept of 'irreversible brain damage' or 'brain death'. This concept has been illustrated dramatically by considering a guillotine victim. Nobody would consider the body, after the head has been severed, to represent an individual living being; yet the body could be resuscitated and the organs kept alive for a considerable period.[4] Thus, whereas in most cases brain death follows the cessation of breathing and heartbeat in the dying process, occasionally the order of events is reversed. This occurs in a minority of cases as a direct result of severe damage to the brain itself, from, perhaps, a head injury or a spontaneous intercranial haemorrhage: instead of failure of such vital functions as heartbeat and respiration eventually resulting in brain death, brain death results in the cessation of spontaneous respiration, this is normally followed within minutes by cardiac arrest. If, however, the patient is supported by artificial ventilation, the heartbeat can continue for some days and this will, for a time, enable the function in other organs, such as the liver and kidneys, to be maintained.

This condition of a 'state beyond coma' or 'irreversible coma' or 'brain death' was advanced as a new criterion of death in 1968 in an influential report of an *ad hoc* Committee of the Harvard Medical School.[5] In such cases a doctor could pronounce as dead a comatose individual who had no discernible central nervous system activity; and then the respirator could be turned off. It was emphasized that judgement of the existence of the various criteria of death was solely a medical issue.

But public opinion did not seem willing to surrender control of such matters lightly to the medical profession! Uneasiness was expressed in connection with the relationship between the attempt to redefine death and the needs of transplant surgeons. From the transplant surgeon's point of view, it is desirable and important that organs taken from a deceased person should be taken as soon as possible after death. In 1975 the British Transplantation Society expressed concern at the poor quality of cadaver kidneys being transplanted, mainly because of the

4. British Transplantation Society (1975) IBMJ, 251, 253.
5. 'A Definition of Irreversible Coma' (1968) 205 JAMA 337.

delay between the determination of death and the removal of the kidneys from the body; more than 17 per cent of kidneys transplanted in Britain were said never to have functioned at all. It was also import-ant, for the purposes of transplantation, that a machine should not be switched off permanently, but rather that the body be kept on the machine to preserve the quality of the organs until they were required. Two major fears were voiced publicly. First, was the pressure to re-define death being made simply to enable transplant surgeons to obtain better results? Could it be said, for example, that potential transplant donors might be designated 'dead' at a point of time earlier than if they were not potential donors? Second, was it ethically or legally permissible to remove organs from a donor before the respirator had been turned off? Indeed, could a doctor be liable for murder or man-slaughter by turning off a machine?

Because of doubts such as these, the British Transplantation Society, as we have seen in an earlier chapter, recommended that the death of a potential organ donor should be certified by two doctors; that neither should be a member of the transplant team and, most important, that the decision to stop a ventilator should be made quite independently of transplant considerations.

In the late 1970s the medical establishment agreed that 'brain death'[6] or, preferably, 'brain-stem death' (which is the 'irreversible loss of brain-stem function') could be diagnosed with certainty; and, in these circumstances, the patient is dead whether or not the function of some organs, such as a heartbeat, is still maintained by artificial means. A Code of Practice for the recognition and confirmation of brain death was endorsed by the DHSS for the benefit of all hospital doctors. However, controversy developed over the Code as a result of the *Panorama* television programme casting doubt on the reliability of the tests. Were patients being diagnosed as brain dead who were not 'really' dead? Or were the few reported examples of such mistakes simply cases where the appropriate criteria for determining brain death had not been properly carried out? Was it possible that organs were being taken for transplantation before a patient had died? In 1986 the continuing anxieties of certain eminent doctors were once again voiced publicly. The validity of procedures to establish 'brain-death' had never, they argued, been rigorously tested. Short-cuts in procedures

6. See I. Kennedy and A. Grubb, op. cit., Chapter 15 and see D. Lamb, *Death, Brain Death and Ethics*, Croom Helm, London, 1988.

were too often prompted by pressure from the transplant team anxious to 'get at' organs swiftly.[7]

Judicial skirmishes

Surprisingly few cases have occurred in English or American courts requiring any extensive discussion of the legal meaning of death. Those cases which have been reported usually involve a scenario where a person suffering from severe injuries is placed on an artificial ventilator which is switched off, after he has been pronounced dead, and then the body is reconnected to a respirator before organs are removed for transplantation purposes. In one case in the United States, the brother of the victim sued the hospital on the grounds that he was not 'properly dead' when the respirator was first turned off, that the surgeons had hastened his death. The standard and successful defence of the surgeons in such cases has been that the victim was 'brain dead' when the respirator was first turned off; and so the removal of the organs at a subsequent stage was not the cause of death.[8] (In this country, of course, it would also be necessary to show that the surgeons had complied with the Human Tissue Act in connection with the measures taken to attempt to trace relatives.[9])

English courts have, on a number of occasions, been faced with cases where a person who is charged with murder claims that it was not he who killed the victim, but rather the hospital team who disconnected the life-support machine. The courts have not reacted favourably to such arguments, even though they have expressly side-stepped the issue as to what, in law, constitutes death. In *R. v. Malcherek*[10] the Court of Appeal had to deal with two such cases. In the first, the defendant had stabbed his wife, who was taken to hospital and put on a life-support machine; when, however, it was found she had irreversible brain damage, the ventilator was disconnected and shortly after that all her bodily functions ceased. The second defendant attacked a girl, causing her multiple skull fractures and severe brain damage; she also was taken to hospital and put on a life-support

7. See the *Guardian*, 6 August 1986, p. 11; in particular, concern was expressed that the twenty-four-hour gap between sets of tests for 'brain death' was not always observed.
8. *Tucker* v. *Lower* (1972).
9. See above, pp. 402 ff.
10. [1982] 2 All E R 422.

machine, which was disconnected when the doctors concluded that her brain had ceased to function. The Court of Appeal upheld the judges' decisions in each case not to leave the issue of causation to the jury, pointing out rather tartly that it was not the doctors but the accused who were on trial. The Court took the crucial fact to be that the original criminal acts by the defendants were continuing, operating and, indeed, substantial causes of the death of their victims. In the ordinary case where treatment is given bona fide by competent and careful medical practitioners, then evidence is not to be admissible to show that the treatment would not have been administered in the same way by other medical practitioners. Thus, without going into any definition of death, the court was not prepared to allow assailants to shelter behind the technical arguments challenging standard medical procedures. But the court did go slightly further than that. Lord Lane CJ said, '. . . whatever the strict logic of the matter may be, it is perhaps somewhat bizarre to suggest . . . that where a doctor tries his conscientious best to save the life of a patient brought to hospital *in extremis*, skilfully using sophisticated methods, drugs and machinery to do so, but fails in his attempt and therefore discontinues treatment he can be said to have caused the death of the patient.'

Should there be a statutory definition of death?[11]

It seems clear, then, that the courts are not yet unduly concerned about the definition of death. There is no statutory definition, and it is usually accepted as an issue of fact established by medical evidence. The law is content to accept the decisions of medical practitioners.

Had there been a legal definition of death, especially a statutory definition based upon the long-standing medical criteria of irreversible cessation of breathing and heartbeat, then the medical redefinitions of death to take into account irreversible cessation of brain function would have no legal effect in those cases where there was a difference in time between the two definitions, until the existing definition was changed by statute or high judicial decision. However, so long as the matter is treated as a question of medical fact, changes in medical approach can be accommodated within the law without any requirement for it to be specifically amended.

11. See Skegg (1976) 2 J. Med. Ethics 190–91; Kennedy (1977) 3 J. Med. Ethics 5.

However, the question must be faced whether there should be a statutory definition of death and of the criteria for its assessment. The Criminal Law Reform Committee thought not in 1980, but had embarked on only a cursory evaluation of the problem.[12] Those in favour maintain that these should not be matters solely for doctors and medical practice but are matters of legitimate public interest and concern. Why should persons who until recently have always been regarded as alive, albeit dying, now be regarded at the same point of time as dead, simply because there is a national need for the use of such organs for transplantation? If there is a case for this new attempt to define death, then surely it is a matter worthy of public debate and statutory enactment. Another reason sometimes advanced for introducing statutory criteria is that the doctors themselves are affected by the considerable uncertainty which exists in the public mind as to the definition of death, and this, in turn, leaves them exposed to the possibility of civil or criminal proceedings in some circumstances. In addition, it is argued that when the matter is raised in a court of law it is not something which should be left for decision either by a judge and jury (in criminal matters) or by a judge alone (in civil matters). Statutory guidance is preferable.

On the other hand, those who argue against the introduction of a statutory legal formula maintain that legislation would be inappropriate: technical clinical matters are not the proper subject matter for statute; it could prove to be inflexible, unable to keep up with medical advances, and there might be difficulty in revising or repealing a definition which became out of date. This debate does at least provide the opportunity to clarify a number of issues which are of major public importance.

First, in connection with switching off life-support machines, the medical authorities and the public ought to appreciate the sharp difference between the situation where the machine is turned off because it is established, medically, that the patient is dead, and the situation where the machine is turned off because, although the patient is still clinically alive, it is thought that there is no further justification in continuing to support life artificially and that, therefore, the patient ought to be allowed to die. In the latter situation, a decision to discontinue 'extra-ordinary' or 'heroic' treatment involves quite different

12. See the 14th Report of the CLRC, *Offences Against the Person*, Cmnd 7844, HMSO, 1980.

considerations, including consent, the quality of life of the patient, and the proper use of scarce medical resources. These are discussed in the next chapter. None of these issues arise where the machine is turned off because the patient has been declared dead. Second, however, it must be appreciated that without proper safeguards, medical changes in the definition of death could conceal policy decisions to introduce limited forms of euthanasia. At present, comatose patients, whether breathing spontaneously or on a life-support machine, who have no hope whatsoever of regaining consciousness – frequently described as 'human vegetables' – are still regarded as living beings because, although irreversible brain damage has occurred, some activity of the brain stem is retained; they are not brain dead in accordance with current medical definitions. It would not be a far cry to modify the definition of death so that some comatose patients in this state are also regarded as dead.[13] Many may believe that this is the most sensible and most compassionate way of dealing with these persons. Criteria based on 'brain-stem death' would be replaced by a concept of 'cognitive death'. If the courts are content to recognize flexible and developing definitions of death as valid if they accord with medical practice, this would in effect be a method whereby without full public debate and without Parliamentary approval a limited form of euthanasia could be introduced directly into medical practice. It does not seem right to accord such power to doctors or judges alone.

Alternative tests?[14]

If a statutory definition of death is introduced which would recognize either the cessation of respiration and heartbeat or the cessation of total brain function, would that mean that in some cases it would be possible to establish the point of death at two or more different points of time? This could certainly have strange implications for a variety of reasons, not the least being the uncertainty of knowing when, for property purposes, an estate passes from one person to another. It was primarily for this reason that the first American legislative attempt to define death, made by the state of Kansas in 1970, was criticized. In setting out alternative definitions, the long-established traditional defini-

13. See the arguments discussed in P. D. G. Skegg, *Law, Ethics and Medicine*, Clarendon Press, Oxford (1984), pp. 213–23.
14. See Kennedy and Grubb, op. cit, pp. 1182–95.

tion and the newer definition, it was said that it would lead the public to believe that there are two separate phenomena of death, one being primarily for transplantation purposes. Notwithstanding the criticisms, many other states adopted similar definitions of death, and the medical profession has also welcomed definitions which are broad enough not to restrict medical discretion and which do not include restrictive medical criteria. More recently, the American Uniform Brain Death Act (1978) has served as a model for a number of states. It provides simply that 'for legal and medical purposes, an individual who has sustained irreversible cessation of all functioning of the brain, including the brain stem, is dead. A determination under this section must be made in accordance with reasonable medical standards.'

It is difficult to see what this, of itself, would add to English law, were it to be enacted. Such a statute would simply repeat and reinforce the Code of Practice[15] currently operated voluntarily by the medical profession. Any doctor violating the Code by, for example, operating for his patients a concept of 'cognitive death' would have difficulty to say the least in justifying his action in any subsequent legal proceedings. The more flexible means of regulation by Code of Practice enable criteria for defining death to be examined and where necessary modified without the need to resort to amending legislation. It is crucial that any such modification is fully and openly discussed if the public is to have confidence in the profession's own Code of Practice. And care must be taken that criteria for defining death are not used as a backdoor means of legalizing active euthanasia. Public confidence in the definition of death is crucial, particularly to the transplant programme. If that confidence is betrayed, legislation will be needed to ensure that medical practitioners see clearly the distinction between duties to a dying patient and the power to remove organs from such a person once that person is properly declared to be dead.

A final problem – the anencephalic baby[16]

In one sad context the current criteria for 'brain-stem death' remain unworkable. An anencephalic baby is born lacking a higher brain. He is bound to die, usually in a matter of days, and were his interests

15. See 'Diagnosis of Death' [1976] 2 BMJ 1187–8, and Addendum [1979] 1 BMJ 332.
16. See Kennedy and Grubb, op. cit., pp. 1206–10A.

alone to be considered such an infant would not be ventilated. However, other babies will be born with intact brains, but defective hearts or kidneys. Doctors may want to use organs from the anencephalic baby to save the life of a baby with other defective organs. If they allow the anencephalic baby to die 'normally' simply by ceasing to breathe his organs will deteriorate so rapidly as to be useless. Thus if the anencephalic baby is to be used as an organ donor he must be ventilated. That poses a problem in defining when he dies. Tests for brain-stem death are not yet properly applicable to newborn babies. And moreover there is some evidence that if ventilated an anencephalic infant's brain stem may remain active, 'alive', for some considerable period of time. If 'brain-stem death' is inapplicable to anencephalic babies should we accept that the lack of any higher brain function renders the baby, so to speak, born dead?[17] Or is that again confusing active euthanasia with defining death? And there is another ethical problem. Anencephalic babies are not ventilated to treat them but to enable them to remain viable organ donors. Can we justify using such infants as means to an end?

17. See the Report of the Working Party of the Medical Royal Colleges, *Organ Transplantation in Neonates* (1988), sanctioning such a course of action.

CHAPTER 21

Death, Dying and
the Medical Practitioner

Society has never been comfortable with issues surrounding the process of dying; and as medical personnel are involved with the dying, they inevitably become involved in the ethical as well as the medical dilemmas which are part of that process. The major contrasting dilemmas are, first, whether efforts should always be made to keep a dying person alive in spite of the additional suffering incurred by that person and the cost in terms of human dignity; and, second, when, if ever, attempts may be made to hasten death when there is excessive suffering and when the cause is hopeless.

The practice of 'striving officiously to keep alive' has been facilitated by the vast increase in high-technology rescue equipment which has become available in different areas of medicine, much of it capable of being used to postpone inevitable death for a time. The benefits of such high-technology equipment are considerable; yet there are those who question the cost, both in economic and in human terms. In economic terms it is maintained that the inappropriate use of such equipment in, for example, intensive care procedures, yields marginal, if any, benefits, while preventing the resources involved being put to better use elsewhere. Of course, this argument cannot be carried too far, since there are others who riposte that such fashionable economic theories are but a device to justify unacceptable reductions in the resources available for health care.[1] Whatever the force of economic considerations, few can deny the personal cost to the patient and to

1. e.g. Green, 'Health Cutbacks and Death with Dignity: A Right Wing Trend in Medicine Today' *Radical Community Medicine* [1985], No. 21, 20–26.

those close to the patient in terms of human dignity. The attention which is now being given to the 'rights' of patients includes the right to human dignity and the right to die with dignity. In preserving and sustaining the life of the patient with a helpless prognosis, it is in the true interests of neither the patient, the family, nor the doctor, always to prolong his suffering (unless this is specifically requested). Unlimited access to high-technology medicine may sometimes be as cruel as the illness itself. Doctors concerned with terminally ill patients may make professional and human decisions to give up *treatment* which may be merely sustaining the function of the organs and turn to appropriate *care* at the terminal stage. But matters of this kind, when discussed openly, raise important and emotive ethical and legal issues: the term 'euthanasia' is sometimes used loosely to challenge those who may contemplate unacceptable ways of easing the suffering of patients, and also to inhibit doctors from courses of action which they might otherwise be prepared to take.

The word 'euthanasia' refers to the means of inducing or bringing about a gentle and easy death; death without suffering. One form of euthanasia, characterized as 'mercy killing', is used where somebody, usually a relative, deliberately and specifically performs some act, such as administering a drug, to accelerate death and terminate suffering. Prosecutions for mercy killing, while rare, are sometimes reported, and the courts usually deal with such cases with compassion. Thus, in one case, a man who had for eleven years devotedly nursed his wife, who suffered from disseminated sclerosis, before killing her, was convicted of manslaughter but received a conditional discharge; and, in another case, a mother who shot her 6-year-old son, who suffered from cystic fibrosis, was simply put on probation for three years. But the courts are not prepared to be as lenient in all such cases. In one case, a woman who was described by a judge as 'caring, sympathetic and compassionate' was sentenced to nine months' imprisonment for attempted murder. She had agreed, reluctantly, to sit with a lonely, elderly woman who was deaf, arthritic and nearly blind, while she committed suicide. Four hours after taking a lethal dose of barbiturates with brandy, she was still breathing; and so the accused placed a plastic bag over the elderly woman's head, and she died soon afterwards. The judge passed sentence in order 'to deter others less altruistic' than her. However, the Court of Appeal did allow for the possibility of alternative approaches to sentencing in these 'shadowy areas' of mercy killing. Sometimes decisions may be taken not to prosecute even where the facts suggest that a case exists. In a much publicized example in 1978, Derek Humphreys, a well-known journalist, assisted his cancer-stricken and dying wife to 'commit suicide'; but in spite of his clear admission of this in his autobiography, no steps were taken against him.

Such cases of mercy killing, where doctors are not usually directly involved, can also be termed active, voluntary or positive euthanasia, in contrast to the term 'passive euthanasia' which might describe, for example, the withholding of life-support treatment so that nature is allowed to take its course.

Official attitudes to euthanasia are fairly consistent. The World Medical Association has declared that voluntary euthanasia is contrary to the Declaration of Geneva, and this has been endorsed by national medical associations throughout the world. For example, in 1969 in this country a medical resolution affirmed the fundamental object of the medical profession as the relief of suffering and the preservation of life, and condemned euthanasia as such. The churches, too, are against voluntary euthanasia, but a report of the Church of England in 1975, *On Dying Well*, following a similar line to various Papal directives, drew a distinction between voluntary euthanasia and a decision not to preserve life by 'artificial' means when it would be better for the patient to be allowed to die; it would be wrong to prolong life at any cost.

It is widely accepted that some medical practitioners from time to time are involved in forms of euthanasia, although inevitably it is impossible to gauge the real extent of this and, indeed, it is questionable whether 'euthanasia' is not a misleading and inappropriate term to use to describe medical conduct in such cases. When a Dr Mair, in an autobiography, *Confessions of a Surgeon*, admitted to carrying out a series of mercy killings on incurable patients during his career, politicians and some doctors attempted to institute private prosecutions against him for murder; although letters of support for Dr Mair appeared in *The Times*. When a Scottish nurse, Miss McTavish, was convicted of murdering geriatric patients by administering massive doses of insulin and sentenced to life imprisonment, Lord Platt, a distinguished physician, publicly stated that he would wish to be on her ward if he ever became senile, demented and incontinent. The contrary view was put by an MP who said that if there had been a verdict of not guilty the case could have become a landmark in establishing the thin end of the wedge to justify the practice of euthanasia.[2]

The uncertainties and doubts which affect public attitudes towards the treatment of the terminally sick and dying are compounded further by widespread misunderstanding about, and lack of clarity of, the relevant law. It becomes appropriate, then, to examine the present state of the law in England and to see how it applies to the various situations in which the medical profession becomes involved. The difficulty with English law is that few of the critical issues have had to be considered by courts, unlike in the United States, where there has been a great deal of relevant judicial activity. Accordingly, some attention will be paid to American cases, although sometimes English legal analysis proceeds on a slightly different basis.

Murder, suicide and assisting suicide

Deliberately taking the life of another person, whether that person is dying or not, constitutes the crime of murder, and causing the death of another by some reckless or grossly negligent act, without any intention to kill, can constitute the crime of manslaughter. Accordingly, any doctor who, no matter how compassionately, practised voluntary euthanasia or mercy killing would be open to charges of murder, attempted murder or manslaughter, if the facts could be clearly established. An important exception to that simple rule was spelt out by Devlin J. in the case *R.* v. *Adams*[3] in 1957. Dr Adams was charged with the murder of an 81-year-old patient who had suffered a stroke; it was alleged that he had prescribed and administered such large quantities of drugs, especially heroin and morphine, that he must have known that the drugs would kill her. In his summing-up to the jury, Devlin J. first restated the law to show that doctors were not in any special category: '. . . it does not matter whether her death was inevitable and her days were numbered. If her life was cut short by weeks or months it was just as much murder as if it was cut short by years. There has been much discussion as to when doctors might be justified in administering drugs which would shorten life. Cases of severe pain were suggested

2. The conviction in that case was eventually quashed because of a misdirection by the trial judge to the jury, and so the issue faded from public notice.
3. *R.* v. *Adams* [1957] Crim. L. R. 773.

and also cases of helpless misery. The law knows of no special defence in this category . . .'

The judge then went on to suggest that perhaps there was a special category for doctors, for he continued: '. . . but that does not mean that a doctor who was aiding the sick and dying had to calculate in minutes, or even hours, perhaps not in days or weeks, the effect on a patient's life of the medicines which he would administer. If the first purpose of medicine – the restoration of health – could no longer be achieved, there was still much for the doctor to do and he was entitled to do all that was proper and necessary to relieve pain and suffering even if the measures he took might incidentally shorten life by hours or perhaps even longer. The doctor who decided whether or not to administer the drug could not do his job if he were thinking in terms of hours or months of life. Dr Adams's defence was that the treatment was designed to promote comfort, and if it was the right and proper treatment, the fact that it shortened life did not convict him of murder.'

This analysis introduces into the law the 'double-effect' principle, much debated in philosophical circles, whereby if one act has two inevitable consequences, one good and one evil, the act may be morally acceptable in certain circumstances. Thus, in the context of abortion, the saving of the life of the mother must entail the 'killing' of the foetus; and here, also, where the giving of morphine to relieve suffering may also accelerate death. Lord Devlin's judgement has been widely accepted as an authoritative statement of the law. However, it will be noticed that the summing-up was not precise, since in one passage he referred to the incidental shortening of life by hours and, in another passage, he referred to the shortening of life by hours or months. It may well be a matter of judgement in each case. Clearly he is dealing with terminally ill patients where, in order to alleviate their pain, it is permissible to disregard the fact that the treatment involved may accelerate the patient's death. But if it could be shown that the administering of the drug was designed to kill, rather than to comfort, that would be a case of murder.

The other area of criminal law which is very important in the euthanasia context is that concerning suicide. Since the Suicide Act 1961 it is no longer a criminal offence to commit, or attempt to commit, suicide. However, the Act does provide that 'a person who aids, abets, counsels or procures the suicide of another or an attempt by another to commit suicide, shall be liable on conviction ... to a term not exceeding fourteen years'. In order to achieve consistency in bringing prosecutions, it is necessary for the consent of the Director of Public Prosecutions to be obtained. It is a crime which may be committed for diverse reasons, ranging from the avaricious to the compassionate. Thus in *R. v. McShane*,[4] a daughter was found guilty of trying to persuade her 89-year-old mother in a nursing home to kill herself so that she could inherit her estate. A secret camera installed by the police showed the daughter handing her mother drugs concealed in a packet of sweets, and pinning a note on her dress saying 'Don't bungle it'! Equally, if a doctor were to be shown to have supplied drugs, with similar intent, whatever his motive may have been, an offence would have been committed. However, in practice, as has been said, it would be very difficult to prove that a doctor who had supplied drugs to a patient was responsible for the patient taking an overdose.

Clear evidence of aiding and abetting a particular act of suicide is, therefore, necessary before a prosecution can be successful. This area of law was examined in *Attorney-General* v. *Able*,[5] where the court was asked to declare that it was an offence for the Voluntary Euthanasia Society to sell a booklet to its members aged 25 and over, setting out in some detail various ways in which individuals could commit suicide. The Society, which campaigned for the introduction of voluntary euthanasia legislation, claimed that, pending such legislation, they saw no alternative to supplying on request the necessary information to enable its members to bring about 'their own deliverance': the Society neither advocated nor deplored suicide; it had a neutral stance and regarded such decisions as matters of personal belief and judgement. Evidence in the case suggested that over a period of eighteen months after the first distribution of the booklet there were fifteen cases of suicides linked to the booklet and nineteen suicides where documents were found which showed that the deceased was a member of, or had corresponded with, the Society. The court concluded that in most cases the supply of the booklet would not constitute an offence. Normally, a member requesting the booklet would not make clear his intentions, and the booklet would be supplied without any knowledge by the supplier of whether it was required for general information, research, or because suicide was contemplated. To establish an offence

4. (1977) 66 Cr. App. R. 97.
5. [1984] QB 795.

it would have to be proved that the Society distributed the booklet to a person who, at the time of the distribution, was known to be contemplating suicide, with the intention of assisting and encouraging that person to commit suicide by means of the booklet's contents, and, further, that that person was in fact assisted and encouraged by the booklet to commit or attempt to commit suicide.

These laws become central to many of the issues now to be discussed. It will be appropriate to consider first the case of the 'competent' patient, that is a person with full legal and mental capacity, who is aware of what is happening and who may wish to make decisions himself about his quality of life: the way he will be treated and how he will continue to live or die. Second, the case of the 'incompetent' patient will be considered: the infant, comatose or mentally handicapped person who does not have the mental or physical capacity to make his own wishes known at the relevant times.[6]

Competent patients: is there a 'right' to die?

The question often posed is whether a person has a legal right to determine that medical treatment be withdrawn so that he be permitted to die. The answer is complex and may turn upon the kind of situation involved. Take first the case where a patient is not terminally ill (a condition which it is often not easy to establish), that is, where the situation is not immediately life-threatening. Here, the legal analysis seems straightforward initially. Patients have a basic right of self-determination: they do not have to seek medical advice and treatment in the first place; and any unconsented interference with them constitutes trespass. Similarly, a patient can discharge himself from medical care; withdrawal of consent would mean that further unconsented treatment would also be trespass. But should this simple analysis apply also where a patient is in, or believes himself to be in, a life-threatening situation? Logically, the wishes of a competent patient, or of a formerly competent patient who had made his wishes known while competent, must similarly be respected. Yet, in such circumstances, patients' wishes often have been overridden and treatment has been given. There are strong medical arguments to suggest that in life-threatening situations

6. It should be noticed, of course, that it may not always be an easy issue to determine whether a person is clinically or legally competent; see above, Chapter 5.

patients are not always capable of making rational decisions: they may no longer be 'competent'.

One study of a number of cases in a medical intensive-care unit showed the complex factors surrounding the request by different patients for cessation of treatment. One patient, whose request seemed clear, was in fact ambivalent. Another's decision was possibly determined by a depressive condition which, if successfully treated, might have affected his general attitude to treatment. Sometimes patients may use a plea for death with dignity to mask other less 'acceptable' problems or complaints; or the request may be based upon misconceptions, on the part of either the patient or the medical staff. Therefore, doctors have argued that superficial and automatic acquiescence to the concepts of patient autonomy and death with dignity threaten sound clinical judgements; and doctors should continue to exercise their professional responsibility for thorough clinical investigation and the exercise of sound professional judgement.[7] The law, however, may be unlikely to consider that the competence of patients is affected in many of these situations. Will it, nevertheless, protect doctors who save or prolong lives of patients against their wishes?

This issue has also been discussed in two related areas: hungerstrikers and Jehovah's Witnesses. In *Leigh* v. *Gladstone*,[8] a suffragette serving a term of imprisonment went on hunger strike and after three days was subjected to daily forcible feedings. Later she sued the authorities, unsuccessfully, for trespass, and the judge, in directing the jury, said that 'it was wicked folly for the plaintiff to attempt to starve herself to death' and ruled: 'as a matter of law . . . it was the duty of the prison officials to preserve the health of the prisoners, and . . . to preserve their lives'. This decision, which stands alone in this area of law, might suggest, if applied to hospital situations, that not only would doctors have a defence of 'necessity' to a trespass action following the overriding of a patient's request to have treatment discontinued, but also that it was a doctor's *duty* to act against a patient's wishes, even outside the situation where medical treatment is imposed upon prisoners.[9] However, this decision has been much criticized, and

---

7. See Jackson and Younger, 'Patient Autonomy and "Death with Dignity"' (1979) 299 New Eng. J. Med. 404.
8. (1909) 26 TLR 139.
9. Cf. *Attorney-General of Canada v. Notre Dame Hospital* (1984) 8 CRR 382; *Freeman v. Home Office* [1984] 2 WLR 130.

it is doubted whether, if medical personnel did so act, they would be able to plead the defence of necessity. Thus, modern prison practice no longer is to forcibly feed hunger-strikers. Similarly when adult Jehovah's Witnesses refuse life-saving blood transfusions, the advice given to doctors is to abide by that refusal regardless of the consequences if the mental and legal competence of the Jehovah's Witness is clear. Where a patient's decision to refuse further treatment does not involve the medical personnel in committing any further positive acts to hasten the patient's death, it would seem that the medical authorities would be liable neither for manslaughter nor for assisting suicide. Moreover, if they do impose treatment on the patient, they may find themselves liable for battery. In *Malette* v. *Shulman*[10] the plaintiff, a Jehovah's Witness, was rushed into Casualty unconscious after a road accident. She carried a card, which staff found, expressly prohibiting any health care professional from administering a blood transfusion. None the less, Dr Shulman went ahead with a transfusion that he considered to be 'medically essential'. He sought to argue that there was no 'informed refusal'[11] of treatment, and he acted out of necessity to save the plaintiff's life. Both arguments failed and the doctor was found to have committed a battery.

More difficult, however, is the situation where positive acts which have the effect of accelerating death, such as turning off a life-support machine, have to be taken by medical personnel. The play *Whose Life Is It Anyway?* concerned a traffic accident victim paralysed from the neck down; his mental faculties were unimpaired and he wanted to die, but he could not turn the machine off by his own efforts. A similar situation arose in America in *Satz* v. *Perlmutter*.[12] An elderly man lay terminally ill in hospital. His affliction had progressed to the point of virtual incapability of movement, inability to breathe without a mechanical respirator, and he could speak only with extreme difficulty. Even linked to a respirator, he would die within a relatively short time. Yet he remained in full command of his mental faculties. He had attempted to 'kill himself' by removing the respirator from his trachea, but hospital personnel, activated by an alarm, had reconnected it. He

10. (1988) 63 OR (2d) 243 (Ontario High Court).
11. He contended that when the plaintiff signed the card refusing blood, she was unaware of the circumstances in which she might actually need blood, and that she may have signed under religious peer pressure.
12. (1978) 379 So. 2d. 359.

451

sought, with the full approval of his adult family, the court's authority to have the respirator removed. Interestingly, the court saw the law's role as involving a balancing exercise between a citizen's right of self-determination and his constitutional right of privacy against the state's interest, in some cases, of overriding such rights. In the USA the right of an individual to refuse medical treatment is tempered by several factors. First, there is the state's interest in the preservation of life generally. But there 'is a substantial distinction in the state's insistence that human life be saved where the affliction is curable, as opposed to the state interest where, as here, the issue is not whether, but when, for how long and at what cost to the individual his life may be briefly extended'. In this case the patient's condition was terminal, his situation wretched, and the continuation of his life temporary and totally artificial; and accordingly there was no compelling state interest on this ground to interfere with the patient's expressed wishes. The second state interest which was not really in point here was said to be the need to protect third parties. The clearest example of this interest would be where the patient was a parent of young children and, by refusing treatment, would be abandoning them; and the state, as *parens patriae*, would be justified in seeking to prevent this. The third factor is the duty of the state to prevent suicide. But is the patient seeking to commit suicide? The court reasoned strongly that a request to turn off a life-support machine in this situation is not necessarily assisting suicide. Its disconnection, far from causing an unnatural death by means of a 'death-producing agent', in fact would merely result in death, if at all, from natural causes. The patient had demonstrated that he really wanted to live but under his own power. This basic wish to live, plus the fact that he did not self-induce his horrible affliction, precluded his further refusal of treatment being classed as attempted suicide. The court found it difficult to distinguish the situation from the case where a mortally sick patient refuses to undergo a further operation which constitutes the only hope for temporary prolongation of his life. The fourth, and last, interest which the state is said to have is the requirement that it should help maintain the ethical integrity of medical practice. In some cases important *medical* decisions should be left as the responsibility of physicians, and there should be no attempt to remove such responsibility from the control of the medical profession and place it in the hands of the courts. It is a matter of medicine only. That interesting and controversial proposition was not applicable in this case. Accordingly, balancing the competing interests, the court, on the facts of this case, came down in favour of the patient being allowed to decide to die with dignity: the right to refuse treatment in the first instance carried with it the concomitant right to discontinue it, even though the withdrawal of the life-support machine would certainly hasten death.[13]

The judgement in *Satz* v. *Perlmutter* was taken a stage further by the California Court of Appeals in *Bouvia* v. *Superior Court*.[14] Elizabeth Bouvia had suffered from severe cerebral palsy since her birth. At 28 she was totally paralysed, and as she also suffered from acute arthritis, she was in continual pain which was only partially relieved by medication. Despite her multiple afflictions she might well have survived a further fifteen to twenty years. Ms Bouvia decided to starve herself to death. Her doctors were determined to feed her and inserted a naso-gastric tube against her will. The California Court authorized the removal of the tube. Elizabeth Bouvia had a right to refuse life-sustaining treatment. Her refusal of treatment was not an act of suicide. Nor was any right to refuse treatment limited to patients who, like Mr Satz, were terminally ill.

On the same facts an English judicial approach would be less flexible and more direct. The central question would be whether a doctor who, at a patient's request, facilitated death by switching off a life-support machine could be liable for aiding and abetting a suicide. The third argument adopted in *Satz* and *Bouvia* would certainly be advanced: the refusal of medical treatment does not necessarily constitute suicide since, first, in refusing treatment the patient may not have the specific intent to die, and, second, even if he did, the decision to switch off the machine is a decision to refuse treatment and not a decision to commit suicide.

Perhaps more problematic than the suicide argument is the question whether those responsible for turning off a life-support system can be liable for murder or conspiracy to murder. In *Bouvia* the California court declared unequivocally: 'No criminal or civil liability attaches to honouring a competent, informed patient's refusal of medical service.' In *Barber* v. *Superior Court*[15] a patient, following an operation, lay in a deeply comatose state, suffering severe brain damage, with little prospect of recovery. After full discussion with his family it was decided

13. See also *Bartling* v. *Superior Court of California* (1985) 209 Cal. Rptr 220.
14. (1986) 225 Cal. Rptr 297.
15. *Barber* v. *Superior Court* (1983) 195 Cal. Rptr 484.

that he should be taken off all life-sustaining machines; but after a few days he was still breathing. Accordingly the intravenous tubes which provided him with fluids and nourishment were removed, and he received only nursing care which preserved his dignity and provided a clean and hygienic environment until he died. The lower court adopted a simple approach and ruled that intentionally shortening life by a period of time was an intentioned, unlawful killing and so constituted murder. The appeal court struggled to avoid this conclusion, in much the same way as an English court would have to, if it were similarly sympathetic to the doctor. First, it looked at the distinction between acts and omissions and concluded that the cessation of 'heroic' life-support measures is not an affirmative act but rather a withdrawal or omission of further treatment.

Even though these life-support devices are, to a degree, 'self-propelled', each pulsation of the respirator or each drop of fluid introduced into the patient's body by intravenous feeding devices is comparable to a manually administered injection or item of medication. Hence 'disconnection' of the mechanical devices is comparable to withholding the manually administered injection or medication.

An alternative argument which has also been used to reach the same conclusion is that a machine is turned off to enable a doctor *during treatment* to decide whether there is any medical advantage in turning it on again. That decision not to turn the machine on again is the omission which leads to death! Having reached the decision that turning off a machine is an omission to act, there is no criminal liability for omissions unless there is a duty to act. Thus the critical issue then turns on the legal duty owed by a doctor to a patient in this situation, which has already been touched upon. Here, whether the patient is competent and refuses further treatment, or incompetent, a doctor is under no duty to continue treatment once it has proved to be ineffective. Thus the court held that the doctors' omission to continue treatment, though intentional and with knowledge that the patient would die, was not an unlawful failure to perform a legal duty. Further, the court decided that there was no difference between switching off mechanical breathing devices such as respirators and mechanical feeding devices such as intravenous tubes.

Medical nutrition and hydration (fluids) may not always provide net benefits to patients. Medical procedures to provide nutrition and hydration are more similar to other medical procedures than to typical human ways of providing nutrition and hydration. Their benefits and burdens ought to be evaluated in the same manner as any other medical procedure.

Can British doctors be confident that a court here would adopt a similar analysis of the doctor's duties and the patient's rights? Or is there a risk that a doctor who switches off a ventilator or removes a feeding tube might face a murder charge? The decisions in the Court of Appeal in *Re C.*[16] and *Re J.*[17] regarding the fate of severely handicapped infants bear some resemblance to their American counterparts. In *Re C.* it was held that there was no duty to feed a dying baby artificially or to resuscitate her should she collapse, and in *Re J.* that reasoning was extended, as in *Bouvia*, to an infant who despite multiple handicap was not in the process of dying. If there is no duty to treat such an infant, and treatment is defined as including administering food or fluids artificially, it must follow that there is no duty to impose such treatment. But the nagging doubt remains whether if, for example, artificial feeding has begun removing the tube or drip will be regarded as different in kind from never inserting it. And in England there is no legislation equivalent to American Natural Death Acts positively asserting a patient's right to die with dignity and to determine the manner of his death.

The unconscious patient

A conscious, competent patient's right to refuse further treatment may provoke problems of distinguishing medical acts and omissions, but is in itself relatively uncontroversial. What of the fate of the patient whose illness or injury has rendered him unconscious and unlikely ever to regain consciousness? This was the issue in the well-known American *Karen Quinlan* case.[18] Karen Quinlan, a young woman suddenly stricken with illness, lay in a coma attached to a life-support machine and presented a terrible dilemma to her family and the hospital authorities. Although she was not dead by the applicable medical criteria for determining brain death, the medical authorities were satisfied that there was no hope that she would ever recover to a cognitive state: she

16. [1989] 2 All ER 782.
17. [1990] 3 All ER 930.
18. *In re Quinlan* (1976) 355 A. 2d. 647.

was characterized as being in a 'chronic, persistent, vegetative condition', kept alive only with the assistance of the respirator.

In those circumstances, the parents of Karen Quinlan decided that it would be best for her to be removed from the life-support machine. Accordingly, her father applied to the court to be appointed her guardian and claimed that, as guardian, he would be entitled to authorize the discontinuance of all 'extraordinary' medical procedures sustaining Karen Quinlan's vital processes and hence her life.

The Supreme Court of New Jersey upheld the father's claim in the following way. First, had Karen Quinlan been conscious and lucid, she would have had a right, by virtue of her constitutional right of privacy, to decide to discontinue life-support treatment in circumstances where it was simply prolonging for a short period a terminal condition. But she was not conscious or lucid. Second, because of her condition, her father was appointed guardian and the question then arose whether he could make a decision of that kind on her behalf. He was entitled to go to the court to seek assistance; and the court was prepared to 'don the mental mantle of Karen Quinlan' to make a decision for her which she would have made had she been able to do so. Thus, by applying a 'substituted judgement' test, the court decided that if, upon the concurrence of the guardian and the family of the patient, the attending physicians should conclude that there was no reasonable possibility of her ever emerging from her comatose condition to a cognitive state and that the life-support apparatus should be discontinued, they should consult with the Hospital Ethics Committee and, if that body agreed, the present life-support system might be withdrawn, without any civil or criminal liability on the part of any participant. Following that judgement, a Hospital Ethics Committee was appointed comprising five lay persons and one physician, and the decision was taken to remove the life-support system machine. It is an interesting reflection on the medical evidence given in the case that withdrawal of the life-support system did not lead to a swift death and Karen Quinlan survived for ten long years after falling into the coma.

The judgement in the *Quinlan* case was greeted with mixed reactions. For every commentator who saw it as a humane and sensitive development in the law there was another who maintained that the 'right to die' had been transformed into a 'right to kill'. None the less, in 1990 the Quinlan judgement was affirmed by the Supreme Court of the United States.[19] Nancy Cruzan, like Karen Quinlan, was a young

19. *Cruzan* v. *Missouri Department of Health*.

woman who had lain for years in a coma, in a 'persistent vegetative state'. By a majority of five to four the Supreme Court sanctioned the removal of all feeding tubes and other life-saving apparatus. Crucial to their decision was the court's acceptance of evidence that Nancy herself would not have wished to survive in such a state.

An English court faced with an English Karen Quinlan or Nancy Cruzan could not rely directly on the American precedents. There is no constitutional right to privacy. There is no means of appointing a guardian to act for an adult unconscious patient, nor any *parens patriae* jurisdiction in the court. We fall back once again on the test in *F. v. West Berkshire HA*.[20] The doctor must act in the best interests of the patient and in conformity with a responsible body of medical opinion. But *F.* does provide that an application may be made to the court for a declaration and it is by this route that the court's guidance could be sought. The possibility that English judges, like their American colleagues, will look to a doctrine of 'substituted judgement' to assist them seems strong. 'Substituted judgement' was referred to with approval by Lord Donaldson MR in *Re J*.[21] It would be tempting to seek to define the interests of the patient by evidence of what that patient would have wanted had he been able to decide for himself whether a ventilator be switched off or artificial feeding discontinued. But is 'substituted judgement' just a comfortable fiction?[22]

Advance directives

One of the major criticisms of the *Quinlan* judgement was that the court imputed to Karen a will to die on what some saw as flimsy evidence. Increasingly in the USA competent men and women seek to direct, in advance of incompetence overtaking them via disease or accident or ageing, how they should then be treated. *Advance directives* take two forms. (1) You may execute a '*living will*' whereby you declare the circumstances in which those caring for you should cease any life-sustaining treatment. For example, a 'living will' may provide, *inter alia*, that if you develop cancer, but are no longer competent and your condition is

20. [1989] 2 All ER 545, discussed fully in Chapter 5 above.
21. [1990] 3 All ER 930 at 938.
22. Particularly in any case where the patient by reasons of mental handicap has never been competent; see *Superintendent of Belchertown* v. *Saikewicz* (1977) ME 2d. 115.

irreversible, you should not be given antibiotics to combat any life-threatening infection, nor should you be artificially fed. (2) You may execute a *durable power of health care attorney*, nominating a proxy to act on your behalf and make treatment decisions for you should you become incompetent. Generally 'living wills' and durable powers of health care attorney will be complementary. The patient will use the 'living will' to indicate his general wishes, and then nominate a proxy to apply the 'will'.

There is nothing to stop any English patient executing a 'living will' and clearly in any subsequent decisions on his 'best interests' the 'will' would be admissible and valuable evidence, albeit it would not be binding on the doctor. For a durable power of health care attorney to have legal force in England, legislation would be required.[23] Most American states have enacted legislation expressly giving binding force to both 'living wills' and durable powers of health care attorney. A Working Party[24] set up by the King's College Centre of Medical Law and Ethics and Age Concern has recommended that similar legislation be enacted in the United Kingdom. In an excellent report the Working Party canvasses all the pros and cons of advance directives.

The advantages of advance directives are pretty self-evident. None the less, there are problems and pitfalls. Over 50 per cent of Britons never execute a conventional will. Will 'living wills' prove more popular? Nominating a health care proxy, someone you trust to take life and death decisions for you, is easy in middle life, less easy in old age. There may be no close friends or family left alive when you actually face terminal disease in extreme age. Is there a risk that proxies would abuse their power? Consider this scenario. A woman of 63 is acting as proxy for her 90-year-old mother who has suffered from senile dementia for ten years. The mother is doubly incontinent, has vicious temper tantrums and no longer recognizes her daughter. Is there an understandable risk that the daughter will refuse treatment for her mother's pneumonia motivated in part by a desire to be rid of an intolerable burden?

However, the greatest problem with 'living wills' and durable powers of health care attorney is this. The advance directive can only authorize any act which the patient if competent can authorize. Thus it may authorize cessation of treatment within the limits, and subject to the

23. The Enduring Powers of Attorney Act 1985 does not extend beyond powers to manage property and finance.
24. *The Living Will*, Edward Arnold, London, 1988.

caveats,[25] earlier discussed. What the advance directive cannot do is authorize an act which would hasten the patient's death, any act of active euthanasia. The nightmare for many of us is that we may end up in a geriatric ward with our mental faculties gone, our dignity destroyed. But patients so afflicted with dementia are often physically fit and able to survive for years. No advance directive can direct the geriatrician to kill you then.

To resuscitate or not to resuscitate

Before going on to examine whether the law should sanction active euthanasia I look at one of the most common problems faced by doctors and nurses, the resuscitation of patients, that is, restoring breathing and heartbeat. Is a decision not to resuscitate a patient whose prognosis is poor a purely medical one, or can that also be challenged as passive euthanasia? Where a patient is under medical care and has not vetoed particular forms of treatment, doctors and medical staff remain under a duty to take proper care of a patient, and may be liable civilly, and possibly criminally, for failing to do so. Thus, what say should a patient have in such decisions?

Because resuscitation decisions have to be taken in emergency situations, guidelines for issuing 'do not resuscitate' orders for individual patients have long been commonplace in America.[26] Some of these codes indicate a scaling down of active treatment for patients who are hopelessly ill by defining several levels of care, including, in some cases, a controversial slow-code procedure, which is a deliberately slow response to a patient who has suffered cardiopulmonary arrest. This procedure has been used when a patient's prognosis suggests that resuscitation is medically inappropriate and the family has refused, or is thought likely to refuse, 'do not resuscitate' status.[27] American courts have recognized the appropriateness of codes of guidance: it would be

25. For example, can a doctor actually remove or switch off the relevant life-saving apparatus? For a view that he should be so allowed see the Institute of Medical Ethics Working Party Report, 'Withdrawal of Life-Support from Patients in a Persistent Vegetative State' (1991) 337 *Lancet* 96.
26. See Jennett, 'Inappropriate Use of Intensive Care' [1985] BMJ and authorities cited therein.
27. Bassom, 'The Decision to Resuscitate Slowly; Troubling Problems in Medical Ethics', *Ethics, Humanism and Medicine*, Vol. 111, 116 (1981).

an impossible situation if every decision not to resuscitate a patient had first to be sanctioned by a court, for that would mean that it would be necessary for attempts to be made to resuscitate dying patients in most cases, without exercise of medical judgement, even when that course of action could aptly be characterized as a pointless, even cruel, prolongation of the act of dying.[28]

In England procedural guidelines whether or not to resuscitate are less frequently available. There is less open discussion, although a recent report on cardiopulmonary resuscitation in the elderly in an English hospital listed a series of circumstances in which this should be withheld.[29] As far as English law is concerned, the uncertain principles which have already been discussed would have to be applied to the specific resuscitation cases.

Attempts to introduce legislation; the euthanasia debate

The relevant English law is imprecise and uncertain. Doctors cannot always be given clear advice about the legality of various procedures. Is this fair to the medical profession? Is it right that some doctors, acting with the best of motives, may under a screen of silence do things which they believe may be unlawful? If what is taking place in medical practice is acceptable to society, should not the law be changed to set out clearly the parameters within which they should be acting? If society disapproves of certain procedures, how can they be controlled? Is it right, again, for the law to be left obscure but that when clear evidence of euthanasia occurs the prosecution may elect not to enforce the law? On the other hand there are those who oppose legislation on the grounds that the current fog allows for maximum flexibility for a caring medical profession.

Furthermore, one must be clear about the type of legislation which may be introduced. Should there be laws relating to certain forms of euthanasia, or more limited provisions dealing, for example, with certain types of high-technology treatment? Proposals for legislation which expressly or implicitly involve euthanasia will immediately come up against all the emotional, religious, social and other objections which are advanced passionately by many people. All kinds of argu-

28. See *Dinnerstein* (1978) 380 NE 2d 134.
29. Gulati, Bhan, Horan, 'Cardiopulmonary Resuscitation of Old People' (1983) 2 *Lancet* 267.

ments can be advanced against voluntary euthanasia legislation. Just how voluntary would such euthanasia be? Would the introduction of such laws result in a change of attitude by society towards the sanctity of life generally, towards the elderly and the infirm and towards the mortally sick? Would the existence of such laws impose pressures upon elderly and terminally ill patients to seek euthanasia rather than remain a burden on relatives or on society? Would the existence of such legislation provide opportunities for fraud and abuse and also undermine the relationship of trust between doctor and patient? How easy would it be to apply such a law? The experience of the Abortion Act shows the danger of imprecise drafting and variability of interpretation by those who wish to go beyond, or retreat from, the rather uncertain compromise which the legislation was designed to provide.

Further, voluntary euthanasia legislation could well contravene Article 2 of the European Convention on Human Rights, which provides that 'Everyone's right to live shall be protected by law. No one shall be deprived of life intentionally . . .'[30] Neither the European Court nor the European Commission on Human Rights has yet been called upon to decide to what extent the consent of a person to voluntary euthanasia procedures would negate what could well be a prima facie violation of the Convention.

Nevertheless, there are strong voices in favour of some clarification of the law. Thus, in connection with the possibility of withholding or withdrawing treatment, it should be made clear whether or not a person who is legally and mentally competent has the right to refuse further treatment, whether ordinary or extraordinary. When that is determined, it should also be made clear whether a person has the right to specify in advance what he would wish to happen in any future situation, when he may not then be competent to make a rational decision. If these matters were clarified, then it would seem natural to move to the next question, which is whether, in cases where there has been a prior indication (for example by a 'living will'), it is possible to use a substituted judgement procedure to enable a decision to be made on behalf of an incompetent patient. In these situations it would also be important to decide whether such decisions could be made only where a patient was terminally ill or in other situations as well. Also important, and in need of major clarification, is the extent

---

30. Although this must be balanced against Art. 3, which includes the right to be safeguarded against inhuman and degrading treatment.

to which the distinction between omissions and positive acts in medical practice should be legally significant. To prohibit doctors from committing positive acts but to allow them to achieve desired objectives by omission may satisfy some who are prepared to accept rather tenuous philosophical distinctions, but in practical terms adherence to such distinctions is capable of working cruelly against a patient and his family. If it is likely that there would be strong objections to empowering doctors to take positive steps to kill upon the request of a patient, then surely it would be far better to decide which positive actions are acceptable and which are not, rather than to draw the line between acts and omissions as such. Procedural matters are also of major importance. Who takes such decisions? Should these be matters of such importance that an objective review by a court of law is required; should there be a quasi-judicial review body such as an American style Hospital Ethics Committee;[31] or is this a matter which should be left primarily as a matter of medical responsibility alone or in consultation with members of the family or a guardian?

Active euthanasia[32]

But should the law go further and sanction active euthanasia in some circumstances? If a patient voluntarily requests help to die, should doctors be authorized to give such help directly by, for example, injecting the patient with a lethal dose of morphine? In the Netherlands an informal agreement between the prosecution authorities and the medical profession has allowed active euthanasia for some years now.[33] Under that agreement the prosecution authorities agreed not to prosecute any doctor who ended his patient's life within the parameters set by agreed guidelines. The patient must have freely requested 'help in dying' and the physician must assure himself that that request is truly voluntary and well considered. The patient and his doctor must be satisfied that there are no other means of relieving the patient's suffering or other incurable condition. A second doctor must be consulted. It is estimated that thousands of patients each year now opt for active

31. No such committees now exist in the UK. Local research ethics committees (see above, Chapter 18) are not concerned with treatment decisions.
32. See generally *Euthanasia*, a Report of BMA Working Party, BMA, 1988.
33. See 'A Report from the Netherlands' (1987) Vol. 1 *Bioethics* 156.

euthanasia in the Netherlands. Response to the Dutch experience is mixed.[34] What is of great interest is that when proposals have been introduced into the Dutch Parliament to give legal, formal effect to this informal policy, opposition to those proposals has blocked any progress.

Nor has the history of euthanasia reform in this country been encouraging for those who are in favour of legislation. The first measure in 1936 was a curious and bizarre Euthanasia Bill, designed to deal with a situation in which the doctor could no longer control a patient's pain. The procedural requirements were that the patient had to be over 21, suffering from an incurable and fatal illness, and he then had to sign a form in the presence of two witnesses asking to be put to death. This form and two medical certificates were then to be submitted to a 'euthanasia referee', whose task it was to interview the patient to ensure that he understood the nature of his request, and the referee might then also question doctors and relatives. Then, if the referee gave his certificate of approval, the matter would go to a special court which had the right to question any parties and consider objections; if the court was then satisfied, it would issue an appropriate certificate which would authorize a practitioner to administer euthanasia, which would have to be effected in the presence of an official witness. This Bill, with its prolonged procedural requirements, was received with no enthusiasm and was quickly rejected. In any event, the primary purpose of such legislation is now less important, since it is possible in most cases to control pain.

Another Voluntary Euthanasia Bill, introduced in 1969, was designed to allow a patient or prospective patient to sign in advance a declaration requesting the administration of euthanasia if he was believed to be suffering from a fatal illness or was incapable of rational existence. Again, the Bill was severely criticized by some as being inadequately thought out, ill-drafted and riddled with loopholes and ambiguities of the most dangerous kind; and above all 'because it failed in what it chiefly sought to do . . . it provided no reliable safeguards for the patient'. Perhaps the *coup de grâce* was applied with the following comment: 'Such a Bill is medically unnecessary, psychologically dangerous and ethically wrong. Unnecessary, because legal rigidity should not be substituted for medical discretion. Dangerous, because this Bill would diminish the respect for life, blurring the line

34. See the BMA Report, *Euthanasia*, pp. 49–52.

between crime and medicine. Ethically wrong, because it infringes on the absolute value of life.'

Subsequent Bills in the mid-1970s were more modest and attempted to avoid being seen as attempts to legalize euthanasia or 'mercy killing'. They were designated 'Incurable Patients Bills' and were described as being attempts to enlarge and declare the rights of patients to be delivered from incurable suffering. Thus, one Bill set out to state the rights of an incurable patient to receive whatever quantity of drugs may be required to give full relief from pain or physical distress, and to be rendered unconscious if no other treatment was effective to give such relief, and also to approve the right of a patient to specify in advance that he should not receive life-sustaining treatment if by reason of brain damage or degeneration he became incapable of giving such directions. Once again, the Bill was seen by its opponents as being the thin end of the wedge and that even if the Bill was strictly not about euthanasia, it could lead to it.

The situation in the United Kingdom appears to be static. The cause of reform was not helped by the adverse publicity received by Exit, the voluntary euthanasia society, when its director and another member were convicted on a number of counts of aiding and abetting suicides in circumstances which cast a major shadow over what had been a highly respected organization.[35] There is little prospect at present of the law being amended.

Conclusions

The effect of the lack of clarity in English law is that in many circumstances the doctor acts at his peril. Yet, as we have seen, enacting fresh legislation is a process fraught with controversy. And critics of American Natural Death legislation doubt the value of legislation, preferring to leave regulation of the treatment of dying patients to codes of practice. Before progress can be made a crucial decision is essential. Should the law ever sanction active measures to end a life? The British Medical Association concluded that it should not,[36] while paradoxically accepting that there might be occasions when a doctor is 'compelled by conscience to intervene to end a patient's life'. What the

---

35. *R.* v. *Reed* [1982] Crim. App. 819; see also *Attorney-General* v. *Able* [1983] 3 WLR 845.
36. See the BMA Report, *Euthanasia*, above, note 32.

BMA adamantly opposed was any law enabling a patient 'to require their doctors to collaborate in their death'. Active euthanasia, while on occasion understandable, is a path the law should decline to follow. The risks of abuse are manifest. Above all, if simple cheap means to end suffering, the one-off lethal dose of morphine, are sanctioned, will society be prepared to continue to fund the invaluable work done in the hospice movement to relieve pain and suffering without violating the dignity of human life?

If active euthanasia is ruled out, legislation to clarify the patient's right to refuse life-prolonging treatment becomes more feasible and likely to succeed. In Canada, a Law Reform Commission has produced an important report in which, first, the right of competent patients to refuse treatment, even if the refusal would inevitably lead to death, was recognized; and, second, the question of discontinuance of medical treatment of the incompetent patient was also considered. While it was stressed that medical treatment of the incompetent patient should be discontinued only for very clear reasons, it was also emphasized that they, too, should have the right to die in peace and dignity, assisted by whatever palliative care is needed at the time. The appropriate mechanism for ensuring consent and protection for patients in such situations was thought to be primarily through the medical profession, after discussion, explanation and consultation with those close to the patients, and it was recommended that there be no criminal liability on physicians for decisions in these situations, including decisions not to treat or to discontinue treatment previously instituted as long as the decision was valid medically; that is, made on reasonable medical grounds under the circumstances, in the best interest of the incompetent patient and in conformity with other standards set by criminal law. When consideration, with a view to possible legislation, is given to these matters in Britain, it would be well to consider seriously such recommendations.

CHAPTER 22

Reviewing and Reforming the Law

The law in England relating to medical practice remains defective, albeit perhaps somewhat improved from the state of affairs prevailing in 1987. The procedures offering patients a remedy when treatment goes wrong are too often still loaded against him. The Court of Appeal has improved the patient's lot by ensuring easier access to medical records,[1] and the Access to Health Records Act 1990 will take this process further. Litigation remains horrendously expensive and usually protracted. The patient tends to feel like David against Goliath. It is too early to say whether NHS indemnity will help or hinder claims. Nor are doctors any happier with the state of medical litigation. Too often for comfort the legal concept of fault is in the doctors' eyes divorced from any real moral culpability. Litigation should be a last resort and is totally inappropriate to many grievances. Effective complaints procedures to ensure that patients' rights are respected and that professionals are accountable to the patients they serve are essential. Little progress in revamping such procedures has been made since 1987.

Nor does the law let patients and doctors down solely in its role as a means to right a wrong. It too often fails at the earlier stage of clarifying the patients' rights and the doctors' obligations. Again and again, in the earlier chapters of this book, I have had to qualify what I say by pleading that the legal rules are unclear and contradictory. On several occasions all I can offer the doctor is a statement that he acts at his peril, because, for example, no one really knows whether switch-

1. *Naylor* v. *Preston AHA* [1987] 2 All ER 353; see above, Chapter 7.

466

ing off a ventilator at the patient's request constitutes the crime of murder. Progress has been made in some areas. The Human Fertilisation and Embryology Act 1990 has clarified the legal status of children born as the result of assisted conception and provided a legal framework for doctors, patients and scientists involved in modern reproductive medicine. Yet legal innovation still tends to be *ad hoc* and usually reactive. In the wake of the scandal concerning the sale of kidneys, Parliament rushed through the Human Organs Transplant Act 1989, but did nothing to sort out the chaos in the rules relating to cadaver kidneys. Nor has proper attention been given to the question of how far law should regulate medicine. Attempts to lay down detailed rules governing every doctor/patient encounter would be as bad for health care as the legal vacuum that often now prevails.

The proper role of the law

The law should have three aims in regulating medical practice. First, it must provide mechanisms for dealing with mishaps and patients' grievances. Sensible and equitable rules and procedures should determine when compensation is payable in respect of medical mishaps. Procedures should exist and be easily available to patients to ensure (a) that individual complaints are fully investigated, (b) that appropriate action is taken to remedy any error found in the course of investigating the complaint, and (c) that any doctor found to be at fault should be dealt with in such a way as to prevent that fault recurring and harming other patients. Second, the law should strive to provide a clearer and more certain framework within which doctors and patients may make difficult and sensitive decisions on health care. Finally, the law must set limits on what medical technology may and may not be used for. The public needs reassurance that *Brave New World* is not just round the corner.

To achieve these aims three steps need to be taken. (1) Either (a) a system of 'no-fault' compensation should be introduced, or (b) radical reform of the procedure in medical litigation should be embarked on. (2) Complaints procedures within and beyond the NHS must be reviewed and rationalized. (3) A Commission on Health Care, Law and Ethics should be established to examine the relationship between law and ethics in health care decisions, and to recommend codes of practice to guide the decision-makers in the future.

1(a) 'No-fault' compensation

At the end of Part II a case for the replacement of the law of negligence by a scheme of 'no-fault' compensation as the primary means of compensating a patient injured in the course of medical treatment was outlined. I recap on just a few of the reasons. For the patient the benefits of a no-fault system are these. Compensation to enable him to take steps to adapt his lifestyle to his disability would be available much more swiftly and easily. The ever-awkward problem of whether his condition resulted from his medical treatment or the natural progression of his original disease or injury would be investigated, and not fought over in a modern version of trial by battle. The patient would be spared the trauma of facing two medical examinations, by his own experts and by the defence experts. Availability of compensation would be more equitable. Resort to law at present depends on whether you are rich enough to pay for legal representation yourself or poor enough to qualify for legal aid. From the doctors' viewpoint, the threat of a judgement in negligence blighting their careers because one mistake is made would be removed. The inhibition about confessing that something has gone wrong to a patient for fear of litigation would go. Frank communication between doctor and patient would be encouraged.

Progress towards introduction of no-fault compensation would take some time and great care. A bad scheme could be worse than no scheme at all. Three major difficulties must be confronted. First, eligibility to claim under the scheme must be defined. Will, or should, no-fault compensation be limited to NHS patients? What must the patient establish to prove that his disease or injury arose from his medical treatment? Second, the funding and administration of the scheme must be worked out. A tribunal to decide disputed cases would have to be established. I made some suggestions on these matters in Chapter 10. The Department of Health should act to create a committee of inquiry, composed of representatives from medicine, the law, patients' associations, the medical defence organizations, health authorities and the drug companies, to consider the options for reform. Their first task may be to weigh the benefits of radical change to no-fault liability against the more limited step of simply reforming existing procedures in medical litigation but keeping the action for negligence. Should they opt for a no-fault scheme, the committee should then take evidence and make recommendations on the funding and general outline of feasible schemes. That excellent report from the King's Fund, *Medical Negligence: Compensation and Accountability*,[2] has already covered much of the ground. Once general proposals are made and accepted by government, those proposals should be referred to the Law Commission for examination and the preparation of a draft Bill on the necessary legislation. One final issue for the Law Commission to consider would have to be whether the system of no-fault compensation should entirely replace the action for medical negligence, or whether resort to the courts should remain an option open to a patient who feels that his case merits public litigation and that compensation alone on a no-fault basis is an inadequate remedy. In deciding this question it must be remembered that a number of 'medical negligence' claims deal not with allegations that something went wrong with the treatment, but that the doctor failed to give the patient sufficient information to make his own decision on treatment. Finally, but most importantly, a no-fault scheme must *not* be introduced unless and until adequate means for ensuring professional accountability are in operation. Compensation for lost income is crucial to many patients who now resort to litigation. All aggrieved patients seek too to find out *why* they suffered injury when they sought care and to ensure that if someone is culpable for what went wrong he is brought to book.

1(b) Reform of existing rules

An alternative and less drastic reform would be to leave untouched the general principles of negligence as they apply to medical litigation and to effect reform of the procedures in medical litigation alone. While I prefer the option of no-fault compensation, albeit with more doubts than afflicted me in 1987, reform of evidential and procedural rules alone would clearly be simpler, and would recommend itself to those who see the sanction of liability for negligence imposed by a court as an important instrument in controlling medical practice, and ensuring medical accountability.

The Lord Chancellor's review of civil justice generally has resulted in some beneficial reforms for patient-plaintiffs. The Courts and Legal Services Act is designed to improve the efficiency of the legal system as a whole and to give the public greater access to legal services. The King's Fund Report on medical litigation called for the following

2. Discussed above, Chapter 7.

improvements to the tort system: (1) Potential claimants should be provided with means of identifying solicitors with expertise in medical malpractice suits. (2) Greater publicity should be given to the availability of legal services. (3) Fee-splitting arrangements should be modified to encourage solicitors to pass on difficult cases to specialists. (4) A system should be instituted to pool risks among health authorities in order to cope with the increasing number of claims. (5) Access to legal aid should be improved. Some progress has been made on 1–4, particularly in proposals for panels of solicitors for medical negligence. But the most crucial proposal (5) to improve access to legal aid remains a pious hope. A patient's ability to seek a legal remedy for a medical mishap remains dependent on the state of his finances.

A more radical reform of the tort system for medical litigation would be to change the rules for expert evidence. The present system is in effect trial by expert. Each party selects his 'champion' and expert evidence is presented in an adversarial fashion.[3] Could questions of what constitutes medical negligence and causation be better determined by an independent, impartial expert chosen by the court? Such a reform, bringing England more into line with practice in Europe,[4] would save time, trauma and money. Only one expert would, for example, have to examine the patient. A panel of experts in the various specialties could be established by the Lord Chancellor's Department. The catch is, would patients trust such a panel? A group of eminent doctors chosen by the medical establishment might be perceived as more likely to protect their peers than the patient. The Lord Chancellor, in recruiting a team of experts, must seek a representative panel from a broad spectrum of the profession. He must consult not just the Royal Colleges but patients' organizations and AVMA as well.

Weighing up the choices of radical reform via no-fault compensation against more limited reform of the existing system is primarily a task for the Department of Health in the first instance. If the government is unhappy, but not totally opposed to the more radical option, they might perhaps refer both options to the committee of inquiry which I

3. See the judicial criticism advanced at the way expert evidence was 'settled' by counsel in *Whitehouse* v. *Jordan* [1981] 1 All ER 287 (in Chapter 7, pp. 154–5).
4. See M. S. Scoggins, 'Expert Evidence: Combat or Conciliation' (1991) 7 *Journal of the Medical Defence Union* 19.

have suggested should be set up to consider ways and means of effecting a no-fault scheme.

2 Complaints procedures

Acceptance of comprehensive and effective complaints procedures is the price doctors must pay for introduction of no-fault compensation. If in the majority of cases the role of the courts in adjudicating on negligence is to cease, then patients must have the means to ensure that any complaint of lack of care, or inadequate or improper care, is fully investigated. Complaints procedures ought to be a much better means of establishing a failure in care than the courts. They will be concerned with finding out exactly what happened. They will be able to distinguish between the understandable error and the blameworthy mistake. The responsibility of the health authority will be properly looked at. Did the medical staff have adequate facilities to provide proper care? What sort of hours had the doctor been working? Procedures will involve the doctors in judging their peers. But they must, if they are to be seen to be fair, involve significant lay representation to assess and evaluate the opinions on medical issues arrived at by the medical investigators.

The Hospital Complaints Procedures Act 1985 required the DHSS to review existing procedures within NHS hospitals. The result was a system not radically different from what went before. Some minor improvements have been made in the complaints procedures relating to general practice. The GMC has shown some initiative. Their role is crucial. The GMC exercises ultimate authority over doctors. Other procedures exist to discipline and warn doctors within the NHS, even to prevent them practising within the NHS, but only the GMC can ensure that a truly incompetent or uncaring doctor never sees another patient. Another issue demanding attention is whether some official body should monitor complaints of malpractice in the private sector. That will arouse political controversy. Now that something like 10 per cent of families are covered by private health insurance, the issue of whether standards of care in the private system are adequately monitored must at least be considered. In Scotland the Medical Practitioners Union backed a review of private hospital practice, after a boy died in the course of a minor operation performed in a private hospital.

Above all, complaints procedures must be rationalized. Whether medical staff should always be obliged to co-operate in an inquiry into

471

a complaint needs consideration. At present compulsion is rare, and, as we have seen, refusal of co-operation can prevent an inquiry achieving any result. Once no-fault compensation is introduced, then the justification that it is unfair to ask a man to incriminate himself will have lessened. Central to review of complaints procedures must be the role of the NHS Ombudsman, the Health Service Commissioner. Should his jurisdiction be extended to embrace questions of clinical judgement? What added resources and support would be needed if this were to be the case?[5]

In view of the crucial importance of the Health Service Commissioner, perhaps the appropriate body to review complaints procedures is the Select Committee of the Commons, which already monitors the Health Service Commissioner's progress. This course of action has the advantage of referring review of procedures to an existing body with substantial experience in the field and the ability to obtain whatever expert assistance is required and to take evidence from all interested parties.

3 Commission on Health Care, Law and Ethics

The first two proposals that I have outlined aim to ensure (1) that an injured patient is offered a fair and simple remedy by way of monetary compensation, and (2) that complaints procedures investigate any alleged failure in medical care. Both are procedures designed to provide a remedy once something has already gone wrong, after the doctor/patient relationship has broken down. My final proposal is intended to improve the framework within which decisions on medical care are taken, to define patients' rights and to outline the limits within which medicine may be practised.

At the heart of many of the problems in medical decision-making discussed throughout this book lies the question of the patient's right to determine what treatment he receives and how to reconcile that right with the doctor's duty to give the patient the best treatment available. This arises in many forms. Did the patient have sufficient information to enable him to decide whether or not to agree to treatment proposed by the doctor? How far may parents consent or refuse consent to treatment of their children? Is a patient asked by his consultant to take part in a research programme genuinely free to refuse?

5. See full discussion in Chapter 9, pp. 209–10.

472

The debate on consent has concentrated on the concept of informed consent. On one side it is argued that it is the patient's fundamental right to decide for himself on health care. To promote that right, the doctor should be under a duty to disclose any unusual and material risks inherent in the proposed treatment and explain any feasible alternative treatment. Deciding whether a risk is unusual or material should be based on what the prudent patient would want to know. Members of the medical profession respond that informed consent is a myth. No unqualified person can adequately comprehend the necessary information relating to the risks and benefits of many procedures and treatments. And, say many doctors, patients do not want to know. They place themselves without qualification in the hands of their doctors.

'Informed consent' is an issue which has been pronounced on by the House of Lords. Their judgement in *Sidaway*[6] appeared at first sight to be a victory for those who maintain that what patients should be told is a matter for medical judgement alone. Careful study of the individual judgements reveals that if there was such a victory, it was partial in effect. And their Lordships' rejection of patient autonomy has been much criticized.

Two other medico-legal *causes célèbres* illustrate the fallibility of the present system of leaving the judges and the common law to develop guidelines for medical practice through contested litigation. Mrs Gillick's campaign to prevent girls under 16 being prescribed contraceptives without parental agreement also reached the Lords,[7] and ended in apparent defeat for her. Yet the judgements of their Lordships left loopholes for further litigation, and the GMC's attempt to interpret their rulings as they affected confidentiality met with bitter criticism. Nor does the law manage to evolve principles relating to the potential criminal liability of doctors any more successfully. The trial of Dr Arthur for murder took place in a glare of publicity. The essence of the charge laid against him revolved around the extent to which parents and doctors together may decide to withhold treatment from a damaged newborn infant. The practice followed by Dr Arthur was disputed but mirrored practices current in many other paediatric units. Dr Arthur was acquitted. The law emerged no clearer for his

6. *Sidaway* v. *Board of Governors of the Bethlem Royal and the Maudsley Hospital* [1985] 2 WLR 480; see Chapter 4.
7. *Gillick* v. *West Norfolk and Wisbech AHA* [1985] 1 All ER 533; see Chapter 15.

ordeal.[8] Subsequent judgements in *Re C*. in 1989 and *Re J*. in 1990 have made some progress in this difficult area, but the case-by-case approach too often proceeds by evading the fundamental issues to achieve a pragmatic solution to the particular problem.

The inadequacy of *ad hoc* case-by-case litigation is a major reason why many commentators are now pressing for a commission to investigate the law as it relates to medical practice. In the USA the President's Commission for the Study of Ethical Problems in Medicine reported in 1982. In Canada the Law Reform Commission reported in 1980 on *Consent to Medical Care*. We should follow suit. We can learn from American experience in deciding on the constitution and membership of a Commission. The Canadian report offers valuable insight into the workings of the common law and its application to consent to medical treatment. But a British Commission must start afresh in evaluating law in the context of medical practice in the UK. Health care here is largely still free of charge. How the existence of the NHS affects the doctor/patient relationship must be carefully evaluated. Many of the factors which influence medical practice and litigation in the USA are absent here. The patient does not pay the doctor directly. The doctor has no profit motive to influence his decision on appropriate treatment. The contingency fee system, whereby lawyers in personal injury cases will act for no charge unless the patient wins and in that case pocket a third of the damages, is not applicable in the UK. Some of the factors which led to an explosion of malpractice claims across the Atlantic exist here. Others do not. Similarly, fears of defensive medicine, of doctors opting for the legally safe rather than the best medical option, may in part have counterparts in England to USA experience. But any similarity is only partial. Doctors who are paid may have financial reasons to opt for an unnecessary series of tests and check-ups and second opinions. British doctors generally have no such financial incentives. The marked differences in law and medicine between Britain and America mean that a British investigation of law and health care must largely start afresh on its task.

Perhaps to suggest that a multi-disciplinary Commission looks at patient autonomy and patients' rights and responsibilities sounds mundane. In the past five years support for some form of multi-disciplinary inquiry has gathered strength. But the terms of reference tend to be grander these days. The Commission should review the ethical prob-

8. See Chapter 14.

lems posed by embryology, by the advances in genetics and all the frightening array of possibilities now laid before us with their potential for good and evil. Rather than waste time on the old chestnut of 'informed consent', what needs consideration is whether parents can be allowed to use the new technology to order their 'designer baby'. Investigation of the ethics of medicine must be proactive not reactive. Such an approach is misguided. Many of the 'problems' posed by advances in medicine are not new – just old problems in a new guise. The implications of our growing ability to screen for genetic disease ante-natally and post-natally simply raise once more the questions of the legal status of the embryo, the rights of its progenitors and, post-natally, the patient's right to information and control thereof. If we can settle the 'old' questions of the law's recognition of autonomy and parental rights, the 'new' problems may for legal purposes settle themselves. The distribution of power and responsibility for decision-making lies at the heart of most medico-legal problems. Of course there will be an added dimension to the Commission's work, to define the limits of what society will tolerate. But that dimension, important as it is, should not obscure the need to define fundamental rights and obligations in health care.

How would any such Commission be constituted? The first question is, who would sit on it? The membership should have a wide base. Clearly the medical profession, doctors and other health professionals, should be represented. The consumers of health care, the patients, should, via representatives of patients' associations, and/or lay members of ethical committees and other existing NHS committees, be given their say. The disciplines of philosophy and theology have a contribution to make, determining proper criteria for decision-making and the formulation of the rights and obligations of those involved in decision-making. And as the legal framework for medical practice and the application of medical ethics would be referred to the Commission, the lawyers cannot be excluded.

In practical terms, even before the selection of members for the Commission comes the issue of its formal establishment and status. Either this could be by means of a statute creating and constituting the Commission, or in the first instance a Committee of Inquiry along the lines of the Warnock Committee could be established by the DoH. That committee could itself consider the appropriate formal constitution for pursuit of its purpose. My preference, tentatively, is for establishment by statute from the beginning, with Parliament giving its

475

seal of approval to the process of review and having a say in the provision for membership and terms of reference of the Commission.

The Commission's terms of reference will need careful drafting. Certain specific issues should be referred expressly to the Commission. Primarily, the question of consent as it affects so many areas of medical care and medical research must be referred to the Commission at once. The problems of confidentiality, where the law at present is extremely superficial, must be addressed. A decision needs then to be taken as to which other of the issues surveyed in Part III of this book require immediate examination. Perhaps those which put the doctor at risk of criminal liability should be given priority. Thereafter the Health Minister should be empowered to refer specific issues to the Commission for consideration and the Commission should be empowered to propose to the Minister problems which it believes require its attention. What I envisage is not a short-term institution which would conduct a limited inquiry, make recommendations and then be wound up. The Commission would remain in existence first to complete its initial review of problems apparent today, then to be there to deal with problems which arise as medicine and technology advance, and finally to keep the law relating to medical practice and medical ethics under constant review.

The Commission's powers should be two-fold, to investigate and to recommend. Investigation is the keynote of its function. It must examine the present constraints the law places on medical practice, the feasibility and application of the principles relating to consent as developed by the courts. It must investigate the claims and counter-claims as to what patients want and need to be told about proposed treatment, and how informed consent will help or hinder good health care. The spectre of defensive medicine must be confronted to see whether it has substance. The Commission must extend its remit beyond the issues already litigated or debated in the context of the common law on consent. The question of payments to research volunteers, the time available for and manner of communications with patients, and the role nursing staff do and can play, must be looked at. From investigation the Commission would move on to reports and recommendations. The Commission would have three options. (1) It may simply issue a report on its findings and outline its views of the appropriate development of the common law. The report should relate general principle to specific practice, distinguishing between and illustrating various spheres of medical practice. Thus a report on consent to medical care would deal with general health care, problems arising out of particular procedures, the question of parents and children, the problems with mentally handicapped adults and the specific difficulties inherent in medical research. (2) The Commission could go further and append to its report recommended Codes of Practice. A Commission created by Act of Parliament could be empowered to make proposals on codes of practice to the Department of Health, so that by ministerial regulation the codes could be given statutory force. (3) Finally, on occasion, the Commission might in appropriate cases recommend specific legislation. For example, were the Abortion Act to be referred to the Commission, new legislation might be called for to amend the law embodied in that Act.

It is the second possibility, that the Commission be empowered to propose codes of practice, which needs some further consideration. Codes of practice have the attraction of introducing a greater degree of practical certainty into health care decision-making. They can distinguish between different areas of medical enterprise, providing, for example, for a separate discrete code on research. They create, too, certain problems for the doctor, the patient and lawyer. A code of practice may represent in the end a negotiated compromise. It offers to the doctor greater precision in the legal framework within which he practises. Its provisions are unlikely to command uniform support for each and every clause in the code. Take the example of therapeutic research on patients. While the common law governs what degree of information is required for the patient's consent to be valid and effective, until and unless a case comes to court it is not clear whether such patients fall within the *Sidaway* rules on disclosure, or some higher standard pertaining to non-therapeutic procedures. Patients and doctors are in a legal vacuum. Within a code of medical research a precise rule will be formulated. The compromise arrived at may not please research teams if they feel it would inhibit their clinical freedom. A high standard of disclosure with exceptions to the standard built in to accommodate the needs of doctors combining health care with research may be unsatisfactory to some patients and potential patients.

Two questions about the legal effect of codes of practice formulated by the Commission call for careful consideration. First, what force would the codes have to bind medical staff in their practice of health care? At the lowest they could be advisory only. Breach of the code would be a factor to be taken into account in investigating complaints and deciding on any disciplinary action against health care staff. If

477

litigation were in progress, the codes would clearly be referred to as evidence of what constitutes proper medical practice. To give further emphasis to the codes, the statute empowering the Minister to give statutory force to a code of practice could expressly require that the codes be taken into account when a court considers questions of medical liability. Finally, it would be feasible but unlikely that a criminal sanction could attach to breach of a code of practice.

The most realistic option, then, may be to construe the codes as guidance as to the civil liability of the doctor. The code would set the legal framework for his relationship with a patient. But if no-fault compensation is introduced, the action for negligence used by Mrs Sidaway and others to litigate the issue of informed consent may be barred in medical claims. The Commission would need to consider whether some new form of civil proceedings to test in the courts the application and interpretation of codes of practice is required. I suggested earlier that the relationship between reform making available no-fault compensation and the existing action for medical negligence will need consideration by the Law Commission. Liaison, perhaps even a formal link, between the Law Commission and the Commission on Health Care, Ethics and Law would be of the utmost importance.

So far I have concentrated on the Commission's role in examining and developing the law. The Commission's task should be wider than this. It must also consider ethical standards, and when it is appropriate for the ethical standard to be set higher than the law. The law can never be more than a crude base-point in deciding what is proper and ethically accepted. Just as the Commission should liaise with the Law Commission in devising a legal framework for decision-making in medical practice, it must also liaise with the General Medical Council in advising on ethics. Nor must the Commission confine itself to formal procedures, whether via legal regulation or the control exercised over professionals by the GMC and other professional bodies. Health Service procedures must be examined. For example, the role of ethical committees in scrutinizing medical research, and of Family Health Service Authorities in supervising general practice, may be crucial in day-to-day decision-making. The Commission offers a forum for general debate, for co-ordination between groups working in this field, throughout the UK. This is an opportunity, which should not be missed, for all those involved in and concerned about health care to co-operate rather than to confront each other.

Since 1987 support for such a Commission has, as I have said, grown apace. Ian Kennedy[9] is no longer a lone voice demanding that society plays its part in ethical decision-making in medicine. The tradition of self-regulation by the profession alone has been eroded; reproductive medicine and transplant surgery are now subject to statutory authorities with substantial lay representation, the Human Fertilisation and Embryology Authority and the Unrelated Live Transplant Authority. Yet the Department of Health appears to remain opposed to a general Commission on Health Care, Law and Ethics, preferring to act on an *ad hoc* basis, reacting to crises as they arise. The Nuffield Trust however is taking decisive action. After extensive consultation and discussions with the Department of Health, Nuffield has established a Bioethics Council which seeks to fill the gap that the government refuses to fill. The unofficial Nuffield Council will for a limited period undertake the role of a Commission on Health Care, Ethics and Medicine. What Nuffield hopes is that they can by example convince the government of the need for such a National Commission.

9. See Ian Kennedy, *The Unmasking of Medicine*, Allen & Unwin, London, 1981.

Some Suggestions for Further Reading

Medical ethics and law is a growing field of interest. In the Notes to the text I refer to several books and articles. In this short bibliography I suggest a few works which will be especially helpful to the reader wanting to extend his or her knowledge of the subject matter of this book.

Dugdale, A., and Stanton, K., *Professional Negligence*, 2nd edn, Butterworths, London, 1989.

Faulder, Carolyn, *Whose Body Is It? The Troubling Issue of Informed Consent*, Virago, London, 1985.

Field, M., *Surrogate Motherhood*, Harvard University Press, Cambridge, Mass., 1988.

Finch, J. D., *Health Services Law*, Sweet & Maxwell, London, 1980.

Freeman, M. D. A. (ed.), *Medicine Ethics and Law*, Stevens, London, 1988.

Gillon, R., *Philosophical Medical Ethics*, Wylie, Chichester, 1986.

Glover, Jonathan, *Causing Death and Saving Lives*, Penguin, Harmondsworth, 1977.

Glover, Jonathan, *What Sort of People Should There Be?*, Penguin, Harmondsworth, 1984.

Harris, John, *The Value of Life*, Routledge & Kegan Paul, London, 1985.

Harris, J. M., and Dyson, A. O. (eds.), *Experiments on Embryos*, Routledge, London, 1989.

Hawkins, Clifford, *Mishap or Malpractice*, MDU, Blackwells, London, 1985.

Hoggett, Brenda M., *Mental Health Law*, 3rd edn, Sweet & Maxwell, 1990.

Jackson, Rupert M., and Powell, John L., *Professional Negligence*, 2nd edn, Sweet & Maxwell, London, 1987.

Kennedy, Ian, *The Unmasking of Medicine*, Allen & Unwin, London, 1981.

Kennedy, Ian, *Treat Me Right*, OUP, Oxford, 1988.

Kennedy, Ian, and Grubb, Andrew, *Medical Law: Text and Materials*, Butterworths, London, 1989.

Keown, John, *Abortion, Doctors and the Law*, CUP, Cambridge, 1988.

Lamb, David, *Death, Brain Death and Ethics*, Croom Helm, London, 1986.

Leahy-Taylor, J. (ed.), *Medical Malpractice*, John Wright & Sons, Bristol, 1980.

Lockwood, M. (ed.), *Moral Dilemmas in Modern Medicine*, OUP, Oxford, 1986.

McLean, S. A. M. (ed.), *Legal Issues in Medicine*, Gower, Aldershot, 1981.

McLean, S. A. M., and Maher, G., *Medicine, Morals and the Law*, Gower, Aldershot, 1983.

McLean, S. A. M., *A Patient's Right to Know*, Dartmouth, London, 1989.

Martin, C. R. A., *The Law Relating to Medical Practice*, Pitmans, London, 1973.

Mason, J. K., and McCall Smith, R. A., *Law and Medical Ethics*, 3rd edn, Butterworths, London, 1991.

Mason, J. K., *Human Life and Medical Practice*, Edinburgh University Press, 1989.

Morgan, D., and Lee, R. G., *Human Fertilization and Embryology Act 1990*, Blackstone, London, 1991.

Nathan, P. C., and Barrowclough, A. R., *Medical Negligence*, Butterworths, London, 1957.

Nicholson, R. H. (ed.), *Medical Research with Children: Ethics, Law, and Practice*, OUP, Oxford, 1986.

Palmer, G., *Compensation for Incapacity: A Study of Law and Social Change in New Zealand and Australia*, OUP, Wellington, 1979.

Phillips, M., and Dawson, J., *Doctors' Dilemmas*, Harvester Press, London, 1984.

Savage, Wendy, *The Savage Inquiry*, Virago, London, 1986.

Skegg, P. D. G., *Law, Ethics and Medicine*, Clarendon Press, Oxford, 1984.

Speller, S. R., *Law of Doctor and Patient*, H. K. Lewis, London.

Speller, S. R., *Law Relating to Hospitals and Kindred Institutions*, 6th edn, H. K. Lewis, London, 1978.

Williams, Glanville, *The Sanctity of Life and the Criminal Law*, Faber & Faber, London, 1958.

Wood, Clive (ed.), *The Influence of Litigation on Medical Practice*, Academic Press, London, 1977.

Index

Visit Penguin on the Internet
and browse at your leisure

◆ preview sample extracts of our forthcoming books
◆ read about your favourite authors
◆ investigate over 10,000 titles
◆ enter one of our literary quizzes
◆ win some fantastic prizes in our competitions
◆ e-mail us with your comments and book reviews
◆ instantly order any Penguin book

and masses more!

'To be recommended without reservation ... a rich and rewarding on-line experience' – Internet Magazine

www.penguin.co.uk

READ MORE IN PENGUIN

In every corner of the world, on every subject under the sun, Penguin represents quality and variety – the very best in publishing today.

For complete information about books available from Penguin – including Puffins, Penguin Classics and Arkana – and how to order them, write to us at the appropriate address below. Please note that for copyright reasons the selection of books varies from country to country.

In the United Kingdom: Please write to *Dept. EP, Penguin Books Ltd, Bath Road, Harmondsworth, West Drayton, Middlesex UB7 ODA*

In the United States: Please write to *Consumer Sales, Penguin USA, P.O. Box 999, Dept. 17109, Bergenfield, New Jersey 07621-0120.* VISA and MasterCard holders call 1-800-253-6476 to order Penguin titles

In Canada: Please write to *Penguin Books Canada Ltd, 10 Alcorn Avenue, Suite 300, Toronto, Ontario M4V 3B2*

In Australia: Please write to *Penguin Books Australia Ltd, P.O. Box 257, Ringwood, Victoria 3134*

In New Zealand: Please write to *Penguin Books (NZ) Ltd, Private Bag 102902, North Shore Mail Centre, Auckland 10*

In India: Please write to *Penguin Books India Pvt Ltd, 706 Eros Apartments, 56 Nehru Place, New Delhi 110 019*

In the Netherlands: Please write to *Penguin Books Netherlands bv, Postbus 3507, NL-1001 AH Amsterdam*

In Germany: Please write to *Penguin Books Deutschland GmbH, Metzlerstrasse 26, 60594 Frankfurt am Main*

In Spain: Please write to *Penguin Books S. A., Bravo Murillo 19, 1° B, 28015 Madrid*

In Italy: Please write to *Penguin Italia s.r.l., Via Felice Casati 20, I–20124 Milano*

In France: Please write to *Penguin France S. A., 17 rue Lejeune, F–31000 Toulouse*

In Japan: Please write to *Penguin Books Japan, Ishikiribashi Building, 2–5–4, Suido, Bunkyo-ku, Tokyo 112*

In South Africa: Please write to *Longman Penguin Southern Africa (Pty) Ltd, Private Bag X08, Bertsham 2013*

READ MORE IN PENGUIN

A CHOICE OF NON-FICTION

Fisher's Face Jan Morris

Admiral of the Fleet Lord 'Jacky' Fisher (1841–1920) was one of the greatest naval reformers in history. 'An intimate recreation of the man in all his extraordinary complexity, his mercurial humours, his ferocious energy and bloodthirstiness, his childlike innocence, his Machiavellian charm' – *Daily Mail*

Mrs Jordan's Profession Claire Tomalin

The story of Dora Jordan and her relationship with the Duke of Clarence, later King William IV. 'Meticulous biography at its creative best' – *Observer*. 'A fascinating and affecting story, one in which the mutually attractive, mutually suspicious, equally glittering worlds of court and theatre meet, and one which vividly illustrates the social codes of pre-Victorian Britain' – *Sunday Times*

John Major: From Brixton to Downing Street Penny Junor

Within a year of a record-breaking general election victory, John Major became the most unpopular Prime Minister ever. With his party deeply divided and his government lurching from crisis to crisis, few thought he could survive. This absorbing biography uses interviews with family, friends, foes, Cabinet colleagues and the Prime Minister himself to uncover the real John Major.

The Bondage of Fear Fergal Keane

'An important source for anyone trying to understand how South Africa achieved its transfer of power' – *Independent*. 'A first-class journalistic account ... likely to be the most memorable account of this terrible, uplifting time' – *Literary Review*

The Oxbridge Conspiracy Walter Ellis

'A brave book that needed to be written ... Oxbridge imparts to our élite values which, in their anti-commerce, anti-technology, anti-market snobbery, make them unfit to run a modern economy. It is the Oxbridge élite which has presided over the decline of this nation' – *Financial Times*

READ MORE IN PENGUIN

A CHOICE OF NON-FICTION

Thesiger   Michael Asher

'Compiled from lengthy interviews with the man himself, meticulous pilgrimages over the same ground, and conversations with his surviving travelling companions, the book both celebrates Thesiger and incorporates what you might call the case against' – *Guardian*

Nelson: A Personal History   Christopher Hibbert

'Impeccably researched and written with Christopher Hibbert's habitual elegance of style, this is a fine biography of a figure genuinely larger than life' – *Sunday Telegraph*

The History of the Ginger Man   J. P. Donleavy

Combining literary history with autobiography, this is the dramatic story of J. P. Donleavy's struggle to create and publish his contemporary classic *The Ginger Man*. 'An endearingly revealing book . . . vintage Donleavy' – *Observer*

Ireland and the Irish   John Ardagh

'He has conducted dozens of interviews in all the provinces of the island, with schoolmasters, poets, nuns, bishops, businessmen, farmers large and small, and anyone else, it seems, in any walk of life, who might have anything to say' – *The Times*. 'This scholarly, balanced and compassionate book ought to be read by every British politician – every British citizen, for that matter' – Jan Morris

South of Haunted Dreams   Eddy L. Harris

In the southern United States, there is an imaginary line – the Mason-Dixon line – that once marked the boundary of the almost unimaginable institution of slavery. Lost behind it is the history of almost every black American. 'Harris went out looking for the face and mind of white racism. What he found wasn't what he expected – at least, not exactly. Harris finds his own very real, and contradictory, history on the highways of the American South' – *Washington Post Book World*

READ MORE IN PENGUIN

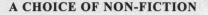

A CHOICE OF NON-FICTION

The Rise and Fall of Popular Music   Donald Clarke

'He attaches a thumbnail biography to everyone he names, he keeps a beady eye on the commercial angles and his capacity to make connections across decades, and sometimes centuries, is consistently invigorating' – *Sunday Times*

Accountable to None   Simon Jenkins
The Tory Nationalization of Britain

'Brings together, with an insider's authority and anecdotage, both a narrative of domestic Thatcherism and a polemic against its pretensions ... an indispensable guide to the corruptions of power and language which have sustained the illusion that Thatcherism was an attack on "government"' – *Guardian*

James Baldwin: A Biography   David Leeming

A unique and outspoken voice in American culture, James Baldwin rose from the Harlem ghetto to international fame with his beautifully crafted novels, short stories and essays. 'Leeming takes us beyond the surface image of the public figure to reveal aspects of the private self that Baldwin masked in even his most personal essays and autobiographical fiction' – *The New York Times Book Review*

From Sea to Shining Sea   Gavin Young
A Present-day Journey into America's Past

'He catches the mind's eye of the reader very deftly ... and, without losing his sense of irony, gives us a genuine account of the tragedy and the pathos, as well as the optimism and bravery, that created American civilization' – *Mail on Sunday*

In Harm's Way   Martin Bell

'A coruscating account of the dangerous work of a war correspondent, replete with tales of Bell dodging, and in one case not dodging, bullets across the globe in order to bring us our nightly news' – *Independent*